A Decade of

Proceedings of the
Portable Antiquities Scheme Conference 2007

Edited by

Sally Worrell
Geoff Egan
John Naylor
Kevin Leahy
Michael Lewis

BAR British Series 520
2010

Published in 2016 by
BAR Publishing, Oxford

BAR British Series 520

A Decade of Discovery

ISBN 978 1 40730723 7

BAR Publishing is the trading name of British Archaeological Reports (Oxford) Ltd. British Archaeological Reports was first incorporated in 1974 to publish the BAR Series, International and British. In 1992 Hadrian Books Ltd became part of the BAR group. This volume was originally published by Archaeopress in conjunction with British Archaeological Reports (Oxford) Ltd / Hadrian Books Ltd, the Series principal publisher, in 2010. This present volume is published by BAR Publishing, 2016.

Printed in England

BAR
PUBLISHING

BAR titles are available from:

BAR Publishing
122 Banbury Rd, Oxford, OX2 7BP, UK
EMAIL info@barpublishing.com
PHONE +44 (0)1865 310431
FAX +44 (0)1865 316916
www.barpublishing.com

CONTENTS

Foreword

In 2007 the Portable Antiquities Scheme (PAS) marked its tenth anniversary by holding a conference at which speakers, both from within the Scheme and outside gave a series of papers that demonstrated the research potential of recording finds of archaeological objects made by members of the public. This volume contains papers given at that conference together with a number of other contributions.

PAS started as six pilot schemes in 1997 and became a national network across England and Wales in 2003. The core aim of PAS has always been to minimise the loss to our heritage caused by the failure to record systematically objects found by the public – metal-detector users, amateur field-walkers and chance finders. The reason for recording these objects is to create a resource that can be used at many different levels as a resource for school projects purposes, for studying the history of one's local area, or for academic research.

One of the first priorities of PAS was to create a database for recording finds and this was made available online at www.finds.org.uk from 1999. It was redeveloped in 2003 as a live online resource and was completely revamped by Dan Pett, PAS ICT Adviser, in spring 2010, at which time he incorporated of two major databases: the Oxford University Celtic Coin Index (CCI) and Iron Age and Roman Coins found in Wales. The database currently (August 2010) contains records of 638,278 objects, 93,789 of which were added over the last year. It is indeed a rich and rapidly growing resource.

Coin experts were probably the first scholars to appreciate the potential of recording finds made by the public: the CCI was established in 1960, before the advent of metal-detecting, while the British Numismatic Journal has been publishing an annual list of stray finds of coins in its Coin Register since 1987. The Early Medieval Corpus of Coin Finds (EMC) was established by Mark Blackburn of the Fitzwilliam Museum, Cambridge in 1997. Many other scholars have published studies of artefact types that include metal-detected finds. It is no exaggeration to say that the distribution patterns of most types of coins and metal artefacts have been totally transformed by the recording of chance finds.

Another fruitful area of research is to use the objects recorded by PAS as part of a study of local landscapes: a study of finds from Lincolnshire has shown that PAS data has added 175 new sites from that county alone. This will be an increasingly fruitful line of study as PAS data is incorporated into Historic Environment Records.

Although PAS has been in existence since 1997, there has inevitably been a time lag before the data gathered by it could become a significant research tool, but it is now established at a major resource for a wide variety of archaeological research projects. Those that we are aware of are listed at www.finds.org.uk/research. These include seven major research projects funded by the AHRC or Leverhulme Trust, 35 PhDs, and 77 MA and BA dissertations. The AHRC's Collaborative Doctoral Award programme has been particularly important and PAS staff are currently supervising eight PhD students.

The papers published here demonstrate clearly the great range of research that can be undertaken from studying such finds. We are very grateful to all the contributors and to the editors, as well as to Claire Costin for her help with typesetting. I would also like to thank all those who helped organise the conference itself, particularly my colleagues in the Department of Portable Antiquities & Treasure, British Museum.

Roger Bland

August 2010

The Portable Antiquities Scheme's Database: its development for research since 1998

Daniel E. J. Pett

In 2003, thanks to Heritage Lottery Fund funding, the Portable Antiquities Scheme (PAS) began to formulate plans to become the national programme for the recording of archaeological finds found by the public. Through the vision of its Advisory Group, the PAS was now in a position to expand to the whole of England and Wales and sought to deliver the fruits of its work via the Internet. There were no models on which to build this project, and the organisation that now exists, is still the pioneer.

In 1996, Tim Schadla-Hall (1996) stated '...how ready is our collections information for the super highway? I suspect the answer is that a lot of it is not ready for the mud track or even the occasionally trodden grassy path!' For a self-confessed computer illiterate this statement was extremely precise. The majority of museums, archives and heritage institutions were not in the position to take advantage of the advent of the web and its vast potential. Indeed, even now, many organisations are still unable to take full advantage of what is an inherently fast paced sector. However, this paper will attempt to demonstrate that this is changing rapidly throughout the Heritage Sector and we are now in a period where disparate resources can potentially be joined up and interrogated easily at the click of a button.

The Scheme's database

In 1997, when the PAS was a fledgling recording programme, the collation of data was extremely fragmentary. In 2001, the Scheme embraced the digital age and produced its first website under the direction of Richard Hobbs and a skeletal database was available for researchers to access online. Data recorded by the original six pilot regions was collected on individual Microsoft Access (devised by Cassely 1998) instances and these data subsequently were collated once a year to a central copy and then published onto the Scheme's website (not fully as some data was retained in the Access instance). The records were the same standard as many found within a wide variety of institutions and, for example, the record would be presented as an outline:

- Object type = coin
- Description = lacking
- Denomination = denarius
- Spatial data = 4-figure National Grid Reference was the normal geo-reference available
- Low resolution image(s)

These data provided a very sparse starting point for any researcher and at the time were heavily criticised by finds researchers who had been asked to assess the value of PAS data, as part of a Review of the Scheme in 2001. Hilary Cool (2001: App. 4.2, 6), for example, stated that 'currently the entries are of variable value, and it is imperative to improve the quality of the poorer ones. If the objects are not identified accurately and in appropriate terminology, then the database will not be used... The input of senior and experienced finds researchers of the type envisioned for the Object Advisor posts will be vital for this'.

The PAS recognised these shortcomings, which helped to devise future recording policy and led to the establishment of the posts of ICT Adviser (that of the author) and the Scheme's Finds Advisers. That said, the genesis of the IT systems was begun beforehand, with Alice Grant Consulting and David Dawson (then Head of Digital Futures, MLA) fundamental in the specifications being drawn up for the development of an online recording application and building on the Access model devised by Victoria Cassely (formerly British Academy). This was granted in December 2002 after a competitive tendering exercise, to Oxford Arch Digital (OAD), and this partnership was maintained until August 2007, when they went into liquidation shortly after this conference closed. The key concepts behind the development of the Scheme's database were:

- Open access to all
- Available 24 hours a day
- Provision of a mechanism for collection of data centrally
- Controlled terminology to standardise entries
- Ordnance Survey based spatial data
- Protection of all sensitive data and compliance with the Data Protection Act (1996)
- Publishing the data online, negation of the Freedom of Information Act (2002)

In April 2003, the Scheme's database went live to the public. Since then, there has been a steady progression of user interfaces and server-side enhancement, including:

- Extensive workflow policy to enable validation of records entered
- Integration of zoom and pan technology for high resolution viewing of images
- Numismatic data entry overhaul
- Search engine overhaul
- Integration with web mapping services (Google and open layers)
- Traffic light workflow indicators to signify status of records
- XML MIDAS schema for Historic Environment Record (HER) integration
- CSV (excel) import/export routine for data manipulation
- Really Simple Syndication feeds (RSS) added for reuse of content by external consumer sites (news, events, blog posts and artefact records)
- OAI-PMH and z39.50 routines for external content consumption (People's Network Discovery Service and HEIRNET (www.peoplesnetwork.gov.uk) (www.britarch.ac.uk/HEIRNET))
- Permissions based access for users
- Email reports for registered users

Sharing archaeological content isn't just for the archaeological community

One of the key aspects that the Scheme identified with regards to broadening its appeal to the potential audience base was to syndicate content and participate in various projects that will reuse and manipulate our collated data. Since 2005, the Scheme has released all of its content via RSS feeds and participated in the following projects using various content dissemination methodologies:

- BRICKS (http://www.brickscommunity.org)
- MICHAEL (http://www.michael-culture.org.uk)
- People's Network Discovery Service
- Sharing content with the signed up partner Historic Environment Records (HERs): 55 current signatories
- INTERFACE: a German led coins network
- Digital Coins Network

As the PAS core funding is from public funds, it is therefore a key principle that its data is shared with anyone that wishes to make use of it (the Data Protection Act 1996 and site sensitivity concerns prevent certain aspects of our data being disseminated to all parties). The concept behind freeing up public funded data gathered momentum with The Guardian newspaper campaigning for open access models via its 'Free our data campaign' (http://www.freeourdata.org.uk).

The PAS has been hampered in its use of Ordnance Survey data as the full license is not cost effective: this is ironic given the Ordnance Survey, like the PAS, is publically funded. At one point the Scheme had a free licence under the Pan-Government Agreement, which was subsequently replaced with a pay for use model. The Scheme is now using a basic outline layer of England and Wales, and is making use of the possibilities offered by Google (www.google.com/apis/maps) and Yahoo (http://developer.yahoo.com/maps) map Application Programming Interfaces (API). Using these mapping facilities reduces costs substantially and common interfaces are being implemented that users will be familiar with.

Uptake in the academic community

In May 2007, the database had attracted over 550 registered users, of which approximately 120 are allowed to enter data directly onto the system; 130 users have access for research. These data are now used by a wide variety of researchers, with respected scholars seeing the value of PAS database in their work. Martin Biddle (pers. comm.), for example, stated: 'the result [of using PAS data in my research] has transformed knowledge of the pattern of Early Anglo-Saxon settlement of central Hampshire, notably of the Itchen valley, more than doubling the number of known sites and emphasising the central role of Winchester. It is a marvelous demonstration of the value of the PAS - if only it had been going from the beginning of metal-detecting!'

As the database matures and more researchers make use of these data, its true merits (together with the efforts of the Scheme's staff and those that offer finds for recording) will be realised. In recent years, several major research topics have been awarded funding to study (in part) the Scheme's data, including:

- Oxford Archaeology's night hawking survey (English Heritage funded)
- The Viking and Anglo-Saxon Landscape and Economy (VASLE) project (Naylor and Richards, 2006) at the University of York (AHRC funded; see also this volume)
- The Tribal Hidage project at University College London (Leverhulme funded; see also this volume)
- AHRC funding for three Collaborative PhDs in 2006-07.
    - King's College London
    - Birkbeck College, University of London
    - University College London
- Over 50 individuals completing research for higher level degrees worldwide (including Australia, Japan USA and the UK).

As the dataset is now rapidly increasing in size, the analysis of de-contextualised find data is now becoming more integral to high level projects. The critical point will be when half a million objects have been recorded and researchers can access a wide variety of information easily for multi-period queries.

Data collection comes at a price

Most pertinent is the upward trend in recording of archaeological objects (Fig. 1). Since 2003, the Scheme has recorded over quarter of a million objects and made them available freely to audiences across the world. The flow of data into the Scheme's database is rising rapidly as shown below. There are several noticeable points to consider when viewing these figures:

- Pre 2003, there were only six recording centres in operation
- 2001-2 saw the Nationwide 'Foot and Mouth' crisis, which restricted access to the countryside
- 2003-4 saw very little activity in Wales due to the Buried Treasure Exhibition: during this period, the Finds Co-ordinator for Wales was engaged in preparation for this installation (Mark Lodwick, pers.comm.)
- 2003-6 saw the inclusion of paper records from Norfolk within these figures
- 2007 saw the import of 10 years of numismatic data from Norfolk in a single batch

Year of recording	Quantity
1998	4,558
1999	8,201
2000	18,106
2001	16,368
2002	11,996
2003	21,684
2004	39,000
2005	52,202
2006	58,311
2007	79,051

Fig. 1: The increase in finds recorded by the PAS since 1998 (after Lewis 2003, 2004, 2005 and subsequent compilation from the database).

The recording of these finds always comes at a cost, something that Tim Schadla-Hall highlighted in his paper to the conference (not published within these proceedings). Analysing the Scheme's return on investment (ROI) in technology, its database can be seen as a widespread and acclaimed success. The embracing of Fully Open Source Software (FOSS) technology has allowed the Scheme to remain free of the shackles of licence fees and proprietary programmes and behave with the flexibility of successful IT companies. If the Scheme had followed the Microsoft or Oracle route, then it would have floundered on a one off product and there would have been less money available for the staffing of the Scheme. Between 2003 and 2007 the Scheme spent just under £162,000 (initial outlay accounted for the majority) on IT development and running costs. Running two servers with dual processors, equivalent licence costs for Microsoft SQL Server would have been around £50,000 per annum for enterprise level service (pers comm. IT department, British Museum). So in those 4 years, the PAS would have spent significantly more than the budget allowed for and impinged upon other activities.

Cost per unit added to the database, when plotted against total IT spending demonstrates a substantial fall with every object recorded. Figure 2 shows the annual IT outlay by the Scheme between 2003 and 2007 (in line with the fiscal year) and the cost per find recorded now stands at £0.84. Added value can also be claimed by the Scheme allowing others to recycle these data into their own applications at no access costs. PAS literally gives away its data at the cost of its bandwidth; external consumers pay nothing.

The usual cost efficiency argument that is discussed in many quarters factors in the costs added for recording each object by using staff salary and associated costs divided by the number of finds recorded. This could be regarded as a false measure of the Scheme's workings. It is extremely difficult to attach a cost element to the 'other work' of the average Finds Liaison Officer (FLO), such as local society talks, finds days, school visits, gallery talks and local museum or authority duties. For example, between 2003 and 2006, 35,668 people attended 1,073 talks and lectures organised by the PAS, and a further 45,225 people attended 1,187 finds days around the country (Lewis 2006). FLO's never spend 100% of their time on data entry and hence the unit cost for each recorded find demonstrates that the Scheme is ultimately extremely cost effective.

The use of a centralised repository has allowed the Scheme to produce statistics on demand with regards to these data and it allows for monitoring of find spot precision and number of finds recorded per region/user/county/parish/type, via the creation of simple or extremely complex computational queries.

The perpetual argument over the lack of provenance of objects recorded in the Scheme's database, versus the archaeological value of finds submitted for recording is now receding. Figure 3 demonstrates the increasing precision to which finds are being recorded. By being able to edit data at any time, these grid references can be improved at any time.

Financial Year	Expenditure	Running total	Finds recorded	Running total of finds recorded	Running cost per find
2003-04	£106,278.25	-	29,344	-	£3.62
2004-05	£18,570.89	£124,849.14	39,851	69,195	£1.80
2005-06	£4,050.36	£128,899.50	57,417	126,612	£1.02
2006-07	£33,017.52	£161,917.02	65,705	192,317	£0.84

Fig. 2: The falling cost for recording items on the PAS database.

These figures show that precision has dramatically increased since the Scheme went National, and are now at a very acceptable level. Data retrieval and analysis can now allow researchers to accurately map trade routes, distribution patterns, anomalies and anachronisms via GIS, for comparison with other historic environment data.

This precision could be further increased by metal-detectorists and field-walkers making greater use of hand-held Global Positioning Systems (GPS) units. It has been suggested that detector manufacturers could produce metal-detectors with built-in GPS units that could log all data as objects are found. These data could then be transferred via USB interface to either the FLO's or the finder's computer for further analysis. High precision data (even with the margin of error accounted for under civilian GPS) will aid studies at all levels and can pinpoint geographical trends or what soils objects are recorded from as landscape characterisation exercises become more developed.

The advent of high tech web mapping resources on the internet, such as Google, Yahoo, MAGIC, Multi-map and the Ordnance Survey's 'get-a-map' (http://www.getamap.co.uk/getamap), have also played a major part in the collection of precise point data. The old adage of 'finds without context are meaningless' is slowly being negated as the more precise mapping of data is adopted and archaeologists are increasingly aware that the majority of detector finds are found in disturbed plough soil contexts.

The Scheme's database allows anyone to access a national rather than county based picture from one central point and is therefore extremely attractive to the researcher. By analysing GIS plots of the data that the Scheme holds on its database, one can see the changing face of its recording patterns. Figures 4–7 demonstrate GIS plots of these point data since April 2003.

The GIS point data for finds recorded through the PAS can now be analysed in conjunction with other datasets, as shown in Figure 8 (the entire PAS Iron Age coin dataset for 2003-6 mapped against finds data recorded on the Celtic Coin Index) and Figure 9 (the PAS Roman coin dataset mapped against the Roman coin finds for Wales database Wells and Guest 2007). Both these maps show considerable additions of data to our known archaeological knowledge base for England and Wales. The Iron Age data is now forming the basis for the Collaborative PhD being conducted by Ian Leins at Birkbeck College, University of London.

Geospatial analysis demonstrates the power of using a variety of sources to analyse patterns and provide the basis for more detailed research. By combination of disparate resources, a much more accurate and informed conclusion can be ascertained and this is demonstrated in the increasing body of work being produced with PAS data as an integral part. Analysis of what the spatial data presented in these maps is outside the scope of this paper and is designed for illustrating the point of synthesising data for greater knowledge.

An archaeological approach

As the PAS database develops, the Scheme is taking a more archaeologically focused approach to the way that data can be analysed within its mechanisms, and also externally. Typologies can now be assembled through image searches. Perhaps the best example of what can be done dynamically from within the database's core is the assignation of 'Reece Periods' to Roman numismatic data that has been collected. (Reece 2002: Appendix).

Year	Total	6-figure NGR and above	Percentage
1998	4,558	2,991	65.62
1999	8,201	6,607	80.56
2000	18,106	14,945	82.54
2001	16,368	14,111	86.21
2002	11,996	11,247	93.75
2003	21,684	18,215	84.00
2004	39,000	30,909	79.25
2005	52,202	43,569	83.46
2006	58,311	50,293	86.24

Fig. 3: Findspot precision between 1997 and 2007.

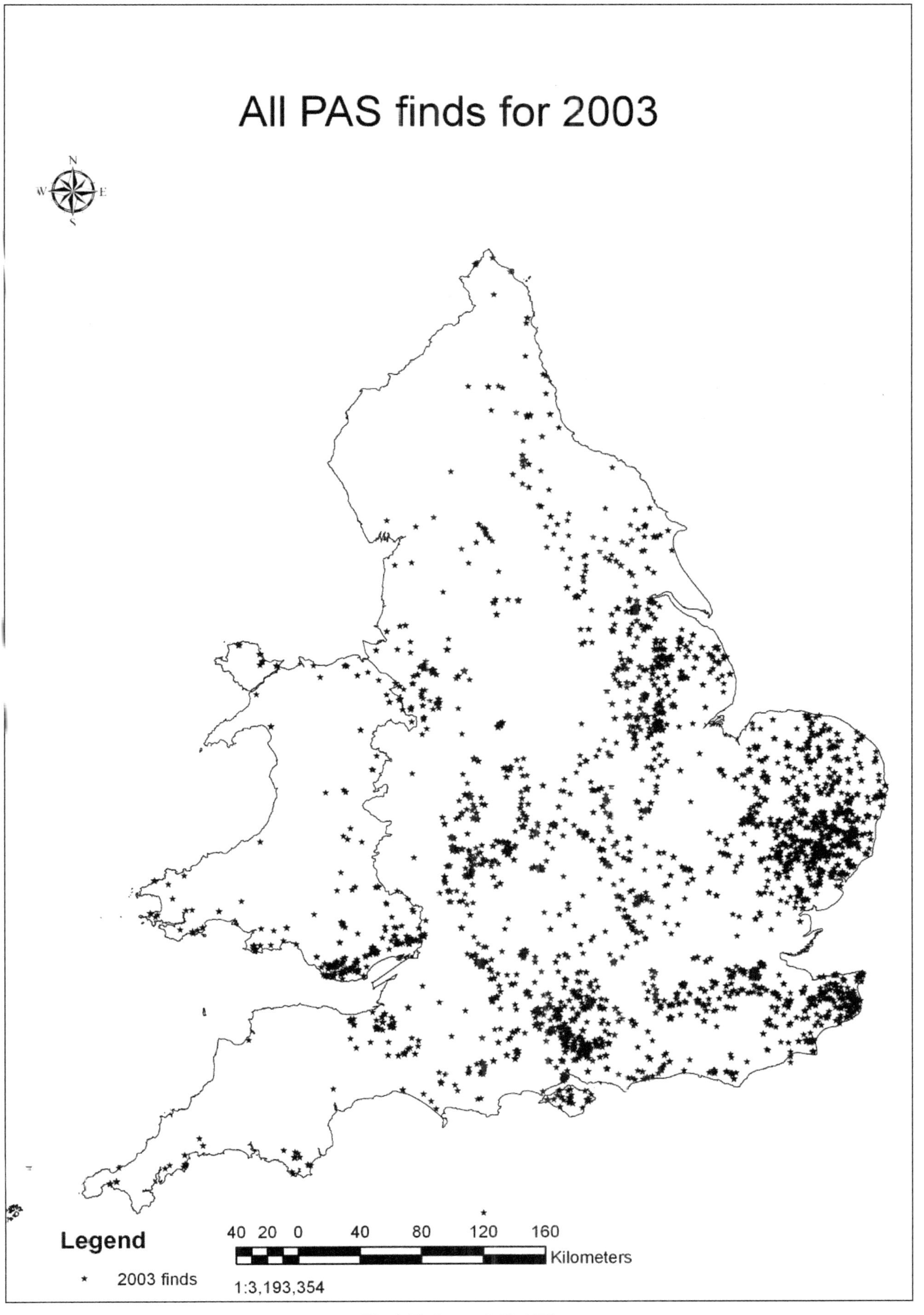

Fig. 4: Finds recorded in 2003.

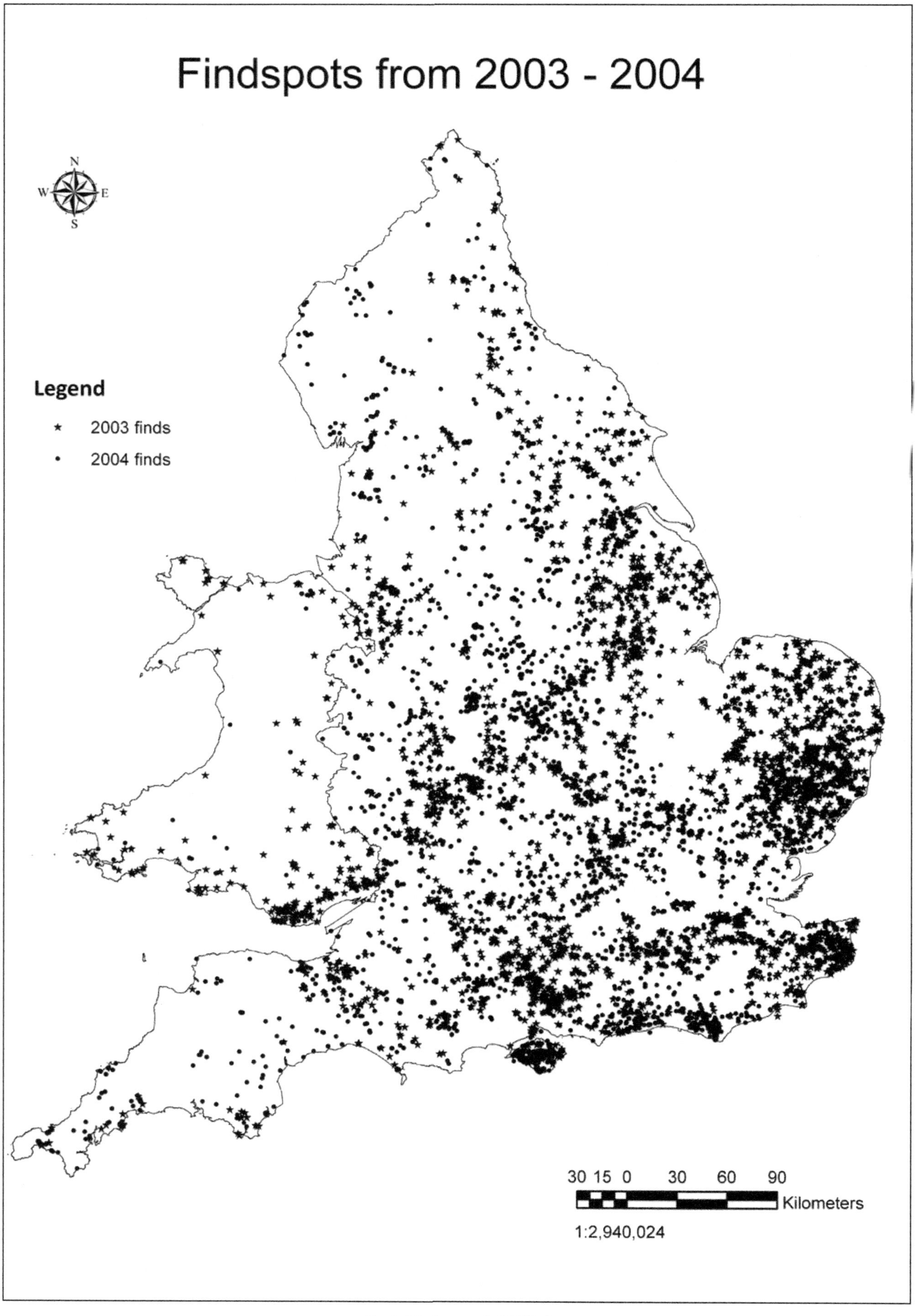

Fig. 5: Finds recorded 2003-4.

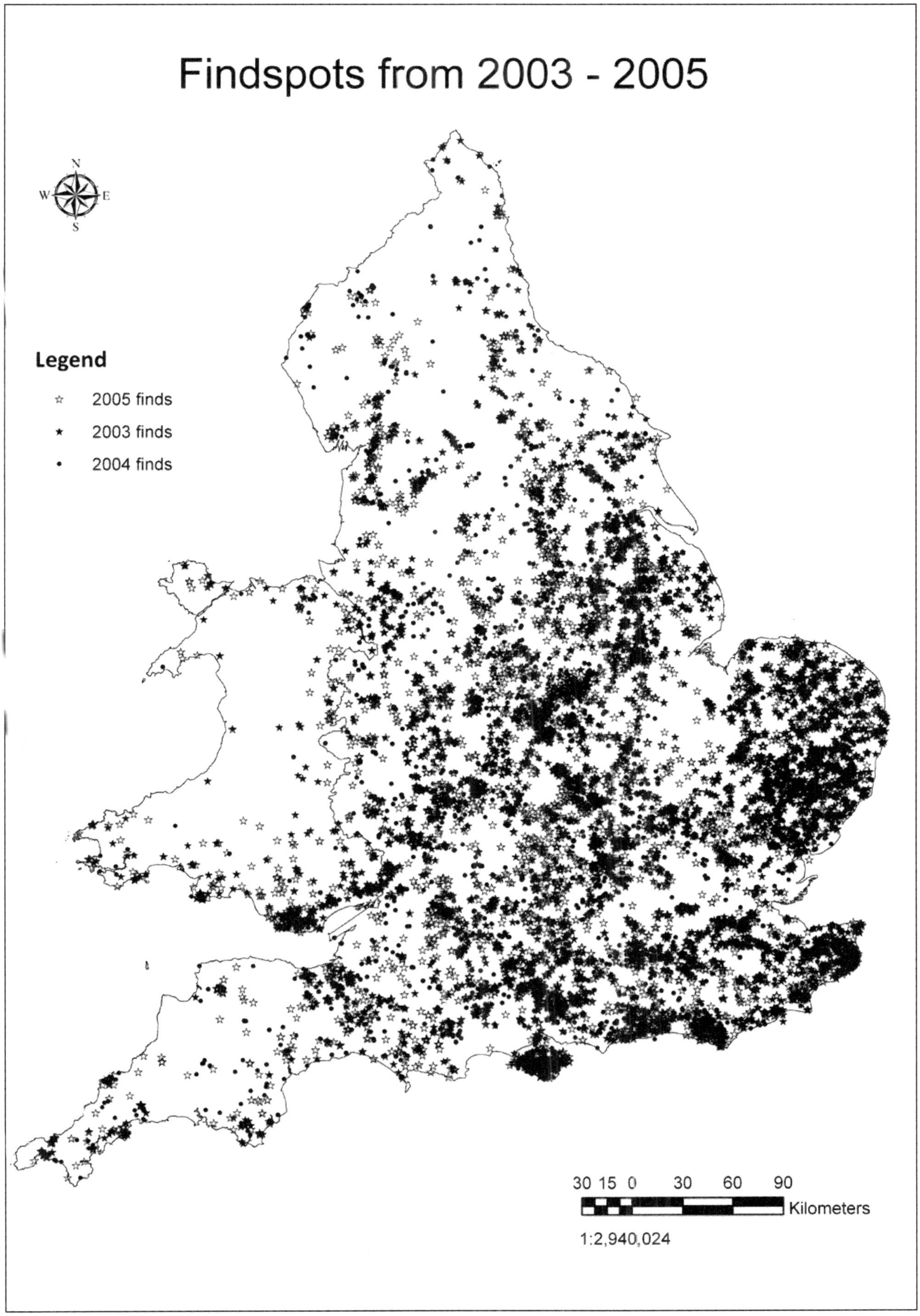

Fig. 6: All finds recorded: 2003-5.

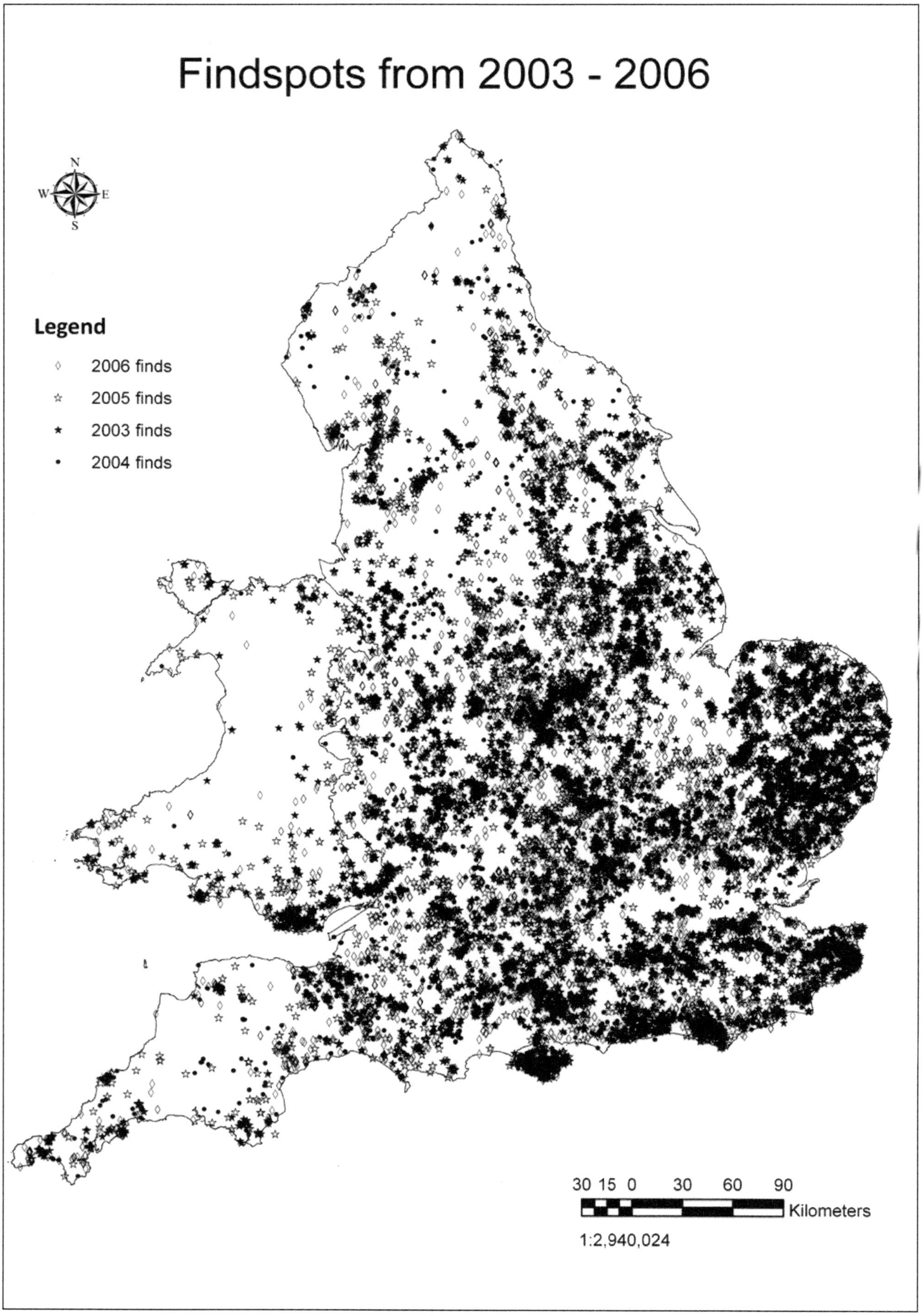

Fig. 7: All finds recorded 2003-6.

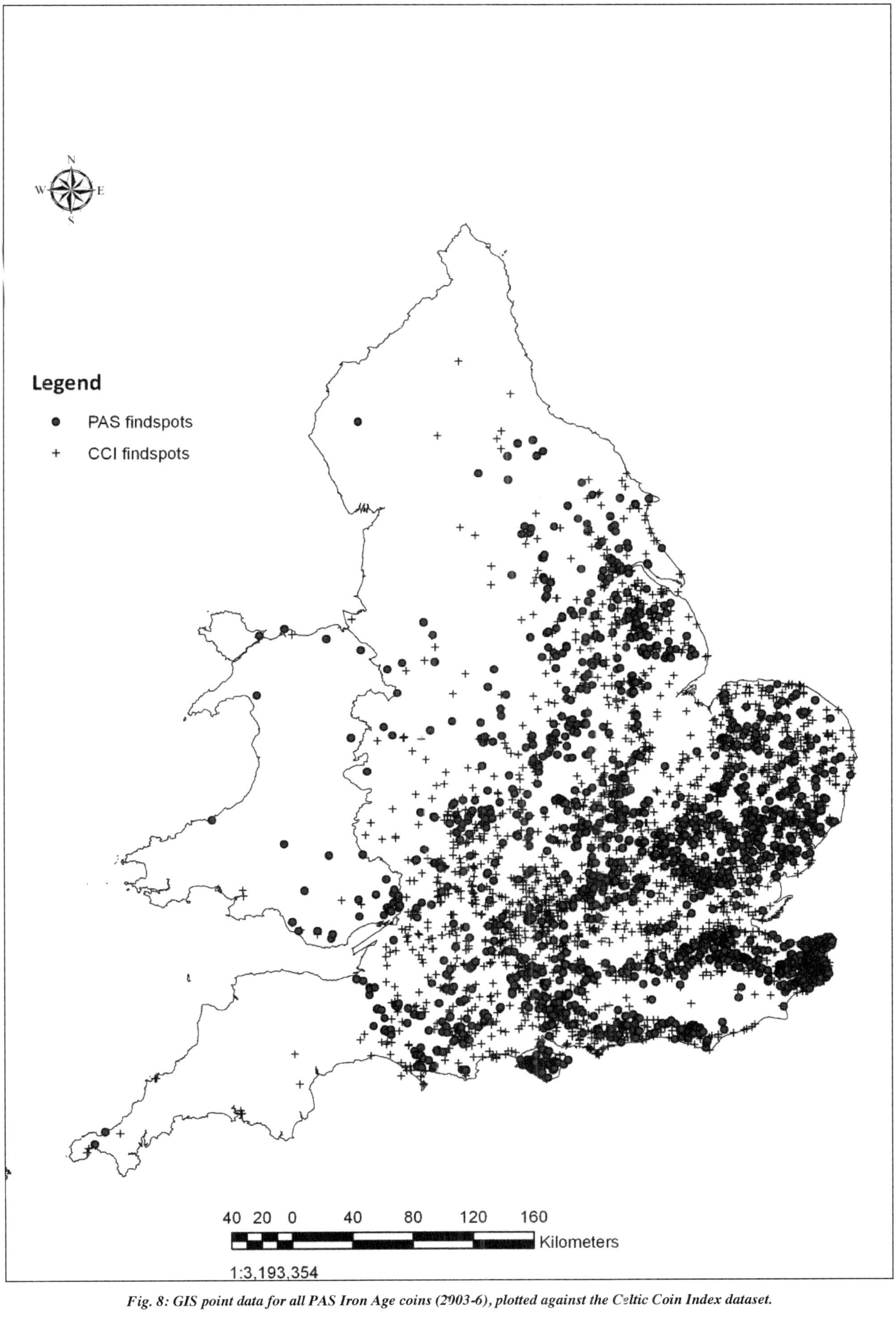

Fig. 8: GIS point data for all PAS Iron Age coins (2003-6), plotted against the Celtic Coin Index dataset.

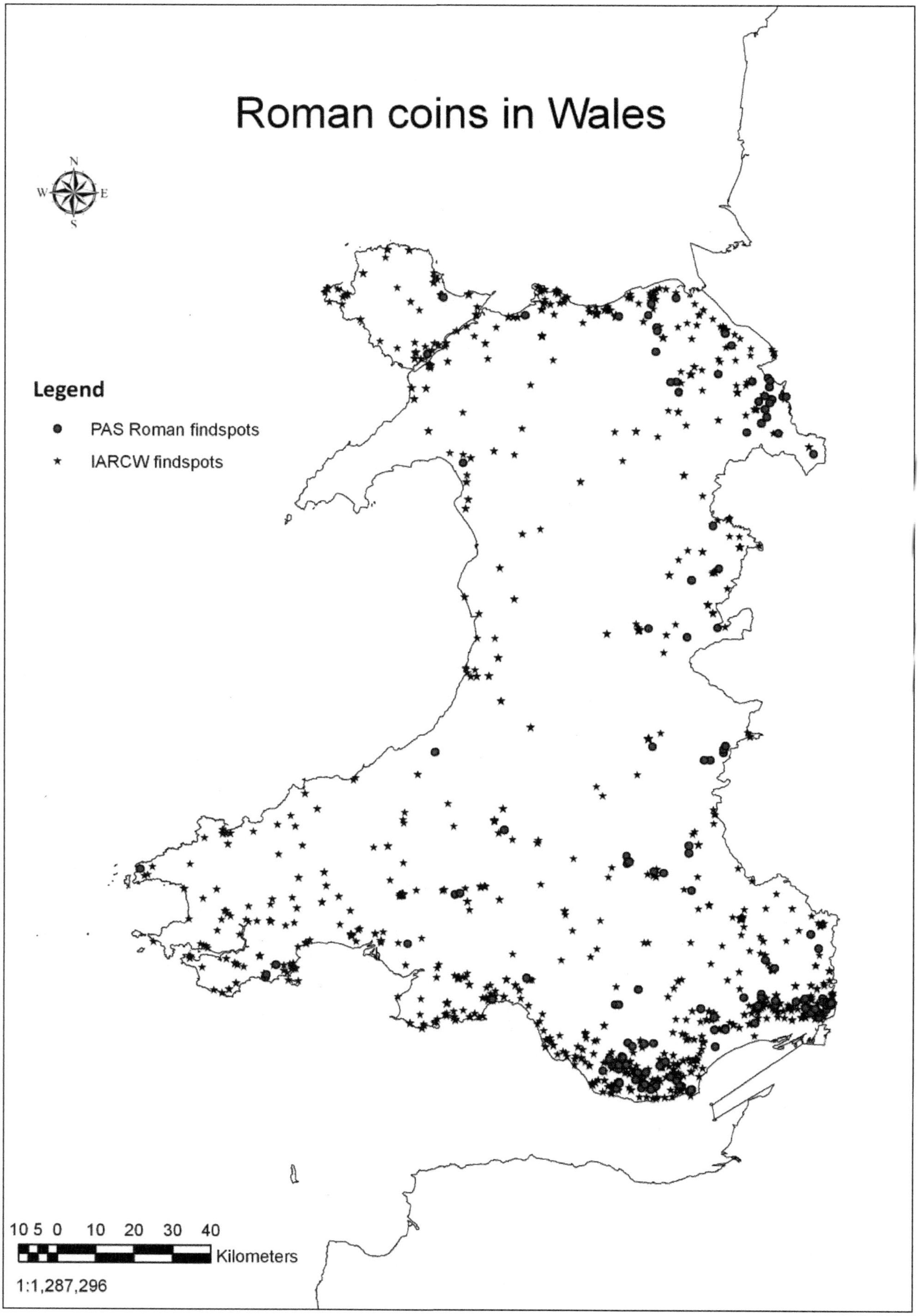

Fig. 9: GIS point data for all PAS Roman coin finds (2003-6), plotted against Guest and Well's 2007 dataset of Roman coins in Wales.

The system now also forces the recorder into implementing a strict relationship model. This presents upon data entry as shown in Figure 10; it should be noted that no methodology currently exists for assigning Rulers to Reece periods 15 and above.

By assigning the Reece period to coins, a better chronological picture can be built up for the study of Roman coin distributions in Britain. This is discussed further by Sam Moorhead (published in this volume). Figure 11 demonstrates the Reece periods for Roman coins recorded on the PAS database.

This is but one example of integrating archaeological theoretical models into the Scheme's database; as more researchers are consulted more archaeological analysis tools will be built into the scripting of the database. This takes time and feedback. Without the latter, there is not the possibility to respond to requests for new features.

The biggest challenge for the PAS (perhaps) is publicising the fact that the data exists, that anyone can use it and highlighting (particularly for under-graduate and post-graduate students) what needs to be studied. Without doubt, greater marketing presences gleaned from prominence on the funding partner websites (British Museum, DCMS and MLA) will further enhance the Scheme's visibility within the public eye. In April 2006, the Scheme became a formal department within the Museum and features more prominently upon the new British Museum website launched in May 2007. It is hoped that there will be a permanent front page link to the Scheme on the British Museum's website at some point in the future.

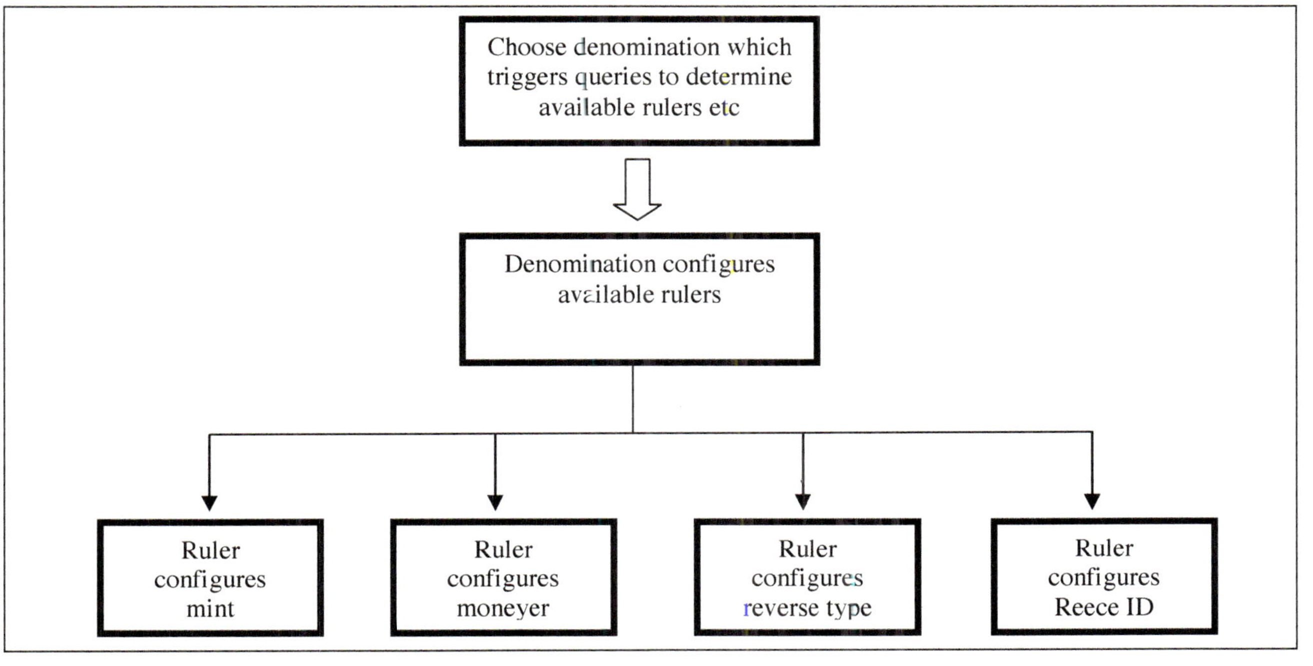

Fig. 10: Flow chart for assigning numismatic data.

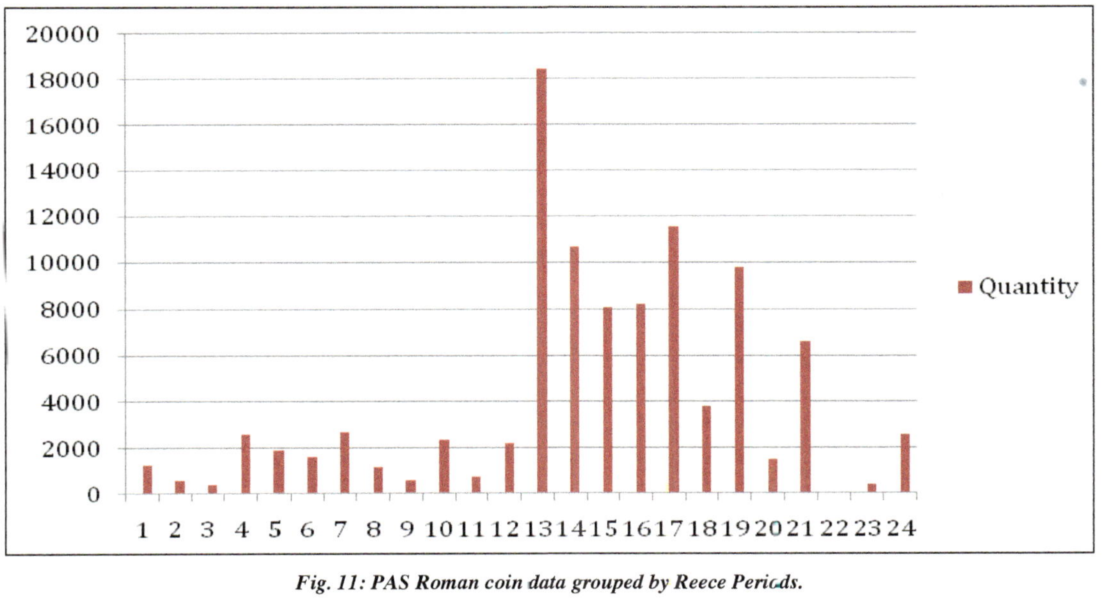

Fig. 11: PAS Roman coin data grouped by Reece Periods.

Experience enhancement

To enhance the experience of people using PAS data the Scheme has implemented various methodologies for studying user behaviour; these include user surveys, the analysis of web logs, behavioural data from Google Analytics, search engine terms and search engine keywords. Figures 13-14 outline the differences between what our registered users want to discover plotted against the unregistered public users. One of the salient points for us is the use of plurality for objects. For example, the plural rather than the singular is a much misused search term. How to communicate this to our users is a challenge. By implementing 'stemming' (Porter 2006) on keyword searching, we can push searches towards a more efficient result. This is one possibility that we can examine for the next iteration of the database.

It is apparent that there is a usability problem within the database for many of our audience. Frequently there have been comments lamenting the impenetrability of the database (which has now been addressed following the redevelopment of the database in 2009-10). Through feedback generated via the Scheme reviews and email correspondence, PAS has enhanced the search mechanism of the database and through this, it is hoped to enhance substantially the user's experience whilst using our facility. A typical user (to remain anonymous for purposes of data protection) comment prior to the re-development of the database was: 'I… wholly support the Portable Antiquities Scheme. However, please try to use the website! Try to access any object that may have been found in your town or county. If you end up as frustrated as I, then please use your influence to ensure that all the wonderful artefacts that have been recorded, are accessible by you and I (and many others)' (pers. comm., May 2007).

The Scheme can use these comments to benefit its work by asking further questions relating to user experience. By working with the user base, the Scheme's online resources can only get better.

What do people look for within our portals?

It is vital that database maintainers analyse the search terms that people enter into their systems. If it is not possible to accurately determine what people are actually looking for then it makes it extremely unlikely that any enhancement to experience can occur. There are several good discussion documents where Museums have analysed fully their database usage, with Chan's (2007) paper at the 'Museums on the Web Conference' an exemplar. The Scheme's database keeps a running log of search terms entered in the different search areas of the website and by different user groups, and this allows for some detailed statistics to be produced. Since the database has been running on Oxford ArchDigital's toadHMS (http://www.oxarchdigital.com) users have performed 93,762 visual searches, 215,865 quick searches and 1,102,049 advanced searches. These can be categorised into the following account groups (not all account types are shown):

Frequency of search	Public users	Percent of total	Registered	Percent of total	FLO group	Percent of total
Quick	190,983	19.2%	24,898	6%	24,269	5.9%
Visual	92,246	9.3%	1,336	0.3%	1,020	0.25%
Advanced	710,240	71.5%	391,879	93.7%	386,655	93.85%
Total	**993,469**		**418,113**		**411,944**	

Fig. 12: Frequency of searches performed on the PAS database.

Search term	Public users	Registered	FLOs
Lincolnshire	37,387	n/a	n/a
Roman	17,812	28,136	28,094
Early Medieval	17,992	25,782	25,751
Coin	34,386	25,023	24,853
Brooch	10,595	17,079	17,031
Edward the Confessor	n/a	12,694	12,690
Medieval	20,464	9,925	9,804

Fig. 13: Frequency of top search terms using advanced search terms entered by the public user group as a baseline.

Search term	Public users	Registered	FLOs
Coin	4,759	94	80
Brooch	1,929	80	77
Roman	1,713	n/a	n/a
Coins	1,433	n/a	n/a
Ring	1,415	31	29

Fig. 14: Frequency of top search terms compared across the three groups using quick search terms entered by the public user group as a baseline.

The above figures (Fig. 12) demonstrate that the visual search is pretty much obsolete for registered users and the FLO group (this aspect of the database has been removed as part of the re-development of the database is rebuilt). The advanced search is used heavily across all user groups (mean use at 86.4% of all searches) with quick search being used evenly for registered users and FLOs. This analysis can then be pursued further to demonstrate what people are actually looking for.

Through the analysis of the search terms entered via the advanced interface, it was surprising to see that the top six terms were pretty much even for registered users and FLOs. What stood out was the high occurrence of searches related to coins of Edward the Confessor for registered and FLO groups. Why are these so popular? Within the public user group, it is demonstrated that a large proportion of users are interested in the county of Lincolnshire, but there is no evidence of an interest in Edward the Confessor…

The interpretation of the quick search terminology highlighted some aspects that users do not comprehend about the PAS recording terminology. For example, the plural of coin is used regularly, whilst every object is recorded in the singular. This could be overcome by enabling the thesaurus look up on the quick term field.

The analysis of the search methods taken by users of the PAS database has allowed for a new set of search interfaces to be developed. This has been long overdue. However, as demonstrated above, the Scheme has very little available money for database enhancement. One can determine from the analysis of search patterns, that the public users utilise the quick search method far more than our other groups, whilst advanced search (despite its critics) appears to be used extensively.

Internet presence: the Scheme's burgeoning audience development

The Scheme recognised (via anecdotal and statistical evidence taken from the Hawkshead Conservation and Arboretum Archaeological Consultancy reviews) that there was a great opportunity for the development of supplementary resources with specific regard to archaeological objects and learning. As the database and website facilities have developed so much since the Hawkshead review, it is probably only relevant to take the figures from the 2006 User Survey (576 responses) in answer to 'why do people visit www.finds.org.uk?' (Fig. 15).

In the 2006 Review of PAS, Rachel Edwards (2006: 29) stated that 'the website has been used by three quarters of respondents, and a fifth uses it monthly or more frequently'. These figures are backed up by web statistical data from Google's analytical program which demonstrates that on average 45% of visitors to the PAS website are returning visitors. If this is compared to the British Museum's website for instance, they consistently return just 25.64% of repeat visitors.

The Hawkshead Review of PAS (Chitty and Edwards 2004: 4) recommended that the Scheme should:

1. Develop web-based resources for adult learning
2. Enhance the website and the database
3. Prioritise making data available to the Historic Environment Record Offices
4. Implement further audience and user research

To implement these recommendations, the Scheme had several things to overcome. The first obstacle was gaining full access to the web server and changing its technology base to become fully open source. This was achieved in March 2004. The website that had been developed by Reading Room was jettisoned and an in-house development was released.

Question	Number responses	Website visitors 2006	Website visitors 2004	Variance 2004-06
To find out about finds from my local area:	299	69%	61%	+8%
To find information about a particular find type:	246	56%	51%	+5%
To report a find or find out contact details	45	10%	8%	+2%
To use the forum	41	9%	10%	-1%
To learn about archaeology and finds in general:	129	30%	30%	+/- 0%
To use the interactive village and education resources	35	8%	n/a	n/a
For general interest	194	44%	43%	+1%
Other	43	10%	17%	-7%

Fig. 15: Reasons why people visit the PAS website (after Edwards 2006: 17-8).

This then allowed for the following features to be developed (Pett 2006: 35):

- PASt explorers website (http://www.pastexplorers.org.uk)
- Creation of a blog (http://www.finds.org.uk/wordpress) with the facility for finders to write about their experiences
- Staff forum and wiki for collaborative working
- RSS feeds for vacancies, news, events, blog posts enabling others to reuse PAS content on their own sites: one example of this can be seen at http://www.ourpasthistory.com where a finder's records have been integrated into their website and automatically update as a new record is added
- Roman coin guide, which has rapidly become the most popular section of the Scheme's web presence
- Medieval coin guide (under development).
- Delivery of the Celtic Coin Index (CCI) in a new format in conjunction with Oxford University
- Google Earth and Google Maps integrations for the CCI
- geoRSS feeds of objects for use in other mapping applications
- Search engine optimisation: over 54% of visitors to the PAS websites are referrals from Google

However, the Scheme has not been afraid to experiment with the creation of a public forum that went live on 23 September 2003 and finally closed in June 2006 due to the strain it was placing on moderation staff. Other experimental aspects that have been implemented include an image gallery and other collaborative social media tools.

The small team size (web development is one person) and proactive attitude of the Scheme's staff has allowed PAS to maintain independence and also the will to try new technology and techniques, which has saved a vast amount of money.

The Scheme has been able to measure the increase in the use of its resources with a great degree of accuracy; an area in which PAS can truly measure our worldwide impact and also measure the user's quality of experience. Since April 2003, the Scheme's web statistics has seen an increase in volume of usage by 3,500%, with length and depth of visit increasing month by month (Lewis 2007: 130-1). Figure 16 demonstrates the upsurge in Scheme website usage between 2004 and 2006.

Month	**Unique visitors**	**Number of visits**	**Pages**	**Hits**	**Mean page views per visit**
April 2004	7,002	21,641	341,784	2,025,978	16
May 2004	7,006	23,089	392,178	1,985,003	17
June 2004	7,429	23,473	460,562	2,624,770	20
July 2004	7,574	25,317	363,102	2,128,634	14
August 2004	5,371	17,130	178,782	987,309	10
September 2004	8,566	29,557	637,456	3,951,582	22
October 2004	8,030	30,629	667,988	3,959,589	22
November 2004	7,912	31,097	620,459	3,440,933	20
December 2004	7,256	30,326	484,497	2,529,853	16
January 2005	9,892	37,650	670,101	3,739,255	18
February 2005	10,789	42,487	680,634	3,924,317	16
March 2005	9,887	39,824	810,655	4,572,750	20
April 2005	9,594	39,722	704,053	3,861,520	18
May 2005	10,710	42,264	799,373	3,813,346	19
June 2005	11,206	42,289	932,994	5,023,172	22
July 2005	11,553	47,298	766,300	4,132,458	16
August 2005	12,590	45,398	846,374	4,119,401	19
September 2005	12,386	43,801	871,472	3,834,717	20
October 2005	20,624	68,566	1,037,937	5,483,918	15
November 2005	16,716	47,950	752,726	3,651,337	16
December 2005	16,764	58,040	767,002	4,604,073	13
January 2006	18,777	71,171	1,416,044	6,164,792	20
February 2006	18,827	69,268	1,131,619	5,297,039	16
March 2006	13,116	29,696	829,173	3,270,043	28
	269,577	**957,683**	**17,163,265**	**89,125,789**	**18**

Fig. 16: Visitors, visits, pages, hits and average pages per visit for the Scheme's websites between April 2004 and March 2006 (during August 2004, the web server was offline for urgent repairs).

Keyword phrase	Visits	Pages per visit
roman coins	7,819	7.19
portable antiquities scheme	3,743	4.73
portable antiquities	1,795	4.8
www.finds.org.uk	1,465	3.77
PAS	1,230	4.26
medieval coins	736	5.82
findsl	721	3.57
portable+antiquities+scheme	666	4.08
identifying roman coins	604	22.54
roman+coins	567	10.76
Antiquities	557	3.84
coin weights	520	1.42
identify roman coins	390	17.94
roman coin	384	4.56
roger bland	383	1.36
roman coin identification	365	21.47
crundale hoard museum	355	4.8
nummus	341	7.43

Fig. 17: Top search phrases that users have entered to discover www.finds.org.uk in the financial year 2006-2007 (These statistics are determined from log file analysis and Google Analytics software).

The average pages-per-visit (PPV) for website visits in the Cultural and Heritage web community is very hard to ascertain. There are no definitive collections of web statistics available for the cultural sector. The average visit to the Scheme's websites, when combined across all three available resources is approximately 18.2 ppv. The depth and range of information and the nature of what the website holds within its portals attracts a quality visit; the nature of the database means that users are retrieving a series of results and often page through these to find what they are after. However, many are frustrated by the complexity of the data that we have collated; an issue continually being addressed internally to make access simpler.

How do our audience find us?

How users of PAS data discover the database and its content is an area worthy of further discussion. This is far easier to accomplish now than it would have been a few years ago. A study of the top keywords that people have entered to discover the PAS websites has also highlighted how the content is now finding its way to the top of the most popular search engines. Figure 17 demonstrates the top search phrases entered to find PAS resources between 1 May 2006 and 31 April 2007. The consistently high ranking and ppv for phrases containing 'Roman coins' has been one very satisfying aspect of our content creation. The Scheme is now seen as an authoritative source for information relating to identification of Roman coins. As time progresses and more resources develop, the Scheme will climb rankings for other artefacts also. By using Google's Webmaster Tools software package, analysis can be made of search rankings for specific words that users have entered to discover the site. By careful manipulation, the important keywords associated with the PAS website, can be harnessed to increase visibility and increase visitors to the website and database.

The PAS has also been monitoring its position on various search engines. The most dominant search engine in the market place at present is Google. Figure 18 demonstrates several keywords and their relative position on Google as at 1 May 2007.

Search phrase	Position on Google
Roman coins	2 out of 1.56 million results
Antiquities	2 out of 6.64 million results
Medieval coins	2 out of 1.27 million results
Nummus	1 out of 70,100 results
Archaeological finds	1 out of 1.22 million results
Conservation advice	1 out of 4.68 million results

Figure 18: Phrase position on Google as at 1 May 2007.

It can therefore be demonstrated that all the website recommendations in the 2004 Hawkshead Review (Chitty and Edwards 2004) have been acted upon and even exceeded with regards to the development of resources and researching our audiences and users. The area in which the Scheme has perhaps made least progress with is the usability of the database, which is currently being addressed.

Social impact: are we in an Ivory Tower?

In 2004 and 2006, the Scheme's ICT Adviser conducted a piece of sociological research (Lewis 2007: 6) into the perceived social class of people recording with PAS. This utilised census data, plotted against postcodes collected from finders. After cleaning the data for valid postcodes, it was possible to plot the estimated class of the recorder and produce a figure that compared favourably against

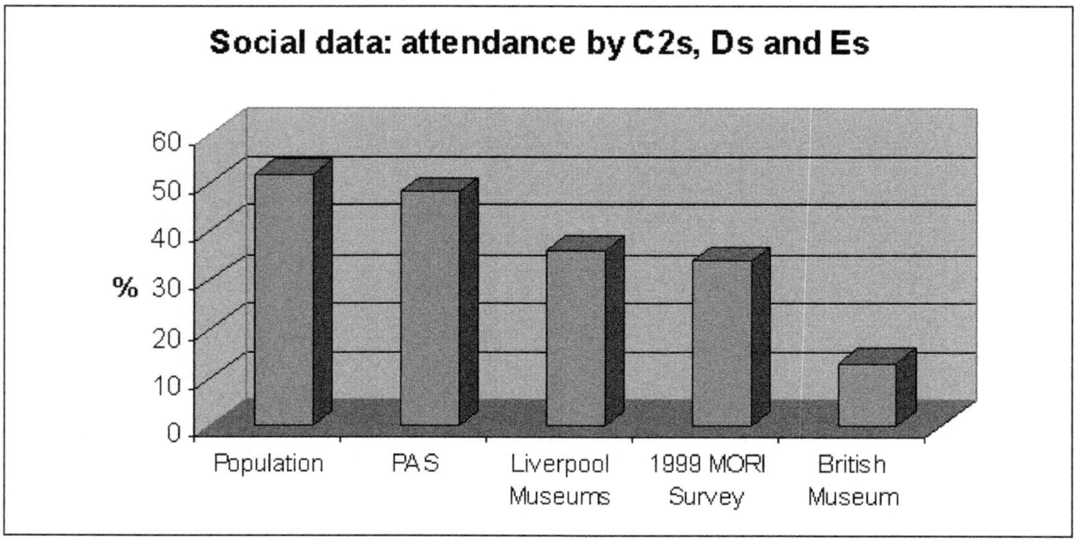

Fig. 19: Comparative analysis of PAS users against various institution and national data sets.

the museum sector and did not show much deviation between the two periods over which the test was conducted. This showed that over 48% of people recording with the PAS come from socio-economic groups C2, D & E, whereas 18% of the British Museum's visitors fall into that category. PAS may be based within an institution that appeals more to the higher social echelons, but it has a penetration into the community that provides a vital cog in the British Museum's 'Partnership UK programme', a principal component of the museum's 'Museum in Britain' section of its annual plan (Hancock 2006: 78, 89, 158-64, and further described by Orna-Ornstein 2010).

Does the Scheme have an International aspect?

Through an analysis of the web statistics, it can also be seen that the Scheme's website serves a wide audience base around the world, comparing well with other British Museum resources. However, it does cater for a majority audience in the United Kingdom, a reflection on the content of the site and the audience that PAS aspires to serve. Figure 19 shows geographical data taken from the 1 January 2007 until the 1 April 2007 and has been compiled from Google's Analytics software.

These figures are calculated by Google's server using a reverse DNS lookup function to approximate the geographical position of the visitor. It is by no means 100% accurate as some users sit behind proxy servers and deliberately conceal their location, others can disable the cookie (Kyrnin 2009) that is used to analyse data and lastly, JavaScript can be disabled to prevent all data collection (Wikipedia 2010).

Website statistical analysis is sometimes seen as an obscure and futile task; there are problems inherent in the collection of 'accurate' data. Kyrnin (2009) stated that 'lots of tools use IP address to assign visitor status, but when a customer is using an ISP such as AOL they are on a dynamic IP. This means that if they come to your site today on IP 'A', tomorrow they might come on IP 'B'. This would be tracked as 2 visitors each with 1 visit, even though it was really 1 visitor with 2 visits' (Kyrmin 2009). Therefore, however web statistics are collected there is always the caveat that they are never 100% accurate and should be just seen as an extrapolated measure.

Figure 20 demonstrates that the Scheme's core audience in comparison to other British Museum websites is very UK focused. Originally, the Scheme's web statistics submitted annually to the DCMS suggested that PAS had a very high proportion of American visitors, but this figure was skewed by a large proportion of users having America Online (AOL) as their Internet Service Provider. The original log file analyser placed these IP addresses into the USA block. This has now been rectified by the implementation of the new data analysis package described above.

In part, these figures are backed up by the range of queries and research requests that PAS receives from around the globe. It is a relatively easy measure to produce and has been touted frequently as one of the measures of success that the Scheme enjoys. However, what will stand the testament of time is the impact that the Scheme's data has on the academic output and lay research that is conducted throughout the world.

Website	UK visitors	USA visitors	China visitors
www.thebritishmuseum.ac.uk The British Museum	47.71	15.33	2.41
www.ancientcivilizations.co.uk Ancient Civilizations	10.82	51.49	<0.25
www.ancientegypt.co.uk Ancient Egypt	23.37	46.43	<0.51
www.pastexplorers.org.uk Past Explorers	78.45	8.11	0.00
www.finds.org.uk Portable Antiquities Scheme	72.64	12.70	0.00
www.mughalindia.co.uk Mughal India	19.90	51.50	0.00
www.earlyimperialchina.co.uk Early Imperial China	8.97	69.84	0.78
www.ancientgreece.co.uk Ancient Greece	29.28	55.06	<0.10
www.britishmuseum.co.uk The British Museum Shop	51.19	17.03	<1.00
www.mesopotamia.co.uk Mesopotamia	5.33	54.32	0.00
Means	34.78	34.18	<0.01

Fig. 20: Visitors by geographic region to various British Museum hosted websites.

What next for the Scheme's web presence?

The coming years will without doubt present the Scheme with a wide variety of challenges with regards to its web presence. These include:

- Keeping pace with increase in data warehousing. The Scheme has already upgraded its storage space twice
- Incorporating other organisation's data sets and presenting them in an accessible format
- Making best use of new innovative techniques developed by the Open Source community. For example, folksonomic tagging (Chan 2007) of objects could be incorporated
- Improving user interfaces to allow users to have the best experience possible
- Improving brand recognition in the research arena, the Scheme needs to make more people aware of these data and how they can make use of them
- Maintaining visibility within the 'search' engine world if the Scheme's technology and distinct URLs change
- Accessing funding streams to allow for redevelopment of our existing site when it reaches end of life

These are but a few of the possibilities ahead, but if the Scheme's web presence and technologies fail to evolve then its IT will fall behind and the use of these data will decline. More funding will allow for greater innovation, but that will always be difficult to access, especially in the current economic climate.

The 'Superhighway' - has it been reached or are we in a muddy rut?

Returning to Schadla-Hall's (1996) statement, when he published his article the majority of institutions had very little idea of what could be achieved by publishing their collections online. Museums and cultural institutions need to study in detail the reasons why they should put their information online, how they should do this, what they hope to gain and what will the end consumer gain from their output Without this research the end result will be poor and the Information Superhighway will have been misused.

The fact that many institutions were not ready for this transition is now changing very rapidly as the online community has shifted dramatically. It is now starting to mash-up data from disparate sources to provide powerful analysis tools that will eventually provide academics and public archaeologists with a very powerful set of tools. For example, one can now take data sources from different institution's websites and produce enhanced maps of the ancient world with prosographic data entwined with geographic information and related archaeological finds, such as the Barrington Atlas project at the University of North Carolina (UNC 2004).

A more holistic analysis can be achieved from the comforts of the researcher's home computer. Nirvana? Maybe, but what is really needed is a wider appreciation of what can be achieved by publishing these data in a format where they can be accessed, used, reused and disseminated to aid research.

Acknowledgements

Thanks are due to the staff of the PAS and the finders who have volunteered their finds for recording, and (as far as the old database is concerned) the technical skills of our supplier at Oxford ArchDigital. Without their efforts, the data would not exist.

Bibliography

Bell, T. W. 2003, Oxford ArchDigital: http://www.oxfordarchdigital.com [now unavailable]

Cassely, V. 1998, 'A database for recording archaeological finds' (unpublished MSc thesis, Birkbeck College, London).

Chan, S. 2007, 'Tagging and Searching – serendipity and museum collection databases', Museums and the Web 2007: the international conference for culture and heritage online: http://www.archimuse.com/mw2007/papers/chan/chan.html

Cool, H. 2001, 'The Iron Age and Roman finds in the Portable Antiquities database' in Chitty, G., Review of the Portable Antiquities Pilot Scheme (Hawkshead Archaeology and Conservation).

Chitty, G. 2001, Review of the Portable Antiquities Pilot Scheme (Hawkshead Archaeology and Conservation).

Chitty, G and Edwards, R. 2004, Review of the Portable Antiquities Scheme (Hawkshead Archaeology and Conservation): http://www.finds.org.uk/news/reviews/2004

Edwards, R. 2006, Portable Antiquities Scheme User Survey (Arboretum Archaeological Consultancy): http://www.finds.org.uk/news/reviews/2006

Guest, P. J and Wells, N. 2007, Iron Age and Roman Coins from Wales (Moneta 66, Wetteren).

Guest, P. J and Wells, N. 2007, 'Iron Age and Roman Coins from Wales': http://ads.ahds.ac.uk/catalogue/resources.html?iarcw_bcs_2007

Hancock, Z.. 2006, The British Museum Plan 2006–2007 (British Museum, London).

Kyrnin, J. 2009, What Web Analytics Can be Tracked: An Overview of Metrics That Can Be Tracked: http://webdesign.about.com/od/analytics/a/what_can_track.htm

Lewis, M. (ed.) 2003, Portable Antiquities Scheme Annual Report 2001/02-2002/03 (Resource, London).

Lewis, M. (ed.) 2004, Portable Antiquities Scheme Annual Report 2003/04 (MLA, London).

Lewis, M. (ed.) 2005, Portable Antiquities Scheme Annual Report 2004/05 (MLA, London).

Lewis, M. (ed.) 2006, The Portable Antiquities Scheme – sharing knowledge about the past (MLA, London).

Lewis, M. (ed.) 2007, Portable Antiquities Scheme Annual Report 2006 (British Museum, London).

Naylor, J and Richards, J. D. 2006, Viking and Anglo-Saxon Landscape and Economy: http://ww.york.ac.uk/depts/arch/vasle/vasleoverview.html

Orna-Ornstein, J. 2010, 'Partnership UK': http://www.britishmuseum.org/the_museum/museum_in_the_uk/partnership_uk.aspx

Pett, D. E. J. 2006, 'Promoting best practice through open access', British Archaeology, March/April 2006, 35.

Porter, M. 'The Porter Stemming Algorithm': http://tartarus.org/~martin/PorterStemmer

Reece, R. 2002, The Coinage of Roman Britain (Tempus, Stroud).

Schadla-Hall, T. 1996, 'What are we groping for?', MDA Information, 2. 4.

University of North Carolina (UNC). 2004, Barrington Atlas of the Greek and Roman World [online],Chapel Hill, North Carolina: http://www.unc.edu/awmc/batlas.html

Wikipedia Google Analytics: http://en.wikipedia.org/wiki/Google_Analytics.

The Portable Antiquities Scheme: the contribution of lithics and lithic scatters

Clive Jonathon Bond

The Portable Antiquities Scheme (PAS) is well known for recording metal artefacts but through field-walking and chance discovery ceramic and lithic artefacts, including stone tools, cores and waste have also been reported. Lithics, mostly in flint or chert, represent a small proportion of the artefacts recorded on the PAS database. These artefacts are the result of prehistoric knapping episodes, mostly discarded during the Mesolithic to Bronze Age. This paper will review the quality and quantity of this data set and assess its research potential. Patterns on the national characteristic of this data will be discussed. The contribution of lithics can be argued to enable the reconstruction of the prehistoric landscapes: peopled places over generations.

Since the introduction of the PAS in 1997, lithics have been recorded by its Finds Liaison Officers (FLOs) with varying quantities, with the largest number of records in 2005 (2,474) and the least in 1996 (6). The PAS is important as it provides a critical resource for understanding change in prehistoric settlement patterns, particularly since the last Ice Age, *c.* 10,000 to *c.* 700 BC. This paper presents a preliminary analysis of the quality and quantity of this lithic data set. Its research potential is highlighted. Only broad trends, compositional and spatial patterns will be reviewed across England and Wales. Further regional analyses will emerge later but are beyond this study.

Importantly, it is argued that the PAS record of lithics and lithic scatters (places where one finds lithic artefacts often brought to the surface by the plough) are important for two key reasons:

- Lithic artefacts represent the result of past individual and group actions, from deep time, for example, from *c.* 500,000 years ago in the Lower Palaeolithic, to the Later Bronze Age, dating to *c.* 1000-700 BC. Each flake, core or tool is an indication of a person working an object and utilising it, then perhaps discarding it once the job is finished. Human agency is at the centre – a very human connection with the past.

- People made these stone artefacts, used, modified and discarded them. In so doing through working stone (mostly flint and chert), these communities left a very tangible trace, a means of understanding changes in land use, people movement and perception in the British regional prehistoric landscapes.

Thus, whether field-walking, metal-detecting or gardening, people in the present can come into close contact with this distant prehistoric world by picking up a flint flake from the ploughsoil. The thousands of lithics recorded on the PAS's database represent communities walking their familiar landscapes, but coming into contact with their past community's landscapes. These were places of work, life and death.

This paper will discuss the following two key aspects:

- Approach: lithics and lithic scatters.
- Lithics: a national overview.

Approach: lithics and lithic scatters

Two elements are important in understanding the contribution of the PAS lithics and lithic scatters. Both cover the importance of systematically recovering artefacts, mapping them accurately spatially and also recording artefacts and their attributes.

Lithic scatters

What are lithic scatters? A short answer is, these are relic features in our regional landscapes; settings where prehistoric people lived, worked, ate, slept and died.

Over the past twenty years research into how lithic scatters – sites come about and what they meant in terms of past human activity has developed. These places represent a particular type of site or 'archaeological record.' They may be indicative of prehistoric settlement areas or places where people extracted stone raw material for working. Initially research focused on how to record artefact 'scatters', including lithic scatters disturbed from their original archaeological context by natural processes (English Heritage 2000: 2; Haselgrove *et al* 1985). This extended into understanding how such sites are created by modern ploughing (Clark and Schofield 1991; Schofield 1991). More recently research has focused on what they may have meant in prehistory, such as the remains of mobile communities (Bond 2004a; b; 2007a; b; 2009a; b; c; forthcoming; Edmonds 1995; Edmonds *et al* 1999; Schofield 1994; 1995; 2000). Essentially, as stone tools were made at a point in a landscape; for example, at a short-term camp on a sand island in the

Somerset Levels, a momentary stop on a river valley terrace or during a foray in the uplands, debris from flaking flint or chert (and other stone) would be discarded. The un-worked raw material lump, or 'core' would be flaked and in addition to the finished 'tool' different types of 'waste' would be discarded and left as a signature of that knapping event. These places represent our main source of evidence for prehistoric activity from the Lower Palaeolithic to the later Bronze Age periods.

Lithics

These lithic artefacts can be classified broadly into three (Fig. 1):

- Retouched forms ('tools').
- Cores (the block from which the tool was made).
- Waste (flakes, blades, chips, etc).

A methodology adopted by the PAS in recording lithics has varied, from recording in detail every lithic artefact provided for identification to recording total assemblages. Individual artefacts, small (<50 artefacts) and large assemblages (>50 artefacts) have been submitted for recording to FLOs. For example, finders may report a single flake, multiple artefacts with a few finely flaked, retouched artefacts such as arrowheads, scrapers or even an earlier Neolithic flint axe. However, less common is a substantial assemblage of several thousand lithics. This bias towards 'small' and 'very small assemblages (<49 artefacts)' was observed in the English Heritage survey of lithic scatter records (Schofield 2000: 50). This indicates a similar phenomenon in collector behaviour within the four sample area of that survey and across England. Importantly, it also suggests all lithic records are significant, no matter how many artefacts are recorded - this point will be returned to later.

The approach adopted by the PAS is reflected in the FLO training programme provided by the author. This provides a framework in which to record and understand all 'lithic scatters'. Advice on lithic artefact identification, recording and analysis has also been circulated (Bond 2004c), synthesising other artefact guides and a range of regional reports on period technology and typology.

A consistent approach towards lithic artefacts and lithic scatters data has been adopted which emphasised the context of artefact recovery and different levels of recording and analysis (Fig. 1). Lithics are considered a product (and by-product, if waste), of the prehistoric flaking process often referred to as the reduction process or 'chaîne opératoire' (Andrefsky 1998: 37; Inizan *et al* 1992: 12). The process referred to records from the beginning to the end of artefact production; from stone raw material nodule, to flaking, reducing the core, to waste, to create a tool. Thus, these three simple categories enable the categorising of any assemblage quickly into: cores, waste and retouched forms, each representing different stages in the manufacture process.

The attributes of lithic artefacts have also been recorded. There are four principal areas for artefact observation, worth considering when identifying lithic artefacts:

- Raw Material (the stone type, its origin, did it travel far to the site where the finder recovered it? Was it procured at distance, or, for example, selected from river gravel flint pebbles down-stream?).
- Condition (the state of preservation; discolouration or treatment of the artefact: patina; burnt; rolled in the ploughsoil).
- Technology (how was it made – by flaking a nodule to make an axe [a core-tool] or by flaking a core to make flakes and blades?).
- Typology (how may it be viewed in a cultural sequence – is it diagnostic of the early or later Mesolithic, earlier Neolithic or Beaker periods; is it characteristically a regional type? For example, a set microlith or scraper form can be highly significant, ascribing this artefact to a specific period or cultural affinity).

Lithic recording and analysis

Lithic artefacts can be analysed as single artefacts, or part of an assemblage. Both approaches are combined in the recording system utilised by the PAS. Critically, rather than simply focusing on the traditional typology and technology, the size and shape of the tools and waste are important, enabling the FLO to ascribe a period range to an artefact and assemblage. This overcomes a traditionally perceived weakness of lithics as a class of artefact; often, only up to 5% of an assemblage may be classified as a stone tool and this, traditionally was the only element that was dated by typology. The radiocarbon dating of typologically discrete lithics from excavated contexts (for example, Clark and Higgs 1960) could occur, but in this way, more than *c*. 95% of a surface derived lithic assemblage was determined as not datable.

A traditional approach to artefact studies, focusing on individual typologies is unhelpful and reductive. In the case of lithics, particularly those derived from lithic scatters, this must be combined with consideration of attributes derived from assemblages. Actually it has been demonstrated that retouched forms ('tools') also relate to a change in flaking technology, from blade to flake production within the British Holocene (Ford *et al* 1984; Pitts 1978; Pitts and Jacobi 1979). Therefore, individual lithic artefacts, including for example, flakes may or may not reflect this global change in lithic industries. Importantly, however, this change does demonstrate that retouched artefacts are not independent of their parent assemblages; the type of waste; technology, shape and size, reflects a changing pattern in flaking technology operating over thousands of years. Therefore, analysis of the total assemblage, making observations on typology, technology and metrics (measurements on size and shape) provides a means of dating broadly lithics artefacts as part of assemblages. This is particularly significant as

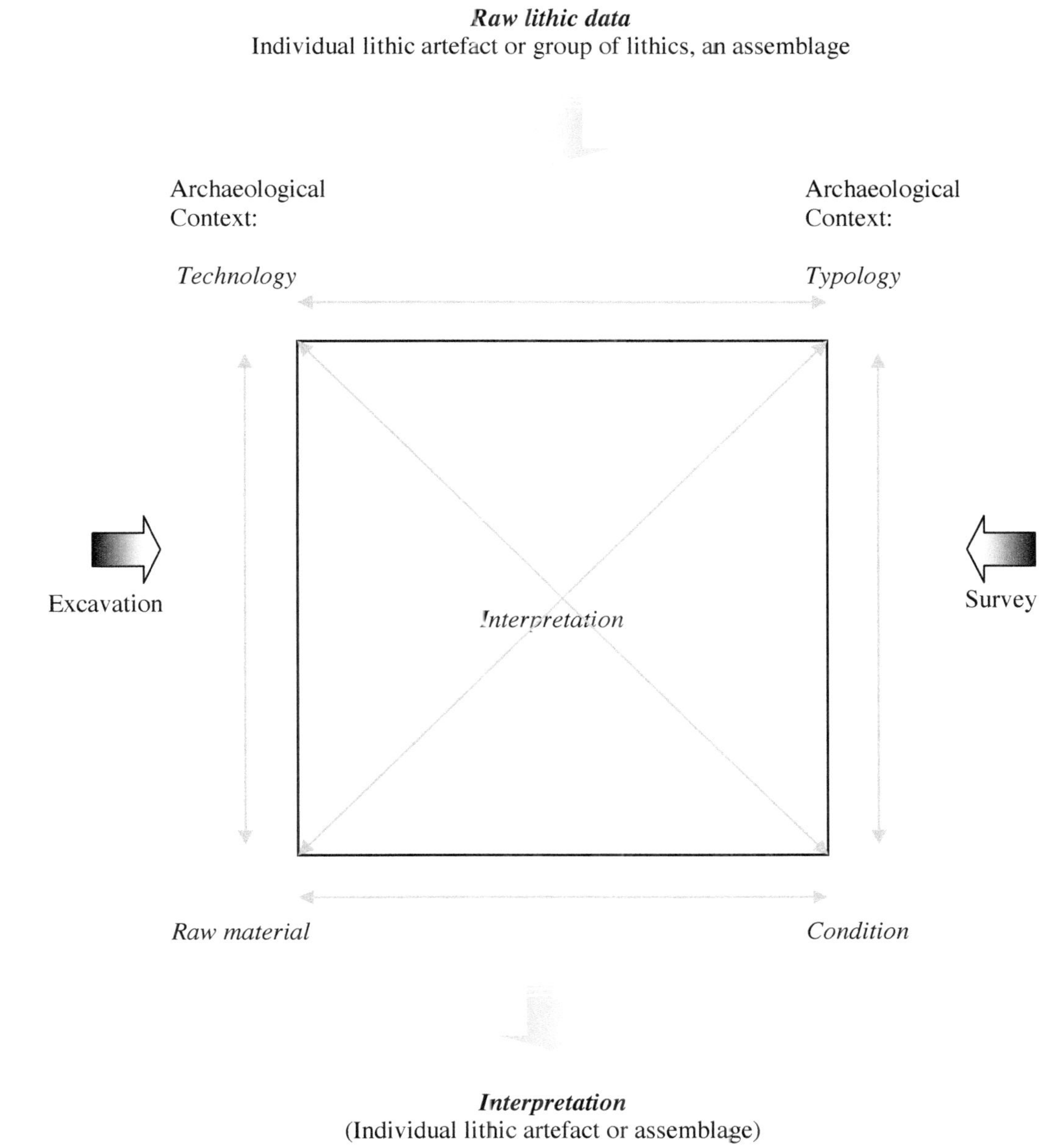

Feedback, direction of interpretive action, around the four principal areas for artefact observations: Technology, Typology, Raw material, Condition

Outcomes:

- Identification of an individual lithic artefact as a Core, Waste or a Retouched form
- Identification of raw material
- Note on condition of the lithic artefact
- Recording of technological attributes per lithic artefact.

Fig. 1: Identification and recording of lithics: an interpretative square, placing the analytical process within a taphomic context and archaeological practice (after Bond 2006: fig. 3.6).

lithics derived from unstratified contexts can thus be dated relative to known long-term technological changes. This approach can be termed a 'whole assemblage' approach (Gardiner and Shennan 1985: 66). It enables the broad dating of any lithics assemblage and many case studies have utilised this approach, enabling broad groupings of lithic artefacts to be attributed to period ranges. These groupings of lithics within period ranges have enabled archaeologists to phase human settlement across sampled transects of a regional landscape. For example, groups may consist of lithic artefacts attributed to the Mesolithic, earlier Neolithic and/or later Neolithic and/or earlier Bronze Age (Ford 1987a; b; Gardiner and Shennan 1985; Healy 1991; Richards 1978; 1990;

Waddington 1999; Woodward 1991). By approaching lithic recording in this way, the Scheme's lithic-based records present an opportunity to understand not just the artefact, but also the place. Lithic records can be regarded as proxy data for human activity; long-term trends in regional settlement patterning. This last and important point raises the high potential for what has been traditionally viewed as a damaged archaeology; with poor research potential (Lisk et al 1998; Schofield 1995). By the near nationwide coverage and same approach to recording artefacts, the PAS provides the first means of obtaining proxy data on regional and national scale on changing prehistoric settlement patterns. This can contribute to other objectives, such as the realising of the variable prehistoric character of the English regional landscapes (Roberts and Wrathmell 2000; 2002).

Lithics: a national overview

The PAS is the first project to provide data on artefact and site assemblages, utilising a uniform recording methodology across England and Wales. Data on lithic records was extracted from the PAS database in October 2006 to April 2007 (the former was the time of initial analysis; the latter was the date of the conference). This research represents a preliminary analysis and interpretation of that data set. This data will be discussed below, analysed at a national level and compared with preliminary results from an English Heritage pilot study on stray finds and lithic scatters (Schofield 1993; 1994; 1995; 2000). Both projects present systematic, different, but comparable methodologies for assessing the significance of lithic artefact and lithic scatter data across the landscape. The result of the English Heritage project was to review lithic data across four counties: Oxfordshire, West Yorkshire, Cornwall and Buckinghamshire (Schofield and Humble 1995). This pilot then prompted the publication of new guidance for this category of site (English Heritage 2000).

The PAS database

The PAS database can enable artefact records to be reviewed in a number of ways including by findspot; finder; county and period. In this research records were reviewed by geographical area and recording areas. The latter refers to the way the staffing of the Scheme cover counties and unitary authorities. There were 34 recording areas over England and Wales covered by 40 FLOs. The approach adopted here will focus on geographical areas, so to emphasise the spatial distribution of artefacts within the landscape.

A quick evaluation of lithic records demonstrated that in most geographical areas lithics were recorded, 45/48 (Fig. 2) from Palaeolithic to Bronze Age. Other periods were also covered including the rare, Iron Age material, perhaps artefacts indicating the presence of late flaking traditions (cf. Young and Humphrey 1999) and the early modern, represented by the presence of gunflints. In October 2006 there were 167,591 records on the PAS database. Of this total lithics-related records accounted for 7,696, some 4.59%. It is important to note, that from October 2006 to April 2007 the total of lithic records increased to 9,550; a c. 20% increase. These 9,550 records represented at that time, 5.37% of the total records in the database (177,557). The total for artefacts recorded by the Scheme more recently has been set at 338,000 (in early 2008). Of this total number of artefacts, some 25,305, or 7.4% equate to lithics (note: lithics-related records may describe more than one artefact).

The largest number of lithic records per geographical area came from Wales, with 2,237 records and 10,941 lithic artefacts. Within Wales, the highest numbers came from Swansea yielding 1,086 records and 6,455 artefacts. In recent years there has been a growth of interest in field-walking within Wales, much of this work has also involved the deployment of projects supported by CADW, the national museum and hosted by regional curatorial agencies and units. In the wake of the English Heritage survey on lithic scatters and stray finds, these projects have sought to investigate and enhance the records of settlements, both in the coastal and interior regions (Cambria 2004; Locock 2000; 2002a; b; Silvester and Owen 2002; Smith 2000; 2005). Many of these projects have engaged with local communities (for example, a survey at Cowbridge in the Vale of Glamorgan in Couper 2005), providing opportunities for amateurs to learn about artefact identification, systematic fieldwalking and the area's landscape history. Officers from the National Museum Wales (Elizabeth Walker) and the PAS (Mark Lodwick) have facilitated these projects. The net result has been to boost lithic records.

This type of cross-agency and amateur engagement can be demonstrated by a few cases. The peak in lithic records from Swansea can in the greater part be said to relate to a prolific fieldwalker, Ron Sanders and his fieldwalking in the years 2002, 2003 and 2005. He has field-walked in the parish of Port Eymon and also the coastal areas of Gowerton. Rod Couper, also a skilled fieldwalker, who marshalled friends and other members of the community, has walked significant parts of the Vale of Glamorgan, but also in Cardiff, Newport and Monmouthshire. Mark Lodwick supported this work. recording artefact scatters using a GPS (Global Positioning System) device (Couper 2005: 87). Another long-term and dedicated collector, who recovered lithics over 25 years of working for the Forestry Commission is Phil Shepherd (Hobbs 2003: 100, figs. 69-72). In Rhondda Cyon Taff and in the parishes of Trearchy, Rhigos and Treherbert his chance finds have recovered rare later Mesolithic scalene triangle type microliths. These small artefacts are difficult to see when walking, they are diagnostic of later Mesolithic hunting forays (or at least preparation for hunts).

These examples demonstrate local traditions of field-walking, access to ploughed land and the knock-on effect of PAS and other linked initiatives have provided some spectacular results. Even the lowest values, from Gwynedd (3 records, each a Neolithic artefact, all from three separate areas) are of interest. Gwynedd has been the subject of the North-West Wales Lithic Scatter Project (Smith 2000, 2005). The rareness of lithics on the

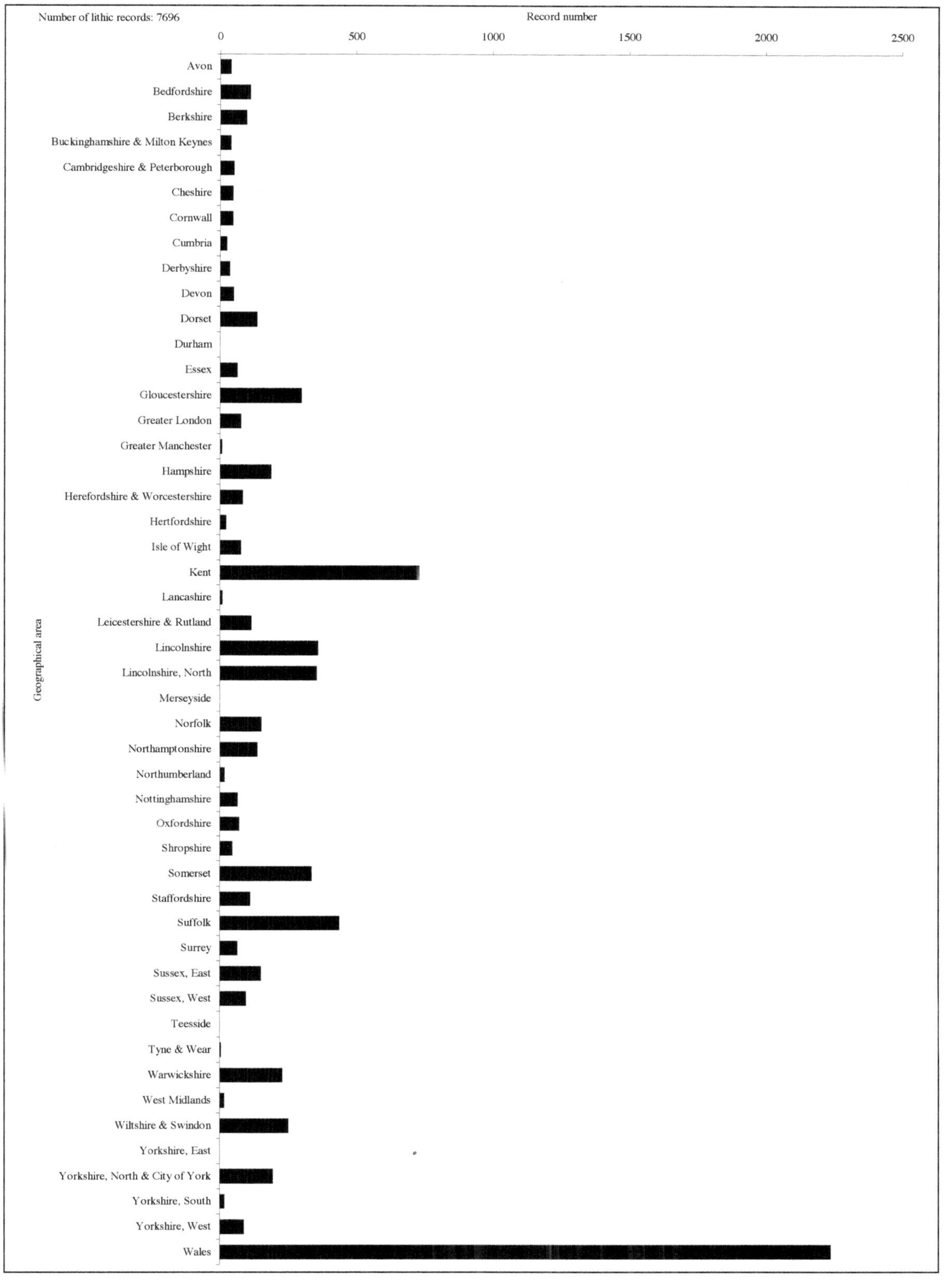

Fig. 2: Lithic records by geographical area.

Historic Environment Record highlighted the need to investigate the potential for the recovery of inland and lowland sites, and hence enhance that record in detecting prehistoric settlement, which prompted the project.

There were only a small number of known sites; 340 lithic findspots, consisting of 126 flint or chert artefacts (Smith 2005: 39). The results of field and monument visits, trial site evaluation and surface collection, indicated that often a low density of lithics existed at sites, assemblages recovered were predominately small (Smith 2005: 52). Hence, even if only a single flake is recovered, as noted for the three records for Gwynedd on the PAS database, these artefacts may represent a low density scatter. These records are important and may be typical, since they may embody all that can be expected to be achieved from a momentary glance, a single walk across a field. However, with more structured fieldwork targeted at these locations with a consideration of the localised landscape, a new, but low density lithic scatter characteristic of the area can be discovered.

Lithic-related records on the PAS database across England consist of tens, or a couple of hundred records per geographical area (Fig. 2). The arithmetic average value for records across England is 116, with a middle value, the median set at 68. But, there are also geographical areas that exceed these values: Kent (728), Suffolk (435), Lincolnshire (358), North Lincolnshire (353), Somerset (334) and Gloucestershire (297). In Kent a group of amateur field-walkers have walked fields across many parishes, generating a corpus of lithic records. Similarly, in Suffolk local people, working with Suffolk County archaeologists have recorded new lithic scatter sites, some as chance finds others as field-walked assemblages. In Breckland, particularly the area on and adjacent the Fen-edge there has historically been a strong tradition of local collecting (Healy 1996). This tradition has been revitalised by strategic field survey, guided by the county Historic Environment Record Officer (Colin Pendleton), in co-operation with the Forestry Commission. As trees are cropped new openings appear in the woodland and these are checked, recorded, with the deployment of a dedicated field survey technique completed substantially by a skilled amateur team (Brooker 2006). This data is mapping afresh this otherwise wooded and not accessible landscape, adding to the findings of recent rapid surveys (Sussams 1996).

In Lincolnshire field-walking across ploughed land has created the majority of lithic records, demonstrating the keen eye and interest of field-walkers. In North Lincolnshire, both field-walking and metal-detecting have been equally used. A project, hosted by the North Lincolnshire Museum, Scunthorpe, has systematically surveyed fields across selected parishes and has been successful in recovering lithic scatters with the recovery also of rare later Bronze Age or early Iron Age artefacts at selected lithic scatters (Kevin Leahy, pers. comm). Also of significance is Bill Bee's contribution. He has diligently walked and re-walked over many years recording lithic scatters, but most importantly has identified previously unknown Lower Palaeolithic sites. These have yielding pointed and ovate handaxes in the Lymn Valley (Bee 2001) and at other sites, for example: Salmonby Carr, on the River Witham; Thimbleby on the Bain, a tributary of the River Witham; Laughterton near the Trent River and Osbournby on sand and gravels, south of Sleaford (Bee 2005).

The relationship between lithic records and the number of total records on the Scheme's database is worthy of consideration (Fig. 3). The highest proportion of lithic records to total records is from Wales. Strategic initiatives and recent field-work may well be the reason for this peak. The majority of geographical areas indicate between 5-10%, as a maximum value. However, West Yorkshire (17.1%), Gloucestershire (15.5%) and Berkshire (14.3%) are significantly higher. A complex suite of causal factors may have created these higher values. Perhaps each area has a strong tradition of field-walking or local communities are more active and more aware of how to identify lithics when field-walking. In Berkshire, particularly on the Downs, the Kennett and Upper Thames, areas have been subject to systematic survey and research projects (Ford 1987a; b; Gaffiney and Tingle 1989). Indeed, more ploughed land available to survey may be a factor, versus pasture. This may or may not be a factor affecting lithic visibility and the volume of records per geographical area.

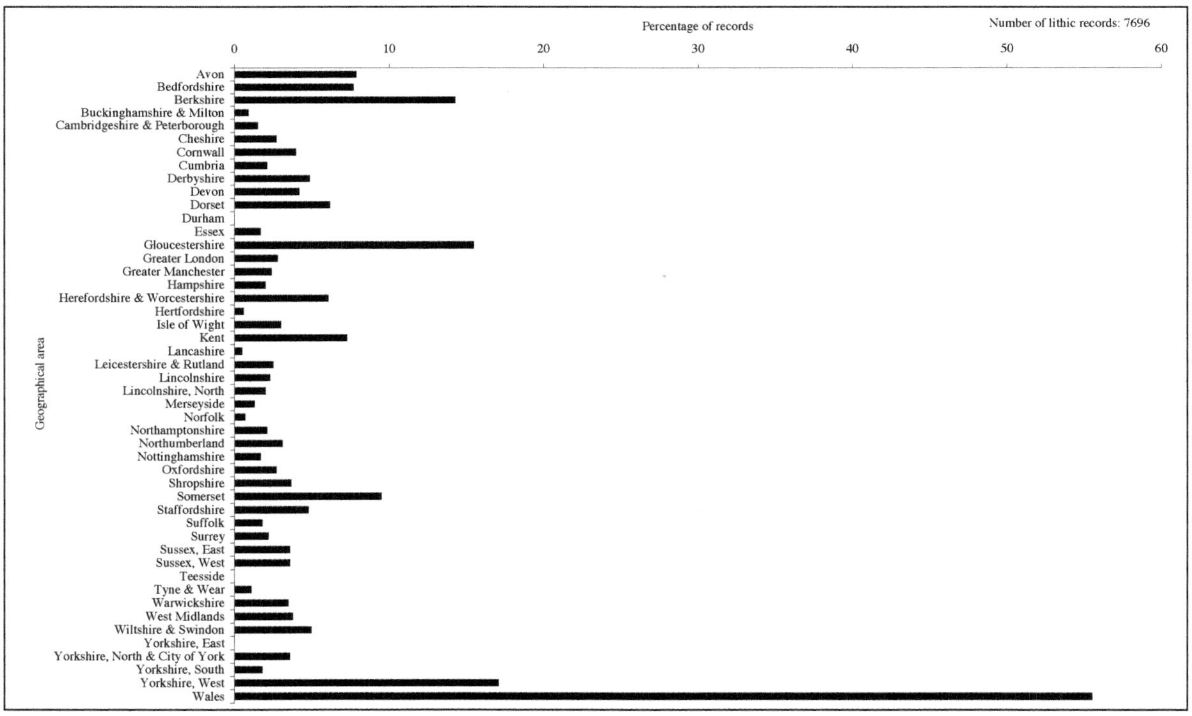

Fig. 3: Lithic records by geographical area, as expressed as a percentage of total records.

A closer look at some of the variables recorded on the lithic records in these areas can demonstrate the complex causes at play affecting the circumstance of discovery. In West Yorkshire the PAS database indicates some 74/86, or 86.04% records suggest field-walking, but this covers ploughed land and grassland or heathland (36/86, 41.86%). Thus, although ploughed fields are available, perhaps the more common leisure activity of walking the pasture and upland landscape has yielded lithics. In Gloucestershire ploughed land accounts for 279/297 records, or 93.93%. Here there is also a high degree of field-walking accorded to find recovery: 182/297, or 61.27%. This may point towards field-work completed off the Costwold plateau, away from the well known pasture areas. This traditional land use for the area (grassland or heathland) provided only three records. Interestingly, a significant proportion of lithics are recorded as chance find during metal-detecting: 71/297, or 23.90%. This is encouraging, implying metal-detectorists are active in recording the total landscape history, not simply focusing on metal objects. For Berkshire, surprisingly, much of the records come from urban areas. Indeed, the discovery of lithics in garden beds is well represented with 77/95, or 81.05%. Chance finds are noted in twelve records, but field-walking only in two.

Often the lithic element of the PAS data set appears slight; some may suggest these records are of little relevance as it is assumed they only represent single artefacts of dubious in-field provenance. This can be viewed as a misconception of the quality of this data which mostly have an accurate spatial provenance. Only 926 out of the total of 7,696 of lithic records, or 12.03%, have no National Grid Reference. Most of these records are from old collections discovered before the Scheme was in place. Thus, 6,770 or 87.96% of records have National Grid References. Most are high resolution: records with 6-figure grid references equate to 83.26% (4,869 records); 8-figure grid references equate to 93.13% (7,168 records); 10-figure grid references equate to 6.64% (527 records).

In total 25,305 lithic artefacts are encompassed within the 7,696 lithics-based records. As with the number of records, Wales covers the greatest number of artefacts at 10,941 or 43.23%. Elsewhere most geographical areas yielded between 50 to a few hundred lithics. But there are also higher values in some areas, exceeding hundreds to thousands: Gloucestershire (3,538), Suffolk (1,922), North Yorkshire and the City of York (951), Kent (864), Lincolnshire (826), Somerset (668) and Warwickshire (631). While it is true that most records represent a single artefact - over *c*. 80% (see Fig. 9), more subtle patterns exist. The application of simple statistical tests, assessing the mean, median and mode values for records indicate a different pattern (Fig. 4). The arithmetic mean value for each geographical area shows a high incidence of values above 1.00: 40 out of the 48 geographical areas, or 83.33%. From this sum, at the top is Gloucestershire (11.90), then the West Midlands (10.42), followed by Avon (7.72). All illustrate the recovery of small assemblages, but all commonly with more than single finds. Four geographical areas provide mean values of 4.00-5.00 (Wales, Yorkshire, North Yorkshire and the City of York, Suffolk, Surrey). Moreover, a further twelve areas yielded mean values between 2.00 and 3.00.

The mode value, the most frequently occurring in the series, clearly matches the presumed assumption that one lithic artefact is most common (Fig. 4). The median value also indicates the individual artefact count. The single exception to this is Gloucestershire where not only is it the highest mean value in the data set, but also it records the only median value of 2. This data can be interpreted to suggest that whilst individual lithic artefacts are most commonly recorded, the data set is not indicating single artefacts as the predominant type of record. Actually, lithics are commonly recovered by finders as numerous artefacts. Therefore, these records illustrate the recording of lithic scatters; locations with more than one artefact (Schofield 1993: 4; 1994: 92). This point to the fact that however recovered - field-walking, chance finds or whilst metal-detecting - the lithic records tend to suggest the presence of lithic scatters, rather than single chance discard. This raises the research potential of each lithic record. As most records tend to be recorded with a high resolution provenance, no matter how poor and non-systematic the field method for recording was, it would theoretically be possible to return to that findspot. That is, these lithic records provide a means of re-assessing otherwise ignored and assumedly poor archaeological data. It is argued here that these lithic records can provide proxy information on the location and character of lithic scatters. If this is the case, then such sites may be returned to and more systematic field survey, perhaps in partnership with curatorial or academic archaeologists. This data set represents thousands of new settlement locales, covering a number of periods across England and Wales!

The importance of lithic records as part of the PAS data set is illustrated by reviewing the composition of the prehistoric material culture data set (Fig. 5). In April 2007 prehistoric material culture represented 9.44% of the total data set (16,825 out of 177,557 records). At that time, from the total of 16,825 prehistoric records lithics accounted for 9,550 or 56.76%. Copper-alloy, mostly of earlier to later Bronze Age objects, constituted the second largest count (4,875 records or 2.74%). Once again, such values emphasise the importance of this at first sight seemingly marginal proportion of the database. Lithics as a proportion of the total database records represents between 9.44% and of the prehistoric material recorded, 5.37%. Granted, this is only a snap-shot in time but, importantly, these percentages of records represent a significant corpus of data currently untapped by researchers.

Geographical Area	*Lithic Finds Recorded*	*Mean*	*Median*	*Mode*
Avon	286	7.72	1	1
Bedfordshire	331	3.03	1	1
Berkshire	157	1.65	1	1
Buckinghamshire & Milton Keynes	42	1.13	1	1
Cambridgeshire & Peterborough	84	1.71	1	1
Cheshire	63	1.40	1	1
Cornwall	45	1.00	1	1
Cumbria	42	1.82	1	1
Derbyshire	92	2.70	1	1
Devon	58	1.23	1	1
Dorset	239	1.78	1	1
Durham	0	_	_	_
Essex	130	2.13	1	1
Gloucestershire	3538	11.90	2	1
Greater London	80	1.08	1	1
Greater Manchester	4	1.00	1	1
Hampshire	276	1.48	1	1
Herefordshire & Worcestershire	129	1.59	1	1
Hertfordshire	47	2.23	1	1
Isle of Wight	76	1.02	1	1
Kent	864	1.18	1	1
Lancashire	7	1.00	1	1
Leicestershire & Rutland	132	1.15	1	1
Lincolnshire	826	2.30	1	1
Lincolnshire, North	359	1.01	1	1
Merseyside	1	1.00	1	1
Norfolk	212	1.41	1	1
Northamptonshire	147	1.08	1	1
Northumberland	33	2.20	1	1
Nottinghamshire	78	1.23	1	1
Oxfordshire	85	1.25	1	1
Shropshire	131	2.98	1	1
Somerset	668	2.00	1	1
Staffordshire	219	2.00	1	1
Suffolk	1922	4.41	1	1
Surrey	249	4.01	1	1
Sussex, East	254	1.70	1	1
Sussex, West	208	2.21	1	1
Teesside	0	_	_	_
Tyne & Wear	2	1.00	1	1
Warwickshire	631	2.77	1	1
West Midlands	146	10.42	1	1
Wiltshire & Swindon	302	1.20	1	1
Yorkshire, East	0	_	_	_
Yorkshire, North & City of York	951	4.95	1	1
Yorkshire, South	26	1.73	1	1
Yorkshire, West	192	2.23	1	1
Wales	10941	4.89	1	1
Total	25305			

Fig. 4: Number of lithic finds recorded by geographical area.

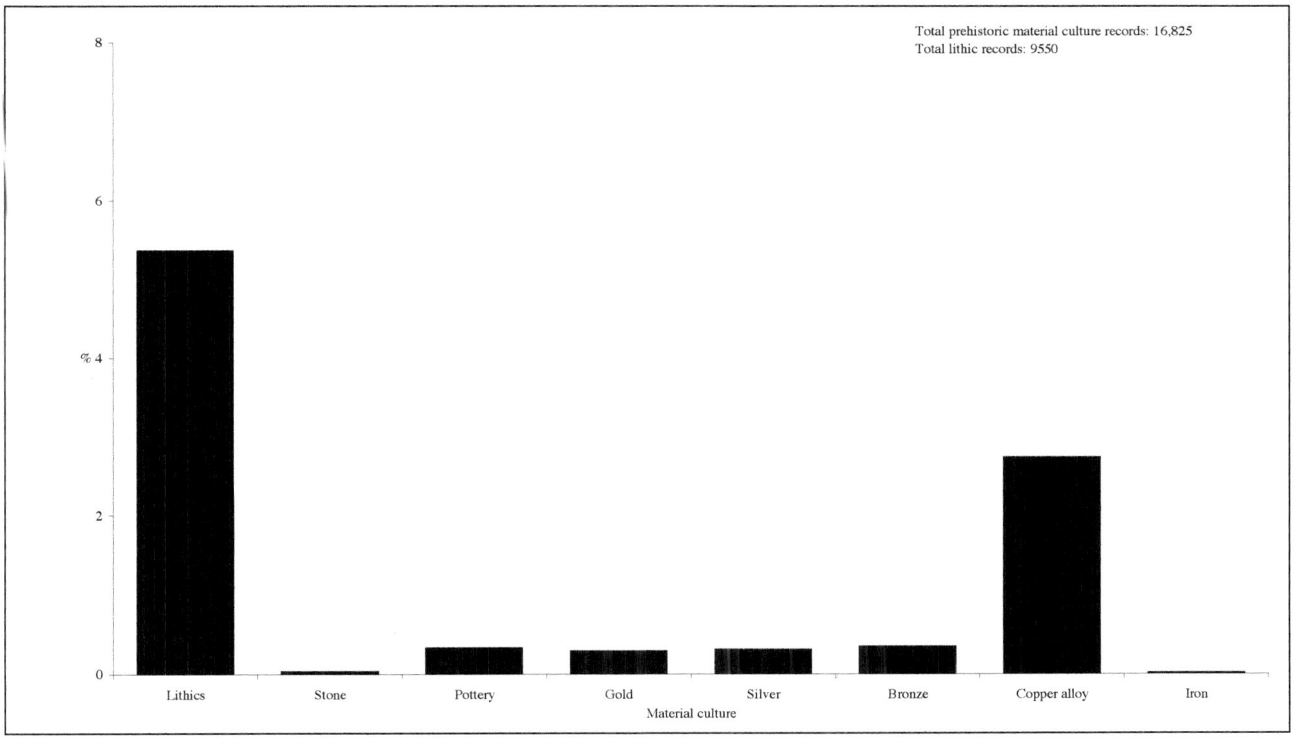

Fig. 5: Total prehistoric material culture within the PAS database.

Comparative Data: English Heritage's Surface Lithic Scatters and Stray Finds Project

A comparative pilot project to evaluate the lithic scatter and stray find resource was completed by English Heritage in 1993-6 (Schofield 1993; 1994; 2000) to evaluate lithic-based records in four sample areas: Buckinghamshire, Cornwall, Oxfordshire and West Yorkshire (Schofield and Humble 1997). In total 2,946 records of lithic scatters were recovered and 1,738 records of stray finds. This data is comparable to the PAS data in two ways: it covered geographical areas (post-1974 government reorganisation) and centred on lithic-based records. A fundamental difference between the two data sets is that the English Heritage project was centred on Historic Environmental Records, with no actual analyses of lithic assemblages (Schofield 1993). A high value of 'unknown' periods in this data may account for the limited quality of records, not actually indicating the lithics are actually of unknown date (Last, pers. comm.). However, comparison between the two data sets is instructive. Both data sets can provide an insight into the qualitative and quantitative record of lithics, one at a nationwide level, the second at a sampled regional level.

The patterning in the aggregate data set across England and the four sampled areas are of interest. Comparing 'lithic scatters' (the English Heritage project) with 'lithic records' that may or may not be 'scatters' by period can act as a cross-check on the quality of this data (Fig. 6). Contrasting both data sets five points emerge:

- Both data sets have similar quantities of Palaeolithic lithics.
- There are also similar proportions of Mesolithic and Neolithic lithics.
- It is noticeable that the PAS records represent between 5 to 10% higher than the English Heritage data.
- There are markedly lower values for Bronze Age lithics in the Portable Antiquities records (c.5%, compared to 15%).
- In the English Heritage data set undated lithics approach c.28%, whereas in the Portable Antiquities data this equates to c.6%. This, as stated above, may relate to the more accurate and quality information provided from analyses of lithic artefacts, as opposed to information from secondary source records.

The strong patterning, between Palaeolithic, Mesolithic and Neolithic values may indicate a shared trend validating the quality of the PAS data set. This trend is perhaps reflecting a real historic presence in the landscape. However, in these periods diagnostic artefacts are perhaps also easier to spot. The separation between the contrasting data sets with the Bronze Age values may denote the limited diagnostic artefacts of that period (or assignment of others to a transitional Neolithic category, for example, that commonly used are the later Neolithic and Beaker groupings). Certainly, the low number of undated records in the PAS data is encouraging. This may illustrate the success of the Scheme's staff and volunteers in identifying chronologically diagnostic artefacts. However, it is more likely that artefacts in the regional records examined by the English Heritage project attributed higher proportions to generic prehistoric dates, with few artefacts indicating typologically and chronologically discrete activity. The 'undated' category is perhaps best interpreted as the mismatch in recording and identifying chronologically diagnostic artefacts.

Further comparison between the two data sets on the presence/absence of certain periods in multiperiod lithic scatters is instructive. A divergence between the two data sets is observed (Fig. 7). Three points emerge:

- Both data sets show a high 'unknown' value (all within *c.* 10% in each category, save that of the 'single' category).
- Single period scatters are much fewer in the PAS data, which may be a reflection on better chronological/typological recording, or at least different recording methods to those surveyed in the English Heritage data set.
- Two and three periods within one lithic scatter/lithic record are higher in the PAS data set by as much as 15%.

The last point is important. Contrasting both data sets it suggests that most lithic scatters/records do demonstrate that more than one period of activity is present at a single location. However, the high in 'unknown' values shared between both data sets also implies that there are a high proportion of records where this presence has not been systematically or fully validated. Clearly, the ability to observe whether a lithic scatter was utilised across periods depends on the presence of typologically and chronologically diagnostic lithics. It is also most probable that the ability to assign waste to set periods, utilising metric approaches on representative samples of any lithic industry (Pitts 1978; Pitts and Jacobi 1979) has not consistently been attempted in the English Heritage data. Many field-workers continue to focus solely on typology for dating surface derived assemblages, rather than following the 'whole assemblage' approach (Gardiner and Shennan 1985: 66). The historic records on lithic scatters studied by the English Heritage project can therefore be assumed to underestimate the actual presence and complexity of phasing. The higher percentage of 'single' period lithic scatters may denote an over emphasis on recording set types of artefact, assigning the scatter to a single period. The overall variation in percentages between categories, PAS versus English Heritage data may also be explained by this bias.

Lithic scatters, as analysed here (Fig. 7), also fit with lithic analyses elsewhere (Bond 2004a; b; 2007a; Ford 1987a; b; Gaffiney and Tingle 1989; Healy 1991; Richards 1978; 1990; Tingle 1991; 1998; Waddington 1999; Woodward 1991) and represent palimpsest activity. Lithic artefacts may have been discarded over days, weeks, months, years, or over hundreds, or thousands of years. It appears that past people revisited the same parts or adjacent places over generations. It has been observed that this activity appears to have changed the size of a lithic scatter which can be seen to contrast in the later Mesolithic to earlier Neolithic and in the later Neolithic to Bronze Age (Edmonds 1995; 1997; Pollard 1998; 1999). Little research has been completed on the actual phasing at such palimpsests. The author's research in Somerset has demonstrated that it is common for two to three periods of activity denoted by the presence of particular lithic artefacts, although more rarely four or more periods are traced in a single lithic scatter (Bond 2006: chapter 8; 2009c). This scheduling of activity may or may not be regionally sensitive. What can be stated is that lithic artefacts are also highly likely to represent activities of re-use within each period. Models and theories on prehistoric settlement more recently have emphasised movement, seasonality and variation in the duration of stays at one locale (Bond 2004a; b; 2007a; b; 2009a; b; c; Bond forthcoming; Edmonds 1997; Whittle 1990; 1997).

Moving from the global comparisons to regional data, the PAS data is important potentially as a means to infer new lithic scatters. The PAS lithic records taken from the sample areas covered by the English Heritage survey may well represent new sites, after that project ended (1996). In the four sample areas of the English Heritage project sizable increases in lithic scatter records are observed: Oxfordshire (503 lithic scatters, increased by 68 or 13.51%); West Yorkshire (948 lithic scatters, increased by 86 or 9.07%); Cornwall (1,173 lithic scatters, increased by 45 or 3.83%); Buckinghamshire (with Milton Keynes: 322 lithic scatters, increased by 37 or 11.49%).

The PAS data: detecting bias?

Contrasting the English Heritage and PAS data sets has risen both similar and different patterning (see Figs. 6-7). Divergent themes have emerged, mostly centred on the differing ways primary and secondary data was recorded from lithic assemblages in the four areas sampled. This need not stem from variation in the quality and reliability of the data. There is little evidence to indicate that the PAS lithic data is of a relatively poorer value. In order to explore bias in this data set, the artefact assemblage representation, quantity of artefacts present, the method of discovery and the land use are analysed below.

Some may consider that what these lithic records represent may be biased towards 'pretty' pieces or more elaborately worked artefacts, rather than representing a sample of the total composition of lithic artefacts present in the ploughed soil. Luckily this type of collection bias can be detected by the weighting of different components of any assemblage, whether it is the composition of newly recorded artefacts from a field-survey or old collections in museums (Gardiner 1987). If finders have little time, or are attracted by more obviously flaked pieces, the assemblage would be biased towards retouched forms ('tools'). An idealised lithic assemblage as a 'balance' would represent this component in less than c.5% of the total assemblage. Therefore, over representation on a record by record basis, or across the total PAS data set would denote a heavily biased collection strategy, and not indicate the actual presence of artefact types at the site. Lithic record composition is presented in Figure 8.

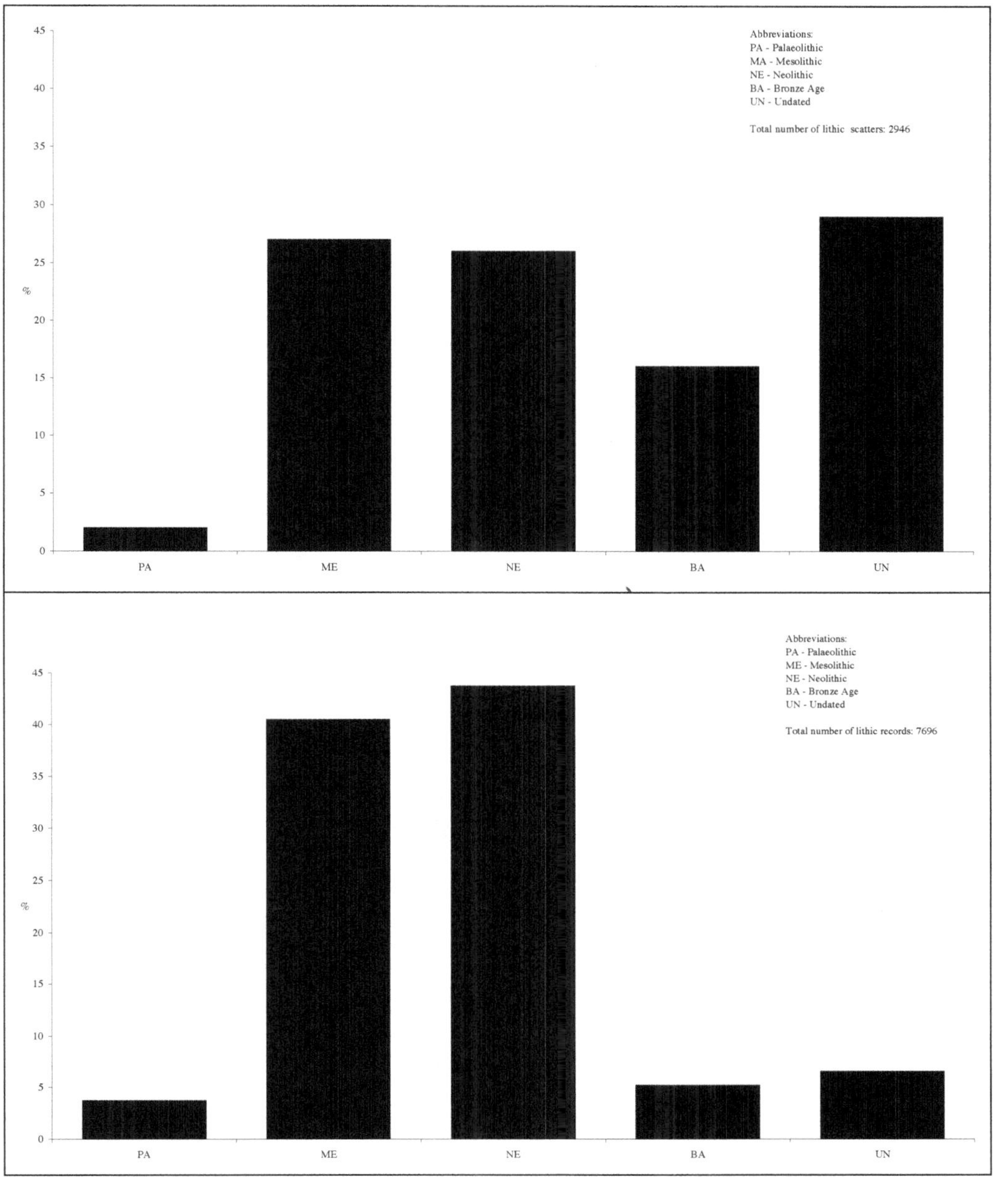

Fig. 6: Lithic Scatters/Records by period. Top: bar chart of scatters arranged by period (after Schofield 2000: fig. 5.2, top). Bottom: bar chart of lithic records arranged by period (PAS database).

From the graph (Fig. 8) four points emerge:

- Most lithic artefacts that are Palaeolithic consist of cores and waste, probably mostly of late Upper Palaeolithic flake/blade material, rather than core-tools such as the rarer pointed and ovate handaxes of the Lower and Middle Palaeolithic.
- Proportions of Mesolithic artefact types are equal, perhaps indicating over representation of cores and retouched forms which are both larger and diagnostic retouched artefacts.
- Proportions for the Neolithic may also indicate a rather skewed pattern with an emphasis on cores and retouched forms.
- Proportions for the Bronze Age are overrepresented, perhaps showing the identification of cores, core/lumps, the commonly occurring 'crudely' worked nodules. It may be that selected retouched forms (for example, arrowheads, scrapers and other flaked 'tools' are recorded in the Neolithic data set). The less diagnostic retouched forms of the middle to later Bronze Age appear not to have been recorded.

Overall a broadly 'normal' pattern is illustrated, with at least proportions of cores, waste and retouched forms present across all periods. Is the composition biased? Yes, to some degree an emphasis on cores and retouched artefacts are more easily identifiable. Critically, elements of the total lithic assemblage are reported: core (the beginning), waste (the middle) and retouched forms (the product). The relative presence of different parts of the flaking process is more problematic.

It would only be possible to make an independent check on artefact representation within the ploughsoil and

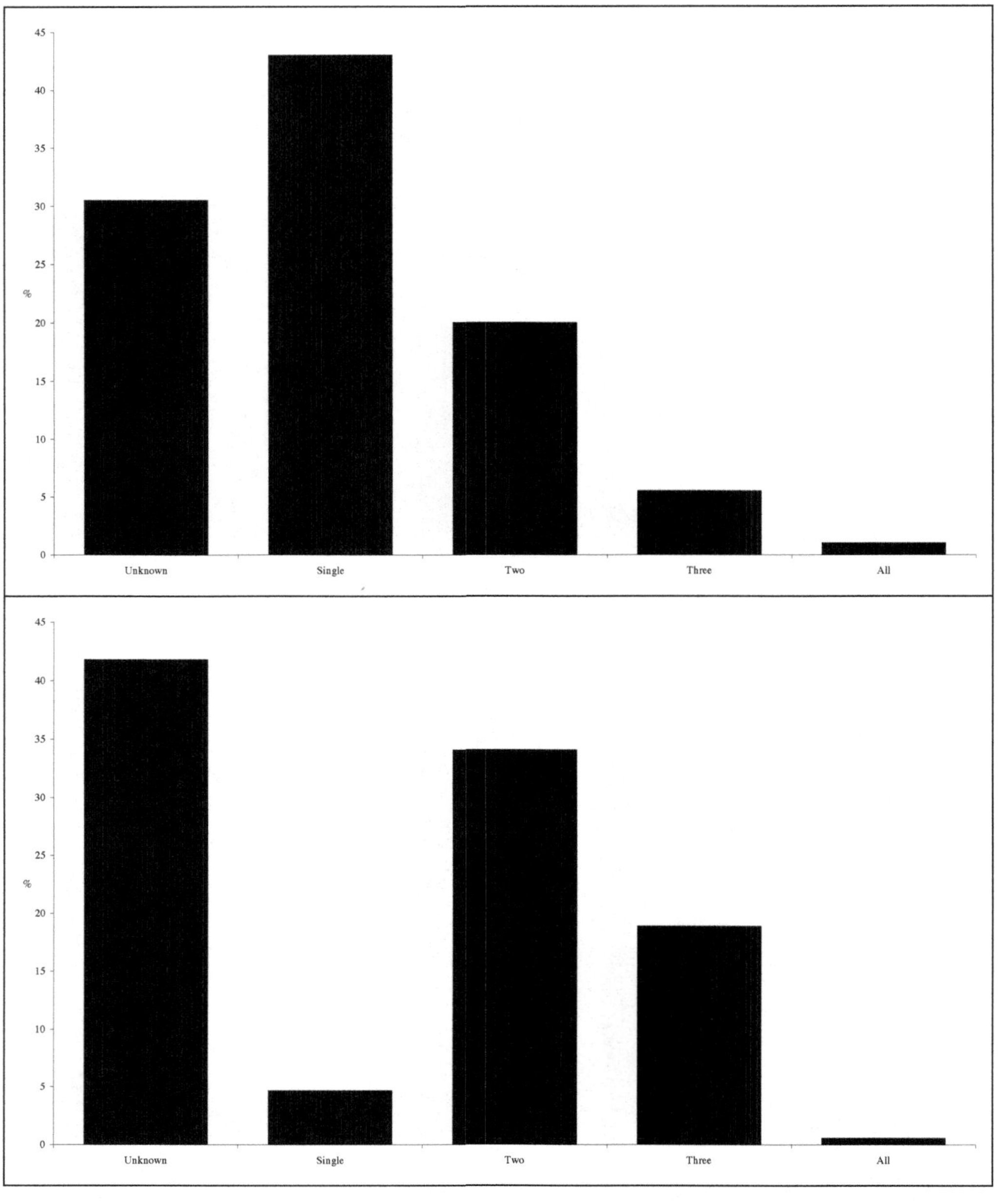

Fig. 7: Multi-period scatters/records by number of periods represented. Top: bar chart of multi-period scatters in which the number refers to the number of these periods represented in multi-period scatters (after Schofield 2000: fig. 5.2, bottom). Bottom: bar chart of lithic records arranged showing the number of periods represented in records that are multi-period (PAS database).

recovered assemblages if fields containing lithic scatters were revisited and re-walked. Such an approach emphasises the incomplete but full research potential of each lithic record. What is demonstrated by this data set is a proxy indicator of the artefacts present at any individual lithic scatter. More precise in-field recording methods have been utilised and those artefacts recorded by the PAS (cf. Coupe 2005); these cases should be assumed to be uncommon. The quality of the survey, the method used, coverage, timing in the field, weather conditions when collecting and knowledge of the walker may all affect the reliability of the artefact sample (Gerrard et al. 2007). It is acknowledged here there is a limit to what extent this type of record can provide a representative sample of lithic artefacts from the plough-soil and this type of question is arguably beyond the scope of the PAS. However, this record still has archaeological value at the local, regional and national level: proxy data is recorded on lithics and lithic scatters from locations equating to the presence of prehistoric people in previously unknown sites.

As mentioned above, most lithic records represent a single artefact. This global patterning is illustrated in Figure 9. Four points are raised by this graph:

- Single lithic artefacts represent the highest proportion of lithic records (over *c.* 80%).
- The second highest lithic records consist of between two to five artefacts (*c.* 9%).
- Lithic records may represent more than one artefact with principally between 2-100 artefacts (see details in Fig. 4).
- Larger scatters do exist (consisting of *c.* 100-*c.* 500 artefacts), but are few and therefore not shown on this graph.

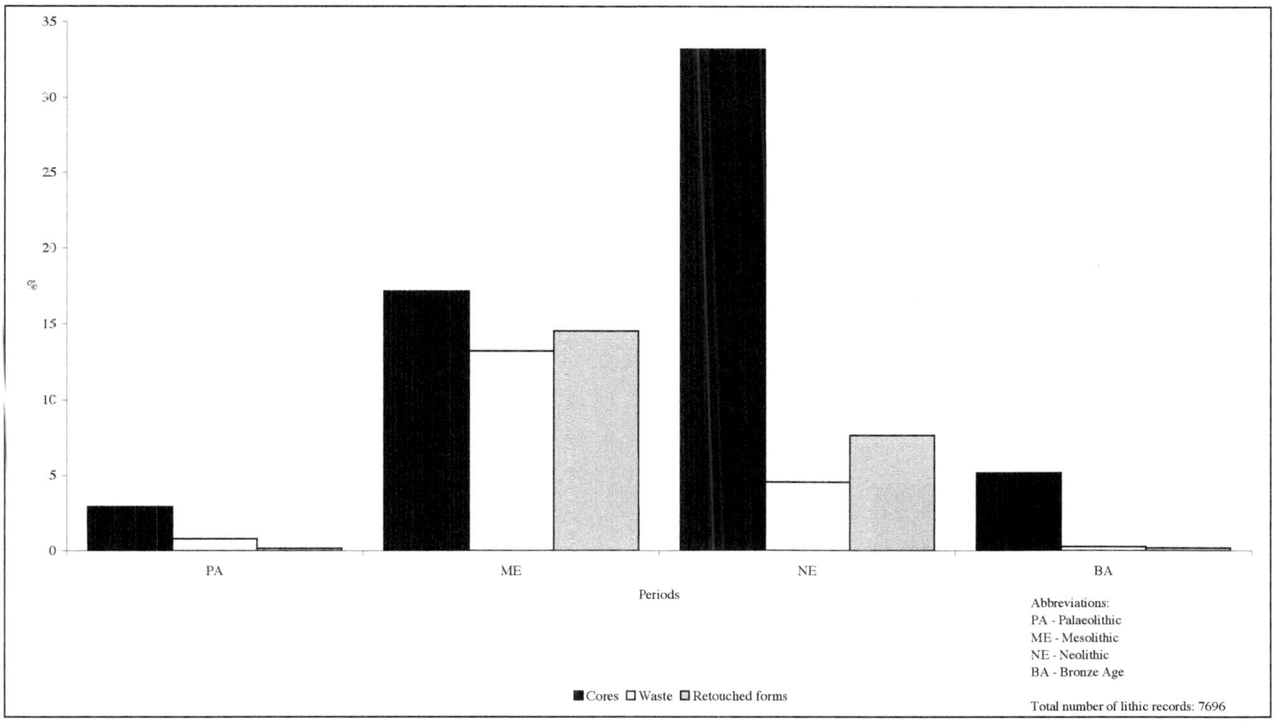

Fig. 8: Technological composition of lithic records (PAS database).

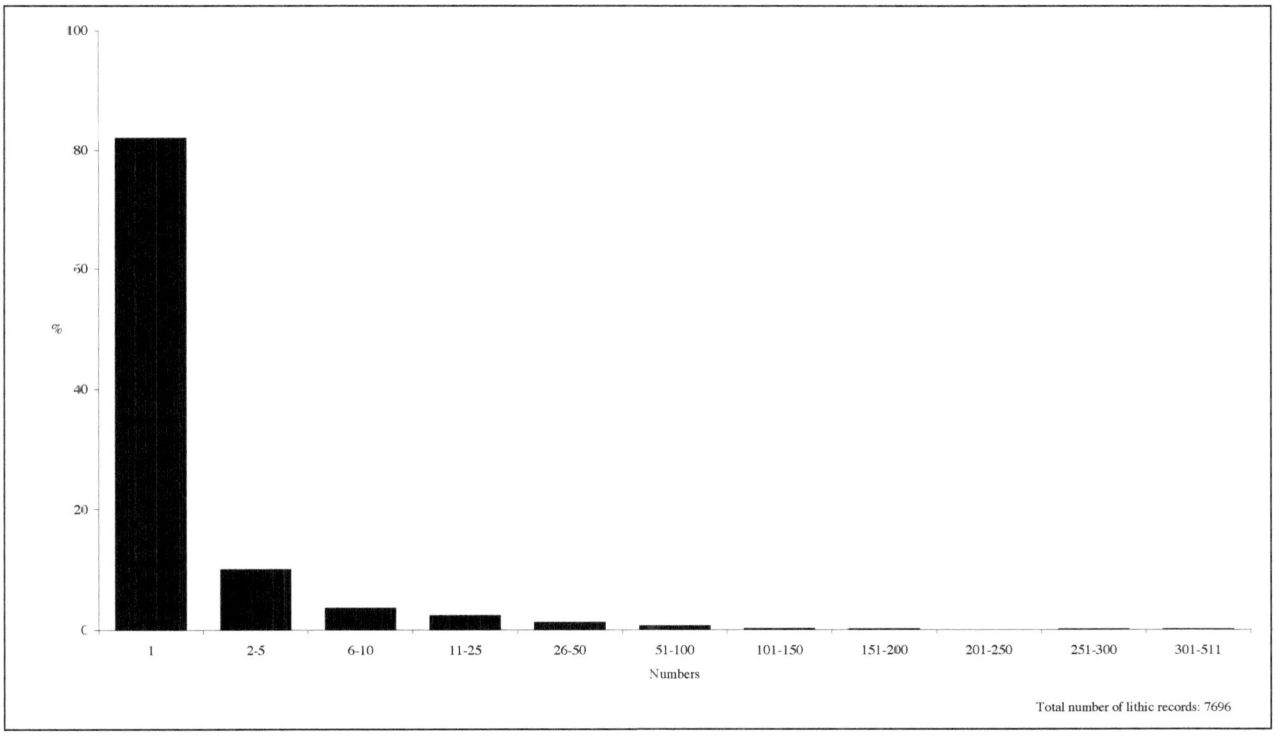

Fig. 9: Number of artefacts per lithic record (PAS database).

The method of discovery, if known, is recorded on the database record (Fig. 10). Three points are raised by this graph:

- Field-walking is the highest proportion of the data set (nearly *c.* 50%).
- Metal-detecting is second highest (nearly *c.* 38%).
- The gardening and 'unknown' categories record similar proportions (less than 5%). Both may relate to ad-hoc discoveries, whilst in the garden, unplanned, but recorded and taken to a FLO for novelty value.

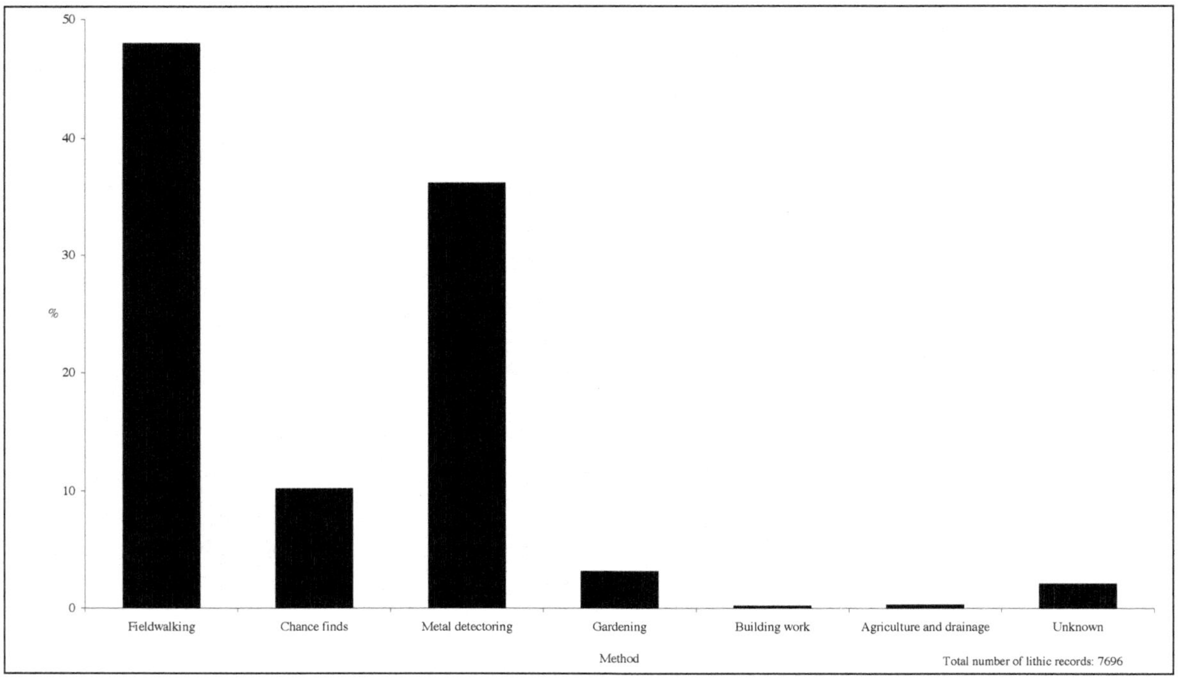

Fig. 10: Lithic records per method of discovery (PAS database).

Field-walking covers both non-systematic and systematic methods. Essentially, at the least an attempt is made to walk a field by the finder and plot accurately using National Grid References the location of the artefacts recovered. This information is then provided to the FLO, where he or she may choose to interview the finder to recover more detail of the findspot. The emphasis on metal-detecting is interesting. This may flag up a change of 'culture' as metal-detector users gain a broader interest in the prehistoric landscape and material culture, beyond a stereotypical emphasis solely on 'treasure hunting'. In line with recent accounts (Hobbs 2003), metal-detectorists appear able and willing to recover all periods and types of artefacts. This has been one critic of the Scheme's data; an assumed bias in representation. In recent years more inclusive field research projects have included metal-detecting, and the win-win strategy of using this as a dedicated technique along with systematic field-walking, may be viewed as paying off. The location of lithics can relate to contemporary or later activities, including the intentional deposition of bronze, copper alloy, gold or iron objects (for example see Healy 1991; 1996). The relationship between lithic and non-lithic data may prove fruitful in future analyses: the spatial and compositional analyses of pottery, metal chance finds and hoards. This poses a potential new regional and national research theme, rather than focusing on single artefact classes or materials. Chance finds represent less than 10% of the PAS lithic records data set. This proportion may mostly relate to ad-hoc visits, the results of afternoon walks, and such like. Once again, with such little emphasis on chance discovery, this implies that lithic records are the result of intentional recovery, mostly by field-walking and metal-detecting. That is, they form part of an intentional strategy by the finder to recover this class of artefact, either as part of the recovery of other artefacts, such as metal objects or singularly. Collecting lithics may therefore be a more common pastime than some may think. In this way lithics represent an untapped resource for both creating records and deploying keen, skilled labour to complete local field survey.

Land use has been discussed above regarding selected geographical areas. The overall pattern in lithic records and land use emphasises cultivated land (Fig. 11). The two other peaks, gardening and the 'unknown' category just below and above c. 10% in each case may simply represent rare discoveries in the garden or elsewhere (see above).

Beyond regional comments, little has been stated of the significance of any spatial patterning. The PAS lithic data has been mapped England and Wales (Fig. 12). Clearly, the importance of the British Isles varies, depending on the presence of ice and the coastline, both elements that had substantial impacts on Palaeolithic to Mesolithic/earlier Neolithic activity.

The Palaeolithic distribution (Fig. 12, top left) maps mostly a southern, central and eastern distribution. For the Lower Palaeolithic (Wymer 1999) and later periods, for example the late Upper Palaeolithic (Jacobi 1991; 1997) and Final Upper Palaeolithic (Barton 1999), river gravels and valley locations have been viewed as important foci. Other global distributions centre on limestone areas, where well known cave sequences are recorded: the Mendip Hills, Somerset, and Creswell Craggs, Derbyshire (Bonsall 1977). Interestingly, the Welsh sites are hardy mapped, save a single site in the Gower region. The difficulty of recovering lithic scatters from pasture landscapes, uplands and coastal sites may have played a part in restricting this distribution. The lack of Palaeolithic activity in the northern English counties may well represent a real historic patterning, denoting the extent of succeeding glacial sheets impacting on the limits of occupation.

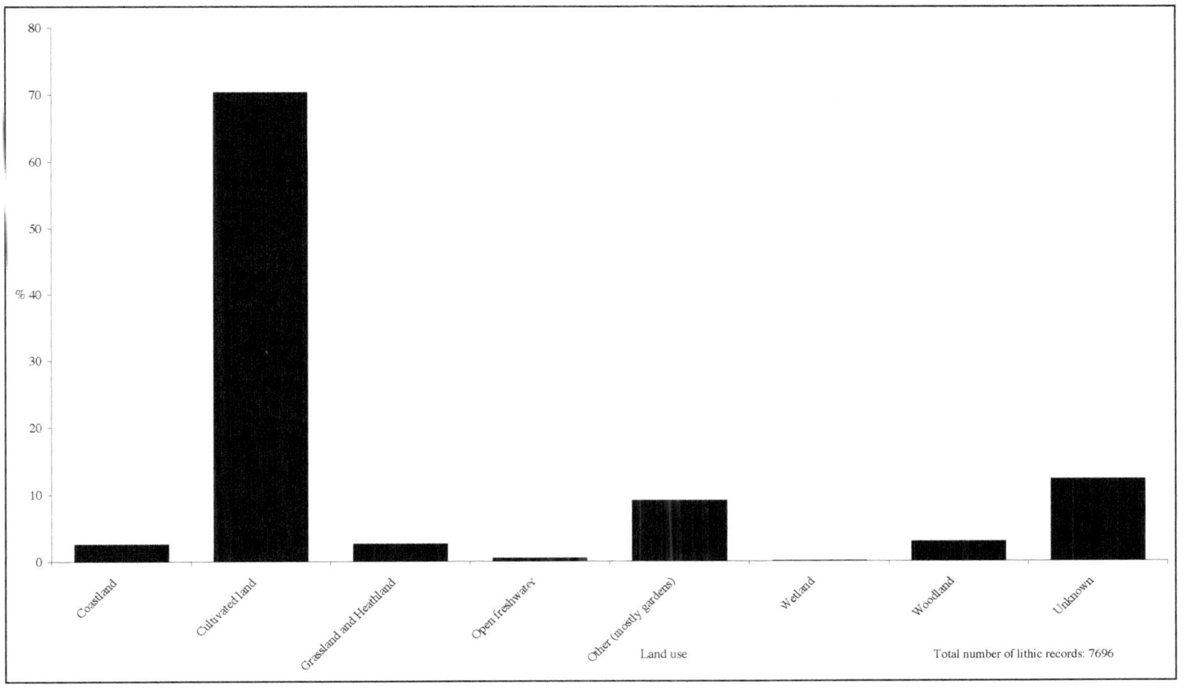

Fig. 11: Lithic records per land use (PAS database).

Lithic records are centred on river-gravels, but also coastal areas, well known for yielding Palaeolithic sites East Anglia (Wymer 1985), the Thames Valley (Wymer 1968), the Solent and Hampshire rivers (Hosfield, 1999) and the Severn and Avon rivers (Lacaille 1954). Few inland locations are mapped and no records south of Mendip. What is highly significant is the distribution of sites away from the known cave sites; open-sites are becoming more apparent (for example, see Scott-Jackson 2000). Most lithic records consist of single or small numbers of artefacts. Given the large scale land changes that have occurred since these artefacts were discarded by hominids; long-term erosion processes, the emphasis of such finds, in private gravel extraction quarries, where earlier river terraces are exposed, it is not surprising that these records are limited and discrete in distribution.

The Mesolithic distribution (Fig. 12, top right) maps, as expected, a much broader distribution compared to that of the Palaeolithic. Traditionally the sites have been interpreted nationally as predominately divided in two: inland and river-based sites are assumed to be dominated by early Mesolithic camps of varied duration. Alternatively, the coastal distribution is regarded as predominately later Mesolithic in date (Palmer 1977; Wymer 1991). The contribution of Phil Shepherd in south-east Wales is registered. Well known locations for recording include the South-East and the Weald (Mellars and Haynes 1986), East Anglia, south-west Wales and the South-West, with sites in the interior of Devon and the coastal Cornwall. A particularly interesting distribution is the recovery of Mesolithic lithic records across the midlands, previously very much a backwater in such studies. Quantities of artefacts are attested per record. But, as with the Palaeolithic record single records with Mesolithic artefacts are very important to opening out, exploring hunter-gatherer lifeways across the landscape, from coast, to river valley and upland.

The Neolithic distribution (Fig. 12, bottom left) maps the denser suite of records across England and Wales but may also impart mirror the previous Mesolithic distribution (at least for the later Mesolithic sites). These lithic records are mostly likely to record transitional assemblage, Mesolithic to earlier Neolithic, often being recorded as discrete patches in the field and the larger later Neolithic, Beaker to earlier Bronze Age assemblages (Edmonds 1995; 1997). Most areas are mapped, save the Welsh interior, only providing a few findspots (this may indicate the lack of field-work as is also the case for the upland landscapes of the northern English counties and South-West). Most records yield quantities of lithics which undoubtedly overlap in space and composition with the Mesolithic records.

The Bronze Age distribution (Fig. 12, bottom right) maps a less broad and dense pattern, compared to the Neolithic. Some degree of spatial and chronological overlap is to be expected, as with the later Neolithic, Beaker and earlier to middle Bronze Age assemblages. Concentrations occur in the East Anglian Fen-edge and Breckland (Healy 1995; 1996; 1998). Other areas, more rarely explored are mapped here – for example the Midlands interior and the claylands of Leicestershire (Clay 1989). But, whether the actual distribution represents less activity, fewer sites than the Neolithic is questionable. If compared to Wessex and the chalkland surveys; generally dating to the post-earlier to middle Neolithic, lithic scatters are seen to increase in size and number of artefacts well into the middle Bronze Age (Gingell 1992; Richards 1990; Woodward 1991). The weakness in this observation is that outside the Wessex chalklands or selected parts of East Anglia where field surveys have been completed, very little information is available. So, it is difficult to assess whether this tend occurs across England and Wales or is actually more regionally unique.

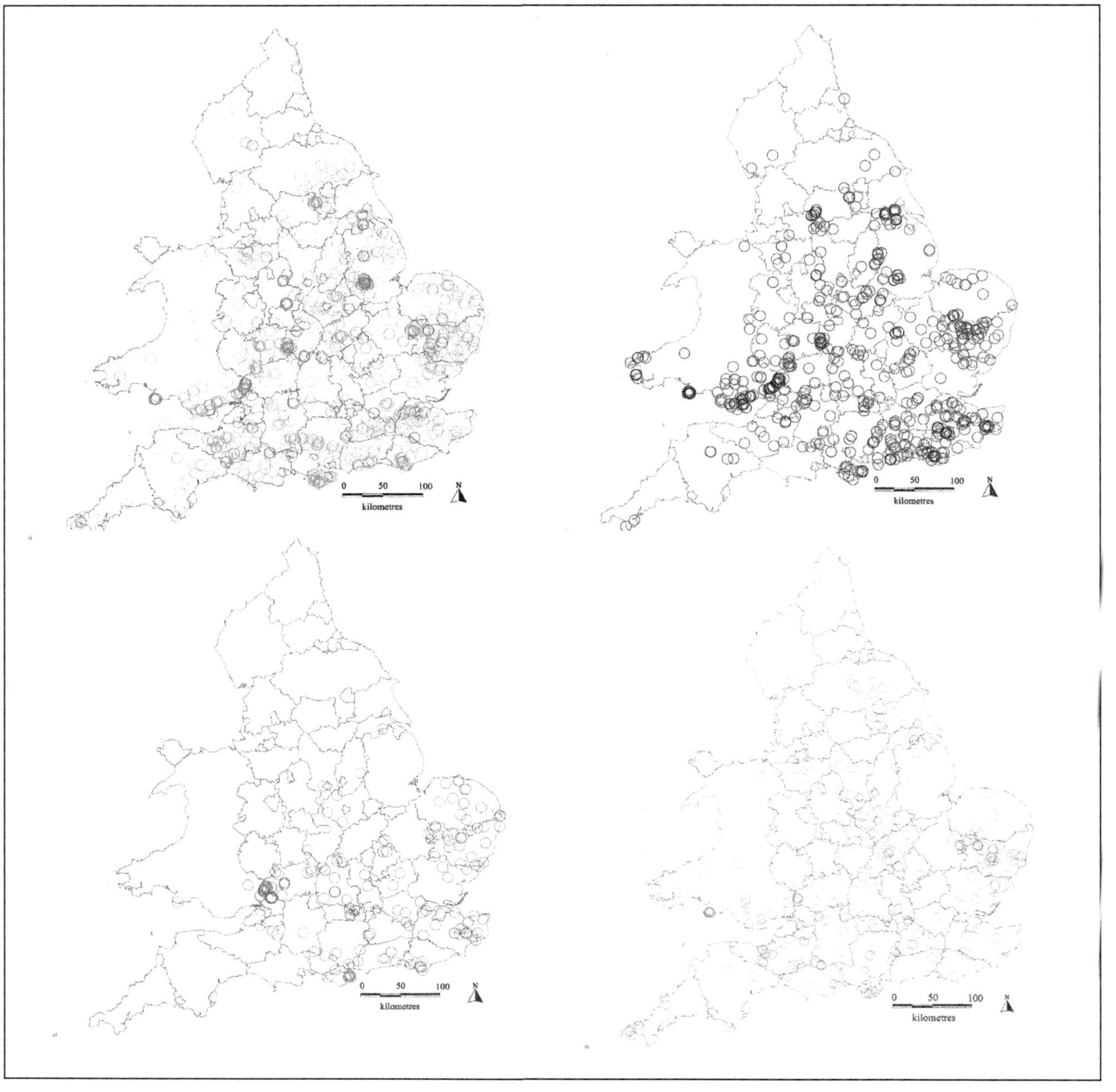

Fig. 12: Lithic records mapped, Palaeolithic to Bronze Age (PAS database). Key: Top left: Lithic records that have been attributed to the Palaeolithic (n=284, 262 mapped); Top right: Lithic records that have been attributed to the Mesolithic (n=3114, 2672 mapped); Bottom left: Lithic records that have been attributed to the Neolithic (n=3363, 2923 mapped); Bottom right: Lithic records that have been attributed to the Bronze Age (n=398, 340 mapped). Digital data source: an Ordnance Survey/EDINA supplied Service.

In central Somerset, the author has noted settlement pattern trajectories are different, with emphasis on the pre- middle Neolithic, even in areas of high concentrations of later Neolithic and earlier Bronze Age monuments on Mendip (Bond 2004a; b; 2005; 2006). Another area raised by this data set, is as to when lithic scatters become less able to trace different types of settlement in the Bronze Age. Recently it has been argued that the flaking of flint and chert moved into the domestic sphere of practice in the middle to later Bronze Age (Edmonds 1995: chapters 6-7; Young and Humphrey 1999). At that time the regional English and Welsh landscapes, from the south western peninsular (Fleming 1979), to Wessex (Barrett *et al.* 1991; Gingell 1992), the Thames Valley (Yates 1999) and East Anglia (Williamson 1987) were subject to the planning of parcel-like land allotments. Such transformation need not have been instantaneous, or implemented by large scale social organisations (Brück 1999; Johnston 2005). However, boundaries; ditches, fences and post alignments, became more indicative of settlement locales, rather than the previous quantities of flaked stone. The relationship with this pan-regional phenomenon and continued use and/or abandonment of flaking stone, a quantitative signature for settlement, is not well understood. Within the PAS data set these records yield few artefacts.

Conclusions

This study presents the first analysis of the lithic records generated by the PAS. Results are necessarily tentative, yet have demonstrated the importance of this nation-wide data set. It may only represent *c.* 5% of the Scheme's overall records, but the systematic recording methodology employed, the consideration of composition and spatial analysis highlight the quality and potential of this data. These records, most usefully can be employed to investigate the presence and absence of lithic scatters across much of the landscapes of England and Wales. Slowly lithics and lithic scatters are becoming recognised as a unique category of site.

'The durability, quantity, and near-ubiquity of knapped flint and stone give them an unique value as the most widely surviving evidence of prehistoric human activity… lithics [are] one of the most reliable indicators of human use of landscape through 9000 years of the Holocene'(Lithic Studies Society 2004: 1). As this states, lithic artefacts are a key resource enabling the finder and the archaeologist to gain access to how past people occupied and perceived much of the British landscape. It is also acknowledged here that this is a class of artefact and site that presents a complex data set to interpret. The quantity and coverage across the regional landscapes does give an, as yet unrealised potential - records of lithics hold the potential to map thousands of years of human settlement. As artefacts, as assemblages and as category of sites within a landscape context, at local, regional and national scale, lithics are highly important, perhaps even more so than more superficially spectacular objects recorded by the Scheme.

The PAS contribution can be defined in three outcomes:

- Lithics, as artefacts – a way of understanding past prehistoric people's craft skills, daily routines and lifeways.
- Lithics, as assemblages in the landscape – as *proxy* data, a means of reconstructing a populated prehistoric landscape, from the Palaeolithic to Bronze Age.
- Lithics, as discarded by all past peoples, but with the facilitation of the PAS, recovered by communities in the present.

Despite recent debate and responses to the protection of rural historic environment (English Heritage 2000; 2003; Schofield 2000; Schofield and Humble 1997; Trow 2004), lithic scatters remain a resource rarely explored by academic researchers. This situation persists although this unique category of site is regularly uncovered in most English and Welsh counties by public and professional fieldwork. Currently, the only project to record and provide nationally significant, measurable outcomes for lithics at rural sites is the PAS. What greater contribution can every finder, FLO and the Scheme as a whole make, but carry on recording this highly valuable, still undervalued and wasting historic asset!

Bibliography

Andrefsky Jr., W. 1998, *Lithics: macroscopic approaches to analysis* (Cambridge University Press, Cambridge).

Barrett, J. C., Bradley, R. and Green, M. (eds.), 1991, *Landscape, Monuments and Society* (Cambridge University Press, Cambridge).

Barton, R. N. E. 1999, 'The Lateglacial or Late and Final Upper Palaeolithic colonisation of Britain', in Hunter, J. and Ralston, I. (eds.), *The Archaeology of Britain. An introduction from the Upper Palaeolithic to the Industrial Revolution* (Routledge, London), 13-34.

Bee, T. W. 2001, 'Palaeolithic handaxes from the Lymn Valley, Lincolnshire', *Lithics: The Newsletter of the Lithic Studies Society* 22, 47-52.

Bee, T. W. 2005, 'New finds of Palaeolithic handaxes from Lincolnshire', *Lithics: The Journal of the Lithic Studies Society* 26, 90-100.

Bond, C. J. 2004a, 'The Sweet Track, Somerset: a place mediating culture and spirituality?' in Insoll, T. (ed.), *Belief in the Past. The proceedings of the 2002 Manchester conference on archaeology and religion*, British Archaeological Reports, International Series 1212 (Archaeopress, Oxford), 37-50.

Bond, C. J. 2004b, 'The supply of raw materials for later prehistoric stone tool assemblages and the maintenance of memorable places in central Somerset', in Walker, E. A., Wenban-Smith, F. F. and Healy, F. M (eds.), *Lithics in Action. Papers from the conference Lithic Studies in the Year 2000*, Lithic Studies Society Occasional Paper 8 (Oxbow Books, Oxford), 128-43.

Bond, C. J. 2004c, *Guide to the Identification, Assessment and Recording of Lithics* (October 2004, version 1) (PAS, London).

Bond, C. J. 2005, 'The Gift was stone: socio-economic complexity and exchange between Neolithic and Bronze Age polities in the South-West and Wessex': paper given at the conference 'Defining Social Complexity: approaches to power and interaction in the archaeological record', University of Cambridge, 11-13 March 2005: http://www2.eng.cam.ac.uk/~djo31/saw33/secure.htm

Bond, C. J. 2006, *Prehistoric Settlement in Somerset. Landscapes, material culture and communities, 4300 to 700 cal. BC* (unpublished PhD thesis, University of Winchester).

Bond, C. J. 2007a, 'Lithics', in Gerrard, C. M. and Aston, M. A. (eds.), *The Shapwick Project, Somerset. A rural landscape explored*, The Society for Medieval Archaeology Monograph Series 25 (Maney Publishing, Leeds), 687-728.

Bond, C. J. 2007b, 'Walking the track and believing: the Sweet Track as a means of accessing earlier Neolithic spirituality', in Barrowclough, D. A. and Malone, C. (eds.), *Cult in Context. Reconsidering ritual in archaeology* (Oxbow Books, Oxford), 158-66.

Bond, C. J. 2009a, 'The power of place and regional identity in the British south-western Mesolithic', in McCartan, S., Schulting, R., Warren, G. and Woodman, P. (eds.), *Mesolithic Horizons: papers presented at the seventh international conference on the Mesolithic in Europe, Belfast 2005* (Oxbow Books, Oxford), 343-51.

Bond, C. J. 2009b, 'A Mesolithic social landscape in South-West Britain: the Levels and Mendip', in McCartan, S., Schulting, R., Warren, G. and

Woodman, P. (eds.), *Mesolithic Horizons: papers presented at the seventh international conference on the Mesolithic in Europe, Belfast 2005* (Oxbow Books, Oxford), 704-14.

Bond, C. J. 2009c, 'Biographies of stone and landscape: lithic scatters'. *Internet Archaeology* 26: http://intarch.ac.uk/journal/issue26/1/toc.html

Bond, C. J. forthcoming, 'The Sweet Track and lithic scatters: walking the land, collecting artefacts and discovering the earliest Neolithic community', in Saville, A. (ed.), *Flint and Stone in the Neolithic Period,* Neolithic Studies Group Occasional Papers (Oxbow Books, Oxford).

Bonsall, C. J. 1977, 'Gazetteer of Upper Palaeolithic sites in England and Wales', in Wymer, J. J. (ed.), *Gazetteer of Mesolithic Sites in England and Wales*, The Council for British Archaeology Research Report 22 (Council for British Archaeology, London), 417-32.

Brooker, P. 2006, *Thetford Forest Archaeology*: http://spamandchips.net/archaeology/index.htm

Brück, J. 1999, 'What's in a settlement? Domestic practice and residential mobility in early Bronze Age southern England', in Brück, J. and Goodman, M. (eds.), *Making Places in the Prehistoric World: themes in settlement archaeology* (University College London Press, London), 52-74.

Cambria 2004, *Prehistoric Undefended Settlements Project, South West Wales. A review of the lithic evidence from the regional SMR*, Report No. 2004/53 (Cambria Archaeology, Llandeilo).

Clark, J. G. D. and Higgs, E. S. 1960, 'Flint industry', in Clark, J. G. D., 'Excavations at the Neolithic Site at Hurst Fen, Mildenhall, Suffolk (1954, 1957 and 1958)', *Proceedings of the Prehistoric Society* 26, 214-226.

Clark, R. H. and Schofield, A. J. 1991, 'By experiment and calibration: an integrated approach to archaeology of the ploughsoil', in Schofield, A. J. (ed.), *Interpreting Artefact Scatters: contributions to ploughzone archaeology*, Oxbow Monograph 4 (Oxbow, Oxford), 93-105.

Clay, P. 1989, 'Out of the unknown. Approaches to prehistoric archaeology in Leicestershire', in Gibson, A. M. (ed.), *Midlands Prehistory*, British Archaeological Reports, British Series 201 (British Archaeological Reports, Oxford), 111-21.

Couper, R. 2005, 'The Portable Antiquities Scheme, mental health and lithics – a fieldwalker's experience', *Lithics: the journal of the Lithic Studies Society* 26, 87-9.

Edmonds, M. R. 1995, *Stone Tools and Society. Working stone in Neolithic and Bronze Age Britain* (Batsford Ltd, London).

Edmonds, M. R. 1997, 'Taskscape, technology and tradition', *Analecta Praehistorica Leidensia* 29, 99-110.

Edmonds, M. R., Evans, C. and Gibson, D. 1999, 'Assembly and collection - lithic complexes in the Cambridgeshire Fenlands', *Proceedings of the Prehistoric Society* 65, 47-82.

English Heritage 2000, *Managing Lithic Scatters: archaeological guidance for planning authorities and developers* (England Heritage, London).

English Heritage 2003, *Ripping Up History: archaeology under the plough* (English Heritage, London).

Fleming, A. 1979, 'The Dartmoor Reaves: boundary patterns and behaviour patterns in the second millennium BC', *Proceedings of the Devon Archaeological Society* 37, 115-31.

Ford, S. S. 1987a, *East Berkshire Archaeological Survey,* Department of Highways and Planning, Berkshire County Council Occasional Paper 1 (Berkshire County Council, Newbury).

Ford, S. S. 1987b, 'Flint scatters and prehistoric settlement patterns in South Oxfordshire and East Berkshire', in Brown, A. G. and Edmonds, M. R. (eds.), *Lithic Analysis and Later Prehistory: some problems and approaches*, British Archaeological Reports, British Series 162 (British Archaeological Reports, Oxford) , 101-35

Ford, S. S., Bradley, R., Hawkes, J. and Fisher, P. 1984, 'Flint-working in the Metal Age', *Oxford Journal of Archaeology* 3(ii), 157-73.

Gaffiney, V. and Tingle, M. 1989, *The Maddle Farm Project: an integrated survey of prehistoric and Roman landscapes on the Berkshire Downs*, British Archaeological Reports, British Series 200 (British Archaeological Reports, Oxford).

Gardiner, J. 1987, 'Tales of the unexpected: approaches to the assessment and interpretation of museum flint collections', in Brown, A. G. and Edmonds, M. R. (eds.), *Lithic Analysis and Later Prehistory: some problems and approaches*, British Archaeological Reports, British Series 162 (British Archaeological Reports, Oxford), 49-66.

Gardiner, J. P. and Shennan, S. 1985, 'The Mesolithic, Neolithic and Earlier Bronze Age Periods', in Shennan, S., *Experiments in the Collection and Analysis of Archaeological Survey Data: the East Hampshire Survey* (University of Sheffield, Sheffield), 47-72.

Gerrard, C. M., Aston, M. A., Gidney, L., Gutiérrez, A and King, A. 2007, 'Fieldwalking', in Gerrard, C. M. and Aston, A. M. (eds.), *The Shapwick Project, Somerset. A rural landscape explored*, The Society for Medieval Archaeology Monograph Series 25 (Maney Publishing, Leeds), 687-728.

Gingell, C. 1992, *The Marlborough Downs: a later Bronze Age landscape and its origins*, Wiltshire Archaeological and Natural History Society Monograph 1 (Wiltshire Archaeological and Natural History Society, Devizes).

Haselgrove, C, Millett, M. and Smith, I. 1985 (eds.), *Archaeology from the Ploughsoil: studies in the collection and interpretation of field survey data* (University of Sheffield, Sheffield).

Healy, F. M. 1991, 'Appendix 1. Lithics and pre-Iron Age Pottery', in Silvester, R. J., *The Fenland Project Number 4: the Wissey Embayment and the Fen Causeway, Norfolk*, East Anglian Archaeology 52 (Dereham, Gressenhall), 116-39.

Healy, F. M. 1995, 'Pots, pits and peats: ceramics and settlement in East Anglia', in Kinnes, I. and Varndell,

G. (eds.), *'Unbaked Urns of Rudely Shape'. Essays on British and Irish pottery for Ian Longworth*, Oxbow Monograph 55 (Oxbow, Oxford) , 173-84.

Healy, F. M. 1996, *The Fenland Project, Number 11: the Wissey Embayment: evidence for pre-Iron Age occupation*, East Anglian Archaeology 78 (The Norfolk Archaeological Unit, Fenland Project Committee and The Scole Archaeological Committee Ltd, Dereham).

Healy, F. M. 1998, 'The surface of the Breckland', in Ashton, N., Healy, F. M. and Pettitt, P. (eds.), *Stone Age Archaeology: essays in honour of John Wymer*, Oxbow Books 102, Lithic Studies Society Occasional Paper 6 (Oxbow, Oxford), 225-35.

Hobbs, R. 2003, *Treasure: finding our past* (British Museum Press, London).

Hosfield, R. T. 1999, *The Palaeolithic of the Hampshire Basin: a regional model of hominid behaviour during the Middle Pleistocene*, British Archaeological Reports, British Series 286 (Archaeopress, Oxford).

Inizan, M.-L., Roche, H. and Tixier, J. 1992, *Technology of Knapped Stone*, Préhistoire de la Pierre Taillée Tome 3 (CREP, Meudon).

Jacobi, R. M. 1991, 'The Creswellian, Creswell and Cheddar', in Barton, R. N. E., Roberts, A. J. and Roe, D. A. (eds.), *The Late Glacial in North-West Europe: human adaptation and environmental change at the end of the Pleistocene*, The Council for British Archaeology Research Report No. 77 (Council for British Archaeology, London), 128-40.

Jacobi, R. M. 1997, 'The 'Creswellian' in Britain', in Fagnart, J.-P. and Thévein, A. (eds.), *Le Tardiglaciaire en Europe du Nord-Ouest. Actes du 119e Congrès national des Sociétés historiques et scientifiques Amiens, 1994* (CHTS, Paris), 499-505.

Johnston, R. 2005, 'Pattern without a plan: rethinking the Bronze Age coaxial field systems on Dartmoor, south-west England', *Oxford Journal of Archaeology* 24(i), 1-21.

Lacaille, A. D. 1954, 'Palaeoliths from the lower reaches of the Bristol Avon', *The Antiquaries Journal* 34, 1-27.

Lisk, S., Schofield, A. J. and Humble, J. 1998, 'Lithic scatters after PPG16 - local and national perspectives', *Lithics: The Newsletter of the Lithic Studies Society* 19, 24-32.

Lithic Studies Society 2004, *Research Frameworks for Holocene Lithics in Britain* (Lithic Studies Society, Prehistoric Society, English Heritage, Salisbury).

Locock, M. 2000, *Prehistoric Settlement in Southeast Wales: the lithic evidence*, Glamorgan-Gwent Archaeological Trust Report No. 2000/024 (Glamorgan-Gwent Archaeological Trust, Swansea).

Locock, M. 2002a, *Prehistoric Non-defensive Settlements in South-east Wales: fieldwork on lithic scatter sites, 2001-2002*, Glamorgan-Gwent Archaeological Trust Report No. 2002/013 (Glamorgan-Gwent Archaeological Trust, Swansea).

Locock, M. 2002b, *Prehistoric Non-defensive Settlement Sites in South-east Wales: further fieldwork, 2002-3 and a review of the early prehistoric evidence*, Glamorgan-Gwent Archaeological Trust Report No. 2002/077 (Glamorgan-Gwent Archaeological Trust, Swansea).

Mellars, P. A. and Haynes, M. 1986, 'Mesolithic exploitation of sandy areas: towards the testing of some hypothesis', in Bailey, G. N. and Callow, P. (eds.), *Stone Age Prehistory: studies in memory of Charles McBurney* (Cambridge University Press, Cambridge), 69-76.

Palmer, S. 1977, *Mesolithic Cultures of Britain* (Dolphin Press, Poole).

Pitts, M. W. 1978, 'On the shape of waste flakes as an index of technological change in lithic industries', *Journal of Archaeological Science* 5, 17-37.

Pitts, M. W. and Jacobi, R. M. 1979, 'Some aspects of changes in flaked stone industries of the Mesolithic and Neolithic of Southern England', *Journal of Archaeological Science* 6, 163-73.

Pollard, J. 1998, 'Prehistoric settlement and non-settlement in two Southern Cambridgeshire River Valleys: the lithic dimension and interpretative dilemmas', *Lithics: The Newsletter of the Lithic Studies Society* No. 19, 61-71.

Pollard, J. 1999, 'These places have their moments: thoughts on settlement practices in the British Neolithic', in Brück, J. and Goodman, M. (eds.), *Making Places in the Prehistoric World. Themes in settlement archaeology* (University College London, London), 76-93.

Richards, J. C. 1978, *The Archaeology of the Berkshire Downs: an introductory survey*, Berkshire Archaeological Committee Publication 13 (Berkshire County Council, Reading).

Richards, J. C. 1990, *The Stonehenge Environs Project*, English Heritage Archaeological Report 16 (English Heritage, London).

Roberts, B. K. and Wrathmell, S. 2000, *An Atlas of Rural Settlement* (English Heritage, London).

Roberts, B. K. and Wrathmell, S. 2002, *Region and Place: a study of English rural settlement* (English Heritage, London).

Schofield, A. J. (ed.), 1991, *Interpreting Artefact Scatters: contributions to ploughzone archaeology*, Oxbow Monograph 4 (Oxbow, Oxford).

Schofield, A. J. 1993, *Pilot Study for the Evaluation of Surface Lithic Scatter Sites and Stray Finds. Project design* (unpublished, Monuments Protection Programme & Central Archaeology Service, London).

Schofield, A. J. 1994, 'Looking back with regret; looking forward with optimism: making more of surface lithic scatter sites', Ashton, N. and David, A. (eds.), *Stories in Stone*, Lithic Studies Society Occasional Paper 4 (Lithics Studies Society, London), 90-8.

Schofield, A. J. 1995, 'Settlement mobility and *la longue durée*: towards a context for surface lithic material', in Schofield, A. J. (ed.), *Lithics in Context: suggestions for the future direction of Lithic Studies*, Lithic Studies Society Occasional Paper 5 (Lithics Studies Society, London), 105-13.

Schofield, A. J. 2000, 'Reflections on the future for surface lithic artefact study in England', in Bintliff, J. L., Kuna, M. and Venclová, N. (eds.), *The Future of Surface Artefact Survey in Europe* (Sheffield Academic Press, Sheffield), 45-55.

Schofield, A. J. and Humble, J. 1995, 'Order out of chaos: making sense of surface Stone Age finds', *Conservation Bulletin* 9, 9-11.

Schofield, A. J. and Humble, J. 1997, *The Evaluation of Surface Lithic Scatters and Stray Finds*, MPP/CAS Project 525 (English Heritage, London).

Scott-Jackson, J. 2000, *Lower and Middle Palaeolithic artefacts from deposits mapped as Clay-with-flints: a new synthesis with significant implications for the earliest occupation of Britain* (Oxbow, Oxford).

Silvester, R. J. and Owen, W. 2002, *Early Prehistoric Settlement in Mid and North-East Wales: the lithic evidence,* Clwyd-Powys Archaeological Trust Report 467 (Clwyd-Powys Archaeological Trust, Welshpool).

Smith, G, H, 2000, *Gwynedd Lithic Scatters Project: evaluation of the early prehistoric landscape through lithic finds*, Gwynedd Archaeological Trust Report 354 (Gwynedd Archaeological Trust, Bangor).

Smith, G. H. 2005, 'The north-west Wales lithic scatters project', *Lithics: The Journal of the Lithic Studies Society* 26, 38-56.

Sussams, K. 1996, *The Breckland Archaeological Survey* (Suffolk County Council, Ipswich).

Tingle, M. 1991, *The Vale of the White Horse Survey,* British Archaeological Reports, British Series 218 (Tempus Reparation, Oxford).

Tingle, M. 1998, *The Prehistory of Beer Head. Field survey and excavations at an isolated flint source on the South Devon Coast*, British Archaeological Reports, British Series 270 (Archaeopress, Oxford).

Trow, S. 2004, 'Saving sites from the plough', *The Institute of Field Archaeologists Yearbook and Directory 2004* (The Institute of Field Archaeologists, Reading), 37-8.

Waddington, C. 1999, *A Landscape Archaeological Study of the Mesolithic-Neolithic in the Milfield Basin, Northumberland,* British Archaeological Reports, British Series 291 (Archaeopress, Oxford).

Whittle, A. W. R. 1990, 'A model for the Mesolithic-Neolithic transition in the upper Kennet Valley, north Wiltshire', *Proceedings of the Prehistoric Society* 56, 101-10.

Whittle, A. W. R. 1997, 'Moving on and moving around: Neolithic settlement mobility', in Topping, P. (ed.), *Neolithic Landscapes,* Neolithic Studies Group Seminar Papers 2, Oxbow Monograph 86 (Oxbow, Oxford), 15-22.

Williamson, T. 1987, 'Early Co-axial field systems on the East Anglian Boulder Clays', *Proceedings of the Prehistoric Society* 53, 419-31.

Woodward, P. J. 1991, *The South Dorset Ridgeway. Survey and Excavations 1977-84*, Dorset Natural History and Archaeological Society Monograph Series 8 (Dorset Natural History and Archaeological Society, Bridport).

Wymer, J. J. 1968, *Lower Palaeolithic Archaeology in Britain as Represented by the Upper Thames Valley* (John Baker, London).

Wymer, J. J. 1985, *Palaeolithic Sites of East Anglia* (Geo Books, Norwich).

Wymer, J. J. 1991, *Mesolithic Britain* (Shire Publications Ltd, Princes Risborough).

Wymer J. J. 1999, *The Lower Palaeolithic Occupation of Britain* (Wessex Archaeology, Salisbury).

Yates, D. 1999, 'Bronze Age field systems in the Thames Valley', *Oxford Journal of Archaeology* 18, 157-70.

Young, R. and Humphrey, J. 1999, 'Flint use in England after the Bronze Age: time for a re-evaluation?' *Proceedings of the Prehistoric Society* 65, 231-42.

Metal Detecting Rallies and Landscape Archaeology: recreating lost landscapes on the Berkshire Downs

Paula Levick and Kate Sumnall

This paper highlights the contribution that a series of large-scale metal-detecting rallies are making to the study of an ancient landscape.

The first of the rallies (at Letcombe) was a three-day event held over August Bank Holiday 2006. It was one of the largest commercial rallies ever held in this country, attracting approximately 2,000 detectorists. It was followed by two further rallies in 2007: the first (at Court Hill), a small one-day event with 100 detectorists, and the second (at Wantage), over two days, with approximately 750 detectorists attending each day. The rallies have produced hundreds of datable finds, from approximately 525 hectares of almost contiguous downland, lying either side of the ancient Ridgeway track. The recorded objects are providing valuable insights into early land-use in this region, challenging previous interpretations and generating a number of new areas for research.

Background

The rallies took place on arable fields on the North Wessex Downs near Wantage and within the environs of Segsbury Camp, an early Iron Age hillfort excavated by Oxford University in the late 1990s (Lock *et al.* 2005). Recently, English Heritage (as part of the National Mapping Programme) used aerial photographs to transcribe all cropmarked archaeological features in this region, revealing a swathe of possible later prehistoric or Romano-British field systems and a number of Iron Age banjo enclosures (discussed below) lying to the south of the hillfort (Small 2002: 17-20, 29-30; Winton 2003: 15-26). The relationship of these features to Segsbury Camp, and to each other, is uncertain, but further investigation is currently being undertaken (by one of the authors of this paper - PL). However, a study using conventional field-work methods is problematic. Today, only 3% of the land within the North Wessex Downs can be classified as 'downland', with the majority of the area under large-scale arable agriculture (M. Conway, pers. comm.). The ancient field systems, settlements, and enclosures, which were once preserved beneath sheep pasture, are now plough-levelled, and monuments and artefacts continue to be lost through attrition. The fields surrounding the hillfort are virtually aceramic, and any surviving pot is in the main abraded and undiagnostic but most probably Roman.

Two seasons of excavations at Segsbury Camp yielded little material culture and the small number of objects recovered suggested minimal domestic activity, with the interior used sporadically or seasonally, possibly for markets or sheep fairs, and with no evidence for long-term or intensive occupation (Lock *et al.* 2005: 144-5). Interpretation of community and land use within the environs of Segsbury Camp owes little of its interpretation to its material culture. Instead, theoretical models have been constructed from the once visible remnants of earlier landscapes and settlements and developed from an anthropological perspective. The overall impression was one of emerging early Iron Age activity on previously unused land with few earlier associations, and possibly abandoned when the banjo enclosures went out of use in the late Iron Age (Miles *et al.* 2003: 265; Lock *et al.* 2005: 135-8, 140-1).

Metal-detecting Rallies: data collection

The rally organiser (Peter Welch) informed detectorists taking part in the rallies of the archaeological research currently being undertaken and asked finders to report all material discovered including ceramic and lithic artefacts. The finds were recorded by staff from the Portable Antiquities Scheme (PAS) who were on site for each of the rallies. Recording follows PAS guidelines, with each find photographed, measured and weighed during the identification and recording stage. This level of recording has allowed detailed post-rally processing to be carried out. In addition to the professional support provided by the PAS, local community volunteers and archaeology students worked with the detectorists in the fields and in the finds tent, recording the location of each find (its findspot), either with handheld GPS (Global Positioning Systems) devices or directly onto Ordnance Survey maps. In order to prevent any bias or subjectivity entering the results, the location of each find was kept separate from the finds identifications and only linked when the finds were entered onto the PAS database. Once on the database, the data are structured in a way that enables queries to be run and the results downloaded. For this study, the downloaded data were analysed and plotted using a GIS (Geographical Information System), which allows for both chronological and spatial analysis to be undertaken.

Interpretation

The rallies have revealed a landscape that is rich in datable objects and while it should be acknowledged that the recovery method lacks the precision of site-dominated archaeological field-work and research, a broad picture has emerged of activities, helping to repopulate the land and revealing a complexity and diversity that was previously unseen in this area.

Metalworking Industry

With no previously known archaeological data to contradict the interpretation of this land as being unused before the early Iron Age, the quantity of Bronze Age artefacts reported at the rallies was unexpected. Twenty objects from this period were recorded during the three rallies, the majority comprising weapons including swords, axeheads and socketed spears of Middle or Late Bronze Age date (1500-800 BC). In addition, a quoit-headed pin, a sickle blade, an ingot fragment and three awls, one from each rally, were recorded.

Following the extension of the Treasure Act 1996 to include hoards of prehistoric base-metal artefacts in 2002 (Treasure (Designation) Order 2002), an increasing quantity of Bronze Age hoards are being reported, particularly from southern and eastern Britain. Bronze Age hoards are usually interpreted within frameworks of utilitarian or ritual activity, seen either as hoards deposited, frequently in the landscape, by a merchant or smith with the intention of later recovery, or as votive offerings in which deposition was a ritual act with no intention or possibility of recovery, such as those laid down in rivers, bogs or in graves (Bradley 1985: 692-704; 1988: 249-60; York 2002: 77-92; Needham 1988: 229-48). It is of interest that a small hoard of four palstave axes dating to the Middle Bronze Age was recovered from Lattin Down, Lockinge in 1872, less than a kilometre from the northern extent of the Wantage rally (Rowlands 1976: 225). Until now this appeared to be an isolated cache of material of this date in this area.

Understanding the context of the unstratified finds recorded at the rallies and the dynamics of what was occurring is somewhat problematic, as today they appear divorced from any social or economic setting. The distribution of the detected finds is difficult to reconcile with the interpretation of a single hoard, even one that has been considerably dispersed through ploughing, and the finds are spatially, and in some cases chronologically unrelated (Fig. 1; Table 1). The possibility that individual objects were dislodged from secure contexts during ploughing, while others remained beyond the range/limitation of the metal-detector, has been considered. However this interpretation, if applied to all the finds, would potentially imply a large number of hoards over an extensive area.

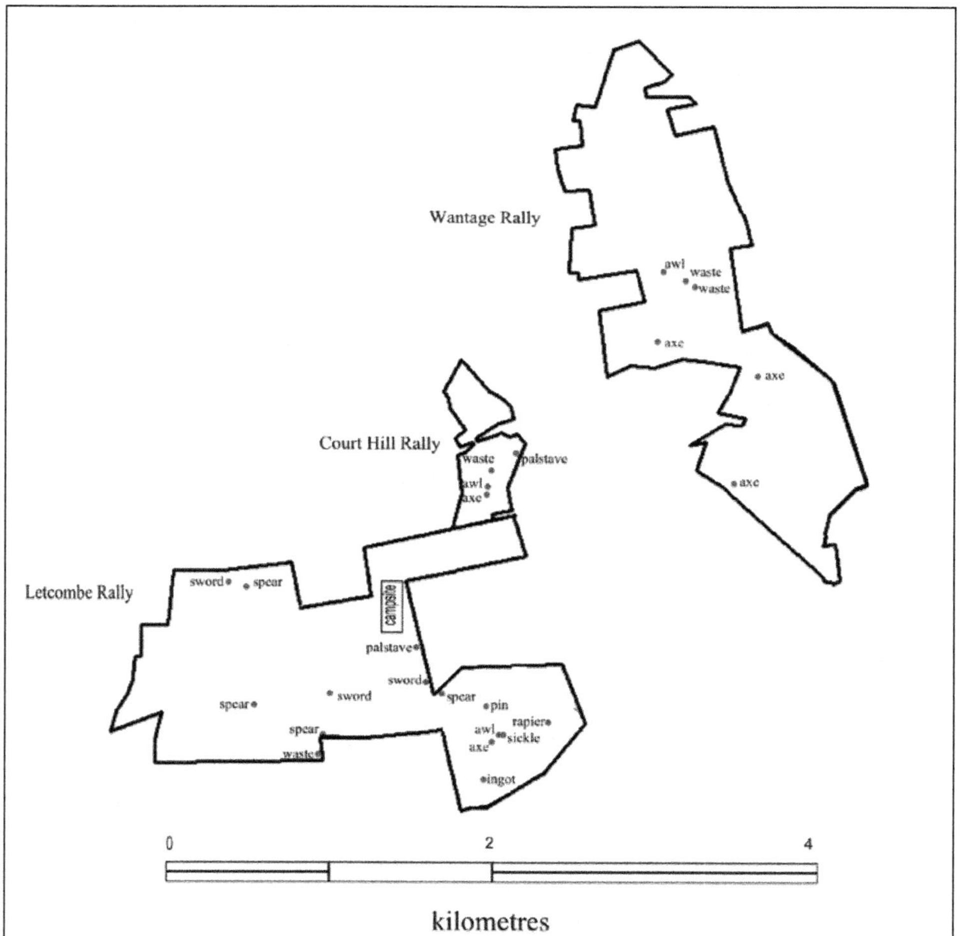

Fig 1: Distribution of Bronze Age artefacts recorded at the Court Hill, Letcombe and Wantage rallies.

Artefact Type	Period	Rally
Flint barbed and tanged arrowhead	Late Neolithic-Early Bronze Age	Letcombe
Socketed spearhead with side loops	Middle Bronze Age	Letcombe
Socketed spearhead with side loops	Middle Bronze Age	Letcombe
Socketed spearhead with side loops (fragment)	Middle Bronze Age	Letcombe
Spearhead (fragment)	Middle Bronze Age	Letcombe
Sickle blade	Middle Bronze Age	Letcombe
Rapier	Middle Bronze Age	Letcombe
Quoit-headed pin	Middle Bronze Age	Letcombe
Sword blade (fragment)	Middle-Late Bronze Age	Letcombe
Palstave axe	Middle-Late Bronze Age	Letcombe
Palstave axe	Middle-Late Bronze Age	Court Hill
Palstave axe (fragment)	Middle-Late Bronze Age	Wantage
Sword	Late Bronze Age	Letcombe
Sword blade (fragment)	Late Bronze Age	Letcombe
Ingot	Late Bronze Age	Letcombe
Socketed axehead (fragment)	Late Bronze Age	Letcombe
?Socketed axe (fragment)	Late Bronze Age	Court Hill
Socketed axehead (fragment)	Late Bronze Age	Wantage
Socketed axehead (fragment)	Late Bronze Age	Wantage
Awl	Bronze Age	Court Hill
Awl	Bronze Age	Letcombe
Awl	Bronze Age	Wantage

Table 1: Bronze Age artefacts recorded by type, period and rally.
Dating follows PAS guidelines: Early Bronze Age (2150-1500 BC); Middle Bronze Age (1500-1150 BC); Late Bronze Age (1150-800 BC).

In addition to the Bronze Age weapons and tools, metalworking waste was also recorded. While this cannot be securely dated, crucible fragments were recovered during excavations at Segsbury hillfort. These are undated, but are possibly residual from earlier activity (Salter 2005: 123; Lock *et al.* 2005: 136). Is it possible then, that this is evidence for several types of event over a large area, within the cycle of metalworking?

The condition of the finds accords well with the interpretation of a metalworking industry. Metal was a restricted resource and a valuable commodity, and objects could have been recycled many times before entering the archaeological record. Few of the metal-detected weapons are complete and often comprised only fragments. Where the objects are incomplete or fragmented (see Table 1) all have a consistent mid-green patina across the broken surfaces, suggesting the damage had occurred in antiquity; possibly during their preparation for recycling, as fragmented objects are a common feature of Late Bronze Age founder's hoards of the Ewart Park phase (1000-800 BC). Although an unfashionable interpretation, some objects might have been hidden individually for safekeeping and their location forgotten. Others were possibly destined for recycling and lost in transit. Recently it has been argued that the ritual-utilitarian distinction might not be so clear-cut as previously thought (Needham 2001: 289, 294), with the vast majority of buried deposits, including 'scrap items', possibly having undergone some form of ceremony or ritual prior to deposition, but which might not necessarily preclude the recovery and reuse of the object at a later date. There are currently many uncertainties in applying these interpretations, but what is now apparent is that this area had a time-depth reaching back further into prehistory than was previously suspected.

Trackways

When plotted, a large number of the finds form distinct linear patterns suggesting corridors of movement across the land (Fig. 2). One of these linears leads towards a break in the southern ramparts of Segsbury Camp (a). The ramparts are now breached in several places, with only the opening in the east considered to be contemporary with the original construction and others later modifications (Cotton 1962: 43; Payne *et al.* 2007: 89-96). Breaches in the north and south-west carry a track that connects the chalk downland with the springs at the foot of the escarpment and the clay vale beyond. This track is shown on John Rocque's map of 1761, but in common with many former tracks and droveways in the region, enclosure and modern large-scale arable farming has removed all traces of it on the ground. Evidence for the origin of this track was fully explored by Bailey (2005: 17-24), who produced a convincing argument for the north and south-west entrances of the hillfort being Iron Age in date, and the track contemporary or possibly Roman. However, he was unable to trace the evidence for this track back further than a report by the antiquarian John Aubrey, written sometime prior to 1693. Also, subsequent excavations were unable to provide conclusive evidence to support this theory (Lock *et al.* 2005: 96-112, 143-4).

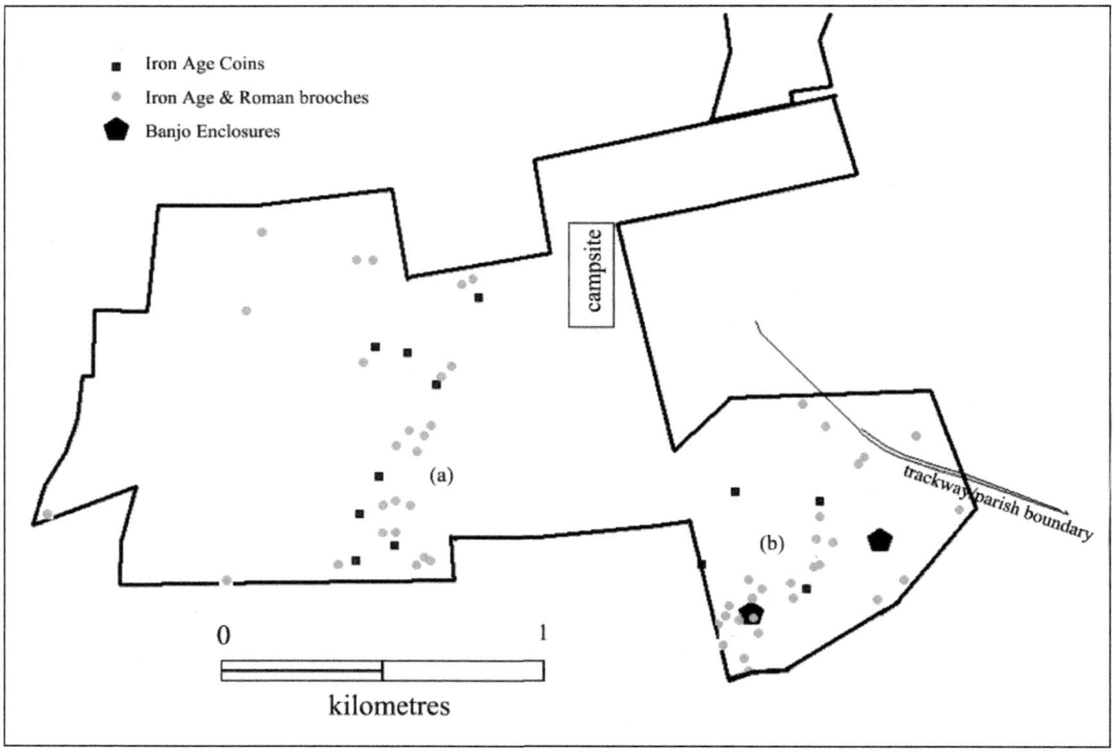

Fig 2: Former trackways

Twelve Iron Age coins were recorded during the Letcombe rally, eight of which lay on or within the vicinity of this trackway; the earliest being an Iron Age gold *stater* dated to the late 2nd to mid 1st century BC. Iron Age and Roman objects, in particular brooches, and finds from later periods, mirror the linear distribution of the coins, suggesting this route had been in regular use for centuries but with its origins dating back to at least the Iron Age.

A second linear arrangement of Iron Age and Roman finds running north-east to south-west in an area where two Iron Age banjo enclosures have been identified (b) but which are now levelled (Winton 2003: 15-26). Banjo enclosures are curvilinear in form with a single entrance approached by double parallel ditches defining a trackway which gives them a banjo-shaped ground plan. Excavated examples date from the middle to late Iron Age (Perry 1986: 35-42; Fasham 1987; Cunliffe and Poole 2000) and they are thought to have continued in use up to the Roman conquest. Their purpose is uncertain but they are believed to have functioned as settlements or used for stock control. The two banjo enclosures face each other across a dry valley. This second possible trackway appears focused on the western enclosure only, passing the one in the east on the opposite side to its entrance and apparently ignoring it. The objects recovered from this track include brooches of Late Iron Age and Roman date and Roman coins. Finds records for the Roman coins are currently being examined but initial interpretations suggest that the use of the western enclosure extended into the 4th century AD. Two supplementary ditched enclosures, one of which is appended to the side of the banjo enclosure, could post-date its original construction and might represent Roman modification and reuse. Based on the finds evidence, both enclosures were in use from the middle Iron Age but the eastern enclosure seems to have seen far less, or a different type of activity and appears to have gone out of use by the end of the late Iron Age.

A final possible linear distribution corresponds to a cropmark described as a possible medieval or post-medieval ditched boundary (Fig. 3), which follows the parish boundary (NMR ref: SU 38 SE 72). The 1881 Ordnance Survey map shows the boundary as a track for some of its way, although it is now ploughed out. Finds from the late Iron Age to early Roman period and later, can be seen to follow the line of this boundary. Early medieval charter bounds have not survived for these parishes, but the fields abut those of a parish for which records do survive. The boundary track can be traced eastwards where it joins bounds described in the charters of AD 939 (Gelling 1995: 657-61) and links to a drove road running to a further banjo enclosure. It is possible therefore that the parish boundary had a much earlier origin than previously suspected and was only formalised at a later period.

Roman Army

Of the 375 Roman finds, 86 have parallels on Roman military sites, suggesting a regular, but possibly transient military presence in the area.

Early Roman coins, including a Republican *denarius serratus* of 79 BC, celebrating the victories of Sulla in the Civil War, and Imperial issues of Nero (AD 54-68) and Vespasian (AD 69-79) suggest a previously unseen Roman military presence in the region from very early in the Conquest period. This interpretation is supported by a

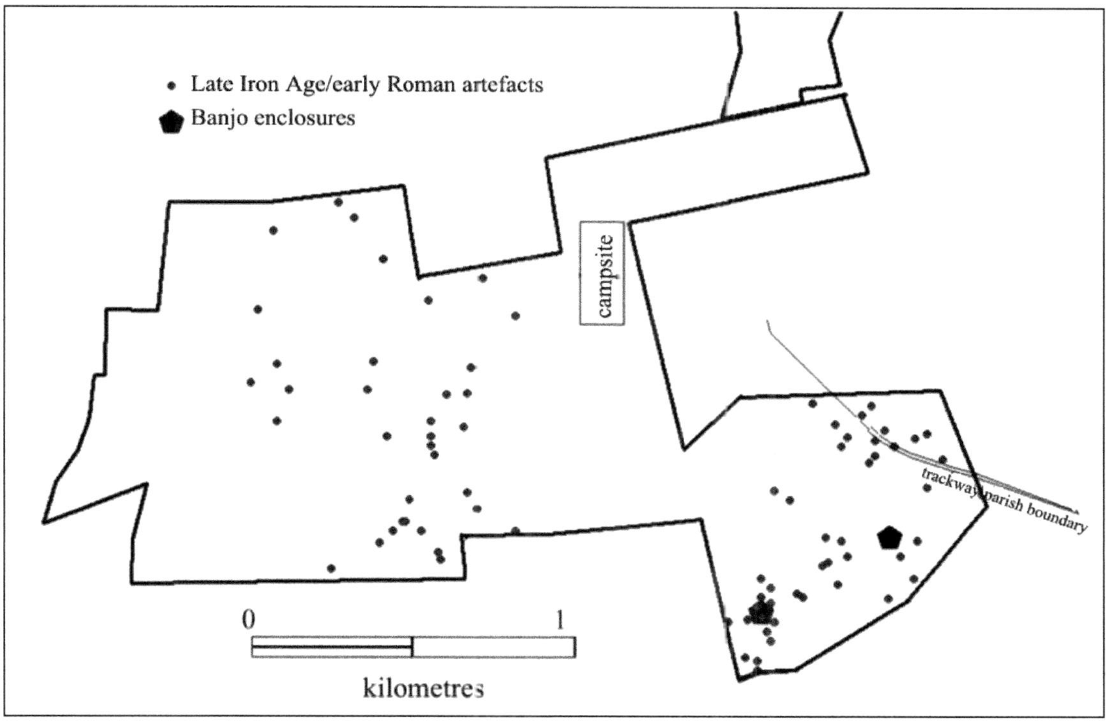

Fig 3: Distribution of artefacts along parish boundary

number of finds recorded, including a lobate hinge from Roman segmented armour (*lorica segmentata*) of the Corbridge type (Allason-Jones and Bishop 1988), military horse gear and Hod Hill brooches, often associated with the early Roman military. A number of these objects lie on the proposed trackways, with a line of Hod Hill brooches plotted along the approach to the western banjo enclosure, suggesting that whatever its function, it was of interest to the Roman army. This area receives no mention in the Antonine Itinerary and although a Roman military way across the Downs has long been suspected (Rodwell 1975; Garnish 1983) its location has never been confirmed. A Roman road enters Wantage from the north but its route beyond this is uncertain. Ermin Street running east-west, and connecting Cirencester with Silchester, lies approximately 12 km to the south. It is probable that an unpaved road crossed the Downs somewhere in the vicinity of where the Letcombe rally took place, with the army making use of pre-existing trackways to connect to Ermin Street, possibly fording the River Lambourn at Great Shefford (Sheep Ford).

Field Systems, Markets and Fairs

All three rallies were dominated by finds from the late Roman period. More than 200 low denomination 3rd- and 4th-century AD coins were recovered during the Letcombe rally, many of which were worn and illegible. The frequency of the coins at Letcombe is exceptionally high for open land with no previously recorded Roman settlement. The distribution of these coins appears to correspond to the field systems mapped by English Heritage (Small 2002) (outlined in Fig. 4). It is probable that a greater number of worn coins were recovered than reported, as these are considered worthless by many detectorists. Studies elsewhere on the distribution of medieval pennies suggests they entered the field with domestic waste during manuring (Sam Moorhead, pers. comm.) in much the same way as pottery, and this might also prove true for the Roman coins. The interpretation of manuring scatters is yet to be fully explored but further studies of this type might offer an additional method for dating Roman fields.

An alternative explanation worth considering is that the coins were lost during communal events such as open markets or fairs. During the Letcombe rally, seven Roman bi-conical lead steelyard weights and a steelyard arm were recovered and with a distribution coinciding with the spread of coinage. Is it possible that this is evidence of the development into the Roman period of the seasonal stock markets or fairs that have been suggested for the Iron Age at Segsbury Camp (Lock *et al.* 2005: 145-9) and possibly for nearby Uffington hillfort (Miles *et al.* 2003: 124). No weights were reported during the Court Hill or Wantage rallies, suggesting that whatever the activity, it was focussed on fields to the south of the hillfort.

Arable fields and markets need not be mutually exclusive. Large-scale seasonal markets or fairs, held on the fields in autumn once the crops were harvested, would give farmers an opportunity to trade their animals before winter, for culling or stock improvement, while animals held temporarily on the fields would provide a source of fertilizer for the thin downland soils. This type of seasonal or annual event might have incorporated smaller markets and fairs from local centres (Henig and Booth 2000: 74-5; Hingley 1989: 112-6), attracting populations from outside the area, with the hillfort providing a prominent landmark for travellers.

Fig 4: Steelyard weights and coin distributions compared to location of field systems (outlined)

Segsbury Hillfort in Context

The scale of the rallies and the data recorded are exceptional. Few of the patterns of activity identified during the Letcombe rally were repeated at Court Hill or Wantage. Instead each rally has displayed a distinct artefactual signature, allowing Segsbury Camp to be placed within a landscape context. Court Hill, the smallest of the rallies, produced only 36 finds. This rally lay to the east of Segsbury Camp on land facing the approach to the eastern entrance of the hillfort. Only one Iron Age find was recorded: a late Iron Age copper-alloy unit of Tasciovanus (20 BC-AD 9), recovered almost a kilometre from this entrance. The paucity of Iron Age finds is surprising if this had been the only entrance to the hillfort during its main period of use (Cotton 1962: 43; Payne *et al.* 2007: 89-96), but helps to support the suggestion that the north and south-western entrances, discussed above, were in use during the Iron Age. No field systems have been mapped in this area and only a small number of Roman coins were recovered. In common with other finds from this rally, the coins are in very good condition and probably represent loss rather than purposefully discarded material. Amongst the finds was a small zoomorphic brooch, probably representing a cockerel, although the head is now missing. Cockerel brooches can be associated with the cult of Mercury and have been recovered from graves, temples and military sites, but are considered rare in rural areas (Crummy 2007: 225-8). Mercury was the god of commerce and trade, especially of grain, which may offer an alternative explanation. This was a time of increasing agricultural intensification as the field systems attest, so could this brooch have been a small offering in the hope of a good harvest. Alternatively, possibly it was the talisman of a merchant, attending markets in the area, or that of a passing soldier.

As with Court Hill, the Wantage rally produced only a small number of Iron Age finds, comprising three coins and two brooches from over 700 finds reported. Instead, finds from the medieval and post-medieval periods were recorded in large numbers. While a further 150 late Roman coins and a number of Roman brooches were recovered during this rally, many of these finds appear to represent a spread of material extending from a possible settlement lying a few metres to the east of the rally area (NMR ref: SU 48 NW 4 and SU 48 NW 67). The remainder of the coins lie in an area for which there is evidence for field systems.

The Artefacts

In this study the artefacts themselves have played a subordinate role to the information they provide about landscape use and re-use. A number of the finds recorded during the Letcombe rally are of types not previously recorded and parallels are still being sought. Others are rare or unusual for the region and in the concluding paragraphs two are considered in brief.

Bronze Comb

A late Roman to early medieval copper-alloy comb of a type rarely recorded in this country (BERK-D2A937; Fig. 5). It is semi-circular in plan, has a triangular hole at the

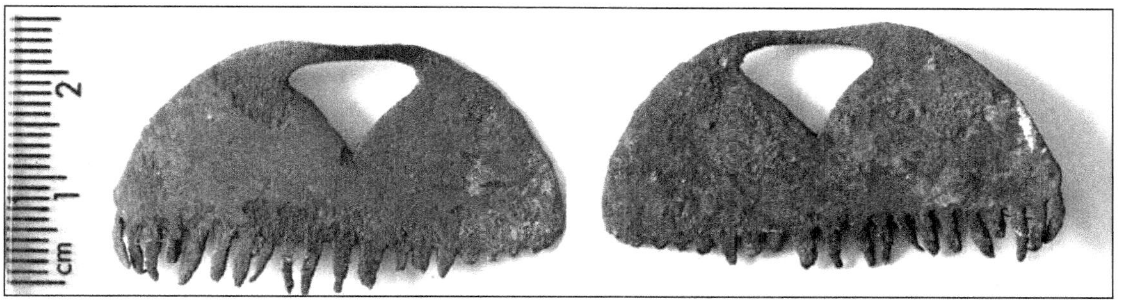

Fig 5: late Roman to early medieval copper-alloy comb (BERK-D2A937).

centre. It has coarse and irregular teeth, which are damaged and incomplete. It is undecorated and in a very poor condition. Although parallels are unknown in this country, in general the form of the comb is very similar to iron combs found in Eastern Europe dating from AD 250-500 (Levada 2000: fig. 2-3). Other examples, also in iron and with a very similar hole at the centre are recorded in rich graves dating from the mid 2nd to late 4th century, from Skovgard and Bregentvel, Denmark (Bo Henriksen 2009: 182, fig. 162), and from other sites in southern Scandinavia.

Other metallic combs recorded by PAS include the highly decorated late Iron Age example from Tanworth in Arden (Ashby and Bolton, this volume). It is suggested that the Warwickshire comb might have been used for dressing horses' manes and tails, owing to the stoutness of the teeth. It is more likely that the Letcombe comb and iron examples of the same form, were used for the preparation of textile fibres rather than as combs for the hair (Mogens Bo Henriksen, pers. comm.). Such an interpretation might provide one explanation for the type of damage seen on the Letcombe example. Whatever its function, the simplicity of its design and the amount of wear suggests the Letcombe comb had a utilitarian use, whereas the Warwickshire example was highly decorated and was perhaps also employed as a display item. It seems reasonable that combs functioned within very different spheres of activity: while one was intended for everyday use, the finer, decorated, example was designed to operate within mechanisms of gift exchange, propitiation or possibly as a grave good.

Terret Rings

Two Late Iron Age to early Roman miniature terret rings, a terret ring fragment and a possible linch pin fragment were recovered in relatively close proximity to the western banjo enclosure. Terret rings were used as rein-rings to secure the reins on a horse drawn vehicle. This suggests that horses might have been corralled or used within the banjo enclosure during that period. Although they are frequent finds in Norfolk (Bates, *et al.* 2000: 229; Hutcheson 2004: 113-5) and amongst the vehicle burials of East Yorkshire, where terrets are also found in association with linch pins (Stead 1991; PASAR 2004/05: 32), they are uncommon finds in Berkshire and Oxfordshire.

Conclusion

Although unstructured, the landscape-wide approach made possible here provides a very different interpretation to that which results from limited, but targeted excavation. Earlier investigations presented this area as a rural backwater, possibly of interest only to Iron Age communities. The spatial distribution of the metal-detected finds has demonstrated that the intense and varied Iron Age and Roman activity to the south of Segsbury Camp was not mirrored in the wider landscape. Approximately 1,300 finds records were created during the three rallies and these are currently undergoing further analysis. While it has only been possible to discuss the major themes at this time, it is sufficient to show that this area of the Downs, and in particular the land to the south of Segsbury Camp, played a much greater role in the later Prehistoric and Romano-British history of the region than previously suspected.

Acknowledgements

We would like to thank all the PAS staff and volunteers who gave their time to assist in this project, and all the detectorists who recorded their finds. Without their help and co-operation this research would not be possible.

References

Allason-Jones, L. and Bishop, M. C. 1988, *Excavations at Roman Corbridge: the hoard*, Historic Buildings & Monuments Commission Archaeological Report 7 (Historic Buildings & Monuments Commission, London).

Bailey, R. 2005, 'The historical background and dating of the road'. in Lock, G., Gosden, C. and Daly, P. (eds.), *Segsbury Camp. Excavations in 1996 and 1997 at an Iron Age hillfort on the Oxfordshire Ridgeway*, University of Oxford School of Archaeology Monograph 61 (University of Oxford, Oxford), 17-24.

Bates, S. 2000, 'Excavations at Quidney Farm, Saham Toney, Norfolk 1995', *Britannia* 31, 201-37.

Bo Henriksen, M. 2009. *Brudager Mark: en romertidsgravplads nær Gudme på Sydøstfyn*, 2 vols (Odense Bys Museer, Odense).

Bradley, R. 1985, 'Exchange and social distance: the structure of Bronze artefact distributions', *Man*, New Series, 20. 4, 692-704.

Bradley, R. 1988, 'Hoarding, recycling and the consumption of Prehistoric metalwork: technological change in Western Europe', *World Archaeology* 20. 2, Hoards and Hoarding, 249-60.

Cotton, M. A. 1962, 'Berkshire hill-forts', *Berkshire Archaeological Journal* 60, 30-52.

Crummy, N. 2007, 'Brooches and the cult of Mercury', *Britannia* 38, 225-30.

Cunliffe, B. and Poole, C. (eds.). 2000, *The Danebury Environs Programme: the prehistory of a Wessex landscape, 2. 5: Nettlebank Copse, Wherwell, Hants. 1993*, English Heritage and Oxford University Committee for Archaeology Monograph No. 49 (English Heritage and Oxford University Committee for Archaeology, Oxford)

Fasham, P. J. 1987, *A 'Banjo' Enclosure in Micheldever Wood, Hampshire,* Hampshire Field Club Monograph 5 (Hampshire Field Club and Trust for Wessex Archaeology, Winchester).

Garnish, L. 1988, 'Is this a Roman road?': www.wantage.com/museum/Local_History/Roman%20Road.pdf

Gelling, M. 1995, *The Place-Names of Berkshire* 3 (English Place Name Society, Cambridge).

Henig, M. and Booth, P. 2000, *Roman Oxfordshire* (Sutton Publishing, Stroud).

Hingley, R. 1989, *Rural Settlement in Roman Britain* (London, Seaby).

Hutcheson, N. C. G. 2004, *Later Iron Age Norfolk: metalwork, landscape and society,* British Archaeological Reports, British Series 361 (Archaeopress, Oxford).

Levada, M. (2000), 'Metal combs of the second quarter of the first millennium AD in Eastern Europe,' in *Die spätromische Kaiserzeit und die frühe Völkerwandrungszeit in Mittel- und Osteuropa* (Wydawnictowo Uniwersytetu Lódzkiego, Lodz), 460-78.

Lock, G., Gosden, C. and Daly, P. (eds.). 2005, *Segsbury Camp. Excavations in 1996 and 1997 at an Iron Age hillfort on the Oxfordshire Ridgeway*, University of Oxford School of Archaeology Monograph 61 (University of Oxford, Oxford).

Miles, D., Palmer, S., Lock, G., Gosden, C. and Cromarty, A. M. (eds.). 2003, *Uffington White Horse Hill and its Landscape: investigations at White Horse Hill, Uffington, 1989–95 and Tower Hill, Ashbury, 1993–4*, Thames Valley Landscapes Monograph 18 (Oxford Archaeology, Oxford).

Needham, S. 1988, 'Selective deposition in the early Bronze Age', *World Archaeology* 20. 2, Hoards and Hoarding, 229-48.

Needham, S. 2001, 'When expediency brooches intention: the flow of metal between systemic and buried domains', *The Journal of the Royal Anthropological Institute* 7. 2, 275-98.

PASAR 2004/5 = Lewis, M. J. (ed.). 2005, *Portable Antiquities Scheme Annual Report* 2004/05 (MLA, London).

Payne, A., Corney, M. and Cunliffe, B. 2007, *The Wessex Hillforts Project: extensive survey of hillfort interiors in central southern England* (English Heritage, London).

Perry, B. T. 1986, 'Excavations at Bramdean, Hampshire 1983 and 1984, with some further discussion of the 'Banjo Syndrome', *Proceedings of the Hampshire Field Club Archaeological Society* 49, 35-42.

Rodwell, K. A. (ed.). 1975, *Historic Towns in Oxfordshire: a survey of the new county* (Oxfordshire Archaeological Unit, Oxford).

Rowlands, M. 1976, *The Production and Distribution of Metalwork in the Middle Bronze Age in Southern Britain*, British Archaeological Reports 31 (British Archaeological Reports, Oxford).

Salter, C. 2005, 'The slag-like material,' in Lock, G., Gosden, C. and Daly, P. (eds.), *Segsbury Camp. Excavations in 1996 and 1997 at an Iron Age hillfort on the Oxfordshire Ridgeway*, University of Oxford School of Archaeology Monograph 61 (University of Oxford, Oxford).

Small, F. 2002, *The Lambourn Downs: a report for the National Mapping Programme* (unpublished survey report, English Heritage, London).

Stead, I. 1991. *Iron Age Cemeteries in East Yorkshire,* English Heritage Archaeology Report 22 (English Heritage, London).

Winton, H. 2003, 'Possible Iron Age 'banjo' enclosures on the Lambourn Downs', *Oxoniensia* 68, 15-26.

York, J. 2002, 'The life cycle of Bronze Age metalwork from the Thames', *Oxford Journal of Archaeology* 21, 77-92.

An Assessment of the Archaeological Research Dividends of the Portable Antiquities Scheme: a case study of Bronze Age metalwork from East Anglia

Nisha Doshi

Established in 1997, the Portable Antiquities Scheme (PAS) celebrated its tenth anniversary in 2007. Although 85% of respondents to a user survey agreed that the Scheme had made 'a positive change by advancing knowledge of the past by systematically recording archaeological objects found by the public' (Edwards 2006: 4), it has been argued that there has been insufficient evaluation of both the use of PAS data in research projects (Chitty and Edwards 2004) and the implications of using the PAS database as a research tool (Cool 2001). This paper investigates the Scheme's potential contribution to archaeological research, taking as a case study Bronze Age (*c.* 2100 to *c.* 800 BC) copper/copper-alloy metalwork recorded in Cambridgeshire, Norfolk and Suffolk (Fig. 1): i.e. East Anglia excluding Essex (with its distinctly Thames Valley character).

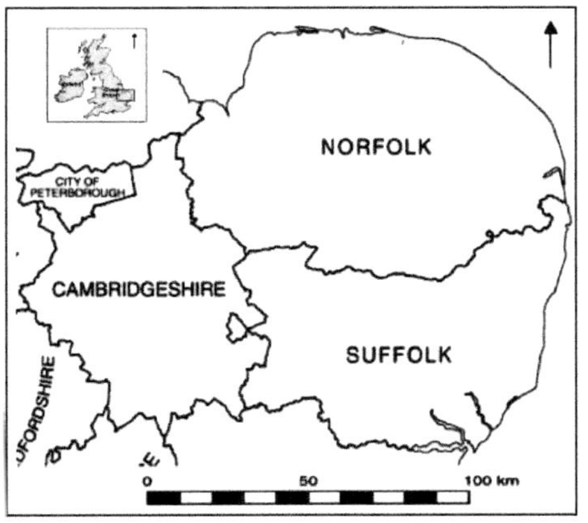

Fig. 1: Map showing research area in East Anglia (adapted from Ordnance Survey 2001).

East Anglia represents an appropriate region for a case study since it is predominantly agricultural and thus characteristic of much of lowland Britain, and a relatively small proportion of East Anglia is inaccessible to detectorists and field-walkers (Holman 1985). The fenland was a key area for Bronze Age metal deposition (Thomas 1999). Furthermore, metal-detected finds have been recorded in Norfolk and Suffolk since the popularisation of metal-detecting in the 1970s (Fletcher 1977; Green and Gregory 1978) and data from these counties should therefore facilitate evaluation of the long-term research dividends of recording chance finds. On the other hand, Cambridgeshire has a short history of recording detected finds and the PAS was only introduced there in December 2003. This is more representative of other counties and should therefore provide a more typical illustration of the Scheme's impact on archaeological knowledge.

To assess the research potential of PAS-recorded Bronze Age metalwork, comparative data were also collected from the Historic Environment Records (HERs) for these counties. To standardise data, records from the inception of each database to 1 October 2007 were examined. Results were analysed in order to address the following questions:

- What effect does the PAS have on the quantity of Bronze Age metalwork data available for archaeological research?
- To what extent does the quality of PAS data impact their utility for academic archaeological research?
- Does the PAS contribute different proportions of artefact types from other datasets? How might any differences be explained and what impact may they have on our understanding of the Bronze Age?
- How does the distribution of Bronze Age metal objects reported to the PAS compare with previous distributions? How might PAS and HER data contribute to analysis of metalwork deposition?

This paper presents the results and conclusions of research with regard to PAS artefact-based data. It also briefly summarises the results of findspot-based and distributional analyses of PAS and HER East Anglian Bronze Age metalwork data (see Doshi 2008 for a more detailed evaluation).

What effect does the PAS have on the quantity of Bronze Age metalwork data available for archaeological research?

It is apparent from Table 1 that the PAS has made a considerable quantitative addition to Bronze Age copper/copper-alloy metalwork, increasing recorded artefacts by 21% overall. This represents a valuable contribution to the pool of data available for research, especially when timescales of data collection are compared: i.e. less than 10 years for PAS data, as opposed to more than 40 years for HER data. However, it

	Cambridgeshire	Norfolk	Suffolk	Treasure	Total
HER	571	3,176	1,788	-	**5,535**
PAS	59	310	596	183	**1,148**
Total	630	3,486	2,384	183	**6,683**

Table 1: ***Total number of copper/copper-alloy artefacts recorded at 1 October 2007 by the HERs and PAS in Cambridgeshire, Norfolk and Suffolk.***

has been argued that the expansion of rescue archaeology has generated an 'information explosion' (Champion 2007; Thomas 1991). Given a potential 'data overload', this paper asks whether PAS-recorded artefacts add anything new to Bronze Age research or simply replicate existing data.

To what extent does the quality of PAS artefact-based data impact their utility for academic archaeological research?

In contrast with HERs, which are predominantly monument-based, PAS records are primarily artefact-centred. The PAS aims to make available as much finds data as possible, whilst simultaneously safeguarding personal information and protecting sites from damage (Bland and Lewis 2004). *Bona fide* researchers can access complete password-protected records and any interested party can access partial records online (including descriptions, images and measurements). Burnett (2000) identifies four principal advantages deriving from online databases: efficiency of publication; ease of searching; ability to link with other databases; and facility to reveal different levels of detail for different purposes. The PAS database also functions across a variety of different operating systems and Internet browsers (Chitty and Edwards 2004) and enables regionally-based Finds Liaison Officers (FLOs) to enter information directly into a national, centralised resource. Furthermore, online resources have a 'democratising impact', broadcasting archaeological information openly, widely and quickly (Hull 2007). This is underlined by the 82 million user-hits on the Scheme's website during 2006 alone (PASAR 2007). It could also be argued that the decentred flexible connections of the PAS relational database encapsulate theoretical calls for a shift from linear text to 'rhizomatics' (cf. Shanks and Hodder 1995).

PAS keyword searches generate summary records with thumbnail images, object identifications and brief descriptions. The database also facilitates searches for similar/related finds, placing in context the object(s) under study (Cool 2001). Data can be exported in xml or csv format, generating readily-usable spreadsheets. Object database fields (Fig. 2) are standardised nationally, thus all PAS records are easily understood and information readily located. Moreover, the PAS database fulfils the requirements of an international, multi-sector agreement (entitled 'Object ID') by including object type, material, measurements, distinguishing features, date/period, short description and photographs (cf. Thornes 1997). This renders PAS data compatible not only with many other records and archives in England and Wales, but also with regional and national databases elsewhere in Europe (Leech 1999).

Stringent PAS data-entry protocols and thesauri maximise consistency, compatibility and retrievability of information without inhibiting flexibility (e.g. Quine 1999). Although researchers must be vigilant since occasional classification errors occur (e.g. CAM-DC93B6 - a PAS rapier recorded as a sword) {1}, PAS object identifications are qualified with 'certain', 'probably' or 'possibly', warning researchers of potential inaccuracies. In addition, PAS records are validated by expert National Finds Advisers and are colour-coded according to their validation status. The facility to modify interpretations and descriptions, coupled with a transparent recording process, ensures that PAS identifications are not 'black-boxed' (cf. Shanks and Hodder 1995) but are open to re-analysis.

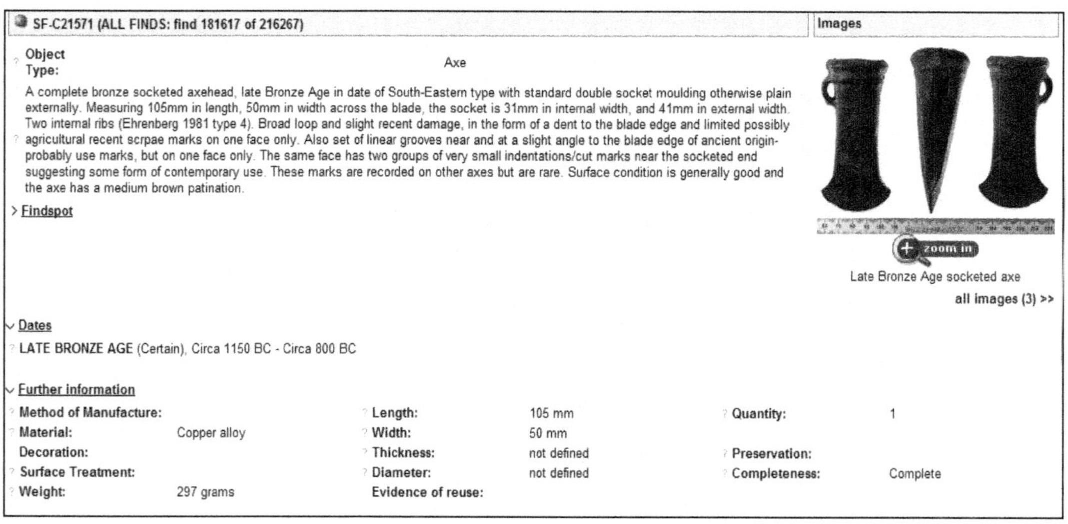
SF-C21571 (ALL FINDS: find 181617 of 216267)

Object Type: Axe

A complete bronze socketed axehead, late Bronze Age in date of South-Eastern type with standard double socket moulding otherwise plain externally. Measuring 105mm in length, 50mm in width across the blade, the socket is 31mm in internal width, and 41mm in external width. Two internal ribs (Ehrenberg 1981 type 4). Broad loop and slight recent damage, in the form of a dent to the blade edge and limited possibly agricultural recent scrpae marks on one face only. Also set of linear grooves near and at a slight angle to the blade edge of ancient origin- probably use marks, but on one face only. The same face has two groups of very small indentations/cut marks near the socketed end suggesting some form of contemporary use. These marks are recorded on other axes but are rare. Surface condition is generally good and the axe has a medium brown patination.

> Findspot

Images

zoom in

Late Bronze Age socketed axe

all images (3) >>

Dates

LATE BRONZE AGE (Certain), Circa 1150 BC - Circa 800 BC

Further information

Method of Manufacture:		Length:	105 mm	Quantity:	1
Material:	Copper alloy	Width:	50 mm		
Decoration:		Thickness:	not defined	Preservation:	
Surface Treatment:		Diameter:	not defined	Completeness:	Complete
Weight:	297 grams	Evidence of reuse:			

Fig. 2: Example of artefact-based data on a PAS record: SF-C21571.

	Cambridgeshire	Norfolk	Suffolk
Total number of PAS records	58	227	381
Number of PAS records for which images are available	47	145	323
Percentage of PAS records for which images are available (%)	81	64	85

Table 2: PAS Bronze Age records with images for copper/copper-alloy objects.

Measurements are provided for 78% of PAS-recorded artefacts and images are available for a substantial proportion (Table 2). Almost all PAS images have scales, supported by measurements, and the majority are high-quality photographs or drawings (e.g. Fig. 2). Since objects cannot be retained by the PAS, images are crucial for both documentation and interpretation of artefacts (cf. Leibhammer 2000). Indeed, as written descriptions depend upon selection and judgement (Shanks and Hodder 1995), images are not merely visual appendages but provide 'summaries' of objects, facilitating re-description and reinterpretation. PAS records' juxtaposition of comprehensive descriptions with high-quality illustrations therefore significantly enhances their usefulness for academic research.

PAS finds grouped as a 'hoard' in the 'Object Type' field represent the principal exception to these observations. Descriptions are often much less detailed, dimensions are rarely recorded and quantities may be ambiguous. Moreover, there appear to be no guidelines for recording hoards in PAS records. In some cases, object type is recorded as 'hoard' and individual artefacts are listed in the description; in others, artefacts are recorded separately and 'hoard' is noted in the description field. Alternatively, some PAS records group artefacts from the same findspot but make no mention of a hoard. Currently, therefore, PAS data appear to be inadequate for analysing the phenomenon of hoarding. {2}

With the exception of hoards, the above analysis suggests PAS records are well suited to artefact-centred research. Such a focus has often been a point of contention between archaeologists and detectorists - professional archaeologists often define their identity and practice in contrast to those who are merely preoccupied with objects (Beith and Flanagan 1981; Wylie 2002; 2005). Artefact-based studies have in fact been neglected in recent Bronze Age research (Burgess 2004; Ben Roberts, pers. comm.). Nevertheless, material culture is increasingly taking centre-stage in archaeological theory (Hegmon 2003; Tilley *et al.* 2006) and many theorists argue that objects form the foci around which networks of interpretations should be built (Barrett 1988; Hodder 2001; Shanks and Hodder 1995). Furthermore, British Bronze Age chronology has recently become firmly grounded using absolute dating techniques (Table 3), facilitating object-based investigations. The next section of this paper therefore utilises chronological and typological frameworks to assess the potential contribution of PAS artefact-centred data to Bronze Age studies in East Anglia.

Period BC	**Metalwork Stage**		**Approximate Dates (cal BC)**	
			Needham *et al.* 1997	Brindley 2007
'Copper stages' *c.* 2700-*c.* 2100	I	Castletown Roche		
	II	Knocknague		
	III	Frankford		
Early Bronze Age *c.* 2100-*c.* 1500	IV	Migdale-Killaha		
	V	Aylesford-Colleonard		
	VI	Willerby Wold		
	VII	Arreton Inch Island		
Middle Bronze Age *c.* 1500-*c.* 1000	VIII	Acton Park 1 (MBA 1)		1575-1400
		Acton Park 2	1500-1400	
	IX	Taunton (MBA 2)	1400-1275	1400-1250
	X	Penard (LBA 1)	1275-1140	1250-1125
Late Bronze Age *c.* 1000-*c.* 600	XI	Wilburton (LBA 2)	1140-1020	1125-975
		Blackmoor	1020-920	975-900
	XII	Ewart Park (LBA 3)	920-800	900-800
	XIII	Llyn Fawr (LBA 4)	800-700	800-600

Table 3: Principal British Bronze Age chronological divisions (after Brindley 2007; Needham 1996; Needham et al. 1997; O'Connor 1980).

Does the PAS contribute different proportions of artefact types from other datasets? How might any differences be explained and what impact may they have on our understanding of the Bronze Age?

Taylor's (1993) study of Bronze Age metalwork in southern Britain defines and compares the proportions of five artefact categories: weapons, tools, ornaments, 'miscellaneous' and ingots/metalworking waste. Although it has been argued that tying artefacts to definitive categories ignores ambiguities (Shanks and Hodder 1995; Hodder 1999), classification remains a fundamental facet of archaeological practice, facilitates comparison between datasets and, if undertaken appropriately, may identify rather than marginalise particularities and rarities (cf. Read 2008). Taylor's categories have therefore been used to group East Anglian PAS and HER data, and these three datasets are compared in Figure 3. The proportions of weapons, tools and 'miscellaneous' artefacts are not substantially different, while the exclusion of gold objects from this analysis of PAS and HER data may explain the under-representation of ornaments *vis-à-vis* Taylor's dataset. However, PAS data clearly contain a higher proportion of ingots and metalworking waste. Prior to the Scheme, detectorists were less likely to retain or report such material (Hobbs *et al.* 2002), whereas they are now encouraged to report all finds. This may enhance knowledge of the scale and distribution of Bronze Age metalworking in East Anglia.

If PAS data are not significantly different from other datasets in terms of broad categories of weapons/tools/ornaments, it may be more fruitful to examine specific artefact types. Since limited space precludes examination of all 1,148 artefacts (Table 1), subsets must be selected for classification and comparison with other studies. Ashwin (1996) predicted that metal-detected finds would contribute particularly to studies of 'utilitarian' objects; indeed, tools are the most abundant Bronze Age metalwork category in East Anglia, and axes are the most numerous tool type (Lawson 1984). Table 4 therefore compares PAS axes and non-axe tools with those in pre-PAS HERs. {3}

Quantitative comparison of axe types suggests that, numerically, the PAS' contribution to pre-PAS HER data is not important (Fig. 4). However, significant numbers of 'non-axe' tools have been recorded in the PAS dataset (<10 years) *vis-à-vis* pre-PAS HER data (*c.* 30 years) (Fig. 5).

Non-axe tools rarely feature in Bronze Age literature. In contrast, spearheads have been studied intensively, both on a national scale (e.g. Davis 2006) and in East Anglia (e.g. Appleby 2003; Bridgford 2000), and are the second most numerous artefact type in East Anglian PAS records (105 at 1 October 2007). Axes, non-axe tools and spearheads are therefore analysed below to assess the PAS' potential contribution to archaeological research.

Analysis: Tools

Axes

Socketed axes are the most common British Late Bronze Age (LBA) artefact (Langmaid 1976) and are three times more abundant than any other metal object in East Anglian PAS records. Many PAS-recorded axes are well-known types e.g. Southeastern (Pearce 1984); however, rare forms such as a shouldered axe (SF11010) are also present - these occur more commonly in Ireland and France, hinting at links with these areas (O'Connor 1980). Particularly notable are ten very late Ewart Park (LBA 3) or Llyn Fawr (LBA 4) socketed axes from Suffolk, including: four Sompting-related forms (SF5748, 9079, 4CB546 and 3739) and one LBA 4 linear-faceted (SF3721) (cf. Burgess 1969; Coombs 1971; 1979; Coombs *et al.* 2003); two very large LBA 4 or LBA 3-4 transitional forms (SF-A66AD4, 988301, the latter with an unusually wide blade of 70mm); and one Armorican form (SF10817). LBA 4 axes are relatively uncommon in Suffolk and much rarer than LBA 3 (O'Connor 1980, 2007). Armorican and Sompting-related types suggest continental links and/or influence (Burgess 1974).

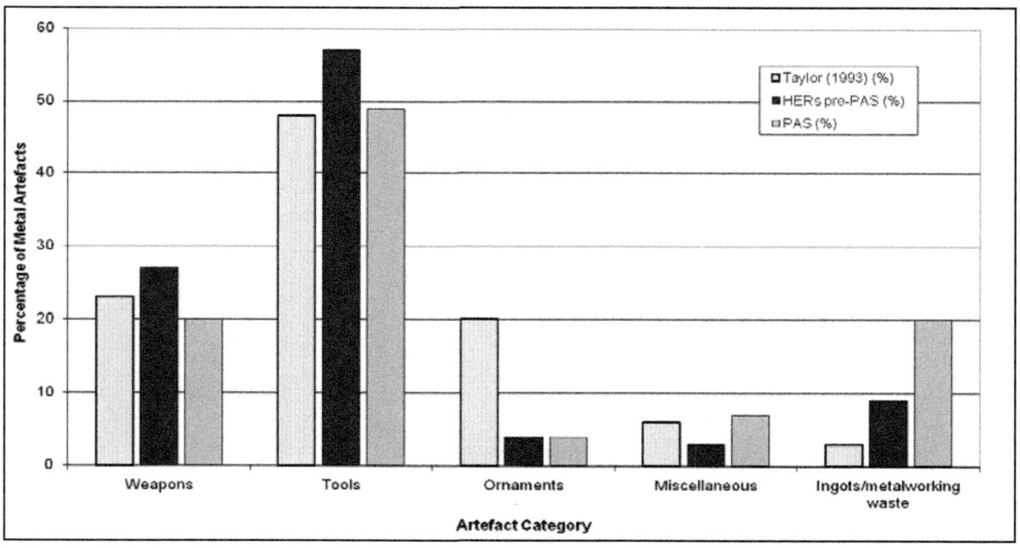

Fig. 3: Comparative proportions of East Anglian Bronze Age metal artefact categories in Taylor's (1993) study, and HER and PAS datasets.

Tool Type	No. of HER Tools (pre-PAS) (*c*.30 years)	No. of PAS Tools (<10 years)	% Increase Contributed by PAS
Axes			
Socketed axe	1,085	346	32
Flat axe	90	16	18
Flanged axe	114	13	11
Winged axe	17	4	24
Palstave	489	30	6
Axe (non-specific)	153	27	18
Adze	2	0	0
Non-Axe Tools			
Awl/tracer	74	55	74
Chisel	80	27	34
Gouge	56	26	46
Hammer	13	7	54
Sickle	10	8	80
'Leatherworking' tool	0	1	100
Saw	2	0	0
Punch	5	2	40
Burin	1	0	0
Point	1	0	0

Table 4: Number of tools in East Anglian HER (pre-PAS) and PAS records at 1 October 2007, and percentage increase contributed by the PAS.

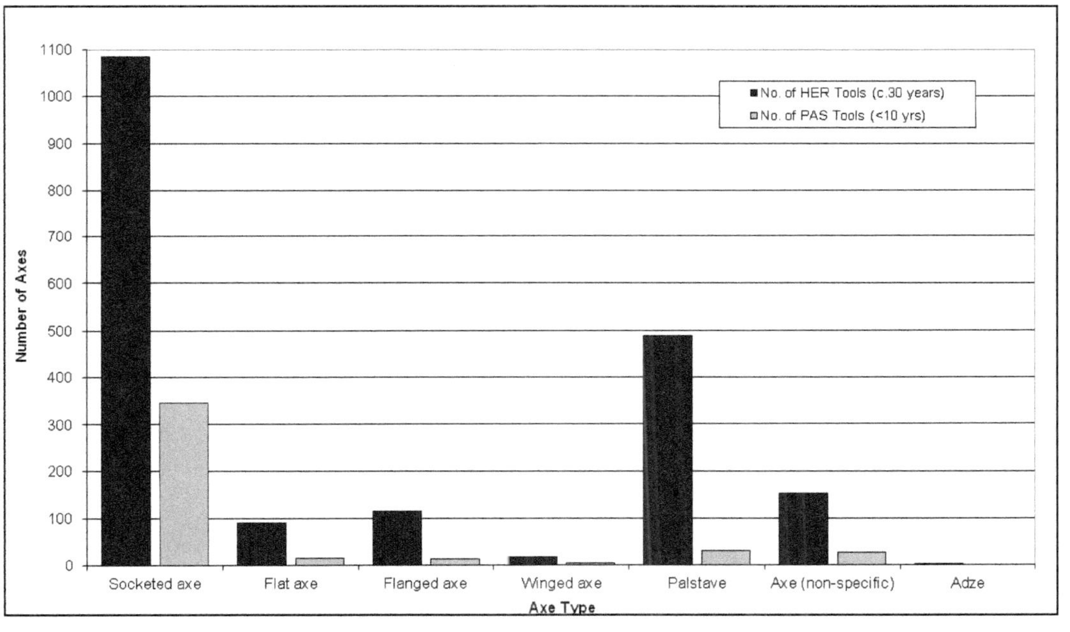

Fig. 4: Number of axes in East Anglian HER (pre-PAS) and PAS records at 1 October 2007.

Although the PAS database contains only sixteen East Anglian flat axes (Table 4), two are characteristic of extremely rare, very early forms (Fig. 6). Of the 13 PAS flanged axes, five (e.g. SF-9072A6) have low flanges and/or punched decoration more characteristic of early or Inch Island (Irish) examples than the high-flanged Arreton axes with hammered decoration considered typical for East Anglia (cf. Burgess 1974; Burgess and Cowen 1972), while one (NMS122) is attributed to the principally Scottish Kirtomy type (Schmidt and Burgess 1981). A haft-flanged axe with short, leaf-shaped flanges, marked stopridge and crescentic blade (SF-DC9112; cf. Rowlands 1976) - a relatively rare form in southern England - may indicate local development of palstaves from flanged axes with stopridges (cf. O'Connor 1980). This would support Burgess' (1980) conjecture that British palstaves developed independently of the continent, possibly in Eastern England.

Despite the comparatively low number of PAS palstaves (Table 4), these strengthen the Scheme's contribution to LBA metalwork: of the 30 recorded, 11 are Transitional/Late types, which are much less common than Middle Bronze Age (MBA) palstaves (Allen *et al.* 1970; Lawson 1984; McNeil 1972), and one is a rare Type Silsden (NMS573; cf. Schmidt & Burgess 1981).

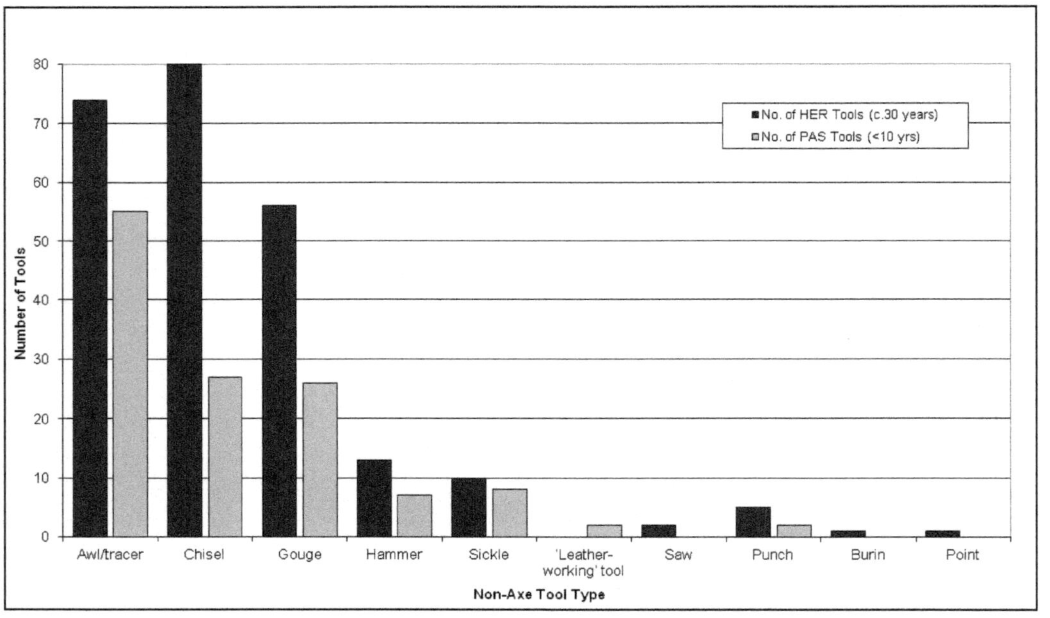

Fig. 5: Number of non-axe tools in East Anglian HER (pre-PAS) and PAS records.

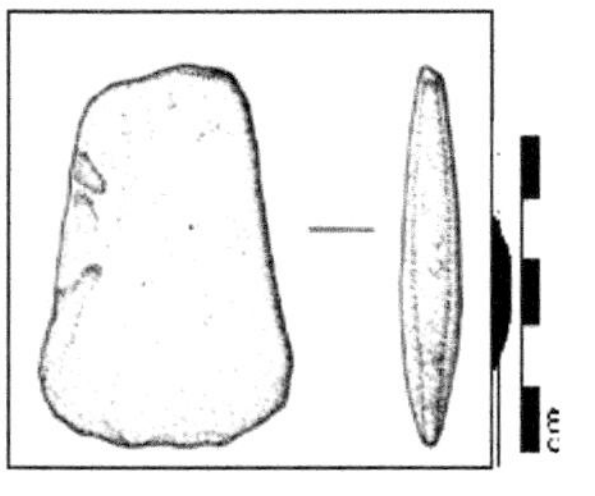

Fig. 6a: Flat axe SF7977.

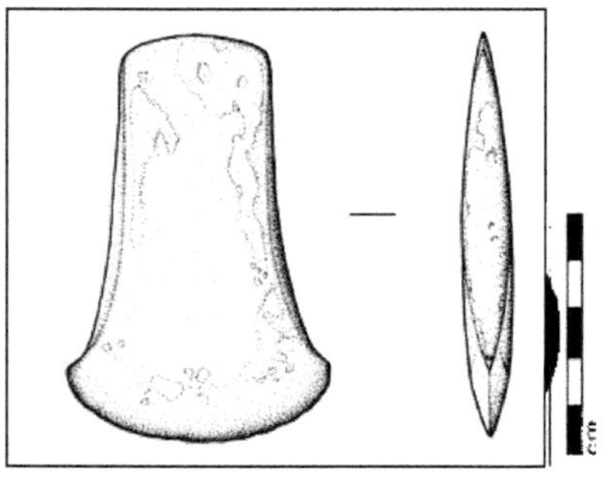

Fig. 6b: Flat axe SF-CDBF47.

Fig. 6: Two very early and extremely rare PAS flat axes (Donna Wreathall): a) copper, relatively straight sides, characteristic of Burgess' (1974) Group A Stage I axes; b) bronze, broad-butted with lenticular long profile, Stage II axe - a type usually made of copper (cf. Burgess 1980; Needham 1996).

MBA palstaves appear to include Rowlands' Class I Group 5b (SF-14BEC5), which is rare for northern East Anglia (being concentrated in the Thames Valley), while the flanges of SF-985D05 are suggestive of the relatively uncommon Class 3 (cf. Rowlands 1976).

Awls/Tracers

Discussion of awls is usually limited to passing comment regarding their presence in Early/Middle Bronze Age (EBA/MBA) burials or settlements, or as an element of the Beaker/EBA 'package' (e.g. Burgess 1980; Butler 1988; Lawson 1986). Indeed, awls are absent from O'Connor's (1980) otherwise thorough discussion of Bronze Age metalwork. However, 55 PAS awls/tracers increase the 61 documented in this area by Pendleton (1999) by 90%, and those in the pre-PAS HERs by 74% (Table 4).

This not only represents a valuable quantitative contribution but also challenges Coombs' (1971) assertion that awls were uncommon in the LBA: analysis of PAS awls shows that 64% are the square-sectioned single-pointed type, characteristic of the later MBA and LBA (cf. Pearce 1983), while 20% are directly attributed to the LBA. If awls are correctly interpreted as leatherworking implements (e.g. Burgess 1980) this attests to the importance of leatherworking throughout the Bronze Age. Furthermore, the PAS corpus contains rarer types, including collared awls (e.g. SF-279D44) and those with hexagonal and octagonal sections (e.g. SF-6923D3, 44D9F7), and an unusual implement (Fig. 7) which may support the hypothesis that some of these tools were used as tracers for incising decoration onto metalwork (Maryon 1938). This could be an important find since the functions of Bronze Age awls/tracers are unclear (Pendleton 2003).

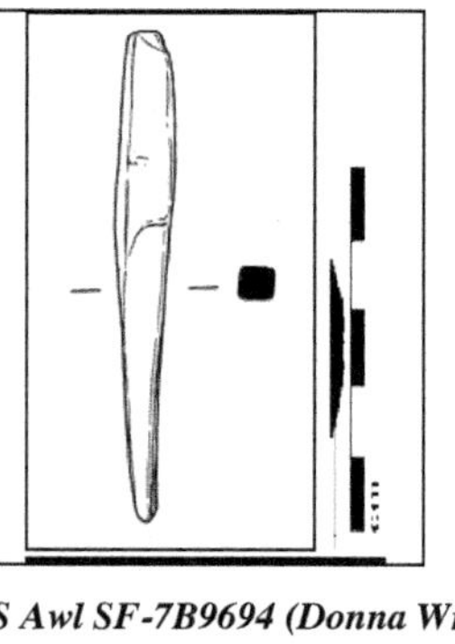

Fig. 7: PAS Awl SF-7B9694 (Donna Wreathall) The mid-point is square in cross-section but both ends are lozenge-shaped in cross-section, and are very worn and twisted in opposite directions, suggesting this tool was used to work a material more resistant than leather.

Class	Characteristics	Length to Edge Ratio	Distribution
I	Plain mouth; narrow blade	4.9	Thames Valley
IIa	Deep collar; narrow blade	5.3	East Anglia
IIb	Ribs/incised lines around mouth	5.6	South England and Thames Valley
III	Small, squat, with wide splayed cutting edge; with/without moulding; never ribbed	2.5	Rare

Table 5: Classification of East Anglian PAS socketed gouges (after Coombs 1971: 251-53).

Chisels

Chisels are also seldom discussed in Bronze Age literature. Pendleton's (1999) survey documented 68 in East Anglia and 80 were recorded in the pre-PAS HERs; PAS data add a further 27 (Table 4). In particular, PAS finds more than double the number of socketed chisels known to O'Connor (1980) and the number of lugged chisels in Pendleton's (1999) survey. Two PAS chisels (NMS-46125, SF3579) have concave-sided blades, a rare form usually confined to Ireland (Burgess *et al.* 1972). The presence of at least one socketed chisel with no clear division between socket and blade may indicate affinities with Breton types (Coombs 1971), while a tanged-and-collared chisel (SF-B480B1) is similar to those found in the Langdon Bay wreck and implies continental connections (Muckelroy 1981).

PAS chisels also exhibit a range of cutting-edge shapes, from almost straight to crescentic, and include flanged, lugged, tanged, socketed and 'palstave' forms. This diversity suggests they span the Bronze Age (cf. Savory 1980) and supports Pendleton's (1999) conclusion that East Anglian chisels were put to a wide variety of uses: those with straight cutting edges (e.g. CAM-A804E6) may have been employed for mortising and those with curved edges for other woodworking tasks (O'Connor 1980); bevelled edges (e.g. NMS-894E92) may have enhanced suitability for carpentry (Maryon 1938). Lastly, six tanged chisels, generally interpreted as leatherworking tools, reinforce the evidence for leatherworking discussed above.

Gouges

The 26 PAS gouges add 46% to pre-PAS HER artefacts (Table 4) and are socketed, supporting contentions that socketed gouges are more common than socketed chisels (e.g. Clough 1979; Coombs 1979). Length to edge ratios of complete PAS gouges range from 4.5 to 5.7 and are therefore more variable than Coombs' (1971) regional classification predicts (Table 5). Furthermore, of the five gouges assignable to a class (on the basis of morphological features) four show more affinities with Class I than Class IIa. PAS data either indicate that East Anglian socketed gouges were more diverse than Coombs believed, or infer influence from the Thames Valley.

Hammers

The seven PAS bronze hammers add 54% to the pre-PAS HERs' total (Table 4), and date to the Ewart Park phase (cf. Britton 1960; Coombs 1971; O'Connor 1980). Bronze hammers played an important role in preparing or re-sharpening metal objects (Taylor 1993) but are marginalised in the literature, which tends to focus on mining at the expense of later metalworking stages (e.g. Ixer and Pattrick 2003, Timberlake 2003). PAS finds may help redress the incongruity between the number of artefacts displaying hammer-marks (including numerous socketed axes in the PAS dataset) and the apparent rarity of hammers (e.g. Pearce 1983).

Sickles

Despite an abundance of Central European Bronze Age sickles (e.g. Maraszek 2000; Nebelsick 2000) and archaeobotanical evidence for the importance of crop production, British sickles are relatively rare; the eight PAS sickles add 44% to Pendleton's (1999) corpus and 80% to those in the pre-PAS HERs (Table 4).

Although most PAS sickles take the form of blade fragments, their weight appears to be centrally concentrated, suggesting they are socketed and supporting the contention that non-socketed sickles are untypical of East Anglia (Fox 1941; Lawson 1979; O'Connor 1980). Surviving sockets appear to represent Fox's (1939) ring-socketed Group I, and support Coombs' (1971) conclusion that ring-socketed sickles are concentrated in Cambridgeshire. In addition, an unusual blade cast at 45° to the socket instead of 90° (SF10118; Fig. 8) may imply local experimentation rather than importation from Ireland or the Thames Valley (cf. Fox 1939), while the range of blades (2.0-7.5 mm thick) supports arguments that several were too thin to be functional and were thus reserved for ceremonial/display purposes (Langmaid 1976).

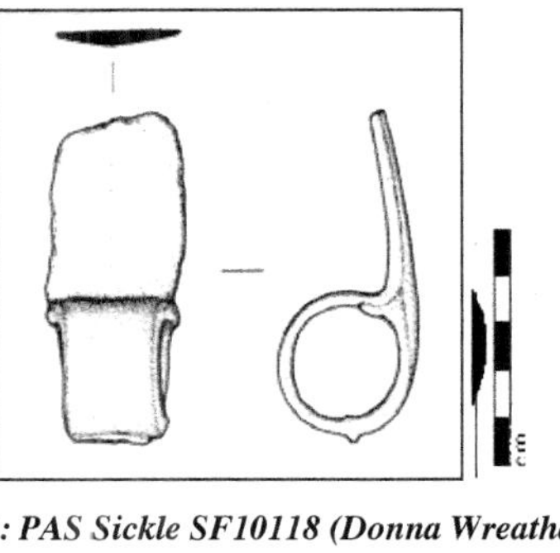

Fig. 8: PAS Sickle SF10118 (Donna Wreathall).

Class	PAS/Treasure No.	No. of PAS Spearheads
Side-looped	NMS-4AE4E1, 936, 470, 174, NLM739, SF-26B707, A75A56, 7EC7E2, 8920, 3835	10
Basal-looped with triangular-shaped blade	SF-A759E5, 8440	2
Rapier-bladed	NMS101, 108	2
Pegged	NMS-O7C165, ESS-O3OCB5, SF9898, 10116, 10241, 10240, 4843, 3753, 2221, 2004 T441, 2005 T234 (23 pegged spearheads), 2006 T10	34
Transitional between kite-shaped and side-looped	SF3547	1
Pegged with vestigial side-loops	NMS-80CE31, SF9908	2
Possibly basal-looped (leaf-shaped blade) and pegged	NMS-53B865	1

Table 6: Classification of 52 PAS spearheads from East Anglia (after Ehrenberg 1977).

Analysis of tools reported to the PAS therefore demonstrates that these artefacts contribute to Bronze Age research in several ways. Not only does a significant proportion of known East Anglian 'small tools' (chisels, gouges, awls, hammers and sickles) {4} derive from PAS data, but several rare types have also been identified and some hypotheses reinforced (e.g. continental links and the impracticality of some sickle blades). However, are contributions limited to artefact types which were previously relatively rare and/or little-studied, or can PAS data also enhance understandings of well-studied artefacts, such as Bronze Age spearheads?

Analysis: Spearheads

A number of classifications have been proposed for spearheads, of which Ehrenberg's (1977) is most closely adhered to by PAS artefact descriptions. Of the 105 PAS spearheads, 53 lack sufficient detail to permit classification and are therefore too limited to contribute to artefact-based research; however, the remaining 52 spearheads can be classified (Table 6), to assess their potential 'research dividends'.

A number of points emerge from this classification. Firstly, a rare form (SF3547), transitional between Irish kite-shaped and side-looped spearheads, may confirm suggestions that side-looped spearheads developed directly from kite-shaped (Davis 2006; Ehrenberg 1977; Rowlands 1976), rather than from continental leaf-shaped spearheads (cf. Evans 1933, Hawkes 1941). Moreover, this artefact implies that side-looped spearheads either developed in East Anglia as well as in Ireland (cf. Ramsey 1989), or indicates movement from Ireland. Local experimentation is also suggested by two pegged spearheads with vestigial side-loops (NMS-80CE31, SF9908), and by one which may be both basal-looped and pegged (NMS-53B865). The distribution of PAS spearheads across typological classes can be compared with Appleby's (2003) data (Fig. 9). This reveals a higher-than-expected proportion of side-looped spearheads in the PAS dataset, and a lower-than-expected proportion of basal-looped types. It is unlikely that these variances are chronological, since the main use-periods are largely contemporaneous (Ehrenberg 1977). However, side-looped spearheads are usually smaller than basal-looped (Osgood 1998), and therefore blade length may be a factor.

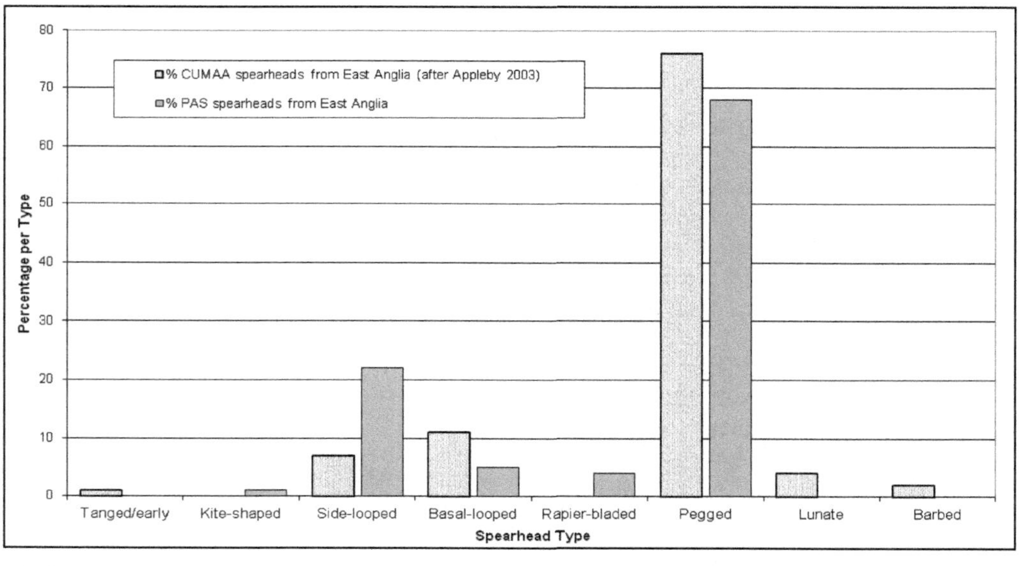

Fig. 9: Comparative proportions of East Anglian spearhead types in the Cambridge University Museum of Archaeology and Anthropology collection (Appleby 2003) and PAS records at 1 October 2007.

Spearhead Class	Average Blade Length (mm)	PAS Record No.	Blade Length (mm)
Side-looped	90–120 (Ehrenberg 1977)	SF-26B707	56
		SF-A75A56	65
		SF-7EC7E2	71
		NLM739	<57
Basal-looped (triangular blade)	120–470 (Ehrenberg 1977); 250 (Davis 2006)	SF8440	85
Pegged	Mostly 100–200, though can be >400 (Ehrenberg 1977)	SF10016	68
		SF10241	50
		SF10240	67
		SF4843	<71
		SF3753	69
		SF2221	<82
		2004-T441	90

Table 7: Comparison of PAS spearhead blades with published average blade lengths, where class and dimensions can be ascertained (Davis 2006; Ehrenberg 1977).

Spearhead Blade Shape	Definition (Bridgford 2000)	Museum Study % (Bridgford 2000)	PAS %
Lanceolate	Sides form continuous convex curve from base to point	75	73
Flame-shaped	Sides form continuous convex curve but, where blade reaches maximum width, become slightly concave or straight, culminating in long, narrow tip	8	5
Ogival	Similar to flame-shaped but blade narrows abruptly before tip; sides are more sinuous	7	8
Barbed	Largely straight parallel sides, abrupt 'shovel' tip, barbed or horizontal base	1	0
Triangular	Straight sides, although base corners may be rounded	8	14

Table 8: Comparison of blade proportions in Bridgford's (2000) East Anglian museum study with PAS spearheads (using Bridgford's blade shape classification). Percentages expressed to nearest integer.

PAS spearhead blades are clearly shorter than published averages (Table 7). Since ogival-shaped blades are typically shorter than lanceolate blades (Burgess *et al.* 1972), perhaps PAS spearheads include a disproportionate number of ogival blades? However, comparison with Bridgford's (2000) study of East Anglian spearheads from museum collections suggests this is not the case (Table 8).

Hence, the smaller PAS spearheads cannot simply be attributed to blade shape. It is often argued that small spearheads were thrown, while larger types were thrusting weapons or had ceremonial/display functions (Ehrenberg 1977; Osgood 1998; Pryor 1991). Perhaps PAS data signify that small, javelin-like spearheads were more common than previously supposed. This conjecture is supported by the under-representation not only of basal-looped spearheads, but also of potentially ceremonial/decorative types, notably barbed spearheads, which tended to be impractical for military use (Osgood 1998), and of spearheads with lunate openings (Davies 1967; Davis 2006). PAS data therefore suggest that previous corpora may have been biased towards larger types.

Discussion

A number of recurring themes emerge. Firstly, small items - both small-sized tool types and spearheads - appear to be over-represented in PAS data *vis-à-vis* previous datasets. Even within tool types, particularly small artefacts seem to be characteristic of PAS material. For example, large flanged chisels are considered the most common MBA form in East Anglia (Rowlands 1976), yet only one PAS chisel is flanged (NMS-894E92). Probable bias towards large objects in existing Bronze Age corpora was observed by Needham and Dean (1987) and Pryor (1992). In contrast, Pendleton (1999) notes the small size of metal-detected finds: 55% of his catalogue are <6cm in length. This rises to 67% for PAS artefacts, as illustrated by Figure 10.

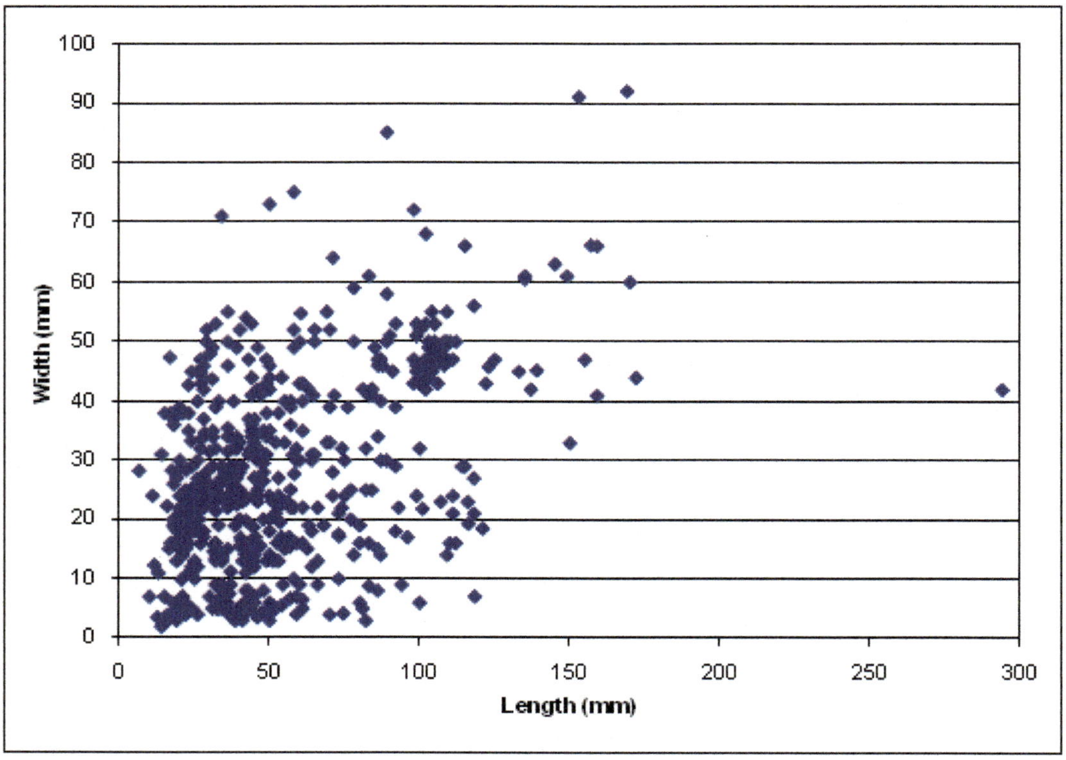

Fig. 10: Size of copper/copper-alloy artefacts in East Anglian PAS records at 1 October 2007.

It has been argued that large objects were selectively deposited in the Bronze Age, due to their enhanced scrap value (e.g. Barrett and Needham 1988); however, PAS data appear to challenge such arguments, adding new colour to our understanding of deposition practices. How might this be explained? Before the inception of the PAS, larger objects were more likely to be recognised and retained by finders, reported to archaeologists and subsequently identified, recorded and acquired by museums (Bridgford 1997). The PAS encourages all finds to be reported, no matter how small or apparently fragmented/unidentifiable (Carr *et al.* 2007), and records all reported objects. Consequently, the predominance of large artefacts in previous corpora probably derived from preferential identification/recording. Are PAS data biased towards small objects, however? This is unlikely: short and thin items are less likely to be found by detectors than those with larger surface areas (Cool 2001; Garrett 1992). Thus, if many small artefacts are found, it is unlikely that larger objects are missed. The number of small objects therefore indicates that the PAS dataset could be more representative of the overall range of artefacts deposited in the Bronze Age than previous corpora.

Furthermore, the absence of large, decorative spearheads in PAS records casts doubt on interpretations that spearheads were primarily symbols of rank and power, employed for display and ceremony (e.g. Gilman 1981; Kristiansen 1998, 2001). Instead, PAS data may support Hodges' (1957) hypothesis that large spearheads were weapons but small spearheads were hunting implements. If weapons are defined as 'objects designed primarily to inflict bodily harm when used by one combatant against another' (Bridgford 2000: 5) the small spearheads prevalent in the PAS dataset may be hunting tools. Indeed, the second theme to emerge is diversity of tool types - a theme related to, but with significance beyond, the proliferation of small-sized artefacts. Much literature relegates 'small tools' to the 'miscellaneous' category (e.g. Davey 1971; Davey *et al.* 1999; Lawson 1980). Where they are mentioned, their rarity is most frequently remarked upon (e.g. Coombs 1971, 1975; Ehrenberg 1981; Pryor 2005). Burgess (1980) and Harding (1976) specifically note the paucity of carpentry tools. However, PAS data suggest that woodworking, leatherworking and metalworking tools may be more common than previously supposed. This should not be surprising: for example, many tools would have been required to create the estimated 12,000 mortice-and-tenon joints in a wooden vehicle, since nails were unknown in Bronze Age Britain (Coombs 1971). Wood was probably the most widely-used material, yet its exploitation is little understood due to its poor preservation and the scarcity of woodworking tools to date (Earwood 1993; Roberts forthcoming). However, the efficiency of bronze palstaves in felling trees has been demonstrated experimentally (Mathieu and Meyer 1997), and the variety of PAS chisels and gouges implies a wide range of woodworking tools and techniques. PAS artefacts therefore provide an opportunity to redress 'the depth of ignorance about most woodworking in the Bronze Age' (Harding 2000: 243).

The rarity of metalworking tools, such as hammers, has been interpreted as evidence for smiths' ambiguous (dangerous/powerful) social position (Barrett and Needham 1988); PAS records suggest that hammers may not have been so uncommon, however. Alongside augmented quantities of metalworking waste and ingots, hammers present an opportunity to enhance knowledge of East Anglian Bronze Age metalworking. Similarly, the abundance of PAS-recorded awls corroborates the large collections of bronze awls from Flag Fen (Coombs 2001; Pryor 1992) and bone awls from West Row Fen (Martin and Murphy 1988), suggesting that these artefacts were also more common than previously believed. In addition, several rare types were noted (e.g. collared awls), and chisels and gouges were more diverse than previous East Anglian studies suggest. Thus claims regarding lack of diversity of British Bronze Age artefacts (e.g. Burgess and Coombs 1979) become untenable, and it can be argued that the broader range of types, in PAS data, increases the probability that patterns are of archaeological significance as opposed to merely reflecting biases in identification and recording. Equally, it can be argued that artefacts whose numbers are not enhanced by the PAS, e.g. adzes, saws and burins (Table 4), were either genuinely rare in the Bronze Age or were not selected for deposition.

A third recurring theme is the presence of larger-than-expected numbers of certain Late Bronze Age artefact types, notably awls, Transitional/Late palstaves, and very late Ewart Park or Llyn Fawr socketed axes. Moreover, the spearheads with measurable blade lengths were all <100mm in length and thus may represent 'short, stumpy' types (Colquhoun 1979; Ehrenberg 1977), which were current during the Ewart Park phase. This supports conclusions reached by earlier studies (e.g. Lawson 1984; Needham *et al.* 1997; Taylor 1993) that substantial quantities of metalwork were deposited during that phase. Therefore, PAS records enhance representations of artefacts dated to the very early and very late Bronze Age (such as Stage I and Llyn Fawr axes), and confirm understandings regarding the broad dynamics of metal deposition over time.

Possible localised development of artefact types is the fourth theme to emerge. It was shown above that some sickle forms and spearhead types hint at local experimentation, and a haft-flanged axe may indicate local development of palstaves from flanged axes. Hence PAS data strengthen the image of East Anglia as an area of innovative metalworking, while the number of transitional types resonates with arguments that new artefacts were most likely to be accepted if they meshed with familiar forms (e.g. Gosden 2005; Sofaer Derevenski and Sørensen 2002).

Lastly, a number of PAS artefacts indicate links between East Anglia and other British/continental regions. For example, gouges and a possible Class I Group 5b palstave (SF-14BEC5) hint at contact with the Thames Valley, early flat axes (e.g. SF7977, DCBF47) and concave-sided chisels (NMS-46125, SF3579) with Ireland, while a shouldered axe (SF11010) may have derived from Ireland or France, and a Kirtomy-type flanged axe (NMS122) may demonstrate Scottish associations. Tanged-and-collared and socketed chisels (e.g. SF-B480B1, NMS-F5F761) also suggest links with France and socketed hammers (e.g. NMS-4D3FD2) may indicate Nordic influence (Burgess 1974).

It therefore appears that PAS East Anglian data do contribute different proportions of some Bronze Age artefact types *vis-à-vis* other datasets, increasing the representation of small tools and spearheads, as well as metalworking waste. Although Mount (2001) argues that metal-detecting only recovers a restricted range of Bronze Age artefact types in Ireland, this analysis has shown that PAS records amplify the diversity of East Anglian types. However, no new types have been recognised and broad category proportions (e.g. tools and weapons) generally mirror those in previous datasets. Some PAS records were insufficient to permit accurate analysis and classification, particularly for spearheads. Furthermore, the above-noted themes largely reinforce previous understandings (such as the predominance of Ewart Park metalwork), or supplement already-identified research topics (e.g. contacts with other regions/countries). Thus, the contribution of PAS data to our research toolkit is most valuable when used alongside detailed chronological and typological frameworks and other artefact records, such as museum catalogues and HERs.

Nevertheless, these conclusions do not diminish the PAS' impact: the above analyses highlight new avenues for detailed research (such as the practices and tools of carpentry, leatherworking and metalworking) and demonstrate that the Scheme can directly provide data with which to commence such research. The PAS' most significant contribution to Bronze Age studies, however, appears to be its representativeness. Since the Scheme is voluntary, it is impossible to ensure that reported objects are representative of all finds; nonetheless, the abundance of small artefacts and identification of rare types suggest that PAS data provide a more rounded picture of the range of metalwork deposited than previous corpora and enable us to approach research with increased confidence that our data more closely represent the dynamics of Bronze Age deposition. As a result, it is possible to broaden the assessment of the PAS' research potential, from artefact-based data to the pivot of Bronze Age deposition studies, namely landscape distribution.

To what extent does the quality of PAS findspot-based data impact their utility for academic archaeological research?

Password-protected PAS findspot data include National Grid Reference (NGR), parish, county, landuse, finder and method of discovery (e.g. metal-detecting or field-walking). Partial information is available on the 'open' website, to preserve the security and confidentiality of findspots and finders. Dobinson and Denison (1995: 27) noted that 'the information on a find's exact provenance provided by detectorists is generally very poor'. As a result of the PAS, the situation appears to have improved considerably in East Anglia (Doshi 2008). For example, a very high proportion of PAS Bronze Age records have NGRs precise to within $100m^2$ (98.1% *vis-à-vis* 77.5% of HER records) and few lack findspot data (1.1% compared with 11.8% HER records). Moreover, the PAS aims to improve NGR precision in future - an important objective for East Anglia, where only 4.5% of findspots are provenanced to within $1m^2$. However, as artefacts can move up to 13m in a single ploughing episode (Campling 2006), precision within $10m^2$ (86.5% of PAS NGRs) may sometimes be adequate.

Variable findspot precision has implications for the types of research question for which these data can be employed. Wide-ranging precision restricts the use of many statistical methods and GIS tools (e.g. buffers) and hinders quantitative analysis of finds recorded within a given distance of waterways - a factor of particular interest to Bronze Age researchers. Topographical analysis is also precluded, as this requires findspot precision within 50m in East Anglia (Pendleton 1999). Nevertheless, these limitations apply to many datasets, including HERs. On the other hand, since 98.1% of PAS NGRs are precise within $100m^2$, spatial analysis can be undertaken in broad landscape terms. Indeed, Chester-Kadwell (2005) advocates the use of metal-detected finds to reveal wide-scale distributions, complementing the small-scale picture provided by excavations.

In addition, archaeologists frequently question the reliability of findspots reported by detectorists (Longworth 1988; Dobinson and Denison 1995) and, unfortunately, PAS FLOs' experience indicates that false provenances are occasionally provided. Although this reduces the utility of PAS provenance data for research, this problem affects most Bronze Age metalwork datasets. Furthermore, FLOs query suspect reports, note inconsistencies, and record on the database subsequent reservations about findspot accuracy. Researchers are therefore made aware of potential problems with PAS data (cf. Ulmschneider 2000).

Impact of metal-detecting and other modern factors on artefact distributions: PAS data as a source of 'calibration'

Other factors may influence the reliability of detector-sourced distributions. Firstly, not all land-types are equally suited to detecting: for example, compacted ground is more suitable than freshly-ploughed soil (Barber 1990). The type of detector may also exacerbate the impact of land-type, e.g. Transmit-Receive detectors are ineffective over mineralised ground (Dobinson and Denison 1995). Despite the potential impact of these factors on finds distributions, detector types and findspot mineral data are not recorded by the PAS, while landuse is often simply listed as 'undetermined' cultivated land, which is too vague for land-type analysis of artefact distributions. Fortunately, however, East Anglian soil is subject to flushing and is relatively mineral-free (Plumridge 2003) and many detectorists revisit fields over several years, reducing variances caused by crop type, tillage and weather conditions (Chester-Kadwell 2005).

Haphazard detecting may also affect findspot distribution. To counter this, FLOs encourage finders to use GPS (Global Positioning Systems) devices and undertake systematic, gridded surveys wherever possible (Amy Cooper, pers. comm.; cf. Wood 2005). Permission to search can be difficult to obtain (Webb 2005; Winter 2007), so detecting is not evenly distributed across the landscape - a problem which is not restricted to the PAS but affects all detector-sourced data. Moreover, it has been argued that the location of metal-detecting clubs and urban areas influence East Anglian artefact distributions (Crowther 1983; Gurney 1997; Pendleton 1999). However, few studies consider the impact of these factors in detail.

PAS data present a means of addressing this issue: since distributions of period-specific finds can be compared with the distribution of finds for all periods, the impact of modern (as opposed to period-specific) factors on finds densities can be investigated. To illustrate this, the distribution of PAS and HER East Anglian Bronze Age metalwork was compared with the distribution of PAS finds for all periods (Doshi 2008). Several areas with few Bronze Age metal finds mirrored those with few finds for all periods and these patterns could be explained by the following factors: Cambridgeshire's short history of recording metal-detected finds *vis-à-vis* Norfolk and Suffolk; detectorists' claims that they rarely search the Fens; and prohibition or restriction of detecting in areas such as the Ouse Washes conservation area, Areas of Outstanding Natural Beauty, The Broads National Park, and scheduled monuments. Distance from detecting clubs (where PAS staff record finds) may also have affected the number of reported finds and low finds densities coincided with some urban settlements.

Spatial data for PAS finds from all periods therefore provides a useful means of 'calibrating' period-specific distributions (cf. Millett 1985; Chester-Kadwell 2005) and indicates that several modern factors influence Bronze Age metalwork distribution, particularly those which affect detectorists' access. Nevertheless, these factors do not exert a uniform effect; for example some areas with little urbanisation had fewer findspots than might be expected, while urbanised areas in central Norfolk and south-eastern Suffolk had more (Doshi 2008). Metalwork distribution in the Bronze Age landscape therefore appeared to be subject to other influences as well, and the next section therefore summarises analysis of PAS and HER findspot data in relation to Bronze Age landscape models.

How does the *distribution* of Bronze Age metal objects reported to the PAS compare with previous distributions? How might PAS and HER data contribute to analysis of metalwork deposition?

Detailed analyses of findspot distributions are presented in the author's MPhil thesis (Doshi 2008); the results are briefly summarised here.

Two trends emerged from comparison of the distribution of PAS and HER Bronze Age metalwork in East Anglia (Doshi 2008). Firstly, whereas published maps (e.g. Evans 2002; Yates 2007) reveal marked concentrations of metalwork on the Bronze Age fen-edge, no such concentrations were suggested by PAS data. This may simply reflect detectorists' avoidance of the Fens (see above). Nevertheless, as fen-edge foci have formed an important element of interpretations of British metalwork deposition, this issue was considered worthy of further examination. Secondly, PAS data filled some apparent 'gaps' in Bronze Age distributions, e.g. flanged axes in eastern Suffolk and hammers in southern Suffolk and central Norfolk. This phenomenon was particularly marked for awls throughout Norfolk and Suffolk, while chisels were more widely dispersed in northern Norfolk, and gouges in Suffolk, than other datasets suggest. Distributional analysis therefore supported the conclusion that the PAS' impact is particularly significant with regard to small artefacts, especially tools such as awls, chisels and gouges. It is argued that these objects are associated with domestic sites (e.g. Butler 1988; Grieg 1972; Pearce 1983); their strong presence in the PAS dataset thus raises the possibility that hitherto unknown settlements may be revealed. Detailed field-based studies would be required to evaluate this possibility; nevertheless, correlations between PAS findspots and known settlements can be examined (see Doshi 2008).

Excluding the wider distribution of small tools and apparent absence of fen-edge concentrations, PAS findspots largely mirrored artefact distributions in HER data and previous studies (Doshi 2008). Furthermore, artefact-based analysis concluded that the contribution of PAS records to Bronze Age research is enhanced when analysed in conjunction with other studies and datasets. Combined PAS and HER data were therefore compared with previous hypotheses and understandings, to consider the extent to which the enlarged dataset may contribute to archaeological research of metalwork distribution in East Anglia.

Recent interpretations of Bronze Age landscapes can be grouped into three principal models, focusing upon zones, boundaries and route-ways respectively (Doshi 2008). To date, however, studies have relied on relatively small datasets e.g. *c.* 650 artefacts from the southern Netherlands (Fontijn 2002), 302 from the Thames (York 2002), and 382 from Lancashire (Barrowclough 2007). PAS and HER East Anglian data overcome this shortcoming, since they represent a combined dataset of 6,683 artefacts (Table 1), of which 80.6% have findspots precise to within 100m^2. To assess the potential contribution of combined PAS-HER data to analysis of Bronze Age metalwork deposition, artefact distributions were examined in the light of the three models. In keeping with recent prehistoric metalwork studies (e.g. Barrowclough 2007; Hutcheson 2004), findspots within 500m of landscape features were deemed to be 'close'.

As in Fontijn's (2002) model of Dutch metalwork, analysis of PAS and HER data suggested that selective metalwork deposition distinguished zones for settlement, burial, routeways and wet/dry areas in the East Anglian landscape (Fig. 11). However, specificities differ. For example, metalwork deposition largely avoided settlement zones in the Netherlands (Fontijn 2002) but ornaments, awls and chisels were spatially associated with settlements in Cambridgeshire. This reinforces the contention that PAS data may contribute particularly to studies of artefacts from domestic contexts. Relationships also differ from those in other regions: e.g. awls were characteristic of dry and rapiers of wet locations in Lancashire (Barrowclough 2007) whereas the reverse appears to characterise East Anglia.

'Rules' guiding deposition seem to have been complex: although distribution of many artefacts correlated with river valley arteries, certain types (e.g. flanged axes and awls) were closely associated with East Anglian waterways but avoided the fen-edge, while others (e.g. rapiers) were often deposited further away from watercourses but associated with the fen-edge. Moreover, although broad East Anglian zones were recognised (Fig. 11), artefacts selected for deposition appear to have varied intra-regionally, e.g. palstaves and spearheads were concentrated in Cambridgeshire, swords and knives in southern Suffolk. On the other hand, some East Anglian traditions resonate with those beyond the region: for example, the close association of swords with waterways parallels relationships in Ireland (Bourke 2001). It could therefore be argued that some understandings of landscape use and artefact deposition extended across Britain (and perhaps near-continental Europe), while specificities of concepts and practices were worked out locally.

PAS and HER metalwork distribution also appeared to correlate with field systems, particularly along the Great Ouse, Cam and Snail and at fenland-river junctions, suggesting that boundaries were also significant in structuring metalwork deposition. However, widespread associations between metalwork deposition and the fen-edge were not upheld, the association between metal artefacts and liminality appeared less prevalent than previously believed, and zones were less spatially-distinct than those in the Netherlands. Indeed, associations between specific objects and zones were not clear-cut and many exceptions were evident (Doshi 2008). Perhaps this derived from imperfect and contested recollections of earlier deposition events (cf. Barnatt and Edmonds 2002). Perhaps, as a result of the interplay between longer-term traditions (e.g. acceptability of objects in particular zones) and the flux of practices in unmarked 'landscapes of memory', boundaries were fuzzy and focal zones shifted through time. The concept of 'taskspace', where specific activities were allocated to designated zones, which were themselves subject to negotiation and reformulation (Ingold 2000), thus seems relevant for the East Anglian Bronze Age landscape.

Combined PAS and HER data therefore differ from previously-known distributions, especially in terms of fen-edge foci, and qualify some understandings of metalwork deposition in the Bronze Age landscape (such as the importance of liminality), while reinforcing others (such as the correlation of small tools with settlements, and axes with routeways). In particular, these data demonstrate ways in which the structure of East Anglian metalwork distribution resonates with that in other regions, and shed light on nuances within the East Anglian landscape, where previous models do not entirely mesh.

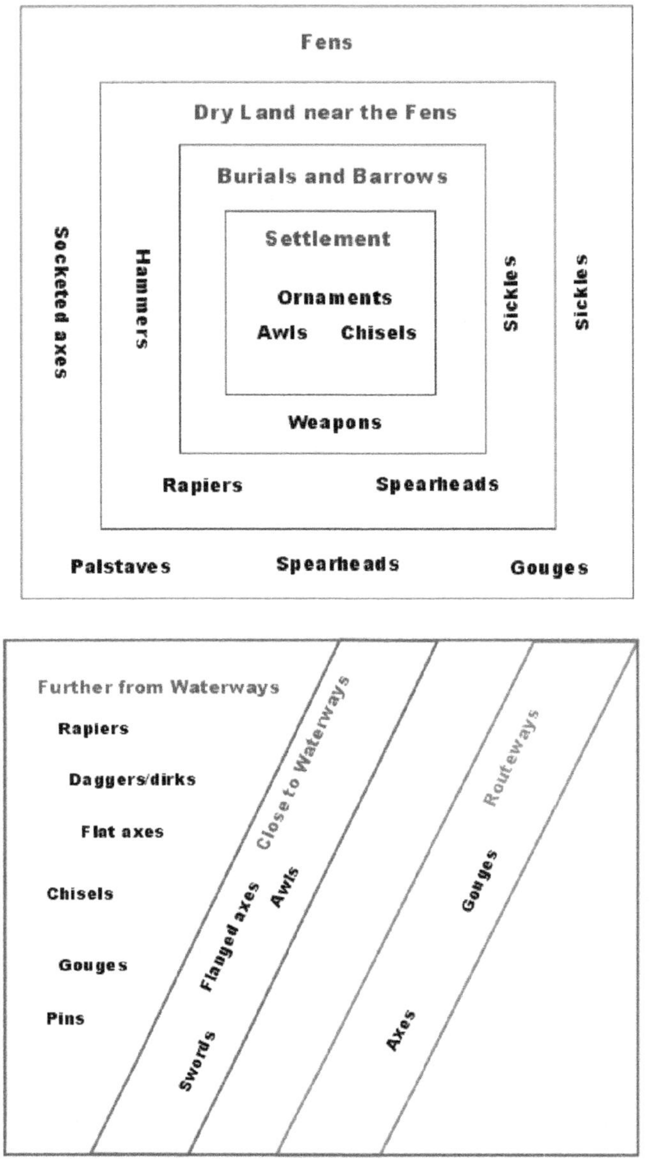

Fig. 11: Associations between metal artefact types and landscape zones in East Anglia.

Analysis indicates that selective deposition reflected 'a structured cultural understanding of the land, in which different places and zones had different and possibly even conflicting meanings' (Fontijn 2002: 271). However, those understandings, structures and practices seem to have been played out in subtly different ways, in different areas and at different times. From PAS and HER findspot data, it can thus be argued that East Anglian zones and boundaries were more ambiguous or contested than previous models have suggested.

Conclusions

'If we are to avoid "drowning in a pollution of unprocessed data" we must do two things. We must ensure that we are able to structure, control and use that information, rather than be overwhelmed by it, and we must ensure that the means are found to exploit the potential of that information to yield new knowledge' (Thomas 1991: 828).

The research for this paper has demonstrated that, through a flexible yet comprehensive online database, the PAS structures and controls information in a manner which is efficient and suitable for archaeological research; it has also shown that PAS data can shed new light on Bronze Age artefact and landscape studies. In the same way that community projects overseas have encouraged archaeologists to answer questions that would not otherwise have been considered (e.g. Marshall 2002; McDavid 2000), so PAS records challenge prevailing assumptions about Bronze Age East Anglia by enhancing knowledge of previously under-represented artefact types and providing data with which to consider little-researched topics.

The PAS' recording system is indeed 'a fluid, systematic and well prepared methodology' (Connolly 2007): systematic in that all records are created using standardised processes, data-entry forms and terminology; and fluid in that each record incorporates detailed object-specific information, benefits from specialist knowledge, can log doubts regarding the certainty of identifications or findspots, and can easily be amended. In addition, the online nature of PAS records renders data and recording processes both transparent and accessible (cf. Pescarin 2007).

The Scheme's relational database facilitates Shanks and Hodder's (1995) dual goals of 'commentary' (interpretation of artefacts in historical context), by identifying contemporary parallels, and 'critique' (building comparisons beyond an artefact's period), by archiving finds from all regions and periods in a single database and enabling a multitude of keyword-based searches. Most PAS records are of a high quality and the Scheme's protocol embodies the widely recognised need for consistency and common standards in archaeological records and archives (e.g. Owen 1995; Perrin 2002). As with all inventories, PAS data require evaluation before they can be applied to research questions (cf. Barber 1999) and, unfortunately, not all records are amenable to detailed academic research (e.g. only 50% of East Anglian spearheads could be classified to a sub-type). Nevertheless, the abundance of high-quality descriptions and images, and the ease with which data accuracy can be cross-checked, offset some of the drawbacks for archaeological investigation.

In their major survey of metal-detecting and archaeology, Dobinson and Denison (1995) found references to only eleven Bronze Age metal-detected artefacts. Thanks to the long-term efforts of Norfolk and Suffolk HER staff and, more recently, the PAS, the dataset used for this paper comprised 6,683 Bronze Age finds from East Anglia alone, the majority of which derived from metal-detecting. Although it is estimated that *c.* 30% of metal-detected finds still go unrecorded (Roger Bland, pers. comm.), it is clear that the proportion of finds which are reported and thus available for archaeological research has increased dramatically since the inception of the PAS.

Contrary to assertions that the PAS merely exacerbates data overload (e.g. Cuddeford 2000), it has been demonstrated that PAS data generate different proportions of artefact types from previous datasets (particularly enhancing the representation of small, rare and transitional types). They also indicate more extensive links between East Anglia and other regions/countries, challenge arguments for deposition bias towards larger objects, and highlight new avenues for research, such as the practices and tools of leatherworking, metalworking and woodworking.

With regard to distribution analyses, combined PAS and HER data complement detailed, small-scale information from excavations, producing images of the broader landscape. Although findspot precision is rarely sufficient for detailed contextual analysis, the PAS has significantly increased the proportion of finds for which grid references are available in East Anglia, particularly the percentage with NGRs precise to within $100m^2$. Several problems with metal-detected data were identified; nevertheless, these also affect other metalwork datasets, and the PAS has taken steps to overcome, or raise awareness of, some potentially distorting factors. Moreover, the facility to map PAS finds for all periods provides a means of 'calibrating' period-specific findspots (cf. Chester-Kadwell 2005; Millett 1985); comparing distributions of East Anglian Bronze Age metalwork with finds for all periods not only indicated areas in which modern factors might account for a paucity of finds, but also suggested that spatial distribution was influenced by other factors which required archaeological analysis.

Indeed, examination of PAS and HER findspots, in the light of three models of Bronze Age metalwork deposition, permitted evaluation of the relevance of concepts of zones, boundaries and routeways, utilising a much larger dataset than researchers had previously employed to address such questions. Although many facets of these models were upheld, PAS and HER distributions qualified previous understandings, revealing more fluid zones, fuzzier boundaries and some dissonance with notions of fen-edge foci and liminality. Spatial analysis has also revealed that PAS and HER data considerably improve our knowledge of awl, chisel and gouge distributions, supporting the conclusion that the PAS presents a more complete picture of Bronze Age metalwork in East Anglia than previous datasets.

Thus, although many academic archaeologists are ambivalent about the research value of finds that lack archaeological context - however well-provenanced they may be (Chitty and Edwards 2004) - and despite the fact that 'issues and value judgements [regarding the PAS, archaeology and metal-detecting]... seem unlikely to be agreed within the archaeological profession, never mind universally' (Renfrew 1995), the Scheme's research potential is manifest. The PAS database is believed to be the largest of its kind in the world (Bland 2009) and this paper has demonstrated that both its artefact-based and findspot-based (provenance) information have significant research value.

Endnotes

{1} This has now been corrected by PAS staff.
{2} This situation should improve dramatically as a result of the systematic incorporation of Treasure finds in the PAS database since 2007 (Dan Pett, pers. comm.)
{3} In some counties, PAS records are now being added to the HERs. Thus, HER data prior to the introduction of the PAS are used to eliminate the risk of duplications in this analysis.
{4} The definition of 'small tools' follows Needham (1988).

Acknowledgements

This paper is based upon my MPhil thesis, submitted to the University of Cambridge in August 2008, and I would like to thank my supervisor, Dr Marie Louise Sørensen, for her advice and support. I am very grateful to Sarah Poppy (formerly Senior Archaeologist, Cambridge Archaeology), Colin Pendleton (SMR Officer, Suffolk County Council), Alice Cattermole (HER Officer, Norfolk Landscape Archaeology) and Dan Pett (ICT

Advisor, PAS) for providing digital copies and/or access to paper archives of PAS and HER datasets and to Roger Bland (Head of PAS and Treasure, British Museum) for providing data from the 2005 and 2006 Treasure Annual Reports ahead of publication. I would also like to thank Amy Cooper (West and South Yorkshire FLO), Helen Geake and Sally Worrell (PAS Finds Advisers), Ben Roberts (Curator, European Bronze Age, British Museum), Ezra Zubrow (University of Buffalo) and Alex Pryor (University of Cambridge) for helpful and stimulating discussions whilst I was undertaking research for this paper.

Bibliography

Allen, I. M., Britton, D. and Coghlan, H. H. 1970, *Metallurgical Reports on British and Irish Bronze Age Implements and Weapons in the Pitt Rivers Museum* (Oxford University Press, Oxford).

Appleby, G. A. 2003, *Warfare or Use-Wear: conflicts in interpretation* (unpublished BA dissertation, University of Cambridge).

Ashwin, T. 1996, 'Neolithic and Bronze Age Norfolk', *Proceedings of the Prehistoric Society* 62, 41-62.

Barber, L. A. 1990, *Metal Detecting for Archaeology* (unpublished BSc dissertation, University College London).

Barber, M. 1999, 'Archaeological monuments: standardization and explanation', in Hansen, H. J. and Quine, G. (eds.), *Our Fragile Heritage: documenting the past for the future* (National Museum of Denmark, Copenhagen), 113-21.

Barnatt, J. and Edmonds, M. 2002, 'Places Apart? Caves and monuments in Neolithic and Earlier Bronze Age Britain', *Cambridge Archaeological Journal* 12, 113-29.

Barrett, J. C. 1988, 'Fields of discourse: reconstituting a social archaeology', *Critique of Anthropology* 7 (3), 5-16.

Barrett, J. C. and Needham, S. P. 1988, 'Production, circulation and exchange: problems in the interpretation of Bronze Age bronzework', in Barrett, J. C. and Kinnes, I. A. (eds.), *The Archaeology of Context in the Neolithic and Bronze Age: recent trends* (Sheffield University Department of Archaeology, Sheffield), 127-40.

Barrowclough, D. A. 2007, *Multi-Temporality and Material Culture: an investigation of continuity and change in later prehistoric Lancashire*, British Archaeological Reports, British Series 436 (Archaeopress, Oxford).

Beith, A. and Flanagan, O. J. 1981, 'Recommendation', in Beith, A. and Flanagan, O. J. (eds.), *Metal Detectors and Archaeology: report on the Committee on Culture and Education* (Council of Europe, Strasbourg), 1-13.

Bland, R. and Lewis, M. 2004, *Draft Transfer of Portable Antiquities Scheme (PAS) finds data to Historic Environment Records (HERs)* (Portable Antiquities Scheme, London).

Bland, R. 2009, 'The UK as both a source country and a market country: some problems in regulating the market in UK antiquities and the challenge of the Internet', in MacKenzie, S. and Green, P. (eds.), *Proceedings of the Conference on Trade in Illicit Antiquities* (Hart, Oxford), 83-102.

Bourke, L. 2001, *Crossing the Rubicon: Bronze Age metalwork from Irish rivers* (National University of Ireland, Galway).

Bridgford, S. D. 2000, *Weapons, warfare and society in Britain 1270-750 B.C.* (unpublished PhD thesis, University of Sheffield).

Brindley, A. L. 2007, *The Dating of Food Vessels and Urns in Ireland* (National University of Ireland, Galway).

Britton, D. 1960, 'The Isleham Hoard, Cambridgeshire', *Antiquity* 34, 279-82.

Burgess, C. 1969, 'Some decorated socketed axes in Canon Greenwell's collection', *Yorkshire Archaeological Journal* 42, 267-72.

Burgess, C. 1974, 'The bronze age', in Renfrew, C. (ed.), *British Prehistory: a new outline* (Duckworth, London), 165-222.

Burgess, C. 1980, *The Age of Stonehenge* (Phoenix Press, London).

Burgess, C. 2004, 'Forty-five years' researches in the chronology and ordering of the British Bronze Age: a personal memoir', in Gibson, A. and Sheridan, A. (eds.), *From Sickles to Circles: Britain and Ireland at the time of Stonehenge* (Tempus, Stroud), 339-65.

Burgess, C., Coombs, D. and Davies, D. G. 1972, 'The Broadward Complex and barbed spearheads', in Lynch, F. and Burgess, C. (eds.), *Prehistoric Man in Wales and the West: essays in honour of Lily F. Chitty* (Adams & Dart, Bath), 211-83.

Burgess, C. and Cowen, J. D. 1972, 'The Ebnal Hoard and Early Bronze Age metal-working traditions', in Lynch, F. and Burgess, C. (eds.), *Prehistoric Man in Wales and the West: essays in honour of Lily F. Chitty* (Adams and Dart, Bath), 167-81.

Burgess, C. and Coombs, D. (eds.) 1979, *Bronze Age Hoards: some finds old and new*, British Archaeological Reports, British Series 67 (British Archaeological Reports Limited, Oxford).

Burnett, A. 2000, 'The scheme for recording portable antiquities in Britain: progress report', International Numismatic Commission Inc., *Compte Rendu* 47, 78-85, http://www.muenzgeschichte.ch/downloads/laws-britain-portableantiquities.pdf

Butler, C. 1988, 'Bronze Age awl from Plumpton, East Sussex', *Sussex Archaeological Collections* 126, 228.

Campling, N. 2006, 'Plough damages henges', *British Archaeology* 90, 26.

Carr, J., Darch, E., Minter, F., Walton, P. and Waters, J. 2007, 'PAS regional feature: a word from the Eastern Region', *Treasure Hunting*, June 2007, 39-40.

Champion, T. 2007, 'Settlement in Kent from 1500 to 300 BC', in Haselgrove, C. and Pope, R. (eds.), *The Earlier Iron Age in Britain and the Near Continent* (Oxbow, Oxford), 293-305.

Chester-Kadwell, M. 2005, 'Metal-detector finds in context: new light on 'Dark Age' cemeteries in the landscape of Norfolk, *Archaeological Review from Cambridge* 20(1), 70-96.

Chitty, G. and Edwards, R. 2004, *Review of Portable Antiquities Scheme 2004* (Hawkshead Archaeology and Conservation Consultancy), http://www.finds.org.uk/documents/PAS_Review_Report_Final.pdf

Colquhoun, I. A. 1979, 'The Late Bronze Age hoard from Blackmoor, Hampshire', in Burgess, C. and Coombs, D. (eds.), *Bronze Age Hoards: some finds old and new*, British Archaeological Reports, British Series 67 (British Archaeological Reports Limited, Oxford), 99-115.

Connolly, D. 2007, 'Thornborough Henges rally report', *The Searcher* 257, 56-57.

Cool, H. E. M. 2001, *The Iron Age and Roman Finds in the Portable Antiquities Database* (unpublished report).

Coombs, D. 1971, *Late Bronze Age Metalwork in the South of England: typology, associations, distributions, chronology and industrial traditions* (unpublished PhD thesis, University of Cambridge).

Coombs, D. 1975, 'Bronze Age weapon hoards in Britain', *Archaeologia Atlantica* 1, 49-81.

Coombs, D. 1979, 'A Late Bronze Age hoard from Cassiobridge Farm, Watford, Hertfordshire', in Burgess, C. and Coombs, D. (eds.), *Bronze Age Hoards: some finds old and new*, British Archaeological Reports, British Series 67 (British Archaeological Reports Limited, Oxford), 197-223.

Coombs, D. 2001, 'Metalwork', in Pryor, F. (ed.), *The Flag Fen Basin: archaeology and environment of a Fenland landscape* (English Heritage Archaeological Reports, London), 255-98.

Coombs, D., Northover, P. and Maskall, J. 2003, 'Tower Hill axe hoard', in Miles, D., Palmer, S., Lock, G., Gosden, C. and Cromarty, A. (eds.), *Uffington White Horse and its Landscape: investigations at White Horse Hill, Uffington, 1989-95 and Tower Hill, Ashbury, 1993-4*, Thames Valley Landscapes Monograph 18 (University of Oxford, Oxford), 202-23.

Crowther, D. R. 1983, 'Swords to ploughshares: a nationwide survey of archaeologists and treasure hunting clubs', *Archaeological Review from Cambridge* 2(1), 9-20.

Cuddeford, M. J. 2000, *Detecting 2000: a new guide to the hobby of metal detecting for the millennium* (Mount Publications, Chelmsford).

Davey, P. J. 1971, 'The distribution of later Bronze Age metalwork from Lincolnshire', *Proceedings of the Prehistoric Society* 37, 96-111.

Davey, P. J., Northover, P., O'Connor, B. and Woodcock, J. J. 1999, 'Bronze Age metallurgy on the Isle of Man: a symposium', in Davey, P. J. (ed.), *Recent Archaeological Research on the Isle of Man*, British Archaeological Reports, British Series 278 (Archaeopress, Oxford), 39-62.

Davies, D. G. 1967, 'The Guilsfield Hoard: a reconsideration', *The Antiquaries Journal* 47, 95-108.

Davis, R. 2006, *Basal-Looped Spearheads: typology, chronology, context and use*, British Archaeological Reports, International Series S1497 (Archaeopress, Oxford).

Dobinson, C. and Denison, S. 1995, *Metal Detecting and Archaeology in England* (Council for British Archaeology, York).

Doshi, N. 2008, *An Assessment of the Archaeological Research Dividends of the Portable Antiquities Scheme: a case study of Bronze Age metalwork from East Anglia* (unpublished MPhil dissertation, University of Cambridge).

Earwood, C. 1993, *Domestic Wooden Artefacts in Britain an Ireland from Neolithic to Viking Times* (University of Exeter Press, Exeter).

Edwards, R. 2006, *Portable Antiquities Scheme User Survey 2006* (Arboretum Archaeological Consultancy, Worcester), http://www.finds.org.uk/news/ac.php

Ehrenberg, M. R. 1977, *Bronze Age Spearheads from Berkshire, Buckinghamshire and Oxfordshire*, British Archaeological Reports, British Series 34 (British Archaeological Reports Limited, Oxford).

Ehrenberg, M. R. 1981, 'The anvils of Bronze Age Europe', *The Antiquaries Journal* 61, 14-28.

Evans, C. 2002, 'Metalwork and the 'cold claylands': Pre-Iron Age occupation on the Isle of Ely', in Lane, T. and Coles, J. (eds.), *Through Wet and Dry* (Heritage Trust of Lincolnshire, Sleaford), 33-53.

Evans, E. 1933, 'The bronze spearhead in Great Britain and Ireland', *Archaeologia* 83, 187-202.

Fletcher, T. 1977, 'Archaeology v Treasure Hunting - the beginning of the end of the war?', *Treasure Hunting*, September 1977, 9-10.

Fontijn, D. R. 2002, 'Sacrificial landscapes: cultural biographies of persons, objects and 'natural' places in the Bronze Age of the Southern Netherlands *c.* 2300-600 BC', *Analecta Praehistorica Leidensia* 33-4, 1-392.

Fox, C. 1939, 'The socketed bronze sickles of the British Isles', *Proceedings of the Prehistoric Society* 5, 222-48.

Fox, C. 1941, 'The non-socketed bronze sickles of Britain', *Archaeologia Cambrensis* 96, 136-57.

Garrett, C. 1992, *Let's Talk Treasure Hunting* (Ram Publishing, Dallas).

Gilman, A. 1981, 'The development of social stratification in Bronze Age Europe', *Current Anthropology* 22.1, 1-23.

Gosden, C. 2005, 'What do objects want?', *Journal of Archaeological Method and Theory* 12, 193-211.

Green, B. and Gregory, T. 1978, 'An initiative on the use of metal-detectors in Norfolk', *Museums Journal* 77 (4), 161-2.

Grieg, C. 1972, 'Cullykhan', *Current Archaeology* 32, 227-31.

Gurney, D. 1997, 'A note on the distribution of metal-detecting in Norfolk', *Norfolk Archaeology* 42, 528-32.

Harding, A. 1976, 'Bronze agricultural implements in Bronze Age Europe', in Sieveking, G. de G., Longworth, I. H. and Wilson, K. E. (eds.), *Problems in Economic and Social Archaeology* (Duckworth, London), 513-22.

Harding, A. F. 2000, *European Societies in the Bronze Age* (Cambridge University Press, Cambridge).

Hawkes, C. F. C. 1941, 'The looped and leaf shaped bronze spearhead', *Proceedings of the Prehistoric Society* 7, 128-31.

Hegmon, M. 2003, 'Setting theoretical egos aside: issues and theory in North American archaeology', *American Antiquity* 68, 213-43.

Hobbs, R., Honeycombe, C. and Watkins, S. 2002, *Guide to Conservation for Metal Detectorists* (Tempus, Stroud).

Hodder, I. 1999, *The Archaeological Process* (Blackwell, Oxford).

Hodder, I. 2001, 'Introduction: a review of contemporary theoretical debates in archaeology', in Hodder, I. (ed.), *Archaeological Theory Today* (Polity Press, Cambridge), 1-13.

Hodges, H. W. M. 1957, 'Some recent finds of bronze implements', *Ulster Journal of Archaeology* 20, 64-9.

Holman, N. 1985, 'Evaluating the contents of Sites and Monuments Records: an alternative approach', *Archaeological Review from Cambridge* 4 (1), 65-79.

Hull, D. 2007, *Too much TalkTalk?* (Theoretical Archaeology Conference, York).

Hutcheson, N. C. G. 2004, *Later Iron Age Norfolk: metalwork, landscape and society*, British Archaeological Reports, British Series 361 (Archaeopress, Oxford).

Ingold, T. 2000, *The Perception of the Environment* (Routledge, London).

Ixer, R. A. and Pattrick, R.A.D. 2003, 'Copper arsenic ores and Bronze Age mining and metallurgy with special reference to the British Isles', in Craddock, P. and Lang, J. (eds.), *Mining and Metal Production through the Ages* (British Museum Press, London), 9-20.

Kristiansen, K. 1998, *Europe before History* (Cambridge University Press, Cambridge).

Kristiansen, K. 2001, 'Rulers and warriors: symbolic transformation in Bronze Age Europe', in Haas, J. (ed.), *From Leaders to Rulers* (Kluwer Academic, New York), 87-104.

Langmaid, N. G. 1976, *Bronze Age Metalwork in England and Wales* (Shire Publications, Aylesbury).

Lawson, A. J. 1979, 'A late Middle Bronze Age hoard from Hunstanton, Norfolk', in Burgess, C. and Coombs, D. (eds.), *Bronze Age Hoards: some finds old and new*, British Archaeological Reports, British Series 67 (British Archaeological Reports Limited, Oxford), 42-92.

Lawson, A. J. 1980, 'A late bronze age hoard from Beeston Regis, Norfolk', *Antiquity* 54, 217-9.

Lawson, A. 1984, 'The Bronze Age in East Anglia with particular reference to Norfolk', in C. Barringer (ed.), *Aspects of East Anglian Prehistory* (Geo Books, Norwich), 141-77.

Lawson, A. J. 1986, 'Notes on three Norfolk barrow excavations at Bridgham, Cockley Cley and Old Hunstanton', in Lawson, A. J. (ed.), *Barrow Excavations in Norfolk, 1950-1982*, East Anglian Archaeology Report No 29 (Norfolk Museums Service, Norwich), 104-13.

Leech, R. H. 1999, 'New approaches to the identification and documentation of the cultural heritage', in Hansen, H. J. and Quine, G. (eds.), *Our Fragile Heritage: documenting the past for the future* (National Museum of Denmark, Copenhagen), 9-14.

Leibhammer, N. 2000, 'Rendering realities', in Hodder, I. (ed.), *Towards Reflexive Methodologies in Archaeology: the example at Çatalhöyük* (McDonald Institute Monographs, Cambridge), 129-42.

Longworth, I. H. 1988, 'Archaeology and treasure trove', in Gough, S. (ed.), *Treasures for the Nation: conserving our heritage* (British Museum Publications, London), 48-57.

Maraszek, R. 2000, 'Late Bronze Age axe hoards in western and northern Europe', in Pare, C. F. E. (ed.), *Metals Make the World Go Round: the supply and circulation of metals in Bronze Age Europe* (Oxbow, Oxford) 209-24.

Marshall, Y. 2002, 'What is community archaeology?', *World Archaeology* 34 (2), 211-9.

Martin, E. and Murphy, P. 1988, 'West Row Fen, Suffolk: a Bronze Age fen-edge settlement site', *Antiquity* 62, 353-8.

Maryon, H. 1938, 'Some prehistoric metalworkers' tools', *The Antiquaries Journal* 18, 243-50.

Mathieu, J. R. and Meyer, D. A. 1997, 'Comparing axe heads of stone, bronze, and steel: studies in experimental archaeology', *Journal of Field Archaeology* 24, 333-51.

McDavid, C. 2000, 'Archaeology as cultural critique: pragmatism and the archaeology of a southern United States plantation', in Holtorf, C. and Karlsson, H. (eds.), *Philosophy and Archaeological Practice: perspectives for the 21st century* (Bricoleur Press, Lindome), 221-40.

McNeil, R. 1972, 'A report on the Bronze Age hoard from Wick Park, Stogursey, Somerset', *Somerset Archaeology and Natural History* 117, 47-64.

Millett, M. 1985, 'Field survey calibration: a contribution', in Haselgrove, C., Millett, M. and Smith, I. (eds.), *Archaeology from the ploughsoil: studies in the collection and analysis of field survey data* (Sheffield University Press, Sheffield), 31-8.

Mount, C. 2001, 'The collection of Early and Middle Bronze Age material culture in south-east Ireland', *Proceedings of the Irish Royal Academy* 101, 1-35.

Muckelroy, K. 1981, 'Middle Bronze Age trade between Britain and Europe: a maritime perspective', *Proceedings of the Prehistoric Society* 47, 275-97.

Nebelsick, L. 2000, 'Rent asunder: ritual violence in Late Bronze Age hoards', in Pare, C. F. E. (ed.), *Metals Make the World Go Round: the supply and circulation of metals in Bronze Age Europe* (Oxbow, Oxford), 160-75.

Needham, S. P. 1988, 'Selective deposition in the British Early Bronze Age', *World Archaeology* 20 (2), 229-48.

Needham, S. 1996, 'Chronology and periodisation in the British Bronze Age' *Acta Archaeologica* 67, 121-40.

Needham, S. and Dean, M. 1987, 'La Cargaison de Langdon Bay à Douvres (Grande-Bretagne): la signification pour les échanges à travers la Manche', in Blanchet, J. C. (ed.), *Les Relations entre le Continent et Les Iles Britanniques à l'Age du Bronze* (Supplément a la Revue Archéologique de Picardie, Amiens), 119-24.

Needham, S., Ramsay, C. B., Coombs, D., Cartwright, C. and Pettitt, P. 1997, 'An independent chronology for British Bronze Age metalwork: the results of the Oxford Radiocarbon Accelerator Programme', *Archaeological Journal* 154, 55-107.

O'Connor, B. 1980, *Cross-Channel Relations in the Later Bronze Age: relations between Britain, North-Eastern France and the Low Countries during the Later Bronze Age and the Early Iron Age, with particular references to the metalwork*, British Archaeological Reports, International Series 91 (British Archaeological Reports Limited, Oxford).

O'Connor, B. 2007, 'Llyn Fawr metalwork in Britain: a review', in Haselgrove, C. and Pope, R. (eds.), *The Earlier Iron Age in Britain and the Near Continent* (Oxbow, Oxford), 64-79.

Ordnance Survey. 2001, *GB Coastline and administrative boundaries*, http://www.ordnancesurvey.co.uk/oswebsite/images/userImages/misc/outlinemaps/outlineb.pdf

Osgood, R. 1998, *Warfare in the Late Bronze Age of North Europe*, British Archaeological Reports, International Series 694 (Archaeopress, Oxford).

Owen, J. (ed.). 1995, *Towards an Accessible Archaeological Archive* (Society of Museum Archaeologists, London).

PASAR 2007 = Lewis, M. J. (ed.). 2007, *Portable Antiquities Scheme Annual Report 2006* (British Museum, London), http://www.finds.org.uk/documents/PAS_2006.pdf

Pearce, S. M. 1983, *The Bronze Age Metalwork of South Western Britain*, British Archaeological Reports, British Series 120 (British Archaeological Reports Limited, Oxford).

Pearce, S. M. 1984, *Bronze Age Metalwork in Southern Britain* (Shire Publications, Aylesbury).

Pendleton, C. F. 1999, *Bronze Age Metalwork in Northern East Anglia: a study of its distribution and interpretation*, British Archaeological Reports, British Series 279 (John and Erica Hedges, Oxford).

Pendleton, C. 2003, 'Rare Bronze Age objects', *The East of England Region Portable Antiquities Scheme Newsletter* 1, 3-4.

Perrin, K. 2002, *Archaeological Archives: a way forward. Documentation, access and deposition* (English Heritage, London).

Pescarin, S. 2007, 'Reconstructing archaeological landscape: interpretation and integration in spatial and real-time open system', in Salisbury, R. B. and Keeler, D. (eds.), *Space - Archaeology's Final Frontier? An intercontinental approach* (Cambridge Scholars Publishing, Newcastle), 69-92.

Plumridge, B. 2003, *Metal Detecting, Portable Antiquities, Law and Later Prehistory* (unpublished MPhil dissertation, University of Cambridge).

Pryor, F. 1991, *Flag Fen Prehistoric Fenland Centre* (English Heritage, London).

Pryor, F. 1992, 'Discussion: the Fengate/Northey landscape', *Antiquity* 66, 518-31.

Pryor, F. 2005, *Flag Fen: life and death of a prehistoric landscape* (Tempus, Stroud).

Quine, G. 1999, 'The CIDOC standard: an international data standard for recording archaeological sites and monuments', in Hansen, H. J. and Quine, G. (eds.), *Our Fragile Heritage: documenting the past for the future* (National Museum of Denmark, Copenhagen), 105-10.

Ramsey, W. G. 1989, *Middle Bronze Age Weapons in Ireland* (unpublished PhD thesis, Queen's University, Belfast).

Read, D. W. 2008, *Artifact Classification: a conceptual and methodological approach* (Left Coast Press, Walnut Creek).

Renfrew, C. 1995, 'Introduction', in Tubb, K. W. (ed.), *Antiquities Trade or Betrayed: legal, ethical and conservation issues* (Archtype, London), xvii-xxi.

Roberts, B. forthcoming, 'The Bronze Age', in Atkins, L. and Atkins, R. (eds.), *The Handbook of British Archaeology* (Constable and Robinson, London).

Rowlands, M. J. 1976, *The Production and Distribution of Metalwork in the Middle Bronze Age in Southern Britain*, British Archaeological Reports, British Series 31 (British Archaeological Reports Limited, Oxford).

Savory, H. N. 1980, *Guide Catalogue of the Bronze Age Collections* (National Museum of Wales, Cardiff).

Schmidt, P. K. and Burgess, C. B. 1981, *The Axes of Scotland and Northern England*, Prähistorische Bronzefunde Abteilung IX, Band 7 (C.H. Beck'sche Verlagsbuchhandlung, Munich).

Shanks, M. and Hodder, I. 1995, 'Processual, postprocessual and interpretive archaeologies', in Hodder, I., Shanks, M., Alexandri, A., Buchli, V., Carman, J., Last, J. and Lucas, G. (eds.), *Interpreting Archaeology: finding meaning in the past* (Routledge, London), 3-29.

Sofaer Derevenski, J. and Sørensen, M. L. S. 2002, 'Becoming cultural: society and the incorporation of bronze', in Ottaway, B.S. and Wager, E. C. (eds.), *Metals and Society*, British Archaeological Reports, International Series, S1061 (Archaeopress, Oxford).

Taylor, R. J. 1993, *Hoards of the Bronze Age in Southern Britain*, British Archaeological Reports, British Series 228 (British Archaeological Reports Limited, Oxford).

Thornes, R. 1997, *Protecting Cultural Objects in the Global Information Society* (J. Paul Getty Trust, Los Angeles).

Thomas, R. 1991, 'Drowning in data? - Publication and rescue archaeology in the 1990s', *Antiquity* 65, 822-28.

Thomas, R. 1999, 'Rise and fall: the deposition of Bronze Age weapons in the Thames Valley and the Fenland', in Harding, A. F. (ed.), *Experiment and Design: archaeological studies in honour of John Coles* (Oxbow, Oxford), 116-22.

Tilley, C., Keane, W., Küchler, S., Rowlands, M. and Spyer, P (eds.). 2006, *Handbook of Material Culture* (Sage Publications, London).

Timberlake, S. 2003, 'Early mining research in Britain: the developments of the last ten years', in Craddock P. and Lang, J. (eds.), *Mining and Metal Production through the Ages* (British Museum Press, London), 21-42.

Ulmschneider, K. 2000, *Markets, Ministers and Metal-Detectors: the archaeology of Middle Saxon Lincolnshire and Hampshire compared*, British

Archaeological Reports, British Series 307 (Archaeopress, Oxford).
Webb, S. 2005, 'Beginners look here', *Treasure Hunting*, June 2005, 70-1.
Winter, J. 2007, 'The ordinary detectorist,' *The Searcher* 258, 26-7.
Wood, S. 2005, 'The day I found Bronze Age gold', *Treasure Hunting,* June 2005, 75.
Wylie, A. 2002, *Thinking from Things: essays in the philosophy of archaeology* (University of California Press, Berkeley).
Wylie, A. 2005, 'The promise and perils of an ethic of stewardship', in Meskell, L. and Pels, P. (eds.), *Embedding Ethics* (Berg, New York), 47-68.
Yates, D. T. 2007, *Land, Power and Prestige: Bronze Age field systems in southern England* (Oxbow, Oxford).
York, J. 2002, 'The life cycle of Bronze Age metalwork from the Thames', *Oxford Journal of Archaeology* 21, 77-92.

Celtic Art, GIS Analysis and the Portable Antiquities Scheme

Duncan Garrow

This paper focuses on the significant contribution that the Portable Antiquities Scheme (PAS) was able to make to the AHRC-funded project entitled 'Technologies of Enchantment: Celtic Art in Britain in the Middle to Late Iron Age and Early Roman periods' (Garrow and Gosden, in preparation). The project as a whole aimed to bring a fresh approach to the study of Celtic Art. At its broadest, it sought to understand the relationship between material culture, aesthetics and power at that time. The central element of this research was a group of objects which have come to be known as 'Celtic Art'. Whilst both words - 'Celtic' and 'Art' - have their own definitional problems (see for example Megaw and Megaw 2005: 7-8; Harding 2007: 1-16; Gosden and Hill 2008), the term was maintained within the project both for convenience's sake and in order to explore the reasons why archaeologists have come to view what might also be termed 'decorated metalwork from *c.* 300 BC to AD 200' as 'Celtic' in its identity, and as 'art' rather than material culture.

The first phase of the project involved the compilation of a database of all Iron Age/Romano-British Celtic Art-related objects in Britain. In doing so, a rich body of material which previously remained relatively widely scattered within a variety of published and unpublished sources was drawn together. Those sources include wide-ranging corpuses of Celtic Art as a whole (Spratling 1972; MacGregor 1976; Jope 2000), specialist studies of particular artefact types (e.g., Palk 1984; Stead 2006), sites (e.g., Macdonald 2007) and regions (e.g., Hutcheson 2004), and information from the PAS and elsewhere. In creating a database of Celtic Art, the project had two aims. The first was to establish a comprehensive understanding of the material at a basic level - what kinds of objects are involved and where they have been found - in order to provide a firm empirical foundation on which to build broader interpretations. The second aim, an outcome of the first, was to provide a readily-available web-based digital resource for others to use in future research. In total, the database contains over 2,500 objects (available to download at: www.britishmuseum.org/research/research_projects/technologies_of_enchantment.aspx).

The main findings resulting from analysis of the project database are described in substantial detail elsewhere (Garrow 2008). For this reason, these broader results are discussed only briefly here. The main intention of this paper is to focus specifically on the different roles that PAS data were able to play in the project's analysis and interpretation.

The PAS contribution

As already mentioned, the compilation of the Technologies of Enchantment database involved gathering together large amounts of information from a variety of different arenas. The primary sources of information were the three previous substantial corpuses of Celtic Art: Martyn Jope's relatively recently published, but not as recently compiled, *Early Celtic Art of the British Isles* (2000), Morna MacGregor's *Early Celtic Art in North Britain* (1976) and Mansel Spratling's unpublished PhD thesis *Southern Decorated Bronzes of the Late Pre-Roman Iron Age* (1972). A number of more recent sources were also used (e.g., Hutcheson 2004; Stead 2006), but as these generally focused on specific regions or specific object types they could not fulfil the much-needed role of bringing knowledge of the whole Celtic Art corpus up to date.

One important question within the project was to explore the extent to which objects found by metal-detectorists and others, normally recorded via the PAS, change, challenge or simply add to what was already known about the distribution and character of Celtic Art and related objects. The potential contribution that these finds can make to the study of Iron Age metalwork has already been demonstrated by work in Norfolk (Hutcheson 2004) and further afield (Worrell 2007). Finds recorded by the PAS certainly made a significant contribution to the corpus of known Celtic Art and related objects. In total, the PAS contributed 337 artefacts to the database, or 13% of the total. Further information about fewer than 100 other artefacts discovered since the 1970s had been recorded by museum curators and other specialists; the majority of these were Scottish finds recorded by the National Museum of Scotland. It is worth noting that the PAS contribution would have been significantly higher, firstly if coins and brooches had not been excluded (coins already have an excellent catalogue in the Celtic Coin Index, while brooches are too numerous and too diffusely reported to include effectively; see Garrow 2008 for a detailed discussion of their omission), and secondly if it had proved possible to incorporate artefacts which had been dated as 'Roman' (as well as 'Iron Age') more easily. The process of filtering objects which might be described as 'Celtic Art' out of the many thousands of

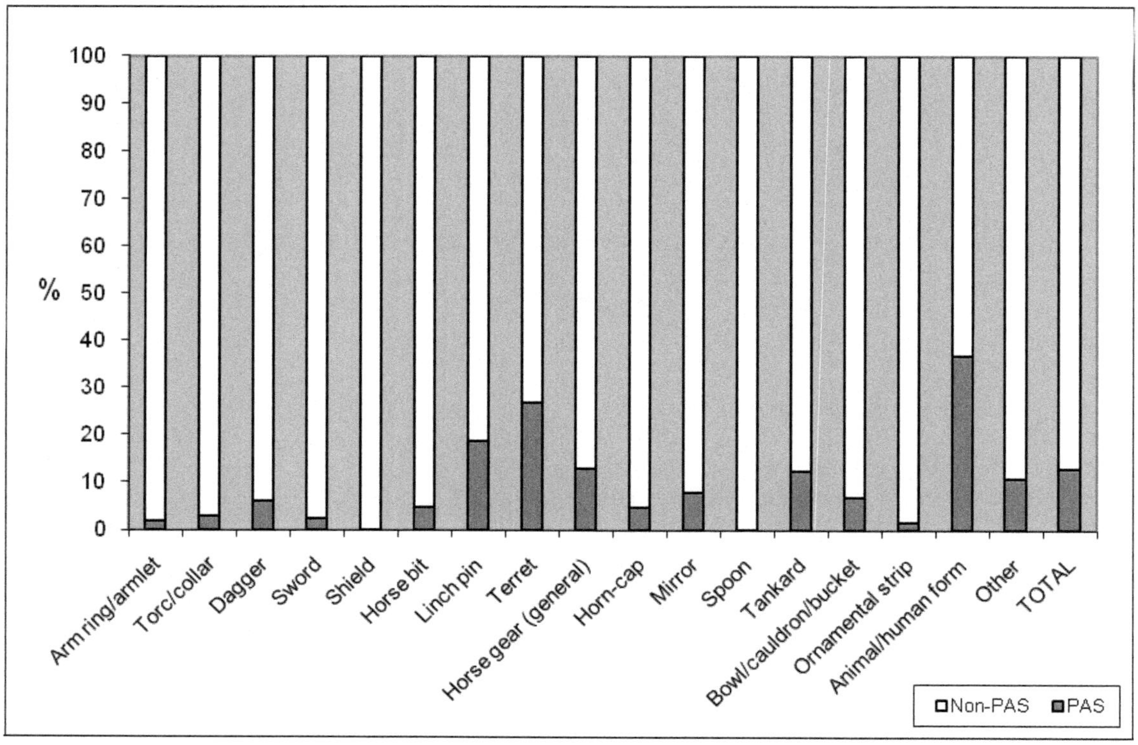

Fig. 1: Proportion of PAS contribution to overall numbers of each object type within the database.

entries within the PAS database dated as Roman would simply have been too time consuming.

Figure 1 gives an impression of the differential contribution of the PAS to each artefact type within the database. It shows very clearly that metal-detecting carried out in recent years has been particularly successful at finding certain artefact types, most notably animal/human figurines, terrets (i.e. rein rings) and linch pins (see also Worrell 2007).

In addition to this sizeable contribution to the overall number of objects, the PAS also proved extremely valuable in enhancing the database in a variety of other ways. In terms of geographical coverage, several gaps within previous distributions were filled, notably in the West Midlands/Cheshire region and southern Suffolk (see Fig. 2). As a result, it became possible to feel much more confident that gaps in the overall distribution were indeed real. The importance of the fact that, from 2003, PAS coverage was extended across the whole of England and Wales cannot be underestimated in this instance.

Unsurprisingly perhaps, given its numerical contribution to the database, the PAS also produced types of artefacts which were previously unknown within the corpus of Celtic Art: Figure 3, for example, depicts a copper-alloy comb decorated in the classic Celtic Art 'mirror style', a type previously known only in bone (Jope 2000: 305 f/g). In addition to new object types, the PAS is also likely to have provided information about a new range of depositional contexts. As Worrell (2007) points out, it is probable that many of the artefacts found as a consequence of metal-detecting would originally have been deposited in contexts different to those recovered by other means. Excavations focusing on known sites, for example, are less likely to recover what would originally have been stray finds and chance losses.

Assessing the reliability of data

In addition to increasing knowledge of the distribution, range and contextual variability of artefact types, the PAS also played an important role in allowing potential biases within the broader database to be assessed. When interpreting broad-scale geographical distributions of this sort, three separate factors must be distinguished in considering the relationship between patterns in the present and 'true' patterns in the past: the actual use/existence of objects in the past, the deposition of objects in the past, and the recovery of those objects in the present. It is important to ask whether the heavy bias towards the south of England in the distribution of mirrors (Fig. 4), for example, is the result of (a) their having been owned and used predominantly in that region and not in the north; (b) their having been used everywhere, but preferentially deposited in visible archaeological contexts such as cremation burials, which are found almost exclusively in the south; or (c) their having been recovered much more often in the south due to the fact that many more excavations have been carried out there overall.

While information from the PAS cannot easily answer all such questions, it certainly can move towards addressing some of them. For example, in the overall distribution map of objects associated with Celtic Art (Fig. 2), the density of artefacts in East Anglia is extremely clear. Again, it is important to consider the three factors mentioned above when interpreting this distribution, asking whether it is the result of use, deposition or recovery. In this case, the role of the latter is particularly

Fig. 2: Distribution of artefacts identified as a result of the PAS (black) in relation to the database as a whole (grey). Note that Scotland is not covered by the PAS.

important, as the east of England has a strong and long-term tradition of co-operation between archaeologists and metal-detectorists (Worrell 2007) which may well have affected records of their recovery.

Using statistical information recorded by the PAS, it was possible to assess the reliability of these broader artefact distributions. For example, in the case of eastern England, the success of the PAS is likely to have skewed results to a certain extent: during 2005/6 for example, almost four times the national average numbers of finds (from all periods) were recorded in Norfolk and Suffolk (*PAS* 2005/6: 113), a pattern seen in previous years as well. However, by comparing numbers of finds between regions, it is also possible to suggest that recovery factors in East Anglia may have merely made clearer a 'real' differential distribution in the past. Overall, closely comparable proportions of metalwork (from all periods) were found in London and the South-East (Fig. 5). As a result, the fact that considerably more Celtic Art-related objects have been recovered in East Anglia can perhaps be taken as a meaningful pattern. Whether due to increased ownership of metalwork, or to different practices (including hoarding), there does appear to have been a reason, to do with the past, why more objects were deposited in the east than elsewhere.

Fig. 3: Decorated copper-alloy comb (WAW-250340).

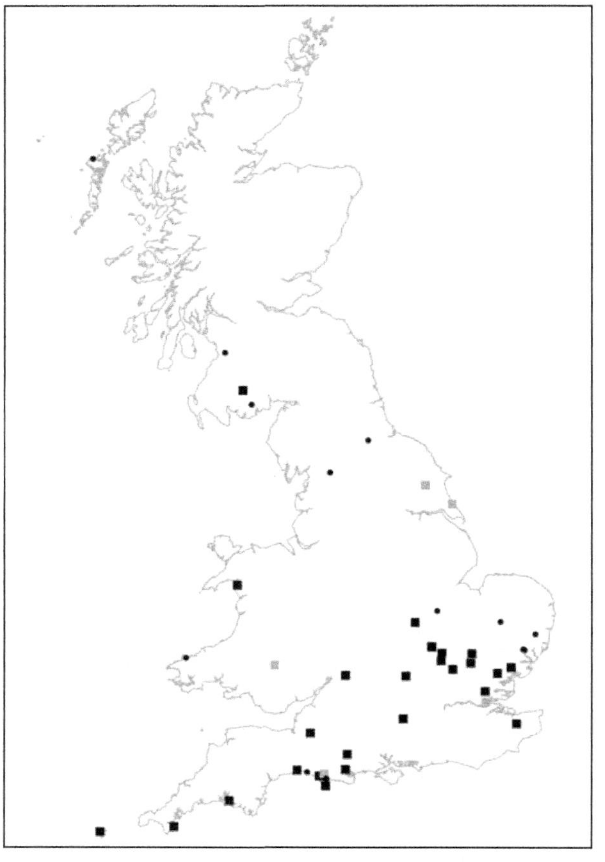

Fig. 4: Distribution of mirrors: bronze plates (black squares), iron plates (grey squares), mirror handles (black dots).

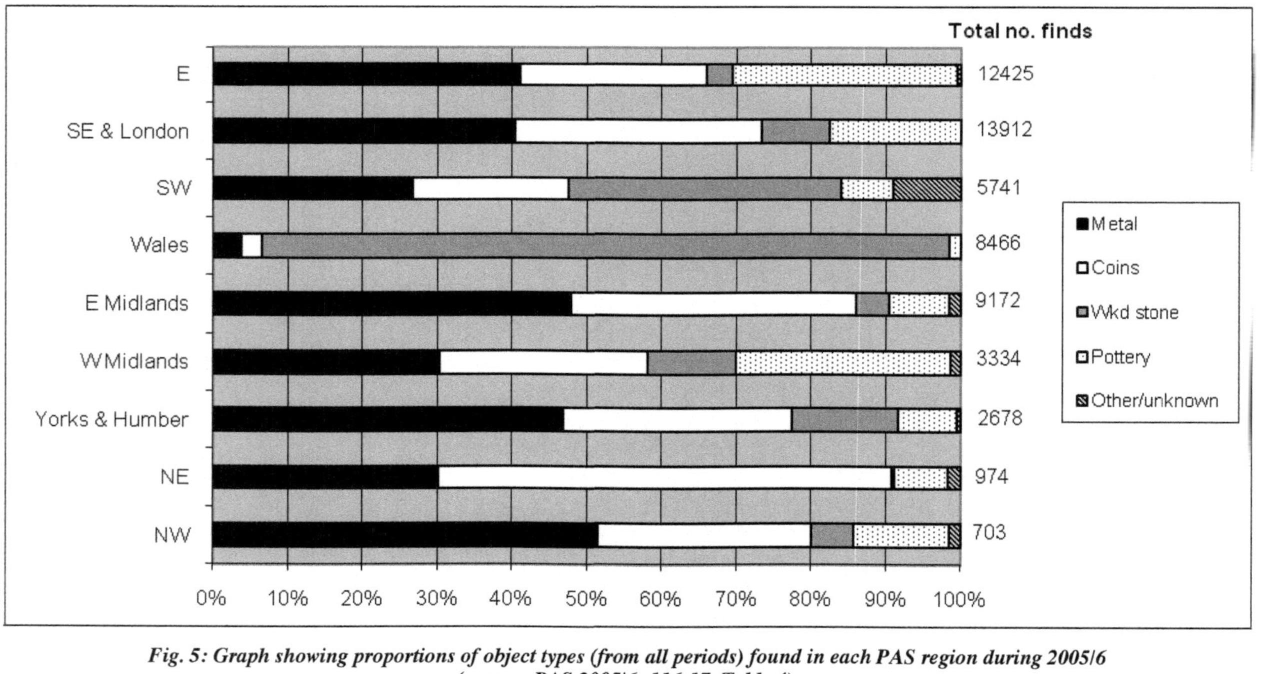

Fig. 5: Graph showing proportions of object types (from all periods) found in each PAS region during 2005/6 (source: PAS 2005/6: 116-17, Table 4).

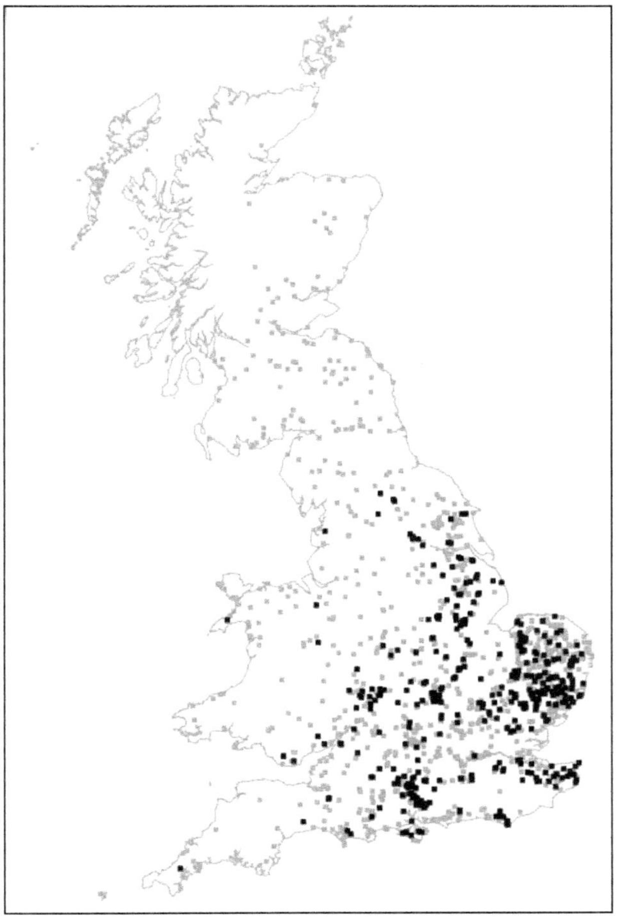

Fig. 6: Distribution of Iron Age brooches recorded by the PAS (shown as black squares) in relation to all objects within the database (note that Scotland is not covered by the PAS).

Opening up new datasets

The PAS also proved extremely valuable in opening up categories of data which otherwise would have remained beyond the reach of the project. As mentioned above, for a variety of reasons brooches and coins were not included in the main project database. Whilst it is possible to obtain distributional information about the latter from the Celtic Coin Index, brooches are rather harder to locate: they have generally been discussed only to a limited extent within the main corpuses of Celtic Art, and otherwise lie largely uncatalogued (as a group) within numerous site reports. Although by no means complete, information about the locations of metal-detected brooches recorded within the PAS database did allow at least an outline comparison of their distribution in relation to other material (Fig. 6). The distribution of Iron Age brooches recorded actually matches that of the database in general fairly closely.

The distribution of Celtic coins is, of course, restricted predominantly to the south-east of Britain. It is interesting to note, however, that within this region, the areas which have produced high densities of coins often appear to match those producing high densities of material generally (Fig. 7). The very high density of coins in Kent is due to the work of one individual, who has collated the results of many others (Worrell 1997). This generalised patterning suggests that the full spectrum of decorated metalwork may possibly have been used or treated in similar ways at this time. Within the densest parts of the plot, linear elements are discernible within the distribution of objects in general and particularly Celtic coins. These linear distributions appear to relate closely to topography, mostly being situated along the interfaces between lowlands and uplands. It is possible, therefore, that they actually reflect the locations of contemporary settlements as a whole (Ian Leins, pers. comm.).

The interpretive potential of distribution analysis

The information available to the PAS - and thus that which is offered up for interpretation when using its information - is of a particular character, essentially being restricted to details of object types and geographical findspot locations. Most notably, in the vast majority of cases, details about the archaeological context of finds are not available from the PAS. Within the Technologies of Enchantment database as a whole, contextual information undeniably aided the interpretation of Celtic Art significantly, facilitating a better understanding of the kinds of place that particular objects were used and deposited, relatively close dating, etc (see Garrow 2008 for a more detailed discussion). However, it is important to emphasise that the level of information which is available from the PAS can certainly be used to develop many other kinds of interpretation, as well as to raise questions which might be answered at a more detailed scale. In conclusion, in order to illustrate the potential of these datasets, a couple of emerging patterns can be noted.

The first example concerns the differential spatial patterning of closely-related artefacts. Certain object categories were found to be distributed right across Britain (such as swords and tankards). By contrast, others were restricted to specific regions (such as 'massive' armlets in the north, and 'horn caps' and mirrors in the south). Intriguingly, while the category of 'horse gear' as a whole displayed a very similar distribution to that of objects generally, once this broad category was broken down into individual object types, a rather different pattern emerged (Fig. 8). While most types (bridle bits, linch pins, etc.) were distributed relatively evenly across Britain, terrets (i.e., rein rings) were significantly denser in East Anglia than anywhere else. The fact that functionally-related objects such as these were deposited differentially in different places raises some interesting questions. Two possible explanations for the discrepancy can be posited. The first is that the 'chariots' or carts with which they were associated were designed or used very differently in the area now known as East Anglia, leading to the largely inadvertent deposition of many more terrets. The second explanation is that, in the east, for some reason terrets were preferentially selected for deposition, being placed in the ground when other horse gear was not. Although it is essentially impossible to distinguish between these two options whilst working at such a broad scale, it might well be feasible to do so if a more detailed, regional study were undertaken following on from these initial findings.

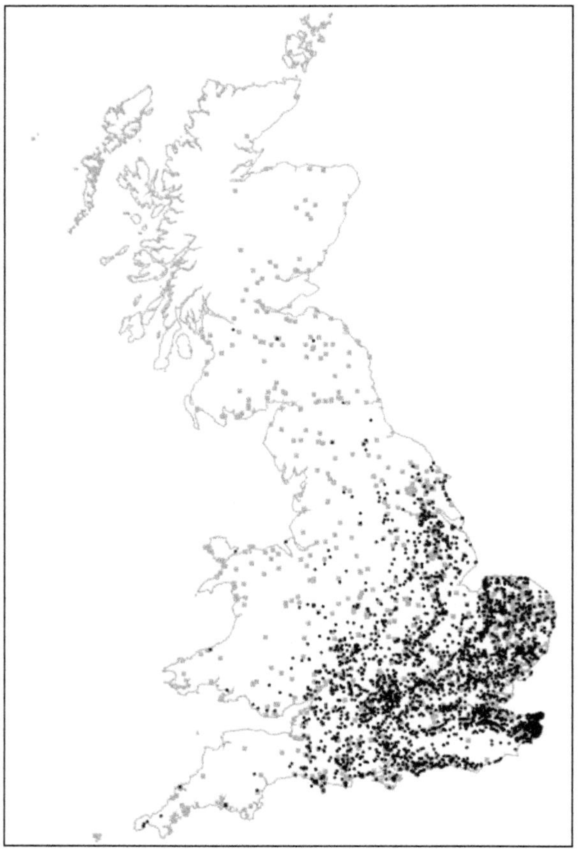

Fig. 7: Distribution of Iron Age coins (shown as black dots) in relation to all objects within the database (coin distribution provided by Ian Leins in conjunction with the Celtic Coin Index).

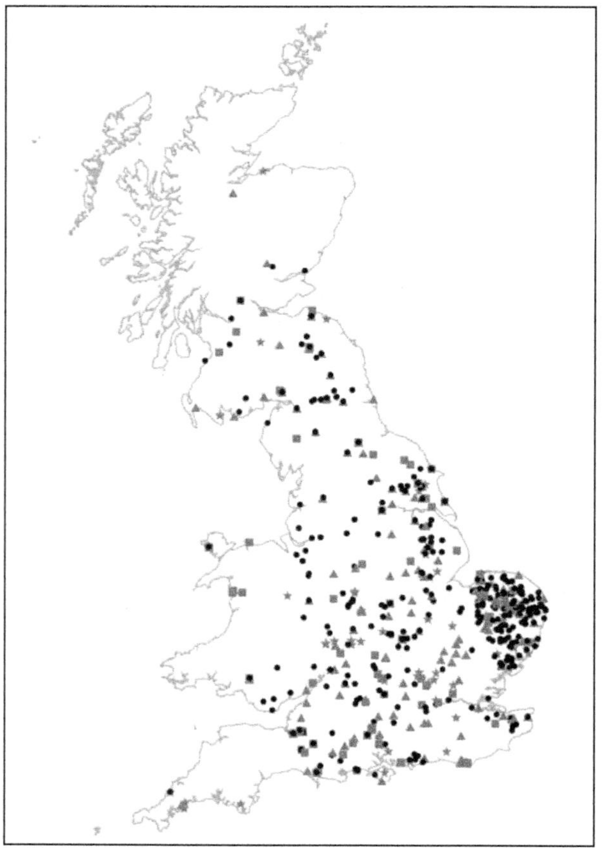

Fig. 8: Distribution of horse gear: terrets (black circles), bridle bits (squares), linch pins (stars) and other horse gear (triangles).

Fig. 9: Location of objects within the database in relation to topography (higher ground is darker).

The second example concerns the topographic location of Celtic Art-related artefacts in general. Figure 9 shows that objects within the database are found right across Britain, from the Isles of Scilly in the south-west, to Orkney and Shetland in the north-east. However, within this widespread overall distribution there are nevertheless some distinct 'blank' areas. A number of the most obvious ones appear to be related to the character of Britain's topography, corresponding closely with upland regions. Dartmoor/Exmoor, the Scottish highlands, and a large proportion of Wales, for example, are notable for their lack of objects. As discussed above, any discussion of finds distributions must take recovery factors into account, as well as variations in depositional practice. It is possible, for example, that the 'blank' areas on high ground may simply be a product of the fact that artefacts are much more likely to be found in the densely-occupied and heavily-ploughed lowlands than in the less-visited and largely undisturbed uplands. The process of distinguishing biases of recovery or deposition from 'real' patterns is undeniably a difficult one. However, it is important not to get too bogged down by that process, as it is only ever possible to make interpretations within archaeology on the basis of the evidence available. Given the relatively low density of Iron Age settlement in upland areas of Britain, it does seem reasonable to assume that despite biases of recovery in the present, gaps in the distribution of objects in these areas may be a genuine reflection of past practice. If indeed people were living predominantly in low lying areas, it seems that they did not make special journeys into the uplands to deposit material, an unsurprising revelation in the case of small fragments perhaps, but a rather more revealing insight in the case of intentionally deposited material such as hoards.

Summary

Within this paper, it is hoped that the vital role played by information from the PAS within the Technologies of Enchantment project has become clear. PAS data enabled the project to update a database which otherwise would have been constructed primarily from sources several decades old, to fill in a number of geographical gaps in previous distribution plots, to include new types of artefacts from different types of context, and to gain easy access to other comparable datasets which would have been very difficult to obtain by other means. Finally, and perhaps most importantly of all, the PAS enabled the project to assess the reliability and biases of information within the database as a whole, allowing for the interpretation of data with much greater confidence.

Acknowledgements

The research upon which this paper is based was funded by the Arts and Humanities Research Council. I would also like to thank Dan Pett and Sally Worrell for making the PAS data so readily available to us, and Anwen Cooper, Chris Gosden and J. D. Hill for their helpful comments on earlier versions of this text.

Bibliography

Garrow, D. 2008, 'The space and time of Celtic Art: interrogating the Technologies of Enchantment database', in Garrow, D., Gosden, C. and Hill, J. D. (eds.), *Rethinking Celtic Art* (Oxbow, Oxford).

Garrow, D. and Gosden, C. in preparation, *Technologies of Enchantment? Celtic Art in Britain c. 400BC-100AD* (Oxford University Press, Oxford).

Gosden, C. and Hill, J. D. 2008, 'Introduction', in Garrow, D., Gosden, C. and Hill, J. D. (eds.), *Rethinking Celtic Art* (Oxbow, Oxford).

Harding, D. 2007, *The Archaeology of Celtic Art* (Routledge, London).

Hutcheson, N. 2004, *Later Iron Age Norfolk: metalwork, landscape and society*, British Archaeological Reports, British Series 361 (Archaeopress, Oxford).

Jope, M. 2000, *Early Celtic Art of the British Isles* (Clarendon, Oxford).

MacDonald, P. 2007, *Llyn Cerig Bach: a study of the copper alloy artefacts from the Insular La Tène assemblage* (University of Wales, Cardiff).

MacGregor, M. 1976, *Early Celtic Art in North Britain* (Leicester University Press, Leicester).

Megaw, R. H. and Megaw, J. V. S. 2005, *Early Celtic Art in Britain and Ireland* (Shire, Princes Risborough).

Palk, N. 1984, *Iron Age Bridle Bits from Britain* (Edinburgh University, Edinburgh).

PAS 2005/6 = Lewis, M. J. (ed.), 2006, *Portable Antiquities Scheme Annual Report* 2005/6 (British Museum, London).

Spratling, M. 1972, *Southern Decorated Bronzes of the Late Pre-Roman Iron Age* (unpublished PhD thesis, University of London, London).

Stead, I. 2006, *British Iron Age Swords and Scabbards* (British Museum, London).

Worrell, S. 2007, 'Detecting the Iron Age: a view from the Portable Antiquities Scheme', in Haselgrove, C. and Moore, T. (eds.), *The Later Iron Age in Britain and Beyond* (Oxbow, Oxford).

New Evidence for Iron Age Sword Strap Fasteners Identified by PAS

Liz Andrews-Wilson

Iron Age scabbard strap fasteners - also referred to as 'buttoned rings' (Stead 2006: 52) or 'baldric rings' - are rare finds in Britain (Collis 1973: 130), but have been recorded in increasing quantities in recent years; a considerable number of which have been recorded by the Portable Antiquities Scheme (PAS). The term 'baldric ring', is derived from the evidence of warrior burials from Owslebury, Hampshire and Whitcombe, Dorset, which indicate that these types of fasteners/rings were used in conjunction with a baldric or harness.

This paper discusses the four Iron Age strap fasteners found by metal-detectorists in West Sussex and recorded by the PAS. It also discusses other examples discovered either through excavation or by metal-detection and found elsewhere in Britain, before ending with theories on the form and workings of the leather straps that would have been use with the suspension of swords and scabbards.

Background

Approximately 300 Iron Age swords are known from Britain (J. D. Hill, pers. comm.). During the Late Iron Age La Téne III period, it is thought that one in five adult males would have owned a sword, but only 17 examples of La Tene III Group D long swords and scabbards are known from Britain (Stead 2006; Montague 1997). In 1973 Collis published a distribution map of late Iron Age scabbard strap fasteners known from north-west Europe. Collis' corpus included only 15 fully authenticated Iron Age warrior burials from Britain (Collis 1973: 131). In contrast, warrior burials with swords and strap fasteners are relatively common finds on the Continent with examples known from settlement and burial contexts across Austria, France, Germany, Poland and Slovakia (Collis 1973: 132, fig.5).

Evidence from late Iron Age inhumation burials confirms that Iron Age warriors carried their swords on their right side. Stead (2006) refers to the winged belt hook found in the Owslebury warrior burial associated with a sword, a wooden scabbard and two copper-alloy suspension rings (Collis 1968; 1973, 126-7, 130, fig. 4-5, 194; Stead 2006: 179, no. 116). Since its discovery, a small number of other interesting fasteners have been found in England through excavation and metal-detection, including the iron, winged belt hook found with a pair of iron brooches and a small iron ring in Grave 20252 at Westhampnett, West Sussex (Montague 1997: 99, no. 27538, fig. 49) and a similar strap fitting from Hayling Island temple, Hampshire (Downey *et al.* 1980), which were excavated from inhumation burial and temple contexts respectively. Since 1999, a further 13 strap fittings, some of which are unparalleled, have been discovered through metal-detection and recorded by the PAS.

Strap fittings or belt hooks are often found associated with suspension rings, in copper-alloy or iron, probably forming a baldric, from which a sword or scabbard was suspended. Stead (2006: 52; Downey *et al.* 1980) lists five burials with Group D swords/scabbards found in association with suspension rings, and a buttoned ring - from Essendon, Hertfordshire, Whitcombe, Dorset, Coleford, Gloucestershire, Owslebury, Hampshire and Hayling Island, Hampshire.

Strap fasteners from West Sussex recorded with the PAS

During 2005, four Iron Age strap fasteners, including two button rings of the winged belt hook form of Stead Type II, an example of Stead Type IV, and an unusual example of unknown type, were found by metal- detectorists in West Sussex at Cold Waltham (SUSS-D82452), Storrington (SUSS-913C68), Houghton (SUSS-4C9825) and Sullington (SUSS-4C8491). Examples of other contemporary strap fasteners have been recorded by the PAS from other counties include two winged belt hook fasteners from Wickham Bishop, Essex (ESS-1D1BC2) and Ripley, Surrey (SUR-122628), a buttoned ring of Stead Type IV and suspension ring from Newchurch, Isle of Wight (IOW-C3C8A6 & C4B3D2), and a baldric fitting from Constantine, Cornwall (CORN-B177A3). These discoveries of unstratified British strap fasteners have been dated against parallels found in excavated and stratified La Téne III contexts from British and Continental sites (Brunaux and Lambot 1987; Collis 1968; 1973; Cunliffe 1987; Stead 2006).

Two of the fittings (Figs. 1-2) may be referred to as baldric rings in the purest sense, due to their parallels with examples found in association with swords and scabbards (Brunaux and Lambot 1987: 129; Collis 1968; 1973; Stead 2006), and Continental examples of this type are dated to 100 BC to 50 AD.

The first, a baldric ring of Stead Type II, was found by Tony Gill at Storrington (SUSS-913C68; Fig. 1) and was an isolated find. The ring is formed from a narrow loop of copper-alloy, with an extending neck from which a stud projects at 90°. Below the neck a decorative scroll draws itself down into the interior of the loop. This high quality artifact, with elegant decoration, remains without a parallel in Britain, although similar examples are known from the Continent in La Tène III (Collis 1973: 127-9, fig. 4:6). An almost exact parallel for the Storrington baldric ring are highlighted by Brunaux and Lambot (1987: 129 & 197).

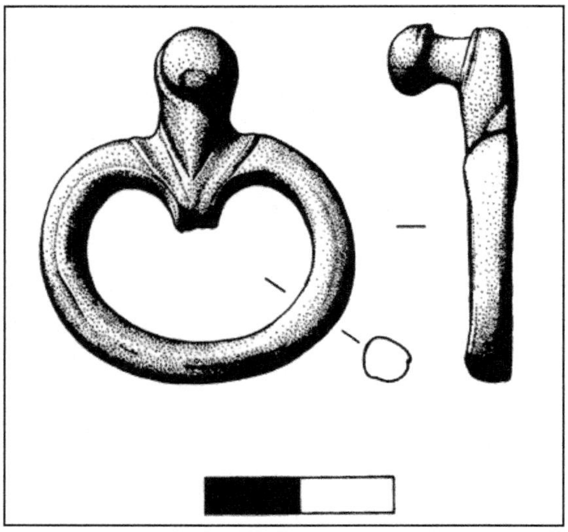

Fig. 1: Baldric ring from Storrington, West Sussex (SUSS-913C68).

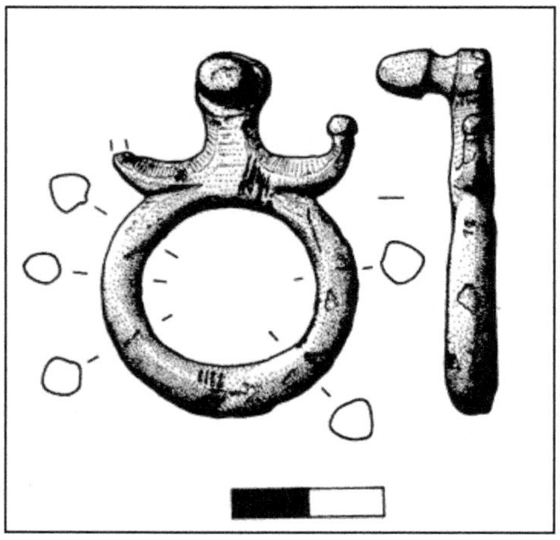

Fig. 2: Baldric ring from Houghton, West Sussex (SUSS-4C9825).

The second, was found by Richard Lyon in Houghton, West Sussex (SUSS-4C9825; Fig. 2), and is also an isolated find. It is a winged belt hook of Stead Type II, with projecting wings from the ring, and a terminating shank. It differs from the baldric ring from Storrington in that it has the wings, with small rounded knops at the terminal of each wing. Fasteners of this type are uncommon and it is rare for them to be found in context, especially as the British warriors tended not to be buried with either weapons or armour (J. D. Hill, pers. comm.). Other examples of winged belt hook fasteners, but without rounded knops at the terminal of each wing, are known from the Owslebury warrior burial, found in association with a sword, wooden scabbard and two copper-alloy suspension rings (Collis 1968; 1973: 126-7, 130, fig. 4-5, 194; Stead 2006: no. 116, fig. 81), at Westhampnett, West Sussex (Montague 1997: 99) and Hayling Island, Hampshire (Downey *et al.* 1980: 293; King and Soffe 1994). At the time of writing, a further two examples of winged belt hooks of Stead Type II were recorded on the PAS database: from Wickham Bishop, Essex (ESS-1D1BC2) and Ripley, Surrey (SUR-122628).

A strap fastener of a more common type was found at Coldwaltham, West Sussex (SUSS-D82452; Fig. 3) by Malcolm Andrews. This fastener of Stead Type IV has a circular hoop with a stud fixed to one side via a neck which projects at about 90° from the loop, and closely fits the classification of strap-fasteners dating to the 1st century BC to 1st century AD. Excavated examples are known from Hengistbury Head, Dorset (Cunliffe 1987: 153, nos. 41-2, ill. 111), Camerton, Somerset (Jackson 1990: 38-9) and Whitcombe, Dorset (Collis 1973: 125; Stead 2006: 178, no. 114). The type is discussed by Minter (2004: 12-14), based on the six similar strap fasteners found in Suffolk and recorded by the PAS. Jackson (1990: 38-9) recognised that rings of this type were ideally suited to the rapid fastening of two ends of a leather strap. By drawing on the modern parallel of a camera bag and strap, he describes how the fasteners may have worked with one end of the leather strap being permanently secured via another loop, with the strap then fed through the strap fastener and the stud pushed through an eyed-slit, enabling the strap to be locked into position, with multiple slots in the leather strap which could either be shortened or extended. It is also thought that these bronze rings may have formed part of a fastener for a handled bag by fastening the flap of the bag to the bag itself, rather than having been a strap fitting (Fuentes 1991: 95).

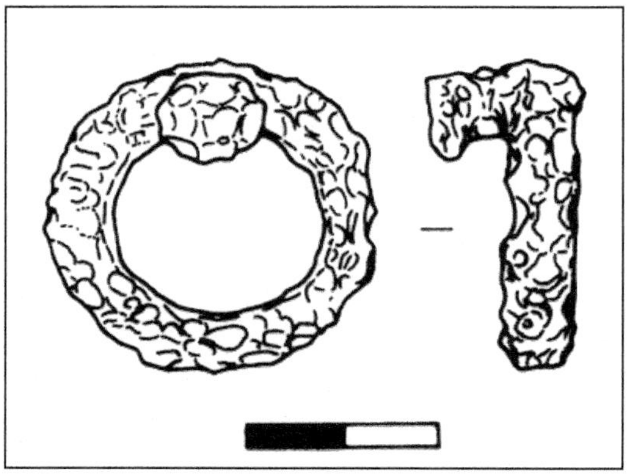

Fig. 3: Baldric ring from Cold Waltham, West Sussex (SUSS-D82452).

No close parallel has been found for the unusual fastener, another isolation find, found in Sullington, West Sussex (SUSS-4C8491; fig. 4) by Frank Kurzeja. The stud is mounted on a stem set above the ring itself with the head in the form of stylised quadrilobed flower. The ring has an iron core which is coated with a high quality copper-alloy sheath. The iron core has broken through the copper-alloy sheath and there are patches of corrosion on the outer surface. The style of the object, its general appearance and the quality of its manufacture places it into the same classification as the baldric rings, but is unusual because it has an iron core with a copper-alloy shell; a practice that was reasonably well-known in the 1st century BC to 1st century AD and which aids the dating of this object. However, the size of the ring is problematic, as it has a much smaller internal diameter than the rings discussed above, which would restrict the size of the strap that could be fed through it. This ring/fastener was likely to have had a less significant function than those discussed above as it would not have been so load-bearing. It therefore may have been purely decorative. The closest published example was found at Welwyn, Hertfordshire (Smith 1911-12: 17). This so called 'bronze ring' is formed from a highly decorated ring with a straight, narrow extension projecting from the side of the ring and terminating with a rounded decorative knop.

Perhaps even more intriguing is the discovery of an incomplete, copper-alloy baldric ring found by a metal-detectorist at Constantine, Cornwall (CORN-B177A3). It is formed of a ring with a straight projection extending and tapering from one side. The terminal stud is now missing. The outer surface of the ring is most unusual in being decorated with multiple triangular cells which are inlaid with chips of deep red, opaque 'sealing wax' glass (enamel). Instead of the lead solder normally used to hold such settings, in place, the solder used on this example is tin-rich which contains lead (Laura Ratcliffe and Anna Tyacke, pers. comm.).

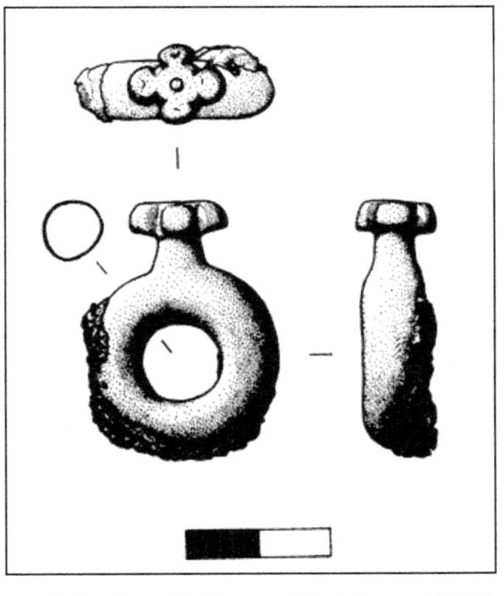

Fig. 4: Strap fitting from Sullington, West Sussex (SUSS-4C8491).

Other fasteners

Over the years, late Iron Age and early Roman fasteners have been assigned to different classifications under various names, including dress or cloak fasteners or button-and-loop fasteners (Brunaux and Lambot 1987: 129; Minter 2004; Wild 1970). Although button-and-loop fasteners are predominantly of Roman date they derived from British Iron Age fasteners. Their function remains obscure, but they are likely to have served as multi-purpose fasteners for clothing and harnesses, with the shank or loop either sewn to a fabric base or attached to it by a thong (Wild 1970: 145; Worrell 2008: 341). Class I fasteners with a double-boss head and other variant forms are in the British Iron Age tradition and date from the middle of the 1st century AD into the early 2nd century. Wild (*ibid.*) also refers to a scabbard found in Mainz, with two fasteners attached to it, suggesting that the fittings were used as a means of fastening the scabbard to the sword-belt Four similar fittings were also found at Manching, Germany (Van Endert 1991: Pl. 7).

Discussion

As stated at the outset, the archaeological evidence suggests that buttoned rings and strap fittings - generally dated to the end of the 2nd century BC to mid 1st century AD - were most probably part of a baldric or harness, from which the scabbard was slung; the strap being placed over the shoulder (Collis 1973: 130; Stead 2006: 52). The exact manner of the strap arrangement, however, remains a matter of debate, since leather straps rarely survive, unlike the metal fittings and the swords themselves.

Earlier in the Iron Age, evidence for swords dating from the early 3rd century BC to the first half of the 1st century BC (La Tène II) survive on the Continent, with the swords suspended from the waist by a series of straps and belt-chains. Much is known about this arrangement as the metal chains, swords and scabbards have often been found in situ - in burials (see Stead and Rigby 1999: Rapin 1991: 321-7). In Britain the belt-chains are not found, and instead the few known La Tène III warrior burials can contain a sword or scabbard, a baldric ring and two copper-alloy or iron rings. A recent metal-detector find from the near Newchurch, Isle of Wight (IOW-C3C8A6 & C4B3D2) consists of a buttoned-ring of Stead Type I which was found in association with a simple belt-ring, presumably used as some form of belt fastener. This discovery provides new evidence that a warrior would have had two or more rings on his baldric (Treasure case: 2006 T396; Minter 2004: 12-4). It is possible that these rings are again similar to examples on the Continent. J. D. Hill (pers. comm.) has suggested that across Britain and the Continent rings made from iron and/or copper alloy may have been used on straps, with as many as five rings used in association.

At the same time that these fittings were being used by the Britons and Gauls, Roman soldiers were depicted carrying their swords on the right hand side and using a baldric to suspend the sword. The major difference between the swords of the Britons and Romans was the sword length. In the 1st century BC to 1st century AD, Roman soldiers were using the *gladius*, a short sword used in close combat (in a stabbing and thrusting motion), whilst the soldier was protected behind a shield. The British style of warfare was different, and used the weight of the long sword to inflict slashing blows on an opponent, in single combat. Long swords, such as that from Owslebury, could be 1,020mm long - including the scabbard (Stead 2006: 179). With such a long weapon, the baldric must have been adjustable to allow them it to be moved up and down.

Based on the practicalities of war, and the need to move quickly and easily, it is possible to theorise how the sword, the baldric and the associated rings might have worked together. For the warrior marching on to the battlefield it seems it would be essential that his long sword was hung high enough, so that the handle could be held in front of the chest with the right hand: this would prevent the sword from hitting the warrior's legs and would enable quicker movement. Whereas if the sword is about to be drawn, it would be preferable for it to be lower slung in order for the warrior to have enough reach to pull the sword out of its scabbard. This pulling action is likely to be done by the right hand, pulling upwards (as demonstrated by re-enactors). In order to have this flexibility, the baldric would need to be adjustable. So this is where the baldric ring (Types I and IV) comes into play.

Based on the burial evidence from Owslebury, it seems plausible that a short, thick leather strap would have been threaded through the back of the scabbard, underneath the suspension loop of the suspension plate, and that each end of this strap would then have been sewn to the copper-alloy (or iron) rings (as found near to the top of the blade); as discussed by Collis (1973: 130; see Fig. 5). The baldric would then have been sewn to the back copper-alloy ring, before the strap stretched up the back and over the shoulder and then down over his chest to where it would have terminated. This strap would have been cut with eyed-slits. A third strap was then sewn to the front copper-alloy ring and stretched upwards over the warrior's stomach to where it terminated. This strap was then sewn onto the 'baldric ring' itself (Fig. 6). The stud of the baldric ring would then be pushed through the eyed-slits on the upper strap enabling it to be locked in place. To make this even more secure the loose end of the upper strap could be knotted around the baldric ring to further secure the fastener.

Of course, it is not possible to prove this hypothesis, unless an intact leather strap is found in situ. Further, there are at least two further possible arrangements of how swords could have been suspended, which have been drawn from helpful discussions with Dominic Andrews who, while drawing the four baldric rings from West Sussex, noticed some of the wear patterns, which might indicate how the rings were held by the different straps (see Figs. 7-8).

Figure 7 shows a simple leather strap going around the waist, incorporating the copper-alloy rings and the suspension plate on the scabbard. The buckle-type fitting that can be seen on the strap is a baldric ring. Its projecting stud would have been hooked through a hole in the strap (as discussed above) and wrapping the end of the strap around would hold it in place.

Figure 8 shows a belt with two short straps sewn to the waist belt. These straps are attached to the rings on the back of the sword scabbard, via a thick leather strap (as at Owslebury). The short straps may have been sewn into place or simply knotted with the second short strap on the back. This arrangement has been depicted on statues, but these two latter arrangements would not have allowed for any adjustment and the belt may have slipped down with the weight of the sword.

Fig. 5: Artist's representation of how the back of the scabbard was connected to the strap fasteners and the baldric strap (Illustration: Dominic Andrews).

Fig. 6: An artist's representation of how the baldric strap was fastened using a baldric ring (Illustration: Dominic Andrews).

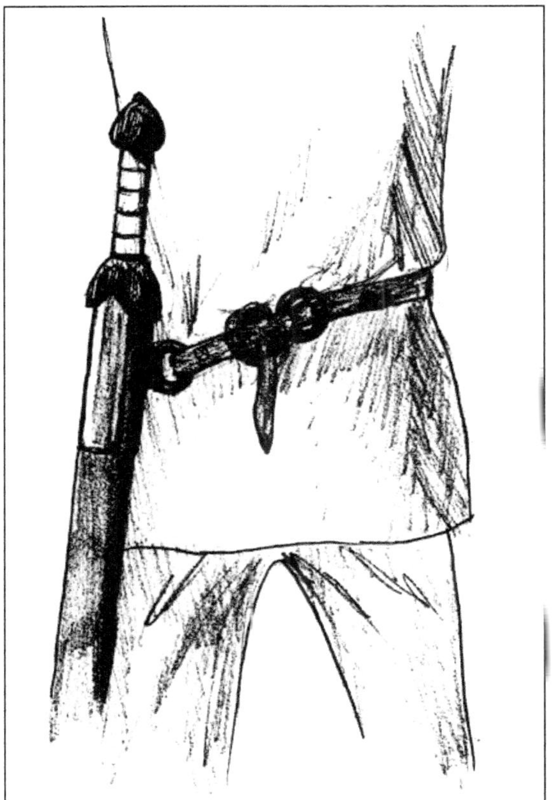

Fig. 7: An artist's representation showing a simple leather strap going around the waist, incorporating the copper-alloy rings and the suspension plate on the scabbard (Illustration: Dominic Andrews).

Fig. 8: An artist's representation showing two short straps are sewn to the waist belt (Illustration: Dominic Andrews).

Conclusions

As discussed above, late Iron Age strap fittings are well-known on the Continent and more are being recognised and recorded in Britain. However, it seems unlikely the same numbers found on the Continent will come to light in Britain, because of the difference in Iron Age society either side of the Channel. In Britain swords and their associated fittings and fasteners may have ended their life by being thrown into a river as offerings, rather than being placed in inhumation burials with their owners, as is the case on the Continent. Swords were also often recycled and very frequently repaired, as they were valued as both expensive and rare possessions. Also, it is likely that the swords may have been passed on from one individual to another, once their original owner had died. Therefore, British swords and their associated fasteners had a very long life expectancy, unlike their Continental parallels. It is therefore extremely important that these strap fasteners are correctly identified and recorded, so that they can be better understood. It is possible that more of these fasteners may have been found and exist in detectorist's collections or in museum stores as either unidentified or misclassified objects. The three unusual Sussex fasteners are intriguing as they were all found inland, in mid to north West Sussex, which could this be significant. As more baldric rings are found and correctly identified, their distribution will be better understood and further conclusions about their origins can be drawn.

Acknowledgements

I would like to thank the finders of the Sussex fasteners, Malcolm Andrews, Tony Gill, Frank Kurzeja and Richard Lyon, who were all at the time members of the Sussex Historical Searchers Society. Once the fasteners had been identified, the finders kindly agreed for them to go on temporary display at Horsham Museum, before donating them to the British Museum. Acknowledgement must also go to J. D. Hill (British Museum), who commented on the text and supplied some very useful discussion points, and Jody Joy (British Museum) and Adam Gwilt (National Museum Wales), who helped gather together the bibliographical references. Laura Ratcliffe (Royal Cornwall Museum Conservator) and Anna Tyacke (Cornwall Finds Liaison Officer) kindly supplied information on the Cornish example. Frank Basford (Isle of Wight Finds Liaison Officer) also supplied information about Treasure case 2006 T396. Thanks also go to Dominic Andrews (reconstruction artist and illustrator) who produced the accompanying finds illustration and the reconstructions.

Bibliography

Brunaux, J-L. and Lambot, B. 1987, *Guerre et Armement chez les Gaulois - 450 – 52 av. J.-C.* (Editions Errance, Paris).

Collis, J. R. 1968, 'Excavations at Owslebury, Hants: an interim report', *Antiquaries Journal* 48, 18-31.

Collis. J. R. 1973, 'Burials with Weapons in Iron Age Britain', *Germania* 51, 121-33.

Cunliffe, B. 1987, 'Other items of bronze', in Cunliffe, B. (ed.), *Hengistbury Head, Dorsey, Volume 1: the prehistoric and Roman settlement, 3500 BC – AD 500*, Oxford University Committee for Archaeology 13 (University of Oxford, Oxford), 151-6.

Downey, R., Soffe, G. and King, A. 1980, 'The Hayling Island temple and religious connections across the Channel', in Rodwell, W. (ed.), *Temples, Churches and Religion in Roman Britain*, British Archaeological Reports 77 (British Archaeological Reports, Oxford), 289-304.

Fuentes, N. 1991, 'The mules of a soldier', *Journal of Roman Military Equipment Studies* 2, 65-99.

Jackson, R. 1990, *Camerton: a catalogue of late Iron Age and early Roman metalwork* (British Museum, London).

King, A. and Soffe, G. 1994, 'The Iron Age and Roman Temple on Hayling Island', in Fitzpatrick, A. P. and Morris, E. L. (eds.), *The Iron Age in Wessex: recent work* (Trust for Wessex Archaeology, Salisbury), 114-6.

Minter, F. 2004, 'Strap fasteners from Suffolk', *Lucerna: the Roman finds group newsletter* 40, 12-14.

Montague, R., 1997, 'Winged belt hook', in Fitzpatrick, A. P. (ed.), *Archaeological Excavations on the Route of the A27 Westhampnett Bypass, West Sussex, 1992. Volume 2: the Late Iron Age, Romano-British, and Anglo-Saxon cemeteries* (Wessex Archaeology Publications, Salisbury), 99.

Rapin, A. 1991, 'Weaponry', in Moscati, S., Frey, O. H., Kruta, V., Raftery, B. and Szabo, M. (eds.), *The Celts* (Thames and Hudson, London), 321-7.

Smith, R. A. 1911-2, 'On Late-Celtic Antiquities discovered at Welwyn, Herts.,' *Archaeologia* 63, 15-18.

Stead, I. M. and Rigby, V. 1999, *The Morel Collection: Iron Age antiquities from Champagne in the British Museum* (British Museum, London).

Stead, I. M. 2006, *British Iron Age Swords and Scabbards* (British Museum, London).

Van Endert, D. 1991, *Die Bronzefunde aus dem Oppidum von Manching: kommentierter katalog* (Franz Steiner Verlag, Stuttgart).

Wild, J. P. 1970, 'Button-and-loop fasteners in the Roman Provinces', *Britannia* 1, 137-55.

Worrell. S. 2008, 'Roman Britain in 2007 II. Finds reported under the Portable Antiquities Scheme', Britannia 39, 337-67.

Iron Age Warwickshire: has the Portable Antiquities Scheme made a difference?

Angie Bolton

This paper represents a preliminary appraisal of the contribution that the Portable Antiquities Scheme (PAS) data has made to study of late Iron Age Warwickshire. It will focus on the copper-alloy artefacts recorded both by the PAS and by the Warwickshire Historic Environment Records (WHER), with two unusual late Iron Age artefacts recorded by the PAS from Warwickshire - a harness mount and a miniature shield - being discussed in more detail. First, it will briefly outline the development of finds recording in Warwickshire.

The WHER includes records of archaeological sites and finds, and is available online (http://timetrail.warwickshire.gov.uk). The information on the WHER is derived from a variety of sources, including documents dating back as far back as 1730 (Dugdale 1730), aerial photographs and excavation and survey reports. Prior to the introduction of the PAS, the Warwickshire Museum had a long history of working with a selection of metal-detector users, identifying and recording their finds and passing data to the WHER. A search of the WHER for late Iron Age artefacts recorded before the introduction of the PAS lists seven copper-alloy artefacts. In addition, a hinged fitting was published by Wise (1997: 71).

The post of West Midlands Finds Liaison Officer (FLO) - covering Warwickshire, Worcestershire, the West Midlands and Staffordshire – was one of six established in September 1997 to record archaeological objects found by the public: the post was funded by the British Museum. In 1999 a further six pilot schemes were created and in 2002 the Heritage Lottery Fund went on to fund an additional 21 Finds Liaison Officer posts, thereby establishing a national PAS, covering the whole of England and Wales. There are now therefore three FLOs for the West Midlands, one for Worcestershire and Warwickshire, one for Herefordshire and Shropshire and one covering the West Midlands and Staffordshire.

By March 2007 over 10,000 finds of all types and periods had been recorded by the PAS in Warwickshire. Forty-eight copper-alloy artefacts (0.77%) date to the late Iron Age, though some are artefact types that continued in use into the early Roman period, such as cosmetic sets and bucket mounts. Comparison shows that this percentage is slightly higher than the percentage (0.51%) of Iron Age copper-alloy artefacts recorded in total by the PAS between 1997 and 2006. The characteristics of these artefacts, including their types and distribution, can be examined through the PAS database (www.finds.org.uk).

The distribution of Iron Age metalwork in the West Midlands

The traditionally held view of prehistory in the West Midlands, including Warwickshire, is that the region represents an 'archaeological desert' (Thomas 1974: 38, quoting an unknown source). Although Thomas (1974) disputes this view, in the main it continues to persist. J. D. Hill (pers. comm. 2002) also commented that the common perception outside the West Midlands is that there is little or no fine Iron Age metalwork in the region. This view is compounded by a lack of published material of finds and sites in the region. Hingley (1996: 2; Palmer 2002) observes that because of the lack of published material, prehistoric Warwickshire is 'drastically under-represented' in national publications. This lack of publication does little to enable people to realise or appreciate the significance of Warwickshire and the West Midlands region in prehistory. As a consequence this area is not given its appropriate significance in regional and national contexts. In contrast, although the PAS database is not a traditional method of finds publication, its data are both dynamic and readily accessible.

The perception of the West Midlands as an 'archaeological desert' is also illustrated by studies of individual types of Iron Age metalwork. Taylor and Brailsford's (1985: 247-272) study of Iron Age strap unions highlights a distribution in the south, east and north of England as well as South Wales. No examples were noted from the West Midlands. However, of the 42 strap unions recorded by PAS between 1997 and 2009, seven examples were found in the West Midlands region (WMID410, WMID5608, WAW-CA0CC0, WAW-C477E6, WAW-7B2AO1, WAW-519897 & HESH-F35BD6), five of which were recorded from Warwickshire, thereby clearly extending both the quantity and distribution of strap unions from the West Midlands.

Jackson's (1985: 176-190) study of cosmetic sets dating to the late Iron Age to Roman periods further illustrates the traditional perception of a dearth of Iron Age copper-alloy artefacts in the West Midlands. Only two of the 99 cosmetic mortars and pestles catalogued were recorded from the West Midlands. Between October 1997 and April 2008, the PAS has recorded 188 cosmetic mortars and pestles (Worrell 2008: 348-349). Of these, 22 examples were found in the West Midlands, seven of which are from Warwickshire (WAW-611301, WAW-4E0706, WAW-3CF170, WAW-0198F7, WAW-FCCE32, WMID-9AA734 & WMID3149).

Worrell (2007: 378-379) also highlights a similar change in understanding of artefact distributions in the West Midlands in relation to horse gear. She notes that prior to the PAS, only four Late Iron Age linch pins were recorded in the region but that up to 2007 the PAS had recorded a further seven linch pin terminals. Study of excavated material shows concentrations of horse gear in Wessex and East Yorkshire (Stead 1979; 1991; Wainwright 1979; Cunliffe 1984; 1995; Cunliffe and Poole 1991). Yet while the PAS data had recorded relatively few horse and vehicle equipment artefacts from Kent (6), Hampshire (8), Dorset (3) and Somerset (1) between 1997 and 2004, 12 horse and vehicle equipment artefacts were recorded in Warwickshire (Worrell 2007: 379).

Garrow (this volume) also makes a further relevant observation in his consideration of the contribution that the PAS has made to an AHRC-funded project, 'Technologies of Enchantment: Celtic Art in Britain in the Middle to Late Iron Age and Early Roman period'. In relation to the West Midlands, he notes the previous geographical gap in the records of Iron Age finds which the PAS data are now filling and that Warwickshire accounts for 36% of late Iron Age artefacts recorded in the region (Garrow 2008: 22).

An assessment of Iron Age artefacts recorded by the PAS

By 2006, the PAS had recorded a total of 48 Iron Age copper-alloy artefacts from Warwickshire, representing a 575% increase in the quantity of objects recorded on the WHER. This quantity excludes coins, the study of which is well-established and the distribution of which is summarised by Cunliffe (1991: fig. 8.2). The object types recorded on the WHER include terret rings, linch pins, brooches, torcs, a spear and an unidentified object. The PAS has broadened the range of Iron Age copper-alloy artefact types recorded in Warwickshire by a further seven object types to include a comb, a miniature shield, strap fittings, toggles, cosmetic sets, and vessel mounts. Graph 1 illustrates the categories and numbers of finds recorded in each category by the PAS, WHER and published artefacts up to 2006.

The objects recorded by PAS have been divided into five broad categories: harness and vehicle fittings, personal accessories, votive, copper-alloy feast related vessels and unidentified objects. These categories designate the primary function of an artefact, though it is recognised that the deposition of an artefact may change the function beyond its primary use; for example an object primarily associated with feasting can later adopt a votive character. The harness and vehicle fittings category contains three object types, terret rings, linch pins and other harness fittings, in total accounting for nineteen artefacts. The personal accessories category includes brooches, torcs, strap fittings, toggles (these can also be harness), cosmetic sets and a comb: 23 artefacts in total. The votive category includes a single miniature shield (Stead 1998: 117) and the feasting category a bucket mount and tankard handle. There are six unidentified objects which cannot be categorised.

The range and quantity of artefacts and categories identified from the PAS and WHER material allow us to identify and discuss the Warwickshire Iron Age finds profile and to assess it by comparison to other regional and county datasets. Worrell (2007: 376) highlights the importance of the PAS data in the West Midlands and uses the Iron Age horse and vehicle equipment as a case study. An interesting detail of the Warwickshire Iron Age horse and vehicle equipment artefact profile is the relatively high proportion of linch pin terminals in comparison to terret rings (Worrell 2007: 378-379). This pattern is reflected across the West Midlands region, whereas the typical pattern is for terret rings to be more common than linch pin terminals; for example in Norfolk and Lincolnshire (Hutcheson 2004: 28-32).

Another distinctive characteristic of the finds profile that is illustrated by the Warwickshire Iron Age artefacts, is the proportion of brooches recorded compared to harness and vehicle fittings. The more common national pattern is for the number of brooches to be greater than harness and vehicle fittings (Worrell 2007: 379), yet in Warwickshire the latter outnumber the former by almost two to one, perhaps suggesting that horses and vehicles were more elaborately decorated with metalwork than people were.

The distribution of artefacts in relation to the landscape is worthy of consideration. The majority of enclosed Iron Age sites and pottery scatters in Warwickshire occur along the Avon Valley and in the Dunsmore area, which transects the county from the north-east to south-west, and there are less frequent sites in the Feldon area (south-east Warwickshire) and in north Warwickshire (Hingley 1996: 14). There are inherent biases in the data collected by the WHER on sites (Hingley 1996: 21; Palmer 2002), and artefacts (Worrell 2007, 373), but it is interesting to note that metal-detecting, the method of discovery of all of the Iron Age artefacts recorded by the PAS in Warwickshire, is in general evenly distributed across the county. Figure 1 illustrates the parishes from which the PAS has recorded artefacts. These cover both high and lowland areas with varying geologies, which may have had an influence on other methods of site discovery, such as aerial photography. In this manner, the finds have been recovered, quite fortuitously, from a more representative sample of the county, including the Avon and Dunsmore areas where enclosed sites and pottery scatters are most frequent.

The distribution of the harness and vehicle fittings can be viewed in relation to prehistoric and Roman major route-ways in Warwickshire. 53% (10) of these artefacts were

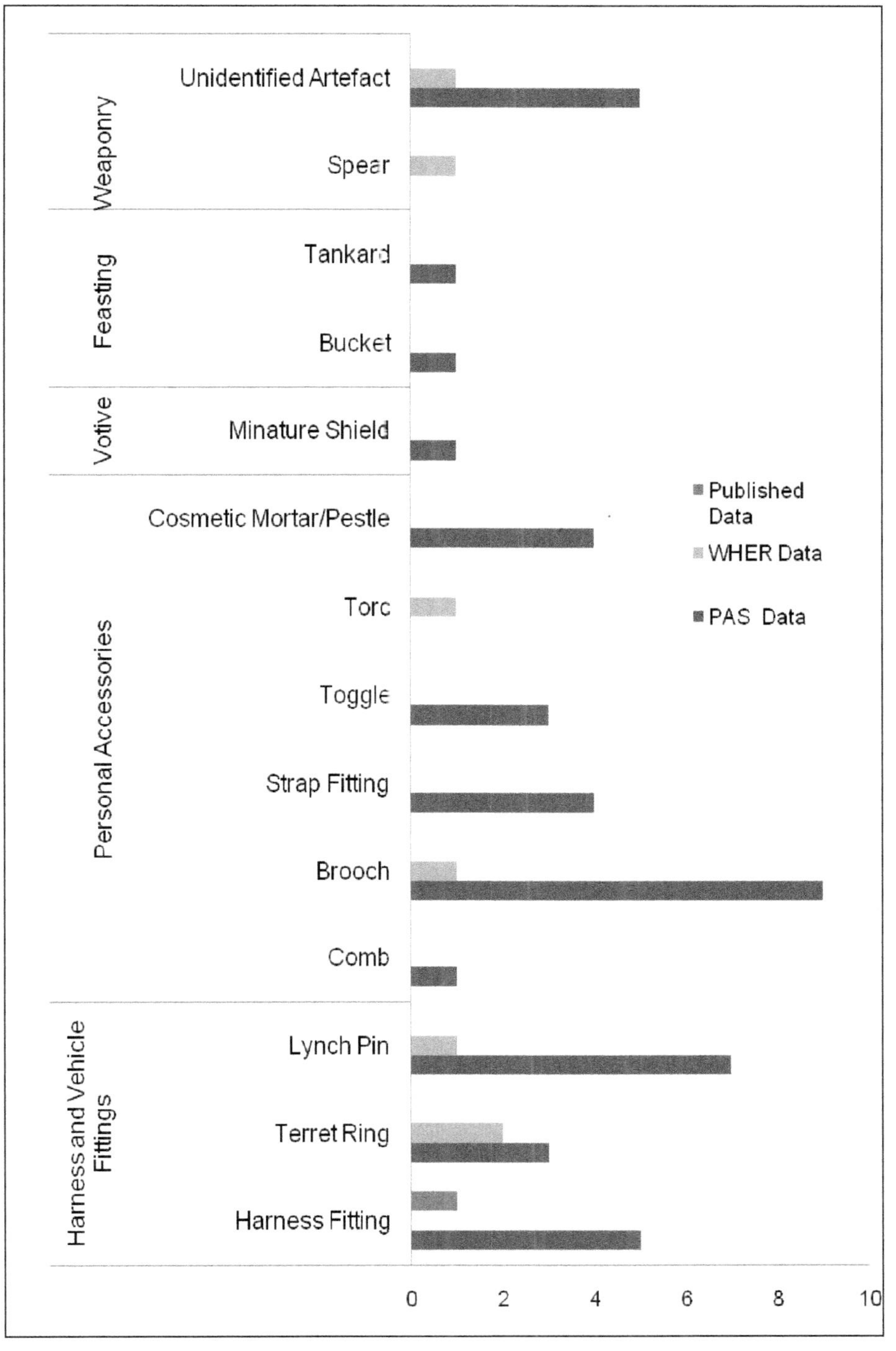

***Graph 1:** Categories and quantities of published finds and finds recorded by the PAS and WHER.*

found close to prehistoric and Roman routeways, seven being close to junctions. Figure 2 illustrates the distribution of harness and vehicle artefacts, sites and major route-ways (information based on HER and PAS data). Presumably, some of these artefacts discovered along the routes were accidentally lost, perhaps sometimes while horses and vehicles were in motion, but some may have been purposefully deposited, as has been proposed for some Norfolk examples (Hutcheson 2004: 85). There are four clusters of harness and vehicle artefacts: near Alcester where there was a Roman fort and large settlement, at Bidford-on-Avon and Salford Priors where there are Roman settlements and a villa. Associated Roman sites are lacking at Tanworth-in-Arden or Kingsbury, although a large Iron Age boundary ditch is documented in the former parish. Natasha Hutcheson's (2004: 40-41) study of Late Iron Age and Roman metalwork in Norfolk, showed that harness and vehicle material was deposited in a diverse range of 'landscape' locations' including clusters of 1st-century material around early Roman forts and camps, has shown the potential for further study of landscape associations of material of this kind.

Fig. 1: Warwickshire parishes where the PAS has recorded finds.

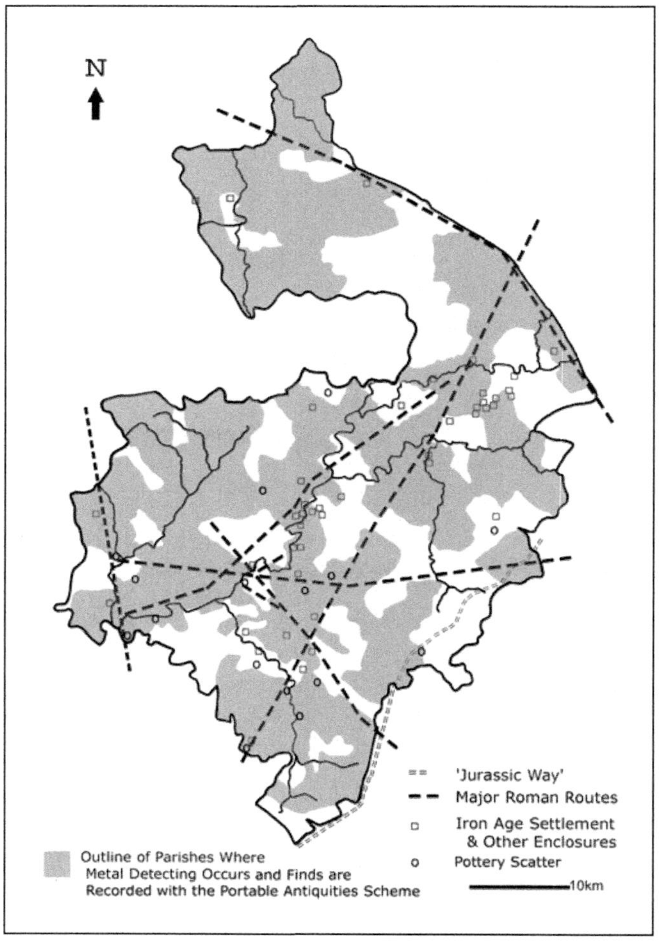

Fig. 2: Distribution of harness and vehicle artefacts, sites and major route-ways (information based on HER and PAS data).

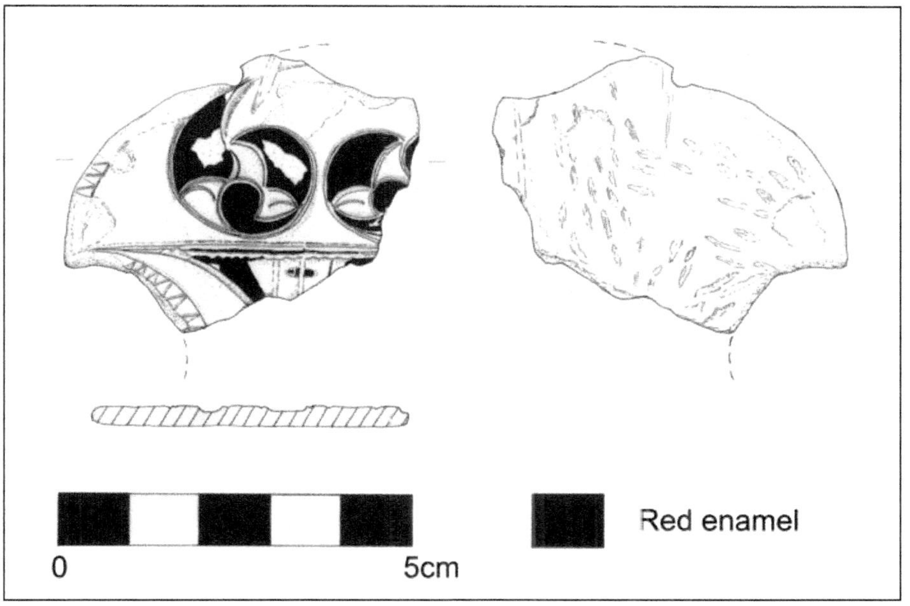

Fig. 3: A copper-alloy harness mount (WMID-9460B5).

An examination of two important artefacts

It has already been shown that Warwickshire was not impoverished in relation to the range and quantity of Iron Age artefacts discovered. As well as the comb found at Tanworth-in-Arden (Ashby and Bolton this volume), two other late Iron Age artefacts found in the county and recorded by the PAS are particularly noteworthy: a copper-alloy harness mount (WMID-9460B5; Fig. 3) and a miniature shield (WAW-9BB642; Fig. 4).

The horse harness mount fragment was found in Stoneleigh by Stephen Quinn and recorded with Duncan Slarke (Staffordshire and West Midlands FLO). In profile the fragment is gently curved across its longer axis and includes portions of two adjoining curved edges. The front is decorated with wavy and zigzag lines and comma-shaped and triangular cells with straight and curved sides, some of which are infilled with opaque red glass. The largest design on the fragment is formed from two spirals, probably originally joined by a now incomplete curved line, all incised. The feature shares some similarities with the 'palmette derivative' designs identified by Fox (1947: 147, group B). Two further incised lines, one almost straight, the other more markedly curved converge towards the point where the two original edges meet. These lines form the corner of a sub-triangular feature. There is also a geometric design of two rows of triangles (Fox 1958: 147, design 48), pointing inwards towards each other, running from the longest side of the sub-triangular design towards the corner opposite. There are a large number indentations, mostly linear and shallow, on the reverse, and a deeper and wider recessed area is visible towards the broadly right angled corner that is the junction between two broken sides. The fragment fragment has a well-developed green patina and has a maximum length of 54.4mm, a width of 33.3mm, and is 3.2-3.8mm thick. It weighs 25.92g.

Two fragments found at the same location over the past 10 years are held at The Market Hall Museum, Warwick. One of the fragments adjoins the mount from Stoneleigh. Based on the shape and parallels, the fragments are likely to be a quadrilobed harness mount. A variation in the quadrilobed harness mount has two larger lobes rather than four eared ones (see the example from Alltwen Neath-Port Talbot, in the National Museum of Wales). The use of geometric elements (triangles) and incised swags and zig zag borders suggest that mount may date to around AD50-80 (Adam Gwilt, pers. comm.). There are similar trends in examples from the Polden Hill hoard, also with red opaque glass decoration (Brailsford: 1975) and similar zig-zag borders on two armour pendants in the Seven Sisters hoard, dated to AD 50-75 (Savory 1976) and the hoards from Westhill and Santon, East Anglia, which have similar mounts (although there are blue and yellow enamels too) are similarly dated. A similar harness enamelled brooch, toggle and bridle bit were found in a burial at King Harry Lane, Verulamium, dated to AD 50-55.

The second artefact to consider is a Late Iron Age bronze miniature shield discovered in the parish of Alcester by a metal detector user, Mr. G. Ross (Fig. 4). The shield is a composite, oval model with a central circular dome representing a boss. Its decoration consists of a single fine linear grooved border and within this border is a series of low-relief dots. Further decoration consists of a roundel, in the field above and below the boss, formed by a circle of low-relief dots with a single dot in the centre. The reverse of the boss is hollow and it has a separate handle attached by two integral rivets either side of the boss. The handle is made from a rectangular sheet of copper-alloy and the long edges have been folded towards each other, forming slightly concave edges.

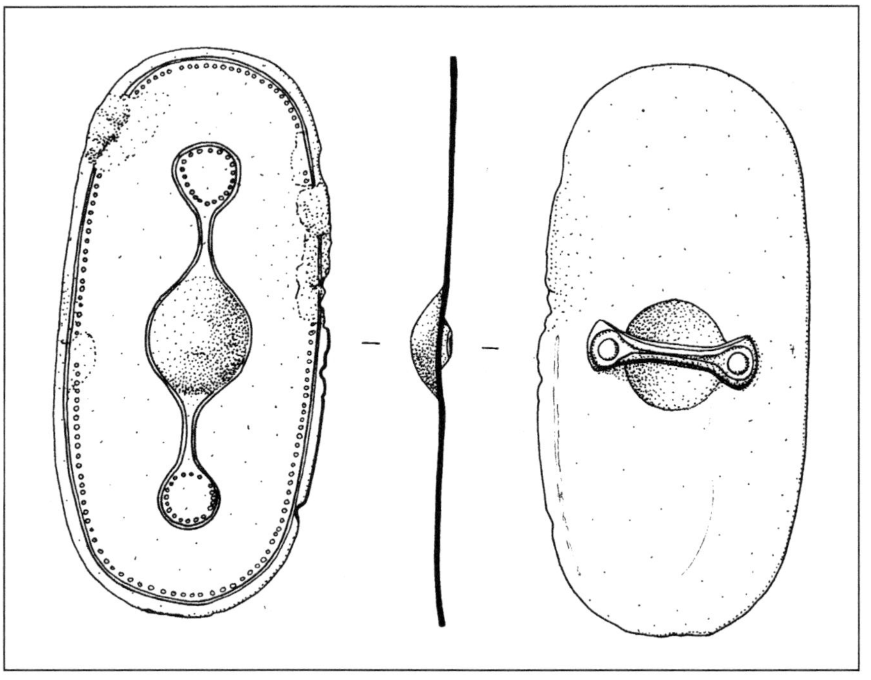

Fig. 4: A miniature shield (WAW-9BB642).

Miniature shields are unusual items, only 15 being known before the discovery of the Salisbury hoard, which contained 24 examples (Stead 1998: 114). Of the previously known 15 shields, two were found on hillforts, five in temples and five were thought to be ritually deposited (Stead 1991: 25). The PAS has recorded a further 22 miniature shields from a site in the Lincolnshire Wolds (LIN-ADDBE4, LIN-ADC107, LIN-ADA9D0, LIN-AD9F17, LIN-D9156, LIN-AD7464, LIN-9EB271, LIN-9E9943, LIN-9E81E4, LIN-9E6944, LIN-9E3CA4, LIN-9E0D82, LIN-9DE863, LIN-9DAE32, LIN-9D9C43, LIN-9D7155, LIN-9D5032, LIN-9D0633, LIN-9CF8E1, LIN-9CEA47 & LIN-9CC832). These were discovered along with miniature axes, spears and swords, all of which suggest a ritual deposition and plausibly this material derives from a shrine, perhaps dedicated to Mars. Another single shield has been recorded by the PAS from Sleaford, Lincolnshire (LIN-BC5A95).

Conclusion

This paper set out to provide a preliminary appraisal of the contribution made by the PAS data to Late Iron Age Warwickshire, focusing on the copper-alloy artefacts recorded by the PAS and WHER. When considering the quantity of artefacts and their associated findspots, it has demonstrated that Warwickshire was not as impoverished as was traditionally viewed. The increased number of recorded artefacts provides the basis of a finds profile, which can be compared with those from other counties.

The PAS data provides an unconventional method to publishing finds and images, allowing on-line access and up to date information. Images are particularly important as they allow the finds to be re-evaluated as new research is produced. The lack of publication of previous finds and sites in general has been highlighted as a possible reason why Warwickshire is under-represented in national studies. It is in this aspect that the PAS can contribute to re-addressing this problem.

This paper has also briefly studied the deposition of the harness and vehicle artefacts by looking at the potential relationships of findspots in relation to major route-ways and settlement sites. This is an area which could be explored further. For a region once described as an 'archaeological desert', a study of the PAS data, particularly in Warwickshire and in combination with the WHER data, is making an important contribution to the study in Iron Age artefact studies at local, regional and national levels.

Acknowledgements

My thanks and appreciation are due in particular to Dave Head and Sally Worrell, who have been patiently giving me advice and encouragement to get this paper started and then completed. Thanks to Alison Hatcher, Emma Jones, Stuart Palmer, Candy Stevens for providing me with data I would not have otherwise seen and answering my many enquiries. Thanks to Phil Watson, Peter Reavill and Sara Wear for their comments on the original poster this paper was based on. Thanks to Jody Joy and J. D. Hill who have commented on previous papers and whose comments have been included here.

Bibliography

Brailsford, J. W. 1975, 'The Polden Hill hoard', *Proceedings of the Prehistoric Society* 41, 222-234.

Cunliffe, B. 1984, *Danebury: an Iron Age hillfort in Hampshire. The excavations 1969-78, Vol. 1: The site; Vol. 2: The finds,* Council for British Archaeology Research Report 52 (Council for British Archaeology, London).

Cunliffe, B. 1991, *Iron Age Communities in Britain* (Routledge, London).

Cunliffe, B. 1995, 'The Celtic Chariot: a footnote' in Raftery, B. (ed.) *Sites and Sights of the Iron Age*, Oxbow Monograph 56 (Oxbow, Oxford) 31-39.

Cunliffe, B. and Poole, C. 1991, *Danebury: an Iron Age hillfort in Hampshire. Vol. 5: The excavations 1979-88: The Finds*, Council for British Archaeology Research Report 73 (Council for British Archaeology, London).

Dugdale, W. 1730, *Antiquities of Warwickshire* (London).

Fox, C. 1947, *A Find of the Early Iron Age from Llyn Cerig Bach, Anglesey* (National Museum of Wales, Cardiff).

Fox, C. 1958. *Pattern and Purpose: early Celtic art in Britain* (National Museum of Wales, Cardiff).

Garrow, D. 2008, 'The time and space of Celtic art: interrogating the 'Technologies of Enchantment' Database', in Garrow, D., Gosden, C. and Hill, J. D. (eds.), *Rethinking Celtic Art* (Oxbow, Oxford), 15-39.

Hingley, R. 1996, 'Prehistoric Warwickshire: a review of the evidence', *Transactions of the Birmingham and Warwickshire Archaeological Society* 100, 1-24.

Hutcheson, N. C. G. 2004, *Later Iron Age Norfolk: metalwork, landscape and society*, British Archaeological Reports 361 (Archaeopress, Oxford).

Jackson, R. 1985, 'Cosmetic Sets from Late Iron Age and Roman Britain', *Britannia* 16, 165-192.

Palmer, S. 2002, 'An archaeological resource assessment for the Middle Bronze Age to Iron Age in Warwickshire and Solihull', in Hurst, D. (ed.), *Westard on the High-hilled Plains: the later prehistory of the West Midlands* (Oxbow Books, Oxford).

Savory, H.N. 1976, *Guide Catalogue of the Early Iron Age Collections* (National Museum of Wales, Cardiff).

Stead, I. M. 1991, 'Many more Iron Age shields from Britain', *Antiquaries Journal* 71, 1-35.

Stead, I. M. 1979, *The Arras Culture* (Yorkshire Philosophical Society, York).

Stead, I. M. 1991, *Iron Age Cemeteries in East Yorkshire*, English Heritage Archaeological Report 22 (English Heritage, London).

Stead, I. M. 1998, *The Salisbury Hoard* (Tempus, Stroud).

Taylor, R. J. and Brailsford, J. W. 1985, 'British Iron Age strap-unions', *Proceedings of the Prehistoric Society* 51, 247-272.

Thomas, N. 1974, 'An archaeological gazetteer for Warwickshire: Neolithic to Iron Age', *Transactions of the Birmingham and Warwickshire Archaeological Society* 86, 15-48.

Wainwright, G. J. 1979, *Gussage All Saints: an Iron Age settlement in Dorset*, Department of the Environment Archaeological Report 10 (HMSO, London).

Wise, P. 1997, 'Alcester, find of Celtic metalwork', *West Midlands Archaeology* 40, 71.

Worrell, S. 2007, 'Detecting the later Iron Age: a view from the Portable Antiquities Scheme', in Haselgrove, C. and Moore T. (eds.), *The Later Iron Age in Britain and Beyond* (Oxbow Books), 371-388.

Worrell, S. 2008, 'Finds reported under the Portable Antiquities Scheme', *Britannia* 39, 337-367.

Changing Objects in Changing Worlds: dragonesque brooches and beaded torcs

Fraser Hunter

As other contributions to this volume indicate, the data available from the Portable Antiquities Scheme (PAS) are making substantial additions to our knowledge of Iron Age and Roman Britain. The aim here is to use case studies based on PAS data to illuminate the transition between these periods. The Roman Conquest was not all blood and guts; there was a necessary adaptation and accommodation between incomers and indigenous groups which took many forms. One way to investigate this is through study of the survival and adaptation of Celtic art styles in Roman Britain. It has long been recognised that much Romano-British art, especially bronzes, shows influence from Celtic art styles (e.g. Haverfield 1923: 48; Collingwood and Myres 1937: 247-60; Toynbee 1964: 9, 333, 341-42; Henig 1995: 103; Megaw and Megaw 2001: 228-41; Hunter 2008a). This provides an avenue to explore the shifting cultures, changing and newly-emerging identities of the Romano-British period. Why did earlier styles persist, and what did they mean? How was material culture used in this time of transition? The PAS data have greatly increased the available information for tackling these questions.

At a general level it can be argued there are three different processes of transition: the continuing production of typically Iron Age styles in the Roman period (such as horse harness and chariot gear; Dungworth 1996: 407-10; Hutcheson 2004; Hunter 2007: 288-94); the decorating of typically Roman objects with styles taken from Celtic art (as on seal boxes and some enamelled vessels; Bateson 1981: 48-50; Casey and Hoffmann 1995: 24; Gardner and Savory 1964: 148-49, fig. 19.10); and the development of hybrid types which are truly Romano-British, combining influences of form and decoration from both Iron Age and Roman contexts to create new kinds of objects. Here two artefact types will be considered which illustrate some of the complexities in these processes: beaded torcs and dragonesque brooches.

Beaded torcs

The torc was one of the 'type-fossils' of the Iron Age in large parts of Europe. Beaded torcs are a distinctively British variant of this broader concept. They come in two parts: a hoop, and a separate front portion (typically about a third of the circumference) with beaded decoration (see Fig. 9 for examples). There are two types, made in very different ways. In type A (Fig. 1.i) the beads are cast individually and threaded onto a rod which slots into the bar- or girder-like hoop. These are complex constructions, and tend to carry more decoration. On the second type (B; Fig. 1.ii), the beaded portion is cast in a single piece, with the ends socketed to receive tenons on the hoop (which is generally circular in section). Typically the beads have a tripartite profile with a central disc and two flankers; both beads and hoop often bear simple geometric decoration, notably transverse ribbing on the beads. Typologically, type B probably developed from type A (MacGregor 1976: 97-99); the dating evidence provides some support for this, although they were in use concurrently (see below).

In 1976 Morna MacGregor pulled together all then-known torcs. These showed a strong concentration in central Britain, between the Humber and the Forth (Fig. 1a). In the subsequent 30 years, excavation and metal-detecting, along with renewed study of old finds, have almost trebled the corpus, from 14 to 44 (as of December 2009; see Appendix 1). Table 1 summarises the find circumstances, which emphasises the contribution of the PAS; it also shows the value of digging in museum stores! There is a clear bias in recording: all the PAS ones are the more recognisable type B beaded portions, while most of the examples found in old publications or museum stores are the less readily-identified type A, suggesting that type A beads are not being recognised in PAS. But what impact does this expanded dataset have on archaeological knowledge?

Method of discovery	Number
Excavation	6
Casual	1
PAS	13
Treasure or Scottish TT	2
Other metal detecting	3
Identified from old discoveries	5

Table 1: Discovery circumstances of beaded torcs since 1976 (as at December 2009).

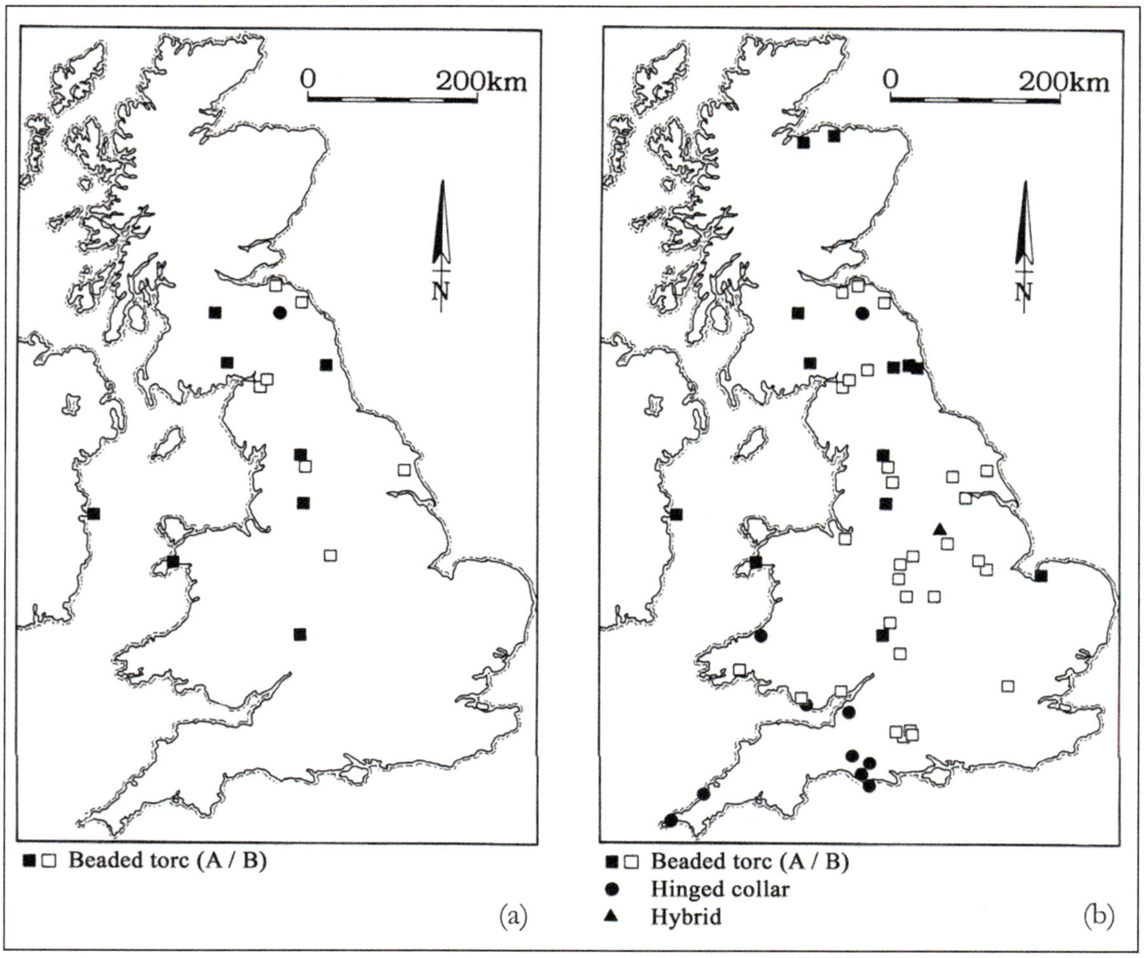

Fig. 1: Beaded torcs a) as known in 1976 and b) as known in 2009;Wraxall-type collars are also plotted (Alan Braby/Fraser Hunter).

Fig. 1.i: Type A beaded torc from Lochar Moss, Dumfries and Galloway (National Museums Scotland).

Fig. 1.ii: Type B beaded torc from Lamberton Moor, Scottish Borders (National Museums Scotland).

Findspot	Type	Dating evidence	Reference
Lambay Island	A	Brooches indicate a mid-C1st date (*c.* 40-75).	Rynne 1976
Hyndford	A	No post-Flavian material from the site.	MacGregor 1976: no. 202
Rickerby Park, Stanwix	B	Pre-Hadrianic (late C1st to early C2nd).	MacGregor 1976: no. 208
Chester (Delamere St)	B	Early C2nd context	Cool forthcoming
Rocester	B	Early C2nd context	White forthcoming
Lamberton Moor	B	Associated with late C1st to C2nd brooch types.	MacGregor 1976: no. 203
Benwell	A	Location suggests Hadrianic or later.	MacGregor 1976: no. 198
Carmarthen	B	Late C2nd context.	Webster 2003: 322-23, fig. 8.6, no. 77
South Shields	A	Antonine.	Croom 1998
Inveresk	B	Early Antonine (*c.* 140-65).	Bishop 2004: 152, fig. 100.3
Corbridge	A	Late Antonine	Croom 1998: 62
Coygan Camp	A	RB phase is late C3rd	Wainwright 1967: 91, fig. 23.7

Table 2: Dating evidence for beaded torcs, arranged in chronological order.

The new excavated finds include a number from secure contexts. When taken with the more circumstantial dating evidence from earlier finds, they support MacGregor's arguments for a 1st to 2nd century date range. The type's origins seem to lie in the early 1st century AD, with some support for type A being the earlier (Table 2).

The numbers from the Hadrian's Wall area and from Antonine contexts elsewhere strongly suggest a 2nd century *floruit*, with both types being found up until the late 2nd century, but very rarely thereafter. While the origins may lie in the late Iron Age, their *floruit* is firmly Romano-British.

These new finds also significantly broaden the distribution, with many of the new finds coming from the Midlands, rather to the south of the former limits. This is seen in both PAS and other data, making the distribution quite robust, with the core area now running from the Forth to the Severn-Wash line, and a cluster in Wiltshire.

This firm evidence for use in the Romano-British period leads to a number of questions. The concept of the torc is not a Roman one, it was presumably an indigenous idea. Yet (with the exception only of the Lochar Moss torc) their decoration owes nothing to Celtic art styles, comprising simple geometric patterns. This and the dating evidence suggests this is not simply the survival of an Iron Age type. Instead, they are a new interpretation or development of the torc tradition in the Roman period.

The form consciously harks back to earlier traditions, but now in much less exotic materials: late Iron Age torcs in Britain, always rare, were overwhelmingly of precious metals. This suggests a much broader social range were now adopting them (although the fact some were deposited in hoards indicates they were still valued).

The distribution is broad, but not pan-British; it is a regional type, albeit over a very broad region, spanning the military and parts of the civilian zone (and thus they are best separated from debates about military decorations or trophies; see Maxfield 1974). This spread is best understood in the wider context of contemporary neck ornaments. The clue comes from a hybrid 'beaded hinged collar' from Dinnington, South Yorkshire, which gives a link to another contemporary type; the Wraxall class of hinged collars (Beswick *et al* 1990; Megaw 1971). In contrast to the beaded torcs, these do often bear Celtic-style decoration; dating evidence points again to a 1st or 2nd century range, and their distribution is essentially complementary to beaded torcs, with a marked concentration in south-west England and an area of overlap in south Wales (Fig. 1b).

Both beaded torcs and Wraxall collars appear regularly in books on Celtic art. Yet their main period and area of use was Roman Britain: regional versions of a habit of neck ornaments which reinterpreted, developed and modified Iron Age traditions to create something new and typically Romano-British. It is notable that these types developed from traditional forms are all but absent from the heart of the civilian zone, in the extreme south and south-east. However, they were not restricted purely to the 'margins' of the province or the military zone: this was not just a phenomenon of the 'periphery' of Roman Britain, but was part of being Romano-British for a segment of the population in a large area of the province. Unfortunately, the evidence does not yet allow discussion of any gender associations.

What did these torcs mean? The distribution of the A-type is much broader than the B-type, with type A examples being found both beyond the frontier in northern Scotland and Ireland, and on Iron Age-tradition sites within the frontier (Fig. 1b). This suggests these more complex forms were more desirable in exchanges, or were the ones identified as most appropriate in an Iron Age context. Yet the type Bs show a clear heritage of earlier traditions; they provide a good example of the reinvention or recreation of that tradition within a new context, modified and made more accessible in this case by their simplification and use of non-precious metals.

In sum, it seems this was a late Iron Age type which saw a new life in the Roman period. The idea of the torc as a restricted, status item (seen in the rare precious-metal torcs of the late Iron Age and reflected in the ornate nature of the type A torcs) was recreated as a wider habit, one regional expression of a broader tradition of neck ornaments which drew on indigenous traditions but reinvented them as part of the creation of Romano-British identities. Wearing a torc became part of being Romano-British, for at least some people in at least some places.

Dragonesque brooches

This theme can be discussed further by examining the dragonesque brooch. While many Romano-British brooches carried Celtic decoration, the dragonesque has caught the modern imagination, and its stylistic links to Celtic styles make it invaluable for study. The key papers are those by Feachem (1951; 1968), with most subsequent workers following his fourfold classification of the enamelled designs (e.g. Bateson 1981: 33-35; Hull type 200, see Bayley and Butcher 2004: 171-72). Kilbride-Jones (1980: 170-83) provided a useful consideration, but his oft-quoted attempt to discern *civitas-* or tribe-based workshops (West and East Brigantian and Parisian types) is flawed, as considered below. Dearne (1998: 59-61) has usefully reviewed the various classifications and their problems, suggesting an alternative typology, while Jope (2000: 116-17, 274-75, pl. 198) viewed the type from a Celtic art perspective. Alloy types were considered by Bayley and Butcher (2004: fig. 147) and Dungworth (1997: fig. 3; 1998: fig. 21), with suggestions of patterning on a modified typology; unenamelled and circular-enamelled motifs had lower zinc and higher tin levels than those with square and lattice decoration. Mackreth (2000: 153-54) has reviewed questions of date and origin, while Jundi and Hill's study (1998) highlights the potential to consider social issues.

Surprisingly, there has been no published synthesis of this material since 1968. Yet the dataset has increased three-fold over the past 40 years, from 83 known to Feachem to over 270 (including S-shaped variants) as of May 2008. This is predominantly due to metal-detecting, primarily recorded through the PAS (Table 3). There will undoubtedly be further examples lurking in journal articles, archives and detectorists' drawers, but this increase allows a much more developed picture of the type. Here the impact of the PAS data will be considered; as this lacks contextual evidence, the focus will be on issues of distribution and classification.

Source	Number
Excavation	36
PAS	103
Other metal detecting	43
Unknown	7

Table 3: Discovery circumstances of dragonesque brooches since Feachem (1968).

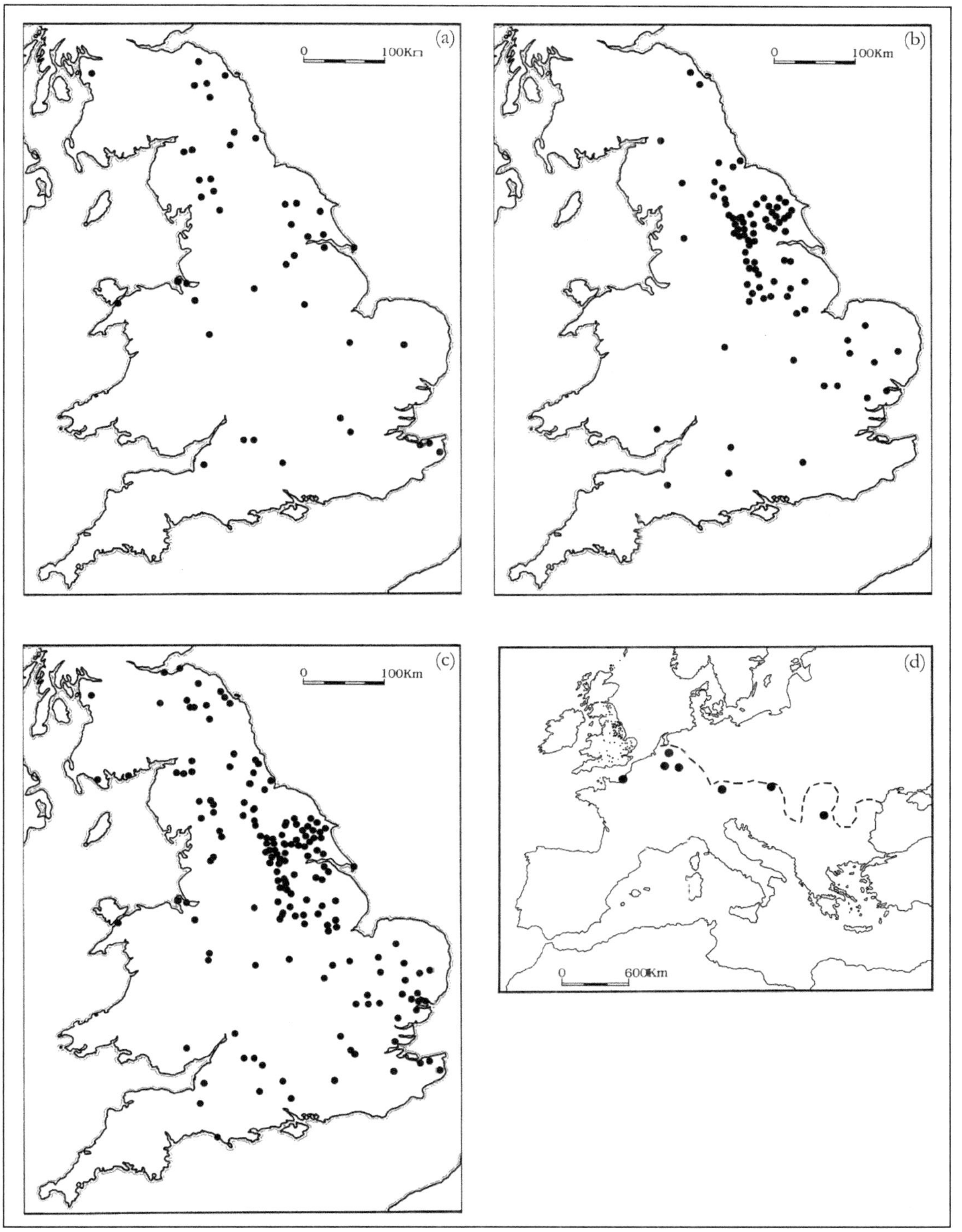

Fig. 2: Distribution of dragonesque brooches: a) as known in 1968; b) distribution of PAS data, 2008; c) overall distribution in 2008; d) European distribution (Alan Braby / Fraser Hunter).

Placing the dragonesque - workshops and locations

One great asset of the PAS data is in providing a much bigger sample for studying the distribution (Fig. 2a-d). In broad terms this supports and fleshes out Feachem's maps (1951; 1968), although PAS does not stretch north of the border with Scotland, and there are biases arising from the frequency of detecting; thus East Anglia is better represented than in Feachem's day, while the Hadrian's Wall zone sees less activity. However, the same core distribution is clear, and when this is combined with other sources of evidence it shows a strongly regional distribution. There is also a thin trickle to the Continent, probably representing two processes: contacts to and fro between adjacent Channel shores, and a spread along the Roman frontier connected to troop movements (Fig. 2d). Figure 3 summarises the distribution, by selecting only (former) counties with five or more brooches. This shows a northern and eastern focus, with a spread from south-east Scotland to East Anglia and a very marked concentration in Yorkshire. There is no doubt that Yorkshire is the homeland of the dragonesque.

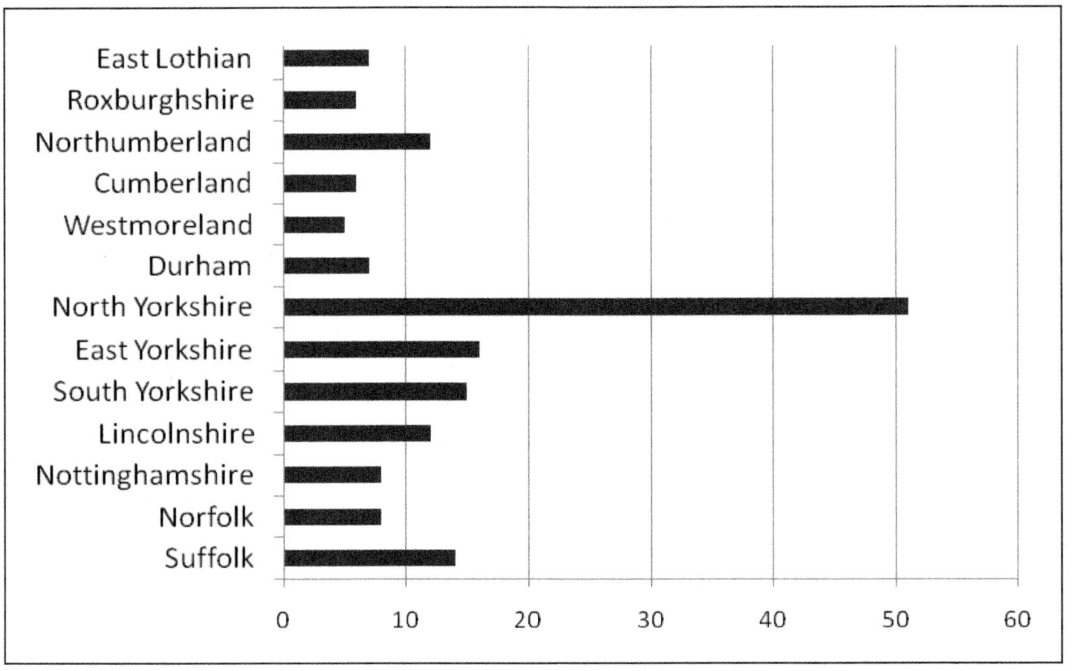

Fig. 3: Counties with more than five brooches, arranged approximately north-south.

This is confirmed by the sparse evidence of its ancestry. The dragonesque did not emerge from nothing in the early Roman period; there are hints of an earlier tradition. Excavations at Wetwang, East Yorkshire have uncovered two iron S-shaped brooches, one from a burial of 3rd century BC date, the other from a settlement apparently similar in date (Hull and Hawkes 1987: 168). This form is otherwise unknown in the Iron Age, and must be a regional type which spawned the later dragonesque; two other iron S-brooches from later contexts may be related (Hull and Hawkes 1987: 168; Stead 1980: fig. 61.17). What is striking is the plainness of these earlier examples; apart from the shape, there is nothing to hint at the decorative developments to come. While its ancestry may lie in the Iron Age, this emblematic piece of Celtic art is essentially a Roman-period development.

Its genesis may lie in the decades around the Roman Conquest. Mackreth (2000: 153-54) has drawn attention to examples from southern Britain in Claudian-Neronian contexts, using this to argue for southern origins. In fact this simply reflects a methodological bias; the inevitable impact of the chronology of the Conquest on our ability to date things. It is impossible to identify such early contexts further north because datable (Roman) material had barely reached these areas at this time. However, these early occurrences (and the good evidence for Yorkshire origins) indicate that the decorative type had emerged by the middle decades of the 1st century AD, with all three major types represented by this date (S-shaped from Longthorpe, Peterborough, non-enamelled from Braughing, Hertfordshire, enamelled from Old Winteringham, Lincolnshire; Dannell and Wild 1987: fig. 21.9; Feachem 1951: fig. 6.1; Stead 1976: fig. 99.11). This puts the dragonesque in a similar time-frame to the explosion of Celtic metalwork in the north (*cf.* MacGregor 1976: 177-78), a phenomenon which may be linked to the increasing need for very visual symbols of display and identity in the face of the threat of Rome (Hunter 2007: 289). The innovations in the dragonesque may thus be part of this wider trend. However, there is no doubt that its *floruit* lay in the Roman period 'proper'; Mackreth's review of the contextual dating evidence puts its currency in the period *c*. 50-*c*. 175 (Mackreth 2000: 154).

A new classification

The three-fold increase in finds allows the classification to be revisited; further examples are now known of most previously unique examples. This is presented as a classification rather than a typology because the dating evidence is too poor to sustain any inferred development sequences; Dearne's (1998: 59-61) suggested typology is more plausible than previous versions (e.g. Bulmer 1938; Kilbride-Jones 1980: 170-83), but still requires more finds from dated contexts to sustain it. The revised classification, building on previous work, is illustrated in Figure 4 and outlined in Table 4. Three basic categories are proposed: A, zoomorphic with enamelling on the body; B, zoomorphic without enamelling on the body; C, S-shaped, lacking clear zoomorphism. A profusion of sub-types is also suggested, with the aim of trying to identify workshop traditions; the validity of this will be tested in further analysis below. At present 165 examples of A, 70 of B and 26 of C (plus eleven recorded only as 'dragonesque') are known; the focus here will be on A and B, the dragonesque proper.

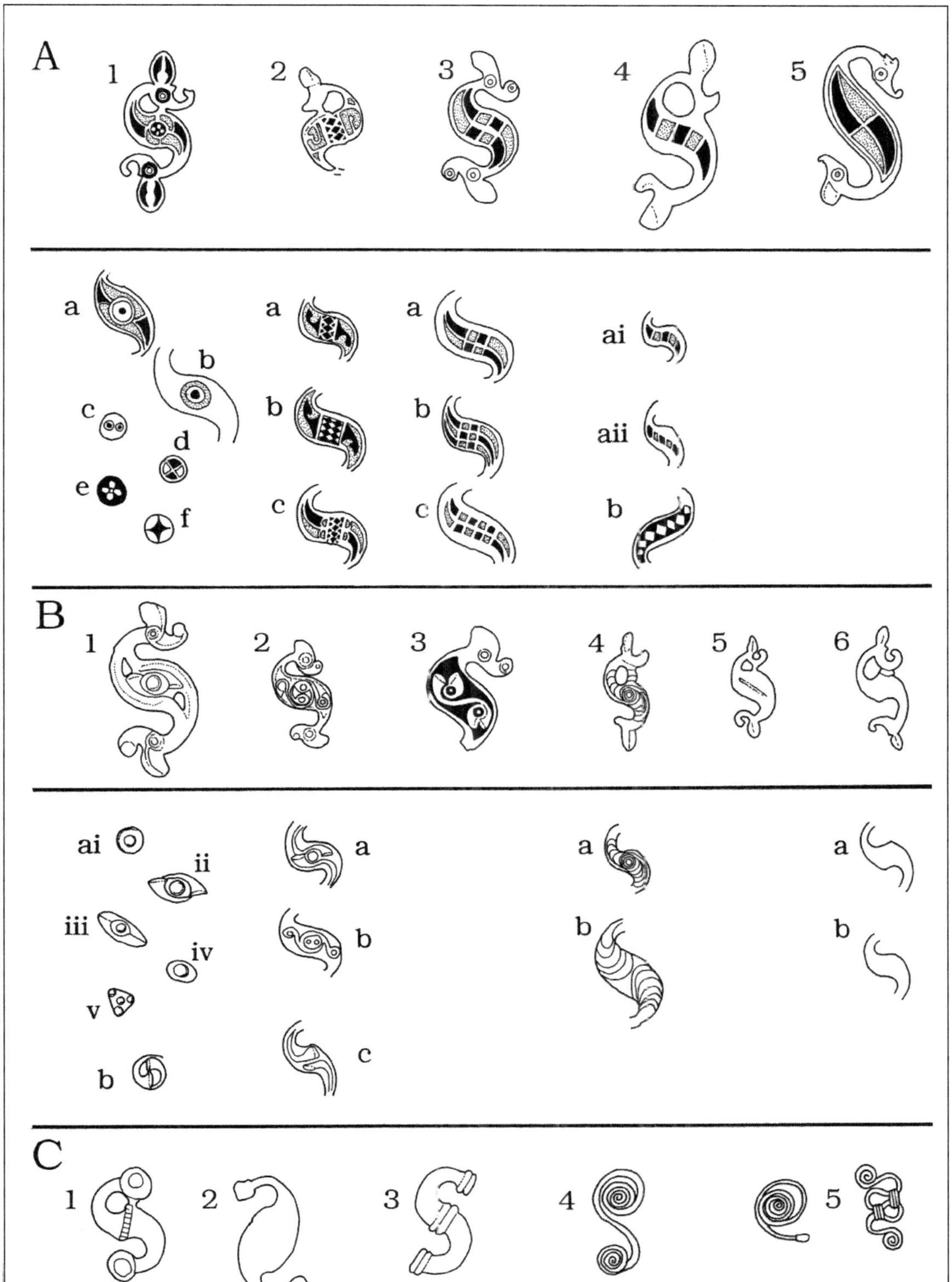

Fig 4: Revised classification of dragonesque brooches. For types A and B, the column below each main type shows subdivisions by lower-case letter and then Roman numerals (Alan Braby).

A	**Enamelled dragonesque brooches** (enamelling on the body) (165 examples)		
	1	Central circular device (43)	
		a	Ring and dot flanked by enamelled zones
		b	Ring and dot on a plain body
		c	Two small ring and dot motifs
		d	Cross
		e	Quatrefoil
		f	Four-point star
		g	Other / hybrid
	2	Lozenges (52)	
		a	Single lozenge row & flanking scrolls
		b	Double lozenge row & flanking scrolls
		c	Single lozenge row, no scrolls
		d	Variants
	3	Panel of squares (22)	
		a	4 squares
		b	6 squares
		c	2 rows of squares
	4	Row of squares (31)	
		a	Squares (i, with triangles at end; ii, squares only)
		b	Other motifs
	5	Curved triangles (body split into four equal-sized curved triangles) (4)	
	6	Other (5)	
B	**Non-enamelled dragonesque brooches** (70 examples)		
	1	Openwork (18)	
		a	Central boss with surrounding elements
			i Ring
			ii Oval formed of two rotationally-symmetric trumpets
			iii Oval formed of conjoined double-ended trumpets
			iv Oval (variant of iii, but trumpets not clearly defined)
			v Triangle
		b	Central circle formed of two ying-yang trumpets
	2	Trumpet-scroll relief decoration (16)	
		a	Trumpet scroll around central boss
		b	Triple-circle trumpet scrolls
		c	Other
	3	Hybrids – relief trumpet decoration and enamelling (5)	
	4	Scalloped decoration (6)	
		a	Scallops radiating from central boss
		b	Scallops radiating from terminals
	5	Ribbed (6)	
	6	Plain body, sometimes with edge demarcation (13)	
		a	Angular body
		b	Rounded
	7	Other (4)	
C	**S-shaped brooches** (26 examples)		
	1	Disc terminals (5)	
	2	Square terminals (4)	
	3	Bar terminals (4)	
	4	Wire S (6)	
	5	Wire variants (4)	
	6	Other (4)	

Table 4: Revised classification of dragonesque brooches (sub-totals do not always add up to totals as some fragments can only be broadly classified).

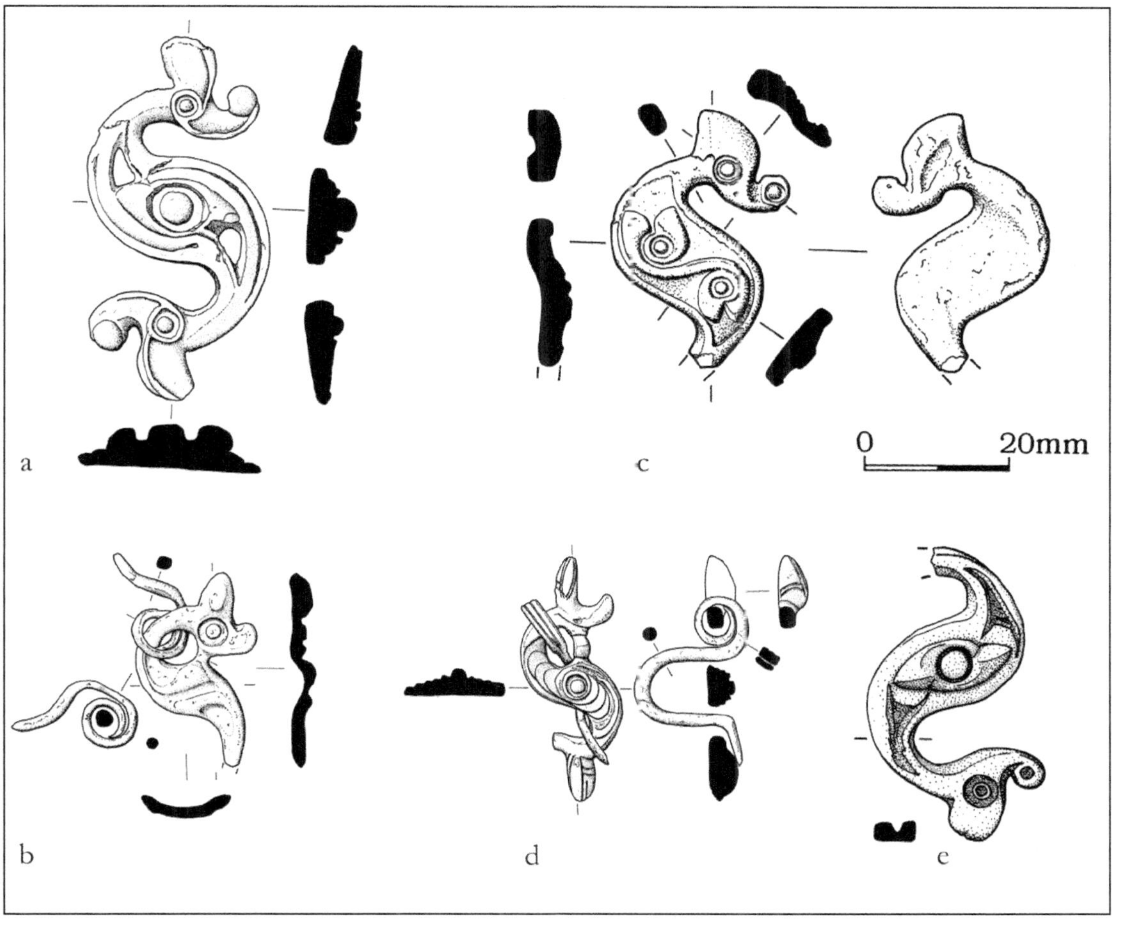

Fig. 5: PAS finds of dragonesque brooches with boss-and-trumpet decoration: a) Norham, Northumberland (NCL-3EABC0); b) East Yorkshire (NCL-4F6884); c) Stillington and Whittington, Cleveland (NCL-2004B5); d) Driffield, East Yorkshire (NCL-9700A8); e) Clitheroe, Lancashire (LANCUM-411DE2) (Alan Braby, apart from e - Adam Parsons).

Before looking at implications, it is useful to consider some details of the classification, for this reveals much. For the enamelled examples, Feachem's four-fold classification has stood the test of time, and is retained here; the vast bulk of material falls into his scheme, with the addition of a fifth sub-division now represented by several examples, and a sixth 'other' category to catch a few variants. Feachem paid less attention to the non-enamelled ones, as they were far less numerous in his time, but their numbers have increased greatly in the intervening years. Most of these have come from PAS, and indeed they are disproportionately represented in the scheme, a phenomenon explored further below.

The non-enamelled ones are predominantly decorated in versions of 'boss style' (Leeds 1933: 54-55, 110), one of the typical late Iron Age art styles of central Britain, characterised by raised bosses and relief trumpets in various combinations. The brooches show a highly imaginative and elegant use of boss and trumpet motifs, in both relief and openwork, with the finest examples having decoration spreading onto the edges as well as the face, using both incised and relief ornament (Fig. 5). This group is characterised by their variety, in contrast to the enamelled ones which can be rather repetitive.

The enamelled and non-enamelled types reflect the two dominant Celtic art traditions identified in this area by MacGregor (1976: 184); these clearly continued as distinctive traditions into the Roman period, adapting to new circumstances (Hunter 2008a). The traditions were not entirely separate; on dragonesques enamelling is regularly found on the eyes and ears of category B brooches; there are also hybrids with strong relief decoration augmented by enamelling (here B3), and enamelling with some subtle low-relief trumpet decoration (especially in A1g; Fig. 6; Hunter 1994: figs. 2-3). However, these latter two categories are rare compared to the bulk of the material. There are also occasional examples of more southerly Celtic art motifs being found on dragonesques, emphasising the experimentation in styles (Hunter 2008b; Hattatt 1987: 167, fig. 54, no. 1026).

This creativity is seen also in the application of dragonesque-type motifs to other objects. The PAS database records a dragonesque strap-fitting (although without an image to confirm this; PAS: YORYMM159), while an unpublished strap-fastener from Rossington Bridge South Yorkshire has a related S-form composed of conjoined trumpets (in Doncaster Museum). More obviously related is the unique penannular brooch from Winterton, Lincolnshire, its terminals clearly dragonesque (Stead 1976: fig. 102, no. 37).

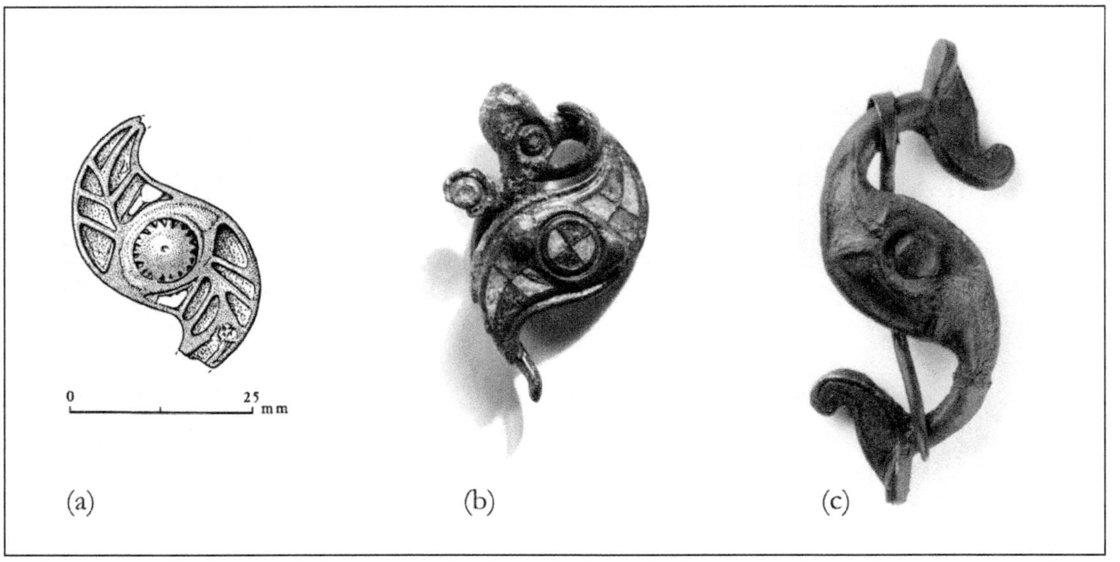

Fig. 6: Brooches combining enamelled and trumpet decoration: a) Boreland of Longcastle, Wigtownshire (Marion O'Neil) b) Castledykes, Lanarkshire (Hunterian Museum); c) ?Lincolnshire (National Museums Scotland).

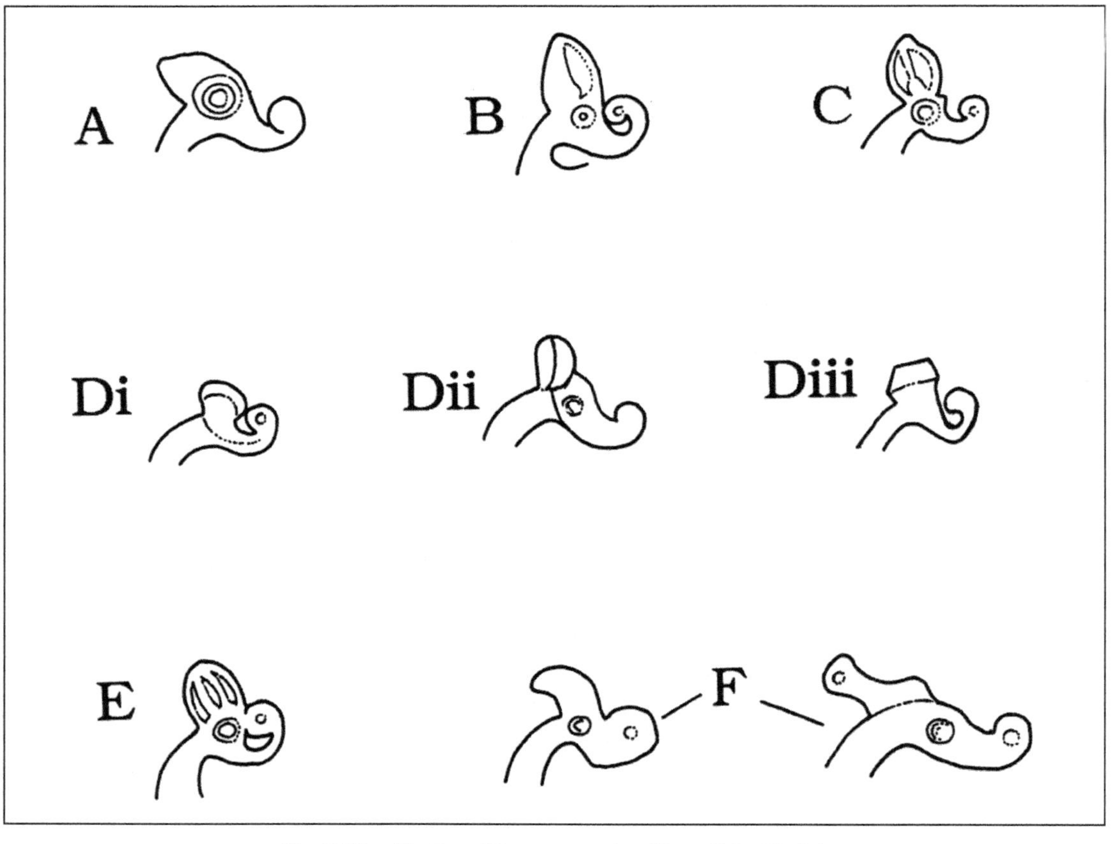

Fig. 7: Classification of dragonesque head types (Alan Braby).

Three other points of classification merit attention. Kilbride-Jones' (1980) division into 'West Brigantian', 'East Brigantian' and 'Parisi' types has been influential, but proves on detailed examination to be illusory. His criteria are rather subjective, but head and ear shape were key: his 'East Brigantian' have upright ear with brow, and often a lozenge pattern, while 'Parisian' ones have back-sloping ears and often a panel of squares; 'West Brigantian' is very mixed. While there are clearly different styles of head, they do not fall into his three regional groups. Instead, four main head shapes may be defined (Fig. 7 A-D); as discussed in more detail in Appendix 2, while there are broad preferences (as Feachem 1951: 32 noted), there are also quite subtle variations, substantially more complex than Kilbride-Jones' threefold division.

The second key point is the issue of regional variety. While Yorkshire dominates the picture, there are certain variants not currently represented there (Appendix 2). Their distribution suggests production of one south of the Humber, the other in southern Scotland. Taken with the evidence of variants and anomalous forms, it indicates that the dragonesque style was adopted quite widely.

The final point is a technological one. There is a noticeable difference (not clear from drawings, but obvious when the objects are handled) between essentially flat, relatively straightforward castings and those with considerable relief decoration; the latter includes not only the boss-and-trumpet designs, but also the raised ears found on many enamelled pieces. There is also a considerable size range, as the illustrations in Feachem (1951) indicate. When taken with the evidence for a diversity of workshops and styles, it indicates a considerable complexity to the type, from fairly simple items to designer pieces.

Interpreting dragonesques

The dragonesque brooch thus provides a good example of the development of a Romano-British form, showing the continuity and development of indigenous art styles within the province, along with experimentation in other styles. It was a successful and popular brooch. But what did it mean? With an object which was (to modern eyes) so obviously linked to indigenous traditions, is it possible to see any patterns in its use? Was it particularly popular in particular areas, or with particular social groups? Was it a symbol of 'non-military, non-Roman identity' as Jundi and Hill (1998: 134) have suggested?

At one level, it is clear this was a generally popular brooch: it is found on a wide range of site types, and few counties in the province lack an example. This makes it hard to interpret as an expression of local identity, resistant to Rome: a considerable number are known from military sites, for instance. However, there are more subtle differences. Using the total sample from known sites, it is possible to define an average dragonesque profile and compare other assemblages to this. This rapidly reveals an interesting difference; enamelled types are markedly more popular on military and urban sites than they are on rural/native ones, which preferred boss-style ornament (Fig. 8; type C are excluded as their numbers are small). This is not a picture of exclusion (more or less all brooch types are found on all site types) but of patterns of preference. Interestingly, this is not part of a general fondness for 'boss style' on native/rural sites, as horse harness in boss style is very common on military sites (Bishop 1998: 63-64). It is thus nothing so simple as a single style being preferred, but more subtle patterns of preference. In this light, it is noteworthy that different styles of enamelled brooch seem to have been favoured in different contexts; A2 were popular in both military and nucleated settlements, but A3 were more popular in the latter.

The patterns in the PAS data reflect these broader trends; when compared to the rest of the data set, they show a higher level of non-enamelled versions (40% compared to 23%), as would be expected if PAS finds come primarily from rural settlements. This could be followed further: there is potential to restore some of these finds to their broad landscape context, but sadly this is rarely attempted. However, an example from Well, North Yorkshire, illustrates the possibility. Here, liaison with the Sites and Monuments Record produced cropmark plots for the findspot of two brooches. This showed they came from an area of field systems close to a rectangular enclosure, linking them most plausibly to a fairly typical rural settlement rather than the villa which is also known in the neighbourhood (Hunter 2008b). The added information gained from this emphasises the value of attempting to place 'stray finds' back in context.

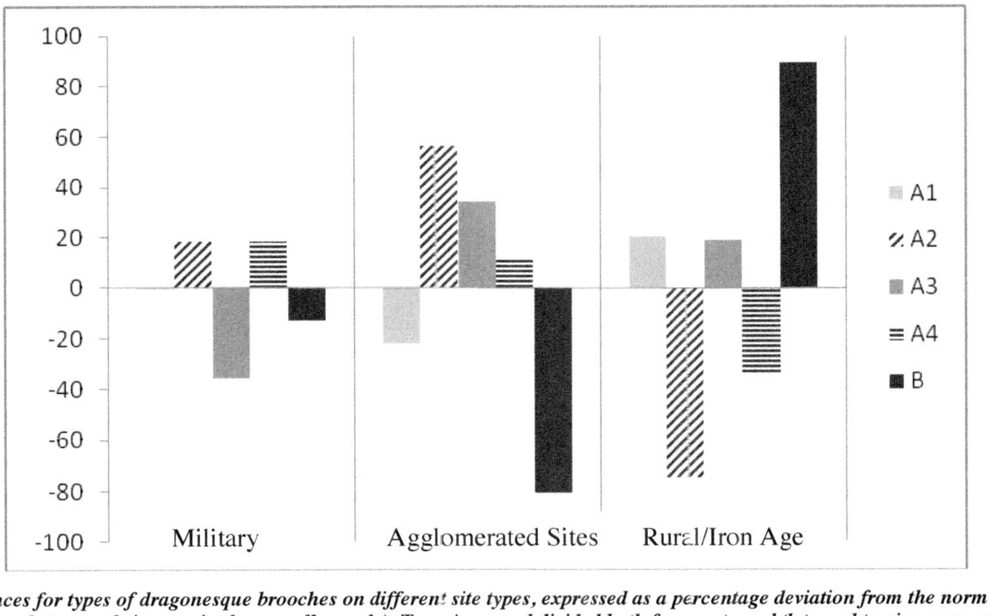

Fig. 8: Preferences for types of dragonesque brooches on different site types, expressed as a percentage deviation from the norm (based on the proportions of brooch type and site type in the overall sample). Type A was subdivided both for greater subtlety and to give near-equal numbers in the different categories (left - Roman military sites; centre - Romano-British agglomerated sites; right - Romano-British rural and Iron Age tradition sites).

The dragonesque thus gives us a picture of a hybrid. The type may have Iron Age roots, but its heart lies in the early Roman period, as part of a wider explosion of metalwork in both traditional and more novel forms. It flourished and developed in the later 1st and 2nd centuries, the main types reflecting the two pre-existing dominant workshop traditions in the area and showing them developing and adapting to changed circumstances. With more subtle study, it is possible to glimpse more subtle choices being exercised in the brooches which people wore, with indications of a difference between military/urban and rural/Iron Age sites. The humble dragonesque clearly has much still to tell.

Towards a Romano-British art?

These case studies have attempted to illustrate something of the complexity of the transition from Iron Age to Roman Britain. Material culture played a key part in this shift; it was one of the main markers people used to signal who they thought they were, or what they wanted to be. In its variability, creativity, adaptation and regional variety, it is possible to see people working out how to live in these changed circumstances. This Romano-British material with earlier overtones was crucial to the processes and negotiations involved in becoming Romano-British, and the PAS provides a key dataset for approaching this problem.

PAS – a northern view

The author was also asked to offer a perspective on PAS from the other side of Hadrian's Wall, and what follows is very much a personal view. On looking south, the main reaction is one of envy. The PAS, and especially its network of Finds Liaison Officers, working closely with detectorists, is a very valuable one; the information being recorded is crucial for research purposes, as this paper has helped to indicate, and this liaison with detectorists can only benefit both sides. Scotland is different, with different laws and different practices. At the time of writing, there is only a single staff member to run the Treasure Trove system. As a result, they can barely keep up with the bureaucracy; to be proactive in outreach is a pipe-dream, and there can be no doubt that much material goes unrecorded.

Yet matters are not so clear-cut; it is important to separate practice from principles. While the practice in England and Wales may be better, the Scottish principles have the edge: in essence, all archaeological objects can be claimed by the Crown, and virtually all pre-seventeenth century finds end up in a museum (the main exceptions are stray coins and stray flints; for further information and complexities, see Saville 2002; 2006). This creates a legacy, an archive of the nation's history; and this is my worry over PAS. The information recorded represents a single moment-in-time record of an object. It cannot readily be studied by anyone else; the decorative details cannot be checked, the alloy cannot be analysed to see how this changed over time, it cannot be put on display to show a community's history, and it is lost to any new approaches. It exists only electronically, with little more reality than an eighteenth-century woodcut of a lost antiquarian object. It may be treasured by a private collector, or it may be sold, but its long-term future is bleak: lost to science, lost to the local community, and lost to future generations. In the course of this study, attempts were made through the PAS to locate and study the brooches of types B1-3; of 28 examples recorded by the scheme, only nine have so far been relocated for study. Every day, the author works with collections gathered by previous generations, with a new eye, new questions and new techniques; every week, researchers come to the museum's stores to study these objects; every month, some of this material goes out to local communities for exhibition. It is important that future generations have the same chance with this marvellous material being recorded by PAS. Whether that is achieved by arguing for enhanced purchase grants for museums, by encouraging finders to leave collections to local museums in their will, or by a change in the law, is a matter for debate. PAS has been a very good thing, and the research value is only beginning to be tapped, but there are concerns. The future is not solely electronic: an object that lives only in digital form is a poor shadow of the real thing, and the real things are a legacy for the future which is slipping between our fingers.

Acknowledgements

I am grateful to Sally Worrell for the chance to develop these thoughts and for considerable assistance with chasing PAS data. A range of Finds Liaison Officers provided invaluable information, but I am especially grateful to Rob Collins and Dot Boughton, for pursuing and procuring brooches for detailed study, to Rachel Atherton for her persistence with beaded torcs, and to those finders who kindly agreed to loan material for study. J. D. Hill and Vincent Megaw commented on an earlier draft to its advantage, while I am grateful to Paul Booth for setting me on the beaded torc trail again with the invitation to work on a recent find from Wishaw Farm, to Hilary Cool, Adam Gwilt and Roger White for information on additional specimens, and to Nina Crummy for information from Hull's corpus. Illustrations are by Alan Braby except where noted.

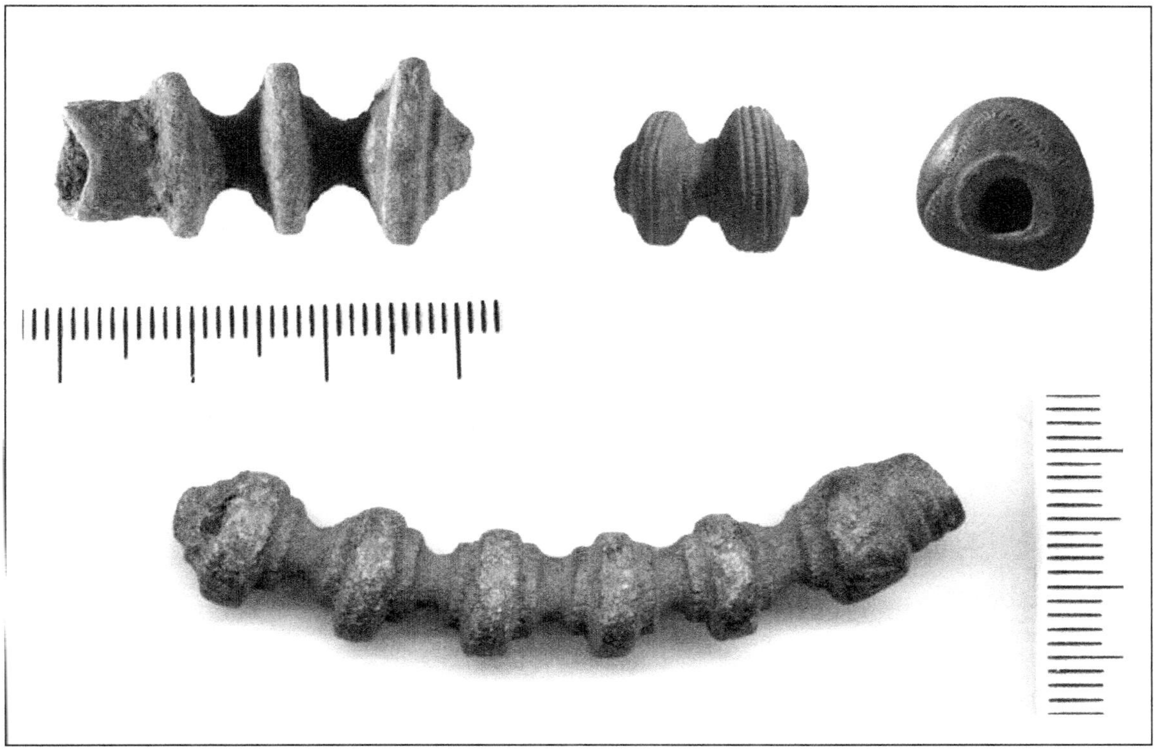

Fig. 9: Beaded torcs recorded by the PAS from: Folkingham, Lincolnshire (LIN-65A032; top left), Wiltshire (WILT-1BCB06; top right) and Wall, Staffordshire (WMID5241; bottom).

Appendix 1: Beaded torcs from PAS

Two of the torcs from MacGregor's (1976: 113-15) list have subsequently been discredited; 197 is the same as 201, while 209 should be dismissed (Leahy 1979: 54). Recent non-PAS finds are listed in Hunter (2008c), to which should be added a type B beaded portion from Chester (Delamere St; Cool forthcoming) and another from Rocester, Staffordshire (Old Shops Site, Mill St; White forthcoming). A summary account of the PAS finds is provided in Table 5; it has only been possible to study three of them first hand.

Appendix 2: the classification of dragonesque brooches

As discussed in the main paper, three basic categories are proposed: A, zoomorphic with enamelling on the body; B, zoomorphic without enamelling on the body; C, S-shaped, lacking clear zoomorphism. Each is further subdivided on morphological or design grounds. For A and B this focuses on the decoration of the body; for C, terminal shape was taken as the key factor. The classification can be investigated further by considering other attributes, notably head form, but also the presence of a junction between one head and the body to retain the pin head, and the occurrence of the reverse-S variant. Other variables (e.g. enamel colours) have not yet been systematically studied, as they require more extensive first-hand examination.

Ear shape was considered by Feachem (1951), who noted persistent differences between types with central devices and types with lozenges. This was taken further by Kilbride-Jones (1980), and was a key element of his influential 'tribal' division of dragonesques. His criteria are rather subjective, and more detailed analysis indicates a far more complex picture than he indicated. There are four dominant forms of head and three less frequent ones (Table 6; Fig. 7).

Table 7 shows that, while there is considerable mixing, certain head types do dominate particular brooch types. However, there is a further complexity which shows the value of more detailed classification; within type A1, different central enamelled motifs are consistently found with different head types. This seems to suggest the practice of different workshops.

A notable feature is the presence of a small percentage of reverse-S form. Feachem (1951) noted about 10% (it is 11% in the current dataset), but this masks considerable variation. Thus, almost a third of type A2a are reversed, whereas none of A2b and A2c are; other notable absences (where there are more than 15 brooches) are noted in Table 8. It is also noteworthy that a significant number of the reversed brooches are otherwise anomalous, with six falling into the 'unusual' or 'hybrid' classifications; there is little geographical patterning beyond an above-expected concentration (perhaps illusory) of four in Suffolk. The significance of the reversal is opaque, but it was clearly not constant among the different kinds of brooches.

The anomalies hold other interesting information, as they show development of the dragonesque tradition outside the Yorkshire heartlands; of the 27 anomalous or unusual specimens, 21 come from outwith Yorkshire. This development of the dragonesque in other areas is suggested also by the existence of rare examples which utilise southern British rather than northern British styles of decoration (Hunter 2008b).

As the maps indicate, the distributions are dominated by Yorkshire. Attempts were made to compare the type spectrum from different regions (on the methodology of Haselgrove 1997: 61-67), but even by amalgamating counties together the numbers are too small for reliable results. Another approach is to look at those few types not currently represented in Yorkshire; while future discoveries may upturn this picture, given the dominance of Yorkshire these may be argued as developments of other regions. Again this shows the value of subdividing Feachem's (1951) enamelled categories, as three of the variants of circle motif are not yet represented in Yorkshire; as with the variability noted in head type, this points to diverse workshops. Their location is unclear, and several are widely scattered, but the balance of the distribution of A1c points to production south of the Humber, while B6a may be a southern Scottish type.

Other features show no obvious patterning - the existence of a head-body join, for instance, is consistently found in around 60% of specimens. Another frequent feature is a stub centrally in the reverse of the brooch. This is best interpreted as the stub of the casting sprue, indicating the metal was poured from the rear.

Site	County	Ref	Brief description
Ockbrook	Derby	DENO-B0A936	Beaded portion, near complete; ten tripartite beads with ribbed flankers; one socketed terminal survives; external diameter *c.* 120 mm.
Dumbleton	Gloucestershire	GLO-41CEA6	Fragment of beaded portion, apparently with a cylindrical terminal and three plain, tripartite, rather low-relief beads.
Huncote	Leicestershire	LEIC-DD6041	Complete beaded portion; 10 plain tripartite beads plus two squared terminals decorated with vertical incisions; internal diameter *c.* 130 mm.
Adlingfleet	Lincolnshire	NLM4339	Fragment of beaded portion, with parts of three tripartite plain beads; iron corrosion implies iron tenon
Ancaster	Lincolnshire	NLM7159	Beaded portion; eleven disc beads; terminals with enamelled triangles.
Folkingham	Lincolnshire	LIN-65A032 (Fig. 9)	Squared ribbed terminal and three surviving plain tripartite beads.
Mansfield	Nottinghamshire	DENO-304F42 & 306A31	Beaded portion in two parts; at least 12 tripartite beads with ribbed flankers.
Wall, Lichfield	Staffordshire	WMID5241 (Fig. 9)	Beaded fragment; tripartite beads with ribbed flankers; terminal bead with grooves and decorated collar.
Durnford	Wiltshire	WILT-DAA276	Fragment of beaded portion with socketed cylindrical terminal and five surviving tripartite plain beads.
?	Wiltshire	WILT-1BCB06 (Fig. 9)	Socketed terminal and two beads; circles with decorated edges (central plain line flanked by ribbed lines); small ribbed collars either side; terminal bead more decorative, with meandering incised line on side.
?	Wiltshire	Not yet fully recorded	Socketed terminal decorated with incised lines; parts of two undecorated barrel-shaped beads.
?	Wiltshire	Not yet fully recorded	Socketed terminal; five surviving tripartite plain beads.
?	Wiltshire	Not yet fully recorded	Socketed terminal, five surviving tripartite beads with ribbed flankers.

Table 5: Summary details of beaded torc fragments recorded by PAS; taken from FLO descriptions, updated from images or objects where available.

A	Backward-sloping ear forming a smooth convex-concave profile with the nose, which generally ends in a scroll; its derivation from a trumpet scroll is clear. The head generally has a marked eye and nose
B	Upright ear; defined eye and nose
C	Upright ear with clear brow separating it from the snout; defined eye and nose
D	The head is formed of a trumpet, and generally lacks a defined eye. i Head of trumpet points forward ii Head of trumpet points to rear iii Trumpet dome is replaced by a conical or truncated-conical terminal iv Variants
E	Nose curls round to join the ear or brow (variants of all the above main types are found with this feature)
F	More naturalistic
G	Other

Table 6: Head forms defined in this study.

	No. (heads)	A	B	C	D	E	F
A unclass	5	1		3		1	
A1	31	16	5	7			1
A2	38	4	5	27		2	
A3	20	9	2	6	1	1	1
A4	29	2	9		14	1	
A5	2						2
A6	4	3					
B unclass	2				1	1	
B1	17	8	2		2	2	
B2	11	7	2			2	
B3	5	3			2		
B4	5	1	1	1	2		
B5	6		3		1	1	
B6	10	1	5	2		1	1
B7	4				1		1
No.	193	55	36	46	24	13	7

Table 7: Distribution of head types across major classes.

	A	**B**	**C**	**D**	**E**	**F**	**Reverse**	**Distribution (types not found in Yorkshire)**
A1a	X							Ayrshire, Cumberland, Derbyshire, Lincolnshire, Wiltshire, Belgium, France
A1b		X						
A1c	X							Lincolnshire, Northumberland, Somerset, Suffolk, Surrey, Holland
A1d			X					Gloucestershire, Norfolk
A1e			X					
A1g	X							
A2			X				1/3 of A2a; none of b-c	
A3	X		X					A3b (Lancashire, Somerset)
A4a		X		X			None	
A5						X		
B1	X							
B2	X						None	
B3	X							Derby, Durham, Lancashire
B5		X						
B6		X						B6a (East Lothian, Roxburghshire, Northumberland)

Table 8: Summary of head form and other key features by category. Dominant head types are marked, but these are rarely exclusive. Type E is not listed as it is found as a variant of all other types; there are only two type G heads. For those types not yet represented in Yorkshire, the counties where they are found are listed, as these may give clues to a non-Yorkshire origin.

Bibliography

Bateson, J. D. 1981, *Enamel-working in Iron Age, Roman and Sub-Roman Britain: the products and techniques*, British Archaeological Reports, British Series 93 (British Archaeological Reports, Oxford).

Bayley, J. and Butcher, S. 2004, *Roman Brooches in Britain: a technological and typological study based on the Richborough Collection* (Society of Antiquaries of London, London).

Beswick, P., Megaw, M. R., Megaw, J. V. S. and Northover, P. 1990, 'A decorated late Iron Age torc from Dinnington, South Yorkshire', *Antiquaries Journal* 70, 16-33.

Bishop, M. C. 1998, 'Military equipment', in Cool, H. E. M. and Philo, C. (eds.), *Roman Castleford, Excavations 1974-85. Volume I: the small finds* (West Yorkshire Archaeology Service, Wakefield), 61-81.

Bishop, M. C. 2004, *Inveresk Gate: excavations in the Roman civil settlement at Inveresk, East Lothian, 1996-2000* (STAR, Edinburgh).

Bulmer, W. 1938, 'Dragonesque brooches and their development', *Antiquaries Journal* 18, 146-53.

Casey, P. J. and Hoffmann, B. 1995, 'Excavations on the Corbridge Bypass, 1974', *Archaeologia Aeliana* (fifth series) 23, 17-45.

Collingwood, R. G. and Myres, J. N. L. 1937, *Roman Britain and the English Settlements* (Clarendon Press, Oxford).

Cool, H. E. M. forthcoming 'The small finds from Delamere Street Chester'.

Croom, A. T. 1998, 'Torc beads from South Shields Roman fort', *Arbeia Journal* 6-7 (1997-8), 60-63.

Dannell, G. B. and Wild, J. P. 1987, *Longthorpe II* (Society for the Promotion of Roman Studies, London).

Dearne, M. J. 1998, 'The brooches', in Dearne, M. J. and Lord, T. C., *The Romano-British Archaeology of Victoria Cave, Settle*, British Archaeological Reports, British Series 273 (John & Erica Hedges, Oxford), 53-66.

Dungworth, D. B. 1996, 'The production of copper alloys in Iron Age Britain', *Proceedings of the Prehistoric Society* 62, 399-421.

Dungworth, D. B. 1997, 'Roman copper alloys: analysis of artefacts from northern Britain', *Journal of Archaeological Science* 24, 901-10.

Dungworth, D. 1998, 'EDXRF analysis of copper alloy artefacts from Victoria Cave', in Dearne, M. J. and Lord, T. C., *The Romano-British Archaeology of Victoria Cave, Settle*, British Archaeological Reports, British Series 273 (John & Erica Hedges, Oxford), 82-4.

Feachem, R. W. de F. 1951, 'Dragonesque fibulae', *Antiquaries Journal* 31, 32-44.

Feachem, R. W. 1968, 'Dragonesque fibulae', *Antiquaries Journal* 48, 100-2.

Gardner, W. and Savory, H. N. 1964, *Dinorben: a hill-fort occupied in early Iron Age and Roman times* (National Museum of Wales, Cardiff).

Haselgrove, C. 1997, 'Iron Age brooch deposition and chronology', in Gwilt, A. and Haselgrove, C. (eds.), *Reconstructing Iron Age Societies* (Oxbow, Oxford), 51-72.

Hattatt, R. 1987, *Brooches of Antiquity* (Oxbow, Oxford).

Haverfield, F. 1923, *The Romanization of Roman Britain* (Clarendon Press, Oxford).

Henig, M. 1995, *The Art of Roman Britain* (Batsford, London).

Hull, M. R. and Hawkes, C. F. C. 1987, *Corpus of Ancient Brooches in Britain: pre-Roman bow brooches*, British Archaeological Reports, British Series 168 (British Archaeological Reports, Oxford).

Hunter, F. 1994, 'Dowalton Loch reconsidered', *Transactions of the Dumfriesshire and Galloway Natural History and Antiquarian Society* 69, 53-71.

Hunter, F. 2007, 'Artefacts, regions, and identities in the northern British Iron Age', in Haselgrove, C. and Moore, T. (eds.), *The Later Iron Age in Britain and beyond* (Oxbow, Oxford), 286-96.

Hunter, F. 2008 a, 'Celtic art in Roman Britain', in Garrow, D., Gosden, C. and Hill, J. D. (eds.) *Rethinking Celtic Art* (Oxbow, Oxford), 129-45.

Hunter, F. 2008 b, 'Two unusual Romano-British dragonesque brooches from Well, North Yorkshire', *Yorkshire Archaeological Journal* 80, 15-20.

Hunter, F 2008 c 'A Romano-British beaded torc fragment', in Powell, A. B., Booth, P., Fitzpatrick, A P. and Crockett, A. D., *The archaeology of the M6 Toll, 2000-2003*, Salisbury: Oxford-Wessex Archaeology Joint Venture, 368-70.

Hutcheson, N. C. G. 2004, *Later Iron Age Norfolk: metalwork, landscape and society*, British Archaeological Reports, British Series 361 (Archaeopress, Oxford).

Jope, E. M. 2000, *Early Celtic Art in the British Isles* (Clarendon Press, Oxford).

Jundi, S. and Hill, J. D. 1998, 'Brooches and identity in first century AD Britain: more than meets the eye?', in Forcey, C., Hawthorne, J. and Witcher, R. (eds.), *TRAC 97: Proceedings of the Theoretical Roman Archaeology Conference,* (Oxbow, Oxford), 125-37.

Kilbride-Jones, H. E. 1980, *Celtic Craftsmanship in Bronze* (Croom Helm, London).

Leahy, K. 1979, 'Some prehistoric finds from the Burton upon Trent area', *Derbyshire Archaeological Journal* 99, 52-57.

Leeds, E. T. 1933, *Celtic Ornament in the British Isles Down to AD 700* (Clarendon Press, Oxford).

MacGregor, M. 1976, *Early Celtic Art in North Britain* (Leicester University Press, Leicester).

Mackreth, D. 2000, 'The Romano-British brooches', in Ellis, P. (ed.), *The Roman Baths and Macellum at Wroxeter: excavations by Graham Webster 1955-85* (English Heritage, London), 144-59.

Maxfield, V. A. 1974 'The Benwell torc – Roman or native?', *Archaeologia Aeliana* (fifth series) 2, 41-7.

Megaw, J. V. S. 1971, 'A group of later Iron Age collars or neck-rings from western Britain', in Sieveking, G. de G. (ed.), *Prehistoric and Roman Studies* (British Museum, London), 145-56.

Megaw, R. and Megaw, V. 2001, *Celtic Art: from its beginnings to the Book of Kells* (Thames and Hudson, London).

Rynne, E. 1976, 'The La Tène and Roman finds from Lambay, County Dublin: a re-assessment', *Proceedings of the Royal Irish Academy* 76C, 231-44.

Saville, A. 2002, 'Treasure Trove in Scotland', *Antiquity* 76, 796-802.

Saville, A. 2006, 'Portable antiquities', in Hunter, J. and Ralston, I. (eds.), *Archaeological Resource Management in the UK: an introduction* (Sutton Publishing, Stroud), 69-84.

Stead, I. M. 1976, *Excavations at Winterton Roman villa and other Roman sites in north Lincolnshire* (Her Majesty's Stationary Office, London).

Stead, I. M. 1980, *Rudston Roman Villa* (Yorkshire Archaeological Society, Leeds).

Toynbee, J. M. C. 1964, *Art in Britain Under the Romans* (Clarendon Press, Oxford).

Wainwright, G. J. 1967, *Coygan Camp: a prehistoric, Romano-British and Dark Age settlement in Carmarthenshire* (Cambrian Archaeological Association, Cardiff).

Webster, J. 2003, 'Bronze objects', in James, H., *Roman Carmarthen: excavations 1978-1993* (Roman Society, London), 289-325.

White, R. forthcoming 'A British beaded torc from the Old Shops site, Mill Street, Rocester'.

The Cult of Totatis: evidence for tribal identity in mid Roman Britain

Adam Daubney

The enigmatic series of finger rings with the letters ToT inscribed on the bezel has been the focus of discussion for some years now (Bédoyère 2002: 127-8). The rings are distinctively Romano-British, dating to the late 2nd to 3rd centuries, and are found especially in Lincolnshire. Each ring bears the letters ToT or slight variations thereof, but one from Hockliffe, Bedfordshire (no. 46; Fig. 1) has an expanded inscription reading DEO TOTA, which convincingly affirms Anne Ross's (1967) suggestion (reiterated by Henig and Ogden 1987) that ToT should be read as an abbreviated form of the name of the god Toutatis, one of the principal deities of Gaul and Britain, who was often identified with the Roman god Mars. The name of the Celtic deity is read as *Toutatis, Toutates, Teutatis, Toutenus, Toutiorix* and *Teutanus* according to a number of inscriptions from the Roman world, and since the name according to the finger rings appears to be rendered Totatis, for consistency's sake this will be the spelling adopted in this paper. The legend DLO TOT on a further recently discovered silver finger ring from Fulbeck, Lincolnshire (no. 26), 'L' presumably being a blunder for 'E' in DEO, provides further evidence that ToT refers to a deity rather than some other phrase. The highly abbreviated name for the god indicates that this deity was well enough known in the region in which these rings occur. This paper discusses the 62 rings known bearing the inscription ToT, which have been found largely by metal-detection and recorded through the PAS (see Table 1 for finds list and references, and also an addenda of rings that have come to light more recently).

Fig. 1: Silver ring from Hockliffe, Bedfordshire (no. 46).

These rings offer a further opportunity to comment on the regional popularity of a Celtic deity in the Roman period. So before the evidence for Totatis is examined further it is useful to briefly look at the religious background in Roman Lincolnshire, where most of the ToT rings have been discovered. The Roman gods represented by limestone inscriptions include Mercury (*RIB* 270), Apollo (*RIB* 271), the Genius of the place (*RIB* 246) and Mars (*RIB* 248). Limestone statuettes known from Lincoln and Ancaster represent the *Deae Matres*, while small bronze figurines representing Mercury, Minerva, Sol, Luna, and Venus have been found in similar quantities (for example, *AJ* 103, 1946: 17; Whitwell 1992: 128; DENO-6AB7C3; NLM-AEA444; LIN-69A207; LIN-A65125; NLM-8EE352). Vulcan, the smith god, is represented on intaglios set in three gold rings and by two figurines (LCNCC 1981.114; LCNCC 1978.215.2; LCNCC 1984.1; NLM1132). Mars is the commonest documented deity, represented by at least seven figurines, numerous miniature shields and votive axes which are probably to be associated with him (*LAASRP* 9.2, 1962: 94-7, pl.1; *JRS* 52, 1962: 192, no. 8; *RIB* 248; *RIB* 270; Whitwell, 1992: 58; May 1996: 264-7, fig. 11.15; YORM-C2A231; NLM-C7BD85; LIN-074A24; LIN-D53ED6), one inscription dedicated only to him, and one pairing with a native deity or epithet *Mars Rigonemetos* (Mars, King of the grove; *RIB* 270). The latter inscription is the only example from the county which bears witness to a conflation of classical with native deities or epithets. Romano-British 'Horse and Rider' brooches are often associated with Mars, but a distribution plot of examples from PAS data revealed no apparent association with TOT finger rings (Ferris 1996: 1-10). The only other native spirit whose name has survived is Viridios, witnessed by two limestone inscriptions from Ancaster (*LAASRP* 9.2, 1962: 97-9, pl. 2; *JRS* 52, 1962: 192, no. 7; *Britannia* 33, 2002: 355-6, no.1; *LHA* 37, 2002: 59-60). Totatis is notably absent from inscriptions in Lincolnshire on objects other than finger rings, although three inscriptions from other regions of Britain bear witness to him and his conflation with the god Mars: silver votive plaque from Barkway, Hertfordshire (*RIB* 219): *Marti Toutati Ti(berius) Claudius Primus Attii liber(tus) v(otum) s(olvit) l(ibens) m(erito)* (Mars Toutatis. Tiberius Claudius Primus, freedman of Attius, willingly and deservedly fulfils a vow); bronze ansate plaque from the Hadrian's Wall area (*Britannia* 32, 2001: 392, no. 20): *Marti Toutati s(acrum) Vinoma v(otum) s(olvit) l(ibens) m(erito)* (Sacred to Mars Toutatis. Vinoma willingly fulfilled a vow); graffito from Kelvedon, Essex (*Britannia* 9, 1978: 478, no. 41; *RIB* 2503.131): *TOVTATIS* (Toutatis). The popularity of Mars in other evidence from the county may therefore compliment the overwhelming evidence for Totatis displayed by the finger rings. It may be worth drawing attention to the popularity of the boar as a symbol on metalwork of the Corieltavi, which features as a number of small life-like figurines (LIN-2CFD83; LIN-90C068; NLM4196; NLM191), on Corieltavian gold and silver tribal coinage, and perhaps most famously, on the Witham shield, now in the British Museum (P&EE 1872 12-13 1). The boar is perhaps a martial emblem and to be symbolically linked to Mars and Totatis.

Only one of the ToT rings shows any association with a religious or ritual scene, a silver ring in the British Museum collection from 'possibly Lincolnshire' (no. 48). The bezel holds a carnelian intaglio depicting a hound chasing a hare, a common scene on Romano-British metalwork, seen on mosaics and on the characteristic Nene-valley ware 'hunt-cups'. This ring is unique in that the letters ToT are located on the shoulders rather than on the bezel. Although clearly a ToT ring, this example appears to have been designed primarily for the hunt-scene and the inscription appears to have been added later: indeed, the hunt-scene is upside-down when the deeply serriefed ToT inscription is read the right way up. {1}

The names of Mars and Toutatis (and Vulcan) are also associated in the hoard from Barkway, Hertfordshire in the British Museum (P&EE 1817.3-8; *RIB* 219). Probably from a temple or shrine dedicated to Mars, the hoard comprised silver votive leaves, a bronze handle and a bronze statuette of Mars. The largest of the leaves is inscribed with a dedication to Mars Toutatis by a Tiberius Claudius Primus, whereas Vulcan, identifiable by his blacksmith's hammer and tongs, is depicted on two of the smaller leaves. One of the geographical outliers of the ToT ring group, the silver ring already mentioned bearing the inscription DEO TOTA, was found like Barkway in the *civitas* of the Catuvellauni, its findspot at Hockliffe, Bedfordshire, being approximately 30 miles to the west of the Barkway find.

Beyond Britain 'Toutatis' is known from stone inscriptions at *Flavia Solva* near Frauenberg, Austria (*CIL* 3: 5320: *Marti Latobio Marmogio Toutati Sinati Mog[e]tio C(aius) Val(erius) [V]alerinus ex voto* (To Mars Latobius, Marmogius, Toutatis, Sinatis, Mogetius. Gaius Valerius Valerinus offers this in fulfilment of his vows); 'Toutati' is interpolated between 'Marmogio' and 'Sinati') and notably at Rome (*CIL* 6: 31182: *Petiganus Placidus Toutati Medurini votum solvet anniversarium*), where he is one of only two Celtic deities honoured. As 'Toutenus' he is paired with Mercury both at Bingen (*AE* 1927: 70: *Merc[urio] Tou[teno]*) and at Hohenburg (*CIL* 13: 06122: *Mercurio Touteno*) in Germany, as 'Toutiorix' with Apollo at Wiesbaden, Germany (*CIL* 13: 07564: *Apollini Toutorigi*) and as 'Teutanus' with Jupiter at Böleske, Bulgaria (*AE* 1991: 1324: *I[OVI] O[PTIMO] M[AXIMO] T[EVTANO]*), Obuda, Hungary (*AE* 1965: 349: *I[OVI] O[PTIMO] M[AXIMO] TEVTANO*) and Alt Ofen, Hungary (*CIL* 3: 10418: *I[OVI] O[PTIMO] M[AXIMO] T[EVTANO]*). Furthermore Toutatis is referred to in the *Bellum civile* written by the Roman poet Lucan (Marcus Annaeus Lucanus, AD 39–65) and the *Berne Scholia*, annotations to a 9th-century manuscript of the *Bellum Civile* (Book I, ll. Lines 498-501: www.omacl.org/Pharsalia/book1.html) described the worship of Toutatis entailing human sacrifice, carried out by the means of plunging the victim headfirst in a vat of liquid until drowned.

The distribution of these eight inscriptions (Fig. 2), all of which are on stone plaques or altars, is closely associated with the frontier zone of the Empire on the Continent.

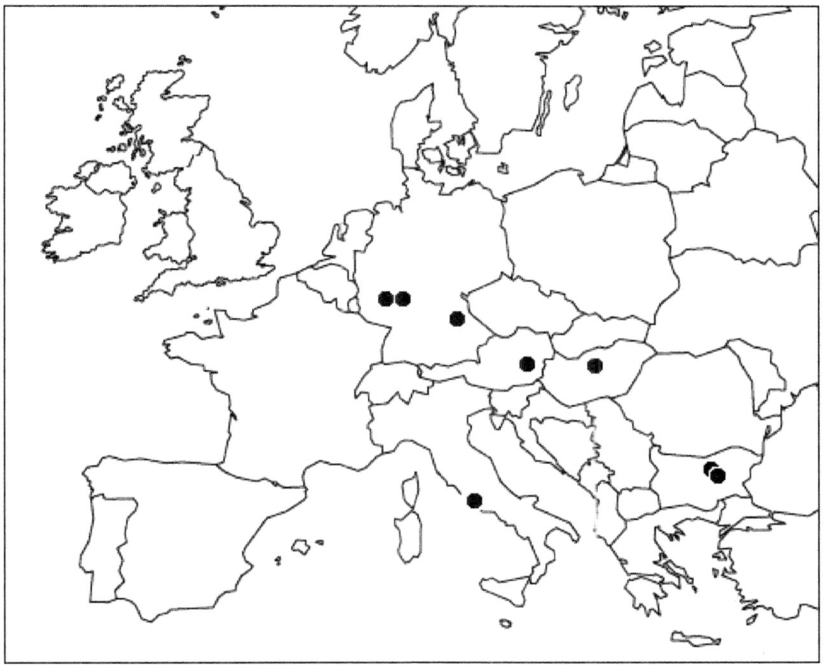

Fig 2: Distribution of stone inscriptions referring to 'Totatis'.

The military-associated distribution is reflected in one of the Romano-British finds from the northern frontier (see above) but the rest of the smaller votive objects dedicated to the deity in England and on the Continent occur at shrine sites away from the frontiers. The votive plaque from Barkway and the sherd inscribed 'TOTATIS' from Kelvedon, Essex both probably derived from a temple or sanctuary. The Kelvedon sherd can be paralleled with five sherds inscribed 'TOTATIS' discovered during excavations of a temple at Beauclair in Combrailles, France, {2} and a single sherd from Cheapside, London inscribed TOT LV[...] (Tomlin 2010). Likewise the TOT finger rings are found away from the frontier zone.

Of the 62 finger rings bearing the inscription ToT from Britain, two are gold, 51 are silver and nine are copper-alloy. These rings are largely confined to two types, Henig Type VIII and Henig Type XI, both dated to the 2nd and 3rd centuries AD (Henig 1978).

Whilst silver rings are known in both types, those in copper-alloy are exclusively of Type XI. The division between the two ring types is fairly even, with 25 rings belonging to Type VIII and 29 belonging to Type XI; the remainder are of uncertain form or have not been seen by the author. 43 of the 62 rings have been discovered in Lincolnshire, the majority being found between a line north of Grantham and south of Market Rasen on the two main areas of higher ground in the county, the limestone uplands on which the important towns of Ancaster and Lincoln are located and the Wolds to the east on which Horncastle and Caistor are situated. There is some clustering in their distribution around Lincoln and to a lesser extent around the Roman town of Horncastle. Of the remaining rings two come from Leicestershire, eight from Nottinghamshire, one from Norfolk, one from East Yorkshire, one from York, one from Bedfordshire and five are unprovenanced. The findspot of the Hockliffe ring is somewhat unusual, being some 70 miles to the south of the rest of the finds. There does not currently appear to be a geographical division between the finger ring types.

While the findspots of the rings (Fig. 3) are predominantly located in a *civitas* based on an Iron Age tribal territory (see below), they do not appear to concentrate in or around traditional pre-Roman Iron Age centres that continued to flourish through the Roman period, such as Old Sleaford and Dragonby (May 1996). Seven of the 62 rings come from urban centres; five rings have been discovered within the *colonia* of Lincoln, three of which were discovered in residual contexts at Michaelgate, Steep Hill and Saltergate, {3} one comes from *Vernemetum* (Willoughby on the Wolds, Nottinghamshire) and one from York. Thirteen rings, five from Lincoln, two from the Trent crossing area at Gate Burton, and individual examples from Ancaster, Old Winteringham, *Vernemetum* and East Stoke are associated with sites with a 1st-century AD Roman military phase, but the rings post-date that phase. Although other continental and British inscriptions are associated with the frontiers, a military connection, even the introduction of the cult of Toutatis by the Roman army, is not impossible but therefore difficult to argue for the TOT rings. The majority of the rings are from rural sites and are metal-detected finds. As such they may derive from a variety of site types including villas, temples or markets: in the majority of cases accurate grid references have been submitted by the finders, enabling future work on further interpretation to be undertaken.

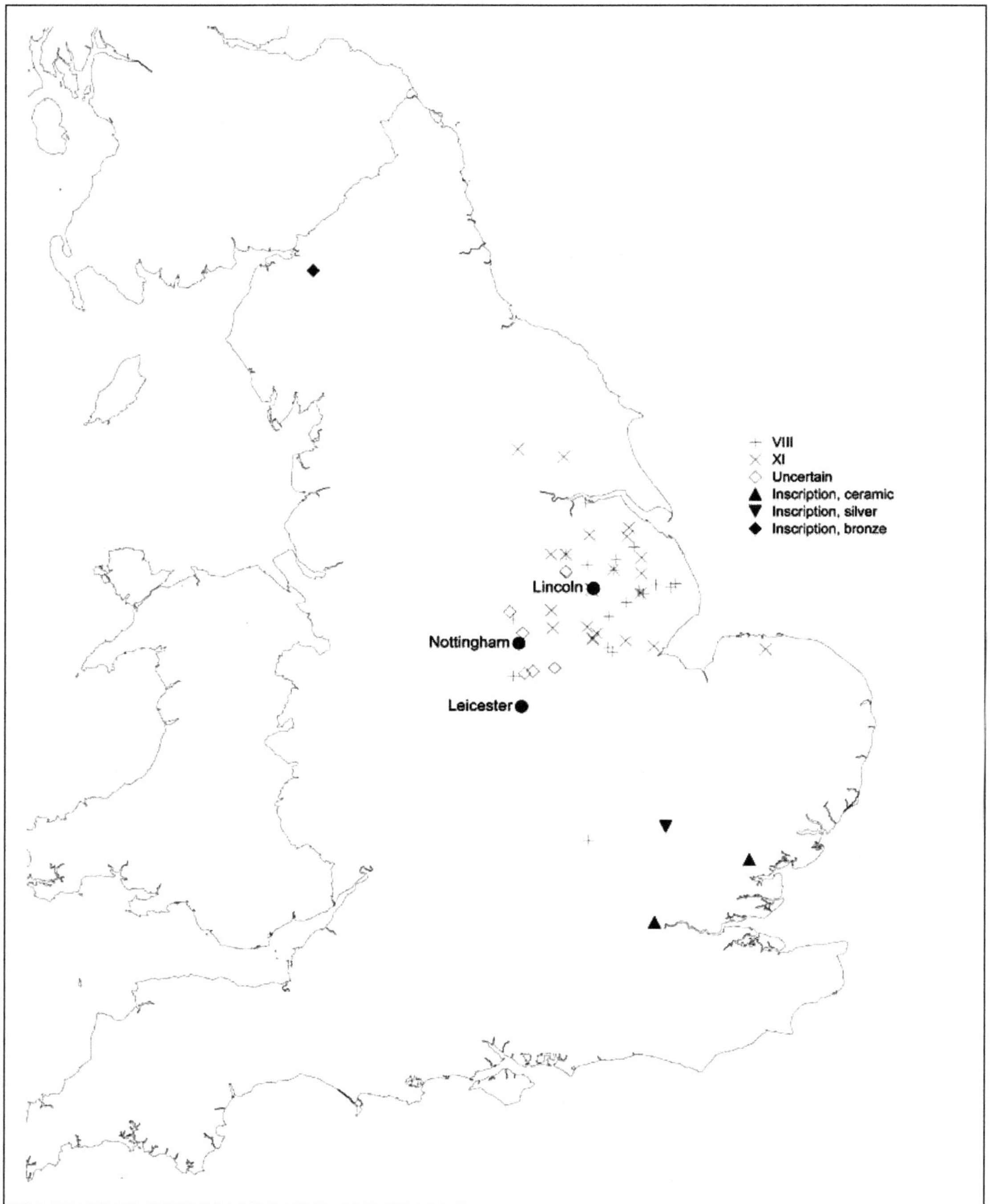

Fig. 3: Distribution of finger rings inscribed 'TOT'.

The findspots appear in all but a few cases to lie within the boundaries hypothesised for the Roman period *civitas* of the Corieltauvi, which are usually thought to be based on the Iron Age tribal area, as reconstructed from coins and major geographical features such as the river Trent (Mattingly 2007: 390), as well as within the *territorium* for the colony at Lincoln, deducted from the tribal territory. Ancient boundaries, whether official or engrained in the minds of generations of locals, may have still determined the sphere of influence of local markets and cult centres. This is a rare instance where we can see a distribution of a specific type of find that correlates so closely with such boundaries. On the basis of his name's etymology - the Proto-Celtic word *teutā* means 'people' or 'tribe' - Toutatis has been interpreted as being the 'tribal protector' (Maier 1997: 263). This interpretation is reinforced by the strong Corieltauvian distribution of the rings.

Form and decoration

Although there is no clear geographical division between the two types of finger ring (Fig. 4) the decorative elements vary greatly. Type VIII has a circular bezel with triangular shoulders, and is often highly decorated with incised lines, swirls, pellets and rope-like divisions. The shoulders often display short rows of perimeter facets. Type XI has a broad, flat bezel with plain, tapering shoulders and is often less decorative, usually only displaying a simple, incised, linear perimeter or a

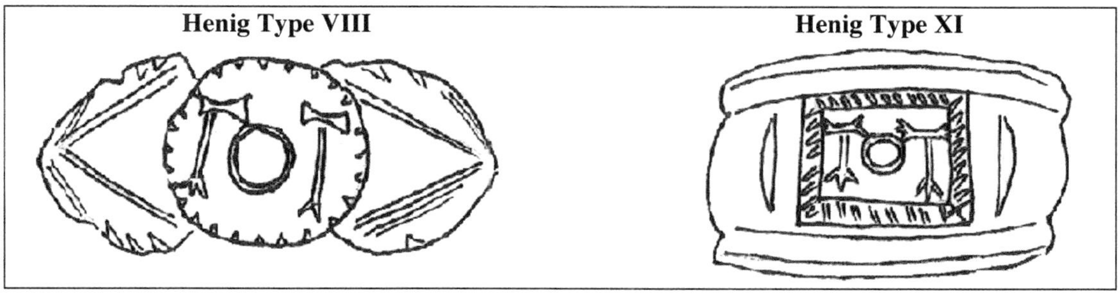

Fig. 4: Types of finger ring inscribed 'ToT'.

rectangular frame of incised, diagonal lines enclosing the inscription. Rings of Type XI can be further divided into two groups from the presence or absence of a deep channel running the circumference of the hoop between the edge and the decoration on the bezel above and below. Of the seven rings displaying this channel, five were found in Lincolnshire (no. 2: Heckington; no. 6: Saltergate; no. 15: Stenigot; no. 17: Lincoln; no. 24: Hibaldstow), one in York (no. 41) and one at Great Walsingham, Norfolk (no. 40).

A triangular decoration appears on the shoulders of three of the Type XI rings, namely one from Stenigot (no. 15), the silver ring from Hayton, East Yorkshire (no. 45), and on an unprovenanced example (no. 47). It appears to mimic the tapering shoulders of the Type VIII rings. The shoulder of ring no. 47 is formed by a simple, incised triangle, the Hayton ring is decorated with a hatched triangle, and the example from Stenigot has a shoulder triangle formed by punched dots.

The standard inscription contains three neat letters across the bezel reading ToT. Quite often the lettering is worn to the point of being almost illegible, but the remaining traces of the letters often make identification possible, in particular the split terminals of the 'T's, which are often engraved slightly deeper and thus survive more often, as does the 'O' when reduced to a single pellet.

In most cases the 'T's have split terminals of either two or three spikes, and the 'O' is usually shown as a smaller letter. Only on a few rings is the letter 'O' reduced to a pellet or indeed a circle of pellets, as seen on the ring from Hayton. The forms of letters 'T' and 'O' are not particular to either ring type, nor is the style of incised decoration exclusive to the series of ToT rings; similar decorative elements to the letter and their borders can be also seen on many other silver rings dedicated to other deities (see Henkel 1913). Unusual forms of the letter 'T' are seen on rings from Great Hale (no. 2), Stenigot (no. 15) and Market Rasen (no. 20). In the case of the Stenigot and Market Rasen rings the lower interior terminal of the letter 'T's are extended, forming an off-balanced 'T'; indeed on the ring from Stenigot the left hand 'T' has an upward kicking inner terminal. Presumably this is either the result of poorer quality workmanship or reflects a lack of desire for accuracy.

The use of indented pellet decoration is a notable feature on a number of rings too. Pellets form the lower terminal of the 'T's on the ring from Great Hale and Market Rasen, whereas, a ring of pellets with a pellet in the centre forms the letter 'O' on the ring from Hayton. The letter 'O' is a single pellet that blends in rather well with the general border of pellets on the ring from Stenigot, and four pellets decorate the bezel of the ring from Market Rasen; three above and one below the text.

Four rings are worth discussing in further detail: a copper-alloy ring from Mansfield, Nottinghamshire (no. 38; Fig. 5); a gold ring from Ulceby Cross, Lincolnshire (no. 23; Fig. 6); a copper-alloy ring from Ancaster (no. 32) and a silver ring from Hockliffe, Bedfordshire (no. 46).

Fig. 5: Ring from Mansfield, Nottinghamshire (no. 38).

Fig. 6: Gold ring from Ulceby Cross, Lincolnshire (no. 23).

The copper-alloy ring from Mansfield is very unusual both in form and decoration. It shows clear native decorative elements and is a variant ring form, being a hybrid of types VIII and XI, combining the circular bezel of type VIII and the broad shoulders and gradual tapering hoop of type XI. The shoulders are decorated in the manner of type VIII rings with a central line of pellets with swirls flanking either side, although notably absent are the side facets commonly seen on type VIII. Punched dots decorate the outer edges at the hoop and of the circular bezel containing the inscription. The ToT inscription is executed in the most abstract style seen on any of the known rings. The letters 'T' both have curved upper and lower crossbars, terminating in three pellets at either end; the letter 'o' is depicted as a pellet in a ring. Similar semi-circular motifs also decorate the shoulders of the ring. Another ToT ring, from Well, Lincolnshire (no. 30; Fig. 7), also shows the practice of creative engraving, this time turning the first letter 'T' into two opposing crescents with pellet terminals. The motifs seen on these two rings might be interpreted as representations of torcs, as might be similar motifs which decorate a miniature votive shield from the Romano-British temple site at Nettleton, Lincolnshire (LIN-9DE863; Fig. 8). In Iron Age Britain the torc, especially the gold torc, was a powerful symbol of authority and nobility. Torc symbols would not be out of place on shields and as a possible attribute of what appears to have been the Corieltauvi's principal deity.

Fig. 7: Silver ring from Well, Lincolnshire showing torc-like letter 'T' (no. 30).

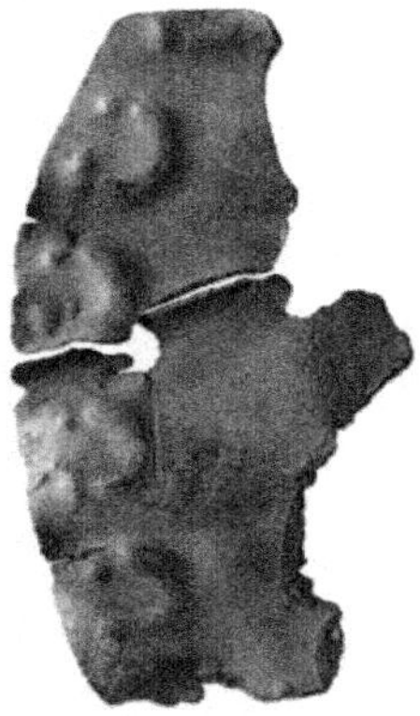

Fig. 8: Miniature shield from Nettleton, Lincolnshire (Height: 40mm).

The Henig Type VIII gold ring from Ulceby Cross, on the Lincolnshire Wolds (no. 23), bears standard decorative features such as incised circles on the bezel and a faceted bezel perimeter. The inscription comprises the standard three letters 'ToT', and in this case the lower terminals of the 'T's are angled inwards. Apart from it being made of gold the ring has no other unusual features. Its surface has a dull yellow patina, and where the ring is broken the cross-section reveals layering, suggesting that the metal is heavily alloyed. Second- and 3rd-century gold finger rings from Britain usually have high bullion contents of over 90% (TAR 1998-9: nos. 19 & 22; TAR 2007: no. 128), and so a low bullion content combined with its relatively crude manufacture may suggest that the ring is the product of a local native workshop.

The copper-alloy rings from Ancaster (no. 32), and Caunton, Nottinghamshire (no. 59) are the only examples that show the inscription TVT instead of TOT. On the continent, the deity's name is spelt in a number of ways, such as TEVT[... and TOVT[..., and so variations in the ring spelling are not unexpected. The Celtic vowel 'ou' which is sometimes spelt 'v', and so in the case of the Ancaster ring the inscription presumably abbreviated Toutatis. {4}

Without doubt the most important finger ring of the series is the silver ring of Henig type VIII with a longer inscription from Hockliffe, Bedfordshire (no. 46), of which the bezel, one shoulder and approximately half of the hoop survive. The octagonal bezel bears an inscription over two lines reading DEO/TOTA. The original existence of a further letter 'T' to the right of the 'A' may be suggested, to judge from a deeply punched or incised triangle on the same line as, and identical to the upper terminals of the other letter 'T's. This would therefore render the inscription 'DEO TOTAT', which can only be an abbreviation of Totatis. The surviving triangular shoulder to the right is decorated with three deep and slightly curved channels on each side. Instead of the decoration continuing down the centre of the shoulders, as seen on most other rings of this type, a further inscription reading 'FELIX' is placed horizontally between two grooves. Although the left hand shoulder is missing, it is very likely that it was also inscribed with the word 'VTERE', thus completing the well known motto VTERE FELIX (use [this and be] happy), known from numerous items of personal adornment (for example, a knee brooch from the Sleaford area (LIN-C355C3), and a silver finger ring from Long Stratton, Norfolk (NMS107; TAR 2000: no. 23; P&EE 82). Perhaps the best known of these is the elaborate, openwork, gold bracelet from the Hoxne hoard discovered in November 1992 (Johns 2010: 51-3, no. 29, figs. 3.48-3.50). The bracelet is unusual not only for the quality of its workmanship, but also because the name of the dedicatee, a certain Lady Juliana also appears in the inscription (DOMINA IVLIANE VTERE FELIX). This was obviously made by the goldsmith to special order.

Rings bearing names of deities are well known and are usually thought of as being dedications to particular gods, who in return were thought to protect and in some cases, heal the owner. The inscription 'To the god Totatis' may therefore be a simple dedication to the god, whereas the 'use this and be happy' may relate to the wearer having luck and enjoying the ring. On the other hand, the inscription may be invoking the god Totatis to use and protect 'this' (i.e. the wearer, not the ring), rendering the wearer as the object of dedication to the service of the god.

The objects studied here also raise questions regarding their manufacture and engraving. Finger rings of Henig type VIII and XI are the most common rings found in the 2nd and 3rd centuries AD, and many examples are inscribed to the various gods of the Roman world. Important differences are seen however between those rings inscribed to Totatis, and those to other gods principally Mercury (for example, finger-rings engraved with MER are known from Vindolanda, and Stonea (*RIC* II, Fascicule 3, 22, no. 2422.9; Johns 1996b: 332, no. 17). Although the decorative bordering, silver content and quality of ring manufacture remains high, the quality of lettering is very varied and the majority of inscriptions appear hastily incised, indicating a lack of skill and, perhaps, that legends were inscribed by the wearers themselves rather than by literate craftspeople. The variation in the abbreviated form in which the god is addressed, including ToT, T.T, TVT, may also suggest that rings were not inscribed by a single or small group of craftspeople. An important silver finger ring of Henig type XI found in Lincoln shows a neatly engraved hatched border as often seen on these rings, but the face of the ring remains uninscribed: this was discovered in the demolition debris of two walls that may have represented part of a mid-Roman building; the latest of the associated pottery dated to the mid- to late 3rd century (LCNCC: 2006.209). Perhaps many of the finger rings studied here were purchased blank and inscribed at a later date with the initials of the chosen deity. The inscription found on the shoulder of the ring bearing the hunt-scene intaglio in the British Museum (see above) clearly shows that a dedication to the deity could be added to existing objects.

The series of ToT rings provides a fascinating insight into the religious and territorial characteristics of the Corieltauvi in the 2nd and 3rd centuries AD. It not only opens up new avenues for research but also offers fresh perspectives on existing Iron Age and Romano-British religious material culture from the region. Although a national survey of dedicatory finger rings has not been undertaken at the time of writing, the number of rings dedicated to Totatis seems to be greater than that any other deity, including Mars, Mercury, Minerva and Jupiter. This trend is certainly true of the finger rings recorded through the PAS and reported under the Treasure Act, which combined has only recorded two rings inscribed to other deities, both of which are dedicated to Mercury (from 'near Halesworth', Suffolk (SF1101) and from Swinderby, Lincolnshire (*TAR* 2002: 24, no. 14). With every new discovery of ring and inscription the deity who was once just an enigmatic abbreviation becomes more established as a key tribal deity in Roman Britain.

Acknowledgements

The author wishes to express thanks to Mark Bennett, Martin Henig, Jenny Mann, John Pearce, Roger Tomlin, Sally Worrell, the various metal-detectorists and archaeologists who discovered the rings, and the Finds Liaison Officers involved in recording them. Special thanks are expressed to Ralph Jackson, for his comments and encouragement, and to Greg Dyer, finder of the Hockliffe ring.

Endnotes

{1} I am grateful to Ralph Jackson for this observation.
{2} The inscribed sherds from Beauclair were discovered during excavations in the 1950s and were 'rediscovered' in the Bargoin Museum of Archaeology by Bernard Clémençon in 2007. Clémençon also notes the existence of a drawing of a vase found in 1882 by Ambroise Tardieu in Beauclair and inscribed 'Totatis', which is now lost. The material is now published by Clémençon and Ganne 2009, *Gallia* 66.2: 153-69.
{3} I am grateful to Jenny Mann for information on the Lincoln rings. The Michaelgate ring came from a dump that, from analysis of the associated pottery, is suggested mainly to comprise redeposited material from elsewhere in the town, deposited in the mid-10th century. The Saltergate ring is from a context that can only be broadly dated to between the very late Roman and middle Saxon periods; associated pottery includes some intrusive early medieval sherds. This context seals a late Roman 'charcoal' deposit that possibly represents the demolition of a timber building, levelled and incorporated into the rampart along the line of the southern defences of the lower city. It is possible that this ring does not necessarily originate from this site specifically, but is from somewhere very close by. The context of the Steep Hill ring is a modern pit; although this disturbed the remains of a Roman building of 2nd-century or later date. Again it is entirely possible that the ring came from elsewhere in the town, as the finds from the site suggest that at least some of the material was brought in during various episodes of terracing.
{4} I am grateful to Roger Tomlin for this observation.

Some additional Toutatis material

i. *AE* 2004: 1204, Drambar, Romania
   Marti / Toutatico / C(aius) Valerius / Hermes pro / salute sua / v(otum) s(olvit) l(ibens) m(erito)
ii. *AE* 1997: 1185, Speyer, Germany
   Deo Toutenc Avento [
iii. IOM Teutano
   There are 17 examples known of the *I(ovi) O(ptimo) M(aximo) Teutano* dedication from Bolske, another certain as well as a probable example from Aquincum (*AE* 2003: 1408-23) and another Pannonian example from Szekesfehervar (*CIL* 3: 3345).

Table 1: Catalogue of 'TOT' rings.

No.	Provenance	Type	Material	References
1	Fillingham, Lincolnshire	VIII	Silver	*TAR* 2003: 50, no. 46 (2003 T259); LCNCC: 2004.230
2	Great Hale, Lincolnshire	XI	Silver	*TAR* 2003: 47, no. 37 (2003 T266); BM: PY2004, 7-2, 1
3	Horncastle area, Lincolnshire	XI	Silver	*TAR* 2000: 21, no. 18; LCNCC: 2002.418
4	Lincoln area, Lincolnshire	VIII	Silver	LIN-949F70
5	Chestnut House, Michaelgate, Lincoln, Lincolnshire	VIII	Silver	Henig 1978: 366; CLAU find: MCH84 (72) <195>
6	Saltergate, Lincoln, Lincolnshire	XI	Silver	Unpublished; CLAU find: LIN73 DI (129) <277>
7	12 Steep Hill, Lincoln, Lincolnshire	VIII	Silver	Unpublished; CLAU find: SH74 (SU) <Ae160>
8	Wickenby, Lincolnshire	XI	Silver	*TAR* 2003: 47, no. 38 (2003 T113)
9	Edlington, Lincolnshire	VIII	Silver	LCNCC: 1957.81.1
10	Tetford, Lincolnshire	VIII	Silver	LCNCC: 1982.80
11	Torksey, Lincolnshire	XI	Silver	LIN-DC7164
12	Frampton, Lincolnshire	XI	Cu alloy	LIN-6773B1
13	Threekingham, Lincolnshire	VIII	Silver	LIN-314215
14	Stenigot, Lincolnshire	XI	Silver	LIN-947B96
15	Stenigot, Lincolnshire	XI	Silver	LIN-944EE5
16	Kelstern, Lincolnshire	XI	Silver	LIN-94B8B4
17	Lincoln area, Lincolnshire	XI	Silver	LIN-9486F6
18	Rowston, Lincolnshire	VIII	Silver	*TAR* 2005 (2005 T196); DENO-DDB0E7
19	Horncastle, Lincolnshire	VIII	Cu alloy	NLM671
20	Market Rasen, Lincolnshire (listed in *TH* as being found near a market town in Lincolnshire)	VIII	Silver	*TH*, March 2001: 45-6, fig. 7; *Britannia* 2001: 396 no. 40.
21	Gate Burton, Lincolnshire	?	Silver	LIN-94E8B5
22	Gate Burton, Lincolnshire	?	Silver	LIN-94FC92
23	Ulceby Cross, Lincolnshire	VIII	Gold	LIN-F98033
24	Hibaldstow, North Lincolnshire	XI	Silver	LIN-9413A1
25	Swinhope, Lincolnshire	VIII	Silver	NLM-869432
26	Fulbeck area, Lincolnshire	XI	Silver	Mills 2000:105; *Searcher* 2002, Issue 207: 18
27	Ancaster, Lincolnshire	XI	Silver	LIN-B319D3
28	Swallow, Lincolnshire	XI	Silver	LIN-B33316
29	Riby, Lincolnshire	XI	Cu alloy	LIN-B340B4
30	Well, Lincolnshire	VIII	Silver	2007 T437; LIN-1901F7
31	Lincolnshire	XI	Silver	LIN-956C56; Bedoyere 2002: 117, no. 72
32	Ancaster, Lincolnshire	XI	Cu alloy	CPAT-DB1042
33	Thimbleby, Lincolnshire	VIII	Silver	2008 T224; LIN-F2BAB4
34	Old Winteringham, North Lincolnshire	VIII	Silver	LIN-9439E6
35	Stanford on Soar, Nottinghamshire	VIII	Cu alloy	LEIC-9AB9F2
36	Vernemetum, Nottinghamshire	?	Silver	Henig 1978: 366-7, endnote 53.
37	East Stoke, Nottinghamshire	XI	Silver	LIN-94DE57
38	Mansfield, Nottinghamshire	Hybrid	Cu alloy	LIN-71BD32
39	Linby, Nottinghamshire	VIII	Silver	2007 T387

40	Gringley on the Hill, Nottinghamshire	XI	Silver	Finder, pers. com.
41	Great Walsingham, Norfolk	XI	Silver	*Britannia* 1999: 32, no.19
42	York, Yorkshire	XI	Silver	RCHM 1962 : pl.65, 141
43	Goadby Marwood, Leicestershire	?	Silver	Found 1982. Peter Liddle, pers. com.
44	Wymeswold, Leicestershire	?	Silver	Found *c*. 1992. Peter Liddle, pers. com.
45	Hayton, East Yorkshire	XI	Silver	Finder, pers.com.
46	Hockliffe, Bedfordshire	VIII	Silver	2007 T357
47	Unprovenanced	XI	Silver	LIN-B29CA1
48	Unprovenanced	1, 2 or 10	Silver	Marshall 1907: 185, no. 1169, fig. 141; BM: GR 1917, 5-1, 1169
49	Unprovenanced	VIII	Silver	LIN-B2ED71
50	Unprovenanced	XI	Silver	LIN-B2BC46
51	Unprovenanced	?	Gold	V&A Museum, London
52	Unprovenanced (noted as 'Lincolnshire?')	VIII	Silver	BM: P1988 11-1, 1; Johns 1996a: 58-9, fig. 3.19.

Addenda

The following rings were recorded after the writing of this paper. These rings are included in statistics of the main text and also in the distribution map.

No.	Provenance	Type	Material	References
53	Ancaster, Lincolnshire	XI	Cu alloy	UKDFD13686
54	Stixwould, Lincolnshire	VIII	Silver	LIN-FA8E72
55	Redhill, Nottinghamshire	XI	Cu alloy	Palyfreyman and Ebbins 2003
56	Lincolnshire	VIII	Silver	LIN-B12288
57	Thonock, Lincolnshire	XI	Silver	NLM2838
58	Thonock, Lincolnshire	VIII	Silver	LIN-361AC0
59	Caunton, Nottinghamshire	XI	Cu alloy	DENO-F16131
60	Osbournby, Lincolnshire	VIII	Silver	LIN-B0B9D4
61	Thonock, Lincolnshire	XI	Silver	LIN-B08B74
62	Wickenby, Lincolnshire	VIII	Silver	2009 T117; SWYOR-6429A2

Addenda 2

The following rings were recorded after the text of this article was finalised. These rings are *not* included in statistics of the main text or in the distribution map.

No.	Provenance	Type	Material	References
63	Caistor, Lincolnshire	VIII	Silver	LIN-B2E964
64	Unprovenanced	XI	Silver	LIN-B34626; 2009 T742
65	Wellingore, Lincolnshire	XI	Silver	LIN-F0E557; 2010 T18
66	Baston, Lincolnshire	XI	Silver	LIN-AF8024; 2010 T200
67	Pewsey, Lincolnshire	VIII	Silver	WILT-AEC221; 2009 T640
68	Unprovenanced	?XI	Silver	LIN-0E52F5

Abbreviations

AE = Anneé Épigraphique
AJ = Archaeological Journal
BM = British Museum collection
CIL = Corpus Inscriptionum Latinarum
CLAU = City of Lincoln Archaeological Unit + site code and context number
JRS = Journal of Roman Studies
LCNCC = 'The Collection' accession number, formerly the 'City and County Museum, Lincoln'.
LAASRP = Lincolnshire Architectural and Archaeological Society Reports and Papers
LHA = Lincolnshire History and Archaeology
TAR = Treasure Annual Report
TH = Treasure Hunting magazine

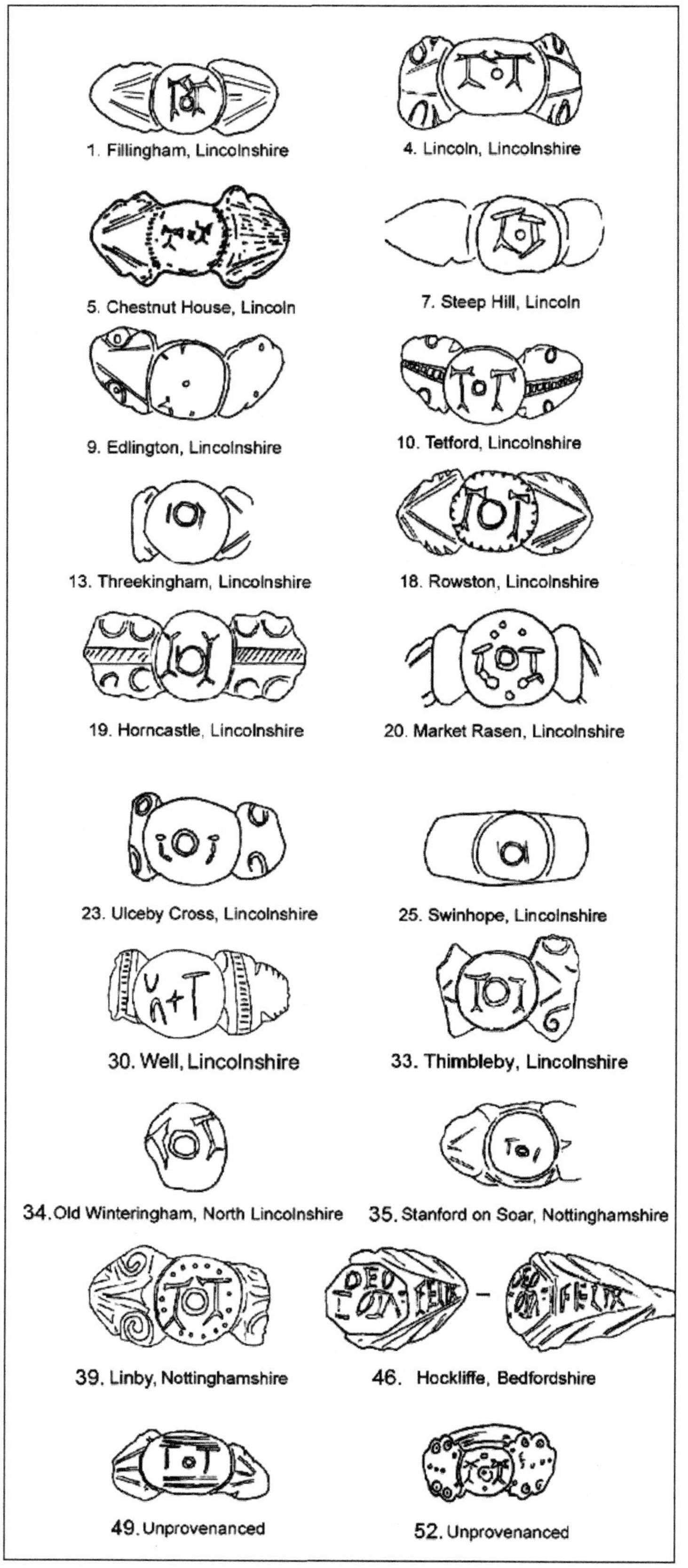

Fig. 9: Catalogue of finger rings, Henig Type VIII (sketched from photographs).

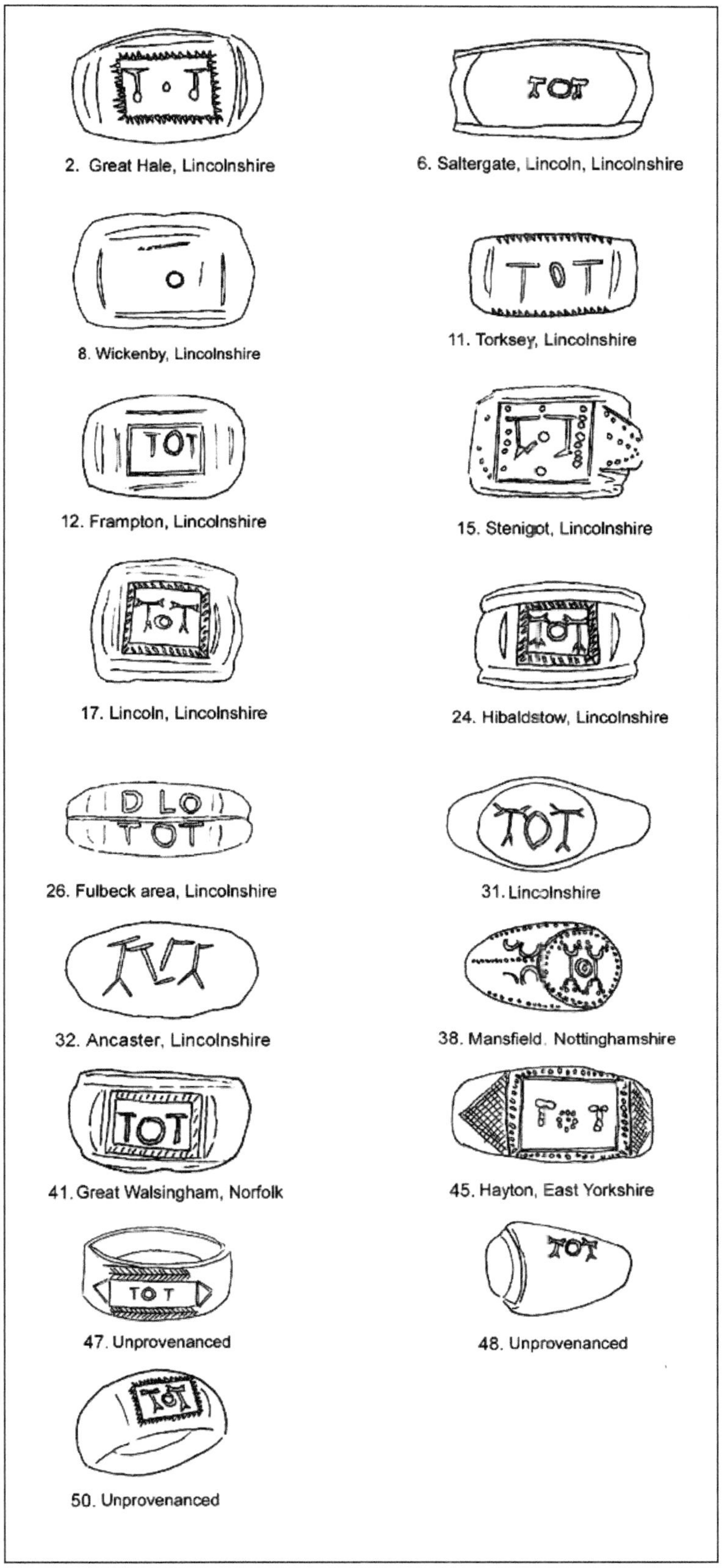

Fig. 10: Catalogue of finger rings, Henig Type XI and misc (sketched from photographs).

Bibliography

Bédoyère, G. 2002, *Gods with Thunderbolts: religion in Roman Britain* (Tempus, Stroud).

Clémençon, B. and Ganne, P. M. 2009, 'Toutatis chez les Arvernes: les graffiti à Totates du bourg routier antique de Beauclair (communes de Giat et de Voingt, Puy-de-Dôme)', *Gallia* 66.2, 153-69.

Ferris, I. M. 1996, 'Horse-and-Rider brooches in Britain: a new example from Rocester, Staffordshire', *South Staffordshire Archaeological and Historical Society Transactions for 1984-1985* 26, 1-10.

Henig, M. 1978, 'A Corpus of Roman Engraved Gemstones from British Sites', *British Archaeological Report* 8 (British Archaeological Reports, Oxford).

Henig, M and Ogden, J. 1987, 'A finger ring', *The Antiquaries Journal* 67, Part II, 366-7, fig. 2b.

Henkel, F. 1913, *Die Romischen Fingerringe der Rheinlande* (Reimer, Berlin).

Johns, C. M. 1996a, *The Jewellery of Roman Britain* (UCL Press, London).

Johns, C. M. 1996b, 'Finger-Rings,' in Jackson, R. P. J. and Potter, T. W., *Excavations at Stonea, Cambridgeshire 1980-85* (British Museum, London), 327-34.

Johns, C. 2010, *The Hoxne Late Roman Treasure Gold Jewellery and Silver Plate* (British Museum, London).

Maier, B. 1997, *Dictionary of Celtic Religion and Culture* (Boydell Press, Woodbridge).

Marshall, F. H. 1907, *Catalogue of the Finger Rings in the Departments of Antiquities, British Museum* (British Museum, London).

Mattingly, D. J. 2007, *An Imperial Possession: Britain in the Roman Empire, 54 BC-AD 409* (Penguin Books, London).

May, J. 1996, *Dragonby, Report on the Excavations at an Iron Age and Romano-British Settlement in North Lincolnshire*, Oxbow Monograph 61 (Oxbow, Oxford).

Mills, N. 2000, *Celtic and Roman* Artefacts (Greenlight Publishing, Witham).

Palyfreyman, A. and Ebbins, S. 2003, 'Redhill Iron Age and Romano-British site, Nottinghamshire: a new assessment', *Transactions of the Thoroton Society* 107, 17-40.

RCHM. 1962, *An Inventory of the Historical Monuments in the City of York, Vol, 1: Eboracum, Roman York* (RCHM, London).

Ross, A. 1967, *Pagan Celtic Britain* (Academy Chicago Publishers, Chicago).

RIB = Collingwood, R. G. and Wright, R. P. 1991, *The Roman Inscriptions of Britain* 2, Fascicule 3 (Alan Sutton, Stroud).

Tomlin, R. 2010, 'Roman Britain in 2009: III. Inscriptions', *Britannia* 41, 313-63.

Whitwell, B. 1992, *Roman Lincolnshire* (Society for Lincolnshire History and Archaeology, Lincoln).

The Portable Antiquities Scheme and Roman Rural Settlement: some preliminary work on Wiltshire

Tom Brindle

This paper is based upon ongoing research into the extent to which Portable Antiquities Scheme (PAS) data has the potential to contribute to our understanding of Roman Britain. This research is in its early stages and this paper is therefore primarily concerned with some methodological issues associated with working with this data.{1} Using data recorded by the PAS from Wiltshire as a case study, this paper considers how such data can be used in conjunction with, and compared to, other bodies of archaeological information. The research is particularly concerned with the extent to which PAS data can enhance understanding of Roman rural settlement.

Rural settlement has traditionally been somewhat neglected in the study of Roman Britain, in favour of the military, ritual and high status sites. However, there has been an increasing awareness that the majority of the inhabitants of Roman Britain would have been low status rural dwellers (Mattingly 2006: 365; Taylor 2001: 46; Millett 1990: 183-86) and there have been recent moves towards a better understanding of this section of society (Taylor 2001; King 2004; Hingley 1989; 2004). After all, the rural population were responsible for the production of the agricultural resources that supplied the army and urban populations within the province, and the lives and activities of the rural population should really be seen as inextricably linked to that of other elements of Roman society. However, whilst there has been a significant increase in the amount of attention given to the rural populace by archaeologists in recent years, rural settlement is still very poorly understood in Roman Britain and there is still significant regional variation in the amount of evidence available.

Massive advances in knowledge have been made as a result of the development of wide-scale survey methods as seen particularly in the field of aerial photography, but there are some areas which are more susceptible to the results of aerial photography than others (King 2004: 362; Jones and Mattingly 1990: 250).

Methodology

The PAS was established in 1997 to promote the reporting of all archaeological finds recovered by members of the public, thus complimenting the reporting procedures for finds under the Treasure Act 1996. Across England and Wales a network of Finds Liaison Officers (FLOs) record finds discovered by the public onto an online database. After ten years, the PAS database now represents a very valuable resource for those concerned with the study of rural settlement in Roman Britain. It has the potential to provide additional information for areas that have not produced good results as a result of programmes of aerial photography, and for areas that have simply been subject to less intensive archaeological investigation. Growing daily, the number of records relating to the Roman period is over 70,000.{2} Rather than considering the impact of all of this data which would be a massive undertaking, the current research is based upon a series of case study regions. In each of these regions the PAS data is to be compared with other forms of archaeological information, chiefly that held by Historic Environment Records (HERs). The case study regions have been selected so as to form a representative sample of the impact of PAS data in different areas. Various factors must be seen to have a potential effect on the impact that PAS data will have in different areas. One such factor is the extent to which archaeological investigation has previously been undertaken in a particular area. It is possible that the PAS data may have less impact in areas that have been well represented by archaeological investigation into the Roman period than areas that have been more marginal in the study of Roman Britain. Consequently, examples of regions that represent both of these circumstances have been included as case studies.

A further consideration is the regional variation in the nature of Romano-British settlement, something that has become ever more apparent as increasing evidence for different types of settlement has been revealed by aerial photography and wide-scale field survey. The traditionally viewed military north/civilian south divide, first suggested by Haverfield (1912) is now recognised as unacceptably simplistic (Hingley 1989: 133; 2004: 327) and within each of these zones there is considerable variation (Corney 2000). Selection of the case study regions has therefore sought to include areas which represent some of the variation in the character of Romano-British settlement evidence.

For various reasons some counties are represented by significantly lower or higher quantities of PAS data for the Roman period than others, partly because the Scheme was rolled out nationally on a gradual basis and FLO coverage started in different areas at different times. There are other factors which affect the regional variation in finds however. Devon and Cornwall, for example, are represented by very low levels of PAS data for the Roman period when compared to others. Aside from having relatively late FLO coverage (both posts were established in 2003), this is a result of apparently genuine lower levels of the use of archaeologically visible Romano-British material culture in these areas, coupled with less availability of arable land for metal-detecting. On the other hand, counties such as Norfolk and Suffolk have very high numbers of Roman data recorded by the PAS. This feature reflects the high incidence of Romano-British material culture in East Anglia, strong traditions of liaison between archaeologists and metal-detector users that predate the establishment of the PAS and higher numbers of staff recording chance finds discovered by metal-detection.

It is important to note that the regions selected as case studies relate to modern administrative units and not to the administrative *civitates* of the Roman period. The decision to employ modern administrative units has been a practical one, as both PAS data and HER data are based upon modern counties and parishes. Attempting to divide this data and relate it to it to the Roman *civitates* would be a difficult task, compounded by the uncertain level of knowledge on the boundaries of the Roman administrative units (Millett 1990: 67).

Case Studies

With the above considerations in mind the regions selected as case studies are Wiltshire, Worcestershire and Warwickshire (two counties as one case study), Northamptonshire, North Lincolnshire and Cumbria. This selection aims to include regions that have been subject to fairly intensive previous archaeological investigation (Wiltshire, Northamptonshire) and regions that have arguably seen less archaeological endeavour (Worcestershire and Warwickshire, North Lincolnshire, Cumbria). The selection of case studies also seeks to capture some of the variability in settlement evidence, and some of the regions are well represented by traditionally viewed Romano-British settlement evidence such as villas and towns (Wiltshire and Northamptonshire), whilst in other areas these features are less common (Worcestershire and Warwickshire, North Lincolnshire and Cumbria). North Lincolnshire was selected as it borders the traditionally viewed north/south military/civilian divide (Haverfield 1912). The region differs somewhat from some of the more southern case studies. Aside from the *civitas* capital at Brough-on-Humber, the urban settlements in this region seem to be linked to military activity and develop differently from the 'small towns' in the south (Hingley 2004: 334). Cumbria was chosen as a case study as it represents an opportunity to explore the potential contribution of PAS data in an area known primarily for its Roman military archaeology. The region is well represented by neither villas nor towns, and it forms a contrasting backdrop to the case studies adopted from further south.

PAS data and HER data

In order to be able to consider the contribution that PAS data can make to the study of Roman settlement, it is crucial to compare it to other available archaeological data. This is most readily available in the form of HER data, although it is apparent that not all evidence available for a particular region appears on the HERs. Table 1 and Figure 1 provide a comparison of the number of records recorded for the Romano-British period on the respective databases for Wiltshire, Worcestershire and Warwickshire.{3}

County	HER Data	PAS Data
Worcestershire	1,054	486
Warwickshire	1,109	2,890
Wiltshire	2,627	2,329

Table 1: Numbers of records on the respective HER and PAS databases.

The table and graph show that Wiltshire has high quantities of HER records with over double the quantity recorded from Worcestershire and Warwickshire. This can largely be explained by the intensity of archaeological investigation in Wiltshire when compared to Worcestershire and Warwickshire (Corney 2000; Booth 2006; Alexander *et al.* 2007). In Wiltshire there are comparable numbers of records on the respective HER and PAS databases. In Worcestershire however, there are approximately twice as many HER records than PAS records, whilst in Warwickshire there are a little over twice as many PAS than HER records.

Since there are intrinsic differences between the two datasets it is important not to draw too much meaning from comparisons of the quantity of records on the two types of database. Generally speaking each PAS database entry relates to a single artefact, although in some cases multiple pottery sherds or lithic artefacts for example, might be recorded under a single record. The total number of PAS records in any given region therefore broadly represents the same number of finds. HER records, on the other hand, generally relate to all aspects of the historic environment and one record could relate to a single find, a large assemblage of finds, or to an entire settlement including evidence for buildings and artefacts. A simple consideration of the quantity of records between a county's HER database and the PAS database is therefore not really a valid comparison.

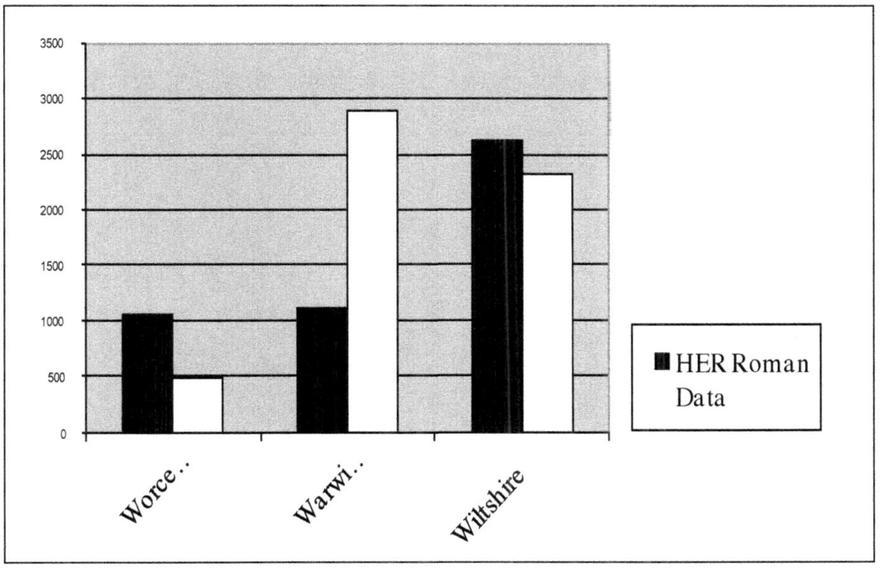

Fig. 1: Numbers of records on the HER and PAS databases.

Density Analysis

When the geographical distributions of the records on the different databases are considered it is possible to make more meaningful comparisons. Figure 2 shows the distribution of PAS and HER data in Wiltshire. Whilst HER data is widely distributed across the county, it is possible to see areas of denser concentration in the north, in the Kennet valley and around Swindon, centrally, around Devizes and in the south around Salisbury. The density map shown in Figure 3 demonstrates this more dramatically.{4} The high density of Romano-British HER records in these areas are largely the result of archaeological material discovered through urban development relating to the Roman towns of *Duroconovium* (Wanborough, near Swindon), *Sorviodunvm* at Salisbury and, in the north, at Cricklade. The high densities of HER data from the Kennet Valley are likely to be the result of the intensity of archaeological investigation into the Avebury prehistoric sites and at Devizes through investigations associated with development.

Figure 4 demonstrates how the PAS data contrasts with the HER data in that as opposed to a fairly even distribution with a few distinct areas of high density, there are instead several areas of fairly dense activity and large areas for which PAS data is not available. This can in part be explained by the nature of metal-detecting as a leisure activity as it is likely that metal-detector users will return to locations that produce high quantities of artefacts. The areas with a high density of PAS data differ somewhat geographically from those with a high density of HER data, and this can largely be explained by the fact that metal-detecting is predominantly undertaken on arable agricultural land, located away from the areas in which urban development has provided much of the information held by HERs. One area from which there is very little PAS data available is the Salisbury Plain; an area used by the military for training and therefore off limits to detector users. What the PAS data has the potential to provide is an enhancement of information from those areas where previous archaeological investigation has been minimal or non-existent.

It is likely that some metal-detector users will seek permission to detect particular areas as a result of the presence of well-known archaeological sites in the vicinity, and some of the areas with a high density of PAS data can perhaps be seen in this light. It is possible that the high density of PAS material from the north-west of the county in the parish of Grittleton is a result of the presence of the Fosse Way Roman Road and of a settlement mentioned in early syntheses of the county's archaeology (Cunnington 1932: 190; Grinsell 1957: 75). Likewise, the dense concentration of PAS data in Chiseldon, immediately south of Swindon may be a result of knowledge of the Roman road between *Corinium* (Cirencester) and *Cunetio* (Mildenhall) (Cunnington 1932: 183; Grinsell 1957: 56-57) and of finds of hypocaust tile noted by Passmore (in Cunnington 1932: 183). At West Lavington, a Romano-British settlement site was identified by Cunnington (1932: 195) and Grinsell (1957: 120) and knowledge of this may have attracted metal-detector users to the area. However, close examination of the extremely dense concentration of PAS data indicates that there are actually a number of distinct sites represented by PAS data in the parish, illustrating how PAS data has the potential to enhance knowledge of an area where there is already some archaeological evidence. One site mentioned on the Wiltshire HER is known solely from information reported by a metal-detector user, and it is clear that there can be some overlap between the two datasets.

Some of the areas with a high density of PAS data appear to occur in areas where very little is known from traditional archaeological sources. To the north of Salisbury, for example, in the parish of Durnford, there is a high concentration of PAS data yet very little HER data and little mention of Romano-British settlement in the syntheses of the county's Romano-British archaeology (Cunnington 1932; Ellis 2001; Grinsell 1957). At Upton

Scudamore, in the west of the county there is, once again, little recorded on the HER beyond records of some unassociated finds and no comments on the parish were made by Grinsell (1957) or Cunnington (1932).{5} The examples above indicate how PAS data has the potential to enhance areas for which our knowledge is slim.

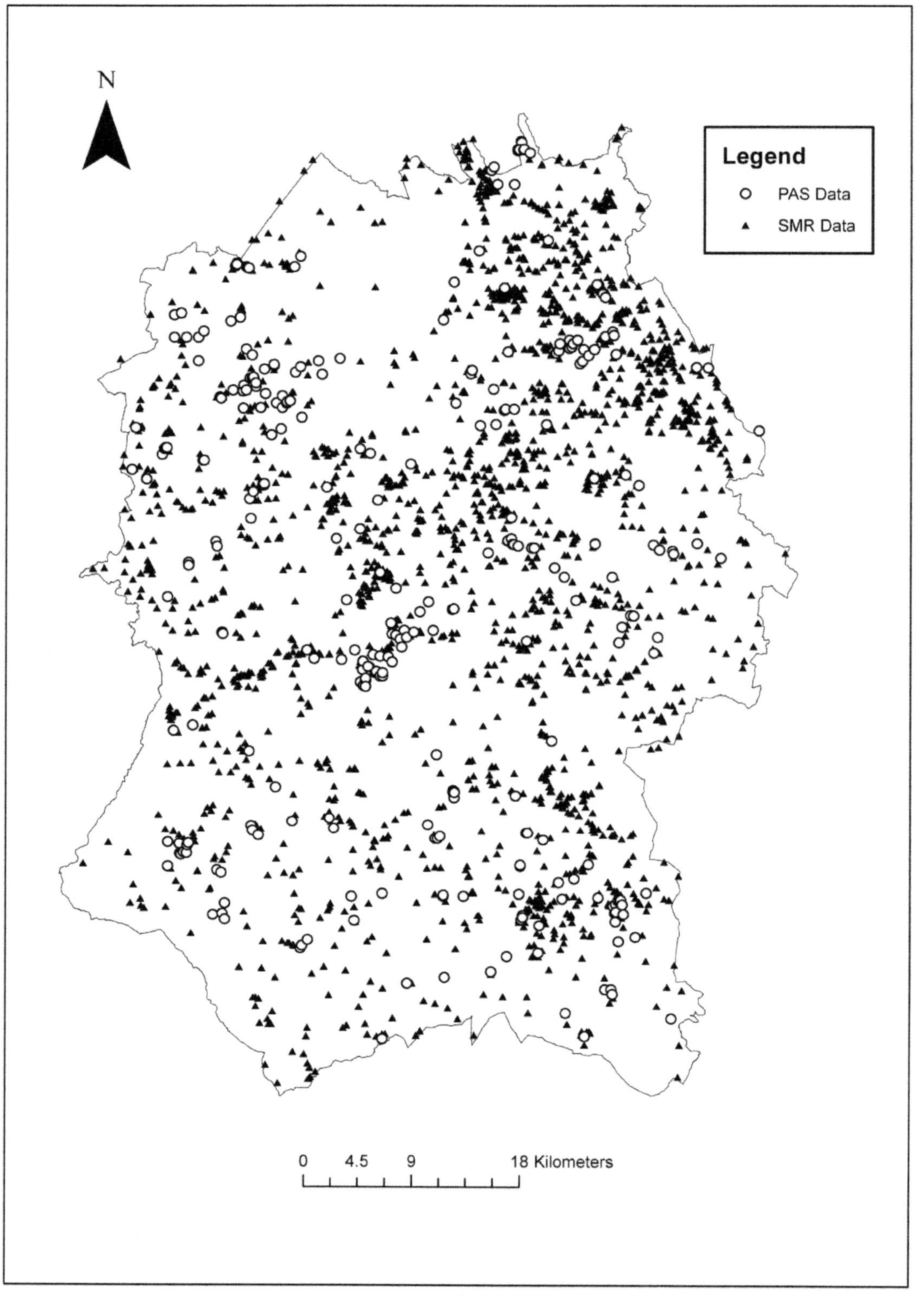

Fig. 2: Map of Wiltshire showing distribution of PAS and HER data.

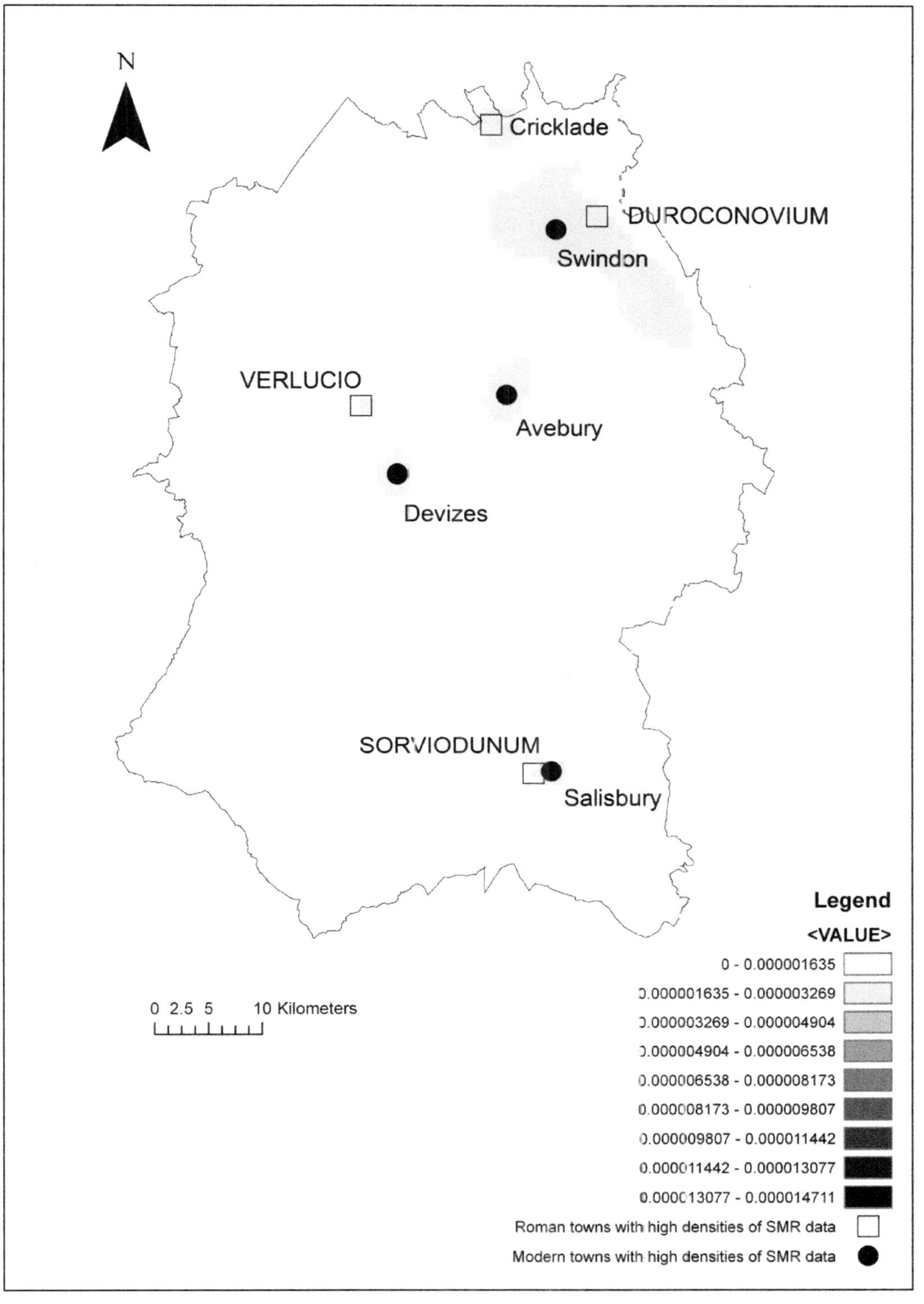

Fig. 3: Map showing areas with high densities of HER data in Wiltshire.

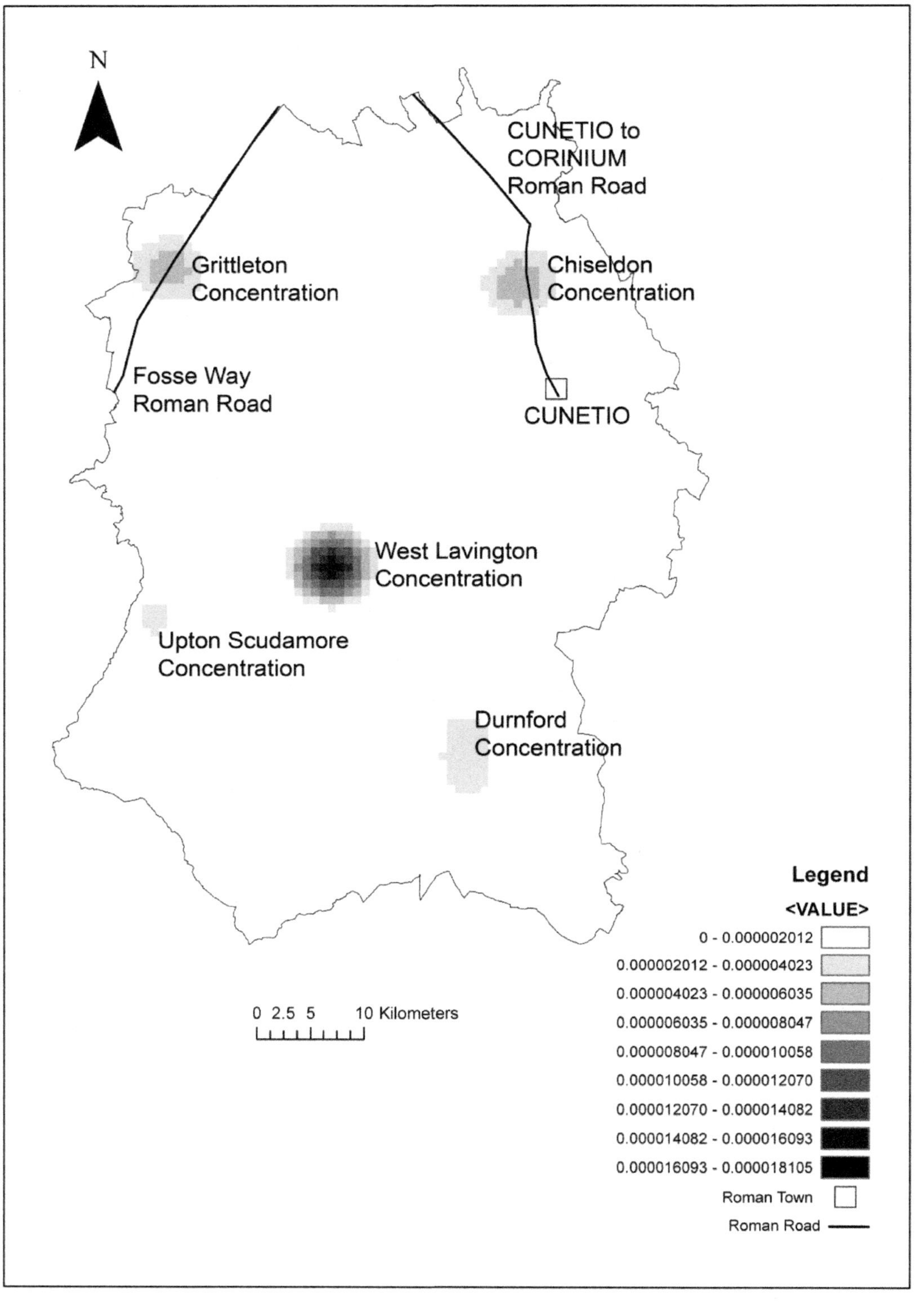

Fig. 4: Map showing areas with high concentrations of PAS data in Wiltshire.

Interpreting PAS data

Whilst provisional density analyses (Figs. 3-4) such as those undertaken above provide interesting information on areas with very dense concentrations of material, they are not so useful for recognising findspots with moderate quantities of finds, but where the composition of the assemblages suggest that they are of interest. However, whilst some findspots represented by small numbers of artefacts must relate to settlement activity, it would be difficult to argue that every single find or small group necessarily represents an archaeological site. The presence of small numbers of artefacts could alternatively be interpreted as casual losses or the result of movement through geomorphological processes, for example. This raises some methodological issues regarding how a site can be recognised.

The problem of interpreting unstratified archaeological material has been given significant consideration (Schofield 1991; Haselgrove *et al.* 1985; Fasham *et al.* 1980) yet this has predominantly been concerned with archaeological field-walking projects that are subject to rigid methodologies and collection strategies; something that clearly does not apply to most metal-detected data. The problem is something regularly encountered by HER officers, who are in a position to interpret archaeological information gathered by a variety of methods, including amateur discoveries. However, there is no national guidance available on the issue and different HERs have their own methods for differentiating between artefacts that relate to settlement or scatters of unassociated finds (Christine Addison, pers. comm.; Jude Plouviez, pers. comm..). At Northamptonshire HER, a group of ten or more Romano-British artefacts discovered within close proximity of one another are considered as potential evidence for settlement, but it is clear that there is always an element of professional judgement involved. A scatter of ten pottery sherds that may relate to manuring would be seen as less likely to relate to settlement than, for instance, a mixed collection of brooches, tile and coinage (Christine Addison, pers. comm.). A further issue is the proximity of finds to one another, and determining whether they are likely to relate to the same episode of activity. At Northamptonshire HER closely datable finds are considered as potentially related if they are found within approximately 250 metres of one another, although once again it is considered important to be able to use one's professional judgement. A large roadside settlement, for instance, may be characterised by a distribution of archaeological material that stretches for some kilometres along the length of a road, whilst a small rural settlement consisting of a few roundhouses set within a circular enclosure is likely to produce a more localised distribution of finds (Christine Addison, pers. comm.). It is also important to stress the use of the term 'potential' here and when dealing with surface assemblages it is crucial to be aware of the fact that the composition of such assemblages is affected by many unknown processes (Haselgrove *et al.* 1985: 9) and interpretation must therefore be somewhat tentative.

It should also be clear that if an arbitrary limit is selected above which the number of finds recovered can be considered as potential evidence for settlement, then this limit will not necessarily be appropriate for different regions. This is because there is evidently wide regional variation in the nature and density of Roman settlement and in the circulation of material culture. Therefore, whilst a collection of seven artefacts of Roman date from Northamptonshire might not be considered particularly unusual, the same number of artefacts discovered in, for example, Cornwall, where finds of Romano-British artefacts are significantly rarer, would warrant particular interest. Any definition of 'site' that relates to the quantity of artefacts found ought therefore to be developed with a specific region in mind, with reference to the background density of Roman finds in that particular area.

One method for considering the background pattern of the distribution of artefacts in different counties would be to compare the total number of artefacts with the size of the county in question. This can be done by dividing the total number of artefact records by the total landmass, allowing a comparison of the number of finds per square kilometre in each county. The results of this exercise are expressed in Table 2 and Figure 5, which compare the results of the five case study regions with the results from Devon and Suffolk.

Devon and Suffolk have been included to compare the results of the five case study regions with counties with very low and very high quantities of Roman records. Of the five regions chosen as case studies, it is possible to see that Wiltshire, Worcestershire and Warwickshire reveal broadly comparable results, whilst Northamptonshire and North Lincolnshire are also comparable. These case study regions fall somewhere between the extremes of Suffolk and Devon. Cumbria has significantly lower numbers of finds per square kilometre however, and is comparable with Devon. It may seem strange to include a county as a case study that is so poorly represented by PAS data, but it was considered useful to include one case study with extremely different characteristics to the others, allowing comparison of the impact of the PAS to be assessed in differing circumstances. Cumbria provides an opportunity to explore the potential usefulness of PAS data in an area poorly represented by Roman finds and with a differing Romano-British settlement pattern to the more southerly case studies.

County	Land Mass	PAS Records	Finds per km2
Northamptonshire	2,364 km^2	3,792	1.6
Wiltshire	3,485 km^2	2,329	0.68
Worcestershire and Warwickshire	3,716 km^2	3,376	0.91
North Lincolnshire	8,46.3 km^2	1,433	1.69
Kent	3,736 km^2	2,311	0.62
Devon	3,487 km^2	291	0.08
Suffolk	3,801 km^2	9,909	2.61

Table 2: Relative quantities of PAS records per county according to landmass.

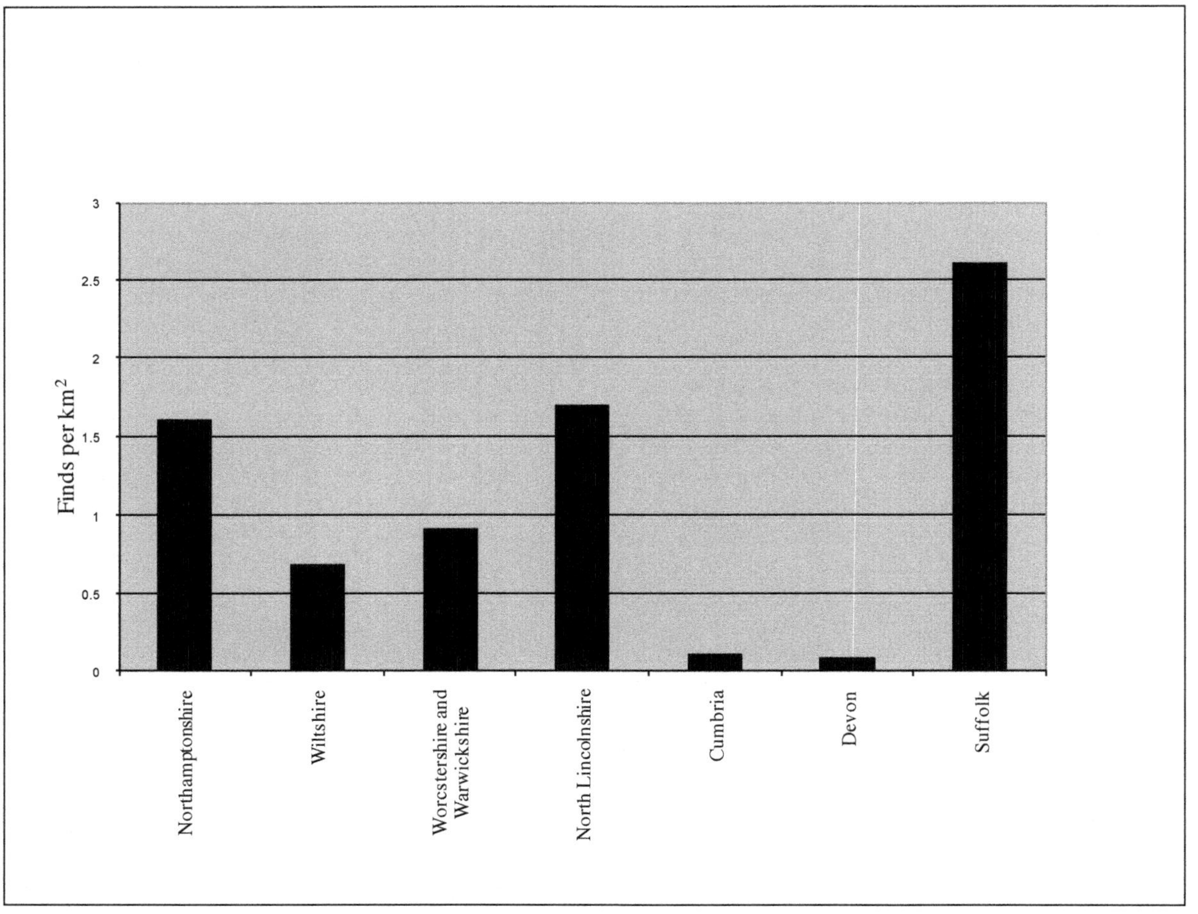

Fig. 5: Relative quantities of PAS records per county according to landmass.

It must be noted that the results of the above analysis should not be seen as a true reflection of the density of Roman settlement in a region, as the number of Roman finds recorded are not evenly distributed across each area. Very little data is available in the Salisbury Plain area of Wiltshire as no detecting occurs on the military training area as a result of the danger of live ammunition. The mountainous terrain of much of Cumbria is restrictive to metal-detector users and this no doubt has some impact on the numbers of finds recovered from this county. Conversely, a vast amount of Northamptonshire is subject to arable farming and there is therefore likely to be more land potentially available for searching than in some other counties. It would therefore be beneficial in the future to base the above analysis on the of amount land under arable cultivation in each region. Such data have not yet been acquired at the time of writing.

For the purposes of this paper the analysis of the background density of finds has been limited to PAS data. A more accurate understanding of the density of Romano-British material available for study in each region would be achievable through analysis of other forms of survey techniques that result in collections of artefacts, notably the results of field-walking projects, and this is also something that will be given further consideration as this research progresses.

PAS data and Roman Wiltshire

It was considered that for the purposes of this paper a minimum of ten finds found within a 250 metre radius can be considered as potential evidence for a Romano-British site in Wiltshire. It is acknowledged that this figure is somewhat arbitrary and it is possible that, as research progresses and the methodology becomes more refined, this threshold will change and that a different figure will be recognised as a threshold for each case study. For the time being this serves as a preliminary means of interpreting Wiltshire's Roman PAS data.

If this methodology is applied to the total of 2,329 records of Roman date on the PAS database, then it is possible to recognise 35 distinct concentrations of material that may represent sites. For the purposes of this exercise the sites have been named based upon the parish in which they are located, with a numerical system applied to parishes with multiple sites.

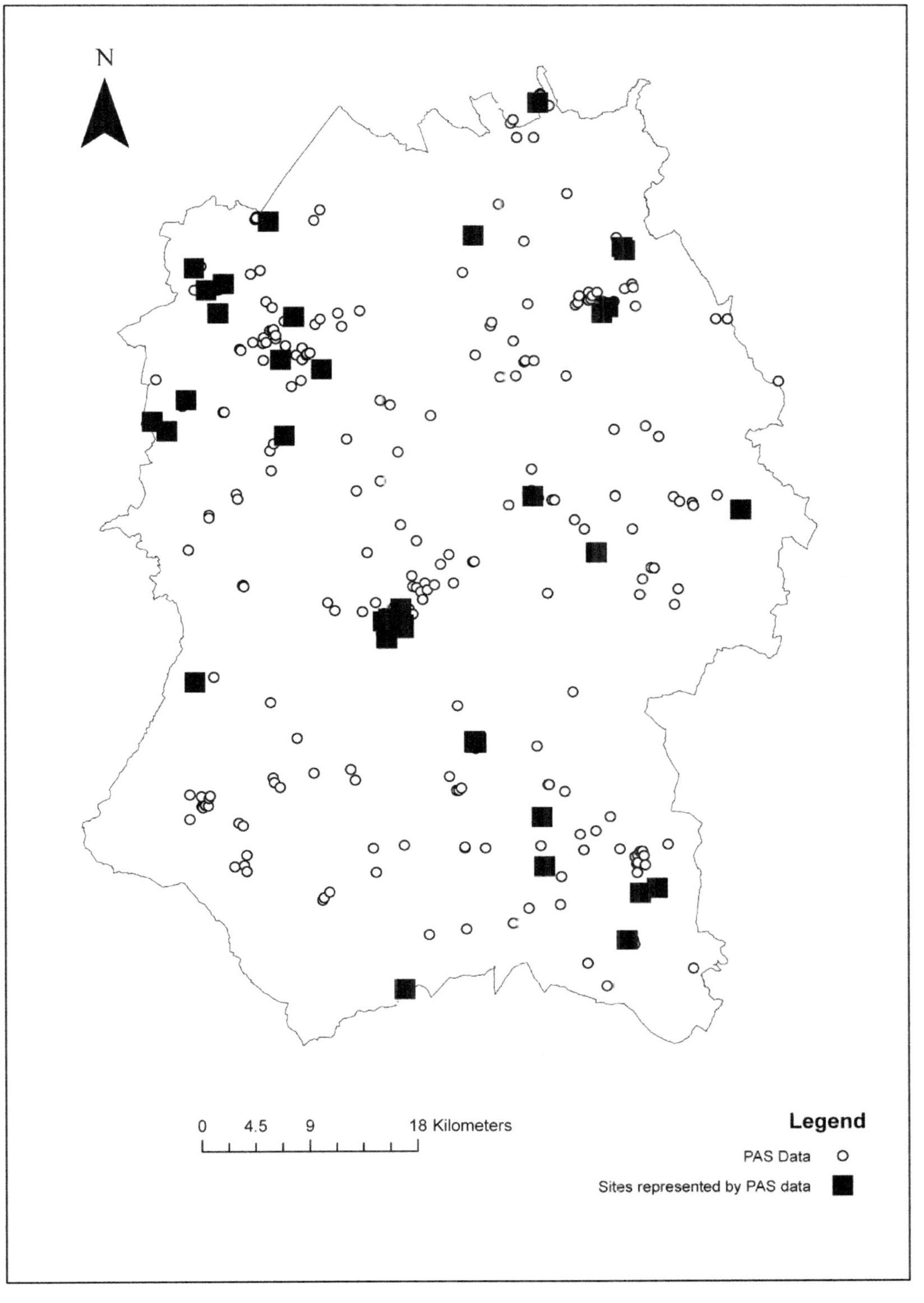

Fig. 6: Distribution of sites represented by PAS data in Wiltshire.

Figure 6 shows the distribution of the 35 sites. Unsurprisingly, the 35 sites are located in areas where the general spread of PAS data indicates that there has been intensive metal-detector use. However, there appear to be no sites associated with the south-west of the county, despite evidence for Romano-British settlement on the HER and activity by metal-detector users. The reason for the absence of sites in this area is currently uncertain, but the distribution of PAS data in this area is represented by single finds or small concentrations of a few artefacts which cannot reasonably be interpreted as evidence for sites when the threshold of ten artefacts is applied. Nonetheless, the findspots do reveal evidence for some Romano-British activity in this part of the landscape and it is worth noting that many activities undertaken by people would have occurred 'off-site' (Gaffney and Tingle 1989: 210; Bintliff 2000: 1; Bintliff and Snodgrass 1988). An absence of determinable sites does not necessarily mean that these parts of the landscape were not exploited.

The number of artefacts recorded on the PAS database for each of the 35 sites varies somewhat, from as few as ten artefacts (the lowest limit as defined by the current methodology) at Bower Chalke, for example, to 147 at West Lavington. Interpretation of the large discrepancy in the number of artefacts recovered from different sites must be undertaken cautiously. Whilst it is possible that the different quantities of artefacts at the different sites genuinely reflect areas of differing intensity of settlement, it is important to be aware of many of the uncertainties associated with haphazardly collected discoveries. In many cases information about the amount of time spent detecting at particular areas is lacking, for example, and about areas of negative activity, where an area was searched, yet yielded nothing. It is also important to be aware of the number of detector users responsible for the discovery of artefacts at a site, as it is likely that a large number of detector users actively searching a site would result in a greater number of records on the PAS database (assuming, of course, that each detector user reported his or her finds). In general, however, it appears that searching (or at least the reporting of artefacts) from each site in Wiltshire is restricted to a single, or perhaps two, detector users. Both Bower Chalke and West Lavington, for example, are represented by finds made by single detector users. However, based upon the information supplied by the PAS database, the finds at West Lavington were made over a period of a number of years, whilst those from Bower Chalke appear to have been discovered during one episode of detecting. The significance of the different quantities of finds from these sites should, therefore, not be overplayed, and it is likely that given an extended period of searching at Bower Chalke greater quantities of artefacts would be discovered.

Site Name	C	V	BM	W/A	DA	TO	TE	G	TR	W	TA	R	Misc	UN	Total
Alton	5	0	0	0	5	0	0	0	0	0	0	1	0	0	11
Bower Chalke	10	0	0	0	0	0	0	0	0	0	0	0	0	0	10
Box 1	0	0	0	0	24	0	0	0	0	0	0	0	0	0	24
Box 2	0	0	0	0	13	1	0	0	0	0	0	0	1	1	16
Bremhill	9	0	0	0	2	0	0	0	0	0	0	1	1	1	14
Brokenborough	10	0	0	0	2	0	0	0	0	0	0	0	0	0	12
Chippenham	0	9	0	0	0	0	1	0	0	0	0	0	0	0	10
Chiseldon 1	72	0	0	0	16	1	0	0	2	0	1	0	0	0	92
Chiseldon 2	27	0	0	0	1	0	0	0	0	0	0	0	1	0	29
Colerne	8	0	0	0	5	0	0	0	2	0	0	1	1	0	17
Downton	18	0	0	0	6	0	0	0	1	0	0	0	0	1	26
Durnford	60	1	0	0	6	0	0	0	1	0	0	0	0	0	68
Grittleton 1	0	16	0	0	0	0	0	0	0	0	0	0	0	0	16
Grittleton 2	81	6	1	0	14	2	0	0	0	0	0	0	0	0	104
Grittleton 3	6	6	0	0	3	1	0	0	0	0	0	0	0	0	16
Kingston Langley	17	8	0	0	0	0	0	0	0	0	0	0	0	0	25
Lacock	11	0	0	0	3	2		0	1	2	0	0	1	0	20
Lydiard Millicent	5	4	0	0	0	3	0	0	0	0	0	0	0	0	12
Market Lavington	15	0	0	0	0	0	0	0	0	0	0	1	1	0	17
Marston Maisey	17	9	2	0	0	0	0	0	0	0	0	0	0	0	28
New Sarum	51	0	0	0	2	1	0	0	0	0	0	0	0	0	54
Pewsey	4	4	2	0	3	3	0	0	0	0	0	0	0	0	16
Pitton and Farley	12	0	0	0	0	0	0	0	0	0	0	0	0	0	12
Pitton Farley 1	4	6	5	0	0	0	0	0	0	0	0	0	0	1	16
Shalbourne	23	0	0	0	6	0	0	0	0	0	0	1	2	0	32
Upton Scudamore	21	12	2	0	28	0	0	0	0	0	0	0	0	0	63
Wanborough 1	0	13	1	0	0	0	0	0	0	0	0	0	0	0	14
Wanborough 2	15	0	0	0	0	0	0	0	0	0	0	0	0	0	15
West Lavington 1	25	17	2	0	5	2	0	0	0	0	0	0	0	0	51
West Lavington 2	9	0	0	0	2	0	0	0	0	0	0	0	0	0	11
West Lavington 3	34	0	0	0	3	0	0	0	0	0	0	0	2	1	40
West Lavington 4	129	2	1	0	10	2	0	0	3	0	0	0	0	0	147
West Lavington 5	23	0	0	0	1	0	0	0	0	0	0	0	0	0	24
West Lavington 6	105	5	0	0	9	2	0	0	0	0	0	0	0	0	121
Winterbourne	15	0	0	0	16	0	0	0	0	0	0	0	0	0	31
Total	841	118	16	0	185	20	1	0	10	2	1	5	10	5	1214

Table 3: Composition of assemblages of sites represented by PAS data in Wiltshire (C = coins; V = vessels; BM = building materials; W/A = weapons and armour; DA = dress accessories; TO = Tools; TE = Textiles; G = Gambling; TR = Trade; W = Writing; TA = Toilet Articles; R = Religion; Misc = Miscellaneous; UN = Unidentified).

The composition of the assemblages of the different sites vary somewhat, and here finds from the sites have been grouped into classes in a method adapted from that used by Crummy (1983) and in subsequent small finds reports (Cool and Baxter 1995; 2002; Worrell 2004) allowing comparison between different sites. Here, the classes of artefact have been defined as coins, vessels (ceramic and non ceramic), building materials (wall plaster, tile and imbrex), artefacts with military associations, dress accessories (brooches, finger rings and hair pins), tools (including items associated with food production and consumption), textiles (spindle whorls), gambling (gaming tokens), trade (weights and steelyards), writing (styli and seal boxes), toilet articles (such as cosmetic sets, nail cleaners, tweezers), miscellaneous artefacts that do not fit into the categories above, including unidentified objects (see Table 3).

In general it is possible to see that coinage tends to dominate the assemblages and in extreme cases accounts for 100% of an assemblage (as at Pitton, Farley and Bower Chalke). After coinage, dress accessories which are primarily represented by brooches, are the most common category of artefact reported. Ceramic vessel sherds are well represented at many sites, but other categories of artefacts occur with considerably less frequency.

Of the sites, only Box 1 and Box 2, Chippenham, Grittleton 1 and Wanborough 1 are entirely unrepresented by coinage. At Chippenham, Grittleton 1 and Wanborough the dominant find type in the assemblages are ceramic sherds and none of the finds recorded from these sites are metallic, indicating that these sites have not actually been metal-detected. The assemblages recorded from these sites therefore reflect the circumstances of recovery, and the database record for the finds at Chippenham reveal that the discoveries were a result of chance finds in a garden. It is very possible that detector use at these sites would reveal the presence of coinage, and other metal artefacts, yet without these additional finds comparison with other sites that are dominated by metal-detector finds is impossible. The identification of these findspots as settlement sites on the basis of relatively small numbers of ceramic sherds is, admittedly, questionable and their interpretation problematic.

However, the assemblages of some of the potential sites are rather more open to interpretation. For instance, at Box 1 and Box 2 the discovery of large quantities of brooches but a complete absence of coinage raises interesting questions about the nature of the site. If coins were present at the sites one would expect metal-detector users to find them. Reece (2002: 99) has demonstrated how late Roman coinage is a relatively common site find, whilst finds of early Roman coinage are considerably more rare. The lack of any coinage on the site may therefore reflect a cessation of occupation in the later Roman period, supported by the 1st- to 2nd-century dates of the brooches. Alternative hypotheses, however, might be that the fairly large numbers of brooches and lack of coinage may represent evidence for a cemetery or perhaps of a votive deposit. The deposition of brooches at shrines is well attested (Aldhouse-Green 2004: 205; Puttock 2002: 74-75; Woodward 1992: 69).

Interestingly, there are a number of HER entries of Roman date from within the parish of Box, including at least two suspected villa sites, one of which was excavated in the 1960s (Hurst *et al.* 1987). However, neither the excavated villa at Box, nor any of the records on the HER are located within close proximity to the sites represented by the PAS data, except a collection of five pottery sherds found 200 metres to the west of Box 1. Clearly there is currently insufficient evidence to relate the sites represented by the PAS data to the other known Romano-British evidence for the parish. However, it is tempting to hypothesise some form of relationship, with possible cemeteries or shrines represented by Box 1 and Box 2, associated with the villa known from Hurst's excavations. Such suggestions, based upon such limited information, are tentative, and substantially more work would need to be undertaken in the parish in order for these hypotheses to be given serious credence, yet they act as an illustration of how PAS material might be used to help interpret areas for which there is already some knowledge.

At Lacock the finds recorded by the PAS are also interesting. Alongside coinage and dress accessories finds include a seal box and a stylus, both evidence for the presence of literacy at the site (Mattingly 2006; Hanson and Conolly 2002; Derks and Roymans 2002). Similar discoveries elsewhere have been suggested as evidence for administration at villas associated with farming estates (Mattingly 2006: 461). Yet the discovery of increasing numbers of styli on low status rural sites has been seen as evidence that literacy spread further down the social scale than hitherto suspected, with many low status rural sites home to at least one person who was literate (Hanson and Conolly 2002: 156-60). No elements of the assemblage at Lacock are suggestive of high status settlement, so the presence of artefacts associated with literacy and writing are important, showing the potential of these data to contribute to the debate on levels of literacy in the Roman Empire.

The two examples above serve as brief illustrations of how PAS data has the potential to contribute to the study of Romano-British settlement in Wiltshire. There is not sufficient space here to undertake full interpretations of each of the sites represented by the data for the county. Instead, the above discussion has sought to introduce the current research, explaining some of the methodological issues being considered and some preliminary results. However, even in the early stages of research it is apparent that PAS data has the potential to provide important new information on Roman rural settlement, as the 24 potential new sites from Wiltshire demonstrate. It is also apparent that the PAS data from the eleven sites for which there are HER records has the potential to considerably enhance what is known.

Interpretation of the potential sites revealed by PAS data has been limited in this paper, but this work is ongoing.

Recent developments in the study of finds assemblages have included the adoption of multivariate statistical techniques such as correspondence analysis (Cool and Baxter 1999; 2002), and these methods provide a useful means of comparing assemblages from different sites. As this research is in its very early stages, the results of the application of such analyses to the PAS data are not presented here, but it is intended that they will appear in future publications as research progresses.

Acknowledgements

I am very grateful to John Pearce, Sally Worrell, Roger Bland and Sam Moorhead who have all provided constructive advice and encouragement throughout my work so far. My thanks are also due to the staff at the HERs for Warwickshire, Wiltshire and Worcestershire who have made data available to me and allowed me to present it in this paper. The HER data displayed in the maps for Wiltshire is owned by Wiltshire County Council, and I am grateful for their permission to display it. The list of individual FLOs who have provided me with information is too long to include here, but I am grateful to all of them for their hard work. I have benefited from the advice of Christine Addison and Jude Plouviez, for which I am also very grateful. Andrew Bevan and Steven Trick provided invaluable advice on GIS. Finally, I wish to thank the AHRC and the British Museum for funding my doctoral research.

Endnotes

{1} The methodology and results presented in this paper represent the very early stages of this research, current in the summer of 2007 when this paper was prepared. Revisions to the methodology have subsequently been made (see Brindle 2009 for a more up-to-date discussion).
{2} Numbers given for the amount of records on the PAS database and on HERs throughout this paper were correct in April 2007, but will have since increased.
{3} The HER data for North Lincolnshire, Northamptonshire and Cumbria had not been acquired at the time of writing.
{4} A GIS density analysis was conducted plotting relative density of HER data and PAS data based upon a search radius of 5,000 square metres. The gradients used in the map are based upon equal intervals of number of records per 5,000 square metres.
{5} However, Cunnington draws attention to Hoare's remarks on the nearby parish of Dilton Marsh, that 'this neighbourhood seems to have been thickly populated in the Roman period' (Hoare cited in Cunnington 1932: 185).

Bibliography

Aldhouse-Green, M. J. 2004, 'Gallo-British deities and their shrines', in Todd, M. (ed.), *A Companion to Roman Britain* (Blackwell, Oxford),193-219.

Alexander, M, Palmer, S. and Chadd, L. 2007, 'Archaeological resource assessment of the aggregates producing areas of Warwickshire', Draft Publication, 1.0 (Warwickshire County Council, Warwick), http://www.warwickshire.gov.uk/Web/corporate/pages.nsf/Links/F9B702ADF1A7738B802571950047EE1D.

Bintliff, J. L. 2000, 'Beyond dots on the map: future directions for surface artefact survey in Greece', in Bintliff, J. L., Kuna, M. and Venclova, N. (eds.), *The Future of Artefact Survey in Europe* (Sheffield Academic Press, Sheffield).

Bintliff, J. and Snodgrass, A. 1988, 'Off-site pottery distributions: a regional and interregional perspective', *Current Anthropology* 29, 506-13.

Booth, P. 2006, 'Roman Warwickshire', *West Midlands Regional Research Framework for Archaeology*, http://www.iaa.bham.ac.uk/research/projects/wmrrfa/seminar3/index.shtml

Brindle, T. 2009, 'Amateur metal detector finds and Romano-British settlement: a methodological case study from Wiltshire', in Driessen, M., Heeren, S., Hendriks, J., Kemmers, F. and Visser, R. (eds.), *TRAC 2008: Proceedings of the Eighteenth Annual Theoretical Roman Archaeology Conference, Amsterdam 2008* (Oxbow Books, Oxford).

Cool, H. E. M. and Baxter, M. 1995, 'Finds from the fortress: artefacts, buildings and correspondence analysis', in Wilcock, J. W. and Lockyear, K. (eds.), *Computer Applications and Quantitative Methods in Archaeology 1993*, British Archaeological Reports, International Series 598 (Archaeopress, Oxford), 177-82.

Cool, H. E. M. and Baxter, M., 1999, 'Peeling the onion: an approach to comparing vessel glass assemblages,' *Journal of Roman Archaeology*, 12, 72-100, (Ann Arbor, Michigan).

Cool, H. E. M. and Baxter, M. 2002, 'Exploring Romano-British finds assemblages', *Oxford Journal of Archaeology* 21 (Blackwell, Oxford), 365-80.

Corney, M. 2000, 'Characterising the landscape of Roman Britain: a review of the study of Roman Britain 1975-2000', in Hook, D. (ed.), *Landscape: the richest historical record*, 33-45, Society for Landscape Studies, Supplementary Series (Society for Landscape Studies, Amesbury).

Crummy, N. 1983, *Colchester Archaeological Report 2: The Roman small finds from excavations in Colchester 1971-9* (Colchester Archaeological Trust, Colchester).

Cunnington, M. E. 1932, 'Romano-British Wiltshire', *Wiltshire Archaeological Magazine* 45 (Wiltshire Archaeological and Natural History Society, Devizes), 166-216.

Derks, T. and Roymans, N. 2002, 'Seal-boxes and the spread of Latin literacy in the Rhine delta', in Cooley, A. E. (ed.), *Becoming Roman, Writing Latin? Literacy and epigraphy in the Roman west*, Journal of Roman Archaeology, Supplementary Series 48 (Portsmouth, Rhode Island), 87-134.

Ellis, P. (ed.) 2001, *Roman Wiltshire and After* (Wiltshire Archaeological and Natural History Society, Devizes).

Fasham, P. J., Schadla-Hall, R. T., Shennan, S. J. and Bates, P. J. 1980, *Fieldwalking for Archaeologists*

(Hampshire Field Club Archaeological Society, Southampton).

Gaffney, V. and Tingle, M. 1989. *The Maddle Farm Project: an integrated survey of prehistoric and Roman landscapes on the Berkshire Downs,* British Archaeological Reports, British Series, 200 (British Archaeological Reports, Oxford)

Grinsell, L. V. 1957, 'Archaeological gazetteer', in Pugh, R. B. (ed.), *Victoria County History of Wiltshire* (Institute of Historical Research, London), 21-27.

Hanson, W. S. and Conolly, R. 2002, 'Language and literacy in Roman Britain: some archaeological considerations', in Cooley, A. E. (ed.), *Becoming Roman, writing Latin? Literacy and epigraphy in the Roman west,* Journal of Roman Archaeology Supplementary Series 48 (Portsmouth, Rhode Island), 151-64.

Haselgrove, C., Millett, M. and Smith, I. (eds.), 1985. *Archaeology from the Ploughsoil: studies in the collection and interpretation of field survey data* (Department of Archaeology and Prehistory, University of Sheffield, Sheffield).

Haverfield, F. 1912, *The Romanization of Roman Britain* (Clarendon, Oxford).

Hingley, R. 1989, *Rural Settlement in Roman Britain* (Seaby, London).

Hingley, R. 2004, 'Rural settlement in northern Britain', in Todd, M. (ed.), *A Companion to Roman Britain* (Blackwell, Oxford), 327-48.

Hurst, H. R. Dartnall, D. L. and Fisher, C. 1987, 'Excavations at Box Roman villa, 1967-8', *Wiltshire Archaeology and Natural History Magazine* 81 (H. F. and E. Bull, Devizes), 19-51.

Jones, B. and Mattingly, D. 1990, *An Atlas of Roman Britain* (Guild Publishing, London).

King, A. 2004, 'Rural settlement in southern Britain: a regional survey', in Todd, M. (ed.), *A Companion to Roman Britain* (Blackwell, Oxford), 349-70.

Mattingly, D., 2006, *An Imperial Possession: Britain in the Roman Empire, 54 BC-AD 409* (Penguin Books, London).

Millett, M., 1990, *The Romanisation of Britain: an essay in archaeological interpretation* (Cambridge University Press, Cambridge).

Puttock, S., 2002, *Ritual Significance of Personal Ornament in Roman Britain,* British Archaeological Reports, British Series 327 (Archaeopress, Oxford).

Reece, R., 2002, *The Coinage of Roman Britain* (Tempus, Stroud).

Schofield J. (ed.) 1991, *Interpreting Artefact Scatters: contributions to ploughzone archaeology* (Oxbow, Oxford).

Taylor, J. 2001, 'Rural Society in Roman Britain', in James, S. and Millett, M. (eds.), *Britons and Romans: advancing an archaeological agenda,* Council for British Archaeology Research Report 125 (Council for British Archaeology, York), 56-59.

Woodward, A. 1992, *Shrines and Sacrifice* (Batsford, London).

Worrell, S. (2004) 'Roman Britain in 2003: II. Finds Reported under the Portable Antiquities Scheme'. *Britannia* (Society for the Promotion of Roman Studies, London), 317-334.

Portable Antiquities in the Roman Frontier

Rob Collins

Since the appointment of full-time Finds Liaison Officers (FLOs) for the North East and Cumbria and Lancashire in 2003, many hundreds of objects have been recorded with the PAS from the former Roman frontier. This paper reviews and summarises the significance of these artefacts, which also provides an opportunity to assess the extent to which Roman objects are recovered outside of scheduled areas and whether or not such finds conform to any typological or distribution patterns.

There are a number of biases and discrepancies associated with PAS data, which must be briefly acknowledged as they will impact on any interpretation of the data. Primarily, PAS data is a record of voluntarily reported artefacts discovered by members of the public. The vast majority are reported by metal-detectorists, who employ varied search methods, target favoured search areas and may not collect non-metallic objects, such as ceramics. Therefore, data is often skewed toward those parishes that are searched frequently. Many parts of northern England are less extensively and intensively searched than the southern counties, and this is reflected in terms of real numbers of finds recorded by county on the PAS database. A further consideration is that many of the Roman sites in the north are Scheduled Monuments upon which metal-detecting is prohibited, and which creates obvious gaps in artefact distribution patterns. Obviously, detectorists who illegally search such sites are unlikely to record any finds from them. There are further biases, of course, related to broader socio-economic issues that impact on the metal detecting hobby, but those mentioned above are the most significant in terms of this study.

The actual area that can be considered or defined as the Roman frontier varied throughout the Roman period (Breeze and Dobson 2000, 5-152). The area examined for this study starts in Cumbria and extends to County Durham and from the Tees north to the Scottish border. This area is referred to as the frontier, following Whittaker's (1994: 84) definition of a frontier as a transitional zone and not a linear boundary or border. Within this defined area of the frontier (from March 2003 to 20 January 2007) 174 coins and 301 artefacts dating to the Roman period have been recorded. It should be stated that some of these unstratified artefacts may in some instances date to the medieval period, notably where objects are fragmentary or generic in character. Figure 1 shows the distribution of findspots of artefacts and coins recorded by PAS in the area considered. Significantly, the distribution of PAS data corresponds to the Roman road network, with the majority of objects found either in proximity to a Roman road or to the coast. Generally speaking, there are relatively few 'blank' swathes of land, with the exception of the Pennines where a lower number of known archaeological sites is also recognised. This blank area is due to the lack of metal-detecting in the uplands. A significant site assemblage recorded by the PAS comes from the River Tees at Piercebridge; this assemblage has not been included due to the many 1000s of artefacts from the site and the extent to which it biases analysis of other Roman finds recorded by members of the public. It should also be noted that Scottish data is not incorporated and therefore the apparent 'blankness' in Scotland should not be taken to indicate anything of significance. Further discussion focuses on tabulations and distributions of Roman objects separated into artefacts and coins for ease of analysis.

Roman Artefacts

The Roman artefacts (not including coinage) have been assessed by material, date and category. The vast majority of recorded artefacts (83%) are made primarily of copper-alloy or ceramic, with lead or lead-alloy as the next most represented material (7%). Geographically, copper-alloy objects are found throughout the study area, while ceramic material is recorded from far fewer locations and there is a notable lack of reported ceramics from north of Hadrian's Wall. Lead objects are only known from findspots with other associated Roman finds. This relates to the frequent difficulty of closely dating lead objects with no other associated finds or information.

When considering the chronological breakdown, 79% of the objects are dated only to the Roman period in general. In most cases, this is due to the lack of well-dated parallels or to the fact that particular object types were made and used over a long period of time. Figure 2 demonstrates the distribution of the 21% of artefacts that can be specifically and broadly dated to a particular century. The 1st- to 2nd-century peak in Figure 2 is created by brooches and ceramics, which apart from coins are classes of objects that are most easily datable. However, the distribution of artefacts by date reveals only one notable trend that all 4th-century evidence is found along Hadrian's Wall or south of it. Initially, this sounds significant, but on closer examination, there are only four finds of 4th century date and all are pottery sherds of East Yorkshire manufacture. The higher incidence of early

Roman finds is not surprising, but the comparative lack of diagnostic 4th-century finds apart from the small quantity of pottery is unexpected.

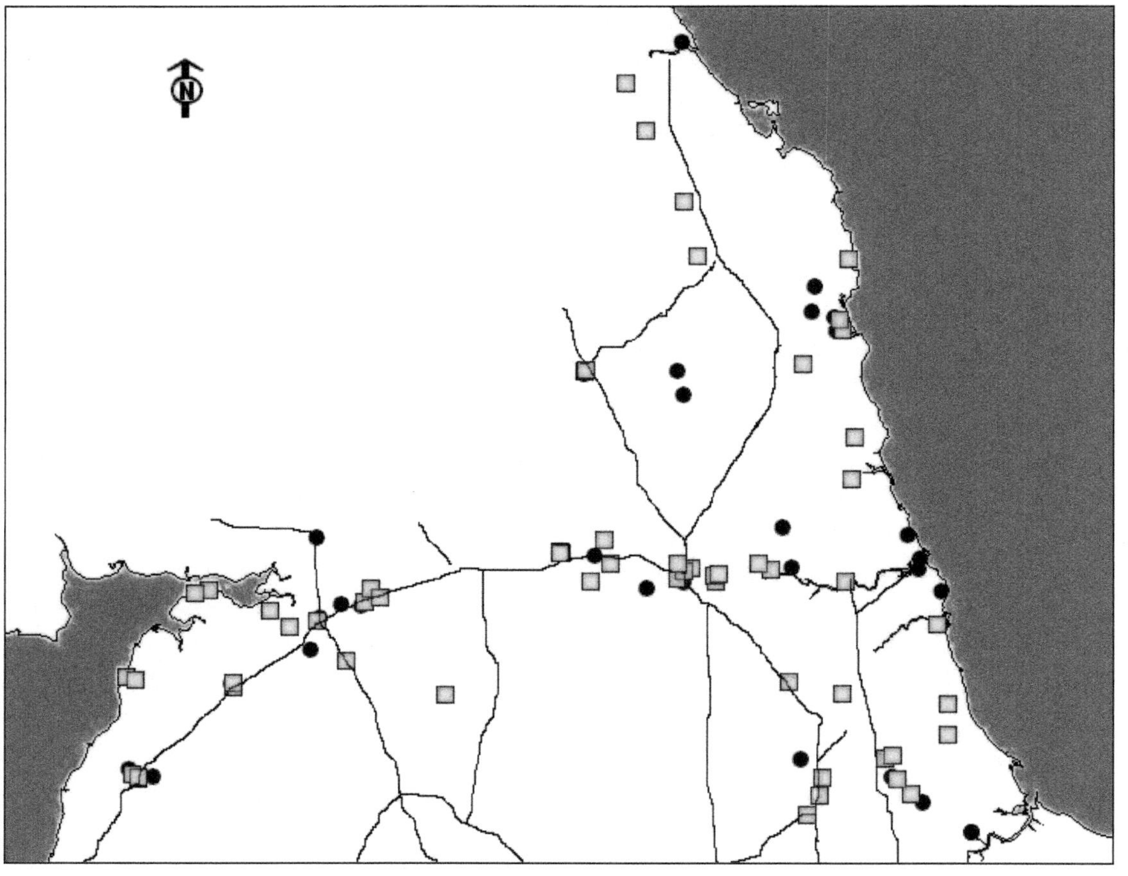

Fig. 1: Roman artefacts (grey squares) and coins (black circles) recorded by the PAS in the frontier in relation to the Roman road system.

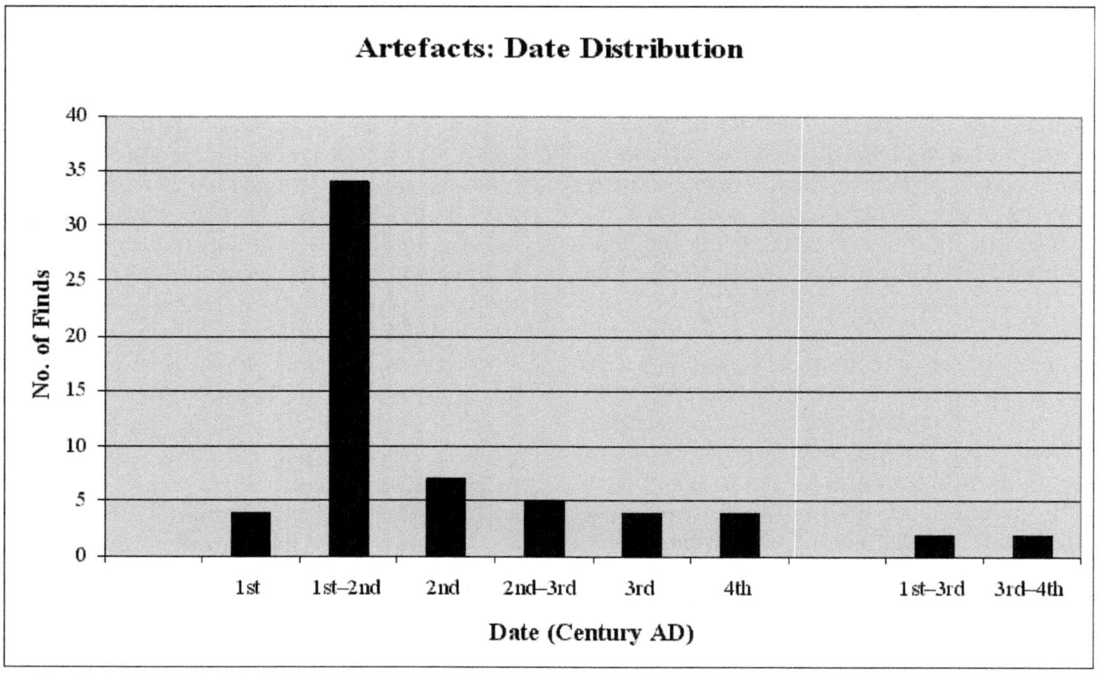

Fig. 2: The date of Roman artefacts by century.

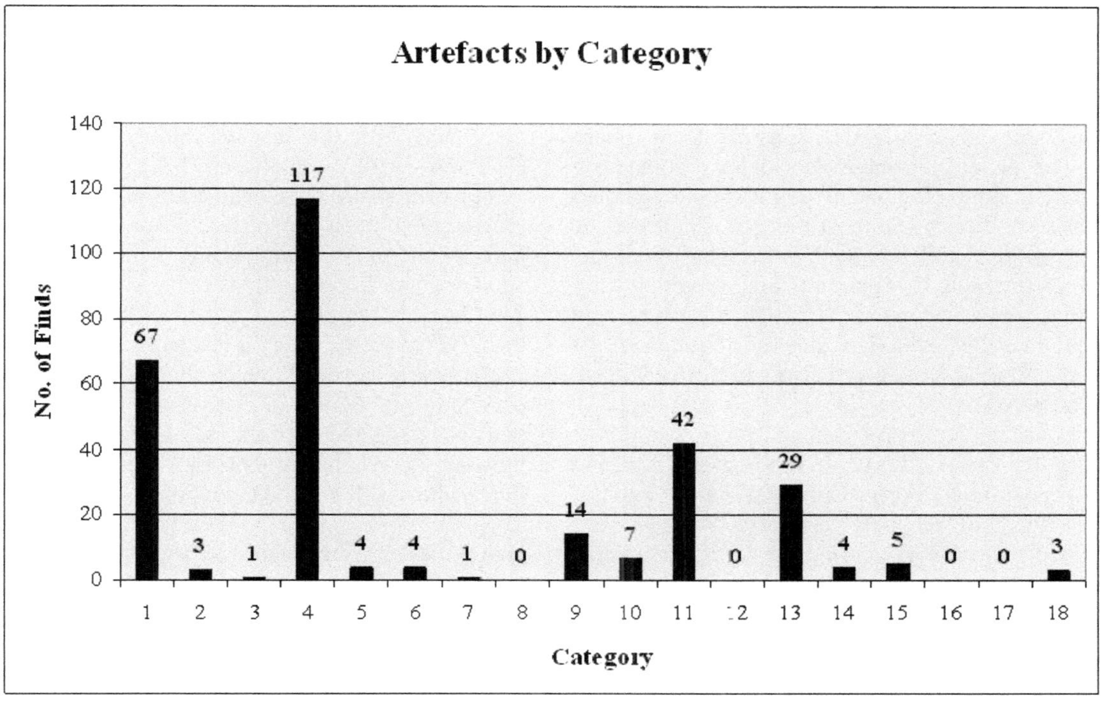

Fig. 3: Numbers of artefacts by functional category: 1) personal adornment; 2) toilet and medical equipment; 3) textile equipment; 4) household utensils and furniture; 5) objects used for recreational purposes; 6) objects used for weighing and measuring; 7) objects associated with written communication; 8) objects associated with transport; 9) buildings and services; 10) tools; 11) fasteners and fittings; 12) objects associated with agriculture; 13) military equipment; 14) religious items; 15) objects and waste associated with metalworking; 16) objects and waste associated with bone working and other skeletal material; 17) objects and waste associated with the manufacture of fired clay objects; 18) miscellaneous objects.

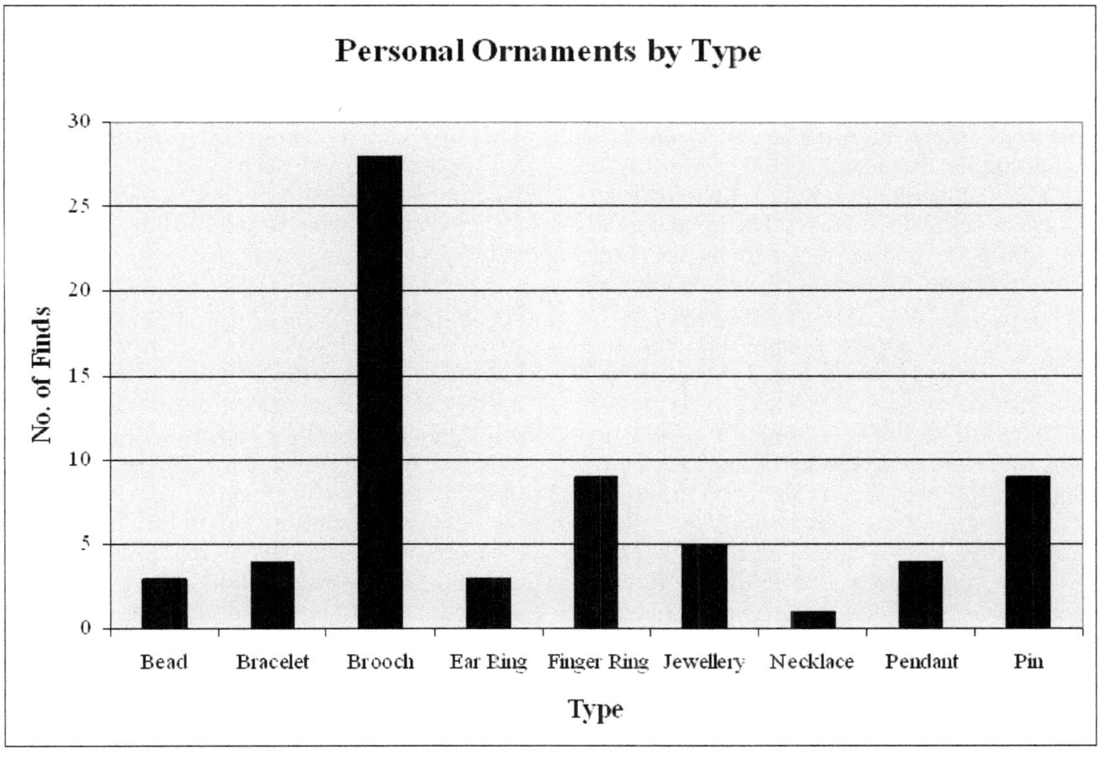

Fig. 4: Numbers of personal ornaments by type.

The non-coin artefacts were also considered according to functional category, adapting Crummy's (1983) divisions (Fig. 3), but also including ceramic sherds. Quantification of artefacts by functional category suggests (in a general fashion) the types of activities that occurred or did not occur in a given area. Such a simplistic analysis can be problematic, particularly given the lack of archaeological context for nearly all the artefacts under consideration, but this functional separation allows for a broad overview of the discoveries made in the frontier. Personal ornaments (category 1) and household utensils and furniture (category 4), dominate the functional categories. Household utensils consist almost entirely of ceramic vessel sherds, though there are a few fragments of copper-alloy and glass vessels, as well as a quern fragment. The personal ornaments category contains a variety of object types (Fig. 4), though it should be noted that brooches are clearly the most numerous and will be discussed in more detail below. The personal ornament category is both the most numerous and geographically widespread artefact category, although fasteners and fittings (category 11), which is generally comprised of unattributed studs and mounts are also widely distributed, but is less numerous.

Interestingly, the ceramic sherds in the household utensil category were all found along Hadrian's Wall or south of it. Other interesting clusters are also notable. For example, tools (category 10) and religious items (category 14) have only been reported in Cumbria with seven and four examples recorded respectively, while there is a cluster of a small number of recreational objects (category 5; 4 items) in the eastern sector of Hadrian's Wall. The greatest diversity in terms of functional categories, has been recorded in proximity to Roman forts or other military installations, notably Corbridge, High Rochester, Papcastle and Irthington.

Given the widespread and long-term military occupation of the region, it is rather surprising that few military objects have been recorded. However, this is typical of frontier assemblages where soldiers were expected to look after their kit; an exception is the Corbridge hoard (Allason-Jones and Bishop 1988). Of the six sites with *militaria* recorded by the PAS (Bowness, Castle Eden, Corbridge, Lanchester, Rochester and Warkworth), four are in very close proximity to forts (High Rochester, Corbridge, Lanchester and Bowness). The remaining two sites where objects have been recorded by the PAS - Castle Eden, County Durham and Warkworth, Northumberland - are not forts or previously known Roman settlements. On closer examination, the finds from these sites include harness fittings (NCL-F74897 and 344F84) that have been considered to be possibly military in nature on the basis of parallels known from military sites. However, the character of these sites might be better suggested by the other finds found in the area, which at Castle Eden include a Headstud brooch (NCL-F5CAD7) and three coins (an unidentified *sestertius* (NCL-F56A58), a *radiate* (NCL-F5A465) and a House of Constantine *nummus* (NCL-F57D82). The interpretation of this small assemblage is not conclusive and could represent either military or civilian presence or both. At Warkworth, in addition to the harness fittings mentioned above, the assemblage contains a lock-bolt (NCL-7F9275), two 2nd-century *denarii* (NCL-8C9294 and 8CE512), one *sestertius* (NCL-4751C4) and one *dupondius/as* (NCL-350130). Although this assemblage is not particularly military in nature, the closest parallels for the lock bolt come from sites in northern England associated with the Roman military as at Birdoswald (Wilmott 1997: 305, no 221). Topographically, Warkworth would have been an ideal position for a small posting of military personnel. There is an excellent local harbour and the modern village (and medieval castle) are sited in an area with high visibility to the north and south. The 2nd-century date of the assemblage could suggest that Warkworth was a staging post for Roman campaigning north of the Wall or during the Antonine occupation of Scotland, but on the basis of the current evidence designation of the site as a civilian settlement is most likely. It is hoped that finds recorded from this area in the future will expand the picture.

Given the high incidence and widespread distribution of personal ornaments recorded by the PAS, this category will now be considered in more detail. A very distinctive pattern can be seen in the brooch distribution, with all brooches occurring either along the line of the Wall or east of the Pennines and Cheviots in the eastern coastal lowlands (Fig. 5). The brooches are all early Roman types dating from the 1st to early 3rd centuries (see Fig. 6 for listing of brooch types by quantity). Within this distribution there are interesting patterns, with the five dragonesque brooches recorded from sites throughout the frontier, while the more numerous Trumpet brooches have a distinctly eastern distribution and a small cluster of headstud brooches in eastern County Durham. This patterning may suggest local differences within the region in respect to dress and personal appearance. More dress accessories are needed to both confirm and further refine any patterning, but such a pattern could provide an interesting backdrop to the archaeological evidence from the frontier, dominated as it is by assemblages from military sites.

Overall, it can be said with some confidence, that the finds recorded by the PAS demonstrate an east-west variation in the distributions in the frontier. This is most notably seen in the brooch distribution, but also in the distribution of religious objects such as the figurines and mounts found in Cumbria (LANCUM-B17ED5 and 0F2255, and LVPL150 and 154). This east-west divide has also been commented upon with other archaeological evidence, notably in the pre- and post-Roman production and use of ceramics (Evans 2000) and environmental evidence (Stallibrass and Huntley 1995; Stallibrass 2000). Unfortunately, a comprehensive comparison of artefact assemblages from archaeological sites has yet to be conducted and this hinders more thorough comparison with excavated data.

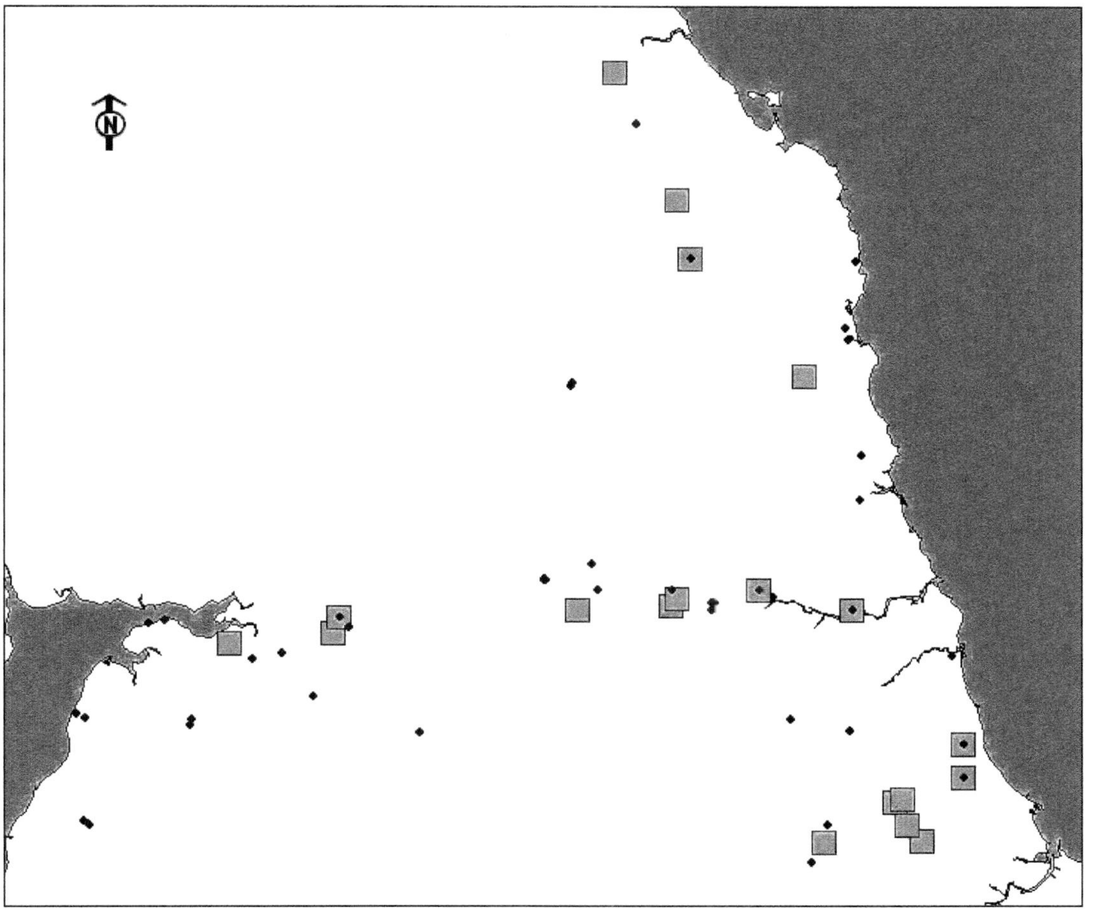

Fig. 5: Geographic distribution of brooches (grey squares) compared to other artefacts (black dots).

Brooch Type	Number of Finds
Bow	6
Dragonesque	5
Headstud	3
Hod Hill	1
Knee	1
Swastika	1
Trumpet	8
Pin	2

Fig. 6: Numbers of different types of brooches.

Roman Coins

174 Roman coins have been recorded from the frontier, 30 (17%) of which are silver and 144 (83%) are copper-alloy. The silver coins are *denarii* of the early Roman period with no *siliquae* or gold coins recorded. Only 78 coins (45%) could be classified according to issue period. The rest were too corroded to date to a specific emperor or issue period, though they could often be dated by century based on size and weight. Figure 7 shows the date distribution of the coinage by century, with a typical peak in the 4th century.

The geographical distribution is most easily distinguished between early and late Roman coinages. The early coinage is more widely distributed throughout the frontier and the late coinage is limited in its northern extent by Hadrian's Wall, with the exception of four *nummi* of the 4th century at Norham (Northumberland), three of which are House of Constantine issues. This feature probably reflects historical circumstances in which large scale campaigning and occupation north of the Wall occurred through the 3rd century, but large-scale military movements north of the Wall in the 4th century were infrequent. The fact that 4th century coinage seems to be less geographically extensive than earlier coinage (despite Constantine's very productive mints), may also indicate a real shift in the use of coinage in the frontier, though this can only be speculation at this point. The other possibility is that coins, particularly those produced in base metal had no function in the economies of the tribal peoples north of Hadrian's Wall. Early Roman precious metal coins north of the Wall in this context can be understood for their intrinsic value and utility as a source of precious metal.

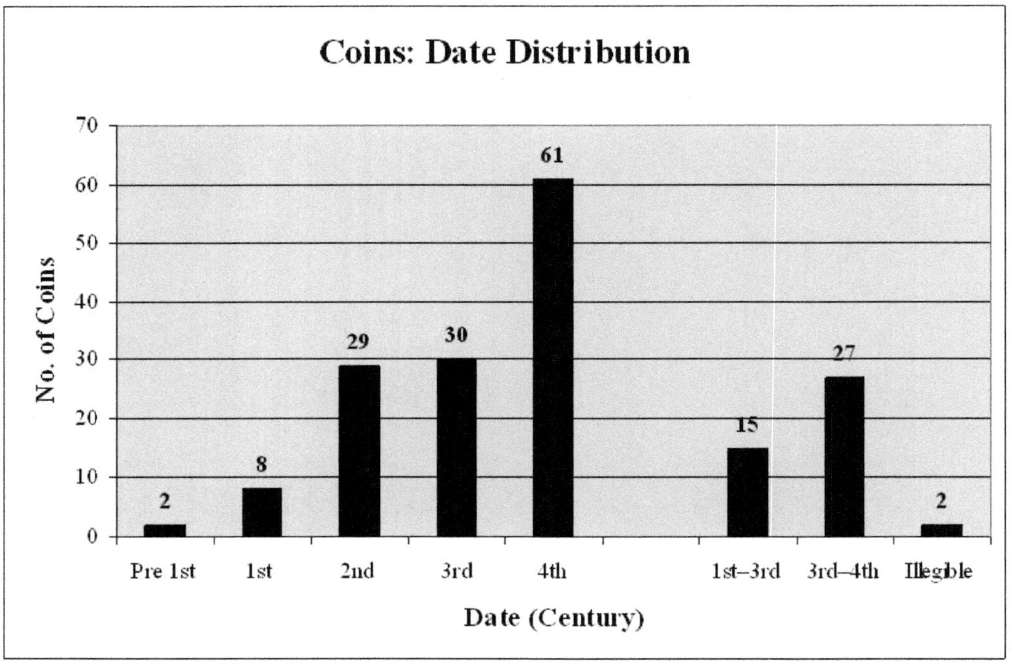

Fig. 7: Numbers of Roman coins as dated by century.

Perhaps the most informative aspect of coin analysis is to examine the distribution of coins by issue period (Reece 2003). Figure 8 presents this data as a bar chart, though it must be noted that the graph does not tabulate coin loss as is typical of numismatic charts. This is due to the unique nature of PAS data, composed here of the records from a number of sites each typically with between 1 and 5 coins scattered across a large area. Under such circumstances, these small samples per site do not allow a calculation of coin loss, let alone a comparison between sites. Therefore Figure 8 represents real numbers, and these numbers have been retained for further comparison of coin loss at the national and regional scales.

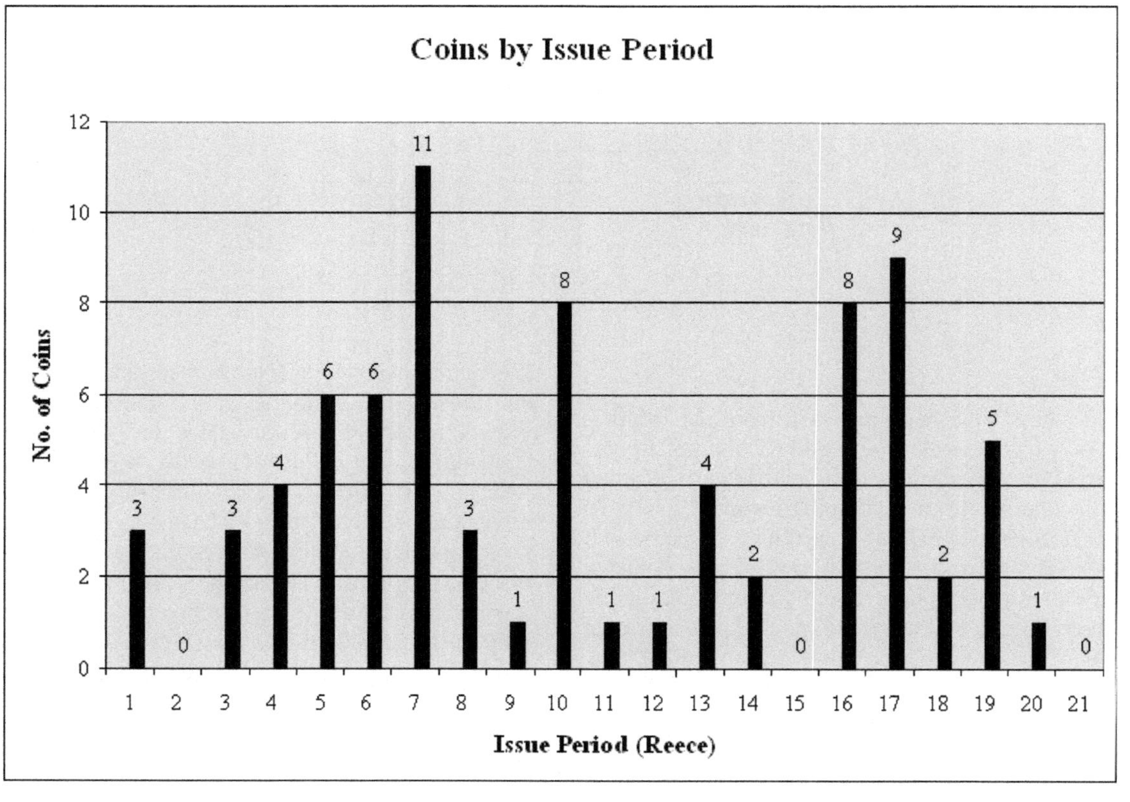

Fig. 8: Numbers of Roman coins by Reece Period: 1) to 41 AD; 2) 41–54 AD; 3) 54–69 AD; 4) 69–96 AD; 5) 96–117 AD; 6) 117–38 AD; 7) 138–61 AD; 8) 161–80 AD; 9) 180–93 AD; 10) 193–222 AD; 11) 222–38 AD; 12) 238–59 AD; 13) 259–75 AD; 14) 275–94 AD; 15) 294–317 AD; 16) 317–30 AD; 17) 330–48 AD; 18) 348–64 AD; 19) 364–78 AD; 20) 378–88 AD; 21) 388–402 AD.

It should be noted that Reece's issue periods were used, rather than the more typical preference for Casey's issue periods for northern sites (Casey 1994; Brickstock 2004). This is because Reece recorded pre-41 AD coins (not provided by Casey) and also because most of the 3rd-century coinage does not retain enough information to make full use of Casey's more specific issue periods for that century.

Plotting coins by issue period allows for a loose comparison to the national average of coin loss (Reece 1995) and the regional average of coin loss (Brickstock 2000) against the numbers of coins recorded by the PAS. The much larger scale of coin loss calculated as the national average distorts the picture and makes comparison difficult, though in general it can be said that proportionally, the numbers parallel each other. The most significant contrast occurs in issue period 21 (388-402 AD) which represents the final period of coin supply to Britain. Removing the national average from consideration demonstrates overall agreement between the regional average and PAS data, but there is a section of potential disagreement. The figures from issue period 3 to issue period 8, covering 69 to 180 AD differ. Notably, where the northern average has a Flavian peak in issue period 4 (69-96 AD), PAS data continues to climb and level out in the Trajanic and Hadrianic periods (issue periods 5 and 6) where the regional average declines. Both the PAS and regional data peak in the Antonine period (issue period 7) with a subsequent decline in issue period 8. This variation is probably distorted to some degree by the difference between the real numbers of PAS data and the calculated coin loss for the region, but there may be an underlying 'real' pattern here. Another pattern that may be worth investigating with PAS data is the northern trend toward lesser numbers of Theodosian coinage than is seen in the South (Brickstock 2000). Tentatively, this difference could be attributed to the northern military economy as it relates to taxation and small goods exchange.

Conclusions

Some basic conclusions can be reached from the analysis of PAS data. There is a clear bias of search areas investigated by metal-detectorists and some of the gaps in PAS findspots may be due either to a lack of searching or a lack of reporting. This is most evident in north-east Cumbria where there are practically no finds reported through the PAS. However, despite these biases PAS data still provides valuable information to the researcher. The basic proximity of PAS data to a Roman road or the coast (Fig. 1) is particularly interesting and continuing discoveries may reinforce or refute such an association. At present, no analysis has been completed on excavated finds assemblages by which to compare PAS data against, but such a comparison may be difficult given the different scales of artefact assemblages from excavations and a 'typical' PAS site in the North. Analysis of certain classes of artefact may prove beneficial, however, as was recently done with late Roman crossbow brooches (Collins 2010). Until more studies of this nature are completed in the region, however, seven basic conclusions have been reached:

1. There is a contrast between higher numbers of artefacts dated to the early Roman period and higher numbers of coins dated to the 4th century, which is a typical feature seen for the Roman period across Britain. Most of the early non-coins finds are brooches and other dress accessories that generally date to the 1st to 3rd centuries.

2. Objects (both coins and artefacts) dated to the 4th century seem to have a less extensive distribution in the area bounded to the north by Hadrian's Wall than objects from the previous centuries.

3. The distribution of different types of personal objects, notably brooches, suggests a possible east-west difference in terms of dress and personal appearance.

4. Despite the highly militarised occupation of the frontier, military objects are not frequently found. When they are found, it is almost always in proximity to military installations.

5. The date of recorded coins generally concurs with Brickstock's (2000) regional pattern of coin use, though not with the national pattern (Reece 1995).

6. Few high denomination coins (of silver or gold) have been found. Those that have been recorded all date to the early empire.

7. Less than half the coins could be attributed to an issue period; a figure that is significantly lower than the percentage from excavated sites. This is probably due to the fact that most PAS data is from land in agricultural use where ploughing and fertilisers regularly destabilise the depositional environment, while most Roman military installations in the north are Scheduled Monuments and protected from agricultural activity.

While these conclusions are rather general, they do offer an important validation of the patterns established through archaeological research in the frontier. More trends and patterns can be discerned through PAS data, but this requires a more focused approach, for example comparing individual classes of artefact from both excavated and PAS data. Future research might highlight the degree to which Roman objects permeated the non-military settlements of the frontier, or look for changes in the economic organisation of the frontier through an analysis of coinage. There are many more potential research topics and it is hoped this paper has demonstrated the value of the data available.

Postscript

Since the data for this paper was gathered, 20 January 2007, more than 850 objects of Roman date have been entered on the PAS database, more than doubling the dataset assessed for this paper. Despite this, many of the broad trends remain the same, though there are some important exceptions and changes that should be noted. A number of new findspots of Roman objects have been recorded, extending the distribution of Roman activity further from the road network, as noted above. There are a greater number of brooch types that have been found, with many of these found in Cumbria, reducing the east-west discrepancy somewhat. There have also been some important late coin discoveries, a clipped silver *siliqua* of the Arcadius or Honorius (395-402 AD) from Kendal, Cumbria (LANCUM-675EC3), and a group of eight *nummi* deposited in the 5th century, in Whittington, Northumberland (Collins 2008).

Acknowledgements

I am grateful to a number of individuals who advised me on various items that contributed to this paper including Sally Worrell, Sam Moorhead, Philippa Walton, Fraser Hunter and Lindsay Allason-Jones. As ever, any mistakes remain my own.

All maps have been produced using Edina digital mapping data and are published in accordance with permission to use such data.

Bibliography

Allason-Jones, L. and Bishop, M. 1988, *Excavations at Roman Corbridge: the hoard* (English Heritage, London).

Breeze, D. and Dobson, B. 2000, *Hadrian's Wall* (Penguin, London).

Brickstock, R. 2000, 'Coin supply in the north in the late Roman period', in Wilmott, T. and Wilson, P. (eds.), *The Late Roman Transition in the North*, British Archaeology Reports 299 (Archaeopress, Oxford), 33-37.

Brickstock, R. 2004, *The Production, Analysis, and Standardisation of Romano-British Coin Reports* (English Heritage, London).

Casey, P. J. 1994, *Roman Coinage in Britain* (Shire, Princes Risborough).

Collins, R. 2008. 'The latest Roman coin from Hadrian's Wall: A small 5th century purse group', *Britannia* 39, 256-261.

Collins, R. 2010, 'Brooch use in the 4th-5th century frontier', in Collins, R. and Allason-Jones, L. (eds.), *Finds from the Frontier: material culture in the 4th-5th centuries* (Council for British Archaeology, York).

Crummy, N. 1983, *The Roman Small Finds from Excavations in Colchester 1971–9*, Colchester Archaeological Report 2 (Colchester Archaeological Trust, Colchester).

Evans, J. 2000, 'The end of Roman pottery in the north', in Wilmott, T. and Wilson, P. (eds.), *The Late Roman Transition in the North*, British Archaeology Reports 299 (Archaeopress, Oxford), 39-46.

Reece, R. 1995, 'Site-finds in Roman Britain', *Britannia* 26, 179-206.

Reece, R. 2003, *Roman Coins and Archaeology: collected papers*, Collection Moneta 32 (Moneta, Wetteren).

Stallibrass, S. 2000, 'Cattle, culture, soldiers and status', in Fincham, G., Harrison, G., Rodgers Holland, R. and Revell, L. (eds.), *Transactions of the Roman Archaeology Conference* 1999 (Oxbow, Oxford), 64-73.

Stallibrass, S. and Huntley, J. P. 1995, *Plant and Vertebrate Remains from Archaeological Sites in Northern England: date reviews and future directions*, Architectural and Archaeological Society of Durham and Northumberland Research Report 4 (Architectural and Archaeological Society of Durham and Northumberland, Durham).

Whittaker, C. R. 1994, *Frontiers of the Roman Empire: a social and economic study* (John Hopkins University Press, Baltimore).

Wilmott, T. 1997, *Birdoswald: excavations of a Roman fort on Hadrian's Wall and its successor settlements* 1987-92, English Heritage Archaeology Report 14 (English Heritage, London).

Expanding the Frontiers: how the Portable Antiquities Scheme database increases knowledge of Roman coin use in England

Sam Moorhead

This paper is intended to highlight the enormous value of the Portable Antiquities Scheme (PAS) database for the study of Roman coinage in Britain. To date (May 2007), over 47,000 Roman coins have been recorded on the database, the largest artefact type from any period. There are numerous ways in which these finds can be studied, from the consideration of particular coins of interest to the use of broad statistical analyses which have been pioneered by scholars like Richard Reece (1972; 1973; 1987; 1995; 2002) and John Casey (1986; 1994; Casey and Reece 1988). This article provides some pointers towards potential research that can be carried out using the PAS data.

Fig. 1: Gold aureus of Carinus (283-5 AD), from Nottinghamshire (DENO-3B3AF6) (diameter: 19mm) (Mattingly et al. 1923-94, RIC V: no. 312).

Fig. 2: Silver denarius of Carausius (286-93 AD) with unpublished VICTORIA AVG reverse, from Norfolk (NMS-784AF4) (diameter: c. 19mm) not recorded in RIC.

Coins of particular interest

The vast majority of the coins recorded are pieces already listed in the standard catalogues (Crawford 1974; Mattingley *et al.* 1923-94; Mattingley *et al.* 1923-94; Carson, Hill and Kent 1965; Besly and Bland 1983; Bland and Burnett 1988). However, a number of new varieties and rare coins have been found. Many of the most interesting pieces are recorded in the annual Coin Register of the *British Numismatic Journal* and in the *Portable Antiquities Scheme Annual Reports.* Recent finds of note include: a gold *aureus* of Carinus (Fig. 1, DENO-3B3AF6), for which only one other specimen (from different dies) is known; an unpublished type for a *denarius* of Carausius with VICTORIA AVG reverse (Fig. 2, NMS-784AF4); a medallion of Antoninus Pius (Fig. 3, SUSS-5C54B2; Gnecchi 1912: no. 66; Worrell 2007: 343, no. 41, fig. 42); and a unique *cliché* coin of Tetricus I (Fig. 4; FASA-FC2B63). Possibly more important is the increasing number of finds of coins which are rarely found outside of hoards, for example Republican silver coins of which over 400 have been recorded from across the country (see Spatial Analysis section below and Map 6). Also, there are many coins which rarely appear in hoards, notably barbarous pieces. There is, for example, scope for an interesting study of the copies of Severan period *denarii* recorded on the PAS database.

The general picture

The publication of site-finds, that is coins from excavations, field-walking and metal-detecting, has until recent decades been less thorough than that for coin hoards (see Robertson 2000; *Coin Hoards from Roman Britain* 1979-2002; Abdy 2002). There are some notable excavation reports, catalogues in county journals, but only a few regional syntheses (see Brickstock 1987; Shotter 1990; Davies and Gregory 1991; Plouviez 1995; Moorhead 2001a; Moorhead 2001b; Guest and Wells 2007). {1} It is fortunate there is a corpus of coins from 140 sites compiled by Richard Reece (1991), which includes 168,828 coins. This work does not by any means cover all of the published site-finds from Britain, but it is still a very large sample. The 45,000 PAS coins might seem rather small against Reece's corpus but initial analysis shows this is misleading. Firstly, one needs to remember that Reece's corpus contains 50,767 coins from Richborough, thus reducing the total to fewer than 120,000. Secondly, and more importantly, Reece's corpus has a heavy emphasis on military and urban sites. The 45,000 PAS Roman coins mostly come from rural sites, many of them undetermined. Reece only records 21,621 coins from rural settlements and 12,821 from temple sites. This presents a total of 34,442 coins from predominantly rural sites which falls way below the 45,000 PAS coins. Therefore, in very broad terms it is possible to argue that the PAS coin data provides a highly significant source of information for the study of coin finds from rural Roman Britain, as well as a complementary dataset to Reece's corpus.

Reliability and validity of the PAS data

Enormous effort has been expended to ensure the quality of the data recorded on the PAS database. Training of the Finds Liaison Officers (FLOs) is core to the activity of the National Finds Advisers. With the added provision of photographs for many objects, experts are able to edit records more effectively. There is also the problem of the presentation of coins to FLOs which have clearly not been found in Britain, but the numbers involved appear to be few - this issue is discussed further below in the section on Byzantine and exotic coins.

However, most important is the validity of the data for statistical analysis. The author has tested the data by comparing PAS assemblages with past research. In an earlier study the author analysed 10,550 coins from 44 sites (in 35 parishes) in Wiltshire (Moorhead 2001b). For Wiltshire, the PAS database records 890 coins from up to 90 sites (in 51 parishes). {2} Immediately, it is clear that the PAS records provide a broader sweep of the county, but the assemblages tend to be much smaller (Maps 1 and 2; Tables 1 and 2).

Consideration of the larger PAS groups shows that they do generally follow the trends expected. Two examples will suffice. The northern half of Wiltshire has a significantly high number of coins of the House of Valentinian which has been discussed in some length elsewhere (Moorhead 2001a: 164-6, 225-34; Moorhead 2001b: 90-5). The site at West Lavington fits perfectly into this pattern when compared with the neighbouring rural settlements at Euridge and Broad Hinton; all sites peaking in Period 19 (364-78 AD) (Figs. 5-8 and Map 4).

Fig. 3: Copper-alloy medallion of Antoninus Pius (138-61 AD) showing the Capitoline Triad, from Sussex (SUSS-5C54B2) (diameter: 38mm).

Fig. 4: Two halves of a copper-alloy cliché coin imitating a radiate of Tetricus I (271-4 AD), from Essex (FASA-FC2B63) (diameter: c. 18mm).

Lacock	50
Verlucio	858
Calstone	135
Mother Anthony's Well	552
Urchfont	372
Eastcroft Farm	12
Total	**1,979**

Table 1: Groups of detector finds published in 2001 (Moorhead 2001b: 100-04).

Kington Langley	21
Wanborough	14
Great Bedwyn	20
West Lavington	384
Winterbourne Stoke (various locations	14
Salisbury (SU 131314)	31
Salisbury (no NGR)	16
Pitton and Farley (various locations)	50
Total	**550**

Table 2: Larger assemblages of detector finds recorded on the PAS database (by September 2006).

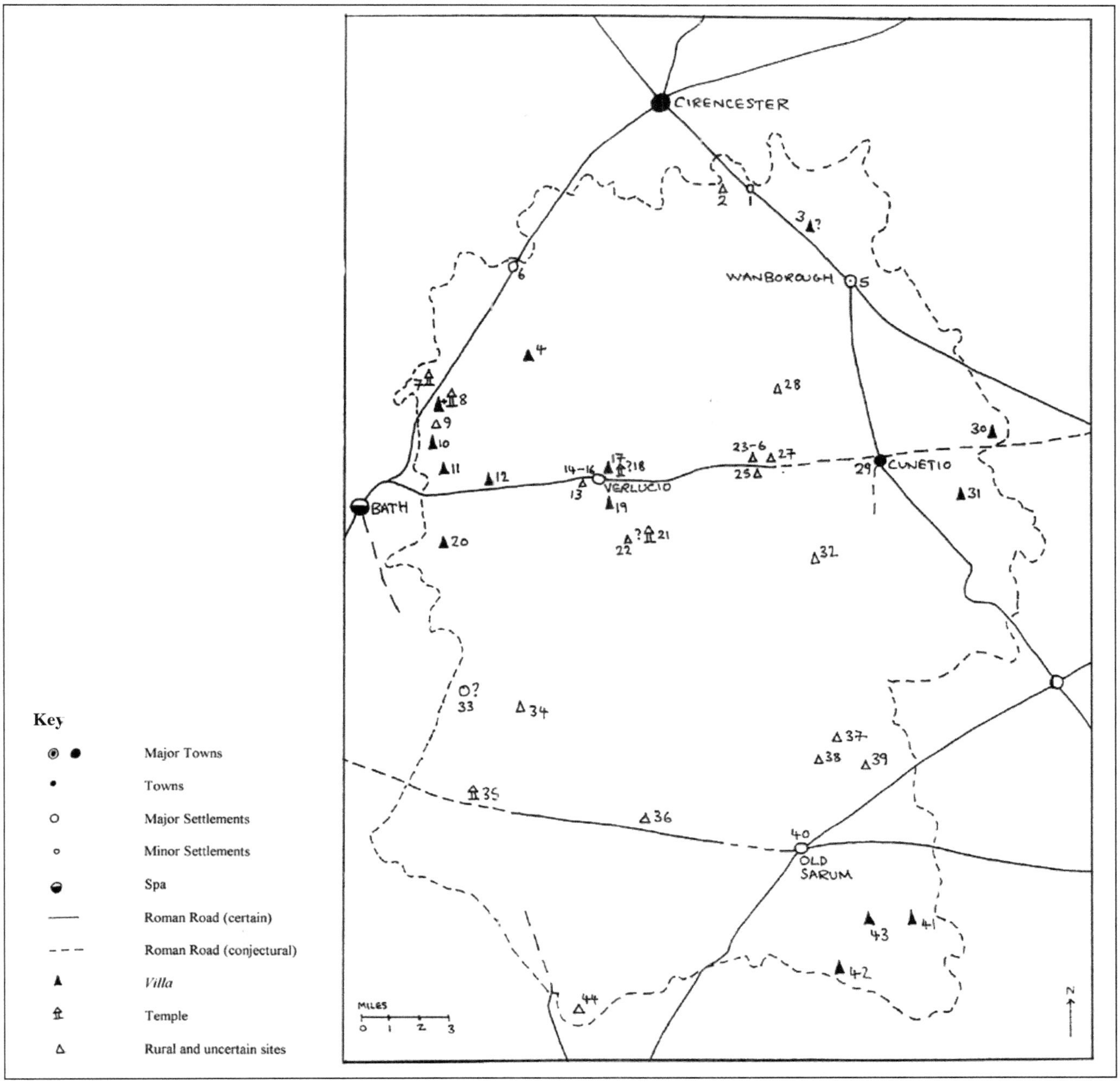

Map 1: 44 sites in Wiltshire used in the study of Roman coins (Moorhead 2001b: 117).

Reece Periods used in analysis for this paper {3}

1	pre-AD 43
2	AD 41-54
3	54-68
4	69-96
5	96-117
6	117-138
7	138-161
8	161-180
9	180-193
10	193-222
11	222-238
12	238-260
13	260-275
14	275-296
15	296-317
16	317-330
17	330-348
18	348-364
19	364-378
20	378-388
21	388-402

Furthermore, moving to south-east Wiltshire there is a trend amongst sites that shows a marked decline in coin-loss after 350 AD; a phenomenon that appears to creep into parts of Hampshire and Dorset (Moorhead 2001a: 167-8, 235-6; Moorhead 2001b: 95-6). This phenomenon is notable at the villas of Downton, West Dean and East Grimstead, but is now also shown by the PAS finds from Pitton and Farley (Figs. 9-11 and Map 3).

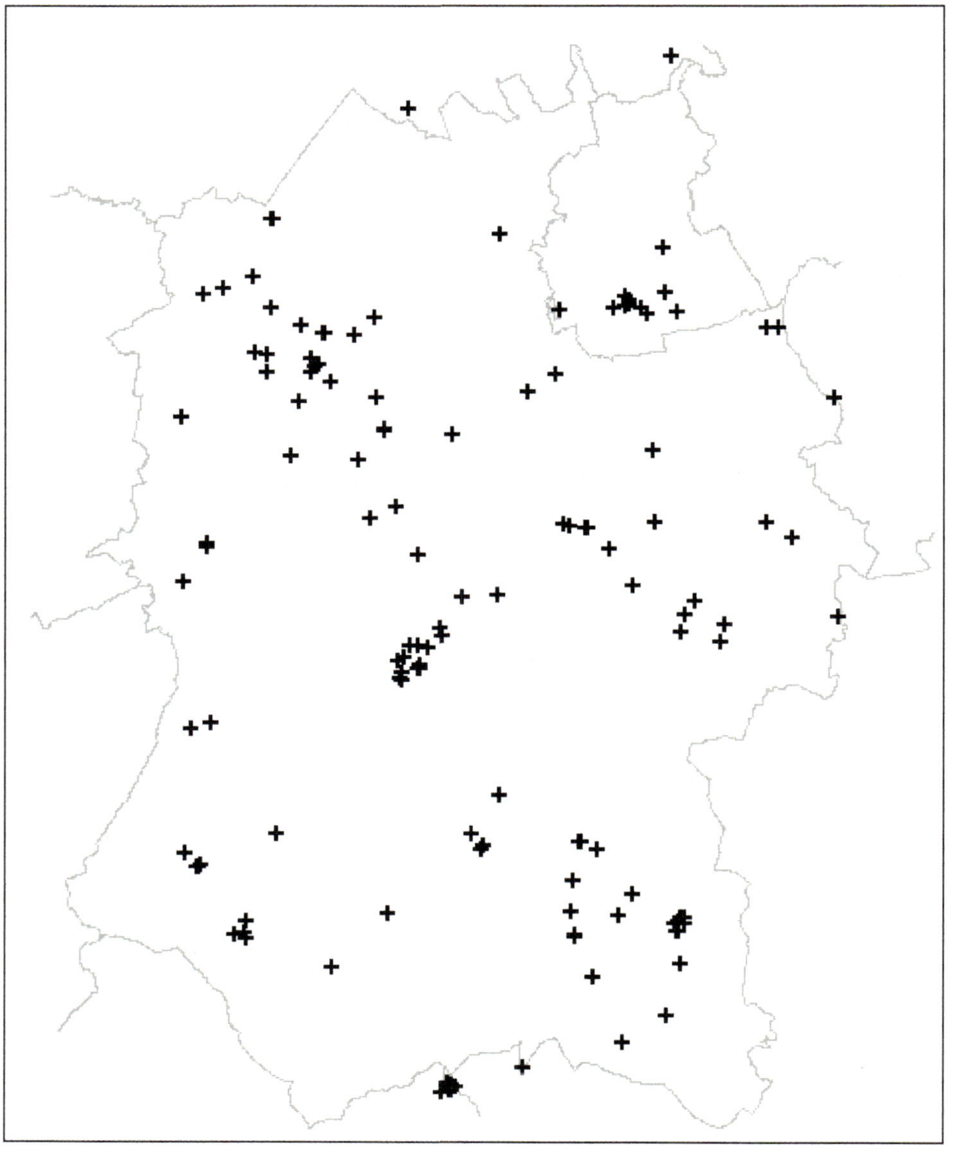

Map 2: 90 sites in Wiltshire that have yielded Roman coins which are recorded on the PAS database (as of September 2006), showing a wider distribution of finds than in Moorhead's study (see Map 1).

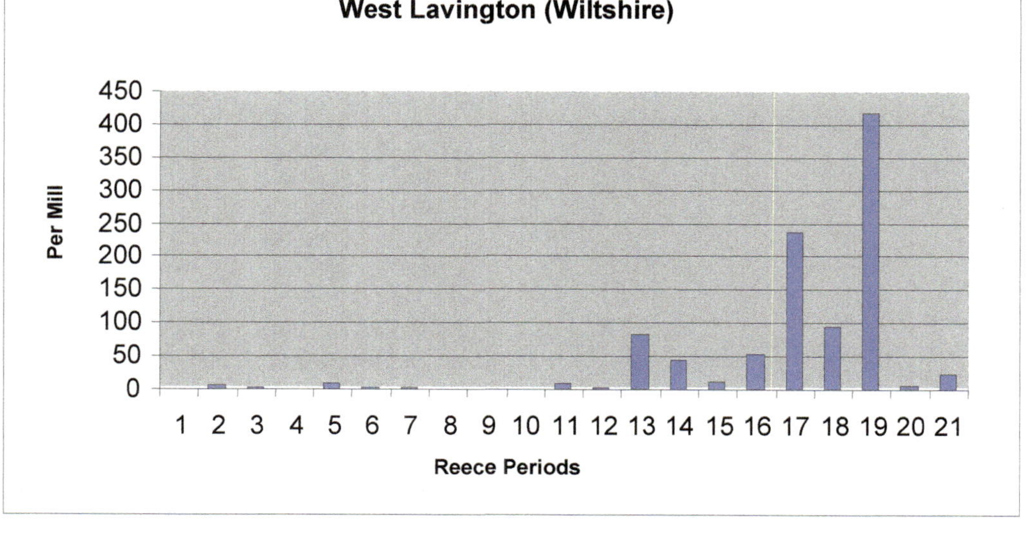

Fig. 5: Bar-chart showing coins (per mill) by period for West Lavington, Wiltshire (PAS; sample size: 384 coins), showing a peak in the Valentinianic period (19: AD364-78).

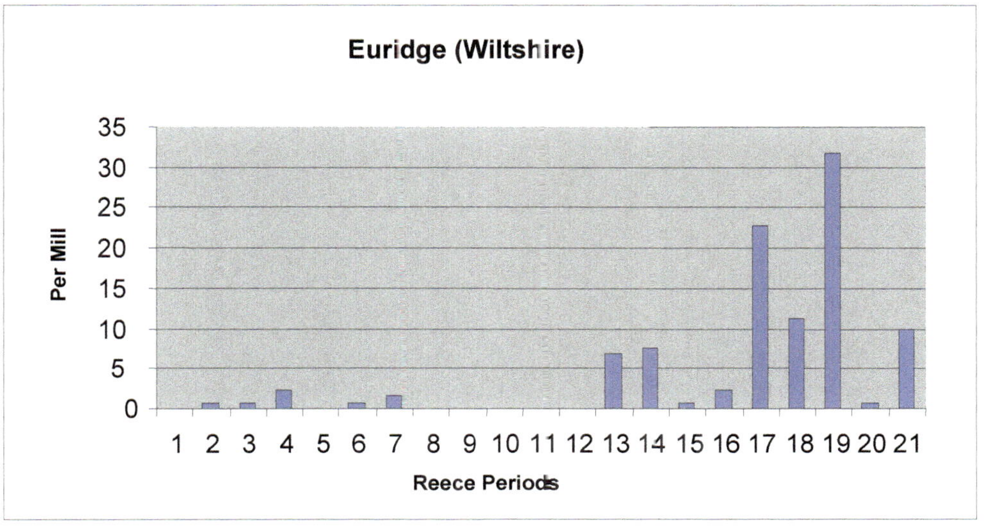

Fig. 6: Bar-chart showing coins (per mill) by period for Euridge, Wiltshire (Moorhead 2001a: 140 (sample size 132 coins), showing a peak in the Valentinianic period 19 (364-78 AD).

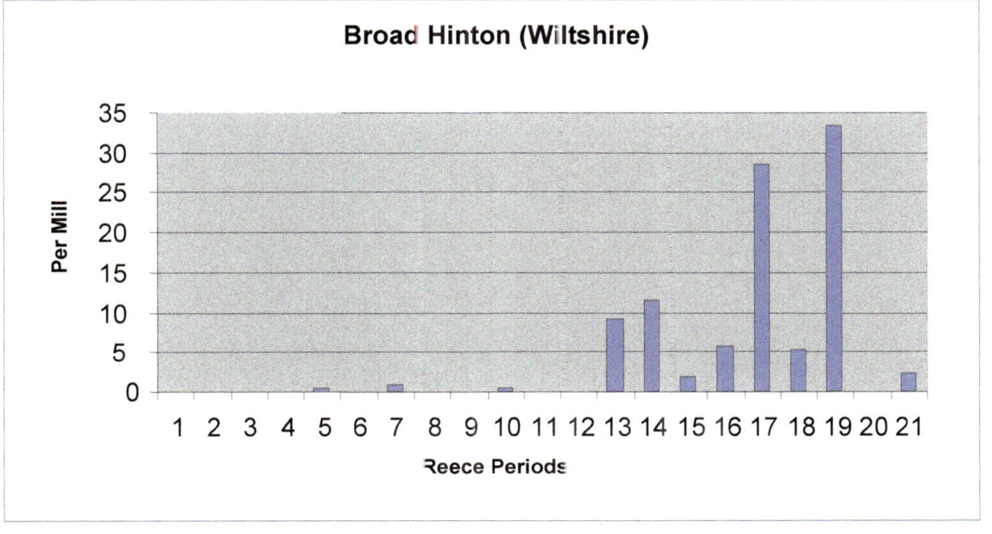

Fig. 7: Bar-chart showing coins (per mill) by period for Broad Hinton, Wiltshire (Moorhead 2001a: 146) (sample size 207 coins), showing a peak in the Valentinianic period 19 (364-78 AD).

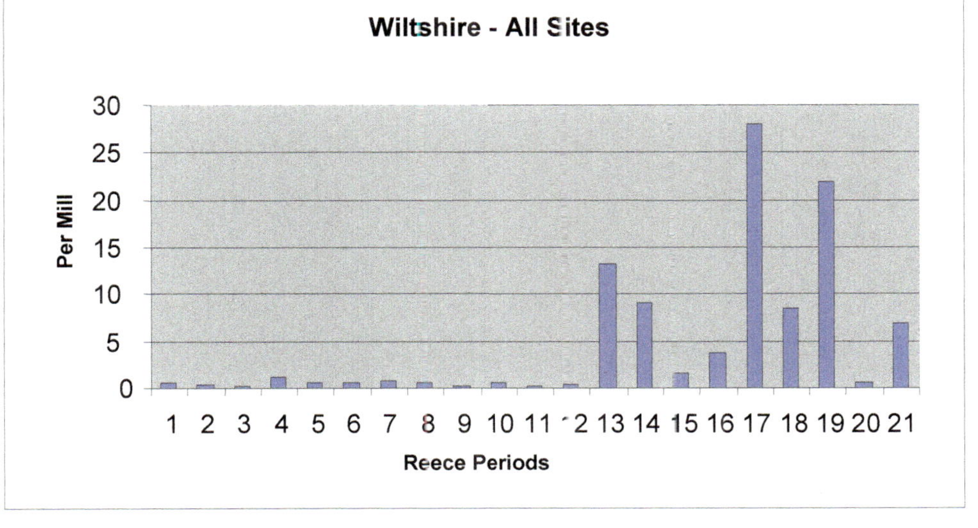

Fig. 8: Bar-chart showing coins (per mill) by period for all Wiltshire sites (Moorhead 2001a: 136) (sample size 10,550 coins), showing a peak in period 17 (330-48 AD) and a significant peak in the Valentinianic period 19 (364-78 AD).

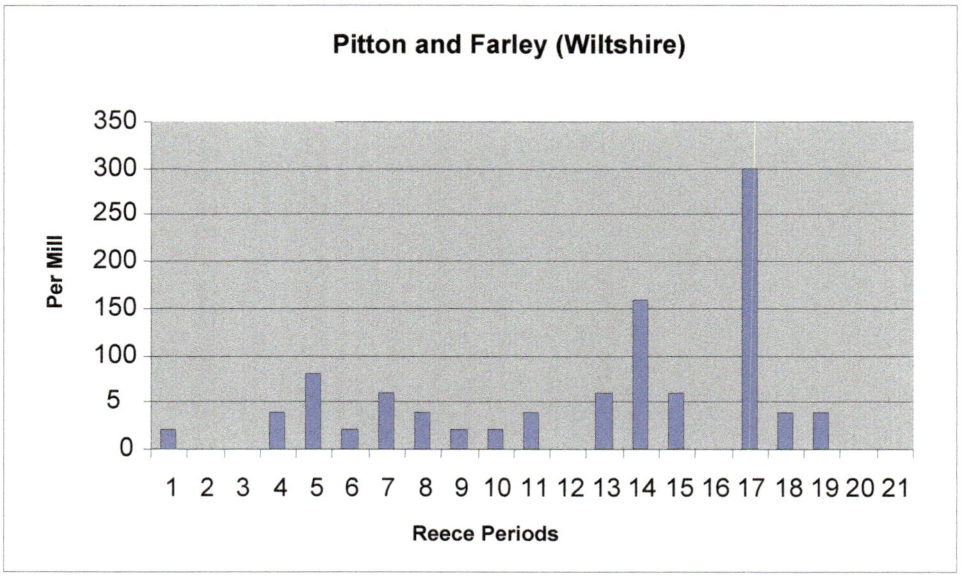

Fig. 9: Bar-chart showing coins (per mill) by period for Pitton and Farley, Wiltshire (PAS: sample size 50 coins), showing a marked decline after period 17 (330-48 AD).

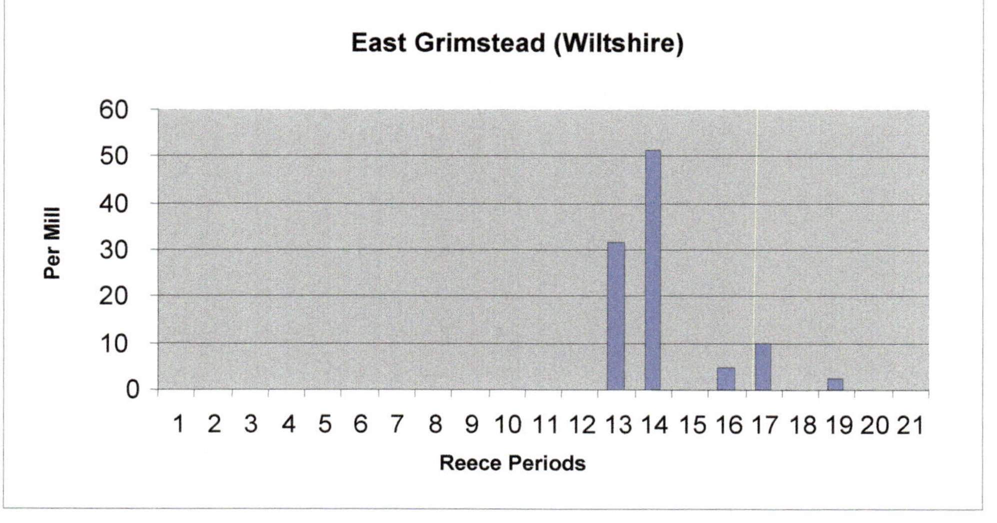

Fig. 10: Bar-chart showing coins (per mill) by period for East Grimstead villa, Wiltshire (Moorhead 2001a: 149) (sample size 41 coins), showing a marked decline after period 17 (330-48 AD).

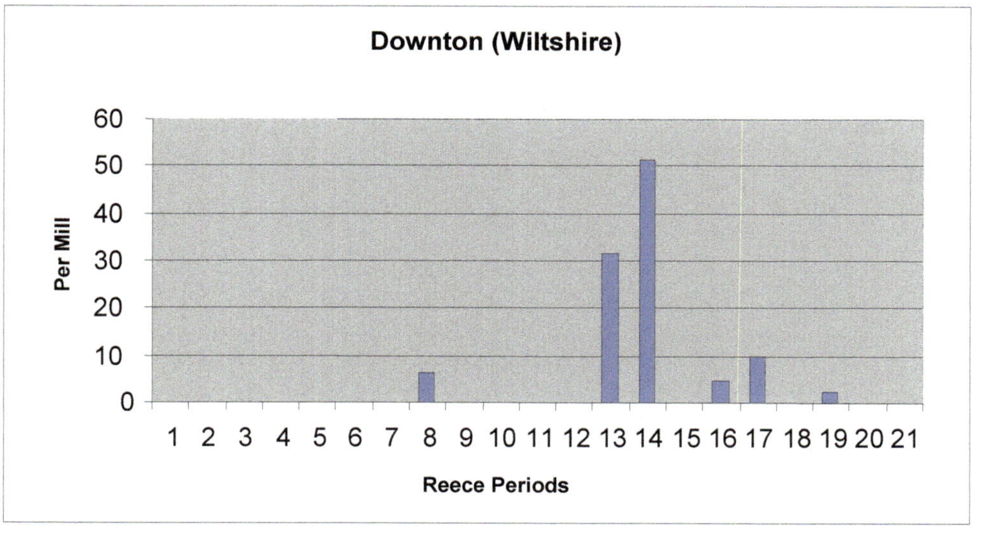

Fig. 11: Bar-chart showing coins (per mill) by period for Downton villa, Wiltshire (Moorhead 2001a: 149) (sample size 16 coins), showing no coins after period 17 (330-48 AD).

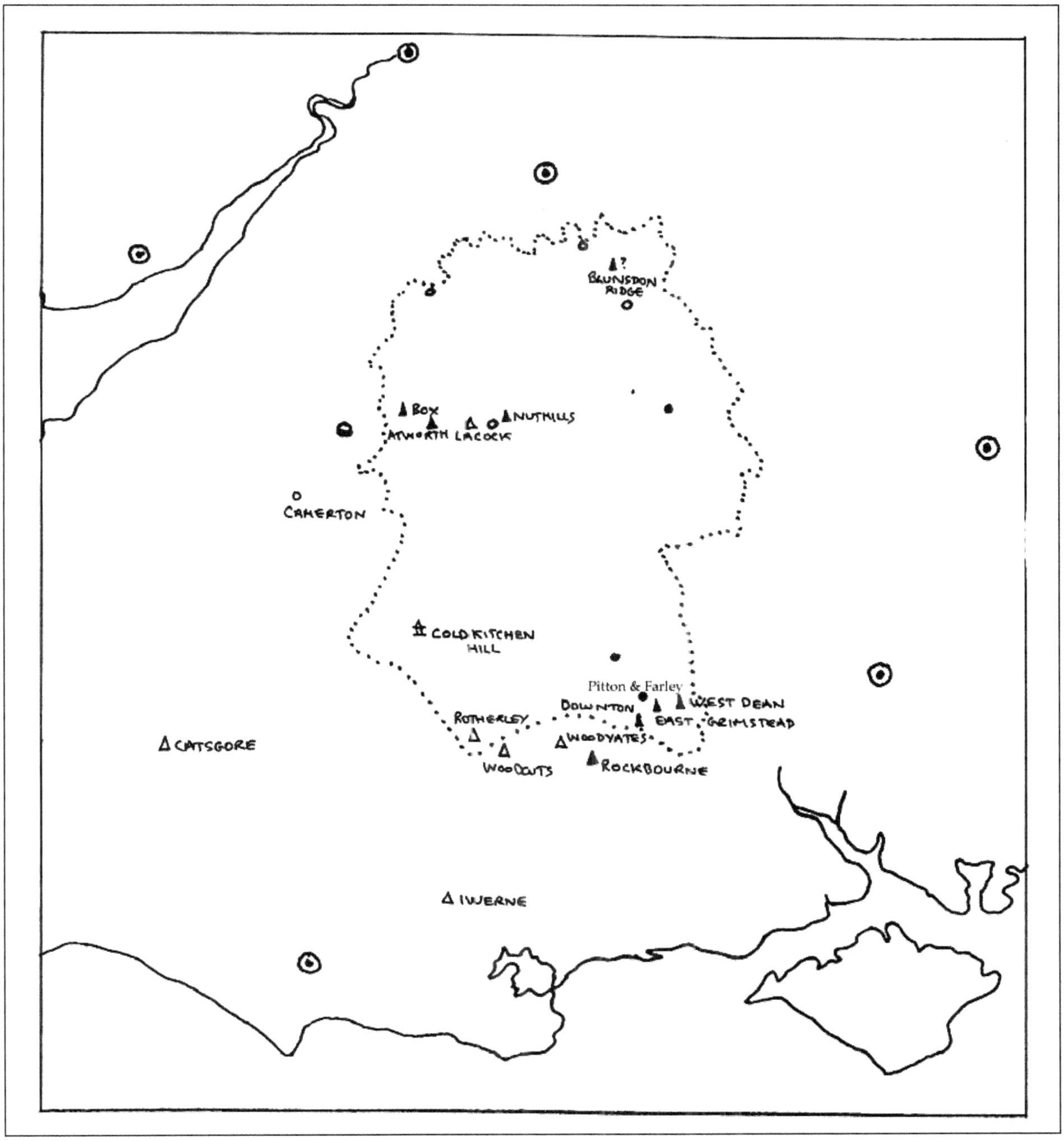

Map 3: Sites in Wiltshire and surrounding counties which show a marked decline in post-348 AD coins found (Moorhead 2001a: 201) with Pitton and Farley added.

Finally in Wiltshire, one anomalous southern site at Butterfield Down was shown to have the north Wiltshire Valentinianic peak.{4} About two miles to the east, over the border in Hampshire, initial analysis of the PAS coins found at Nether Wallop show the same phenomenon (Figs 12-13, Map 4). {5} Both these sites appear to be large sprawling rural settlements that flourish until late in the 4th century, as opposed to villa sites like Downton, West Dean and East Grimstead which decline earlier. Across Britain, the PAS records are identifying large, poorly defined rural settlements which have previously lain undetected.

These examples from Wiltshire do show that larger assemblages (at least of 12 coins; preferably over 20) do suggest that the data is valid when tested against previous research. The same is the case in Suffolk where a comparison of PAS finds from Wenhaston with Mells Hamlet with published finds from Hacheston show a similar profile with a peak in Period 17 and swift decline thereafter (Figs. 14-5). This is a phenomenon which Judith Plouviez (1995; identification work by Faye Minter) has identified in East Suffolk.

It is clear that where there are significant samples, statistical analysis is possible. However, it is clear from the study of the PAS data in Wiltshire that there are many cases where only a few (generally better preserved or more collectable) coins have been recorded from a parish or site.

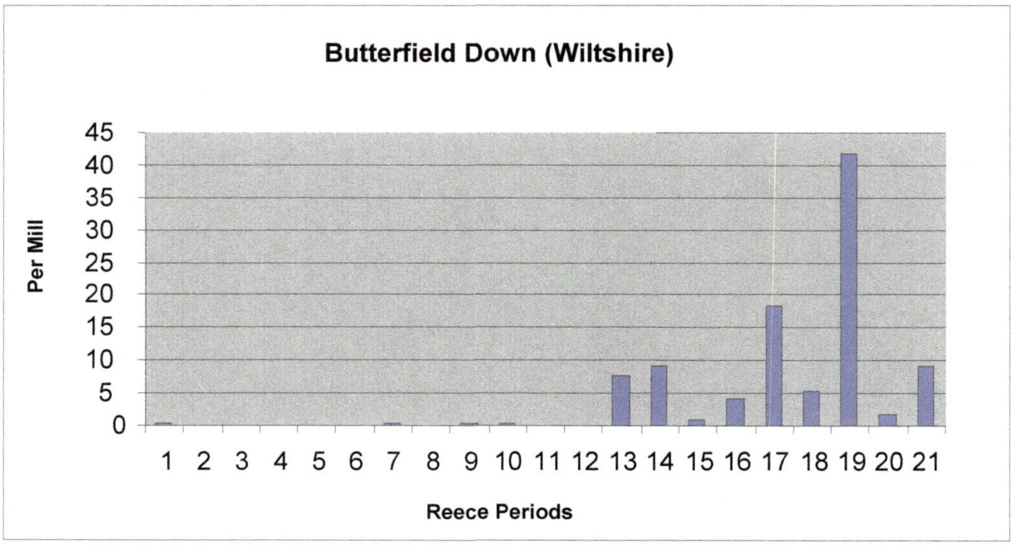

Fig. 12: Bar-chart showing coins (per mill) by period for Butterfield Down, Wiltshire (Moorhead 2001a: 1489) (sample size 692 coins), showing a peak in the Valentinianic period 19 (364-78 AD).

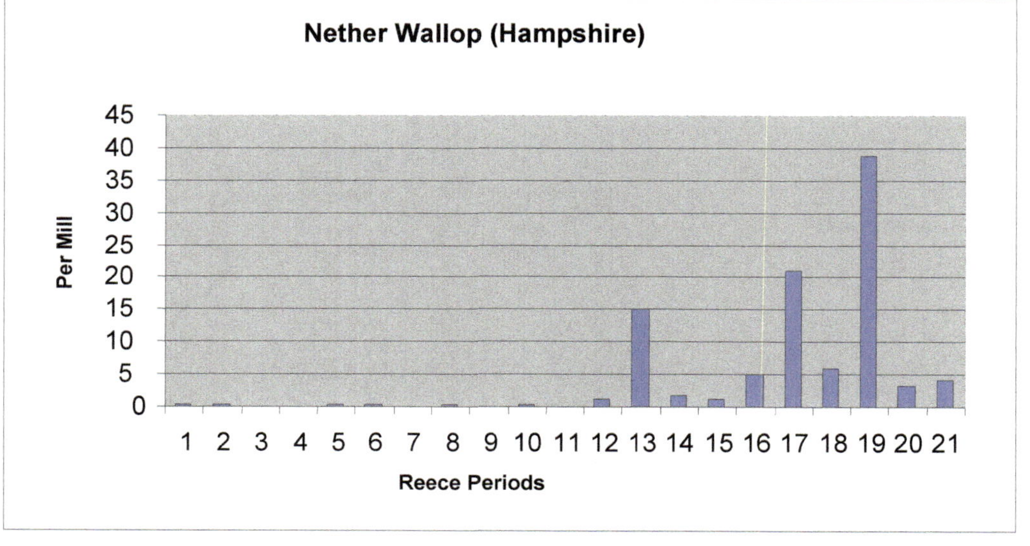

Fig. 13: Bar-chart showing coins (per mill) by period for Nether Wallop, Hampshire (sample size 265 coins), showing a peak in the Valentinianic period 19 (364-78 AD) similar to that at Butterfield Down (see Fig. 7).

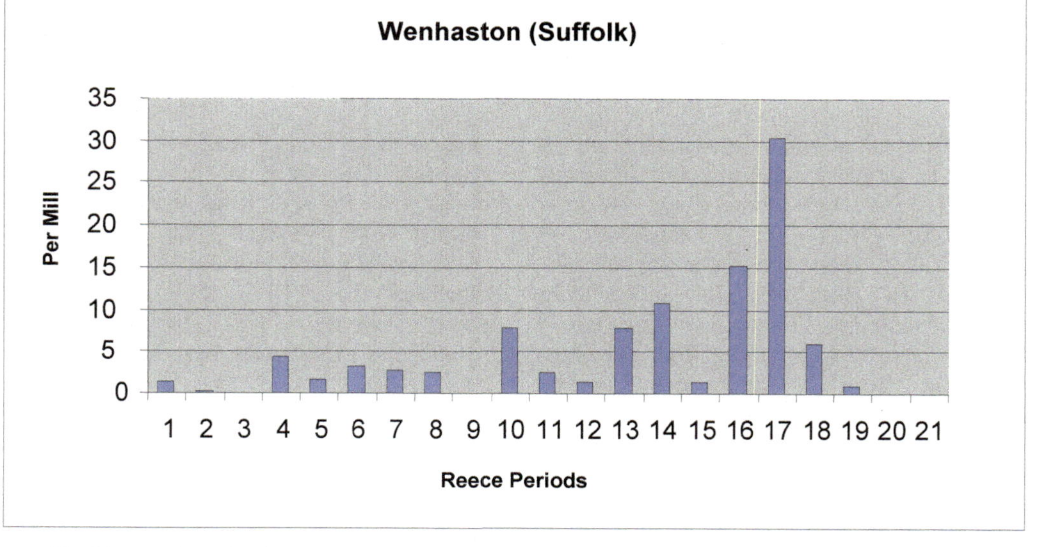

Fig. 14: Bar-chart showing coins (per mill) by period for Wenhaston, Suffolk (PAS sample size 369 coins), showing a marked decline after period 17 (330-348 AD).

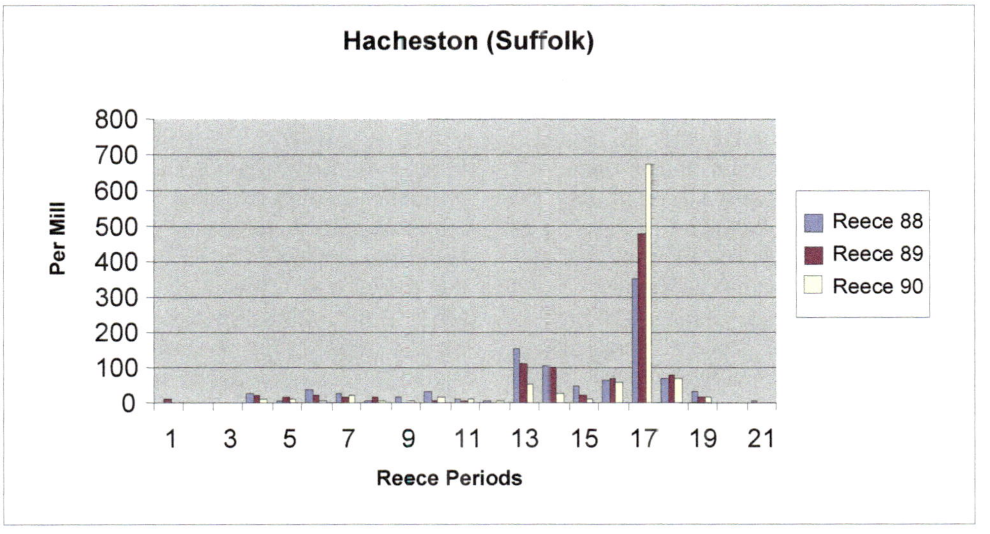

Fig. 15: Bar-chart showing three groups of coins (per mill) by period from Hacheston, Suffolk (Reece 1991: nos. 88-90), showing a marked decline after period 17 (330-48 AD).

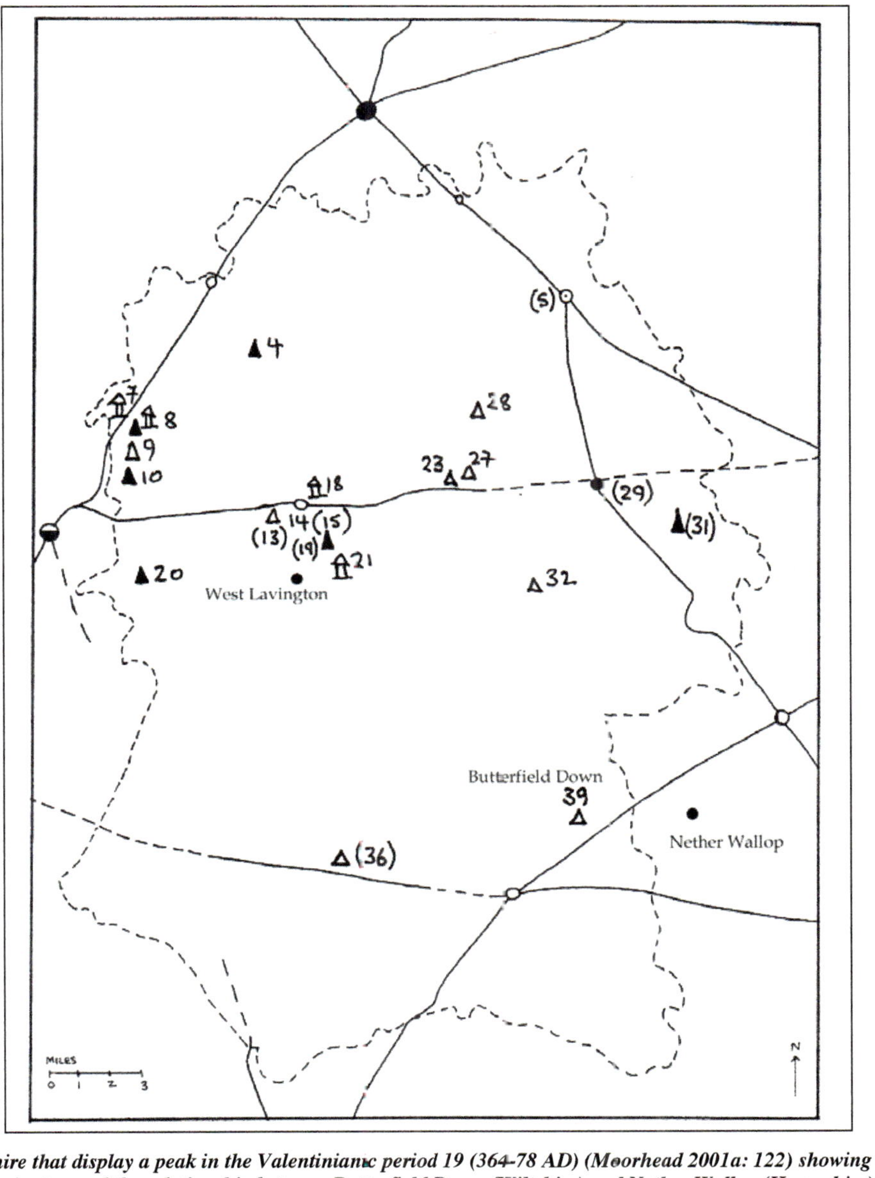

Map 4: Sites in Wiltshire that display a peak in the Valentinianic period 19 (364-78 AD) (Moorhead 2001a: 122) showing the new site at West Lavington and the relationship between Butterfield Down (Wiltshire) and Nether Wallop (Hampshire).

Following this up with Katie Hinds (Wiltshire FLO) and then discussing with other FLOs, the presence of an enormous number of poorly preserved (generally 260-402 AD) coins (normally termed 'grots') which were not being declared by finders or recorded onto the database was recognised. It is essential that these coins are recorded where possible, especially if they can be assigned to Reece periods. The exclusion of 'grot' will often lead to a blank for periods 20 and 21 (378-402 AD) when the coins are small, often poorly struck, and generally worn. Furthermore, these coins often have a high lead content and are therefore prone to a high degree of corrosion. The author has mounted a major campaign to have these coins recorded and it is already reaping benefits - over 300 coins from an important villa site in Hertfordshire have already been secured. {6} There is also another potential advantage for detectorists in declaring such coins - an unrecorded coin that had been deemed unimportant by its finder has turned out to be an extremely rare *denarius* of Augustus of which there is only one published example (from Paris) (IOW-0D5931) (*RIC* vol. I, no. 542). The author has been addressing detector clubs about the need to record all coins so as to add more sites with statistically valid assemblages.

Spatial Analysis

Because so many coins are recorded with precise findspots, often to 8-figure National Grid References (NGRs), it is possible to use GIS technology to construct distribution maps. The applications will be limitless, but two general examples with suffice.

It is interesting to note strong similarities between the distribution of the PAS Roman coin finds with the distribution of villas in England (Maps 5-6). This, given the rural nature of the PAS data, is as might be expected. However, there are areas, such as East Anglia and central Kent, where the patterns do differ.

For a long time there has been generally informal debate about the circulation of Roman Republican *denarii* in Iron Age Britain. We know from hoards that these coins could circulate as late as the 3rd century AD, although most were driven from circulation by debasements in the 1st and 2nd century. However, it is strongly stated that there was no mining of silver in Britain prior to the Roman Conquest and, indeed, the presence of a significant amount of silver in Iron Age Britain only seems to start with the contacts with the Roman world from the time of Caesar's campaigns in the 50s BC (Craddock 1995: 214; Northover 1992: 253ff.; Matthew Ponting, pers. comm.) {7}. Furthermore, other than the use of the odd piece of silverware, like the cup found in the Welwyn Garden City burial, the major source of silver in Iron Age Britain would have been continental silver coins, the *denarius* becoming the major denomination from the later 1st century BC. Therefore, we might assume that Republican and early Imperial *denarii* were melted down to provide the large silver coinages of rulers like Cunobelinus, Tincomarus and Verica, not to mention the massive silver issues of database, other voids will undoubtedly also be filled.

regions further north such as the Iceni. However, there still appear to be no Roman *denarii* in a secure pre-Conquest context. Can the PAS data help? Map 7 shows all the Iron Age coins recorded on the Celtic Coin Index (CCI, which includes PAS finds: http://www.finds.org.uk/CCI). Map 8 shows all of the Republican coins recorded on the PAS database. Upon initial inspection, the patterns are similar with the bulk of the coins coming from the 'lowland zone' to the east of the Fosse Way. However, looking more closely at the Republican coin distribution it is possible to see a larger, more distinct, group of coins in the Cheshire/Lancashire region, and another group moving up the Vale of York towards a scatter on the Hadrianic frontier. When one then compares the Republican map with a map showing all Roman coin finds (Map 5), it is possible to see that these two groups fit neatly into the Roman coin finds pattern. This does not mean that all the Republican coins were lost in the Roman period, but it suggests that a large number were.

Filling the Void

The author was asked by Rachel Atherton (Derbyshire and Nottinghamshire FLO) to comment upon the Roman coin finds from Nottinghamshire in November 2006. There were then 1,535 Roman coins from the county on the PAS database. Six sites were identified, totalling 917 coins: Sutton (29), Thorpe (53), East Stoke (85), Orston (72), Thoroton (574) and Shelton (104) with substantial assemblages to analyse, although time precluded a thorough edit of the material.

Taken individually all of these sites have profiles which are plausible for Roman Britain with few pre- 260 AD coins and peaks in periods 13, 17 and 19. Figure 16 shows the profile for Thoroton which has the largest assemblage of the group. However, what became clear was that there was a dearth of comparative material: there are no Nottinghamshire sites in Reece's corpus. Therefore, the PAS data was helping to fill an apparent void in evidence for Roman coin loss in this part of Britain. This led the author to combine these six sites and to construct Figure 17, which provides a profile for Nottinghamshire, set against Reece's national profile. What it shows is interesting. Although the Nottinghamshire region was incorporated into the Province in the Flavian period, it lacks the significant peak for coins in period 4 (69-96 AD). In fact, there are very few coins prior to the expected peak of coins in period 13 (260-75 AD). There is a slight peak in period 7 (138-61 AD) a phenomenon which occurs on many rural sites and is discussed below (see Flavian and Antonine peaks, below). The interpretation of the coin finds from these six sites suggests a region which is only heavily monetised in the later Roman period (330-78 AD), a phenomenon shared with many rural regions in other parts of the Province. Thanks to the PAS data, we are at least able to start considering a county for which there are few previous records. As work progresses with the PAS database, other voids will undoubtedly also be filled.

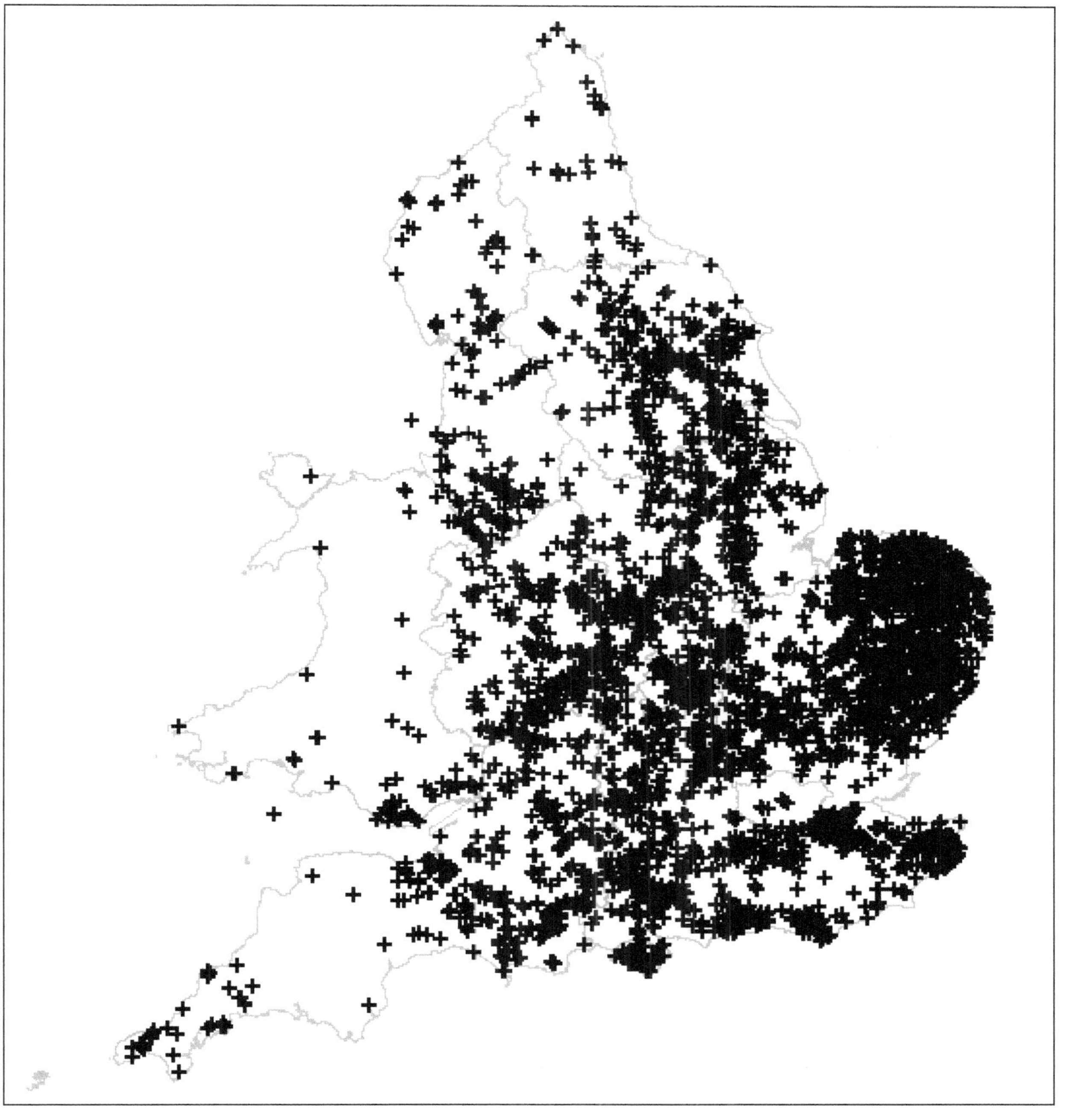

Map 5. Distribution of all Roman coins on the PAS database (April 2007; sample size c. 46,000 coins).

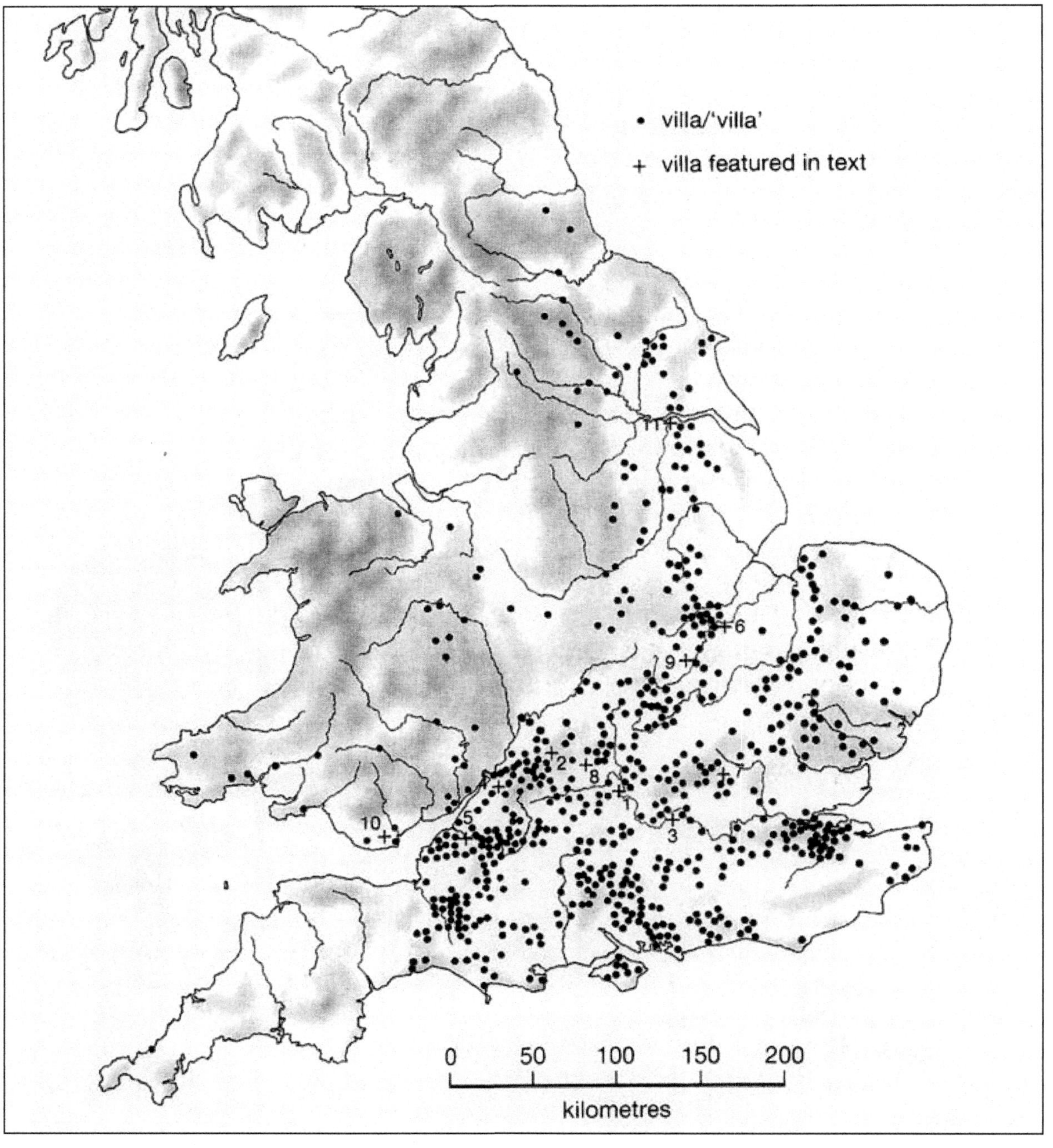

Map 6: Distribution of villas in Roman Britain (taken from Jones and Mattingly 2002: Map 7:6).

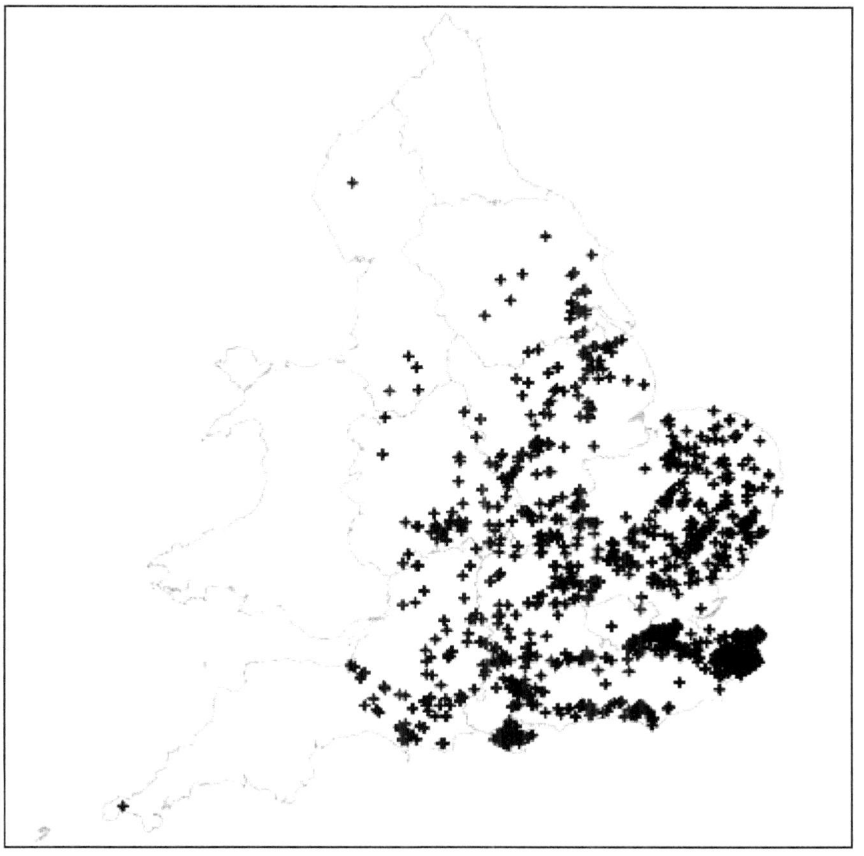

Map 7: A map showing the find-spots of all Iron Age coins on the Celtic Coin Index (April 2007; sample 37,839 coins).

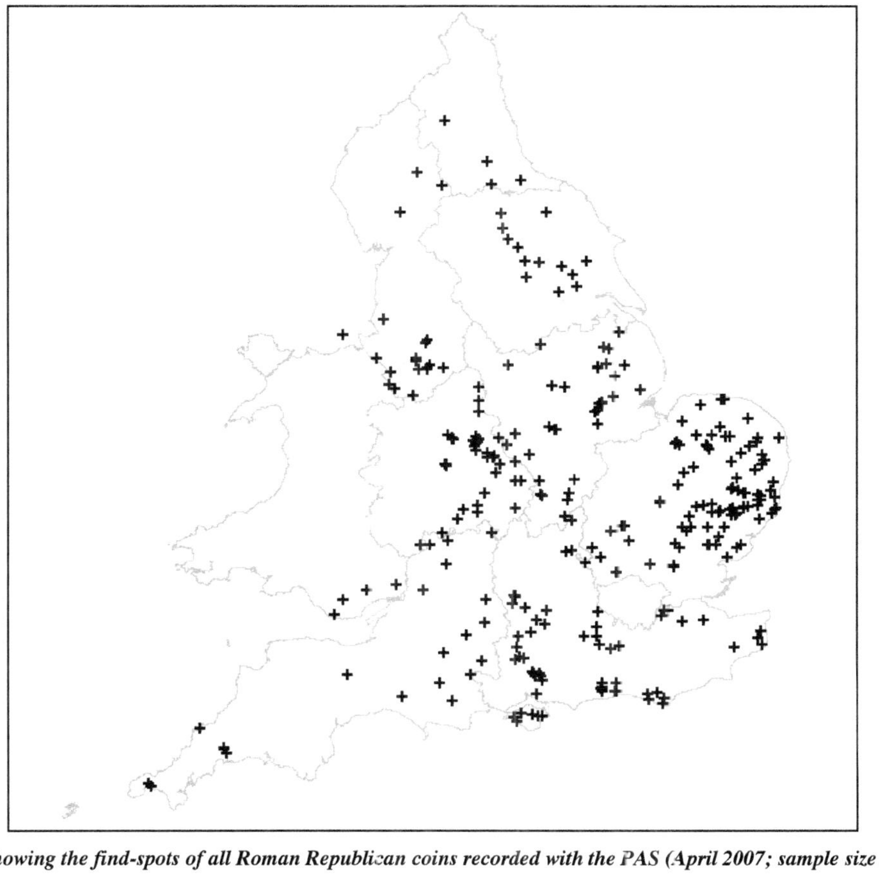

Map 8: A map showing the find-spots of all Roman Republican coins recorded with the PAS (April 2007; sample size c. 415 coins).

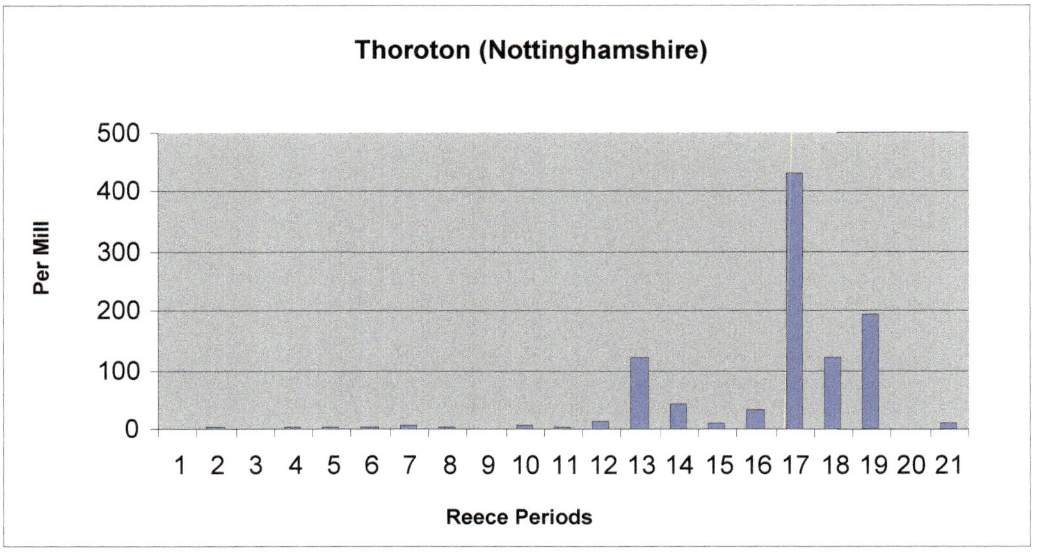

Fig. 16. Bar-chart showing coins (per mill) by period for Thoroton, Nottinghamshire (PAS sample size 574 coins).

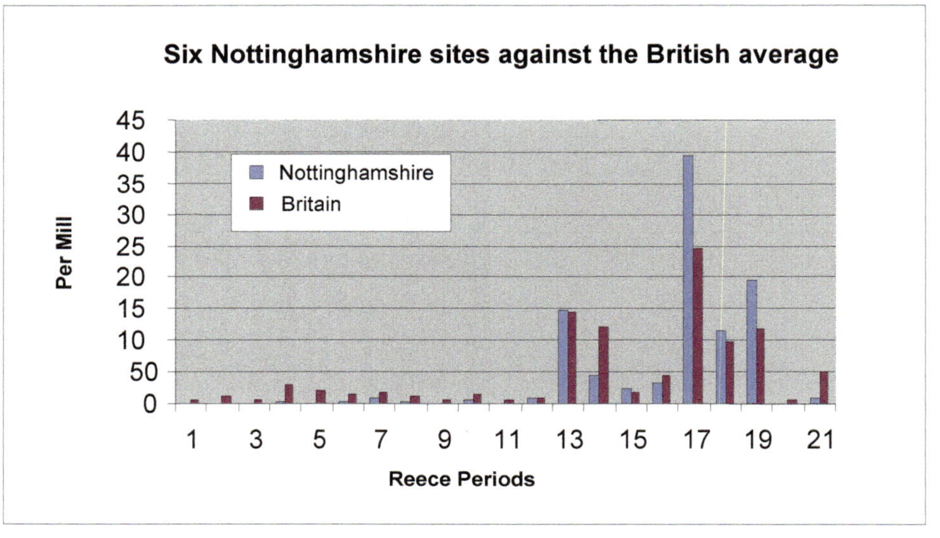

Fig. 17: A bar-chart comparing coin profiles (per mill) of Nottinghamshire (PAS sample size 917 coins) and the British average (Reece 1995: 183).

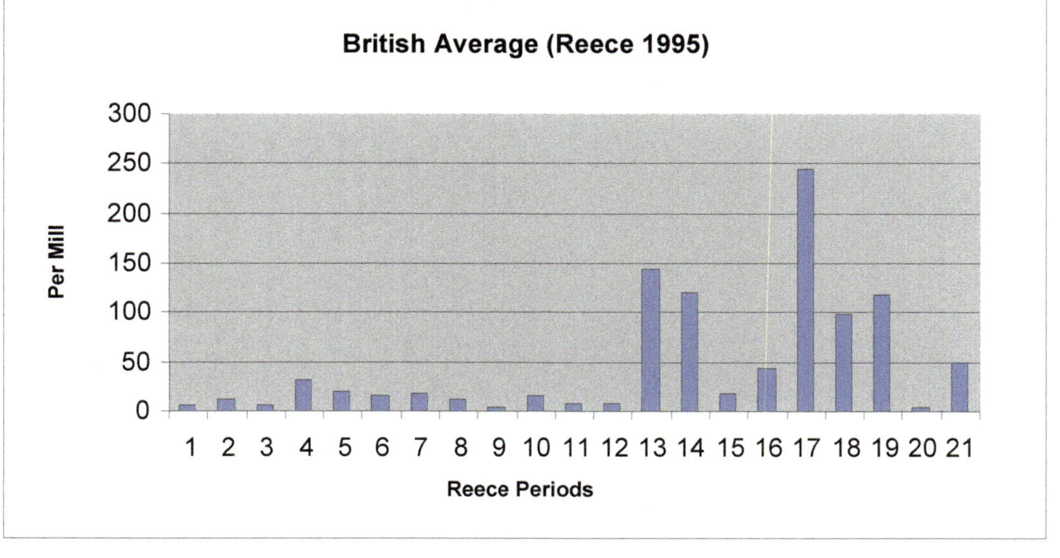

Fig. 18: Bar-chart showing number of coins from all British sites (per mill) by period (Reece 1995: 183), which shows an early peak in period 4 (69-96 AD).

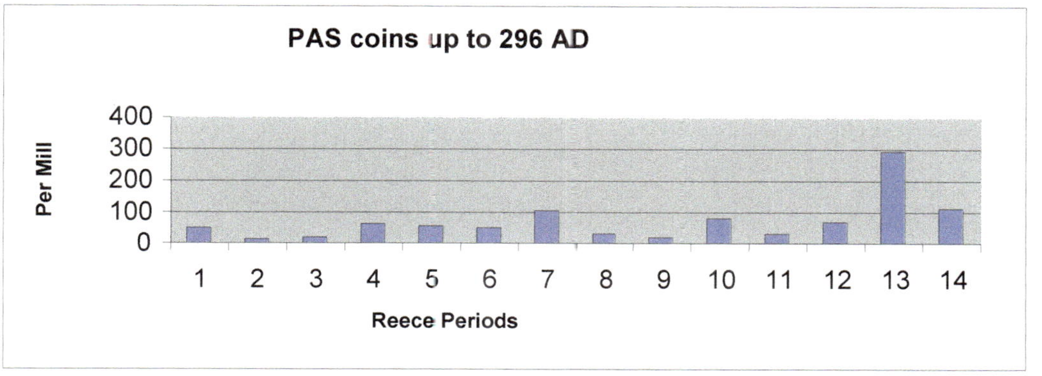

Fig. 19: A bar-chart showing number of coins from Reece Periods 1 to 14 (up to 296 AD) (per mills) on the PAS database (sample size 8,545 coins), showing the peak in period 7 (138-61 AD).

Flavian and Antonine peaks

When one looks at a graph of Reece's coin-loss for all sites in Britain (Fig. 18) the first significant peak is in the Flavian period 4(69-96 AD). Indeed, this is often the case at military and urban sites which were founded in the half century or so after the conquest in 43 AD.

However, initial analysis of the PAS data from up to 296 AD (periods 1-14) shows that the most significant early peak is in the Antonine I period (7: 138-61 AD), not the Flavian. Why is this the case? As mentioned above, the PAS data comes from mainly rural sites, sites which were not Romanised to the extent of forts and towns in the 1st century AD. Indeed until the middle of the 2nd century they appear to have been on the periphery of coin-use. However, with the massive influx of coins of Antoninus Pius, Aurelius Caesar and Faustina II in the 150s there appears finally to be a more plentiful supply of low denomination coinage to the Province. In fact, David Walker (1988: 288ff) noted in his seminal report on the coins from the Sacred Spring at Bath that many of these coins were of types common only to Britain, coins he called 'Coins of British Association'. He suggested tentatively at the time that this was a time when coin use became more widespread, as did Reece (1986: 37) in a paper on coins from villas. Although more work needs to be done to breakdown the coins by denomination and type, what the PAS data seems to prove is that indeed it was in the mid-2nd century that coin use expanded significantly in rural regions in Britain. Obviously, this peak in period 7 (138-61 AD) does not compare with the explosion of coin use across the Province in period 13 (260-75 AD).

Important new sites

Any site with a large assemblage of coins (numbering over 100) is important; for example West Lavington (Wiltshire), Wenhaston with Mells Hamlet (Suffolk), Thoroton (Nottinghamshire) and Nether Wallop (Hampshire), all mentioned above. It is hoped that further investigations can be carried out at Nether Wallop to determine more accurately its nature, and to compare it with the excavated site at Butterfield Down, only a couple of miles away. However, there are other sites with an added importance.

Rigorous spatial recording of over 550 Roman coins by David Hunt at Godstone (Surrey) interested the PAS so much that a Channel 4 *Time Team* excavation tried to determine the nature of the site in 2006-7. {8} Because of the large proportion of pre-260 coins, Richard Reece and the author reckoned that the site was a religious centre, as the profile was similar to assemblages from the Sacred Spring at Bath and Coventina's Well. Excavation has not proven this and it has been suggested that the site was a roadside settlement that also held periodic markets. However, the jury is still out and the debate continues.

Another PAS assemblage of enormous importance has been found by divers in the River Tees at Piercebridge, the site of an important Roman fort and *vicus*. Philippa Walton's meticulous recording of the numismatic and other finds has shown this to be a votive deposit on a par with ritual deposits from Bath and Coventina's Well. However, the Piercebridge coins peak, very unusually, in the Severan period (10-11: 193-235 AD). This apparently coincides with a major expansion of the fort.

Coins and trade routes

In most periods and regions, the use of coin mintmarks to argue for particular trade routes is not valid. This is because when there were several mints feeding coins to Britain, there was a homogenous mix of coins. For example, in the Valentinianic period (364-78 AD) coins are found in hoards and as site-finds with roughly the same percentages from the different mints: Arles, Lyons, Trier, Rome, Aquileia and Siscia (Moorhead 1997: 407, Table 2). However, a recent group of metal-detector finds from Hayle, east of St Ives, in Cornwall might indicate a distinct trade route. These coins came from a coastal settlement and include pieces from central and eastern Mediterranean mints - Sirmium, Heraclea, Nicomedia and Alexandria - coins which only occur rarely in British assemblages. In this case, it might be possible to argue with a direct maritime link with the Mediterranean. This is apparently supported by the finding of Byzantine coins in the south west (see below) which probably also came on ships directly from the Mediterranean. Whether it is possible to extend this argument to cover other coins on the south coast is debateable, but a recent Constantinian coin from Heraclea found on the Isle of Wight (IOW-AF2D45) might be a contender.

Byzantine and exotic coins

For long it has been argued that Byzantine coins recorded as being found in Britain were in fact recent losses, for example coins bought back by troops after the two World Wars (Casey 1986: 108). In many cases, this might be true, especially when the coins have no patina or *verdigris*. However, there are a number of recent Byzantine finds from Britain, ranging from a gold *solidus* of Phocas (602-10 AD), found in North Yorkshire (Fig. 20), to 6th-century copper issues found in the south west.

Fig. 20: Gold solidus of Phocas (602-10 AD) minted in Constantinople, found in North Yorkshire (NCL-6A6EF5) (diameter: 21mm). Hahn 2000: vol. II, no. 9.

Fig. 21: Copper decanummium of Justinian I (527-65 AD), probably minted at Cyzicus, found in Cornwall (CORN-72D1D7) (diameter: 13mm). C.f. Hahn 2000: no. 123a.

Fig. 22: Four copper Byzantine folles of the 6th-century AD found in east Devon (DEV-464726) (approximate diameters: c. 32mm).

Byzantine gold coins did reach Britain, as is shown in a recent gazetteer of early medieval continental coins found in Britain (Abdy and Williams 2006: 30ff). Furthermore, given the large amounts of 6th-century Mediterranean ceramics from Tintagel, Cornwall and Bantham, Devon the finding of Justinianic *decanummium* in Cornwall (Fig. 21) and four 6th-century *folles* from east Devon (Fig. 22) is perhaps not that surprising. The PAS is therefore already beginning to present supportive evidence for continued contact between the South West and the Mediterranean in the 5th and 6th centuries.

There are a number of other 'exotic' coins which the PAS records. The authenticity of findspots for a number of later 3rd-century Alexandrian *tetradrachms* struck for Roman emperors should not always be doubted. Such coins with a plausible patina or *verdigris* can be entered on the PAS database with some confidence, given the fact that other Roman provincial coins are now being found (see below). However, it is still necessary to be wary of intruders as John Casey warns (1986: 108). Furthermore, the finding of Roman provincial coins from Eastern mints in Britain can also be countenanced. For a long time, Roman provincial silver coins from Lycia and Cappadocia have been found in hoards. Now, examples of bronze issues are known, notably two specimens of the same issue for Elagabalus (218-22 AD) from Cius, north-west Turkey - one from near Ashford, Kent, and the other from Hertfordshire (BH-9909C7; Fig. 23).

Fig. 23: Copper-alloy coin of Elagabalus (218-22 AD), minted at Cius, north-west Turkey (BH-9909C7) (diameter: 23.5mm). Wroth 1889: no. 41.

All of the above said, there are cases where coins are brought in for identification which do not seem to have been found in Britain. These are often Greek or Roman Provincial coins without patina or *verdigris*, or with patina and *verdigris* more typical of finds from the Mediterranean. These are often 'found' in gardens, and often were 'found' by a friend or an ancestor. It is not an envious task for a FLO or National Finds Adviser to suggest that a coin is not a genuine ancient loss. In cases where we cannot prove that the coin was not found in Britain, we can only enter a strong statement about the condition of the coin and its unlikely provenance in the 'Note Box' on the database. Other, more disturbing, activities are the 'salting' or 'seeding' with coins on detector rally sites or fellow detectorists' patches, and the invention of a findspot to add 'value' to a particular coin. In the great scheme of things, the number of coins involved is very small and in most cases the experience of the FLOs and National Finds Advisers can at least enable qualifying statements.

Conclusions

This paper has attempted to show the importance of the PAS Roman coin data for the study of the currency, archaeology and history of Roman Britain. Amongst the 47,000 Roman coins recorded so far (up to September 2007), there are a number of highly important pieces which are of enormous numismatic interest. However, possibly more importantly, it is clear that the PAS records will greatly enhance our knowledge of coin-loss on rural sites, many of them otherwise unknown; this will help to redress the balance which has tended to be in favour of military and urban sites.

There is an important issue about the validity of the PAS data. It can be argued that large assemblages, which include the poorly preserved coins, are valid and that they can be researched alongside existing assemblages. There is a serious need to emphasise the importance of recording all coins from a site and the author is leading a major publicity campaign on this front. We all need to be aware of non-ancient losses which creep on to the database, but experience and vigilance should be able to identify the more suspect finds.

When analysed, the PAS coin data are already enhancing our knowledge of coin-use in Britain. New assemblages are extending trends that have already been identified, such as the high incidence of Valentinianic coinage in parts of Britain. The PAS database is also confirming speculative comments made by scholars, notably the suggestion that the quantity of coins in circulation in rural regions increased substantially in the mid-2nd century. In some regions with few recorded coin finds, like Nottinghamshire, the PAS is providing a wealth of new material which enables one to fit the county into a broader, national, picture.

A considerable number of scholars have devoted much time to the study of Roman coinage in Britain. The PAS not only offers them a feast of new data, it also provides an overarching, national, framework for the analysis of coin finds. This paper highlights only a few avenues of potential research, but with the assistance of an Arts and Humanities Research funded PhD student (Philippa Walton), it is intended to make substantive progress on a major research programme analysing the PAS data against existing material. In future years, it is hoped there will be numerous reports highlighting the importance of the Roman coins recorded with the PAS.

Endnotes

{1} Peter Guest is editing a volume on Roman coins from Cornwall recorded by the late Roger Penhaligon.
{2} The Wiltshire data has been mainly recorded by Katie Hinds (Wiltshire FLO) and David Algar (Salisbury and South Wiltshire Museum).
{3} Note that the author has added two more periods on the PAS database: 22: 402-45 AD; 23: 445-98 AD.
{4} The Butterfield Down coins are listed by Mark Corney in Rawlings and Fitzpatrick 1996.
{5} For Nether Wallop, I am grateful to the finder, Peter Barker, and the three FLOs for Hampshire, Sally Worrell, Jodi Puls and Robert Webley.
{6} Articles about recording 'grot' have appeared on the PAS website.
http://www.finds.org.uk/wordpress/index.php/246, and in the South West and Eastern Region Newsletters for 2007.
{7} I am also grateful to Catherine Johns and the late Tim Potter with whom I had lengthy discussions about silver in Ancient Britain.
{8} The Godstone coins will all be added to the PAS database when the final report is completed.

Acknowledgements

I would like to acknowledgement the assistance of Richard Reece, John Casey, Judith Plouviez, Richard Abdy, Ian Leins, Roger Bland, Daniel Pett and all of the FLOs in the preparation of this paper.

Bibliography

Abdy, R. A. 2002, *Romano-British Coin Hoards* (Shire, Princes Risborough).
Abdy, R. A. and Williams, G. 2006, 'A catalogue of hoards and single finds from the British Isles, c. AD 410-675', in Cook, B. and Williams, G. (eds.), *Coinage and History in the North Sea World, c. 500-1250* (Brill, Leiden).
Besley, E. and Bland, R. 1983, *The Cunetio Treasure* (British Museum Press, London).
Bland, R. and Burnett, A. 1988, *The Normanby Hoard and other Coin Hoards*, Coin Hoards from Roman Britain VIII (British Museum Press, London).
Brickstock, R. 1987, *Copies of the Fel Temp Reparatio Coinage in Britain*, British Archaeological Reports, British Series 176 (Archaeopress, Oxford).
Carson, R., Hill, P. and Kent, J. 1965, *Late Roman Bronze Coinage* (Spink, London).
Casey, P. J. 1986, *Understanding Ancient Coins* (Batsford, London).
Casey, P. J. 1994, *Roman Coinage in Britain* (Shire, London).
Casey, P. J. and Reece, R. 1988, *Coins and the Archaeologist* (Seaby, London).
Craddock, P. T. 1995, *Early Metal Mining and Production* (Edinburgh University Press, Edinburgh).
Crawford, M. 1974, *Roman Republican Coinage* (Cambridge University Press, Cambridge).
Davies, J. and Gregory, A. 1991, 'Coinage from a *Civitas*: a survey of the Roman coins found in Norfolk and their contribution to the archaeology of the *civitas icenorum*', *Britannia* 22, 65-101.
Gnecchi, F. 1912, *I Medaglioni Romani* (Ulnco Hoepli, Milan).
Guest, P. J. and Wells, N. 2007, *Iron Age and Roman Coins from Wales* (Moneta 66, Wetteren).
Hahn, W. 2000, *Money of the Incipient Byzantine Empire* (University of Vienna, Vienna).
Jones, B. and Mattingly D. 2002, *An Atlas of Roman Britain* (Oxbow, Oxford).

Mattingly *et al.* 1923-62, *Coins of the Roman Empire in the British Museum* (British Museum, London).

Mattingly *et al.*, 1923-94, *Roman Imperial Coinage* (Spink, London).

Moorhead, T. S. N. 1997, 'All Cannings', in Bland, R. and Orna-Ornstein, J. (eds.) *Coin Hoards from Roman Britain* 10 (British Museum Press, London), 406-9.

Moorhead, T. S. N. 2001a, *Roman Coin finds from Wiltshire* (unpublished MPhil thesis, Institute of Archaeology, University College London).

Moorhead, T. S. N. 2001b, 'Roman coin finds from Wiltshire', in Ellis, P. (ed.) *Roman Wiltshire and After* (Wiltshire Archaeological and Natural History Society, Devizes), 85-105.

Northover, P. 1992, 'Materials issues in the Celtic coinage', in Mays, M. (ed.), *Celtic Coinage: Britain and beyond*, British Archaeological Reports, British Series 222 (Archaeopress, Oxford), 235-99.

Plouviez, J. 1995, 'A hole in the distribution map: the characteristics of small towns in Suffolk', in Brown, A. E. (ed.), *Roman Small Towns in Eastern England and Beyond* (Oxbow, Oxford).

Rawlings, M. and Fitzpatrick, A. W. 1996, 'Prehistoric Sites and a Romano-British Settlement at Butterfield Down, Amesbury', *Wiltshire Archaeological and Natural History Magazine* 89, 1-43.

Reece, R. 1972, 'A Short Survey of the Roman Coins Found on Fourteen Sites in Britain', *Britannia* 3, 269-76.

Reece, R. 1973, 'Roman Coinage in Britain and the Western Empire', *Britannia* 4, 227-52.

Reece, R. 1986, 'Coins and Villas', in Branigan, K. and Miles, D. (eds.), *The Economies of Romano-British Villas* (University of Sheffield, Sheffield), 34-41.

Reece, R. 1987, *Coinage in Roman Britain* (Seaby, London).

Reece, R. 1991, '*Roman Coins from 140 Sites in Britain*', Cotswold Studies 4, (Cotswold, Cirencester).

Reece, R. 1995, 'Site-finds in Roman Britain', *Britannia* 26, 179-206.

Reece, R. 2002, *The Roman Coinage of Britain* (Tempus, Stroud).

Robertson, A. S. 2000 (Hobbs, R. and Buttrey, T. V. eds.), *An inventory of Romano-British coin hoards*, Royal Numismatic Society special publication 20 (Royal Numismatic Society, London).

Shotter, D. 1990, *Roman Coins from North-West England* (Centre for North-West Regional Studies, Lancashire University, Lancaster).

Walker, D. R. 1988, 'Roman Coins from the Sacred Spring at Bath' in Cunliffe, B. (ed.), *The Temple of Sulis Minerva, II: finds from the sacred spring* (Oxford University Committee for Archaeology, Oxford).

Worrell, S. A. 2007. 'Roman Britain in 2006 II. Finds reported under the Portable Antiquities Scheme', *Britannia* 38, 303-44.

Wroth, W. 1889, *Catalogue of the Greek Coins in the British Museum, Pontus, Paphlagonia, Bithynia, and the Kingdom of Bosporus* (British Museum, London).

Early Anglo-Saxon Brooches in Southern England: the contribution of the Portable Antiquities Scheme

Laura McLean and Andrew Richardson

This paper is a summary of preliminary findings and interpretation regarding early Anglo-Saxon brooches, dating from the 5th to 7th centuries AD, recorded through the Portable Antiquities Scheme (PAS) in southern England. It will be argued that metal-detected finds from this period are not for the most part derived from burials, hitherto the primary source of early Anglo-Saxon brooch finds. This has implications both for our understanding of Anglo-Saxon brooch types, as well as for interpretations of landscape and cultural identity.

For the purposes of this study, southern England is defined as England south of, and including, the counties of Gloucestershire, Oxfordshire, Buckinghamshire, Hertfordshire and Essex. A number of interim reports on this project were published during the period 2001-2006 when the majority of data was compiled (Lewis 2001; Richardson 2004a; Richardson 2004b; Richardson and McLean 2006). The data and figures used are accurate up to the end of January 2007, by which time a total of 439 Early Anglo-Saxon brooches had been recorded by the PAS across southern England. These finds mostly exist in the private collections of a large number of amateur metal-detectorists (few detectorists have more than two or three Anglo-Saxon brooches in their collection, and many have none). Undoubtedly, unrecorded examples exist in collections across the study area and there are also areas of the landscape where metal-detecting is not possible. The authors are confident, however, that the sample on which this study is based is large enough and, set against a backdrop of widespread metal-detecting activity, and willingness to record finds with the PAS, its findings as reliable as any other archaeological distribution across such a large area.

The origins and development of the Anglo-Saxon Brooch Project

The origins of this research date back to the early to mid-1990s, before the advent of the PAS. During this period a number of large-scale metal-detecting rallies, known as the 'South of England Rallies', were held in east Kent and attended by many hundreds of metal-detector users. Efforts were made to record finds at these rallies, with volunteers from Dover Museum and the Dover Archaeological Group in attendance. Whilst involved with recording finds from these events Keith Parfitt noted apparent disparities between the range of Anglo-Saxon brooch types being recovered by detectorists and those occurring as grave goods in east Kentish cemeteries. Parfitt, who had excavated large numbers of burials of 5th to 7th century date in east Kent, notably the cemeteries at Mill Hill, Deal and Buckland, Dover (Parfitt and Brugmann 1997; Parfitt and Anderson, forthcoming) commented on this pattern to one of the present authors (AR), in particular mentioning the frequency of cruciform brooches amongst Kentish detector finds (Richardson 2005: I, 254). Parfitt referred to this pattern in his discussion of the landscape around the Mill Hill cemetery (Parfitt and Brugmann 1997: 9).

Kent became one of the pilot areas of the PAS in 1997. Through this, the opportunity arose to obtain systematic data on metal-detector finds of early Anglo-Saxon brooches across the county and the Kent Anglo-Saxon Brooch Project was launched in 2001 by Keith Parfitt, Martin Welch (University College London) and Michael Lewis (then Finds Liaison Officer, Kent). An attempt was made to include as many brooches as possible, both new and old finds and from non-funerary as well as funerary contexts, to provide as comprehensive as possible a corpus of detected and settlement finds of brooches from Kent. By the end of January 2007 a total of 198 early Anglo-Saxon brooches from the county had been entered in the PAS database.

By 2005 it was becoming apparent that the contrasts between archaeologically recovered brooches and detector finds were not confined to Kent and extended across southern England, which was distinct from the midlands and East Anglia in terms of the proportions and diversity of brooch types present. It was clear that a wider geographical context was needed to understand the patterns of brooch types present in the Kentish landscape, therefore the scope of the study was extended to cover the whole of southern England. In 2006 Laura McLean agreed to jointly undertake the research and writing up of the project, the aim being to produce an overview of the contribution that PAS records could make to the understanding of the brooch types and use across the south of England during the 5th to 7th centuries AD. This paper encompasses brooches of all types (including imported examples) manufactured between circa 400-700 AD, found within the study area and recorded by the PAS between 1997 and January 2007. At the time of writing the number of brooches recorded in the study from outside Kent is low in comparison with the number of Kentish records: Kent finds account for just over 45% of the sample. Also, no attempt has yet been made to incorporate brooches archaeologically recovered from non-funerary contexts outside of Kent. Nonetheless, the sample is now producing consistent patterns of brooch recovery and distribution across the study area and it therefore seems timely to present an update on the current dataset along with initial interpretations of its significance.

Preliminary discoveries in Kent

The brooch types recovered during the metal-detector rallies in Kent did not match the proportions of brooch types from excavated east Kentish burials. Parfitt (pers. comm.) observed that the most numerous type being recovered by detectorists in this area appeared to be cruciform brooches. This class of brooch only accounted for just over 30 brooches out of a total brooch corpus for Kent of several hundreds. A sample of 400 brooches from 216 burials of 5th to 7th century date was dominated by square-headed brooches (19%), Kentish, plated and composite disc brooches (16.5%) and, to a lesser extent, by radiate-headed brooches (9.75%), annular brooches (8.75%) and button brooches (7%) (Richardson 2005: 142-43). In contrast, cruciform brooches made up only 1.75% of the brooches from this sample, occurring in only four graves. At the time of writing, fewer than ten recorded burials in Kent (all inhumations) have produced cruciform brooches, from a total of several thousand recorded graves.

By the end of January 2007, cruciform brooches recorded by the PAS in Kent totalled 39 (plus four fragments that may be parts of cruciform brooches), more than doubling the known corpus for the county, but more significantly amounting to nearly 20% of PAS records of early Anglo-Saxon brooches from the county, making them the largest single early medieval brooch type recorded by the PAS in Kent, a pattern that has remained consistent since the early days of the Scheme. When all brooch types are considered, a clear discrepancy between the proportions of brooches recorded through metal-detecting and those excavated from cemetery contexts in Kent is apparent (Fig. 1). An attempt to understand and interpret the reasons for this discrepancy is a key theme of this paper, in which the PAS brooch data from across the extended study area, encompassing all of southern England, is compared with the established archaeological brooch corpus, mostly derived from excavated burials. At the time of writing it has not been possible to compare specific numbers of over or under represented brooches in the PAS and cemetery data, as has been done for Kent, since a detailed break-down of brooch types from burials in the south is not yet available. It is intended that further comparative work will be possible in future once a comprehensive corpus of known brooches for each county has been compiled. In the meantime, the data from Kentish cemeteries has been used as a benchmark against which the PAS data from the study area can be compared (Fig. 2), thus providing some overview of over- and under-represented brooch classes throughout southern England. Although the Kentish cemetery material cannot be considered representative of the whole of the south, it does provide a starting point in comparing the PAS and archaeological datasets, and available archaeological distribution maps of brooch types (see below) provide a further comparative source.

Interpreting PAS brooch data

At the time of writing (mid-July 2007), the PAS, across the whole of England and Wales, has recorded 13,246 brooches of all periods. Early medieval brooches make up 2,330 of this total, whilst there are 916 Iron Age, 8,913 Roman and 1,036 medieval brooches recorded by the Scheme. It is clear that the majority of these brooches are not derived from burials. Roman brooches, the most numerous represented in the PAS data, are interpreted as being from a wide range of sites, including domestic, ritual and funerary, and may also be interpreted as having been accidentally lost or casually discarded. Brooches in general appear to be one of several artefact classes (including many dress accessory types) which occur frequently as metal-detector finds and this is likely to be due in some part to the propensity of dress accessories to be lost as a result of everyday wear and activity.

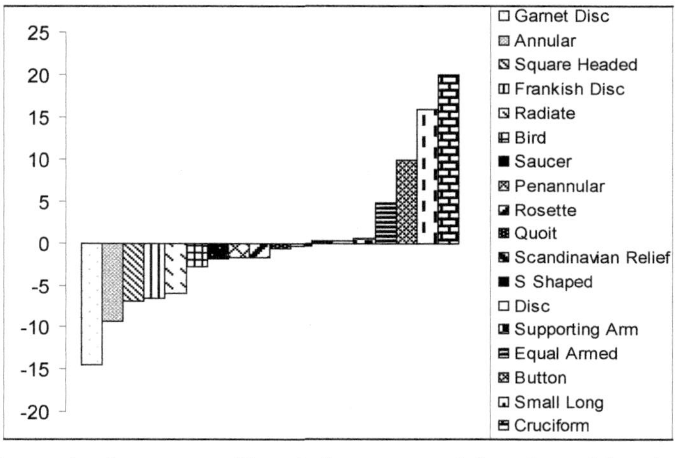

Fig. 1: Over- and under-represented brooch classes recovered through metal-detecting in Kent, compared with a sample of brooches recovered from graves in Kent ('0' on the vertical axis).

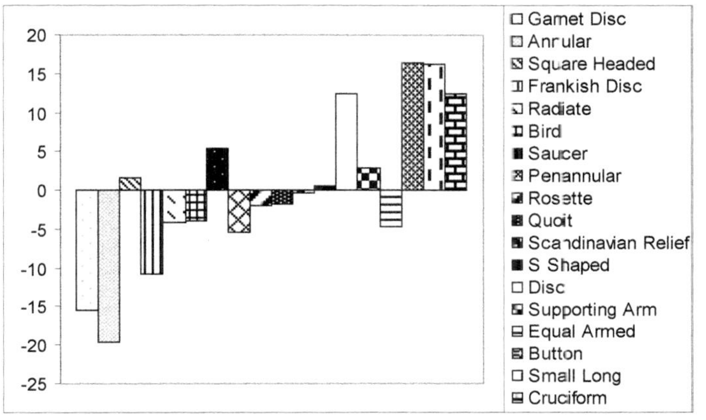

Fig. 2: Over- and under-representation of brooch classes recovered through metal-detecting in Southern England, compared with a sample of brooches recovered from graves in Kent ('0' on the vertical axis).

Within the early medieval period, brooches dating to the 8th century or later are never found in burials, and clearly post-date the custom of fully clothed burial (as do, of course, the many brooch finds of later medieval date). In general, it is clearly the case that deposition of a brooch in a grave (whether an inhumation or cremation) is only one possible route by which a brooch may enter the ground and subsequently be recovered by archaeological excavation or metal-detecting. However, in the case of the early Anglo-Saxon period, brooch finds have usually been interpreted as indicators of cemetery or burial sites, with other possible interpretations being largely ignored or dismissed. Clearly at least a proportion of early Anglo-Saxon brooches recovered by metal-detectorists are derived from burials (usually those that have been disturbed by cultivation), but it is the premise of this paper that a significant proportion have entered the ground in other ways. Before going on to consider what these ways may have been, it is worth considering why it is that early Anglo-Saxon brooches are often interpreted only as being derived from graves.

Prior to the advent of systematic recording of metal-detected finds, the great majority of recovered early Anglo-Saxon brooches were excavated examples found within a funerary context, with a much smaller number recovered from settlement and occupation contexts.
Analyses of metalwork from early cemeteries and settlement/occupation sites have consistently shown brooches, along with other dress accessories, to form a high proportion of the metal finds from cemeteries, but a very low proportion (indeed, they are often completely absent) of the finds from settlement/occupation sites (Mary Chester-Kadwell, pers. comm.). As a result, individual finds of early Anglo-Saxon brooches are often interpreted as indicating the presence of a cemetery or individual burial, it usually being assumed that the objects have been removed from their original context (a burial) by cultivation. It is clear that a proportion of the early Anglo-Saxon brooches recorded by the PAS are so derived from (usually plough-damaged) graves, for example the scatter of brooches (found in association with other dress accessories such as buckles) located further down the hill from the known cemeteries of Chessel Down and Shalfleet, the Isle of Wight (Arnold 1982: fig. 2, and appendix). Such brooches will generally have been deposited more or less complete, attached as dress accessories to the costume the deceased was buried in, although some brooches also occur in graves as detached finds in purses or bags. Some brooches recorded by the PAS are clearly identifiable as former grave goods. Characteristics that would suggest such an identification include the presence of textile remains (indicating that the brooch was attached to a garment when it entered the ground), a largely intact spring/pin (these are usually of iron and are unlikely to survive a prolonged period in a cultivated horizon), the close proximity of multiple finds of similar date (especially if any are of precious metals), a landscape location that fits local patterns of cemetery placement and, of course, the findspot being a known cemetery site (although the possibility that an individual find on a cemetery site may in fact equate to an accidental loss cannot be ruled out, as may be the case for a button brooch recovered from the topsoil above the cemetery at Ringlemere, near Woodnesborough, Kent; Keith Parfitt, pers. comm.). Examples of metal artefact scatters in Kent that fit some, or all, of the above criteria are interpreted as probable cemetery sites include Dover Elmswood Farm, Eastry Ham, Eastry Highborough Hill, and Hollingbourne Broad Street. In Kent, however, apparently clear cases, such as these, relate to only a small proportion of PAS records. Of the cases cited, only one, Eastry Highborough Hill, has seen any excavation (by Channel Four's 'Time Team' in 2005), which failed to locate any burials, although a heavily disturbed cemetery remains the most likely explanation for the artefact scatter at this site. Conversely, isolated or very dispersed finds of broken or heavily abraded copper-alloy brooches, with no traces of textile or surviving springs or pins, in landscape locations (for example the base or lowest slopes of valleys) not paralleled locally by known cemetery sites cannot be assumed to indicate the presence of burials. Given that in other periods, when furnished burial and the deposition of brooches in graves was rare or non-existent, brooches are nonetheless common metal detected finds, it has to be accepted that at least some early Anglo-Saxon brooch finds entered the ground by similar mechanisms as the many Roman and medieval brooches recovered by detectorists. What, then, are the most likely alternative mechanisms by which such brooches enter the ground?

Isolated finds are sometimes referred to as 'stray finds' or 'casual losses', neither term being particularly well-defined. The approach followed here is to approach this question by considering deposition (by whatever means) within the wider context of the overall 'lifecycle' of an artefact.

Artefact lifecycle

All man-made artefacts undergo various stages in their existence, from conception through production to eventual deposition or destruction. Figure 3 is a diagrammatic representation of the possible stages any artefact, once conceptualized, can go through, from the sourcing of raw materials through to several possible end results. This serves to illustrate that there are numerous possible outcomes for any given artefact.

Clearly there are several possible routes, leading to several different outcomes, that an early Anglo-Saxon brooch could take through this 'lifecycle', and equally clearly the brooches which have been recovered (and, crucially, recorded) represent only a subset of the total originally produced. What then are the most likely routes by which the known extant brooches have survived?

All started as raw materials before being fashioned (usually through casting in a two-piece mould) into brooches intended for use as part of (usually adult) female costume. Both precious and non-precious metals were a valuable commodity in the early Anglo-Saxon period. Although more numerous than brooches of silver or gold in both excavated and metal-detected assemblages, it would be wrong to assume copper-alloy brooches of this period as being produced from plentiful raw materials. British sources of copper ore are all located in western upland areas that were under British, rather than Anglo-Saxon, control in the 5th to 7th centuries (Leahy 2003: 136). Metal analysis has demonstrated that a wide range of copper alloys were used in the production of early Anglo-Saxon brooches (Mortimer 1988) and it seems clear that the main source of metal for their production were recycled artefacts, probably including available Roman coinage and artefacts, some of which would have been imported from the continent, the rest locally sourced. This is in clear contrast to contemporary artefacts produced by British (or 'Celtic') craftsmen, which seem to have been manufactured from new metal (Leahy 2003: 136). Sources of precious metals were even more restricted, with metal analysis demonstrating that one source of gold was Byzantinian coins, and it has been suggested that Frisian coinage was used as a source of silver (ibid.: 153).

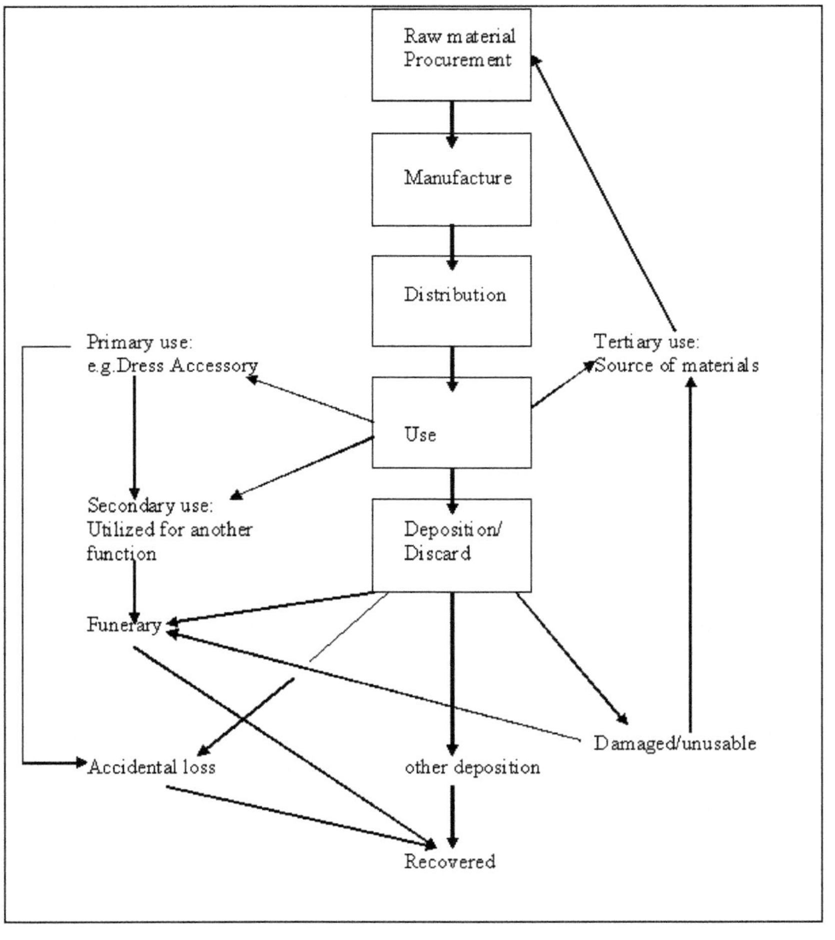

Fig. 3: Artefact lifecycle.

Recycling, refuse and loss

Given the importance of recycling to the early Anglo-Saxon production of copper alloy, silver and gold artefacts, two key points may be inferred that are relevant to this paper. Firstly, a substantial proportion of brooches produced during the early Anglo-Saxon period are likely to have been recycled once they reached the end of their useful life, thus removing any chance that they would survive to be recovered and recorded in the modern period. Secondly, that the likely value of even fragments of brooch for recycling purposes means that the deliberate discard of brooches is unlikely to have been a frequent occurrence. Nonetheless, casual disposal of broken brooches has in the past been offered as one explanation for scattered finds, perhaps via their inclusion in manure heaps that are then spread across adjacent fields (Keith Parfitt, pers. comm.; Parfitt and Brugmann 1997: 9). Hinton (1998: 6) commented that small luxury goods were common enough to be casually broken or lost, citing the excavation of discarded brooches at Mucking. Most early Anglo-Saxon settlement sites, however, have produced very little in the way of brooches (or indeed other copper-alloy, silver, or gold finds) and this is probably due to the twin factors of the intrinsic value of these artefacts, meaning they were frequently recycled rather than discarded, and to the increased chances for contemporary recovery that existed within settlements (see below). The brooches at Mucking seem to be the exception, rather than the rule.

Casual discard is often linked as an explanation with accidental loss but, in fact, the two are quite separate processes, one representing deliberate, conscious behaviour, the other accidental or unconscious behaviour. It is accidental loss which the present authors believe is likely to be the factor by which many (and perhaps most) metal-detected finds of early Anglo-Saxon brooches entered the ground. Indeed, many of the artefact types recovered in large numbers by metal-detectorists, and recorded via the PAS, are likely to have been accidentally lost during the course of their use. Late Anglo-Saxon harness and stirrup fittings are an obvious example of a class of finds that were prone to accidental loss. Dress accessories form a major proportion of detected finds, from the prehistoric to modern periods, and the majority of these were probably also lost rather than deliberately deposited or discarded. It is not difficult to see why early Anglo-Saxon brooches, worn, often in multiple sets, by women as part of their costume, would have been lost as women carried out their daily activities. Aspects of brooch design and use on the costume (for example a design flaw which makes a type prone to breakage or to becoming detached from the costume) are likely to have been important factors in whether or not a brooch was lost in the first place. The location of the loss is likely to be a factor in whether it is recovered at the time or not; a brooch lost within a building or even within a settlement will stand a higher chance of being recovered, either at the time of loss or sometime later within the contemporary use of the site, than a brooch lost in grassland, standing crops or woodland. Also a factor in whether a brooch is recovered at the time of breakage may be the role of the brooch on the costume. The loss of some brooches (for instance those securing a *Peplos*-type dress) may be more instantly noticeable to the wearer than the loss of those playing a more decorative or peripheral role in the costume (for instance those fastening an outer cloak or dress to the inner dress, see below). In the former case it might be expected there is a higher probability of the brooch being recovered at the time of loss and therefore not (at that point anyway) generating a potential modern find. Those brooches that were lost and not recovered, however, will have entered general upper soil horizons, rather than any discrete archaeological features such as pits, ditches or, indeed, graves. Only the advent of metal-detecting will have allowed more than a very few such brooches to have been recovered in the modern period.

The probability that lost brooches with a high precious metal content would have been recovered at the time of, or soon after, loss is likely to be higher than that for copper-alloy (or iron) brooches. At the time of writing less than 2% of early medieval brooches recorded in the national PAS database (and reported through the Treasure Act 1996) were of gold or silver. It seems probable that a more concerted effort would be made to recover a lost brooch of precious metal than would be the case for other types. It is also highly unlikely that objects of such high intrinsic value would be discarded once out of fashion or after they became damaged and broken. Thus, deposition in a burial (albeit sometimes in an old or damaged condition) is by far the most likely explanation for any silver or gold brooches recovered by metal-detecting; although a silver relief brooch (KENT-3A7463), deposited in a pit at Grange Farm, Gillingham, possibly represents a rare case, for England, of votive deposition.

Comparative case study: annular and cruciform brooches

A comparative study of annular (Fig. 4a) and cruciform brooches (Fig. 4b) offers an opportunity to draw together some of the issues discussed above. These two brooch classes exhibit very different patterns of recovery. Annular brooches, mostly produced in copper alloy, are common finds in burials. The narrow-banded copper-alloy examples have been described as 'sturdy' and typifying '…the Anglian region in the first three quarters of the 6th century, when they were mostly worn as matching pairs on the shoulders…' (Walton Rogers 2007: 117). In Kent they accounted for just under 10% of brooches from the comparative burial sample used in this study. Yet as metal detector finds they remain surprisingly rare; in Kent only one example (PAS: KENT-5A1466) has been recorded by the PAS to date, with only a further five in the whole of southern England, respectively representing just 0.5% and 1.4% of the PAS brooch sample in Kent and the south as a whole.

Even more surprisingly, a similar pattern holds across England as a whole, including those areas where the cemetery evidence suggests that annular brooches were amongst the most common brooch types in use.

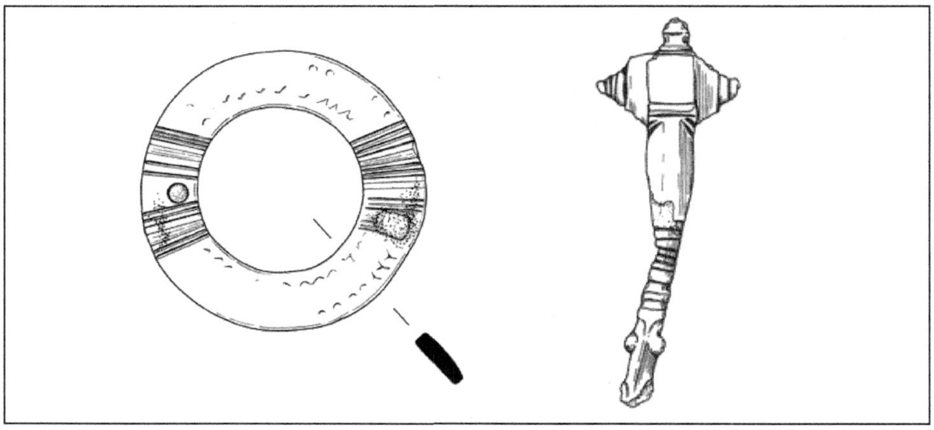

Fig. 4: a) annular brooch (missing pin) (PAS: SF-74C243) and b) cruciform brooch (PAS: KENT4438).

In Suffolk, for example, annular brooches account for only 2.3% of PAS records of early medieval brooches and across England annular brooches accounted for only 2.9% of all PAS early medieval brooch records at the time of writing. An initial theory that this under-representation was due to metal-detectorists failing to recognise annular brooches as Anglo-Saxon has had to be abandoned. Detectorists frequently recover and record superficially similar items such as medieval ring brooches and buckles, and many are also conscientious in retaining even small fragments of unidentified metal. Exhaustive searches through finders' 'scrap boxes' have failed to reveal more than a few annular brooches or fragments. For whatever reasons, it does appear that metal-detectorists rarely find Anglo-Saxon annular (or quoit) brooches.

Cruciform brooches, in contrast, represent the largest single class of early medieval brooch recovered by metal-detectorists in England and seem to be frequently over-represented compared to their occurrence in burials. As mentioned above, they make up nearly a fifth of PAS Anglo-Saxon brooch records from Kent (the largest single type), despite being rare in burials in Kent. In the study area as a whole they comprise 13.7% of the brooch sample, making them the third commonest type after Small Long and Button brooches. Cruciform brooches have long been recognised as one of the main brooch types of the 5th to 6th centuries in Anglian regions and their frequency as metal-detector finds in the Midlands and East Anglia especially reflects this. Overall, at the time of writing they made up over 27% of PAS records of early medieval brooches from England and Wales.

The same pattern of low numbers of annular and high numbers of cruciform brooches amongst metal-detector finds has been observed in Norfolk and Mary Chester-Kadwell (pers. comm.), in the course of her research, has offered some theories as to why this may be the case. Processes of sorting and breakage under cultivation are offered as one explanation, it being suggested that cruciform brooches (and presumably bow brooches in general) are more prone to being brought into the higher levels of the plough soil (thus making them more susceptible to discovery by metal-detecting) than annular brooches. The tendency of cruciform brooches to fracture at or near the junction of the bow, or for detachable knobs to become separated, is also seen as a factor which may increase the chances of any one part of the brooch being recovered as a detector find, since multiple fragments represent multiple chances of an individual part being located and recovered by a detectorist. Conversely, there is some evidence that annular brooches have a weak metal-detector signature, especially when broken and effectively transformed into a penannular brooch (Jude Plouviez, pers. comm.).

It is possible that these factors do play some part in the pattern of metal-detector finds of annular and cruciform brooches, but a number of considerations suggest that they are not the only (or even the most significant) factors. Square-headed and radiate-headed brooches ought to display much the same characteristics as cruciform brooches in plough soil. If detector finds of brooches are mostly coming from representative inhumations then these types should proportionately out-number cruciform brooches in areas like Kent, which they do not. Looking beyond the Anglo-Saxon period, detectorists appear to have little difficulty finding large numbers of Iron Age, Roman and medieval coins and small finds, many of which are far smaller than annular brooches. These finds frequently include extremely small fragments of metal (for example, medieval cut quarter pennies), as well as many copper-alloy rings, brooches and buckles that are superficially very similar to Anglo-Saxon annular brooches and might be expected to behave similarly under conditions of cultivation.

If accidental loss is accepted as a significant factor in the deposition of brooches recovered by metal-detecting, then another set of factors can be considered which may explain both the prevalence of cruciform brooches in the metal-detected sample, both in England as a whole and in areas like Kent where they do not frequently occur in identified burials, and the under-representation of annular brooches. As was mentioned above, the primary function of annular brooches was to secure the early Anglo-Saxon tubular (or *Peplos*) dress, though it might be assumed that the loss of a *Peplos* brooch might more immediately be noticed by the wearer than with other brooch types. Furthermore, annular, quoit and penannular brooches differ from other brooch types by passing a section of the garment through the central hole of the brooch and locking this in place using a (often substantial) pin, sometimes (as iron pins are common on annular brooches in eastern England) manufactured in the same metal as the main brooch. In contrast, most other brooch types rely on an iron pin and spring, passed through the textile and fitted into a catch-plate on the reverse. It seems possible that this fundamental design difference renders annular brooches less prone to becoming accidentally detached from a garment than other brooch types. That this was the case is supported by anecdotal evidence from re-enactment and living history groups: one manufacturer of replica brooches informs the authors that whilst he frequently repairs or replaces broken or lost brooches, annular brooches very rarely need replacing since '....they never come off...' (Peter Butler, pers. comm.). If this theory is correct, and if most metal-detector finds of brooches are of examples that have been lost, then we should expect annular brooches to be significantly under represented as detector finds, despite their prevalence in burials. If cruciform brooches, on the other hand, were particularly prone to loss, either due to a tendency to break or due to their position on the costume (several of those excavated in burials in the south and elsewhere had been used to pin an outer cloak or mantle to the inner dress; Walton Rogers 2007: 173) then it might be expected that they at least match or exceed their frequency in burials.

In addition we should not necessarily assume that any particular brooch type was in use as a dress accessory for the living in the same numbers as it was in use as a dress accessory in burials. The selection of costume, and associated brooches, used in a burial could reflect many aspects of a person's life, or indeed the constructed memory (for more on social construction of memory see Williams 2006) of that person through those performing the burial rites. Social status, affiliations to particular groups, constructed social phenomena such as ethnicity as well as personal preferences are among many factors that will have determined what was deposited in a burial. In short, the choice of what costume and associated accessories are deposited in a grave is likely to have been deliberate and selective, and may not accurately reflect choices of costume in life. With regard to the unexpectedly high frequency of detector finds of cruciform (and some other) brooch types in Kent and elsewhere, compared to a low (or non-existent) frequency in burials, there may also be a chronological factor to consider. Relatively low numbers of 5th-century inhumations have been identified in Kent; it is only during the 6th century that the well-furnished inhumations characteristic of the county become numerous and widespread. It has been remarked that burial in 5th century Jutland was characterised by a fairly minimalist inhumation. Most if not all of the cruciform brooches recovered from Kent (by any means) date to the 5th or very beginning of the 6th century. The class did not go on to be produced throughout the 6th century as it did in Anglian regions. The same can be said of the cruciform brooches found in West Sussex, Hampshire and the Isle of Wight. It may be that whilst sufficient numbers of these and other 5th-century types were in use to generate artefact scatters as a result of accidental loss, their use largely predates the widespread adoption in some areas of well-furnished costumed inhumation characteristic of the 6th century, therefore explaining their relative under-representation in burials. In east Kent in particular, furnished inhumations during the latter half of the 5th century may have been restricted to a relatively small elite, perhaps operating as much under Frankish as southern Scandinavian influence. Certainly differences in the range of materials deposited as grave goods in this period compared to the 6th century are apparent in this area, male burials being characterised largely by the wearing of belt sets rather than the deposition weapons for example. The bulk of the east Kentish population in the 5th century was apparently being disposed of in other, less visible ways, be that minimalist inhumations, urned and un-urned cremations (both now recorded from east Kent, albeit still in small numbers) or by some other means. The possibility that cremations, especially un-urned, were present in east Kent but were not being archaeologically detected, is something that has been postulated for many years and low visibility burials have sometimes been suggested as a source of metal-detected material. In this context it is worth mentioning that few if any of the brooches (of any type) from the PAS southern sample, show any signs of having been cremated, in contrast to many examples from further north.

In summary, a number of factors may lie behind the patterns of brooch (and other artefact) types recovered by metal-detectorists. In the case of the early Anglo-Saxon period, the custom of depositing brooches in burials provides one major source of metal-detector finds. However, it is suggested here that accidental loss is also a major (perhaps the major) source of early Anglo-Saxon brooches found by metal-detectorists, and that the different processes of deliberate deposition in burial compared to accidental loss produce different patterning, both as regards types of brooches and their spatial distribution, at both local and regional levels. It is questions of regional spatial distribution that are considered next.

Distribution and zones of brooch use and loss

The spatial distribution of an artefact type will be dependent on the location of the production sites (which may not be fixed), the mechanisms by which it is distributed and used, and the factors leading to its deposition. In the case of early Anglo-Saxon brooches, their distribution across southern England could have been affected by many factors including control of resources, trade, social relations, the place of craftsmen within society and who controlled craftsmen. The status of craftsmen within society (élite specialists or high value slaves controlled by an élite), and whether they were travelling craftsmen or based in settled workshops, will be relevant factors affecting production and distribution. Many of the brooches considered here were imports, produced abroad. Most, however, were probably manufactured within the study area.

Of these, most were probably produced by itinerant workers; only for the Kentish range of square-headed and garnet-inlaid disc brooches is there circumstantial evidence for production being based in a fixed, specialist, location, in this case Faversham (Richardson 2005, I: 33-34).

Cultural, social, ethnic, tribal or other aspects of group identity are also likely to have been factors affecting the distribution of brooch types, brooches being an archaeologically visible aspect of different costume styles that seem, in the 5th and 6th centuries at least, to have reflected local and regional identities within Germanic society. In the past attempts were often made to relate particular brooch (and other artefact) types directly to historically attested Anglian, Saxon and Jutish (or other) identities. However it is now generally accepted that in few, if any, cases can specific artefact types be directly equated with a particular ethnic (or other) identity; a saucer brooch within a grave is no longer considered to be an indication of that individual's Saxon ethnicity, nor a cruciform brooch an indicator of an Angle. Rather, suites of artefacts were employed in different ways by different groups, with often considerable overlaps both between artefact suites and areas of distribution. Strong regional patterning is, however, apparent, especially within southern England, although it seems unlikely that there was ever a straightforward correlation between brooch types and ethnic affiliation. Prior to the advent of the PAS, established distribution patterns for most brooch types had been identified, most of these being based on brooches recovered from burials. A summary of these distribution patterns can be found in Lucy (2000: 134-37, figs. 5.5-5.7).

The PAS data on early Anglo-Saxon brooches has been used to generate distribution maps (Figs. 5-7) providing preliminary comparisons of the distributions of the different brooch types within this data set. This was then used to define a number of broad zones of brooch use, loss and recovery (see Fig. 8 for provisional map of these zones). These zones were then compared with the established brooch distribution patterns derived from archaeological sources (primarily cemetery excavations). The aim was not to define zones of ethnicity (or any other form of cultural identity), but simply to identify and highlight areas in which certain brooch types, or ranges of brooch types, appeared to be most common. In fact, it could be argued that the resulting zones do correlate to some extent with attested historical tribal and/or ethnic boundaries.

The commonest brooch types from the study area, for which established archaeological distribution maps were also available, were saucer, button, cruciform and small long brooches. A brief summary of the distribution of each of these types is outlined below.

In the case of saucer and button brooches, the distribution pattern of the PAS records correlates well with the established archaeological distribution pattern. Tania Dickinson (this volume) highlights the fact that the PAS data has increased the corpus of saucer brooches available for study, but has not shown any discrepancy with the established distribution patterns, either in terms of overall distribution or in terms of stylistic distribution within the saucer brooch class. Both the excavated and PAS datasets suggest the Upper Thames region as the likely production area for most insular cast saucer brooches due to the high concentration of brooches in this area.

The PAS data has greatly increased the known corpus of button brooches. Button brooches are an insular development, but with strong Scandinavian influences. The face masks can be found on square headed and cruciform brooches, and an even more direct link to Scandinavia is the face-mask motifs on the round Scandinavian button clasps (Welch 1985: 145), although the origin of their development in England is still unclear. By January 2007, the PAS had recorded 62 button brooches in the study area considered by the paper, increasing Avent and Evison's 1982 corpus by over 50%. This data supports the overall distribution pattern of the class as a whole established by the excavated examples from burials. However, the distributions of sub-classes of button brooches do not always match that of the distribution patterns established from burials. Due to the limits of this paper, the typologies and distributions of individual classes will not be discussed in full. In summary, however, the more naturalistic button brooches, Class A, which Avent and Evison attributed to a Kentish origin (1982: 79) are no longer limited to Kent, and the more stylised brooches, such as class C, D and E, which were not recorded in Kentish graves have now been recorded in Kent through the PAS. Class B brooches maintain their wide distribution across the whole of southern England. Beyond the distribution of individual classes within the button brooch corpus, it is interesting to note that the two areas containing the most diverse range of classes are Kent and Hampshire, and these are also the only two areas to record 'button-type' brooches (of button brooch size without a face-mask motif) through the PAS. The diversity and numbers of button brooches in Kent and Hampshire suggest two likely areas for this brooch type's origin and development.

It has already been noted that cruciform brooches have been recovered in greater numbers than expected as metal-detector finds in east Kent. The PAS records now also include a number of examples of cruciform brooches from Kent west of the Medway valley, in an area usually characterised as having a Saxon cultural background distinct from that of east Kent. In general the brooches found in west Kent do reflect this, with higher proportions of saucer and disc brooches than are found in the east, for instance, but the picture is not as clear cut as might have been expected; in particular, detector finds around Cliffe-at-Hoo, north-west of the Medway estuary, include several cruciform (as well as some Kentish square-headed) brooches. Cruciform brooches have also been recorded further west in the Darenth Valley. It is in the east, however, and particularly around the southern inlets of the Wantsum Channel, that cruciform brooches occur in the greatest numbers. Beyond Kent, metal-detectorists have also begun to record examples of

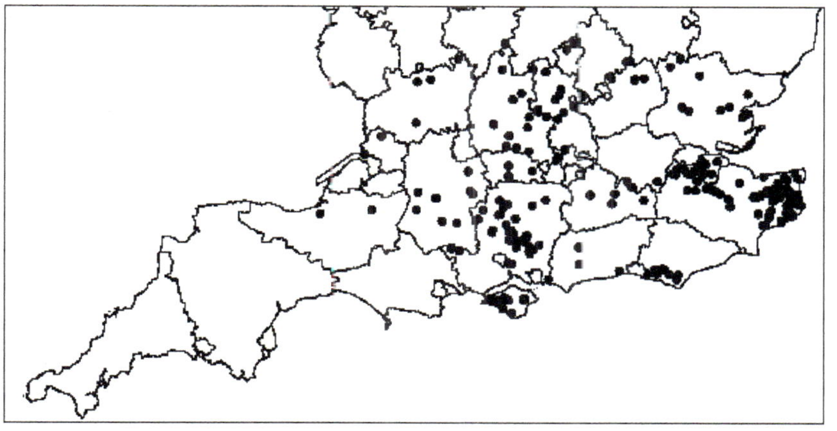

Fig. 5: Distribution of early Anglo-Saxon brooches recorded by the PAS in southern England.

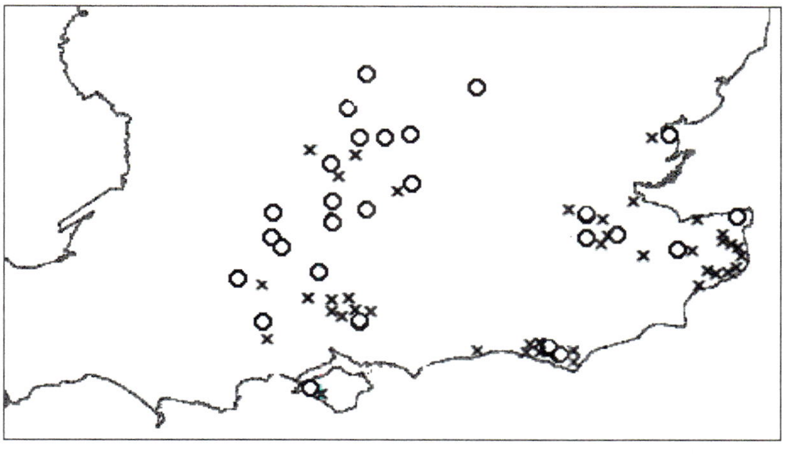

Fig. 6: Distribution of saucer brooches (circles) and button brooches recorded by PAS.

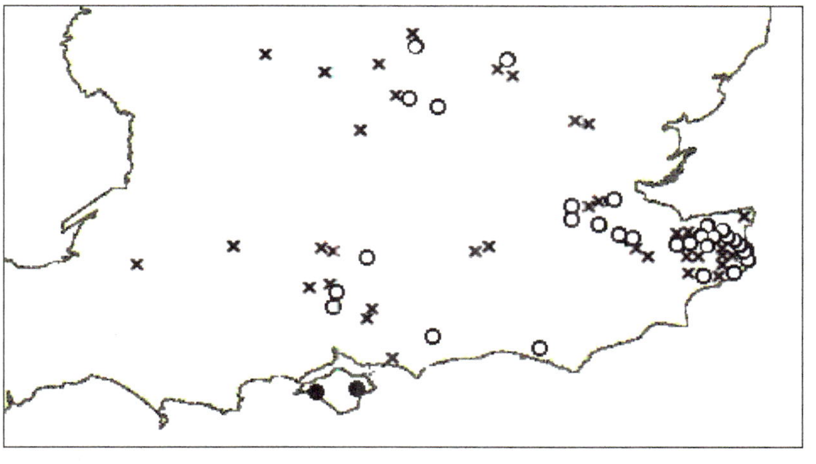

Fig. 7: Distribution of cruciform brooches (circle) and small long brooches (cross) recorded by PAS.

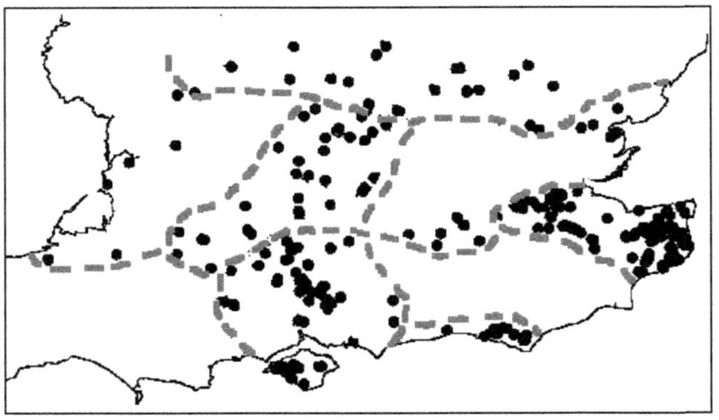

Fig. 8: Zones of brooch use/loss/recovery based on PAS data.

cruciform brooches in Hampshire, the Isle of Wight and the westernmost part of Sussex. A number of other cruciform brooches are recorded from within the study area, but these are from the northern edges of the area and represent the southern extent of the midlands and East Anglian distributions. The examples recorded in Kent, Hampshire, the Isle of Wight and West Sussex are, without exception, examples of Åberg's Groups I-III (Mortimer's types A-C). Most, if not all, probably date from the mid to late 5th century, or very early 6th century, and are probably imports rather than local products. Certainly there is no evidence of production (or indeed use) of cruciform brooches continuing in these areas much into the 6th century, in clear contrast to more northern areas, where insular production and use of cruciform brooches continues for most of the 6th.

The distribution of excavated finds of small long brooches, whilst displaying a midlands and East Anglian bias, does extend across most of the study area, with a very few examples in Kent and more significant scatters along the Thames estuary and down into Hampshire and Wiltshire (Lucy 2000: 133-34, fig. 5.5). The PAS data, however, reveals a significant over-representation of small long brooches across the study area; they are in fact the most numerous type of early Anglo-Saxon brooch recorded by the PAS in southern England. However, it should be noted that the term 'small long' is something of a catch-all for small bow brooches that do not clearly fit into other established classes. The 'small long' category therefore covers a variety of brooch forms; including simplified copies of other brooch types, for example cruciform and square headed brooches, but also brooches that are likely to be a discreet development in themselves. Future research on the different sub-types of small long brooch may enable clearer patterning behind their spatial distribution to emerge.

A number of other brooch types, though not so numerous in the PAS records as the types discussed above, also seem to have quite discreet distributions within the study area. These include small and/or Kentish square-headed brooches, which seem confined to Kent, the Isle of Wight and Hampshire and its immediate environs, and Kentish garnet-inlaid disc brooches, which have a similar distribution, with a small number of copper-alloy imitations in the Hampshire/Wiltshire border area, perhaps indicating a localised production. Overall, comparison of the different brooch type distributions has enabled a provisional sub-division of the study area into seven zones, illustrated in Figure 8. The Kent and Isle of Wight/Hampshire zones are characterised by broadly similar proportions of brooch types, with a diverse range present, whereas other areas show much more limited ranges of brooch types. Some zones, such as the Wealden zone, have yet to produce any detector finds of brooches, and clearly correlate either with areas of low scale human activity (such as woodland), or with areas that were culturally British, rather than Germanic. The divisional zones will be explained in more detail in a subsequent paper.

Conclusions

This paper has summarised initial analyses of spatial distribution patterns created by PAS data compared with established distribution patterns derived from excavations. At the current stage in this research project a number of broad patterns are apparent. It has been argued that whilst some metal-detected early Anglo-Saxon brooches are derived from burials, the majority represent accidental losses. This realisation has fundamental implications for the interpretation of early Anglo-Saxon metal work scatters. It follows that the areas of the landscape most likely to produce finds of brooches are those areas which saw regular and relatively intensive human activity, but which were not subject to frequent or effective retrieval. The latter areas, it is suggested, are more likely to represent the zones immediately around settlements (and cemeteries perhaps) than areas within settlements themselves.

Where costume in life matched costume worn in death (at the funeral), and where brooch types are all equally prone to accidental loss, then it might be expected that metal-detected finds of brooches closely correlate with the pattern of brooch use from excavated cemeteries. However, in areas (or periods) where the range of brooch types in use differs from the range deposited in furnished burials, or where aspects of brooch design, or use make, some types significantly more or less prone to accidental loss, the pattern of types recovered by metal-detecting will differ from excavated evidence derived from graves.

The study to date demonstrates that bow brooches principally small long brooches and cruciform brooches, have a wider distribution pattern across southern England than would have been expected based upon the funerary evidence. In contrast, the PAS distribution of other, mostly circular, brooch types more closely correlates with established distribution patterns, although the distribution of some sub-types (notably amongst button brooches) in the PAS data may indicate a need to revise existing interpretations of the development and production of those types.

Future Research

Further work as part of this research project should enable refinement and more detailed analysis of the spatial distribution of brooch types and the zones of brooch use/loss/recovery, and hopefully a clearer understanding of the cultural behaviour and identities that lie behind them. Specifically, future work will focus on:

- metal work scatters around known and excavated cemetery sites.
- metal work scatters that could be interpreted as potential cemetery sites.
- metal work scatters/individual finds which are unlikely to represent a cemetery site, and reflect accidental loss or other means of deposition.
- the integration and correlation of the PAS brooch records with the overall brooch corpus for the study area, or selected parts of it.

In relation to these case studies, brooch classes and individual brooches will be studied in more detail, with consideration given to condition, wear and breakage patterns, to assess which brooch types seem more prone to breakage, and thus may be over-represented as metal-detector finds due to accidental loss. The condition of the pin attachments and textile remains will also be taken into account when assessing whether or not brooches were from a non-funerary or funerary context when deposited.

Brooch classes with a wider than expected distribution and frequency as metal- detector finds will be examined in particular detail, in terms of their propensity to accidental loss, their chronological correlation (or not) with the local adoption of furnished burial rites and their use in costume. Consideration will also be given to whether brooches used as dress accessories in life were not selected (or, conversely, were over-represented) as dress accessories in the funeral rite.

The recording of metal-detected finds by the PAS has increased the corpus of known early Anglo-Saxon brooches and has produced some rare and unusual additions to that corpus. This data has considerable potential to help develop, refine and reinterpret typologies, however much of that work lies outside the scope both of this initial summary and of the forthcoming paper. The primary aims of this project are not to reinvent, bolster or amend established typologies of brooch classes. Rather, they are to consider the mechanisms by which brooches entered the archaeological record, and how those brooches were used in life and in death. Although individual classes of brooches will be discussed in the forthcoming paper, with references to typology, new, or substantial revisions to, typological sequences are beyond the scope of this research project; any future studies would be best undertaken as a separate research project which can incorporate all available data, including both PAS and excavated evidence, within a wider context.

Bibliography

Arnold, C. J. 1982, *The Anglo-Saxon cemeteries of the Isle of Wight* (British Museum, London)

Avent. R. and Evison, V. I. 1982, 'Anglo-Saxon button brooches', *Archaeologia* 107, 77-124.

Hinton, D. A. 1998, *Anglo-Saxon Smiths and Myths*. The Toller Memorial lecture, reprinted from the Bulletin of the John Rylands University Library of Manchester, vol. 80, no. 1. Manchester Centre of Anglo-Saxon Studies (University of Manchester, Manchester).

Leahy, K. 2003, *Anglo-Saxon Crafts* (Tempus, Stroud).

Lewis, M. J. 2001, 'Kent Anglo-Saxon Brooch Project', *FLO Kent: the newsletter of the Finds Liaison Officer* 3 (Kent County Council, Maidstone), 1.

Lucy, S. 2000, *The Anglo-Saxon Way of Death: burial rites in early England* (Sutton Publishing, Stroud).

Mortimer, C. 1988, 'Anglo-Saxon copper alloys from Lechlade, Gloucestershire', *Oxford Journal of Archaeology* 7, no. 2, 227-33.

Parfitt, K. and Brugmann, B. 1997, *The Anglo-Saxon Cemetery on Mill Hill, Deal, Kent,* Society for Medieval Archaeology Monograph Series 14 (Society for Medieval Archaeology, London).

Parfitt, K. and Anderson, T. forthcoming, *Buckland Cemetery Report* (Canterbury Archaeological Trust, Canterbury).

Richardson, A. F. 2004a, 'The Kent Anglo-Saxon brooch project', in Lewis, M. (ed.), *Portable Antiquities Scheme Annual Report* 2003/04 (MLA, London).

Richardson, A. F. 2004b, 'Kent', in Geake, H. (ed.), 'The Portable Antiquities Scheme', *Medieval Archaeology* 28, 236-38

Richardson, A. F. 2005, *The Anglo-Saxon Cemeteries of Kent*, British Archaeological Reports, British Series 391, 2. vols. (John and Erica Hedges, Oxford).

Richardson, A. F. and McLean, L. A. 2006, 'Kent' in Geake, H. (ed.), 'The Portable Antiquities Scheme', *Medieval Archaeology* 50, 286-87

Walton Rogers, P. 2007, *Cloth and Clothing in Early Anglo-Saxon England*, CBA Research Report 145 (Council for British Archaeology, York).

Welch, M. G. 1985, 'Button brooches, clasp buttons and face masks', *Medieval Archaeology* 29, 142-54.

Williams, H. 2006, *Death and Memory in Early Medieval Britain* (Cambridge University Press, Cambridge).

Beyond the Tribal Hidage: using portable antiquities to explore early Anglo-Saxon kingdoms in southern England

Sue Harrington and Martin Welch

'Beyond the Tribal Hidage' is a project based at the Institute of Archaeology, University College London (UCL), and funded from 2006 to 2009 by the Leverhulme Trust. It is researching the origins of the first Anglo-Saxon kingdoms in Britain south of the Thames Valley within the period 400-750 AD. A primary objective is to draw together the relevant data from both archaeological and written sources (including place-names) into a coherent whole in the form of an electronic database. The Portable Antiquities Scheme (PAS) database has proved to be a particularly significant and valuable resource that assists the project in testing and confirming current perceptions of the transition from Roman Britain to Anglo-Saxon England.

State formation in southern Britain

The dynamic cultural changes in central, southern and eastern Britain involved decline, disruption, migration and invasion. These eventually saw localised 'tribal' groups coalescing into visible, organised and documented kingdoms (or provinces to use Bede's terminology). This change in social organisation is captured in one of the few early medieval texts available to us, the *Tribal Hidage*. This survives in 11th-century copies that list polities existing in the 7th century. These political units were expressed as peoples, such as the Cantwarena (Kent), the Suþsexena (Sussex), the Gyrwe (Fen Dwellers in Cambridgeshire), who owed annual tribute renders to a then dominant king, whether Northumbrian or Mercian overlords (Brooks 1989: 159-61). The evidence suggests that the Anglo-Saxon kingdoms mentioned in this and other early written sources such as Bede's *Ecclesiastical History* were comparatively recent creations of the late 6th and early 7th centuries (Yorke 1990: 4).

The project systematically explores three neighbouring kingdoms listed in the *Tribal Hidage*. There are the Jutes of Kent (Cantwarena), the South Saxons (Suþsexena) and the West Saxons (Westsexena). Interestingly, Surrey falls between them, but apparently does not develop into a kingdom (Blair 1991: 12-24). Although located within a single geographical zone and contiguous with one another, these three kingdoms exhibit contrasting characteristics when they emerge into the historical record of the seventh century. The South Saxons form a standard-sized kingdom, Kent has expanded to more than double its original standard-sized core in East Kent, while the West Saxons represent an amalgamation of several former kingdoms, including the Jutish province in Hampshire and the Isle of Wight (Yorke 1990: 137).

A central question is whether the formation of kingdoms in the post-Roman period was a top-down process - the result of centralised leadership, militarism and control of inter-regional trade - or was rather a bottom-up process. The latter would be characterised by patterns of exchange between pre-state social groups, the differential use of resources and shifting models of landscape exploitation, eventually re-deployed to underpin the consolidation of regional power. It is the bottom-up process that the project explores.

Through processes of data collection and GIS mapping, fundamental and interconnected issues are being addressed in this research. Firstly, it will consider how incoming migrants from north-western Europe utilised Late Roman landscape structures and communication networks in southern Britain, such as roads and major settlements. Secondly, it identifies changes in production, consumption, exchange and cultural identity accompanying the formation of our three kingdoms. In particular the project will explore evidence for environmental exploitation, wealth creation and contacts with the Germanic homelands, Frisian traders along the North Sea littoral and the Frankish kingdom.

The primary sources of data are furnished burials and, to a lesser degree, excavated settlements, making it possible to map the scale and extent of the kingdoms. Here, discrete artefacts are central to this analysis, in terms of their type, provenance, raw material and weight. These are all aspects that the PAS also records as a matter of course. It has been established already that access to resources was unevenly distributed between populations, with the clearest evidence coming from earlier research on East Kent, with its preponderance of ironwork and imported goods. These tail off in volume for those communities furthest from major trading networks or beyond the Kentish sphere of influence (Brookes 2007: 146-50). The teleological element at work here is that social and economic change appears to be stimulated by competition between communities. Nevertheless, the formation of kingdoms was clearly not a uniform and coherent process over time and it is by examining both broad trends and local-scale interactions that a more nuanced view of the period will be realised.

The archaeological evidence for the early Anglo-Saxon kingdoms

The Beyond the Tribal Hidage Electronic Database (THED) has been built up initially from the Anglo-Saxon Kent Electronic Database (ASKED); now freely available as a special online collection through the Archaeology Data Service. ASKED was a research tool developed by Sue Harrington and Stuart Brookes at the Institute of Archaeology, UCL between 1998 and 2001. For the new project ASKED has been extended using the same format to cover the rest of Kent, East and West Sussex, Hampshire, the Isle of Wight, Dorset, Wiltshire, Somerset, Gloucestershire, Berkshire, Oxfordshire south of the Thames, Surrey and Greater London south of the Thames. In addition we have recorded those parishes bordering the Thames on its north bank. Data collection was closed with effect from August 2007, with the final totals of 2,055 locations for early Anglo-Saxon material, burial records for approximately 11,500 individuals and 29,300 objects. All of these have been mapped over space to 12-figure National Grid References using GIS technology.

The PAS data, available in the public domain, is additional to these totals. Excluding coins, there are in the region of 900 new location spots of relevant metalwork objects within the study area as a whole, representing an increase of 44% on the total given above. This rather startling percentage increase in the number of locations is not evenly spread geographically, however, as Table 1 illustrates.

The recorded location totals from the project database presented here for each county comprise only the cemeteries, burial sites and certain other findspots, i.e. those sites producing metalwork comparable to the items listed through the PAS. This deceptively rosy picture of enhancement by the PAS should be qualified by three observations:

- some of these entries may represent duplications in both datasets, as the amalgamation of the PAS data into county SMR/HERs is uneven, adding to the difficulties of producing a definitive early Anglo-Saxon listing for each county;
- some of the PAS entries may relate to already known sites, such as on the Isle of Wight, where significant additional material and indeed several grave groups have been retrieved from beyond the limits of the scheduled area of the Bowcombe Down Anglo-Saxon cemetery (Arnold 1982: 89-96);
- the numbers of entries in each county may be indicative of the density of metal-detectorist activity and also reflective of the effectiveness of working relationships built up with the PAS's Finds Liaison Officers (FLOs).

Taking the southern, coastal part of our study region as a case study, the contribution to the total number of metal objects recorded appears to be somewhat unbalanced in terms of the constituent material of the finds. The project database record of approximate totals of iron and copper alloy objects by county is shown in Table 2.

As might be expected, the greatest number of artefacts comes from Kent, with its particularly well-furnished inhumation cemeteries of the 6th and 7th centuries. There is a considerable fall off in terms of object numbers moving westwards county by county. Table 2 also highlights the imbalance between the background noise represented by the overwhelming number of iron objects in the archaeological excavation record and the emphasis on copper-alloy artefacts, and indeed also gold and silver items, from the metal-detector retrieved finds.

County	Recorded locations	PAS locations	Percent increase
Kent (East and West, including Greater London)	334	397	118%
Sussex	178	65	33%
Hampshire	153	115	75%
Isle of Wight	49	99	202%
Dorset	69	14	20%
Wiltshire	253	34	13%
Somerset	30	12	40%
Berkshire (including Vale of the White Horse, Oxon)	139	46	33%
Surrey (including Greater London)	124	17	14%

Table 1: Findspots of metalwork by county (those falling wholly within the study area).

County	Iron	PAS iron	Copper-alloy	PAS copper-alloy
Kent	6,000	7	2,000	309
Sussex	1,000	2	500	56
Hampshire	1,000	0	400	110
Isle of Wight	250	1	200	86
Dorset	150	0	10	13

Table 2: Iron and copper-alloy objects by county, from excavations and PAS finds.

County	Gold objects	PAS gold	Silver objects	PAS silver
Kent	97	15	342	29
Sussex	3	1	20	0
Hampshire	6	0	24	2
Isle of Wight	2	3	17	5
Dorset	5	[illegible]	3	0

Table 3: Gold and silver objects by county (precious metal as the major component, not including gilded objects).

It seems probable that the absence of ironwork in the PAS corpus may be a direct consequence of the search methods used by detectorists. Apparently habitually they set their equipment to filter out iron and presumably only encounter it when it is associated with copper-alloy objects.

New finds in Dorset

Nevertheless, these new finds reported via the PAS through the Treasure Act 1996 have a key role to play in shifting our perceptions of the distributions of relatively high-status metalwork objects in copper alloy and precious metals over the landscape. This is evident in the example of Dorset, where as a direct consequence of metal-detectorist activity, it now appears that the material culture of the early Anglo-Saxon period may have shared more similarities with that of its neighbours to the east than had been considered previously.

Indeed, the recovery of even small numbers of gold and silver artefacts has added significantly to the total number of recorded objects made from these materials in a relatively short space of time (Table 3). Clearly there are potentially important variables in the distribution of high-status metalwork objects over geographical space between the early Anglo-Saxon kingdoms. The well-established similarities during the 6th century between burial sites in east Kent and the Isle of Wight (Arnold 1982: 102-9; Welch 2007: 192) are demonstrated by the comparability of access to precious-metal items, an aspect supported by the finds reported Treasure through the PAS.

Once again, Dorset appears as something of an anomaly. Although notionally located on the edge of the Anglo-Saxon zone of settlement at an interface with potentially hostile British peoples to the west (Eagles 2004), it has produced a significant collection of gold objects now recorded in the THED. Admittedly, each of these items is small in size and light in weight, but the find of a rare, early 7th-century pyramidal gold-and-garnet sword mount, reported Treasure via PAS and recently purchased by Dorset County Museum, adds credibility to this distribution pattern and suggests that revisions to earlier perceptions are required.

Case study: Sussex

It is useful at this point to consider one coherent regional dataset in greater detail in order to assess the impact of the PAS reported finds. The example of early Anglo-Saxon Sussex (the kingdom of the South Saxons) is pertinent here. Meaney (1964: 246-56) recorded just 47 burial locations for the early Anglo-Saxon period in Sussex, while Welch (1983: 333-508) extended this to 135 discrete sites. The amalgamated SMRs for East and West Sussex, incorporating the excavations recorded in the 'grey literature' of reports generated by archaeological contractors, particularly since the 1990s, together with the most recent work published in its county journal (Sussex Archaeological Collections) and personal communications with local researchers, now brings the total number of sites up to 235, of which 178 have produced metalwork. During the last six years the PAS has added a further 65 findspots to this list, representing a further 27%, bringing the grand total to 300.

The county sites list comprises:

- 79 cemeteries of various types (single and mixed rite).
- 55 isolated burials.
- 125 individual findspots.
- 21 settlements.
- 20 miscellaneous sites.

Within the cemetery and isolated burials category, there are some 1,400 recorded individuals and also approximately 2,700 associated artefacts.

The historical background to Saxon Sussex

There are continuing debates around the relationship between the late Roman and post-Roman landscape and the Anglo-Saxon settlement of the south coast of Sussex. These are centred on concerns about transition and both continuity and discontinuity between two distinct material cultures. The historical framework is not drawn from contemporary source material and many historians would regard it as unreliable myth and legend. There are the stories recorded in 9th-century sources, notably the *Historia Brittonum* in which a 5th-century British overlord (Vortigern) is treacherously captured by a Saxon warlord (Hengest). As a result Essex and Sussex are ceded to the Saxons. There are three matching entries in the *Anglo-Saxon Chronicle* relating to another Saxon warrior (Ælle). Landing in three ships at Cymenesora he drives the opposing British into the Weald. A Cumeneshora occurs in the boundary clause of a supposedly 7th-century charter fabricated in the 10th century that grants land on Selsey. This provides the only reason for placing Ælle's landing in the Chichester-Selsey area. Textually and geographically a more plausible location would be further east in the Ouse estuary near Lewes, as this is physically close to the Weald. Next comes a battle with the British at Mearcredesburna (a 'river on the frontier (mark) agreed by treaty'), probably the Ouse, but perhaps the Cuckmere. Although no victor is named, in the final entry Ælle storms the Roman fort at Anderida (Pevensey Castle) massacring the British there. This is an unusual achievement for any early Saxon warlord and suggests that the Saxons had acquired a territory adjacent to the Ouse that had come under threat from a military force protected by stone defences. The capture of Anderida seems to represent the final consolidation of Saxon control over the East Sussex downland as far east as Eastbourne. Additionally the early 8th-century historian Bede knows of Ælle as an important war leader in the 5th century, listing him as the first of those with authority over other kings south of the Humber (Welch 1983: 258; 1989: 81).

The archaeological evidence of Late Roman material

Interestingly, the PAS data and all other archaeological evidence supports an initial Saxon settlement in East Sussex and in particular the region between Lewes and Eastbourne. Overall archaeological evidence for the South Saxons is represented by major cemeteries between Eastbourne in the east and the Chichester region in the west. Only six of the Anglo-Saxon sites could be attributed fairly secure starting dates within the 5th century, however, and only one of these was in West Sussex (Welch 1971: 232-37; 1983: 163-88). The Highdown cemetery and settlement site near Worthing was located within and adjacent to the ramparts of a Late Bronze Age hillfort, whose defences were possibly re-commissioned in the late Roman period. The remaining five cemeteries, one of which at Rookery Hill, Bishopstone is adjacent to its settlement, were located in a restricted block of downland between the rivers Ouse and Cuckmere, with the Weald to the north and the sea to the south.

The contrast with the Roman site distribution, in which the greatest numbers of the major sites occur in West Sussex within a 20 mile radius of Chichester, the walled *civitas* capital (Noviomagus Regnensium), is marked. It seems plausible that the earliest Saxons were settled as *foederati* (troops engaged on the basis of a treaty or *foedus*) in territory well to the east of Chichester. This might have been land that was disposable in the eyes of the principal Romano-British landowners.

The existence of the isolated Highdown site then needs some explanation. It dominates the coastal plain near Worthing and might represent a strategic station for Saxon troops employed by the British to both control and defend the coastal plain on the exposed coastline of West Sussex. The nearby, but further inland mid-5th-century coin hoard from Patching was discovered in 1997 by metal-detectorists and reported under the Treasure Act (White *et al* 1999). This hoard suggests that at least one wealthy British landowner lived in the vicinity of Highdown at a time that overlapped with the Saxon presence there. The coins included 23 Roman or pseudo-Roman gold *solidi* and 27 Roman or pseudo-Roman silver coins, all of which were minted between 333 and 461 AD. A proposed deposition date of *c.* 465 AD seems to be confirmed by a silver sword-chape fitting of a continental type that would be in circulation in the second half of the 5th century. The owner of the Patching hoard may either have died or been forced to flee before he or she had an opportunity to recover it. The presence of this hoard may fit with the suggested identification of a few inhumations within the Saxon cemetery on Highdown as British individuals (Welch 1983: 183). This would suggest that the hilltop settlement originated as a community under British control.

Distinctively 5th-century artefacts, particularly Quoit Brooch Style dress fittings, have been excavated from some Saxon burials in East Sussex, within the dense cluster of sites between the Ouse and the Cuckmere and adjacent to a network of Roman roads. On the other hand, the graves of Saxon warriors buried with 5th-century 'simple' belt sets of the type found at Dorchester-on-Thames, Croydon and Milton Regis are so far missing from the south coast region (Böhme 1986: 498; Welch 1993: 269-78). These belt sets are common at sites along and behind the Rhine frontier, but also occur in significant quantities with inhumations in north-west Germany between the estuaries of the Weser and the Elbe, the continental homeland of the Saxons. Admittedly there are a couple of still later Roman belt fittings of the small fixed-plate buckle type from Sussex. These are recorded from Alfriston in East Sussex (heavily worn from a burial) and Highdown in West Sussex (as an isolated find). Overall, however, evidence for first-generation Saxon military leaders, the equivalents of those named in the written sources, is distinctly limited in Sussex compared to Thames valley sites in Kent, south London and Oxfordshire.

The archaeological evidence of early Saxon material

Returning to the archaeological evidence for East and West Sussex, it can be seen from Table 4 that there are other real differences between the two areas emerging, to put alongside those hinted at in the historical sources.

There is a general parity in terms of site type numbers between East Sussex and West Sussex and in the number of recorded individuals, except for the number of settlements. There are only two settlement sites recorded in East Sussex, though one of these is the extensively-excavated settlement on Rookery Hill, Bishopstone. This was established within the 5th century and includes the presence of at least one probable 7th to 8th-century building (Bell 1977: 224-26; Gardiner, pers. comm.). The remaining 19 settlements (often represented by just a single building) are all located in West Sussex and in general are dated later within the study period. The other unexpected feature is that comparable numbers of burials in relation to the number of cemeteries have produced almost three times as many artefacts in East Sussex as occur in the West Sussex sites. It is this disparity in the deposition of wealth that requires further consideration and explanation. For now it is possible to comment on the relative rarity of richly furnished 6th-century cemeteries in West Sussex, apart from Highdown and Apple Down (Down and Welch 1990).

Sites	East Sussex	West Sussex
All types	121	114
Cemeteries	47	32
Isolated burials	31	24
Find spots	26	34
Settlements	2	19
Other	15	5
Individuals in burials	800	600
Objects in burials	1,900	700

Table 4: Comparison between East and West Sussex by sites, individuals and objects.

There is also the generalised spread across Sussex of poorly-furnished cemeteries secondary in barrows that may be contemporary, but more probably date later in the 7th and 8th centuries.

So there is now a pattern of evidence that can be tested against the PAS data for illustration of comparable or divergent trends. For the period 400 to 600 AD only five new findspots of material are recorded from West Sussex compared to 18 from East Sussex and this reflects the imbalance in the numbers of objects already noted. The West Sussex material comprises three brooches and two mounts, whilst the East Sussex finds include several early brooch types, mainly coming from the lower Ouse valley and between the Ouse and Eastbourne. Kentish-made and Frankish imports dating to the 6th century also occur here. The latter include fragments of Kentish small square-headed brooches and Saxon-type great square-headed brooches, a Frankish bird brooch and a continental Frankish radiate-headed brooch. Such items match finds from relatively recent excavations at an Eastbourne cemetery. Admittedly a single female grave (Eastbourne 655) contains most of the comparable items here, but, on examination of the finds, this woman's dress assemblage would not have looked out of place in a mid-6th century cemetery in east Kent, such as at Sarre on Thanet. Her burial demonstrates the wider cultural and diplomatic links of communities along the south coast between the emerging kingdom of Kent and the Jutish province of Hampshire and the Isle of Wight (Yorke 1990: 27; Welch 2007: 192). This point is reinforced by the metal-detected finds, firmly entrenching these links in East Sussex, but surprisingly not in West Sussex, with exception of the Highdown (Grave 19) assemblage with a pair of Frankish bird brooches.

Importantly, metal-detectorists have recovered a small number of particularly early Saxon metalwork objects, all probably imported from the Elbe-Weser coastlands within the first half of the 5th century. It is unfortunate that nothing is known of their buried contexts in Sussex. A supporting-arm brooch (Perlberg type) from the Willingdon/Jevington downland to the west of Eastbourne is matched by a hybrid supporting-arm brooch from the Keymer area (Welch 1988). For the purposes of dating, the manufacture of such brooches is likely to be within the first third of the 5th century (in Böhme's Stufe II), but deposition in burials in lowland Britain could well occur later within the first half of the century. A metal-detected chip-carved decorated supporting-arm brooch said to be from Hamsey, just to the north of Lewes and adjacent to the Ouse, would also be an import from northwest Germany. It is matched in Riensförde and was probably associated with the Nesse Type equal-arm brooch found there, both being attributable to Böhme's Stufe III in the middle third of the 5th century. Deposition within the second half of the 5th century seems probable for this Hamsey find (Welch 1999: 36). These items hint at the potential for other early finds to come to light, that may match those recorded from excavated cemetery sites in the lower Thames valley as at Dartford (Temple Hill), Orpington and Mucking (Welch 2007: 230). As contexts for the Sussex finds are lacking, it is difficult to extrapolate from this material. On the other hand, these are female dress fitments, so it is possible to conclude that they may represent mixed-sex settled kin groups, rather than single-sex military adventurers who intermarried with the indigenous population.

To conclude, the Saxon settlement of former Roman territory of the Regni within East Sussex, but no further east than Eastbourne, appears to be a homogenous event of short duration. There is no reason to dismiss the concept of territory being ceded to the first Saxons by the remaining Roman hierarchy, first proposed in 1971 (Welch 1971: 232-7; 1983: 257). The core area remains the Ouse-Cuckmere block of downland and present evidence implies a high density of sites, perhaps at intervals of 1km. The communities represented by these sites would have exploited similarly-sized parallel tracts of chalk landscape, but with access to further resources northwards towards the Weald. The first East Sussex sites seem to be founded early within the second half of the 5th century, but there is the exceptional isolated West Sussex site at Highdown possibly containing a small group of post-Roman British inhumations. The unique small group of Highdown women buried wearing early applied disc brooches (unmatched in East Sussex) and its wide range of Quoit Brooch Style metalwork, typical of the earliest horizons of Anglo-Saxon burial in southern England, are significant here. Other sites in East Sussex were perhaps founded a generation or so later than the earliest group.

Figure 1 presents a distribution map of Sussex sites for the whole period (early 5th to mid 8th centuries) as recorded in the project database, but not differentiated by site type.

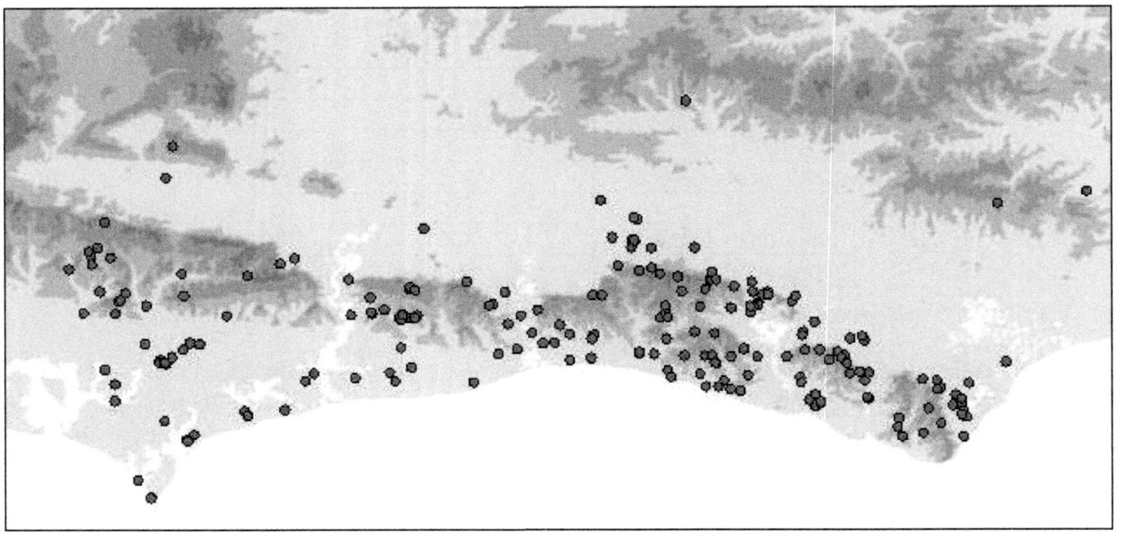

Fig. 1: Map of all non-PAS sites in Sussex from early 5th-mid 8th centuries.

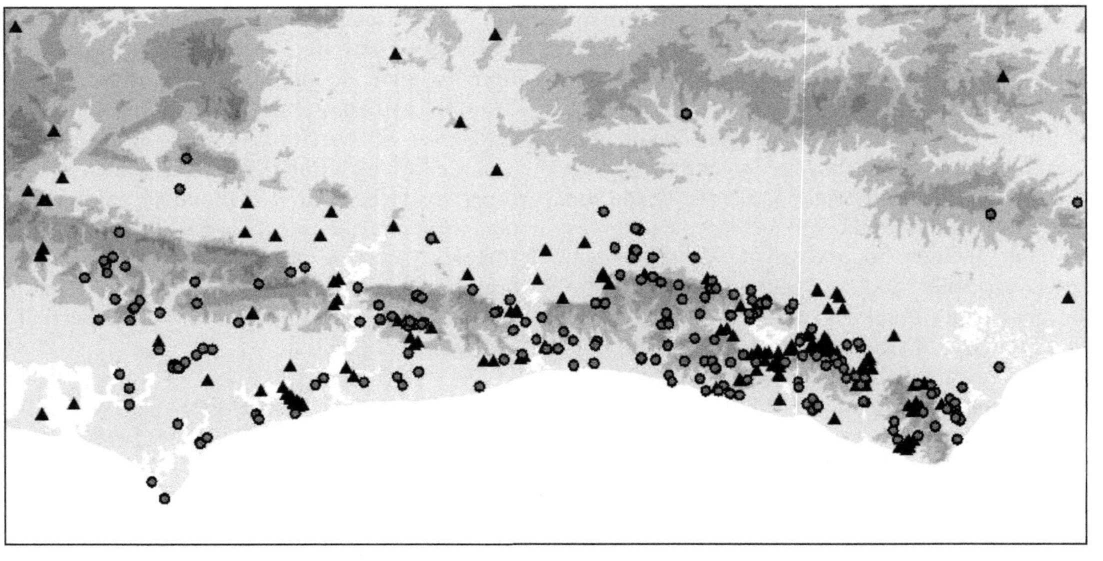

Fig. 2: Map comparing non-PAS (circles) and PAS-derived sites (triangles) in Sussex from early 5th-mid 8th centuries.

The map on Figure 2 combines these sites with the new PAS-generated locations. This new set of locations begins to extend geographically the distribution of Anglo-Saxon material, as evidenced by the small cluster of sites to the north of Chichester and on the southern edge of the Weald. It also confirms the known site distributions, with nearly all of the locations associated with the chalk of the South Downs or with the river valleys cutting through them between Eastbourne and the Chichester region. What is new here is the sheer density of settlement that is emerging through metal-detected find reporting.

Conclusions

The PAS data has supported the exploration of the 'Beyond the Tribal Hidage' project research questions in a number of ways and has the potential to assist us further. For example, any examination of the interplay between late Roman sites and their early Anglo-Saxon equivalents is hampered by the relative paucity of overlapping evidence from conventional excavation. Nevertheless, the distribution of metal-detected late Roman coinage can be mapped against that for the known early Anglo-Saxon sites for comparative distributive purposes. The detection of increasing numbers of high-status metalwork objects is also crucial in developing our understanding of the changing access to and control of such materials over time and space.

The 'Beyond the Tribal Hidage' project has mapped the parameters of the extent of early Anglo-Saxon material culture in southern Britain, parameters that have been hinted at throughout earlier phases of research into this period. Indeed, it would be very surprising if any radical and different indicators were to emerge now, but if any such data is to make an appearance, the most likely source will be through the activities of that most mobile army of object gatherers - the metal-detectorists - rather than through conventional rescue excavation carried out by contract units based in already established locations and reacting to modern development pressures.

Finally it is now possible to raise tentatively the potential for the identification of new site categories - ones that are not simply casual losses of metal artefacts or indicators of abandoned settlements or furnished cemeteries. Instead some of these finds might represent evidence for ritual hoards. Certainly in Scandinavia, deposits consisting of a decorated brooch and bracteates, coins or other pendants do occur (Hines 1989: 29), but as yet the project has failed to identify convincingly any such assemblages in England. Admittedly it has been suggested that finds of iron weapons and parts of shields in rivers might represent another contemporary type of religious deposit here. Nevertheless precious metal hoards are not normal, though isolated finds of bracteates do occur in England.

Archaeological researchers are ready to reassess all aspects of early Anglo-Saxon material culture and examine it in new and innovative ways. Here, the standard of recording of the PAS material sets a benchmark. The PAS material can act as a new reference collection for the types, weights and material content of many object types. It is clear that critical comparison of datasets from conventional archaeological sites with the PAS finds is crucial in forcing us to reappraise our understandings of the origins of the early Anglo-Saxon kingdoms.

Bibliography

Arnold, C. J. 1982, *The Anglo-Saxon Cemeteries of the Isle of Wight* (Trustees of the British Museum, London).

Bell, M. 1977, 'Excavations at Bishopstone', *Sussex Archaeological Collections* 115, 1-299.

Blair, J. 1991, *Early Medieval Surrey: landholding, church and settlement before 1300* (Alan Sutton/Surrey Archaeological Society, Stroud).

Böhme, H. W. 1986, 'Das Ende der Römerherrschaft in Britannien und die Angelsächsische Besiedlung Englands im 5. Jahrhundert', *Jahrbuch des Römisch-Germanischen Zentralmuseums Mainz* 33.2, 469-574.

Brookes, S. 2007, *Economics and Social change in Anglo-Saxon Kent AD 400-900: landscapes, communities and exchange*, British Archaeological Reports, British Series 431 (Archaeopress, Oxford).

Brooks, N. 1989, 'The formation of the Mercian kingdom', in Bassett, S. (ed.) *The Origins of Anglo-Saxon kingdoms* (Leicester University Press, Leicester), 159-70.

Down, A. and Welch, M. G. 1990, *Chichester Excavations 7: Apple Down and the Mardens* (Chichester District Council, Chichester).

Eagles, B. N. 2004, 'Britons and Saxons on the eastern boundary of the civitas Durotrigum', *Britannia* 35, 234-40.

Hines, J. 1989, 'The military context of the adventus Saxonum', in Hawkes, S. C. (ed.), *Weapons and Warfare in Anglo-Saxon England* (Oxford University Committee for Archaeology, Oxford), 25-48.

Meaney, A. L. 1964, *A Gazetteer of Early Anglo-Saxon Burial Sites* (Allen and Unwin, London).

Welch, M. G. 1971, 'Late Romans and Saxons in Sussex', *Britannia* 2, 232-37.

Welch, M. G. 1983, *Early Anglo-Saxon Sussex*, British Archaeological Reports, British Series 112 (British Archaeological Reports, Oxford).

Welch, M. G. 1988, 'A Saxon equal-arm brooch from Keymer, Sussex', *The Antiquaries Journal* 67, 364-65.

Welch, M. G. 1989, 'The kingdom of the South Saxons', in Bassett, S. (ed.), *The Origins of the Anglo-Saxon Kingdoms* (Leicester University Press, Leicester), 75-83.

Welch, M. G. 1993, 'Archaeological evidence for federate settlement in Britain in the fifth century', in Vallet, F. and Kazanski, M. (eds.), *L'armée romaine et les barbares du IIIe au VIIe siècle* (Association Francaise d'Archéologie Mérovingienne et Musée des Antiquités Nationales, Rouen), 269-78.

Welch, M. G. 1999, 'Relating Anglo-Saxon chronology to continental chronologies in fifth century AD', in Freeden, U. v., Koch, U. and Wieczoreck, A. (eds.), *Völker an Nord- und Ostsee und die Franken* (Römisch-Germanische Kommission Reiss-Museum, Mannheim), 31-38.

Welch, M. G. 2007, 'Anglo-Saxon Kent to AD 800', in Williams, J. H. (ed.), *The Archaeology of Kent to AD 800* (Boydell Press/Kent County Council, Woodbridge) , 187-248.

White, S. Manley, J., Jones, R., Orna-Ornstein, J., Johns, C. and Webster, L. 1999, 'A mid-fifth century hoard of Roman and Pseudo-Roman material from Patching, West Sussex', *Britannia* 30, 301-15.

Yorke, B. 1990, *Kings and Kingdoms of Early Anglo-Saxon England* (London, Seaby).

The Changing Face of Saucer-brooch Distribution, 1912 - 1977 - 1997 - 2007

Tania Dickinson

The most numerous and widely distributed type of gilded and relief-decorated brooch in Early Anglo-Saxon England is the saucer brooch. It is best known as an element of burial dress, with the brooches usually worn in pairs to fasten an adult female's overdress at the shoulders. Composite saucer brooches, decorated with applied *Pressblech* or cast faceplates, first appeared in the earlier 5th century in north Germany and the Netherlands, whence they were introduced to England. The fully cast form emerged during the 5th century, but is rare on the Continent and seems to be an essentially English product, persisting here until the late 6th century (Dickinson 1993; Inker 2006). During this time, the form of saucer brooches varied little except in size, but their decoration varied a lot. From the end of the 5th century onwards the initial repertoire of late antique geometric motifs was supplemented by and integrated with motifs taken from Salin's Style I, the complex animal art that had developed in southern Scandinavia (Dickinson 2002).

The potential wealth of data that saucer brooches offer - typologically and contextually - has made them an attractive target for archaeological study. In 1912 E. T. Leeds based his first systematic essay into the dating and distribution of the Anglo-Saxon settlement on them, and later they formed a major component of my doctoral study of the Upper Thames Region (Dickinson 1976), which included an attempt to use minor differences in the decoration of pairs to explore questions about the methods and contexts of brooch-production (Dickinson 1982). More recently, they have been used to explore social and ideological meanings behind the decorative designs (Dickinson 1991; 2002). In all these analyses, mapping findspots played a significant role, and it is therefore important to know whether they reflect genuine patterns of past activity or merely the accidents of survival and modern recovery. In general, a findspot must be taken to represent the place of final usage or deposition, whether that was a deliberate discard, as in a burial, or an accidental loss, since, as yet, there is little good evidence for where saucer brooches were actually made.

One way to test whether the distribution reflects past reality or not is to monitor changes over time in the rate and/or pattern of discoveries, an analysis which I had in mind in 1977 when starting to compile a corpus of cast saucer brooches. Among the data recorded was a 'date of discovery'. In many cases this was the actual date of discovery, but in others it could be only approximate or a *terminus ante quem* given by the date of the first public reporting. No record, however, was made of what occasioned discovery - be it, for example, agricultural or industrial intervention or, especially since the 1980s, metal-detecting - nor was a distinction made between casual finds reported through the Portable Antiquities Scheme (PAS) and those reported through the provisions of the 1996 Treasure Act, to a local Sites and Monuments (SMR) or Historic Environment Record (HER), to a museum or by some other means. In fact, of the 700 entries in my database as at January 2007, on which the analyses in this paper are based, only thirty-eight were derived from the PAS database (though it is always possible that more existed there undetected; by March 2007 the number had gone up to 40 out of 708 entries). Whilst so far the contribution of the PAS to saucer brooches seems relatively modest, these data make it possible to assess how the rate of discovery and its geographical range have changed over the long term, and in particular to judge whether new finds are providing new information - on types and locations - or are merely reinforcing existing knowledge.

Growth in numbers

First, then, what has been the rate of discovery? If a straight count of discoveries by decade is taken (Fig. 1), then the variously fluctuating peaks can be explained by the excavation of individual cemeteries, sometimes with largish numbers of saucer brooches apiece: these start in the mid-19th century, when archaeological reporting and investigation as a whole took off. The figures can also be presented as a cumulative frequency diagram (Fig. 2), and again the cemetery excavations appear as slightly sharper steps in what is otherwise a fairly consistent rate of discovery. At this scale, neither metal-detecting nor PAS seems to register much of an impact.

If, however, the discovery of saucer-brooch sites rather than of saucer brooches is considered, then the last twenty-five years or so have seen a significant increase (Figs. 3-4). In other words, there has been a change in the ratio of finds to sites. Most sites produce only one or two saucer brooches, whilst large numbers at one site are exceptional and always reflect substantially excavated cemeteries (with the 32 excavated at Lechlade, Glos, in 1985 still the largest single assemblage: Boyle *et al.* 1998; Dickinson, forthcoming). Since 1977 one- or two-brooch sites have become ever more common: they accounted for 61 per cent of sites up to 1976, but 85 per cent of sites between 1977 and 2007. As a corollary, the ratio of brooches in pairs or twos to singles has also altered (Fig. 5): up to 1976 pairs accounted for 64 per cent of the finds in the corpus, but for finds made between 1977 and 1996 this declined to 50 per cent, and since then it has tumbled to just 37 per cent. Yet if only those brooches from recorded burials are taken, then the proportion of matching or non-matching pairs is over 80 per cent. So while the number of sites has grown considerably, the quality, or complexity, of the data has tended to degrade - unless the new sites represent not burials as are conventionally expected, but some other type of context, as Laura McLean and Andrew Richardson (this volume) suggest might be the case for some brooch-finds in southern England, although it is doubtful that this is so for saucer brooches.

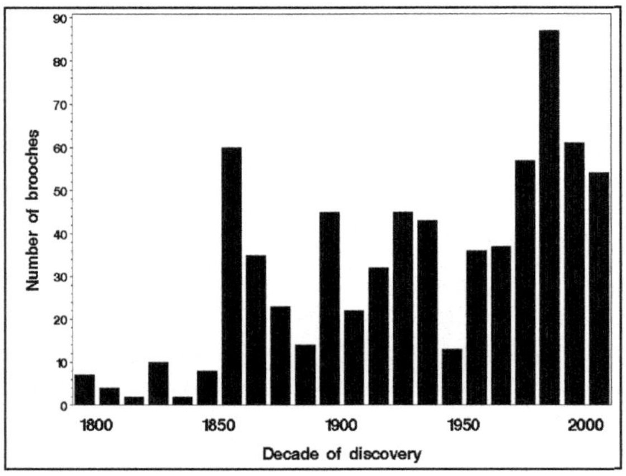

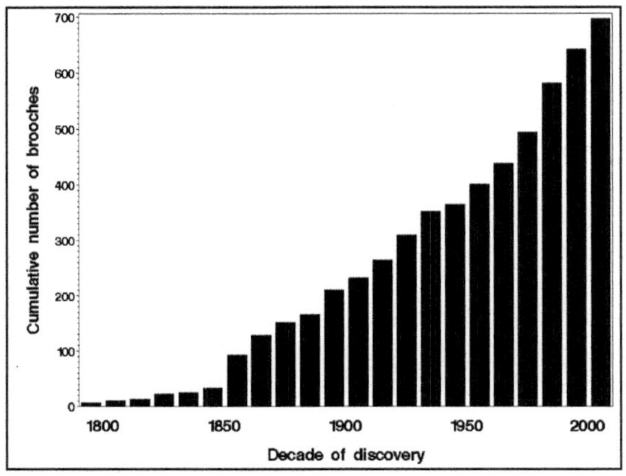

Figs. 1-2: Histogram of discovery of saucer brooches by decade and cumulative frequency histogram of discovery of saucer brooches by decade.

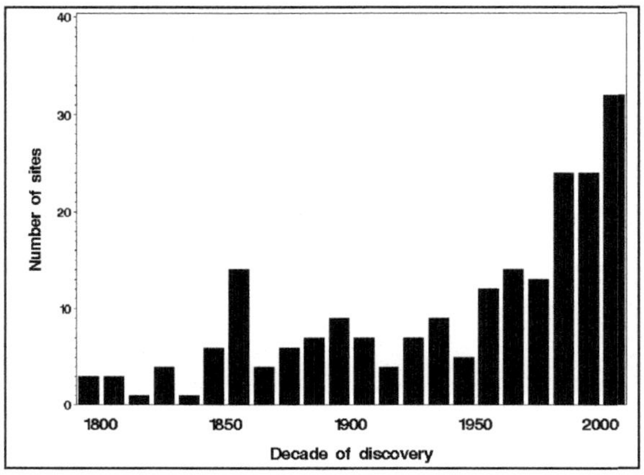

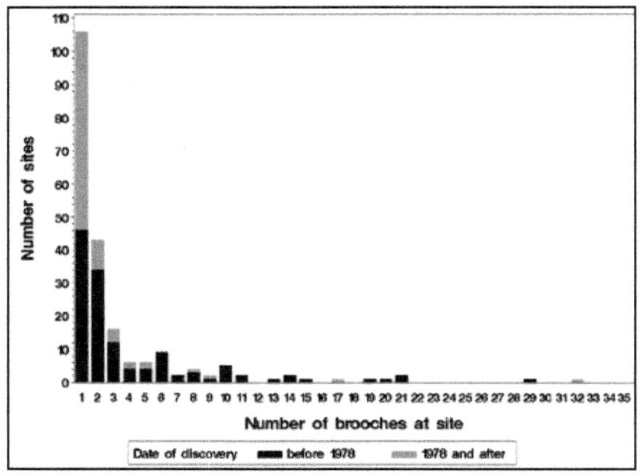

Figs. 3-4: Histogram of discovery of saucer-brooch sites by decade and histogram of ratio of number of brooches to number of sites.

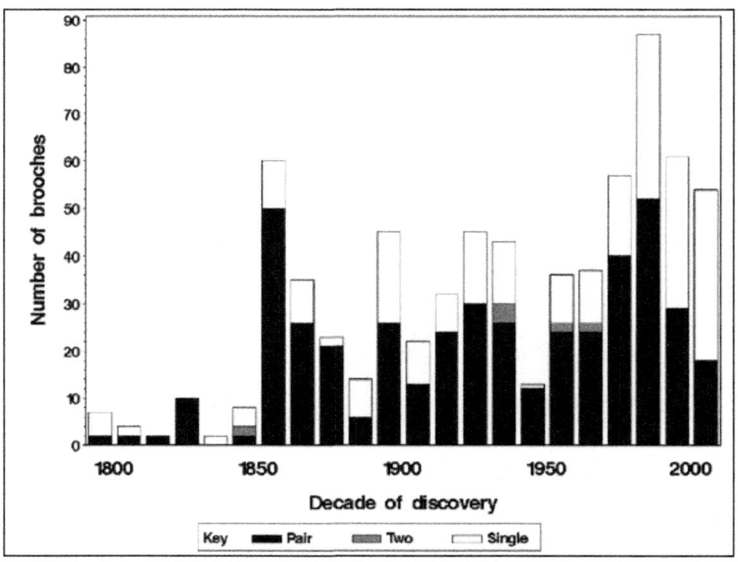

Fig. 5: Histogram of saucer brooches discovered in pairs, twos or singly by decade.

Changes in overall distribution

Second, how have these new sites affected the geographical range of saucer brooches? In 1912, Leeds catalogued 223 cast saucer brooches, so this makes a good starting date for the analysis, though using corrected data from my corpus (Fig. 6; cf. Leeds 1912: 197-202 and fig. 4). The core area of distribution was clearly the Upper Thames and south Midlands, with lesser scatters along the lower Thames and along the south coast from south-east Kent to Sussex. In the years up to starting the corpus in 1977 (Fig. 7), the core areas became increasingly marked, especially the Warwickshire Avon valley. A scatter in South Wessex was becoming evident, whilst a thin spread of new finds from Essex through Norfolk to north Lincolnshire showed that eastern England was not totally outside the saucer-brooch using world. Over the next twenty years (up to and including 1996) the basic picture remained the same (Fig. 8): south Wessex, West Sussex and the Lambourn valley became yet more sharply defined (especially the last, thanks to the good offices of West Berkshire Heritage Services) and Suffolk entered the peripheral distribution in eastern England.

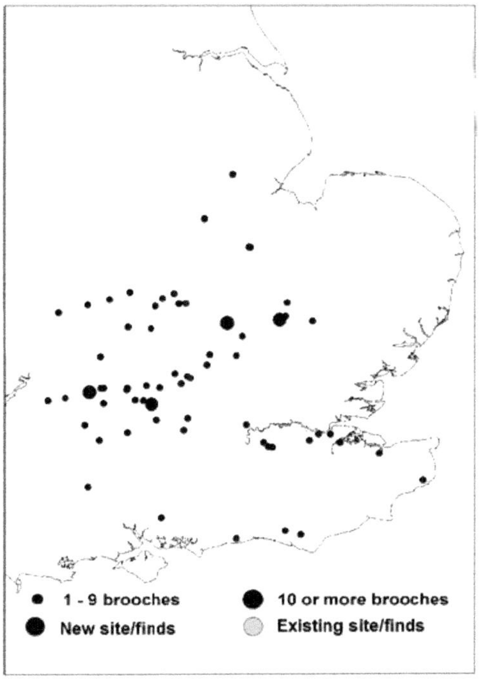

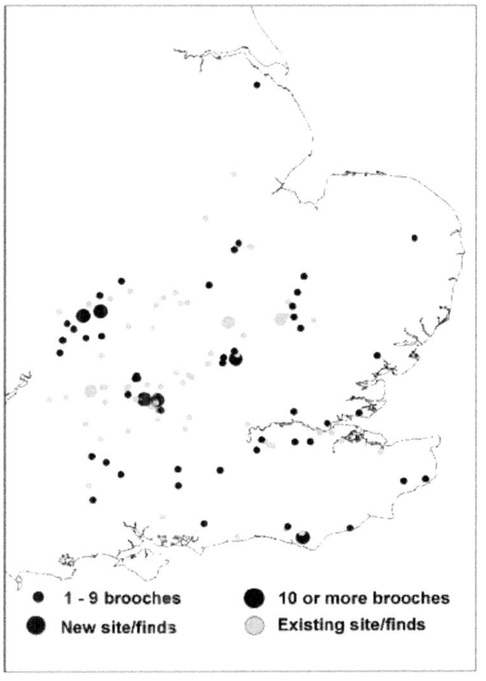

Figs. 6-7: Distribution map of saucer brooches before 1912, and before 1977.

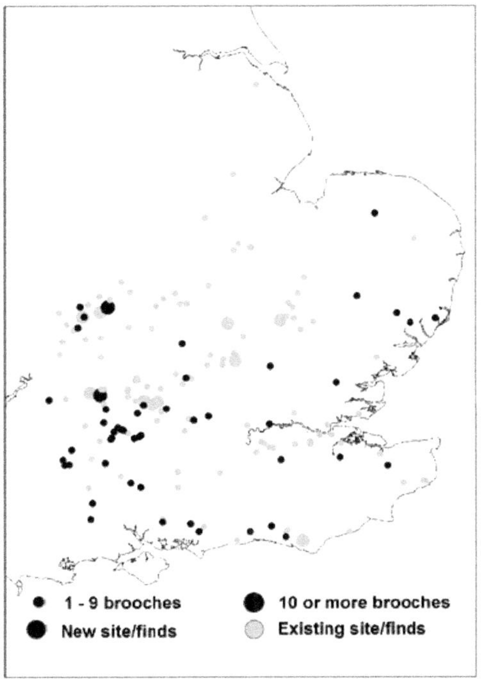

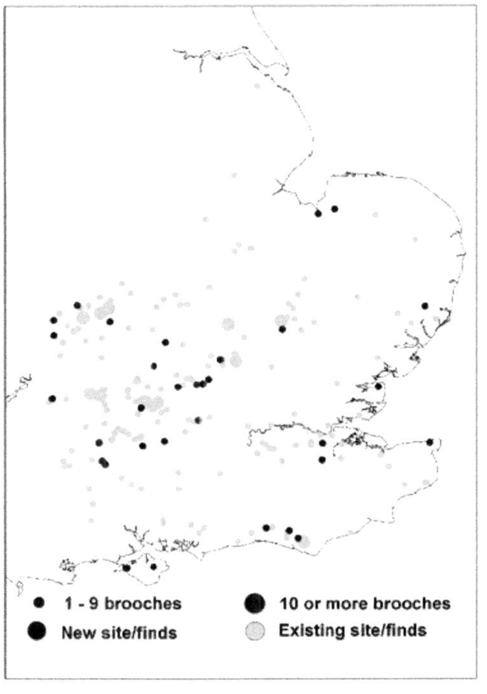

Figs. 8-9 Distribution map of saucer brooches before 1997, and up to January 2007.

The last ten years (Fig. 9) - the PAS years (though the first saucer brooch in the PAS was found in 1995) - are not really long enough to show a significant change, especially given that between 1997 and 2002 the Scheme operated in only six regions, none of which covered core saucer-brooch areas and two (the North-West and Yorkshire) were quite outside them. Nonetheless, the place of north Norfolk in the distribution has been confirmed, and for the first time the Isle of Wight has been registered as a saucer-brooch using district.

Taken together, the maps show how a distinctive 'thumb-print' of saucer-brooch distribution has been progressively revealed: the areas of greatest use - the core areas - have simply become ever more represented, whilst areas of more limited use - the peripheral zones in eastern England and round the southern coastlands - have more slowly become evident (Fig. 10). That this is a real pattern and not a consequence of modern-day factors is supported by the way it contrasts with the distribution of PAS finds in general and, for example, with the particular patterning of many Middle and Late Saxon artefacts, both of which are represented far more heavily in eastern England (Naylor and Richards 2006; Naylor 2006, interpretation and results: figs. 3 and 5).

Changes in distributions of types

Lastly, to illustrate how new finds and locations relate to the repertoire of decorative designs the discussion will focus on the 65 brooches in the corpus discovered between 1995 and January 2007. Here the impact that the PAS has made can be more truly seen: 39 of the finds were reported to the PAS or as an obligation under the Treasure Act 1996; eleven were casual finds reported or publicised by other means; only 15 were archaeologically excavated finds.

Well-known design-types

Thirty of the new finds belong to well-recognised design-types, an outcome which is exemplified by all three of the saucer brooches now known from the Isle of Wight. The brooch from Arreton (IOW-AD1B74) belongs to the largest group of all, the five running spirals design (Fig. 11). In 1988 these comprised 13 per cent of the corpus (Dickinson 1991); since then their representation has increased, accounting for 18 per cent of subsequent finds, and now stands at 14 per cent overall. Moreover, almost all new finds can be assigned to one of the detailed subgroups presented in Dickinson 1991: the most common subgroup then (IIB5) has continued to account for the largest number of new finds - including Arreton.

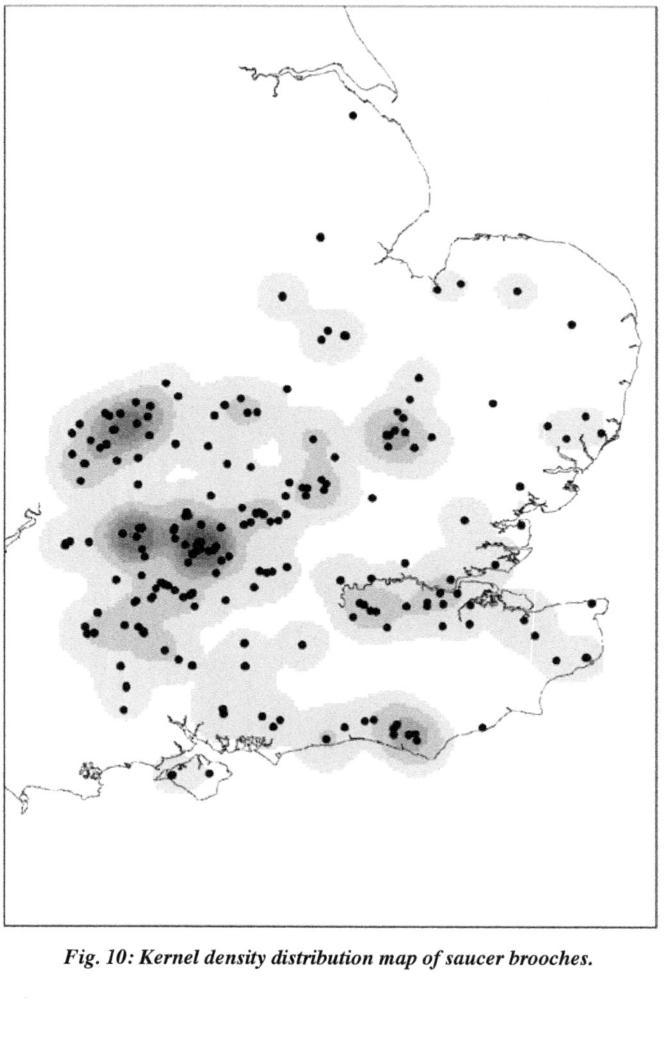

Fig. 10: Kernel density distribution map of saucer brooches.

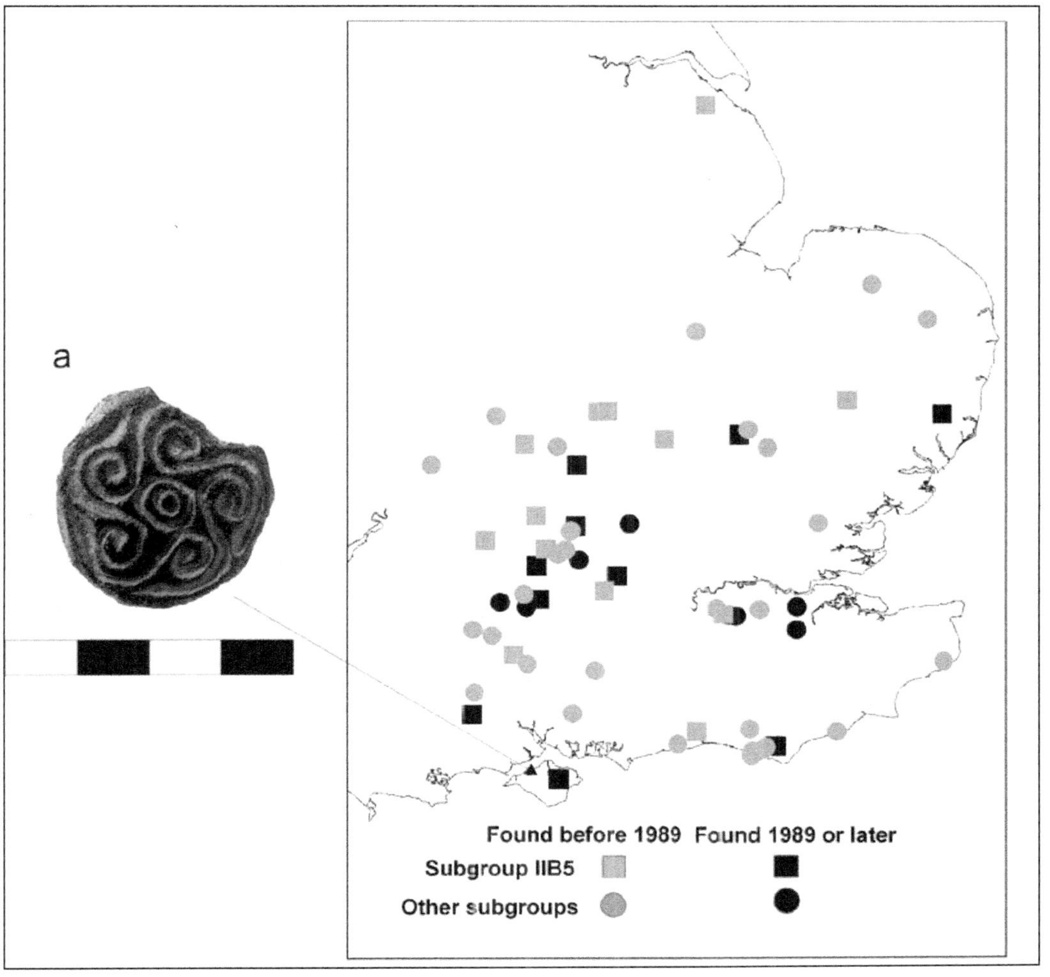

Fig. 11: Saucer brooches with five running spirals design, distinguishing subgroup IIB5 (Dickinson 1991). a. Arreton (IOW-AD1B74). Scale 1:1.

The fragmentary brooch from Yarmouth (IOW-235E85), with two decorated fields of astragal motifs, belongs to another easily recognisable and widely distributed type (Fig. 12; Dickinson 1981). It appears, curiously, to have been cut down in antiquity to a rectangular shape, so might be a candidate for a find from a non-standard context of deposition.

The third Isle of Wight brooch comes from a cemetery known as West Wight (Ager 2004). Although fragmentary and uncleaned, it can be recognised as belonging to a design-type hitherto known only from the core Upper Thames/Warwickshire Avon area (Fig. 13). It is distinguished by three trapezoidal pseudo-inlays, which separate pairs of Style I heads (with coils at the nape of the neck) set back-to-back between bundles of lines. This design appears to be based on Kentish inlaid disc brooches of Avent's Class 3 (Avent 1975: 30-33; Dickinson 1993: 26, fig. 49), which on current understanding would now be dated to the late 6th century. That dating seems corroborated by another new find of the saucer-brooch design-type, a pair from grave 12 at Tring Hill, Aston Clinton, Buckinghamshire (John Hines in Masefield 2008: 138-39). The associated skeleton has yielded a radiocarbon date of 1517 +/- 19 years BP (UB-4975), for which dates of cal. 539-578 AD at one sigma and 1.000 probability, and cal. 533-602 AD at two sigma and 0.914 probability are provided by Calib 5.0.2, using IntCal04.14c (http://calib.qub.ac.uk, consulted June 2007; Stuiver and Reimer 1986-2005; Reimer *et al.* 2004). This seems an important contribution to confirming the late dating of this type of saucer brooch, and with publication of IntCal07 the radiocarbon date is likely to be yet further refined (at two sigma the calibration curve also offered dates of cal. 442-455 AD at 0.025 probability, and cal. 460-484 AD at 0.060 probability, but these are manifestly wrong for this burial).

New variants of well-known design-types

Ten of the recent finds represent variations of well-known designs. For example, metal-detecting at Earwig Corner, near Lewes, East Sussex, on the edge of the Anglo-Saxon cemetery at Malling Hill, South Malling, disturbed further graves, some of which fortunately were then excavated professionally (Welch 1983: 404-5; Thomas 2002; Harrington, Thomas and Merkel, in preparation).

Among the nine saucer brooches found were two pairs of very fine quality, which were decorated with a central Style I leg-swastika and a border of egg-and-tongue in negative relief. The basic design is well known and widely distributed (Fig. 14; Dickinson 1993: 22), but in all examples hitherto the feet have two simple, bifurcated

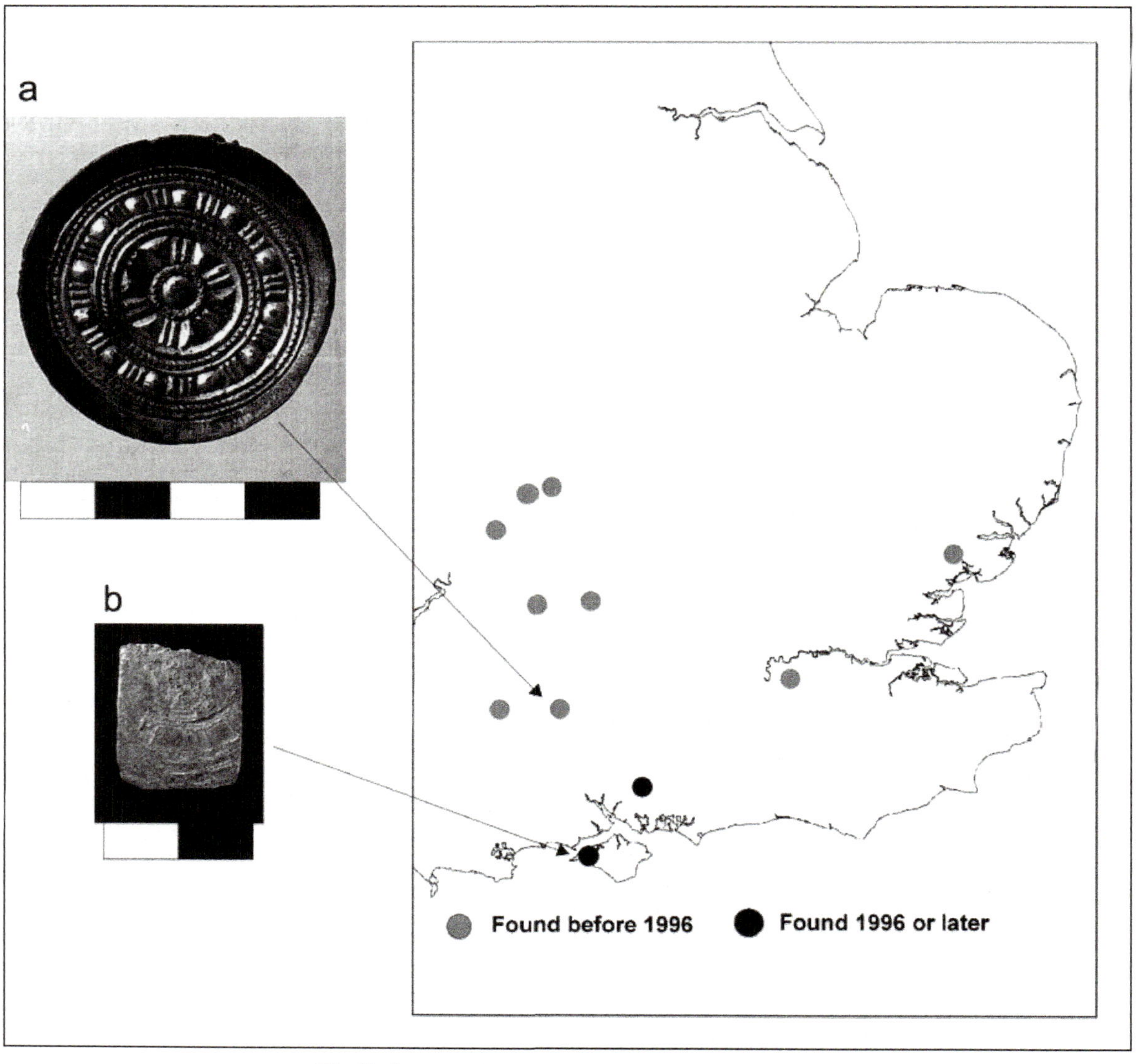

Fig. 12: Saucer brooches with two fields of astragal design.
a. Collingbourne Ducis grave 20, Wiltshire (photograph: T. M. Dickinson);
b. Yarmouth, Isle of Wight (IOW-235E85). Scale 1:1.

toes (Fig. 14a), whereas on the Earwig Corner brooches they have a plain forward-pointing toe and multiple recurved toes (Fig. 14b), a detail in Anglo-Saxon Style I which is particularly characteristic of the high-rectangular belt plates worn by some high-status men in late 5th- and early 6th- century southern England (Fig. 14c-d; Marzinzik 2003, Type II.14a: 42-43). Possibly, this Style I trick was transmitted from the belt-plates to saucer brooches in Sussex, which in turn inspired the less accomplished but more widely distributed versions elsewhere.

The diffusion of designs in style and in space is also illustrated by a design with central 'quatrefoil' disc and a surrounding field of two Style I animal-men with helmet-like heads (Fig. 15). The southern instances from Alfriston grave 101 (Fig. 15c) and Apple Down grave 10, West Sussex, and Mitcham grave 208, Greater London (Welch 1983: 52; Down and Welch 1990: 35, fig. 2.17; *cf.* Dickinson 2002: 172 and fig. 4e) are now joined by a very flat copy from Newbury, West Berkshire (Fig. 15b; NMGW-4B6573), and a quite accomplished piece, though with plain centre, from Ettington, Warwickshire, close to the Avon valley (Fig. 15a; WMID-CDDDF1).

Corroboration of a design-type

Seven new finds have provided valuable evidence that a design previously known only from one or two examples really is a recognisable 'type'. In particular, the floriated cross motif, as it occurs on early 5th-century, continental, applied disc brooches and derivative, Anglo-Saxon, applied saucer brooches, is now represented in cast copper alloy from Firle, East Sussex (SUSS-8C1187) and Earwig Corner grave 2 (Fig. 16d-e), which can be set beside the silver specimen long known from Merton, Greater London (Fig. 16c; cf. Inker 2006: 23, 33, 45, 48 and 50, Types Aiii, Bix and Diii; by March 2007 the PAS had logged another cast example from Puddletown, Dorset, SOMDOR-EB4897). Likewise, a derivative of the floriate cross motif, the four-pelta design, which is found occasionally on the Continent on applied saucer brooches with a cast faceplate and on fully cast saucer brooches, has been known in England only from Luton, Bedfordshire (Fig. 16a). It is now joined by yet another

Fig. 13: Saucer brooches with back-to-back Style I heads between pseudo-inlays. a. Stretton-on-Fosse grave F102, Warwickshire (photograph: T. M. Dickinson); b. West Wight (Treasure: 2004 T187). Scale. a: 1:1; b: not to scale.

Sussex find, a rather crude version from Hassocks, West Sussex (Fig. 16b; KENT5309; Inker 2006: 50). The distribution in England of cast saucer brooches with early floriate cross motifs thus comes much more clearly into alignment with the predominantly south-eastern distribution of the cognate applied brooches (there is no comprehensive, published map for the latter, however: cf. Welch 1975: fig. 1, Evison 1978: fig. 4, and Inker 2006: fig. 6, though this last is selective of the types discussed and classified therein).

New designs

Since 1995 totally new designs have been recorded on only eight brooches. In all cases, however, the designs involve Style I motifs and/or multiple fields of decoration, attributes which are less easily reduced to archaeologically orderly types because of their greater capacity for variation and permutation. Nevertheless, the affinities of their general designs and individual motif-elements are not in doubt. For example, a pair excavated from Croydon Park Lane grave 231, Greater London, decorated with two chasing animal-men are related to a large group of brooches with two or three such creatures (McKinley 2003: 76), whilst finds from Cherington, Gloucestershire (NMGW-0DB6C6), Mildenhall, Wiltshire (WILT-0521F3) and Chesterton, Oxfordshire (NCL-351555) typify the extra-large brooches with multiple geometric and/or highly debased Style I motifs that characterise the last phase of saucer-brooch production, especially in the core areas (Dickinson 1993: 34).

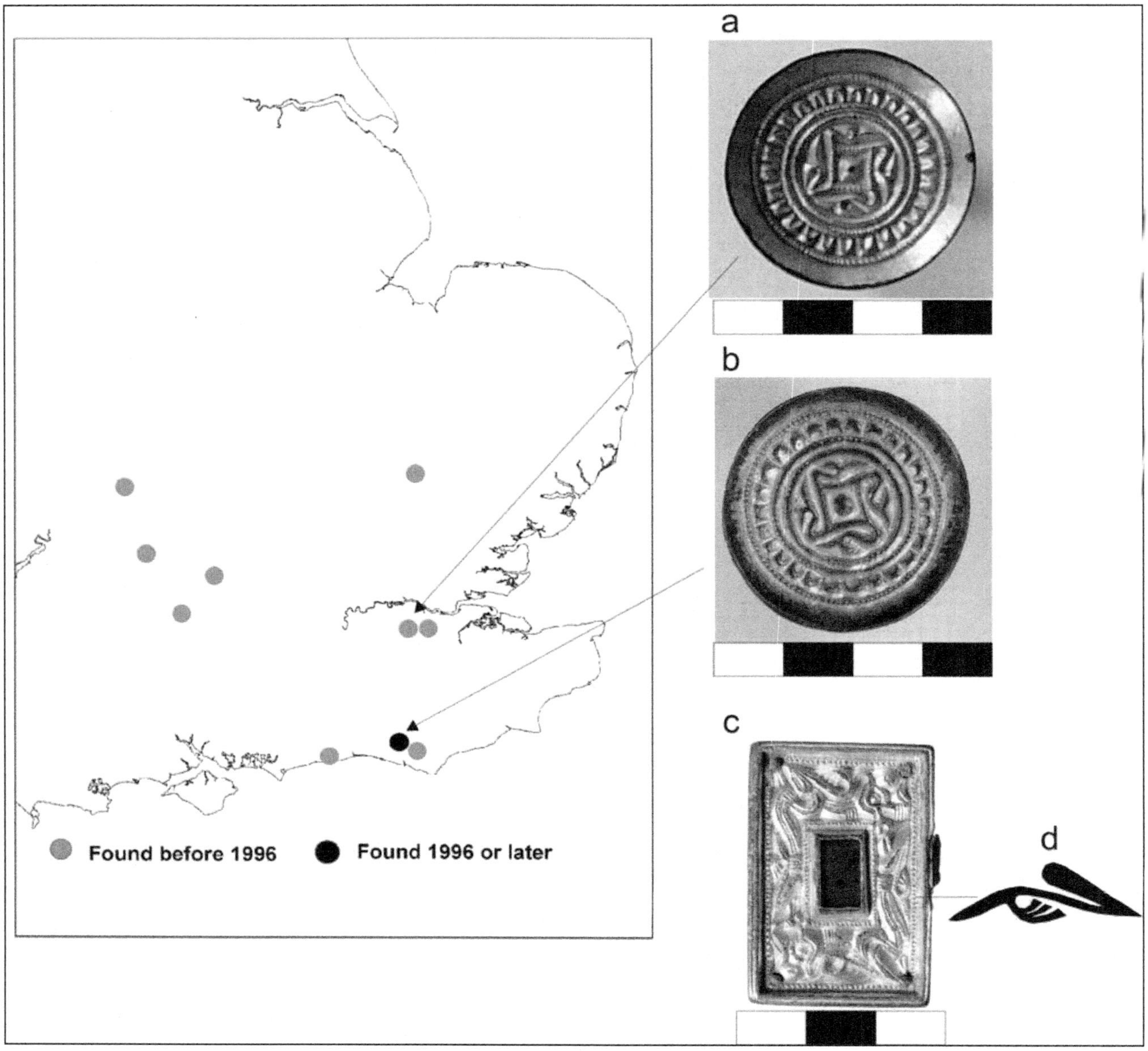

Fig.14: Saucer brooches with leg-swastika and egg-and-tongue design.
a. Horton Kirby II grave 97, Kent; b. Earwig Corner grave 4;
c. Blacknall Field (Pewsey) grave 22, Wiltshire, high-rectangular belt plate;
d. Foot motif from (c) (photographs and line-drawing: T. M. Dickinson). Scale. a-c: 1:1; d: 2:1.

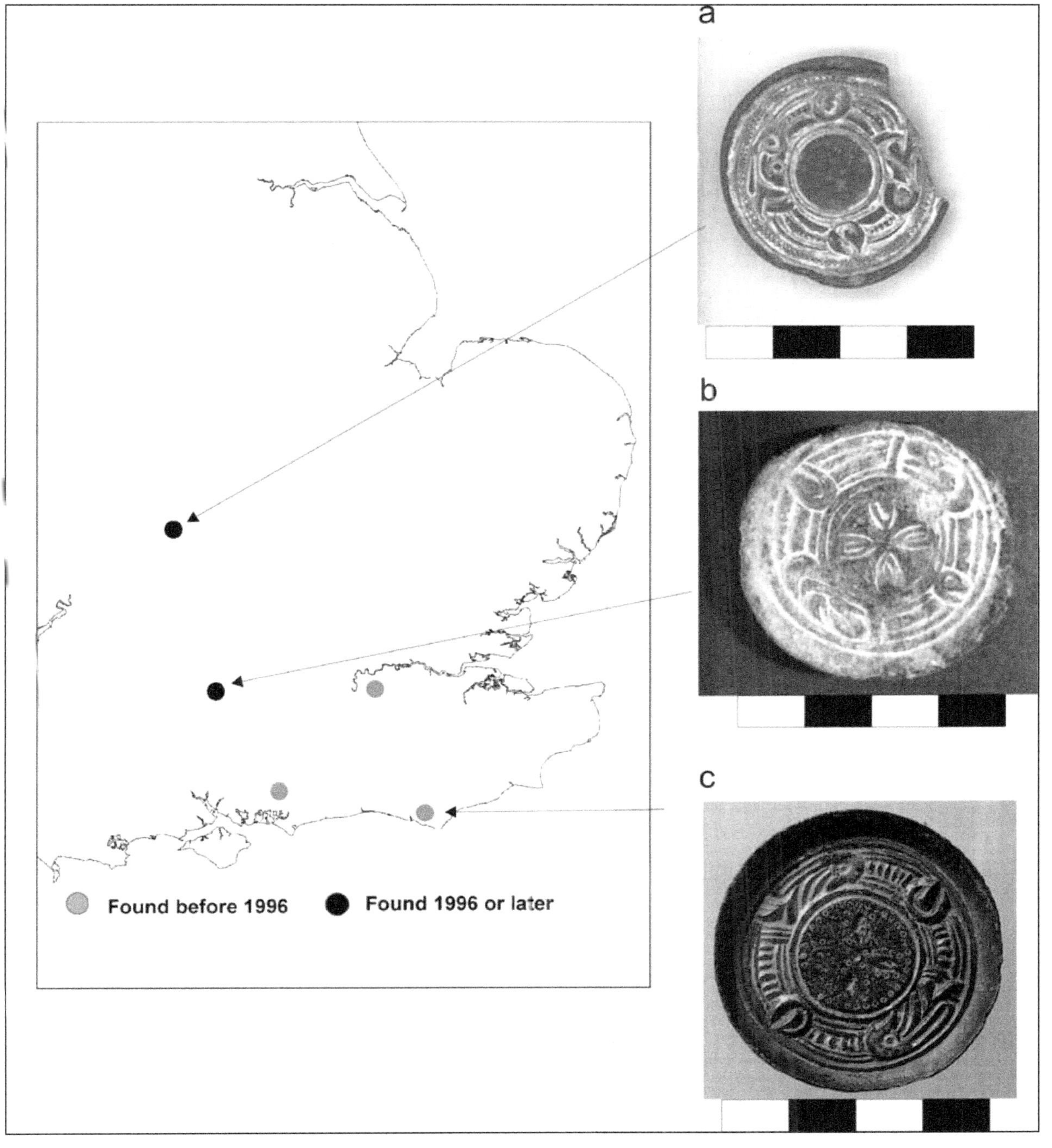

Fig. 15: Saucer brooches with Style I animal-men with helmet-like heads. a. Ettington (WMID-CDDDF1); b. Newbury (NMGW-4B6573); c. Alfriston grave 101 (photograph: T. M. Dickinson). Scale. 1:1.

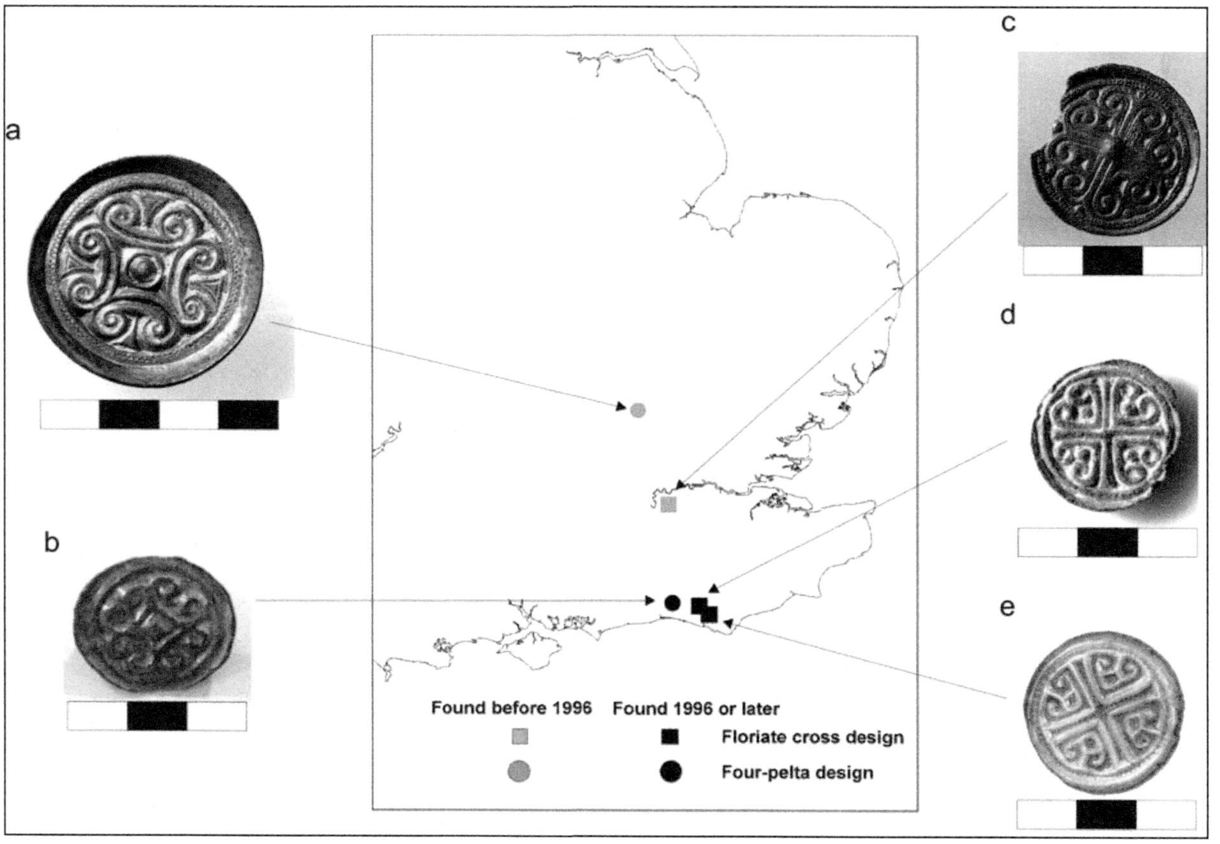

Fig. 16: Saucer brooches with early floriate cross designs. a-b: Four-pelta design; c-e: Floriated cross. a. Luton (Luton Museum 40/41/27); b. Hassocks (KENT5309); c. Merton; d. Firle (SUSS-8C1187); e. Earwig Corner, grave 2 (photographs a, c and e: T, M. Dickinson). Not to scale, measure = cms.

Conclusion

The analysis demonstrates that cast saucer brooches have a clear and distinctive spatial signature in the archaeological record, a signature which has merely become denser and more surely defined as more finds have been made and reported. There seems no reason why this cannot be taken as a real reflection of past deposition. Moreover, given that so few recent finds surprise with a novel decorative design and that most are only 'more of the same', it might be possible to argue that a representative sample of past decorative output has also now been achieved. These gains have been associated, however, with a shift from finds made through excavation to finds made casually and/or with the use of a metal-detector. While this has generated many more findspots - dots on the map - the contextual data that might be expected for this class of material, whether from a burial or a settlement site, and which should support more sophisticated research questions than those addressed here, have mostly been lost.

Acknowledgements

I am deeply indebted to Charles Whyte, who generated the statistics, diagrams and maps used in this paper as part of his work for an MSc in Archaeological Information Systems at the University of York. I am also most grateful to Robert Masefield, Alex Bayliss, John Hines and Chris Scull for enabling me to access the radiocarbon date from Aston Clinton grave 12 and for permission to cite it ahead of their own publications, and to Helen Geake and Dan Pett for facilitating my access to the PAS database.

Bibliography

Ager, B. 2004, 'West Wight, Isle of Wight: Anglo-Saxon grave assemblages', in Hitchcock, F. (ed.), *Treasure Annual Report* 2004 (Department for Culture, Media and Sport, London), 68-71.

Avent, R. 1975, *Anglo-Saxon Disc and Composite Brooches*, British Archaeological Reports, British Series 11 (British Archaeological Reports, Oxford).

Boyle, A., Jennings, D., Miles, D. and Palmer, S. 1998, *The Anglo-Saxon Cemetery at Butler's Field, Lechlade, Gloucestershire, Vol. 1: prehistoric and Roman activity and Anglo-Saxon grave catalogue*, Thames Valley Landscapes Monograph 10 (Oxford Archaeological Unit, Oxford).

Dickinson, T. M. 1976, 'The Anglo-Saxon burial sites of the Upper Thames Region, and their bearing on the history of Wessex, c. AD 400-700' (unpublished DPhil thesis, University of Oxford).

Dickinson, T. M. 1981, 'The saucer brooch', in Crummy, P., *Aspects of Anglo-Saxon and Norman Colchester*, Council for British Archaeology Research Reports 39 (Council for British Archaeology, London), 8-9.

Dickinson, T. M. 1982, 'Ornament variation in pairs of cast saucer brooches: a case study from the Upper Thames Region', in Webster, L. (ed.), *Aspects of*

Production and Style in Dark Age Metalwork: selected papers given to the British Museum seminar on jewellery AD 500-600, British Museum Occasional Paper 34 (Department of Medieval and Later Antiquities, British Museum, London), 21-50.

Dickinson, T. M. 1991, 'Material culture as social expression: the case of Saxon saucer brooches with running spiral decoration', *Studien zur Sachsenforschung* 7, 39-70.

Dickinson, T. M. 1993, 'Early Anglo-Saxon saucer brooches: a preliminary overview', in Filmer-Sankey, W. (ed.), *Anglo-Saxon Studies in Archaeology and History* 6 (Oxford University Committee for Archaeology, Oxford), 11-44.

Dickinson, T. M. 2002, 'Translating animal art: Salin's Style I and Anglo-Saxon cast saucer brooches', *Hikuin* 29, 163-86.

Dickinson, T. M. forthcoming, 'Cast saucer brooches', in Boyle, A., Miles, D. and Palmer, S. *The Anglo-Saxon Cemetery at Butler's Field, Lechlade, Gloucestershire, Vol. 2* (Oxford Archaeology, Oxford).

Down, A. and Welch, M. 1990, *Chichester Excavations 7: Apple Down and the Mardens* (Chichester District Council, Chichester).

Evison, V. I. 1978, 'Early Anglo-Saxon applied disc brooches: Part II: In England', *Antiquaries Journal* 58, 260-78.

Harrington, S., Thomas, G. and Merkel, J. in preparation, 'The Anglo-Saxon cemetery at South Malling, Lewes: new finds and new perspectives', *Sussex Archaeological Collections.*

Inker, P. 2006, *The Saxon Relief Style*, British Archaeological Reports, British Series 410 (John and Erica Hedges Ltd., Oxford).

Leeds, E. T. 1912, 'The distribution of the Anglo-Saxon saucer brooch in relation to the battle of Bedford, AD 571', *Archaeologia* 63, 159-202.

Marzinzik, S. 2003, *Early Anglo-Saxon Belt Buckles (late 5th to early 8th centuries A.D.): their classification and context*, British Archaeological Reports, British Series 357 (Archaeopress, Oxford).

Masefield, R. 2008, *Prehistoric and Later Settlement from Chiltern Scarp to Aylesbury Vale: the archaeology of the Aston Clinton Bypass, Buckinghamshire*, British Archaeological Reports, British Series 473 (Archaeopress, Oxford).

McKinley, J. 2003, 'The Early Saxon cemetery at Park Lane, Croydon', *Surrey Archaeological Collections* 90, 1-116.

Naylor, J. 2006, *Viking and Anglo-Saxon Landscape and Economy* (http://www.york.ac.uk/archaeology/vasle/index.html, consulted May 2007).

Naylor, J. and Richards, J. D. 2006, 'Viking and Anglo-Saxon landscape and economy', in Geake, H. (ed.), 'Portable Antiquities Scheme', *Medieval Archaeology* 50, 275-76.

Reimer, P. J. *et al.* 2004, 'IntCal04 terrestrial radiocarbon age calibration, 0-26 cal kyr BP', *Radiocarbon* 46, 1029-58.

Stuiver, M. and Reimer, P.J. 1986-2005, *Calib Radiocarbon Calibration: executable version 5.0.2* (www.calib.qub.ac.uk/calib, consulted 12 June 2007).

Thomas, G. 2002, '"Teeth worn down like Iguanadons": new evidence for Early Anglo-Saxon Lewes', *Sussex Past & Present* (Sussex Archaeological Newsletter) 96, 4-5.

Welch, M. G. 1975, 'Mitcham grave 205 and the chronology of applied brooches with floriate cross decoration, and a note on the pot by J. N. L. Myres', *Antiquaries Journal* 55, 86-95.

Welch, M. G 1983, *Early Anglo-Saxon Sussex*, British Archaeological Reports, British Series 112 (British Archaeological Reports, Oxford).

A 'Productive Site' at Bidford-on-Avon, Warwickshire: salt, communication and trade in Anglo-Saxon England

John Naylor and Julian D. Richards

Since the recording of portable antiquities by museum curators and archaeologists began about two decades ago, and especially after the instigation of the Portable Antiquities Scheme (PAS) in 1997, thousands of new archaeological sites have been recorded. Virtually all of these have been found through the efforts of metal-detector users and their interpretation is not straightforward. Most assemblages predominantly consist of copper-alloy artefacts, plus precious metals and lead on occasion, as well as coinage. Iron is notably lacking, owing to the bias in recovery against ferrous objects, and little pottery or stonework is generally collected (Naylor 2004: 79-80). The lack of excavation on the vast majority of these 'productive sites' compounds the problem leaving us, essentially, with a scatter of metalwork from which archaeologists must try to interpret a site's nature and function. These problems of interpretation have most affected early medievalists who have traditionally lacked much data regarding domestic rural settlement. They have been keenest to accept and utilise portable antiquities data, especially in socio-economic research (although see Brindle and Moorhead's contributions in this volume for a Roman perspective). Much has been made of the location of early medieval 'productive sites' on communication routes, and finds scatters are often interpreted within the frame of evolving settlement hierarchies and increasing internal trade (Ulmschneider 2000; Pestell and Ulmschneider 2003; Naylor 2004). In general, the finds of large amounts of coinage have been seen as an indicator of economic significance, and precious metals a possible elite presence, often seen as ecclesiastical authority, although this is by no means certain (Ulmschneider 2000: 66-72; cf. Naylor 2004: 131-32).

However, few have attempted to analyse 'productive sites' quantitatively and in relation to both other sites and general finds in the region, although an attempt was previously made by one of the authors (JN) which has proven useful in discussion of the circulation of coinage (Naylor 2007). The work of the AHRC-funded project 'Viking and Anglo-Saxon Landscape and Economy' (VASLE) at the University of York, though, was designed to provide an in-depth exploration of Anglo-Saxon portable antiquities across England and Wales (Naylor and Richards 2006). Briefly, this has shown that, with care, portable antiquities can be confidently used to explore ancient settlement patterns, and that in some cases at least interpretation of sites is possible so long as a broad, interdisciplinary approach is taken (Richards *et al* 2009). This paper presents a short case study illustrating one method for the interpretation of portable antiquities data, using the middle and late Saxon data for the parish of Bidford-on-Avon, Warwickshire, where there is a long history of scholarly attention, excavation and metal-detection. In this case, the locations of the 'productive sites' are well-known and have been previously published (Wise and Seaby 1995; Palmer 1999: fig. 2).

The parish of Bidford-on-Avon

Bidford-on-Avon (Fig. 1) lies in the Avon Valley at the crossing point of the River Avon with Ryknild Street, the Roman road running south from Watling Street to the Foss Way and a major medieval saltway (*Sealt Stræt*) which runs east from Droitwich through Bidford towards the Chilterns (Margary 1973: 15; Maddicott 2005: 46-47; WSMR 8217). Finds dating from the neolithic onwards are known from across the parish, and Iron Age settlement at Bidford-on-Avon village is attested (Booth and Hodgson 1990). To date, about 1,400 portable antiquities have been recorded within the parish by the PAS, two-thirds of Roman date, with the Anglo-Saxon period accounting for three-percent of all finds (Angie Bolton, pers. comm.). These Anglo-Saxon finds dot the parish (Fig 2), with the main concentration to be found to the east of Bidford village and north of the river. This site covers an area of about 1000m x 400m (Seaby and Wise 1995: 57; WSMR 4027; Palmer 1999).

Early medieval activity is well known within the village's immediate surroundings (Fig. 2). In the village itself, excavations have revealed a 6th to 7th-century mixed rite cemetery containing *c.* 320 burials (200 inhumations and *c.* 120 cremations), the largest known early Anglo-Saxon cemetery in the Avon Valley (Humphries *et al* 1923). Middle and/or late Saxon occupation is evidenced by possible enclosures cut by a later ditch, structural evidence and a pit (Meaney 1964: 258; Booth and Hodgson 1990; Ford 1995: 69; Webster and Cherry 1980: 233). Early Anglo-Saxon material has also been found by metal-detector users and excavations to the south-west of the village, and excavations outside Broom (on the A46) uncovered evidence for early Anglo-Saxon burial and settlement evidence respectively (Palmer 1999: 197-208;

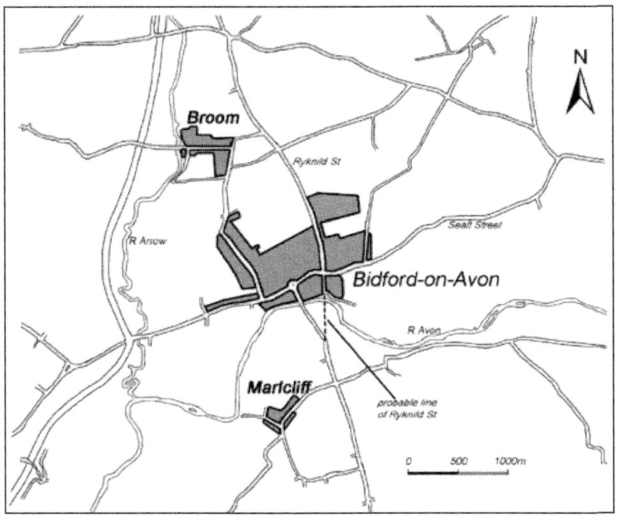

Fig. 1: Bidford-on-Avon village and its environs.

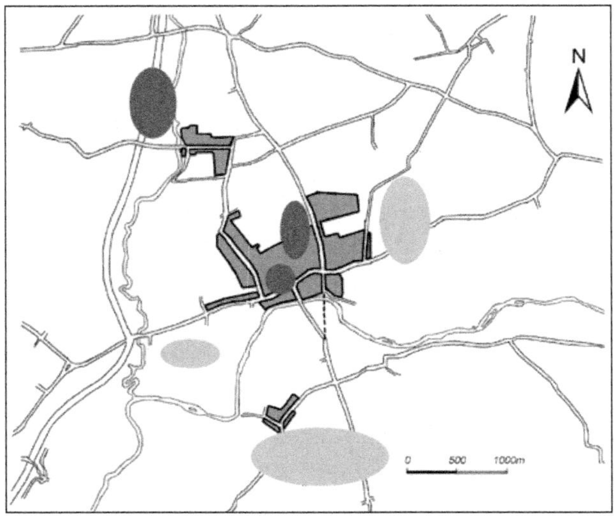

Fig. 2: Approximate locations of the known Anglo-Saxon activity at Bidford-on-Avon (dark grey oval = excavated sites light grey oval = metal-detected sites).

WSMR 605, 303). At Marlcliff, 1.5km south of Bidford-on-Avon, early and middle Anglo-Saxon finds have been made around Ryknild Street including at least four sceattas (Wise and Seaby 1995: 57; WSMR 5687, 5688, 4046, 5101, 4012). Bidford-on-Avon was clearly of some importance during the Anglo-Saxon period and has received scholarly attention on a number of occasions in connection with the trade in Droitwich salt in the early and middle Anglo-Saxon period. The location of Bidford-on-Avon at the intersection of Sealt Stræt, Ryknild Street and the River Avon has lead to the convincing argument for the site being a distribution point for salt, and the presence of Continental coinage may be indicative of the presence of foreign traders in the area in the early 8th century (Maddicott 2005: 47; Metcalf 2003: 42). However, no quantitative analysis has been made, especially in comparison to the region around it. Such investigation will help to highlight any differences which, in turn, may be used to provide a more nuanced interpretation of the site.

The 'productive site'

The site lies to the east side of Bidford-on-Avon village on low-lying land which rises up from the River Avon, the current course of which runs c. 500m to the south (Fig. 2). It is unclear if the site extends underneath the modern village. The Roman road, Ryknild Street, runs north-south through the village, c. 500m west of the metal-detected area, and once forded the river immediately east of the church. Detecting on the site began by 1984, when a saucer brooch was discovered and the first coin was found the following year. Finds continued to be made regularly and the site was first published by Wise and Seaby (1995), since when many more have been reported to the PAS and others to the Warwickshire SMR (www.timetrail.warwickshire.gov.uk).

No archaeological interventions are known for the site.

The finds assemblage

The dataset is an amalgamation of records from the PAS, the Early Medieval Corpus of Coin Finds, 410-1180 (www.fitzmuseum.cam.ac.uk/dept/coins/emc/), the Warwickshire SMR and published material (Wise and Seaby 1995: 58-64). Of these, the PAS data is well located, often with 6 or 8-figure National Grid References, and the published material can be located with reference to the Warwickshire SMR. The location details on the EMC relate to the midpoint of the parish and not particular findspots. The online records from the Warwickshire SMR have provided more accurate grid references for some of these EMC and previously published finds, all of which correspond to concentrations of finds as mapped by Palmer (1999: Fig. 2). By examining the nature of the distribution of finds (Fig. 2), several concentrations of material can be seen, alongside the main areas east and south of Bidford-on-Avon village. A total of 61 metal objects dating c. 650-c. 900 AD have been recorded in the parish, comprising 27 coins and 34 artefacts. The 'productive site' itself has produced 28 artefacts and 19 coins. All coins are of silver, whilst all of the artefacts, with the exception of a gold mount, are predominantly of copper-alloy (Fig. 3). The basic chronology of all of the material (Fig. 4) indicates a broad spread of middle-late Saxon material, but only a single strap-end can be definitely dated to the 10th century or later.

The coinage

The overall coinage assemblage from Bidford-on-Avon parish comprises 17 late 7th- to mid 8th-century sceattas and ten pennies dating from Offa of Mercia to Baldred of Kent, c. 765-c. 825 AD. Three Primary phase sceattas, including one copy, are the earliest known coins dating c. 680-c. 710 AD. These coins, two Series C and one A/C imitation, are rare finds in the Midlands.

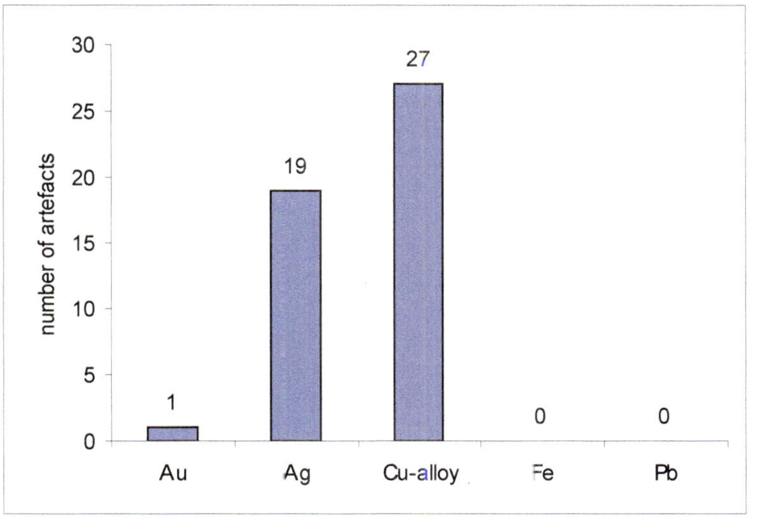

Fig. 3: The finds assemblage by metal type.

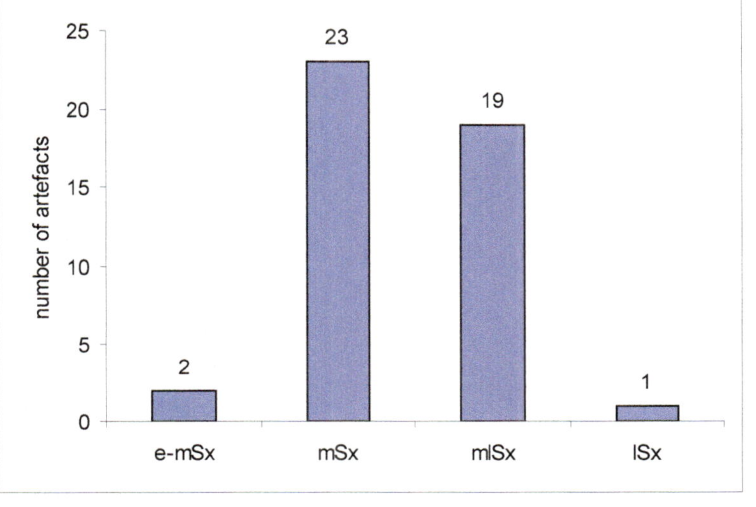

Fig. 4: The outline chronology of the site.

There is a small cluster of eight Primary phase *sceattas* in the region south of Birmingham, which could be seen as a loop around Droitwich, coming out from the main distribution, and there is no reason to suppose that they are not associated with the salt industry. Three of these, however, are at Bidford-on-Avon, and a fourth is *c.* 2km north at Wixford (EMC1998.2057) attesting to the early importance of the site and the routes around it. There is also a cluster of earlier 7th-century gold coins and Primary phase *sceattas* stretching south along the Ryknild Street from Bidford-on-Avon towards and along the Foss Way through Gloucestershire. Seven *sceattas* are of Continental origin (either Series D or E), as is another a few kilometres south at Bickmarsh (WAW-02E056). This has lead Metcalf (2003: 42) to describe the parish as a 'hot spot' for Continental Series E and interpreted these as most likely being deposited in the area only due to the presence of foreign traders. Of four Series E *sceattas*, three are early types, dated to *c.* 695-*c.* 715 AD. The remaining coin belongs to the Secondary phase (*c.* 710-*c.* 750 AD), as do four others, a Series J (type 72), possibly of Low Countries origin, a Kentish Series K (type 20/18) and two Series L (type 15a) from London.

The comparatively high numbers of late 8th-century coins, three of Offa, one of Coenwulf with Æthelheard, Archbishop of Canterbury, and three of Eadwald of East Anglia are of interest and attest to the continued wide-ranging contacts at the site. All appear to be stray losses, with the distributions of finds not consistent with a dispersed hoard activity (Wise and Seaby 1995: 60). Two of these pennies are not included in the original publication (EMC1996.5002 and EMC2005.0006) but their location is also only approximately known (in published literature).

The distribution of coinage around the parish sees a line of finds following Ryknild Street from its north at Wixford to its southern boundary around Marlcliff, and further finds are known immediately to the south in Bickmarsh. Given the published accuracy of the finds' locations, it is unclear whether there is any patterning in the distribution of coins at the 'productive site' but those coins found until 1995 were described as 'widely scattered' (Wise and Seaby 1995: 60). This brief assessment of the Anglo-Saxon coin assemblage illustrates that coin finds appear to cluster around the routes on which Bidford-on-Avon lies, although the main impetus for their presence in the region was most probably the Droitwich salt trade. However, we are limited in what can be interpreted from the distributions alone and a quantified, in-depth analysis of the coin data is required if more is to be understood of Bidford-on-Avon's role in the region: the analysis of patterns of coin loss through time is based on the comparison of coin data quantified by a calculated date group for individual sites against data for an entire region. In this case the region used can be considered the Southern Midlands, using the counties of Gloucestershire, Warwickshire, Worcestershire and Oxfordshire. This takes account of the changing patterns of coin loss to the north and south of the site. See Naylor (2007) for details of date groups and methodology.

Figure 5a shows the overall nature of coin loss on the parish from the 7th to the 10th centuries. The peak of coin loss comes early in the 8th century (*c.* 680-*c.* 710 AD) dropping off dramatically around *c.* 710-*c.* 740 AD, at a point when coin loss greatly increases around the rest of the region (Fig. 6), and remains at these levels until the end of the 8th century. The period *c.* 790-*c.* 810 AD produced a massive increase in coin loss, the opposite of the calculated regional average. Fewer early 9th-century coins are known, and none dated after *c.* 840 AD, when settlement may have coalesced in the present village location (Webster and Cherry 1980: 233). The 'productive site' itself (Fig. 5b) shows high activity at an early date, and again *c.* 790-*c.* 810 AD. The early peak around 700 AD is much above average, and the number of late 8th-century pennies vastly exceeds expected losses.

The early peak in coin loss and subsequent decline is interesting when considered against the regional historical background (Fig. 6) and previous interpretations of the site in the remit of the salt trade emanating from Droitwich, *c.* 15km to the north-west. The likely relationship between this and the location of Bidford-on-Avon has been confidently asserted previously (Maddicott 2005: 46-47), but the apparent decline in activity around *c.* 710 AD brings interesting possibilities. During excavations at Upwich, Droitwich's main brine spring, thick alluvium dated to the early 8th century indicated that a large number of major floods may have seriously impeded salt production for a period of time (Hurst and Hemingway 1997: 27-28). If so, it is entirely likely that less salt was distributed via Bidford-on-Avon and its economic significance diminished. Salt production had likely returned to its previous high levels by the time the Offan and East Anglian pennies were lost.

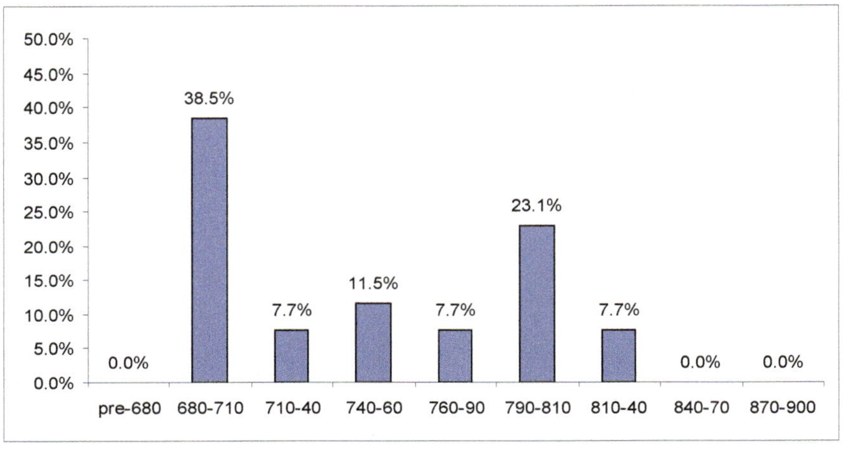

Fig. 5a: The coin assemblage in the parish shown as proportions by date group.

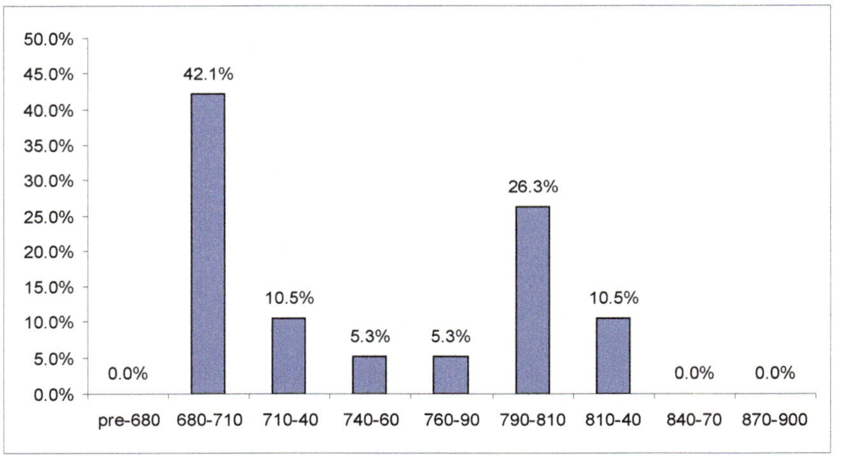

Fig. 5b: The coin assemblage at the 'productive site' shown as proportions by date group.

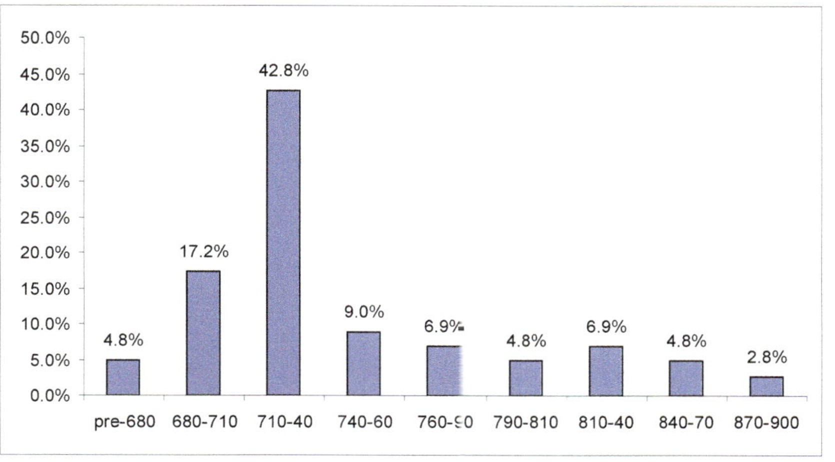

Fig. 6: The regional coin assemblage shown as proportions by date group (this chart is made up from data from Gloucestershire, Oxfordshire, Worcestershire and Warwickshire).

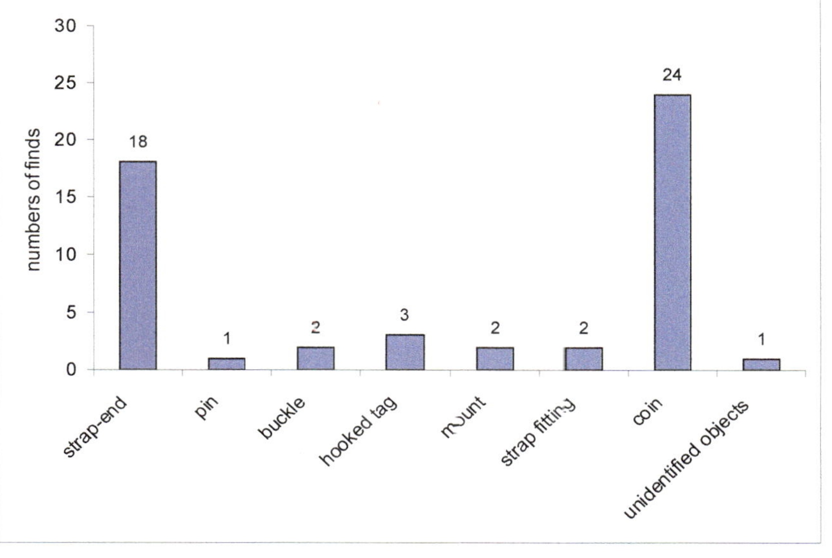

Fig. 7: Chart showing the artefact assemblage at the 'productive site'.

The artefacts

A range of personal-related items have been recovered from the parish, with strap-ends providing by far the largest portion of the assemblage (Fig. 7). No weaponry, horse-related or domestic material has been found, the latter probably owing to the lack of archaeological intervention, although some pottery, described as 'Anglo-Saxon' was seen on fields metal-detected in Marlcliff (WSMR 5101 and 4046). Chronologically, the site is anchored in the middle Anglo-Saxon period (Fig. 8), with only a single definite late Saxon piece, a Thomas Class I strap-end. A single pin, of polyhedral-headed type, is typically middle Anglo-Saxon. Identifiable types from the eighteen strap-ends comprise 11 belonging to Thomas's 9th-century Class A, and three Class B, belonging more broadly to the later 8th to 11th centuries (Thomas 2003: 2-5). The three hooked tags cannot be dated closer than the middle-late Saxon periods at present. However, the fact none of the larger, Carolingian-derived strap-ends of the 10th century are known nor any horse-related items, generally datable from the later 10th through the 11th century would suggest that abandonment of the site by the later 9th to early 10th century is likely.

The artefacts themselves are within the typical remit of middle-late Saxon types known from across England, including four 9th-century Trewhiddle style strap-ends and the polyhedral-headed pin, which can be readily paralleled across the country. The 8th-century gold mount is the only piece of particularly high quality metalwork from the site and is stylistically comparable to several well-known examples, including the hanging bowl from Witham, Lincolnshire and trefoil brooch from Kirkoswald, North Yorkshire (Wise and Seaby 1995: 59).

The basic patterns of artefacts found in the region (Fig. 9) is reflected at the 'productive site' (Fig. 10), although it is immediately apparent that there is a dearth of later material across the parish. This perhaps indicates a shift of settlement to the present village location, as the archaeological evidence hints at with late Saxon features found within the present village (WSMR 605), and is a situation seemingly typical in the region (Dyer 1995, 121).

The low numbers of finds obviously affects the proportions of material present and, for example, the excessive levels of strap-ends and low numbers of pins may simply reflect recovery patterns with larger objects likely to found with greater ease (Dave Haldenby, pers. comm.). However, it is interesting to note the presence of three hooked tags, a rare find in the Midlands, but much more common in eastern counties. Like much of the coinage, it is entirely likely that these reached Bidford-on-Avon from travellers coming west along *Sealt Stræt* from the Chilterns and beyond.

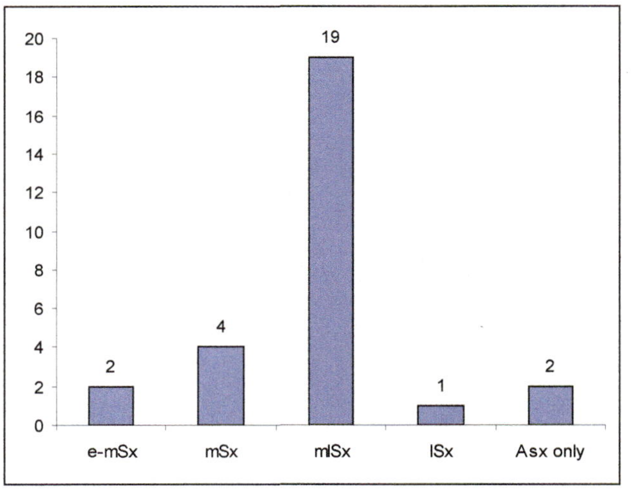

Fig. 8: Chart showing the outline artefact chronology for the 'productive site'.

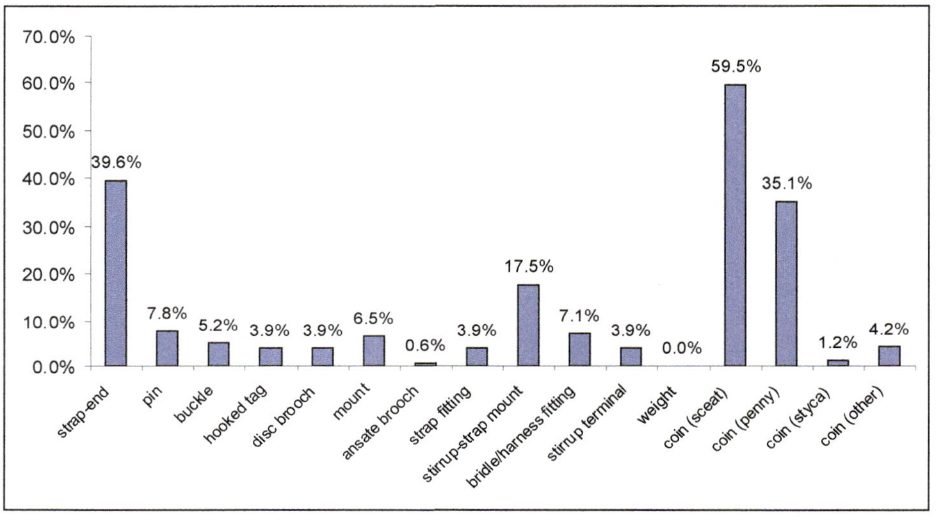

Fig. 9: The regional artefact and coinage 'fingerprint'
(this chart is made up from data from Gloucestershire, Oxfordshire, Worcestershire and Warwickshire).

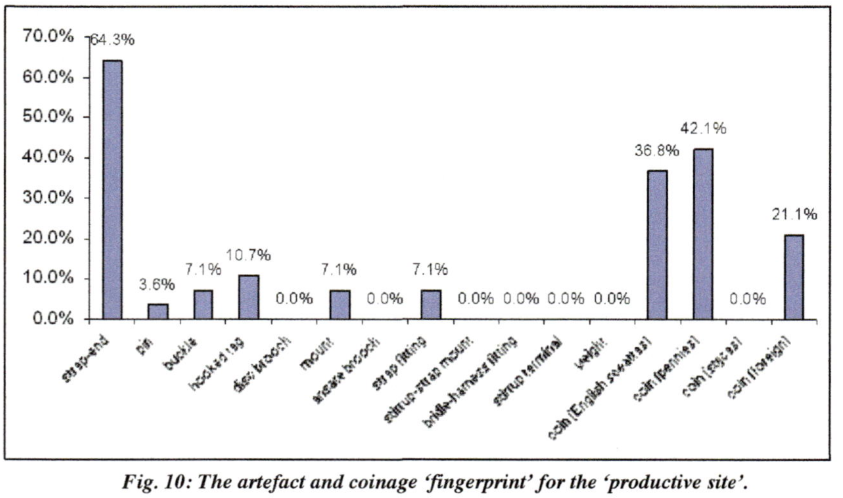

Fig. 10: The artefact and coinage 'fingerprint' for the 'productive site'.

Discussion

The methods outlined above as an interpretative framework for the archaeology of 'productive sites' has illustrated the usefulness of considered, quantitative analysis for assemblages made up entirely, or predominantly, of portable antiquities. Such sites can only be investigated adequately with reference to the general loss patterns around the region, and an understanding of the nature of portable antiquities in general (Richards *et al*, 2009). The methodology has confirmed previous work in considering Bidford-on-Avon as an area of undoubted regional importance during the 7th and 8th centuries (Maddicott 2005: 46-47), but has also provided a more nuanced interpretation, providing additional information on the internal chronology of the site and how this may relate to broader issues in the region. From this, the evidence connecting Bidford-on-Avon to the salt trade is strengthened and the fluctuations in the nature of coin loss in the parish can be adequately explained with reference to flooding at Droitwich itself (*ibid.*; Hurst and Hemingway 1992: 27-28).

The coin finds provide a rather restrictive chronology, with issue dates from *c.* 680-*c.* 825 AD, but it is possible that the lifespan of the site can be extended further into the 9th century at least with the Trewhiddle style strap-ends and ornamental fragment. The other strap-ends are typical of mid-late Saxon deposits across the country, although the fact that none of the larger, Carolingian-influenced types from the 10th century are known may provide support for the abandonment of the site in the 9th century, probably in favour of the present village location. The lack of horse-related items of later Anglo-Saxon type also suggests pre-Conquest abandonment.

The junction of Ryknild Street and the River Avon as a long-term focus settlement at the must be considered as predominantly strategic given the archaeology of Bidford and its immediate environs. The addition of *Sealt Stræt* only adds to this (Fig. 1). The wealth and extensive contacts witnessed in the parish is clear from the finds assemblage indicating lines of communication running to the east of England, although there is little in the assemblages, except the single gold mount, to suggest much of an elite presence at the site. Maddicott's (2005: 47) contention that Bidford may have been some kind of transhipment point for Droitwich salt is sensible and the resulting cosmopolitan assemblage of finds would not be unexpected. Alongside such trade, the lines of communication represented by river and roads make it likely that a range of travellers must also have passed through the village, possibly on royal or ecclesiastical business in London or the south-east. It must be noted, however, that Ryknild Street is only a documented saltway further south, on the Warwickshire/Gloucestershire border (Hooke 1985: fig. 31), and any suggestion that it continued to the north can only be made on archaeological grounds. Extending Ryknild Street as a saltway further north to Alcester at least, though, would make far greater sense in linking routes to Droitwich. Certainly there is a line of early coinage spreading north and south from Bidford along the Roman road, which must suggest something of the route's importance in early medieval communications. It is interesting to note that the junction of Ryknild Street and the Foss Way at Lower Slaughter, Gloucestershire is also the site of middle Anglo-Saxon settlement with evidence for long-distance contacts, and at Lechlade, Gloucestershire where another saltway met the River Thames, extensive early to middle Anglo-Saxon settlement and a rich cemetery have been excavated (Kenyon and Watts 2006; Bateman *et al* 2003; Boyle *et al* 1998). It may be possible that through the integration of portable antiquities and excavation data in this region we are witnessing an early system in the regulation of inland trade in Anglo-Saxon England, with these sites on junctions possibly representing the locations where traders in the later 7th to 9th centuries stopped en route to their destination, or paid toll to the king. It is only by adopting an integrated regional approach that we will ever find an answer.

Acknowledgements

This paper was produced with financial support from the Arts and Humanities Research Council, under grant award APN18370, for the University of York-based project 'Viking and Anglo-Saxon Landscape and Economy'. The authors would like to thanks the Warwickshire SMR for permission to use their data, downloaded from the Warwickshire County Council's 'Timetrail' website (www.timetrail.warwickshire.gov.uk), Angie Bolton (PAS) for taking time to discuss the nature of portable antiquities in the village and its environs, and the finder of many of the artefacts studied here, Robert Laight.

Bibliography

Bateman, C., Enright, D. and Oakey, N. 2003, 'Prehistoric and Anglo-Saxon settlements to the rear of Sherborne House, Lechlade: excavations in 1997', *Transactions of the Bristol and Gloucestershire Archaeological Society* 121, 23-96.

Booth, P. and Hodgson, J. 1990, 'Bidford-on-Avon, excavation of part of an Anglo-Saxon cemetery', *West Midlands Archaeology* 33, 85.

Boyle, A., Jennings, D., Miles, D. and Palmer, S. 1998, *Anglo-Saxon Cemetery at Butler's Field, Lechlade, Gloucestershire: Volume I: prehistoric and Roman activity and grave catalogue*, Thames Valley Landscapes Monograph 10 (Oxford University Committee for Archaeology, Oxford).

Dyer, C. 1995, 'Rural settlements in medieval Warwickshire', *Transactions of the Birmingham and Warwickshire Archaeology Society* 100, 117-32.

Ford, W. J. 1995, 'Anglo-Saxon cemeteries along the Avon Valley', *Transactions of the Birmingham and Warwickshire Archaeology Society* 100, 59-98.

Hooke, D. 1985, *The Anglo-Saxon Landscape: the kingdom of the Hwicce* (Manchester University Press, Manchester).

Humphries. J. M., Ryland, J. W., Barnard, E. A. B., Wellstood, F. C. and Barnett, T. G. 1923, 'An Anglo-

Saxon Cemetery at Bidford-on-Avon, Warwickshire', *Archaeologia* 72, 89-116.
Hurst, J. D. and Hemingway, J. A. 1997, 'The excavations', in Hurst, J. D., *A Multi-Period Salt Production Site at Droitwich: excavations at Upwich*, Council for British Archaeology Research Report 107 (CBA, York), 9-67.
Kenyon, D. and Watts, M. 2006, 'An Anglo-Saxon enclosure at Copsehill Road, Lower Slaughter: excavations in 1999', *Transactions of the Bristol and Gloucestershire Archaeological Society* 124, 73-109.
Maddicott, J. R. 2005, 'London and Droitwich, c. 650-750: trade, industry and the rise of Mercia', *Anglo-Saxon England* 34, 7-58.
Margary, I. D. 1973, *Roman Roads in Britain* (Baker, London).
Meaney, A. L. 1964, *A Gazetteer of early Anglo-Saxon Burial Sites* (Allen and Unwin, London).
Metcalf, D. M. 2003, 'Variation in the composition of the currency at different places in England', in Pestell, T. and Ulmschneider, K. (eds.) *Markets in Early Medieval Europe: trading and 'productive' sites, 650-850* (Windgather, Macclesfield), 37-47.
Naylor, J. 2004, *An Archaeology of Trade in Middle Saxon England*, British Archaeological Reports, British Series 376 (Archaeopress, Oxford).
Naylor, J. 2007, 'The circulation of early medieval European coinage: a case study from Yorkshire', *Medieval Archaeology* 51, 41-61.
Naylor, J. and Richards, J. D. 2006, 'Detecting the past: interpreting early medieval settlement patterns through portable antiquities', *Medieval Settlement Research Group Annual Report* 20, 19-24.
Palmer, S. C. 1999, 'Archaeological excavations in the Arrow Valley, Warwickshire', *Transactions of the Birmingham and Warwickshire Archaeology Society* 103, 1-231.
Pestell, T. and Ulmschneider, K. (eds.) 2003, *Markets in Early Medieval Europe: trading and 'productive' sites, 650-850* (Windgather, Macclesfield).
Richards, J. D., Naylor, J. and Holas-Clark, C. 2009, 'Anglo-Saxon landscape and economy: using portable antiquities to study Anglo-Saxon and Viking Age England', *Internet Archaeology* 25, http://intarch.ac.uk/journal/issue25/vasle_index.html.
Thomas, G. 2003, *Late Anglo-Saxon and Viking-Age Strap-ends 750-1100: part 1*, Finds Research Group Datasheet 32 (Finds Research Group).
Ulmschneider, K. 2000, 'Settlement, economy and the 'productive' site: Middle Anglo-Saxon Lincolnshire A.D. 650-780', *Medieval Archaeology* 44, 53-79.
Webster, L. E. and Cherry, J. 1980, 'Medieval Britain in 1979', *Medieval Archaeology* 24, 218-64.
Wise, W. A. and Seaby, P. J. 1995, 'Finds from a new 'productive site' at Bidford-on-Avon, Warwickshire', *Transactions of the Birmingham and Warwickshire Archaeology Society* 99, 57-64.

Medieval Copper-alloy Mace-heads from England, Scotland and Wales

Adam Daubney

Copper-alloy knopped mace-heads are relatively uncommon finds in England, Wales and Scotland. This paper concerns the 29 examples known to the author at the time of writing (see catalogue): 16 of which were previously listed by Geake (2005: 334-37). Thirteen of these have been recorded through the Portable Antiquities Scheme (PAS). Three further ones have been discovered through excavation, which may be residual finds. No.28 from Perth, Perthshire, was found in the floor of a c.14th-century bakery (Holdsworth 1987), No. 25, from Dryslwyn Castle, Carmarthenshire, was found deep within the fill of a latrine pit dated to 1250-60 (Jessop, forthcoming) and No. 11 came from a waterfront excavation in the City of London (there is no full publication of the site sequence).

It is perhaps correct to stress that some degree of caution needs to be exercised when using the term 'mace-head', as the word has military, political and ecclesiastical connotations. It is the writer's opinion that although many of the copper-alloy knopped varieties were used in combat, some of these are likely to have had an ecclesiastical function. The distinction between the two classes is not clear at present and it is possible that some maces had dual purposes. Iron knopped maces, known from Britain and the continent are thought to have been used exclusively in combat. A detailed study of the iron examples is beyond the scope of this paper.

The knopped mace-head is simply a cast, hollow cylinder of copper alloy, sometimes leaded,{1} and usually with three rows of pyramidal or half-pyramidal knops. The only clear divisions within the knopped group are those with integral shafts and those without (Fig.1). Both varieties were mounted on long wooden staves, as evidenced by many examples retaining wood within their sockets. Those with integral shafts were secured by an iron nail through a small hole at the bottom of the socket, and those without may well have been secured by an iron nail through the top of the socket. Iron corrosion has been noted around the socket on a number of mace-heads, notably No. 6 from Fiskerton, Lincolnshire. Indeed, one unprovenanced iron knopped mace-head (seen by the author on the internet) is known with an iron nail still through the socket.

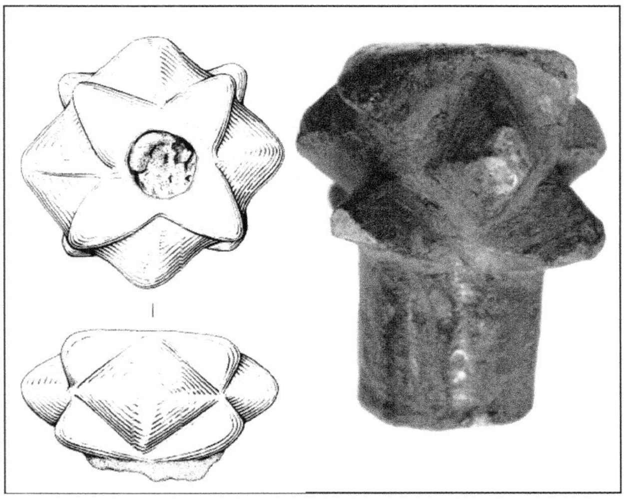

Fig. 1. Mace-head a) without shaft (No. 2); height 24mm (drawing D. Watt) and b) with shaft (No. 20); height 52mm.

The distribution of the mace-heads is very much centred on the east of England, with Lincolnshire having produced a relatively large quantity. The distribution map (Fig. 2) also shows that a significant number of maces are found in coastal counties, at inlet locations and along major waterways. Although the dataset is few in number and obvious biases can be thought of, it seems likely that this distribution is representative.

Knopped mace-heads are better known in Ireland, Scandinavia, and continental north-eastern Europe, where many examples are decorated with moulded motifs, openwork shafts and in some cases silvering (Fig. 3). The Irish and European knopped copper-alloy mace-heads have been the focus of attention of a number of scholars, in particular Halpin (1988: 168-200) and Kirpichnikov (1966: 47-57). According to Kirpichnikov, copper-alloy knopped mace-heads developed in north eastern Europe, perhaps centred on Kiev in the 9th century. The earliest forms of mace found in the Baltic area are undecorated and have no integral shaft. It seems that decorated examples did not appear until the 12th century. The peak in usage occurs between the 11th and 14th centuries on the continent, with broad 13th- and 14th- century dating for those from the British Isles.

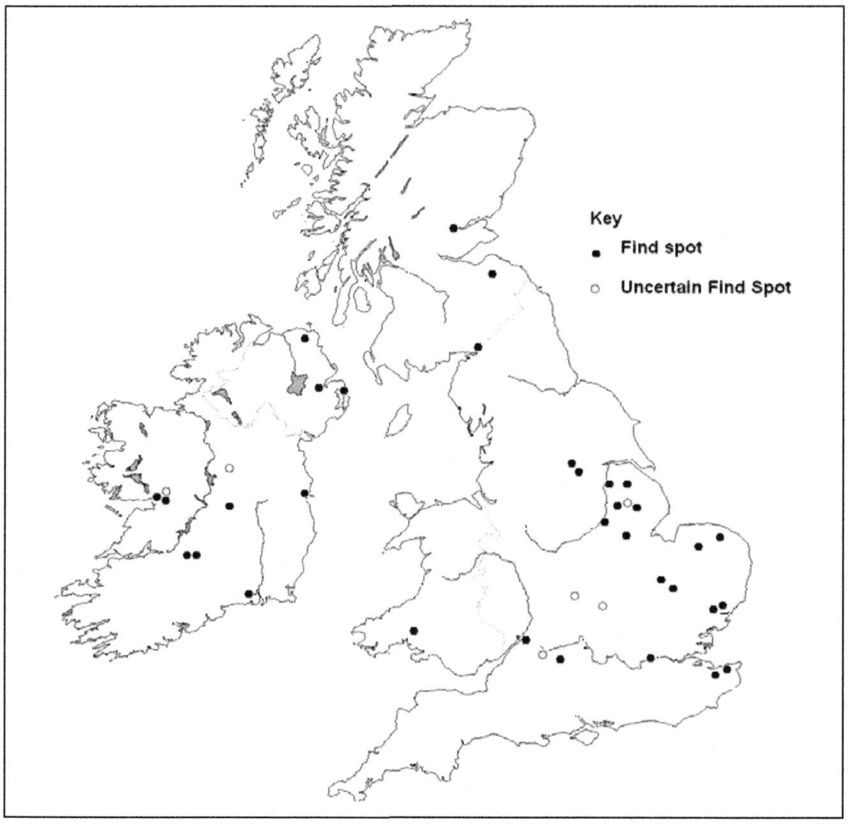

Fig. 2: Distribution of copper-alloy mace-heads in Great Britain and Ireland (Irish finds cf. Halpin 1988: 192, fig. 11).

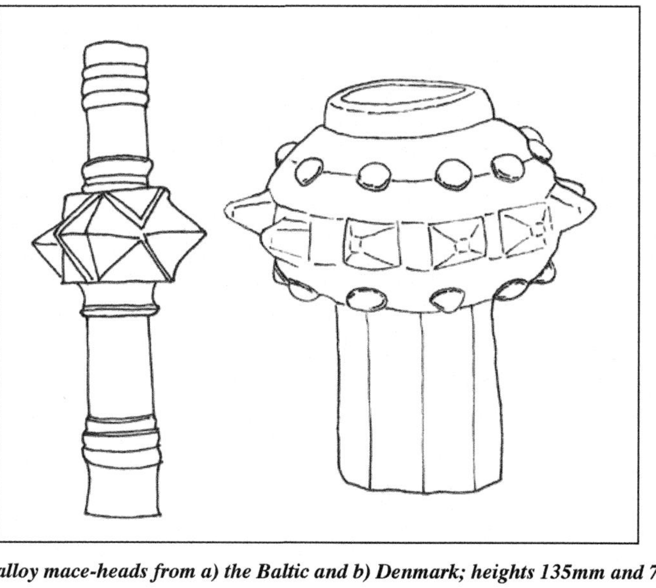

Fig. 3: Decorated copper-alloy mace-heads from a) the Baltic and b) Denmark; heights 135mm and 79mm (Adam Daubney).

The writer knows of no knopped mace-heads from France or southern Europe; instead, these areas tend to produce iron-flanged mace-heads, which are firmly at home in a military context. There are notable concentrations of early decorative and plain knopped mace-heads in Scandinavia, in particular Denmark and Gotland, Sweden. Two maces were found in probable Christian graves dated to *c.* 1000-1100 AD at a cemetery site in Barshalder, Gotland (Rundkvist 2003: 67 - graves nos. Bhr 1962:14:1 and Bhr 1963:01), and a third mace is documented from a grave at Hemse Annexhemman, also on Gotland (*ibid.*: 67). Other burials within the Barshalder cemetery contained small, ornate axes that were interpreted as being ceremonial rather than martial, symbolically linking the owner to armed conflict. This interpretation is supported by the evidence from one grave where the length of the haft seems to have been too long for practical use (*ibid.*: 65). The maces from the Barshalder cemetery were found at the feet of the deceased, with the hafts originally orientated towards their heads (*ibid.*: 65 and 67). Rundkvist (2003: 67) suggested that because the mace-heads were set further from the head of the deceased than the axes, the hafts of the former may have been longer. This is not in keeping with contemporary illustrations of maces used in battle, which were mounted on short staves. A small mace-head on a long shaft does not readily lend itself to combat, whether used for fighting on foot or on horseback. The absence of other components within the graves shows that there were no metal bindings, studs or other decorative elements on the shafts. In the 11th and 12th centuries religion on Gotland was significantly influenced by the eastern Christianity of Russia (Lagerlöf 1999). Staecker (1997: 77-81) has suggested that the early Christian graves containing jewellery and dress fittings found in churchyards on the island and at Leksand in Dalecarlia, and even those with pottery at Grodby on Bornholm (Denmark), might be seen as indicators of historically undocumented missionary work on the part of the Eastern Church. Perhaps the same can also be suggested for the British maces.

Some of the Scandinavian mace-heads are extremely elaborate and were clearly not intended to be employed in physical warfare. A few have silver decoration and others are decoratively moulded, occasionally as openwork. One in Finland shows a figure, possibly a saint, holding a book that is probably a bible, standing beneath an arch which may represent a church or monastery (Fig. 4), which suggests an ecclesiastical association. Further possible evidence for the knopped mace being an item employed in spiritual, rather than physical warfare is seen in a stone sculpture of a figure who holds one in his right hand at the 12th- or 13th-century church at Horsne, Gotland (Fig. 5).

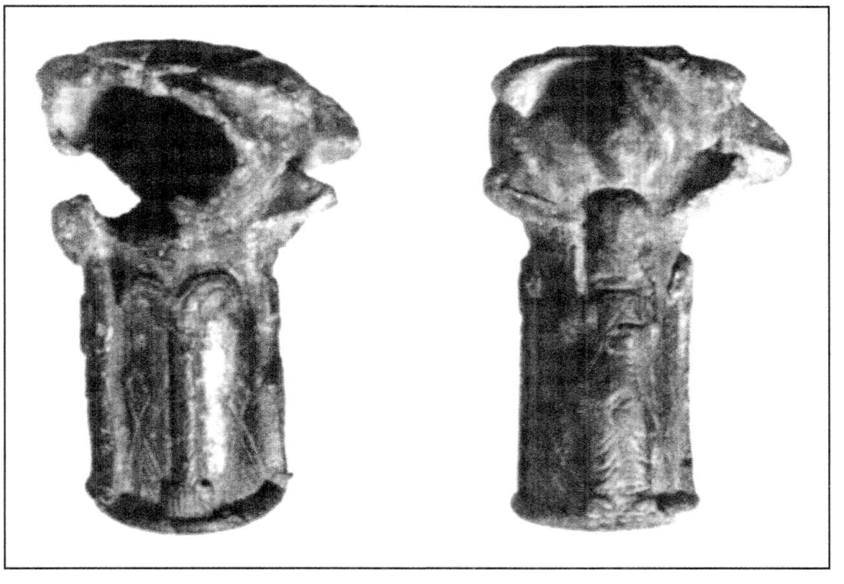

Fig. 4: Mace-head from Finland with moulded arcade and (possible) praying figure (National Museum of Finland).

Fig. 5: Figure holding mace at Horsne church, Gotland (Adam Daubney).

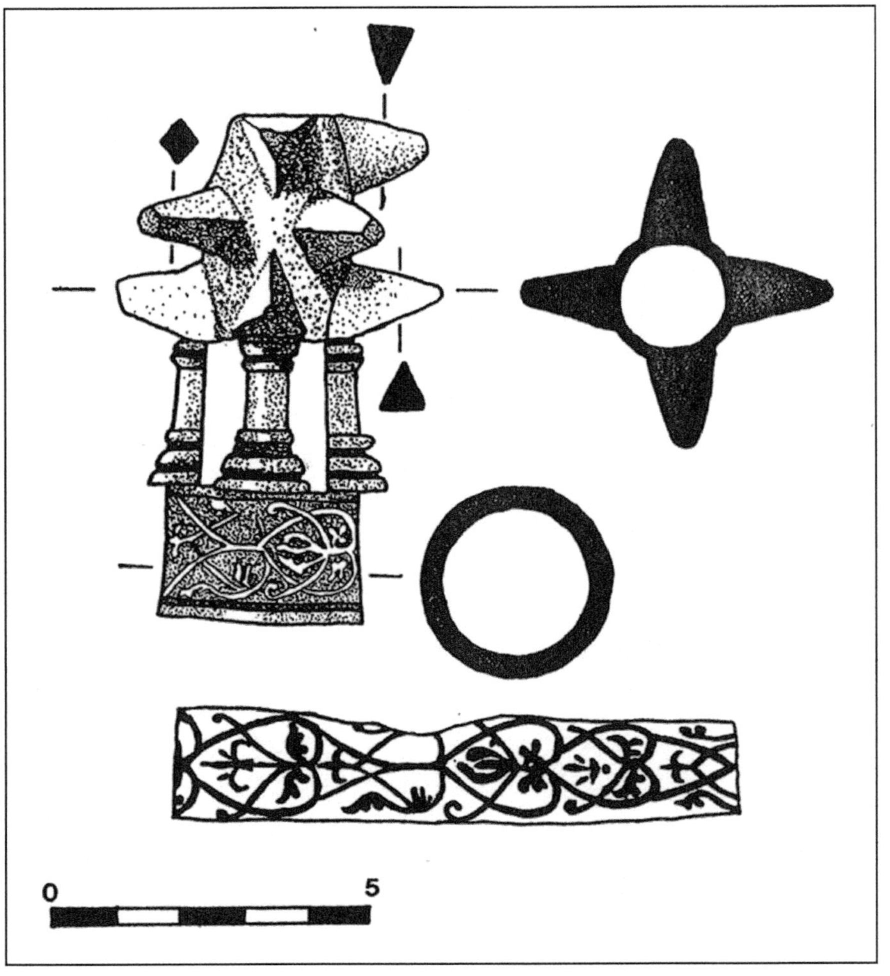

Fig. 6. Openwork mace-head from Athenry, Galway. Height 101mm (Andrew Halpin).

The movement of mace-heads (or more accurately those who were carrying them) turns to Ireland, which has produced a sizeable collection of the knopped variety. In his detailed study Halpin (1988) lists 19 examples. Many of these are decorative, including one from Athenry, Galway, with an openwork socket formed of four pillars (ibid.: 182, fig. 1 and pls. 2 and 3; Fig. 6), which brings to mind the arch on the Finnish example. The openwork socket and obvious high quality suggest non-military useage for this particular item. On the other hand, Halpin (ibid.: 174) notes that many of the Irish maces have damaged, down-turned prongs that could well be the result of service in battle. Similar traits are also seen on the English, Scottish and Welsh maces, particularly on the most prominent upper and middle rows of prongs. Although damage to the upper prongs could have been caused by general wear, damage to the middle row implies that the maces were swung horizontally, which in turn suggests aggressive intent.

It may be significant that England and Wales are yet to produce a decorated copper-alloy knopped mace-head. Scotland has some: No. 27 from Millsteads Farm, Canonbie, Dumfries and Galloway is decorated with a moulded fleur-de-lis on the shaft and No. 28 from Perth, Perthshire has traces of corroded silver in some areas. This was originally thought to be contamination of the copper (Holdsworth 1987: 125, no. 29), however in the light of the silver on continental examples it is more likely to represent surface coating.

The findspots of maces found at Soutra, Midlothian and Perth, Perthshire maces (Nos. 26 and 28) may also hint at ecclesiastical associations. The Perth mace-head was discovered at a location known as 'Kirk Close' (Church Close) and Soutra was the site of a large and important hospice founded in 1164 by King Malcolm IV, which includes an Augustinian church (the site lies just off Dere Street, which remained the only major highway between England and the north until the 18th century and it was the principal pilgrim route to St Andrews across the Lammermuir Hills.{2}

It seems appropriate to make a tentative link between the undecorated and decorated knopped mace-head and a group of smaller, openwork copper-alloy staff fittings which are gradually becoming better known in England (Fig. 7). These hollow fittings were originally described as sword pommels (Ward Perkins 1940: 23, fig. 2, nos. 1 and 2) but they have more recently been re-identified as cross-staff bases by Simon Bailey (1994: 171-75). Ten of these fittings have been recorded through the PAS to date. {2}

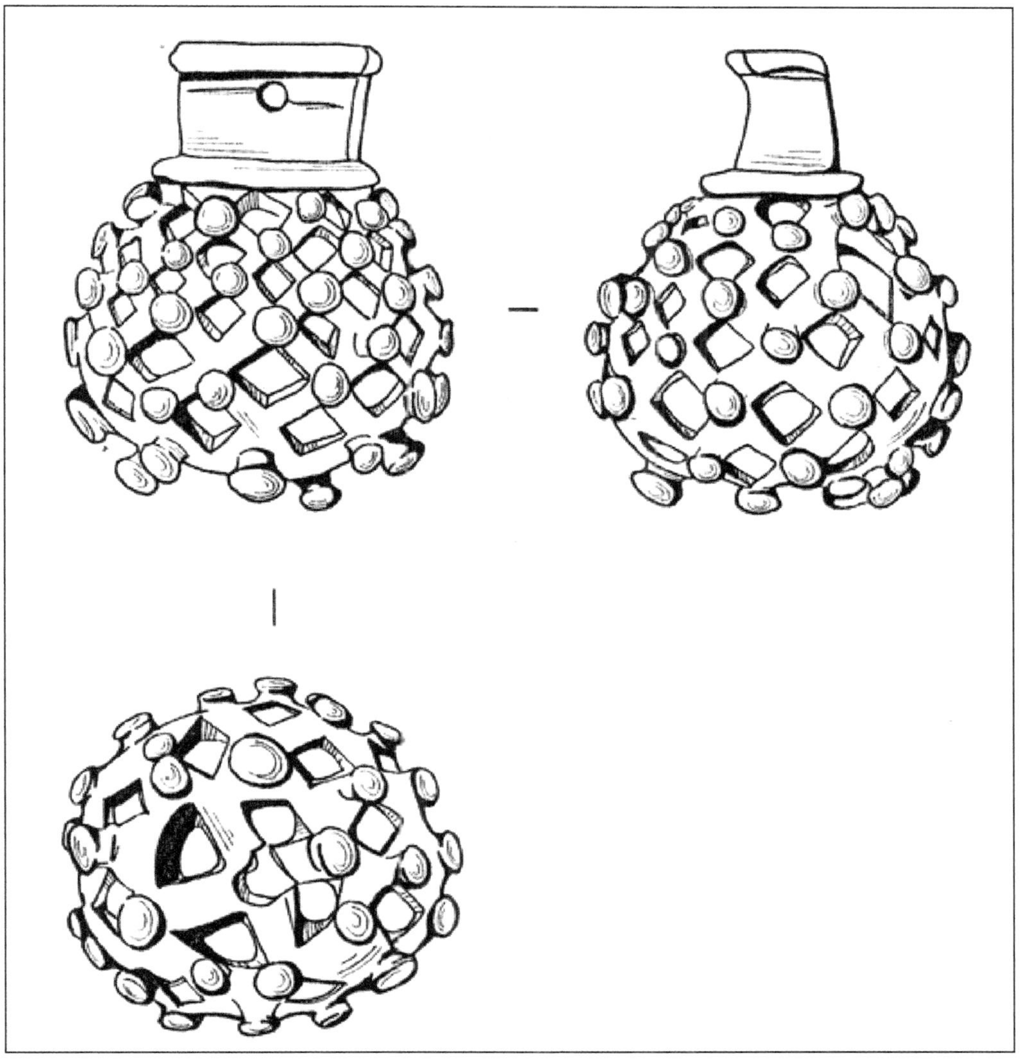

Fig. 7: Cross-staff fitting from Sharnbrook, Bedfordshire (BH-B64636); height: 45mm (Garth Denning).

They are of two main types: the first group is discoid and the second globular. Both groups are socketed and were secured to a wooden staff by means of a small nail at the top of the socket.

Although these cross-staff fittings are smaller in size, many of them are strikingly similar in basic form to the undecorated knopped mace-heads, often including three rows of globular knops similar to the arrangement of pyramidal and half-pyramidal knops seen on undecorated British mace-heads. If the openwork cross-staff fittings did indeed follow the form of undecorated mace-heads, then the latter must be earlier in date or at least contemporary with the openwork fittings. This does, however, not appear to be the trend currently seen in the excavated examples. Two cross-staff fittings excavated at Dublin and Canterbury, Kent were dated to the mid- and late-11th century respectively (*ibid.*: 171-75), whereas the two stratified knopped mace-heads noted above are dated to the mid 13th century. The undecorated mace-heads from Britain relate to Kirpichnikov's Group III and IV from the Baltic region, which he dates between the 12th century and the first half of the 13th century (1966: 49). From this evidence and also the lack of openwork fittings from the continent, it would appear that, despite the similarities, the openwork fittings are English artefacts that developed independently from, and indeed earlier than the knopped mace-head.

The date at which the knopped copper-alloy mace-heads entered England is still very much open to debate and awaits new finds with reliable close dating. At present it seems likely to have been in the later 12th century at the earliest. Some examples may be local products based on Scandinavian or north-eastern European types. It is clear that the majority of copper-alloy knopped mace-heads were manufactured as weapons of war, particularly larger ones that are heavily leaded and have knops that have fractured or become down-turned through the application of considerable force. The available evidence does point to some of them having a non-martial function, in which case they may have been used as ecclesiastical staff terminals. If the knopped mace-head evolved quickly from a weapon into an object employed as a ceremonial or ecclesiastical staff fitting, then it might be possible to see remnants of 12th- and 13th-century maces in later ecclesiastical material. Some 15th-century candlesticks and processional crosses have knopped collars that are remarkably similar to the mace-heads, with common details such as three rows of pyramidal knops and integral shafts extending below but not at the tops, along with various other decorative elements (Oman 1962: 195, pls. 15-16 and 18). The staffs on the 12th- and13th-century maces are however unlikely to have continued up beyond the head, as the knops on later processional crosses did. As noted above, iron corrosion on several sockets indicates the use of nails as a method of securing the heads to the shafts, and some of the mace-heads have closed tops, particularly Danish examples. Finally the mace-heads from the graves in Gotland indicate that they formed the terminal for the shaft. This evidence does not necessarily go against the knops on processional cross developing from them.

The mace-like knopped collars on the processional crosses may well point back down the evolutionary line of metalwork motifs, ultimately to the mace-head. Depending on the closeness of this connection, the maces are of interest not only to finds specialists, but potentially to those who study the movement of missionaries and the spread of the gospel throughout medieval Europe as well.

Catalogue of copper-alloy knopped mace-heads from England, Wales and Scotland:

No.	Findspot	Reference
1	Wicken, Cambridgeshire.	Anon 1850: 302.
2	Stroud, Gloucestershire.	Anon 1861: 163.
3	Ramsgate, Kent.	LIN-7778D6
4	Canterbury, Kent.	LIN-772E80
5	Edlington, Lincolnshire.	LIN-1EC113
6	Fiskerton, Lincolnshire.	LIN-871975; Geake 2005: 336, fig. 5b.
7	North Kelsey, Lincolnshire.	LIN-6DD211.
8	Sleaford area, Lincolnshire.	LIN-9CB1B8; Daubney 2005: 336, fig. 5a.
9	Thonock, Lincolnshire.	NLM2851.
10	probably Lincolnshire.	For sale on internet.
11	78 Upper Thames Street, City of London.	Museum of London archive: TEX88 acc. no. <7286>
12	Burgh and Tuttington, Norfolk.	NMS-AE5497.
13	Burgh with Tuttingham, Norfolk.	Norfolk HER: No. 33592.
14	Saham Toney, Norfolk.	Norfolk HER: 34101.
15	Coddington area, Nottinghamshire.	LIN-9570B5.
16	possibly Ipswich, Suffolk.	Anonymous, *The Searcher Magazine*, November 2002, 18.
17	Lidgate, Suffolk.	Anon 1849: 181; Evans 1881: 271.
18	Tunstall, Suffolk.	SF3643.
19	Warwickshire.	BERK-7DF537.
20	Great Bedwin, Wiltshire.	Anon 1849: 411; Evans 1881: 271.
21	possibly Swindon, Wiltshire.	For sale on internet 2006.
22	Marr, Doncaster, South Yorkshire.	SWYOR-F30727.
23	Tickhill, Yorkshire.	LIN-1A5260.
24	'A DMV site in Northamptonshire'.	For sale on internet 2006.
25	Dryslwyn, Carmarthenshire.	Jessop, forthcoming.
26	Soutra, Midlothian.	Treasure: 2005/11
27	Millsteads Farm, Canonbie, Dumfries and Galloway.	Dumfries Museum accession number: DUMFM:1969.18 (Caldwell 1981: 306-7).
28	Kirk Close, Perth, Perthshire.	Holdsworth 1987: 44-45.
29	Unprovenanced, presumably UK.	ESS-897423.

Endnotes

{1} X-ray fluorescence analysis of the Millsteads Farm, Canonbie mace-head showed the occurrence of copper, lead and tin (Holdsworth 1987, 125). The heavy mass of many of the other maces seen by the author also suggests the addition of lead, although none has been scientifically analysed at the time of writing. No. 11 weighs 521g.

{2} Sharnbrook area, Bedfordshire (BH-B64636); Billington area, Buckinghamshire (BUC-69D596); Tarrant Hinton area, Dorset (SOMDOR-AF3CC7); Wickham Bishops Area, Essex (SUSS-3C8EA4); Isle of Axholme area, North Lincolnshire (NLM2712); Catton Hall, Staffordshire (PAS: BUC-5F9404); Shenstone, Staffordshire (WMID-20EEE6); Finningham area, Suffolk (SF-E1DB04); Great Barton area, Suffolk (SF-A69D93); Fillongley, Warwickshire (WAW-8E2FA3).

Acknowledgements

I am extremely grateful to the Finds Liaison Officers involved in recording mace-heads, and to Helen Geake

(PAS), Andy Halpin (National Museum of Ireland) and Jenny Shiels (National Museums of Scotland) for their assistance and encouragement. Thanks also to Geoff Egan (PAS) for alerting me to the TEX88 mace-head and for sharing his thoughts and comments regarding these finds with me, to Anne Pedersen (National Museum of Denmark) for her help with the maces in the Danish and Finnish National Museums, and to Shawn Caza (independent researcher) for bringing the Kirpichnikov article to my attention. Much gratitude is expressed to the finders who reported their mace-heads.

Bibliography

Anon. 1849, 'Proceedings at meetings of the Archaeological Institute', *Archaeological Journal* 6, 175-200 and 395-416.

Anon. 1850, 'Proceedings at meetings of the Archaeological Institute,' *Archaeological Journal* 7, 295-302.

Anon. 1861, 'Proceedings at meetings of the Archaeological Institute,' *Archaeological Journal* 18, 147-92.

Anon. 2002, 'The identification and valuation desk', *The Searcher* (November) 207, 18.

Bailey, S. 1994, 'Two copper-alloy cross-staff heads from Warwickshire,' *Medieval Archaeology* 38, 171-75.

Caldwell, D. H. 1981, *Scottish Weapons and Fortifications 1100-1800* (John Donald Publishers Ltd., Edinburgh).

Evans, J. 1881, *The Ancient Bronze Implements. Weapons and ornaments of Great Britain and Ireland* (Longman, Green and Co., London).

Geake, H. 2005, 'Medieval Britain and Ireland, 2004: Portable Antiquities Scheme', *Medieval Archaeology* 49, 334-37.

Halpin, A. 1988, 'Irish Medieval Bronze Maceheads', in MacNiocaill, G. and Wallace, P. F. (eds.), *Keimelia. Studies in medieval archaeology and history in memory of Tom Delaney* (Galway University Press, Galway), 168-92.

Holdsworth, P. 1987, *Excavations in the Medieval Burgh of Perth* 1979-1981. Society of Antiquaries of Scotland Monograph 5 (Society of Antiquaries of Scotland, Edinburgh).

Jessop, O. 2007, 'Weapons', in Caple, C. (ed.), *Dryslwyn Castle Excavations* 1980-1995. Society for Medieval Archaeology Monographs 26 (Manley Publishing, Leeds).

Kirpichnikov, A. N. 1966. 'Drevnerusskoe oruzhie. Vyp. II: Kopia, sulitsy, boevyetopory, bulavy, kisteni, IX-XIII vv', *Arkheologiia SSSR. Svod Arkheologicheskikh Istochnikov* (Nauka, Leningrad).

Lagerlöf, E. 1999. *Gotland och Bysans. Bysantinskt inflytande på den Gotländska kyrkokonsten under medeltiden* (Ödins Förlag, Visby).

Oman, C. 1962, 'English medieval base metal church plate', *Archaeological Journal* 119, 195-207.

Rundkvist, M. 2003, *Barshalder* 2, *Studies of Late Iron Age Gotland* (University of Stockholm, Stockholm).

Staecker, J. 1997, 'Searching for the unknown: Gotland's churchyards from a gender and missionary perspective', *Lund Archaeological Review* 1, 77-81.

Ward Perkins, J. B. 1940, *London Museum Medieval Catalogue* (HMSO, London).

Widespread Devotion: new insights from the Portable Antiquities Scheme into medieval pilgrim trinkets

Geoff Egan

The publication of the large corpus of medieval pilgrim souvenirs found in London (Spencer 1998) for some time seemed almost to have rendered further work by archaeologists on this fascinating subject redundant. While there might be a limited number of previously unrecorded badges, the great majority of future finds looked as if they would readily be fitted without difficulty into the wisdom received from this masterful synthesis, perhaps with a few minor supplements. A great expansion in university studies of medieval pilgrimage as a broad social phenomenon, with the significance of individual cults given fresh consideration, and the badges themselves considered from a range of art-historical viewpoints has subsequently given fresh impetus. At the same time, far more single provincial finds have been recognised from right across the country. The majority of these have been recorded by the Portable Antiquities Scheme (PAS), and detailed information is available on them individually through the Scheme's database. They are mainly of lead/tin but include several of copper alloy and a very few precious-metal items that may be regarded as more expensive pilgrim souvenirs (the latter have been recorded under the Treasure Act 1996 and are detailed in the *Treasure Annual Reports* from 1996 onwards, and are now being systematically also added to the PAS database). The listing below includes all of those in the Treasure reports (apart from crucifixes that may not relate to a specific shrine). A couple of copper-alloy pendants which relate to the cult of St Antony have also been included below.

The great majority of the recorded *ampullae* (holy water containers of lead/tin), of which there are several hundred on the PAS database, are probably late-medieval. These containers for potentially healing liquid, mainly from the end of the medieval tradition of religious trinkets are rarely found in urban areas, and may represent a new manifestation of religious or superstitious interest in rural 'holy' wells (cf. Spencer 1998: 203-6). In contrast with a relatively tiny number of earlier *ampullae* on the database (which can usually be associated with known cults) few of these later ones can even tentatively be assigned to a specific source. *Ampullae* are therefore not considered in this present paper.

The first step in this present piece of work, given 284 items recorded as 'badges' put on the PAS database in its first decade (1996-2006) was to identify and eliminate from consideration a number of early-modern retainers' and livery badges, various mounts, a fire-insurance badge and a few 20th-century military badges (there were also some outright misidentifications, optimistically identified in part because of the popularity of pilgrim souvenirs among many searchers, for whom these are aspirational finds). A few early lead/tin toys, which can often also appear very similar, were also weeded out. It was then possible to identify among the remaining items those which related to pilgrimage, and separate them from the stylistically very similar secular ones (also of medieval date). Several items are simply too fragmentary or otherwise damaged to differentiate from medieval and early-modern confusabilia - a very few among these which seem most likely to have been pilgrim souvenirs but cannot be definitively identified are not considered in the main text but are summarily listed in Appendix 1. This left 103 items, which can be identified with some confidence as pilgrim badges for specific cults (Fig. 1).

The picture established largely by Brian Spencer's work was of important groups of base-metal badges from a limited number of towns - Canterbury, London, Kings Lynn, Salisbury, etc. with smaller assemblages from other urban centres – this is now being supplemented, mainly through single finds from rural areas put on the PAS database. This important new information largely confirms the received 'league table' which can be extrapolated from Spencer's work of the popularity of the national leading cult centres, with Becket at Canterbury still way out in front (Fig. 2; cf. Spencer 1998: 103). The Becket-head souvenirs (comprising both the large reliquary souvenirs of *c.* 1320-*c.* 1420 and a range of smaller versions originally in frames, or part of a complete equestrian figure of the archbishop returning from exile) retain their status as the most popular of all the lead/tin pilgrim souvenirs judging from finds from the ground (Fig. 3). Cast copper-alloy or lead brooches of St Barbara newly emerge as widespread, with seven very similar finds in at least two versions, one the mirror-image of the other: at least a further half dozen not on the PAS database have been recorded locally in Norfolk (Steven Ashley, pers. comm.), and they are also known on the Continent in the Netherlands (van Beuningen and Koldeweij 1993: 126-27, figs. 39-40).

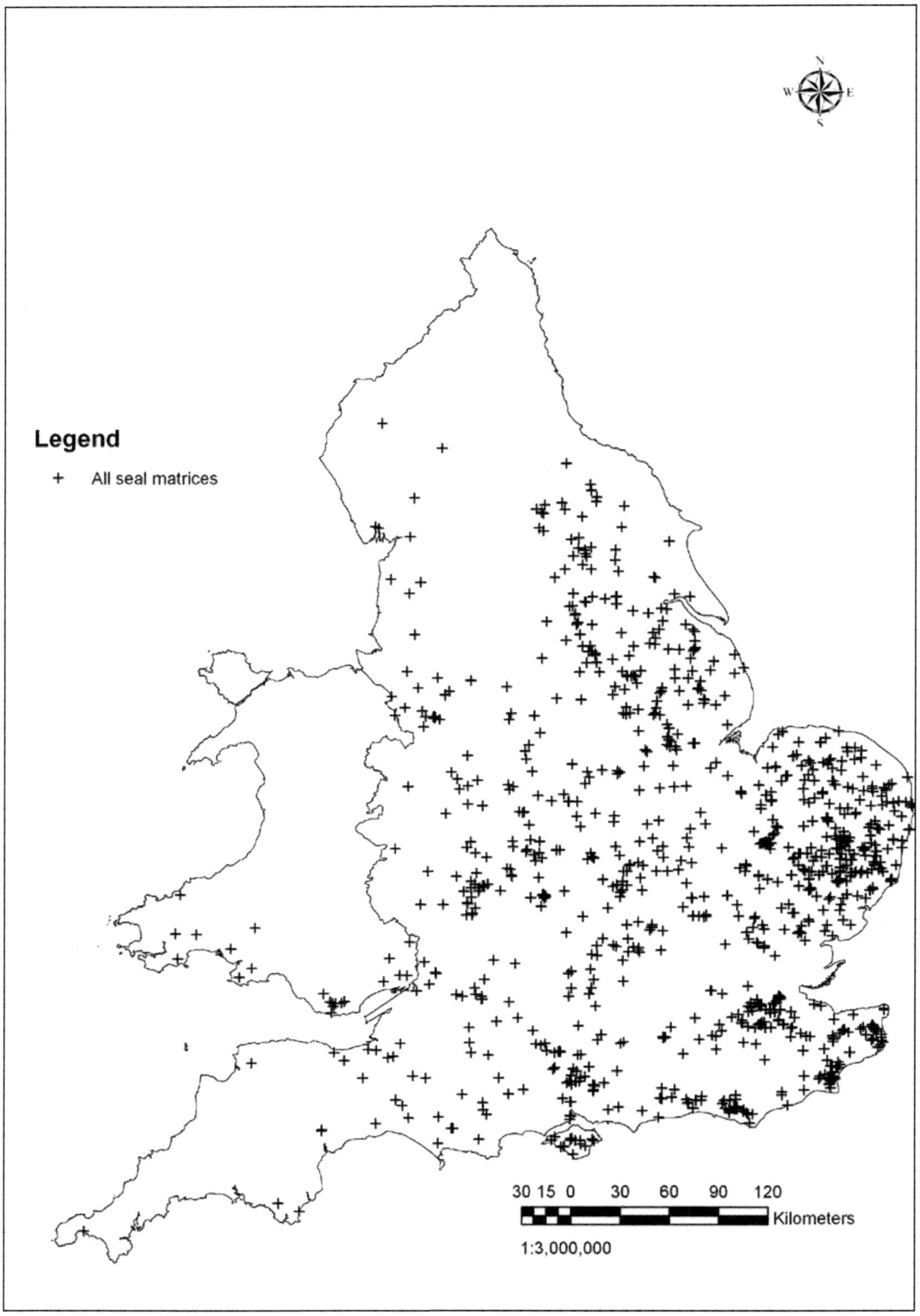

Fig. 1: Map showing medieval pilgrim badges found in England and Wales recorded by PAS 1996-2006.

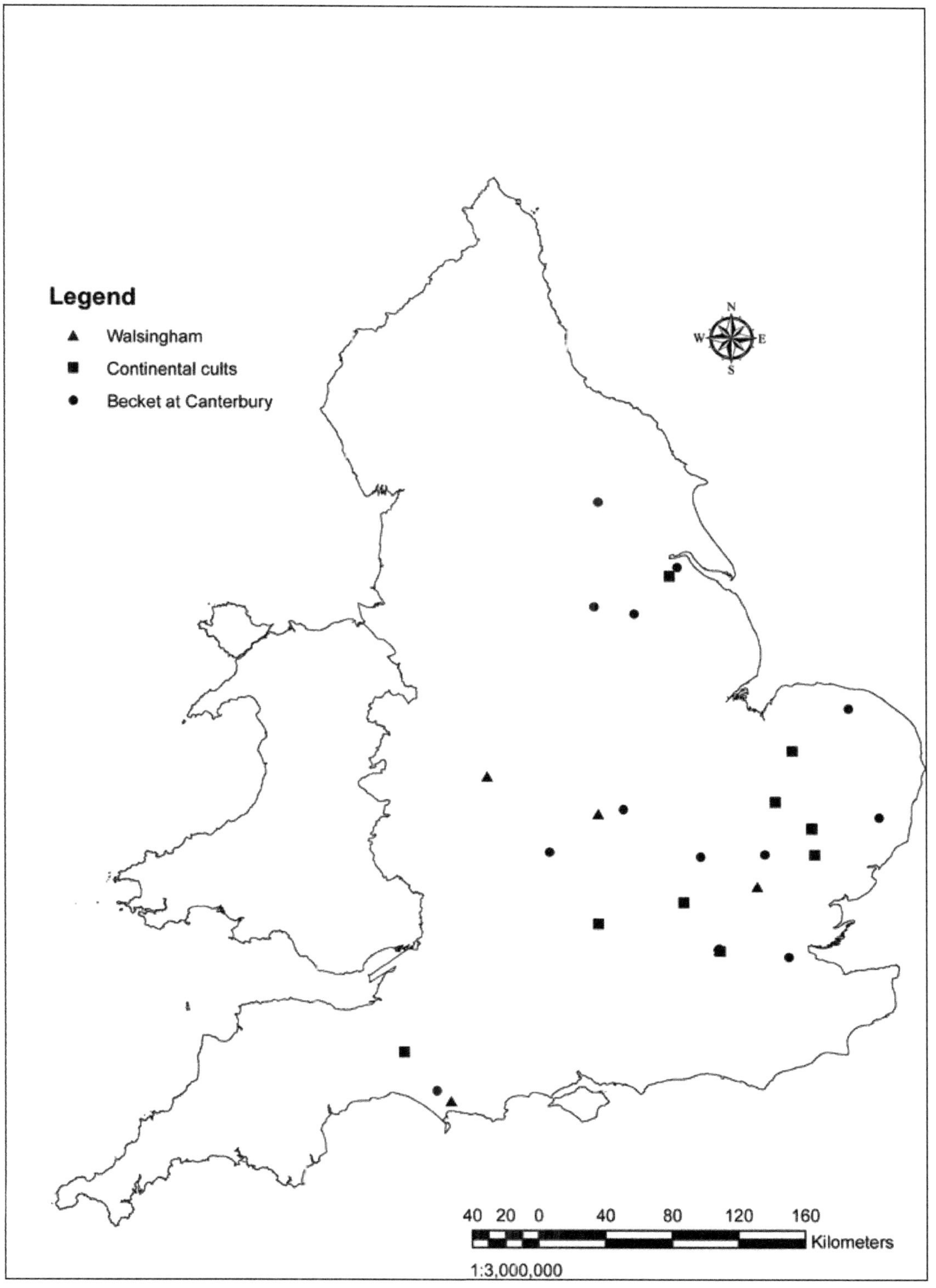

Fig. 2: Map showing PAS Database finds recorded of souvenirs of the most popular English cults, and all Continental cults, as recorded by PAS 1996-2006.

Fig. 3: Head-reliquary Becket souvenir from Canterbury (No. 8, found in Frampton, Dorset; SOMDOR-29F941).

There is an overall pattern of the largest concentration of recorded badges (about 40% of the identified ones listed from the PAS database below) in central London, with usually much more scattered finds across much of a southern and eastern (lowland) zone, and relatively few from the northern and western (highland) zone, where soils are generally less kind to flimsy objects of lead/tin. Finds from East Anglia in general are relatively prolific, with large numbers from Norfolk, where the long tradition of the public reporting finds continues to be built on (about 20% of the total listed below) and some from Cambridgeshire beginning to emerge for the first time. The emphasis in Norfolk is on the many local shrines, with ones in London and on the Continent also relatively well represented; as indicated above, the badges on the PAS database that were found in Norfolk do not include all of the very large number recorded there over the years (Steven Ashley, pers. comm.). It is the remarkable range, with a heavy emphasis on foreign cults that makes Suffolk stand out. A focus on local northern cults suggested by a few finds unearthed in north-eastern England before the PAS began recording in 1996 (for example, St William of York and Thomas of Lancaster; information from York Archaeological Trust and Martin Foreman of Hull Museums) is not reinforced by the small number of trinkets from that area recovered subsequently and put on the database. Some other regional differences are beginning to be suspected from fresh information. The known pilgrim-related finds from Wales are currently being collated (Redknap, forthcoming). So far, few found there are on the PAS database, and as with almost all of the saints of the Celtic Church more widely in Britain, the absence of pertinent souvenirs implies some apparently unstated avoidance of this means of supplementing funds. So far no specific focus is suggested by increasing numbers of finds there (most numerous are anonymous, late *ampullae*).

Although none of the finds considered here has any definitive context dating, they virtually all are assignable from parallels for which this is known or on stylistic grounds to the 14th to early 16th centuries. The possible exception is the unparalleled No. 4, which may be 13th-century (this would make it exceptional for an English badge, as the received wisdom is that the mass-produced pilgrim souvenirs made in this country at least were exclusively *ampullae* up to the 1300s). The apparent absence from the PAS database at the time of writing of any of the extensive series of possible late 12th/13th-century *ampullae* or of comparably early foreign badges like those recovered from excavation sites, mainly in London, seems strange overall. No obvious explanation has been forthcoming. It is not the case that soils in rural areas are almost universally unsuitable for the long-term preservation of fragile objects of thin lead/tin, in which case some of the earliest souvenirs that have been recovered might have been expected to be much more corroded than they are: this pattern is, however, evident in London away from waterlogged sites. It seems improbable, too, that only a major urban centre would have had the excess wealth for the earlier trinkets to be common enough in the population's possessions to figure in the record of buried material culture (cf. the range of Continental souvenirs found at the fishing village of Meols on the Wirral: Egan 2007: 152-56).

Several identified cults are represented by two or more finds listed below. Seven categories of Becket souvenirs are recorded, making his the most popular of all - the head reliquary (the most common), more-ornate head souvenirs, the equestrian return-from-exile figure (sometimes represented by a smaller version of the head), martyrdom scene, assailant's sheathed sword, assailant's shield, and Becket's gloves. Of the total of 18 souvenirs from this most prolific of cults, London has produced six,

Kent, Lincolnshire and Yorkshire two each, and Bedfordshire, Dorset, possibly Essex, Norfolk, Northamptonshire, Suffolk and Warwickshire one each. Walsingham comes next with five (none is fully certain), from Dorset, Essex, London, Northamptonshire and West Midlands, along with four badges of the (possible) Man of Sorrows, which have been recorded from Cheshire, Derbyshire, possibly Nottinghamshire and possibly Yorkshire (so far unknown in London).

A couple of celebrated medieval preachers were also popular in a time of radical religious thinking. Three badges each are listed for John Schorn (Shorne) and Richard Caister (all London finds except one of the former from Oxfordshire). The badges identified as the Five Wounds are most unusual in being symbolic representations (two from London, and another possibly from Yorkshire). Those of (possibly) Our Lady of Willesden (three, all found in London) and St Anne with the Virgin (Cambridgeshire, two from Lincolnshire, and Somerset) all have multiple records. Saint George badges are also of varied metals, with versions in precious metals putting in more than one appearance (copper-alloy, with the saint standing from Staffordshire, and on horseback from London; silver, on horseback from Essex and Norfolk, and standing from Yorkshire). The politically contrived, briefly very popular cult of Henry VI (never officially sanctified) has produced badges from London, Warwickshire, possibly Yorkshire and possibly Oxfordshire (the last could instead be another John Schorn souvenir). The capital also produced two souvenirs of St Alban and one of St Bridget (Syon Abbey), both within a day's journey, as well as one thought to be for the more distant St Osmund of Salisbury. A smallish group of cast copper-alloy badges share the similar design traits of more emphasised three-dimensionality than most of those of lead/tin, and simple openwork making a tripartite whole often with a curving base and more complex upper profile, all of which suggests a common origin. They seem to be emerging as a popular and widespread series, which comprises brooches for St Barbara (total seven, in at least two versions: tower to right from the Isle of Wight, Northamptonshire, Somerset and Surrey; tower to left from Dorset and Gloucestershire; position unrecorded from Kent), ones showing the Piéta (three in total from Kent, Northamptonshire and Surrey; the lead/tin badges from Norfolk and Yorkshire are completely different), and St Edmund/Sebastian flanked by two archers (one example of copper-alloy from Norfolk - cf. Spencer 1998: 182, where several others are noted. Another published as lead/tin was found in the Netherlands: van Beuningen and Koldeweij 1993: 191 fig. 331). It is possible that St Edmund is significant and these all originated at Bury St Edmunds.

Two cults that seem previously to have been unknown from souvenirs in England have emerged. 'Aedgar, saint and king,' presumably the 10th-century King Edgar, appears on an early looking, Continental-style looped badge found in Cambridgeshire. Despite his renown for a leading role in developing the minster at Winchester, the origin of this badge is more likely to be from Glastonbury, where he is buried (Teresa Hall, pers. comm.). A badge probably showing St Agnes found in Wiltshire would be the first recorded for this saint in Britain. The possible Salutation badge would be a further newcomer to the known repertoire.

From the Continent, St Roche appears to be another new addition to the cannon of saints attested by finds in England, though similar finds were already known in the Low Countries. Foreign travel is implied by this badge (found in Somerset), finds of two souvenirs of St Andrew from Scotland (both Suffolk finds), one possibly for St Giles (Gilles du Gard in the South of France, found in Suffolk) and three for St Leonard of Noblat also in France (from Norfolk, Oxfordshire and Suffolk), and from beyond the Alps two for Saints Peter and Paul, from Rome (Norfolk and Suffolk finds), one possibly for the Vernicle would also be from Rome (found in Norfolk), and there are three for St Nicholas of Bari also in Italy (from Lincolnshire, Oxfordshire and Suffolk). A silver badge of St Michael (found in Kent) may be from Mont St Michel, France or perhaps St Michael's Mount, Cornwall (the former is favoured by the present tradition of interpretation, though his popularity as a protector was such that this badge might have been acquired almost anywhere). Relatively robust scallop shells of lead/tin, perhaps forms of mount rather than brooches, but nevertheless possibly representing the cult of St James of Compostela, northern Spain, have been recovered in Cambridgeshire, Hertfordshire and Kent (a silver fragment with a scallop motif is too fragmentary to determine what form of accessory it is from).

The total of ten badges and devotional pendants of silver (Fig. 4) and one of gold in the list recorded after ten years (several were recorded as Treasure) is perhaps more than might have been expected in precious metals: only three have been published from London (Spencer 1998: 117-18, fig. 108e; 176 and 178, fig. 198d; 186 and 188, fig. 206f, respectively for Becket, St George and St Barbara). Featuring a range of saints and the Virgin (Nos. 2 and 83 in the following list), those on the Database are all rural finds.

They presumably reflect the greater purchasing power of rich travellers. The growing numbers of finds of brittle silver outside towns may perhaps be a function of loss while on horseback (contemporary recovery from lush vegetation would have been far less likely than for losses in populous centres where streets were constantly walked by the poor, who would have kept eager watch for anything valuable). The identified saints represented are St Michael (from Kent), St Nicholas with the boys/girls he saved from drowning or provided dowries for, represented by a foil badge (from Suffolk, complementing a cast one of lead/tin from Lincolnshire and another in copper-alloy from Oxfordshire), and St George (three, as noted above), whose popularity among all classes as the national hero knight in the late 14th and 15th centuries is not surprising. The sole gold item (No. 84 in the list, from Suffolk) served probably for both Becket and the Annunciation may be more accurately described as a devotional aid than a pilgrim souvenir, though the later remains a possibility.

The discovery of any pilgrim souvenir remains uncommon, and of enough significance still to be notable in itself. It has taken some time to put the fresh information on pilgrim souvenirs available through the PAS into a meaningful synthesis. There is now a sizeable new corpus, constantly being added to, which can furnish significant new information in this popular subject.

Fig. 4: Precious metal accessories:
Top: Both sides of gilded copper-alloy pendant of Thomas Becket and the crucifixion (No. 16 found in Hampshire);
Middle left: cast silver brooch of St Michael (No. 22 found in Kent);
Middle right: silver gilt sheeting fragment of a button brooch of St Nicholas of Bari protecting three boys (No. 89 found in Suffolk);
Bottom: Gold pendant featuring Becket and the Annunciation (No. 84 found in Suffolk).

Fig. 5: New cults: Top left: St Edgar the peacemaker king (No. 4 found in Cambridgeshire); Top right: ?St Agnes (No. 95 found in Wiltshire); Bottom left: Man of Sorrows (No. 6 found in Cheshire); Bottom right: St Roche of Montpelier with dog (No. 81 found in Somerset).

With cast copper-alloy badges: Left to right: two St Barbaras (Nos. 18 and 80, respectively found in the Isle of Wight and Somerset), Pieta (No. 91 found in Surrey) and St Christopher carrying Christ (No. 15 found in Gloucestershire).

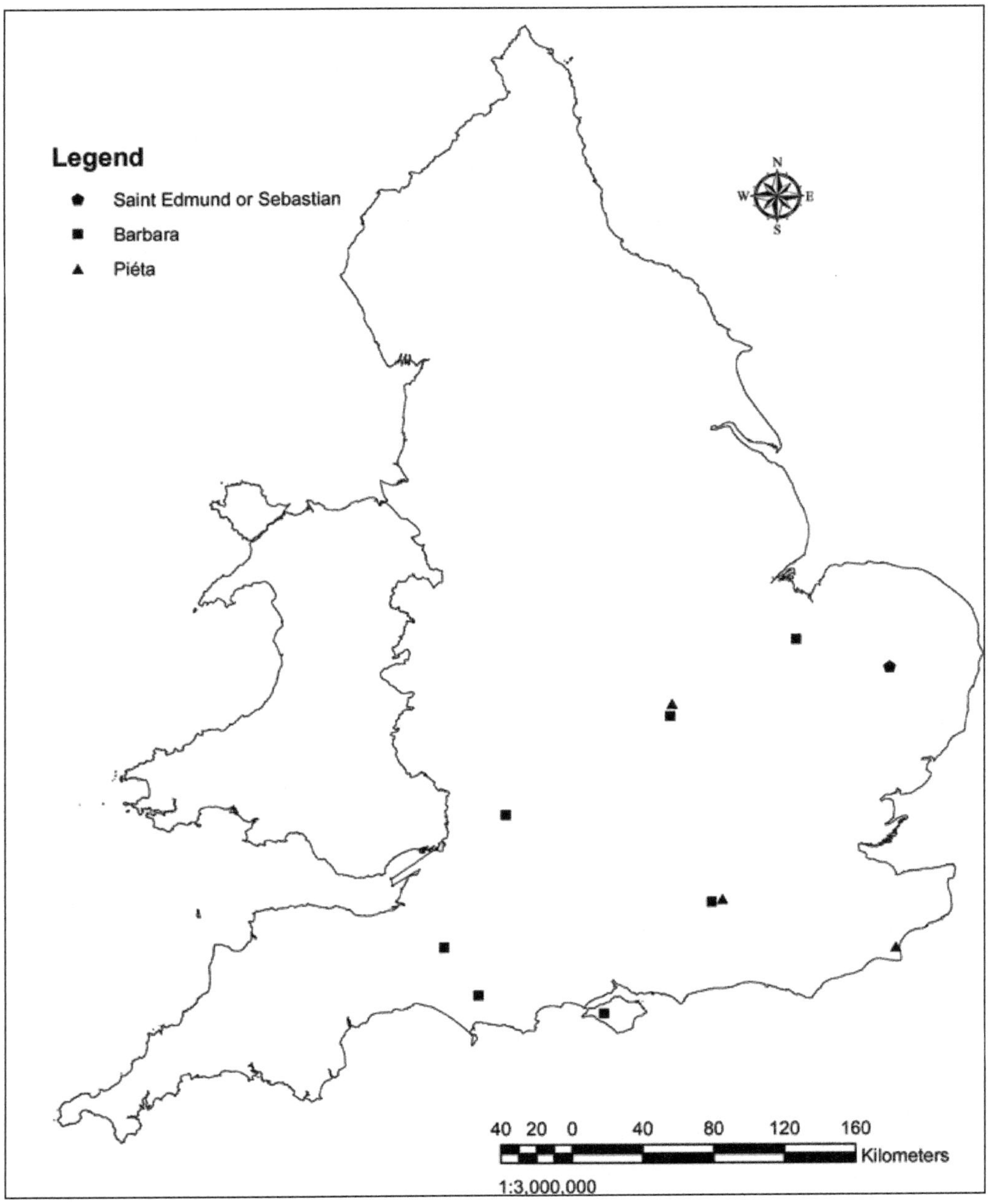

Fig. 6: Map showing PAS database finds recorded 1996-2006 of cast copper alloy souvenirs possibly produced at the same workshop: Piéta, St Barbara and St Edmund/ Sebastian.

Fig. 7: New variants: Left to right: Annunciation oval (No. 38 found in London; height: 38mm), John Schorn (No.58 found in London; also Richard Caister preaching in the pulpit (No. 61 found in London; height: 44mm).

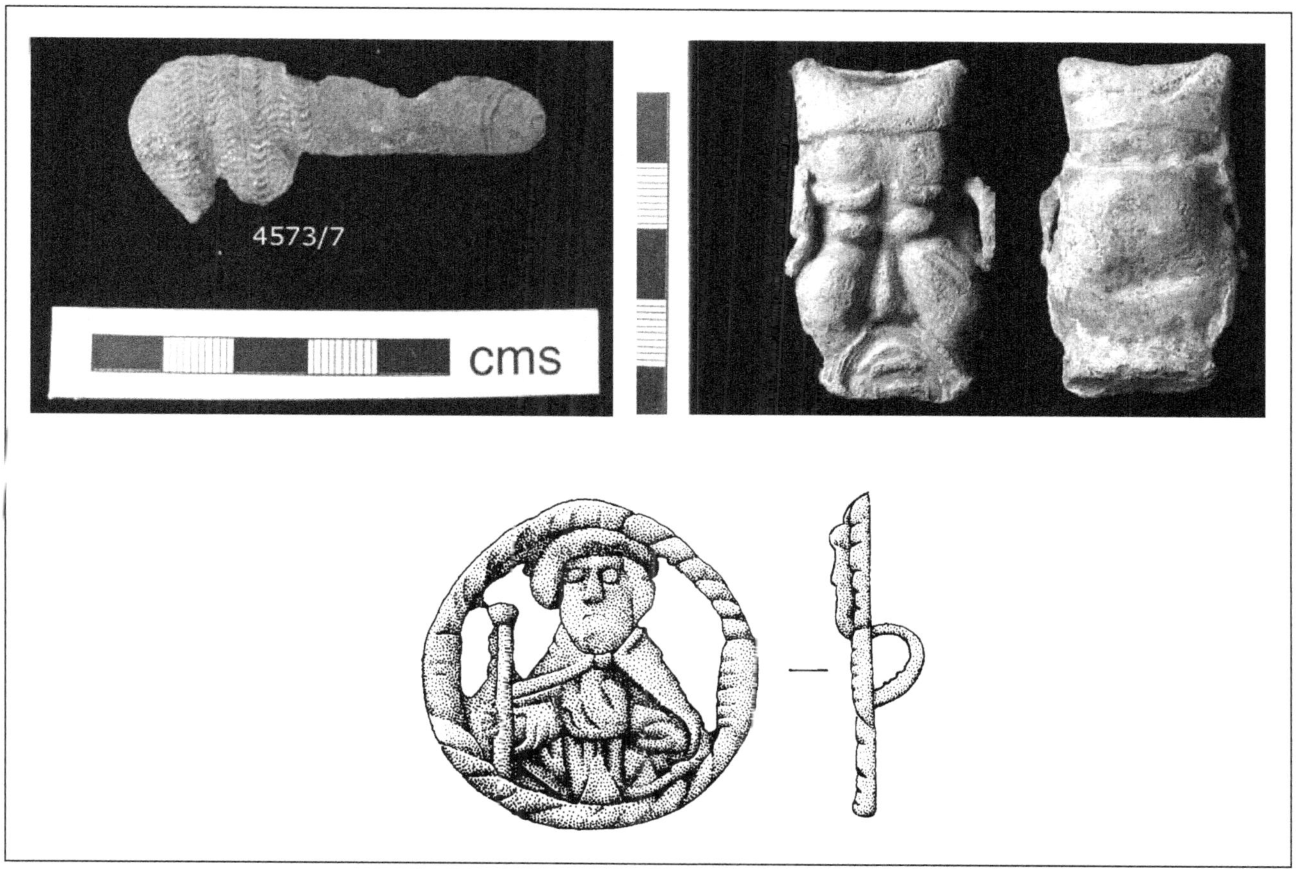

Fig. 8: Related Items (not in main list): secular badge, curious ampulla and (?)16th-century brooch:
Top left: Secular phallic brooch found in London (LON-1F9E84);
Top right: Unusual ampulla in form of grotesque head, found at Henhull, Cheshire (LVPL1993);
Bottom: Copper-alloy button brooch of ?pilgrim with staff, found at East Meon, Hampshire (HAMP2202; diameter: 27mm).

Listing of Pilgrim Badges

The listing, within county (etc.) findspot locations, follows the conventions used in Spencer 1998. Not all items were recorded in the county in which they were found.

Key:

(...) = inference by recorder.
[...] = inference by present writer (image of object or detail not seen).
'...' suggestion by recorder that appears questionable or likely to be erroneous.
Some other identifications are by the present writer from considering the image and other data on the PAS database
No. - reference to item in the following list
no. - number reference not in the following list

Bedfordshire (1 item):
1: BH-19C0B6. Lead/tin, frame fragment with censing angel (from side of Becket head), Astwick, Bedfordshire. Variant of Spencer 1990: 22, no. 26 and 72, fig. 32.

Buckinghamshire (1 item):
2: Treasure item. Cast silver, crowned M, found at Haddenham. Published, *TAR* 2003: 93 and 221, no. 131. Acquired by Buckinghamshire County Museum, Aylesbury. Mary Queen of Heaven.

Cambridgeshire (3 items):
3: NMS-552096. Lead/tin, lower half of standing figure, St Anne, from badge of her together with the Virgin (cf. nos. 27-28 and 79 etc.; details of the drapery make the identification certain). Found at Elm. Cf. Spencer 1998: 176-77, fig. 196c.
4: SF10740 (Fig. 5). Lead/tin, Aedgar, = Edgar the Peaceful (r. 943-75), king and saint (active in promoting the church, especially the Minster at Winchester). Found at Fordham; presumably a souvenir from Glastonbury Abbey, where Edgar was buried.
No other souvenir for this saint seems to have been recorded.
5: CAM-28B7A7. Lead/tin, scallop (?Compostela), ?mount; found at Shudy Camps.
Cf. Nos. 13 and 18A and Spencer: 1990: 42-43, fig. 87, and 80, fig. 113.

Cheshire (1 item):
6: LVPL-F6D514 (Fig. 5). Lead/tin, ?Man of Sorrows. Found at Nantwich.
Cf Nos. 7, 76 and 99; the resemblance to Spencer 1998: 162 and 166, no. 180b, a John Scorn badge, is presumably coincidental. The notion of Christ as 'the Man of Sorrows' presumably comes from Isaiah: 53: 3.

Derbyshire (1 item):
7: DENO-B7F1D4. Lead/tin (incomplete). ?Man of Sorrows. Found at Whitwell.
See on preceding item.

Dorset (3 items):
8: SOMDOR-29F941 (Fig. 3). Lead/tin, Becket-reliquary head. Found at Frampton.
Cf. Spencer 1998: 78. Published, *PAAR* 2005/6: 90.
9: SOMDOR-7514C8. Lead/tin, roundel, Annunciation (?Walsingham). Found at Whitcombe. Cf. Spencer 1998: 142-43 (fig. 150b differs).
10: SOMDOR-FF50A2. Cast copper-alloy, (incomplete) St Barbara with tower to left. Found at Piddlehinton. Published, *PAAR* 2004/5: 74-76, no. 142. Cf. Nos. 14, 18, 66, 75, 80 and 92.

Essex (3 items):
11: ESS-80AFE7. Lead/tin, (?)Becket head (mitre only). Found at Roxwell.
Cf. Spencer 1998: 102-9 [mitre H: 40mm].
12: ESS-57FB48. Lead/tin, Virgin and Child in ornate frame (?Walsingham). Found at Takeley. Cf. Spencer 1998: 150 and 152, fig.159c (not a precise parallel).
13: Treasure item. Cast silver gilt, mounted St George and dragon, found at Takeley. Published, *TAR* 2004: 116-17 and 284, no. 229. Cf. No. 102.

Gloucestershire (2 items):
14: GLO-D4BD11. Cast copper-alloy, St Barbara with tower (to left) and martyr's palm. Found at Minchinhampton. Cf. Nos. 10 etc.
15: GLO-ECFFB2. Cast copper-alloy, haloed (?)St Christopher, carrying the Christ Child across a river with foliage to each side. Found at Minsterworth. No parallel traced; see Spencer 1998: 181.

Hampshire (1 item):
16: WILT-B4CF25 (Fig. 4). Gilded cast copper-alloy, tau-cross pendant engraved with St Antony seated // crucifixion. Found at Broughton. Published *PAAR* 2004/5: 74-75, no. 139. The second design is described there as ?St Catherine with wheel but the main figure has been misinterpreted, as the drawing from the following reference shows, and the 'wheel' may be the conventional skull; Geake 2002: 136 and 138, fig. 3e. No parallel traced; see Spencer 1998: 177-78.

Hertfordshire (1 item):
17: BH-048794. Lead/tin, scallop, ?mount. Found at Redbourne. Cf. No. 4 etc. and Spencer 1990: 42-43, fig. 87, and 80, fig. 113.

Isle of Wight (1 item):
18: IOW-2A0A40 (Fig. 6) cast copper-alloy, St Barbara with tower (to left) and martyr's palm branch. Found at Calbourne. Cf. No. 10 etc.

Kent (5 items):
19: KENT-F04B93. Lead/tin, Becket head. Found at Cliffe. Cf. Spencer 1998: 102-9.
20: KENT345. Lead/tin, Becket-head reliquary. No findspot given: finder frequented Thames in London among other locations. Published *PAAR* 1997/8: 30. Cf. Spencer 1998: 102-9.
21: KENT4898. ?Cast copper-alloy (no image), Pieta. Found at New Romney. Cf. Nos. 65 etc.
22 KENT680 (Fig. 4) Cast silver, St Michael spearing the devil. Found at Canterbury.
No parallel in this metal traced; see Spencer 1998: 231.
23: KENT-82EAD4. Lead/tin scallop (fragment), ?mount. Found at Newchurch. Cf. No. 4 etc. and Spencer 1990: 42-43, fig. 87, and 80, fig. 113.

Lincolnshire (8 items):
24: NLM667. Lead/tin, Becket-head reliquary. Found at Thornton Curtis, North Lincolnshire.
Cf. Spencer 1998: 102-9.
25: NLM-BE7AB7. Lead/tin, (?)Becket head, bearded (crude). Found at Gainsborough. Cf. Spencer 1998: 102-9.
26: NLM-66F7F3. Lead/tin, oval button form, two standing figures (? one of the Magi with halo, and an angel) flanking a seated Virgin (?) and Child and presenting gifts. Found at Swinhope. No parallel traced.
27: NLM-D36812. Lead/tin, fragment or St Anne with the Virgin, crowned and with rosary (?Buxton); this image, with the Virgin held so close as possibly to be across her mother's lap (though the definitive lower part is missing), is reminiscent of some Pieta badges, though there Christ's upper torso is invariably unclothed (see Nos. 65 and 101). Found at Braceby and Sapperton. Cf. Spencer 1998: 176-7.
28: NLM4718. Lead/tin, [?St Anne and the Virgin (?Buxton)]. Found at Thimbleby.
Cf. Spencer 1998: 176-77, fig. 196c.
29: NLM2903. Lead/tin, incomplete ('?tent') = female figure (headless), (?)St Catherine in frame with bosses. Found at Elsham. (?) Cf. Spencer 1998: 179-80, fig. 198j (which shares a similar pelleted frame). No precise parallel traced.
30: NLM5728. Lead/tin (oval pendant), St Margaret standing over dragon // HIS. Found at Binbrook. Cf. Mitchiner 1986: 174, no. 551 (there assigned from a Midlands/East Anglian distribution to St Margaret's Church at Lynn).
31: NLM2914. Lead/tin, fragment (drawing only): two boys reading in front of incomplete larger figure, ?St Nicholas of Bari. Found at Elsham. Cf. No. 78; see Spencer 1998: 255 and 257.

London (40 items):
32: LON-974287. Lead/tin, Becket's head in quatrefoil in square (no image). Found in City of London. ?Cf. Spencer 1998: 112 and 114, fig. 108a.
33: LON-A9F210. Lead/tin, Becket head. Found in City of London. Cf. Spencer 1998: 102-9.
34: LON-400806. Lead/tin, Becket head, ?from equestrian figure or ornately bordered souvenir. Found in City of London. Cf. Spencer 1998: 102-9.
35: LON-CD2C70. Lead/tin, (fragment) Becket martyrdom scene (base fragment with legs of assailants and slumped Becket). Found in City of London. Variant of Spencer 1998: 92, fig. 64.
36: LON-CF5770. Lead/tin, Becket murder weapon (sword and scabbard). Found in City of London. Cf. Spencer 1998: 95-97.

37: LON-B92301. Lead/tin, Becket's episcopal glove (Canterbury). Found in City of London.
Cf. No. 63 and Spencer 1998: 120-21, figs. 120 etc. (no precise parallel).
38: LON-69C4E5 (Fig.7). Sheet copper-alloy oval, Annunciation (?Walsingham). Found in City of London.
Cf. Spencer 1998: 142-44, figs. 151a etc.
39: LON- B88A97. Lead/tin, Our Lady of Willesden (incomplete). Found in City of London.
Cf. Spencer 1998: 149-52, figs. 155-56.
40: LON-840972. Lead/tin, Our Lady of Willesden (no image). Found in City of London. See on preceding item.
41: LON-D7E724. Lead/tin, fragment, Our Lady of Willesden (no image). Found in City of London. See on No. 39.
42: LON-0D6BB3. Lead/tin, fleur de lis in roundel (?symbol of the Virgin). Found in City of London. Cf. following two items; cf. Spencer 1998: 158-59, fig. 176; these fleur brooches had a variety of apparently secular pendants attached (e.g. bagpipes, purses).
43: LON-893C42. Lead/tin, openwork fleur de lis in roundel. Found in City of London.
See on preceding item.
44: LON-473472. Lead/tin, openwork fleur de lis in roundel. Found in City of London.
See on No. 42.
45: LON-50F233. Sheet copper alloy (incomplete), crowned figure on a scallop-shell background - (?)Christ holding cross. Found in Southwark. No precise parallel traced, but for the form and background scallop cf. Spencer 1998: 246, fig. 250d, identified as St James of Compostela (Spain), and said to be too flimsy to be a badge in its own right - possibly a composite or a mount.
46: LON-A7B2B4. Lead/tin, (?)The Five Wounds. Found in City of London. See next item and No. 101; cf. Spencer 1980: 24, fig. 103 – 'perhaps connected with the cult of the Five Wounds of Christ', and *idem* 1990: 38 and 79, nos. 74-6, figs. 99-101, where they are given this attribution with less reservation. If correctly interpreted, the highly stylised symbolism stands almost alone among the canon of popular pilgrim trinkets.
47: LON-0DC910. Lead/tin, (?)The Five Wounds. Found in City of London. See No. 46 etc.
48: LON-8F52D2. Sheet copper-alloy roundel, instruments of the Passion. Found in City of London. Published, *PAAR* 2004/5: 79, no. 149. Cf. Spencer 1998: 173-74, fig. 194a.
49: LON-C95623. Lead/tin, (fragment), blackletter Ihc or s. Found in City of London.
Differs from Spencer 1998: 173-74, no. 194.
50: LON-4240A85. Lead/tin, (fragment) scroll with blackletter ... in Ihc. Found in City of London. No precise parallel traced; cf. Spencer 1998: 173-74.
51: LON-E75417. Lead/tin, St Alban (fragment with part of executioner). Found in City of London. Published *PAAR* 2004/5: 79, no. 149. Variant on Spencer 1998: 175-76, figs. 196 and 196a.
52: LON-0E5057. Lead/tin, St Alban (frame fragment). Found in City of London.
Cf. Spencer 1998: 175-76, fig. 196a.
53: LON-F5F957. Lead/tin, roundel (some of edge missing), crude, St Bridget at lectern (Syon Abbey, Isleworth). Found in City of London. No close parallel traced, cf. Spencer 1998: 178-80.
54: LON-D3A3E3. Cast copper alloy (headless; no image), 'mounted St George over slain dragon'. Found in City of London. Recorder compares this with lead/tin badge Spencer 1998: 186 and 188, fig. 206d.
55: LON-FF30A5. Lead/tin (no image), 'bishop' holding staff and orb. Found in City of London, [Henry VI (Windsor) presuming the 'staff' is a sceptre]. Cf. Spencer 1998: 189-92.
56: LON-0ADE06. Lead/tin, (incomplete) headless, standing figure holding missing object - John Schorn (with devil in boot - North Marston/Windsor). Found in Southwark. Cf. Spencer 1998: 193-95, fig. 208k.
57: LON-322DF6. Lead/tin, headless fragment - John Schorn (North Marston/Windsor). Found in City of London. Cf. Spencer 1998: 192-95, fig. 208j.
58 LON-0E51B1 (Fig.7). Lead/tin, (crude) roundel with head of John Schorn with (?)'SZCHOrN' (North Marston/Windsor). Found in City of London. Published, MacGregor 2007: 333, fig. 6.4. No close parallel traced; see Spencer 1998: 192-95. Acquired by Ashmolean Museum, Oxford.
59: LON-C98694. Lead/tin, roundel with bishop's bust, possibly St Osmund (Salisbury). Found in City of London. Cf. Spencer 1990: 13-14 and 69, fig. 6, and idem 1998: 194 and 196, fig. 208p; these and other parallels have been found in London, but so far none has turned up in Salisbury.
60: LON-408022. Lead/tin, Richard Caister (Norwich), Putney. Found in Greater London.
Variant on Spencer 1998: 196-8, figs. 209 etc. (larger dove of Holy Spirit).
61: LON-931D60 (Fig.7). Lead/tin, (incomplete) Richard Caister preaching from the pulpit, the Holy Spirit in the form of a dove, sent by God the Father (missing apart from a hand) from above the clouds to inspire him, blackletter 'soli deo honor:/et:gloria/ioh(?kais)' along border (Norwich). Found in City of London. Cf. Spencer 1998: 196-97, fig. 209b (not a precise parallel).
62: LON-324B84. Lead tin, fragment with body of Richard Caister, who is preaching in the pulpit (Norwich). Found in City of London. Cf. Spencer 1998: 196-98, figs. 209b-d.

Norfolk (20 items):
63: NMS-D0D287. Lead/tin, Becket's episcopal glove. Found at Corpusty. Cf. No. 37 and Spencer 1998: 120-21, figs. 120 etc.
64: NMS-B76D74. Lead/tin, roundel with seated Virgin and Child on background of rays. Found at Cawston. Spencer 1998: 150, fig. 159b, has similar rays, though there the figures stand in a crescent moon.
65: NMS-E48254. Lead/tin, crude, Pieta. Found at Upwell. Cf. No. 101.
66: NMS962. Cast copper-alloy, St Barbara (no image). Found at Upwell. Cf. No.21 etc. Cf. Spencer 1998: 178.
67: NMS-1FC390. Lead/tin, St Blaise, comb pendant (Canterbury). Found at Emneth. Cf. Spencer 1998: 176 and 178, fig. 198f.
68: NMS906. Cast copper-alloy (no image on database), St Edmund/Sebastian found at Quidenham/Kenninghall.

Published, Geake 2003: 210-11, fig. 3a. See Spencer 1998: 181-82.
69: NMS-24DDF3 [was NMS539]. Cast silver gilt, mounted St George and dragon. Found at Briston. Published, *TAR* 2001: 67, no. 116; Norfolk Archaeology and Environment Annual Review 2005-6: 10. See Spencer 1998: 186-87.
70: NMS-5F9BB2. Lead/tin, (no image) fragment, St Leonard standing with kneeling chained prisoner. Found at West Walton. ?Cf. No. 10.
71: NMS-58AE57. Lead/tin, (?) head of Christ, possibly the Vernicle, Rome (the cloth which on the way to the Crucifixion was used to wipe Christ's face and which then bore its image). Found at Beachamwell. Cf. Spencer 1998: 250-52 (in contrast with figs. 254 a-c there the present head has no frame).

Northamptonshire (4 items):
72: NARC1754. Lead/tin, Becket-head reliquary (fragment). Found at Pitsford. Cf. Spencer 1998: 102-9.
73: NARC866. Lead/tin, '?mother and child sitting in roofed structure' (no image). Found at Norton. [?Our Lady of Walsingham]. ?Cf. Spencer 1998: 137-39.
74: NARC-7A4A72. Cast copper-alloy, Piéta. Found at Overstone. Cf. Nos. 21 etc.
75: NARC-B9F6E5: Cast copper-alloy, (incomplete) St Barbara with tower (to right - lacks palm branch). Found at Grendon. Cf. No. 10 etc.

Nottinghamshire (1 item):
76: LVPL-D75692. Lead/tin, Man of Sorrows. Found at Collingham. Poorly registered version of Nos. 6 etc, with lower part of beard missing.

Oxfordshire (2 items):
77: BERK-186AD6. Lead/tin, (crude) John Schorn or Henry VI (North Marston/Windsor); these cults resulted in some closely similar souvenirs at the cruder end of the respective ranges - it is not possible to differentiate between the two for this damaged accessory, though it is possible the devil in a boot is intended on the left side and no discernible crown for the main figure, both of which would point to the former. Found at Islip. ?Cf. Spencer 1998: 192-95, cf. no. 2081 (or 189-90 for Henry VI).
78: BERK-A95AE5. Cast copper-alloy, St Nicholas blessing three children (?)in tub (?Bari). Found at Drayton St Leonard. See on No. 31.

Somerset (3 items):
79: SOMDOR148. Lead/tin, upper half of St Anne teaching the Virgin to read (?Buxton). Found at Sampford Brett. Published, *PAAR* 1998/9: 40, fig. 43. Cf. Spencer 1998: 176-77, fig. 196c (here the figures are standing).
80: SOMDOR-9E68C2 (Fig. 6). Cast copper alloy, St Barbara with tower (to right) and martyr's palm. Found at Kingsdon. Cf. No. 10 etc.
81: SOMDOR905 (Fig. 5). Cast copper alloy, St Roche (Montpelier, France). Found at South Petherton. Published, *PAAR* 1999/2000: 42, fig. 40; Geake 2003: 245-46, fig. 3b. Cf. van Beuningen and Koldeweij 1993: 190, fig. 327, cat. no. 1837. St Roche was a pilgrim who suffered from a disease which resulted in a sore on his thigh, which he is shown exposing, and he is flanked by a kneeling ?angel helper (Fig. 5) and a dog standing on its hind legs.

Staffordshire (1 item):
82: WMID-FB76D0. Cast copper-alloy, standing St George and incomplete dragon. Found at Ilam. Cf. No. 102 and Spencer 1998: 186-89 (no precise parallel).
Suffolk (8 items):
83: SF-725306. Cast silver, crowned MARIA ligature. Found at Palgrave. Spencer 1998: 155-58 mentions only crowned 'M' badges, though figs. 170-71 (respectively of lead/tin and copper alloy) have similar ligatures.
84: Treasure item. Gold, lozenge pendant with bishop's head and S T (lombardic lettering) // Annunciation, (?) Becket (Canterbury). Found Framlingham. Published, *TAR* 2003: 114 and 232, no. 214. No parallel traced.
85: SF2266. Lead/tin, rectangular - figure holding staff or crozier (limited record; no image). Found at Freckenham (same field as following item); [??St Giles - Gilles du Gard, France].
?Cf. Spencer 1998: 236-39.
86: SF1834. Lead/tin, rectangular (no image), standing saint with crozier, kneeling prisoner with shackle at side, '[S]CI LE[ON]ARDI SIGILLVM', St Leonard (Noblat, France). Found at Freckenham (same field as preceding item). Cf. Spencer 1998: 230 and 232-33.
87: SF3. Lead/tin, rectangular - St Andrew (St Andrews, Scotland). Found at Polstead. Cf. Spencer 1998: 270-72, fig. 265.
88: SF9179. Lead/tin (bent), rectangular - St Andrew (St Andrews, Scotland). Found at Bradfield Combust with Stanningfield. Cf. Spencer 1998: 270-72, nos. 265 etc. (no precise parallel).
89: SF8047 (Fig. 4). Silver-gilt sheeting, (incomplete, loop on back), St Nicholas of Bari (headless) with three boys in crescent. Found at Bradfield Combust with Stanningfield. Published, *TAR* 2001, 67 no. 115. No parallel traced in the same metal; see Spencer 1998: 255 and 257.
90: SF8205. Lead/tin, rectangular - St Peter & St Paul (Rome). Found at Badingham. Variant on Spencer 1998: 248-51, figs. 251 etc.

Surrey (2 items):
91: SUR-B57856 (Fig. 6). Cast copper-alloy, Pieta. Found at West Horsley. Cf. Nos. 21 etc.
92: SUR-7865B6. Cast copper-alloy, St Barbara with tower (to left) and martyr's palm. Found at West Clandon. Cf. No. 10 etc.

Warwickshire (2 items):
93: WAW-632026. Lead/tin, (fragment) head ?of Becket. Found at Brailes. Cf. Spencer 1998: 102-9.
94: WMID286. Lead/tin, roundel with Henry VI (Windsor). Found at Coleshill. Cf. Spencer 1998: 189-91, fig. 208.

Wiltshire (1 item):
95: WILT-DD6D34 (Fig. 5). Lead/tin, naked female figure with abundant hair, presumably St Agnes. Found at Durnford. No parallel traced. St Agnes rejected overtures of marriage from the son of a powerful official, for which she was condemned to death, but as Roman law did not

allow the execution of virgins she was dragged naked through the streets to a brothel. As she prayed her hair grew to cover her body. The prominence of her breasts on this badge was presumably to identify the hirsute figure as female, and hence St Agnes.

Worcestershire (1 item):
96: WMID-6FEEB1. Lead/tin, 'man and woman facing each other, staff between'. Found at Dudley; [? = Walsingham Annunciation]. ?Cf. Spencer 1998: 141-43.

Yorkshire (?6 items):
97: SWYOR-C9A808. Lead/tin, Becket head. Found at Tickhill, South Yorkshire. Cf. Spencer 1998: 102-9. [H of face only 20mm].
98: YORYM347. Lead/tin, rider (headless) on horseback (no image) [?Becket on horseback]. Found at Wilberfoss, East Yorkshire. ?Cf. Spencer 1998: 81-89.
99: YORYMM328. Lead/tin (no image), 'bearded, probably long-haired saint with rope-like hair'; [? Man of Sorrows]. Found at Knaresborough, North Yorkshire. ?Cf. No. 6 etc.
100: SWYOR-2133C1. Lead/tin, Pieta (fragment). Found at Hooton Levitt, South Yorkshire.
Cf. No. 65.
101: SWYOR-AEAAF5. Lead/tin, (no image) circular, with openwork four holes and central circle of pellets; [?The Five Wounds]. Found at Market Weighton, East Yorkshire.
?Cf. Nos. 46 etc.
102: Treasure item. Cast silver, (incomplete) St George standing over dragon. Found at Sherbourne-in-Elmet, North Yorkshire. Published *TAR* 2000: 83, no. 154. Cf. No. 82 (the absence of wings for the upper figure argue the present figure is not an archangel though it was published as St Michael). Acquired by Yorkshire Museum.
103: SWYOR-E2D028. Lead/tin, lozenge with Henry VI (Windsor). Findspot not given (?South Yorkshire). Variant on Spencer 1998: 189-90, fig. 208a.

Uncertain Identifications

While some of the nineteen items and scrappy survivals listed here may well be medieval pilgrim badges, in the present state of knowledge they cannot be identified with a specific cult and so this cannot be confirmed (suggestions are made for a limited number. For others identifications are altogether far less certain). A few simply lack detailed enough descriptions for an identification to be possible.

Bedfordshire (1 item):
BH-B903E5. Lead/tin, (crude, sub-triangular outline) standing figure - (?)'St George with dragon' (the latter is noted by the recorder, though it is difficult to make out in the record photograph, as is any armour on the human figure), series of crosses along each side. Found at Bletsoe. Not necessarily a pilgrim badge; no parallel traced.

Buckinghamshire (1 item):
BUC-823A02: Lead/tin, 'pilgrim badge' (no image or further details). Found at Creslow.

Humberside (1 item):
YORYM-7FC646. Lead/tin, (crude) roundel with male head facing (headgear of uncertain character, most likely a mitre); ?St Osmund (Salisbury). Found at Brantingham. (?)Cf. Spencer 1990: 13-14 and 69, fig. 6, and *idem* 1998: 194 and 196, fig. 208p. Not a precise parallel - see on No. 59 above.

Kent (2 items):
KENT1681. Sheet copper-alloy, three-dimensional brooch in form of cross crosslet, 'knights of Holy Sepulchre'. Found at Otford. The dubious identification probably derives from Mitchiner 1986: 244, nos. 939-41; this cross may be part of the arms of Jerusalem; possibly a post-medieval brooch.
KENT3618. Copper-alloy (?cast or sheet), 'saint with lamb' (no image). Found at Aylesford. [?St John the Baptist].

Lincolnshire (1 item):
DENO-08C020. Cast silver, crown (no image), found at Norton Disney. [?St Edward - this cannot be considered more than a possibility]. See Spencer 1998: figs. 202-4.

London (5 items):
LON-864DE5. Lead/tin, (fragment) stylised leaf in scrolled stem. Found in City of London.
Possibly too three-dimensional for a badge; could be from a mount. No precise parallel traced, though cf. the tracery (half the scale of the present item) in Spencer 1998: 104, fig. 76a (a Becket head-reliquary badge), and Egan and Pritchard 1991: 321-22, pendant no. 1603, which is also stylistically similar.
LON-0E4208. Lead/tin, (fragment) broad, squared frame with round central aperture. Found in City of London. No parallel traced.
LON-45C0B4. Lead/tin, (?)foliate-stem frame (fragment). Found in City of London. Although some St Alban badges have similar frames, no precise parallel has been traced to confirm this possible identification.
LON-9EA5F0. Lead/tin, 'four-petalled rose' (image not available). Found in City of London.
LON-2C5AD2. Lead/tin, (tiny fragment). Found in City of London. Scrap, possibly showing clothing.

Northamptonshire (4 items):
NARC-69D2A6. Lead/tin, (fragment) wavy ray (perhaps from Becket-head or other badge with star-like rays, though it is coarser than the potential parallels cited - length 21mm). Found at Tiffield. Cf. Spencer 1990: 79, fig. 107 (fragments there compared with star badges for Christ's birth) and *idem* 1998: 110, nos. 91-2 (fragments there compared with Becket head badges with a star surround), and 144 and 147, fig. 153 (a Walsingham badge with a pair of rays, showing Sir Ralph de Boutetorte, who was miraculously transported, while being pursued by his enemies, to the safety of sanctuary at the shrine by being transported through a gateway normally far too restricted for his access).

NARC-91D456. Lead/tin, (fragment) drapery of figure(s) with (?...SCI:S...) on scroll. Found at Little Houghton. No parallel traced.
NARC-921961. Lead/tin, (fragment) bifacially bevelled main part with blackletter legend (E etc.) and two lateral tabs. Found at Overstone.
NARC-424E60. Lead/tin, (fragment) ?purse. Found at Farthingstone. Cf. Spencer 1998: 313-15 and 317 for a variety of different purse-form accessories thought to bring good luck charms.

Suffolk (2 items):
SF6115. Virgin and Child (no image or further information). Found at Packenham.
Treasure item. Cast silver (?)badge or dress hook, (incomplete) scallop on bar, ?St James (Compostela). Found at Covehithe. Published, *TAR* 2004, 117 and 284, no. 230.
NMS-E446A6. Lead/tin, (fragment) leaf. Found at Flixton. Although tripartite leaves serve as finials on some pilgrim badges with ornate frames, no parallel has been traced in the same style, and the present fragment at *c*. 20mm+ long seems too large for this. Perhaps not from a badge.

Warwickshire (1 item):
Treasure item. Sheet silver, roundel (folded) with bishop's head, possible shackles and legend to side. Found at Alcester. Published, *TAR* 2002, 101, no. 123. Shackles could indicate St Leonard.

Yorkshire (1 item):
YORYM-C0C077. Curved, slightly trapezoidal, with crowned head (no image), lug on back. Found at Kellington, North Yorkshire.

Selected other badges

Pornographic badge:
LON-1F9E84 (Fig. 8). Lead/tin, (?incomplete) phallus, found in City of London. Cf. Spencer 1998: 317-18 notes the paucity of these from London, with references; see also Jones 2002, 248-68, fig. 12.8; Gaimster 2000; Koldeweij 2006, 114-16; comparable examples have two human-form legs and sometimes a man pushing a wheelbarrow loaded with penises along the top, or are winged, some combining this with a crown and bell, or a pecking bird.

The following are probably Reformation- period developments from the medieval tradition:
CAM-466AB8. Lead/tin, roundel with majority of edge missing, bust of (?)Henry VIII, pelleted border. Found at Shudy Camps, Cambridgeshire. Published, *PAAR* 2005/6: 99.
Cf. a copper-alloy version from Sherriff Hutton, North Yorkshire (J. Halliday datasheet record).
HAMP-2202 (Fig.8). Cast copper-alloy openwork roundel, ?pilgrim with staff (it is difficult to see this particular, hat-wearing figure as St James of Compostela). Found at East Meon, Hampshire. No parallel traced. Published, Geake 2003: 205-6, fig. 1h.

Acknowledgements

First, to the finders for making their objects available, to the many Finds Liaison Officers and other recorders across England and Wales, and to Helen Geake for a series of correct identifications; to Anne Pedersen for help checking PAS database numbers for captions, to Dan Pett for help with the database and for providing the distribution maps; to Steven Ashley (Norfolk Archaeology and Environment), Mark Redknap (National Museums of Wales) and Martin Foreman (Hull Museums) for making information on finds from their areas available, to Arthur MacGregor for his paper on John Schorn(e), to Teresa Hall for information on St Edgar; finally to the late Brian Spencer for his generous encouragement in the subject he had made his own.

Bibliography

Egan, G. 2007, 'Later medieval non-ferrous metalwork and evidence for metal working,' in Griffiths, D., Philpott, R. A., and Egan, G. (eds.), *Meols: the archaeology of the north Wirral coast: discoveries and observations in the 19th and 20th centuries, with a catalogue of collections.* Oxford University School of Archaeology Monograph 68 (Institute of Archaeology, University of Oxford, Oxford), 77-188.

Egan, G. and Pritchard, F. 1991, *Dress Accessories.* Medieval Finds from Excavations in London 3 (HMSO, London).

Gaimster, D. 2000, 'Sex and sensibility at the British Museum', *History Today* (September), 10-15.

Geake, H. 2001, 'Medieval Britain and Ireland 2000' in *Medieval Archaeology* 45, 236-51.

Geake, H. 2002, 'Portable Antiquities Scheme', in James, T. B. (ed.), 'Medieval Britain and Ireland 2001', *Medieval Archaeology* 46, 128-45.

Geake, H. 2003, 'Portable Antiquities Scheme', in James, T. B. (ed.), 'Medieval Britain and Ireland 2002', *Medieval Archaeology* 47, 202-17.

Geake, H. 2004, 'Portable Antiquities Scheme', in James, T. B. (ed.), 'Medieval Britain and Ireland 2003', *Medieval Archaeology* 48, 239-46.

Jones, M. 2002, *The Secret Middle Ages: discovering the real medieval world* (Sutton, Stroud).

Koldeweij, J. 2006, *Foi et Bonne Fortune: Parure et Dévotion en Flandre Médiévale* (Terra Lannoo, Arnhem).

MacGregor, A. 2007, 'The cult of Master John Schorne', in Gilmour, L. (ed.), *Pagans and Christians - From Antiquity to the Middle Ages: papers in honour of Martin Henig,* British Archaeological Reports, International Series 160 (British Archaeological Reports, Oxford), 327-36.

Mitchiner, M. 1986, *Medieval Pilgrim and Secular Badges* (Ravenshill Publications, Sanderstead).

Norfolk Archaeology and Environment Annual Review 2005-6 (Norfolk Museums and Archaeology Service, Norwich).

PAAR 1997/8 = Bland, R. F. (ed.) 1999, *Portable Antiquities Annual Report* 1997-98 (DCMS, London).

PAAR 1998/9 = Bland, R. F. (ed.) 2000, *Portable Antiquities Annual Report* 1998-99 (DCMS, London).

PAAR 1999/2000 = Bland, R. F. (ed.) 2001, *Portable Antiquities Annual Report* 1999-2000 (DCMS, London).
PAAR 2004/5 = Lewis, M. J. (ed.) 2005, *Portable Antiquities Annual Report* 2004/05 (MLA, London).
PAAR 2005/6 = Lewis, M. J. (ed.) 2006, *Portable Antiquities Annual Report* 2005/06 (MLA, London).
Redknap, M. forthcoming, 'Pilgrim souvenirs and secular badges found in Wales'.
Spencer, B. 1980, *Medieval Pilgrim Badges from Norfolk* (Norfolk Museums Service, Norwich).
Spencer, B. 1990, *Pilgrim Souvenirs and Secular Badges.* Salisbury and South Wiltshire Museum Medieval Catalogue 2 (Salisbury Museum, Salisbury).
Spencer, B. 1998, *Pilgrim Souvenirs and Secular Badges.* Medieval Finds from Excavations in London 7 (The Stationary Office, London).
TAR 2000 = Bland, R. F. (ed.) 2002, *Treasure Annual Report* 2000 (DCMS, London).
TAR 2001 = Bland, R. F. (ed.) 2003, *Treasure Annual Report* 2001 (DCMS, London).
TAR 2002 = Bland, R. F. (ed.) 2004, *Treasure Annual Report* 2002 (DCMS, London).
TAR 2003 = Bland, R. F. (ed.) 2005, *Treasure Annual Report* 2003 (DCMS, London).
TAR 2004 = Hitchcock, F. (ed.), 2006 *Treasure Annual Report* 2004 (DCMS, London).
van Beuningen, H. J. E. and Koldeweij, A. M. 1993, *Heilig en Profaan: 1000 Laat Middeleeuwse Insignes uit de Collectie HJE van Beuningen.* Rotterdam Papers 8 (Cothen, Rotterdam).

Personal and Impersonal Impressions: identity revealed through seals

John Cherry

Seal matrices were created in metal, stone or ivory for sealing legal agreements or letters in wax. Sometimes they show the name of the owner, which may help date them. Otherwise seal matrices can sometimes be dated by reference to dated documents with wax seals attached.

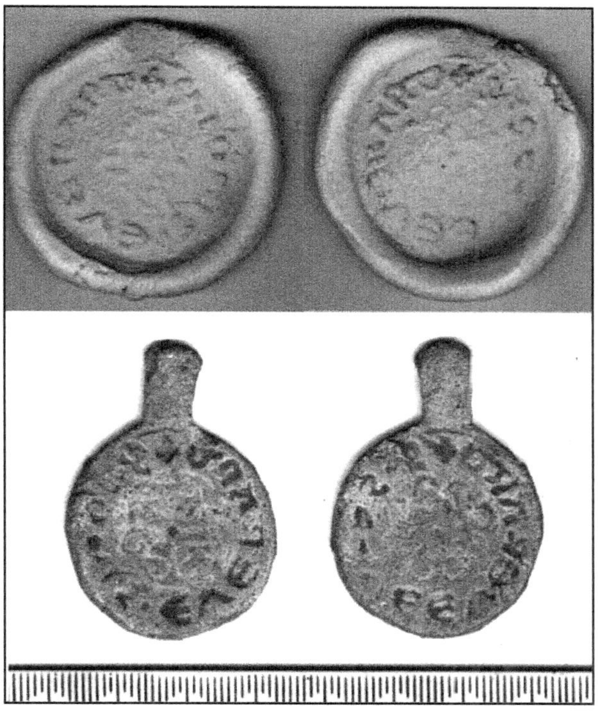

Fig. 1: Seal and matrix of John and Selve Everard, Suffolk (SF-7872).

Sometimes there are two wax seals on a document. For instance, a document relating to an exchange of property at Welton, Lincolnshire in the 13th century, owned by Henry of Bishopthorpe and his wife Matilda, is sealed by both. The two seals are exactly alike in shape size and style of engraving and form of the legend, differing only slightly in the design. When published, it was thought that they were made as a pair (Harvey and McGuinness 1996: 84, fig. 76). However, the Portable Antiquities Scheme (PAS) database shows a seal matrix found at Blaxhall, Suffolk, of John and Selve (Sylvia) Everard, which has similar identity of engraving on both sides (SF-7872; Fig. 1). It is the single seal matrix of a husband and wife. Henry of Bishopthorpe and Matilda are more likely to have had one double-sided seal matrix, and not a pair of matrices.

Seal matrices can be either personal, such as the Everards, or impersonal, with only a central device, such as a lion, and an impersonal legend, such as 'wake me no man' (PAS: SOMDOR-BB1AD2 is a typical example; Fig. 2). Sometimes personal seals show a person's status employment or craft or status. The central image is often simple and repetitive, but occasionally full of interest.

They have a life after their initial use. Some were worn as amulets or pieces of jewellery. Since they had a legal significance, they were often destroyed after use, either by cutting in half, defacing or simply throwing them away. Sometimes seals recorded on the PAS database have been deliberately cancelled, by being scored through or by being cut in half, and this data offers the opportunity of conducting research on this practice (Cherry 2002: 81-97).

The Portable Antiquities Scheme database

The PAS database is an excellent source of information about the seals of lesser people. Past study of seals has focussed on kings, nobles, towns, monastic houses or bishops. Seals found by metal-detectorists, although occasionally significant, are mostly of less important people, whose documents are rarely preserved.

How important is the find place of the seal? The seal of Cecily of Kingsdone (SOMDOR106) was found at Kingsdon, Somerset, from which village she took her name, and where she presumably lived. Another example is that of Geve of Calston (Cherry 1996: 134-36). It is likely that her seal too was engraved in Somerset, and lost where she lived. On the other hand, the seal matrix, undoubtedly engraved in England, of Geoffrey of Hastings, was lost in the castle of Grossau bei Raabs, Austria, near the border with Bohemia (Cherry 1997, 21-22). His presence there, always assuming that he was there when it was lost, is unknown.

Between those two extremes, there is the seal of William of Hereford found at Waterperry with Thomley, Oxfordshire (WAW-BFA280; Fig. 3). It is not known whether he lived in Waterperry, or not. That might be ascertained by examining all the documents related to the village. He might have been from Hereford and migrated to Oxfordshire. But he might also have lived in Oxfordshire all his life and been called of Hereford, since his family came from there. Its find place in Oxfordshire may have no real significance, since he may have lived elsewhere.

Some seals were lost near where their owners lived or worked, while others were lost far away. The PAS database enables that question to be explored, whereas in the Schøyen catalogue of seal matrices (Linenthal and Noel 2004), mostly found in England in the 1980s and early 1990s with metal detectors, the association of object and find place has mostly been lost.

Important seals have been found and recorded by the PAS or reported under the Treasure Act 1996, such as the that of William of St. Donats, Abbot of Neath (1326-41) found at Aberavon, and now in the National Museum of Wales (Redknap 2000: 170; Cherry 2004: 55); the silver seal set with a Roman intaglio found at Swanley, Kent (KENT-683033; Treasure: 2005 T75 Fig. 4), now in the British Museum; the silver heraldic seal of Walter of Thornton found at Hamstall Ridware, Staffordshire (*TAR* 1998/9, no. 168, 173) now in the Potteries Museum, Stoke-on-Trent (Fig. 5); and the seal of the Deanery of Hertismere, Suffolk (SF-9157).

The importance of the PAS database is the large number of seals (1,779 on 26/6/2007). In 2001, the database had only 136 seal matrices out of a total of some 18,000 finds. Although some are too worn to be useful, one can study the distribution of categories and types of personal and impersonal seal matrices. It is worth noting that other recording of seal matrices proceeds in parallel with the PAS. In Norfolk, for instance, there have been eight reports published in *Norfolk Archaeology* by Andrew Rogerson and Steven Ashley and others. The reports include 479 matrices, and the tenth report in the series will contain an overall analysis of the group (Steven Ashley, pers. comm.).

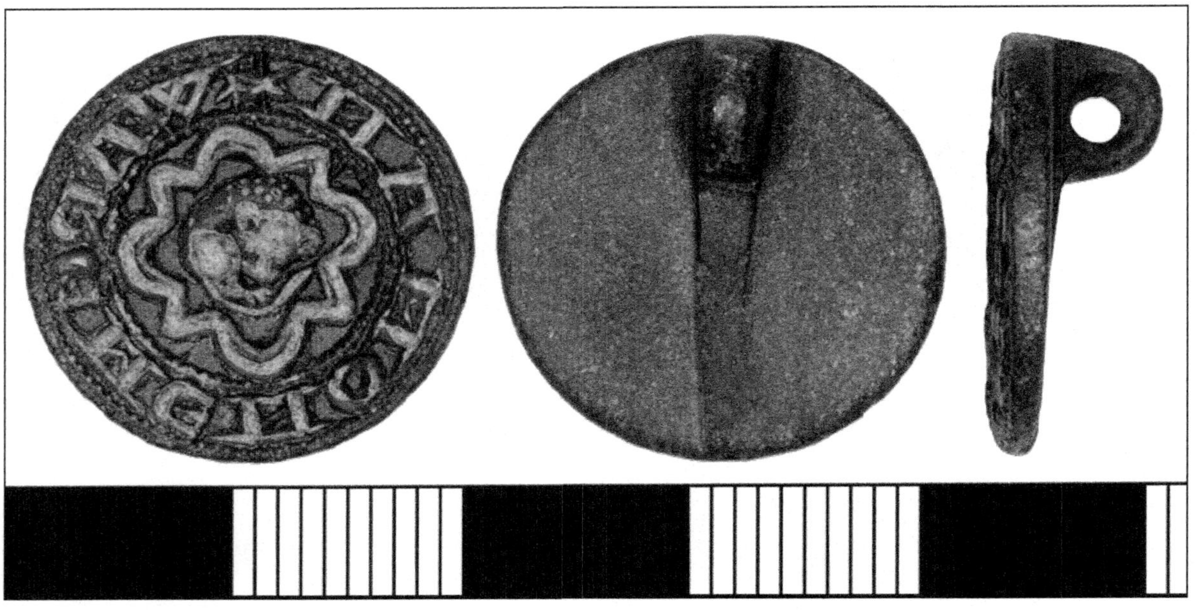

Fig. 2: Matrix with the inscription 'wake me no man' (SOMDOR-BB1AD2).

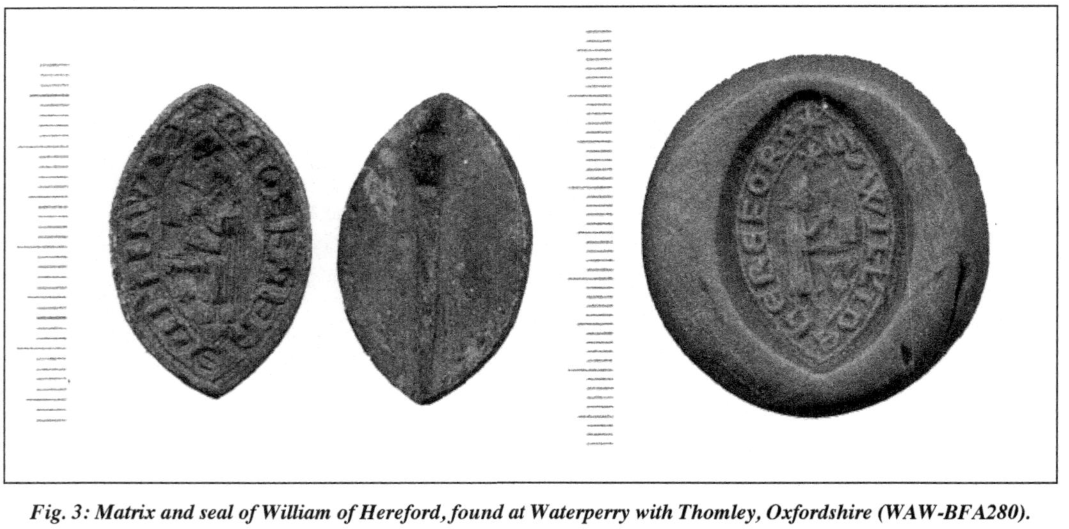

Fig. 3: Matrix and seal of William of Hereford, found at Waterperry with Thomley, Oxfordshire (WAW-BFA280).

Fig. 4: Silver matrix with a Roman intaglio, found at Swanley, Kent (KENT-683033; 2005 T75).

Fig. 5: Silver matrix of Walter of Thornton, found at Hamstall Ridware, Staffordshire.

On numbers, there has never been a survey to count all the existing medieval wax seals in the country. It is worth noting that some 60,000 medieval and early modern seals are thought to exist in the Public Record Office, of which fewer than 9,000 have ever been catalogued (New 2002: 47). If one adds other record offices and collections in England and Wales, one might guess that there may well be about 200,000 medieval and early-modern wax seals.

Another survey of some seals from Yorkshire, now on the PAS database, was made by Irene Szymanski (2005: 143-67). Otherwise there has not been a general survey, and, while this article will touch on only one limited aspect of the finds, it will hopefully indicate something of the potential.

The county distribution is very varied. Many counties have no seals or only one or two recorded. The greatest concentration is in Suffolk with 221 (Fig. 6), followed by Kent with 207, Lincolnshire comes third with 173, and Norfolk fourth with 145. The only other county recording more than 100 is North Yorkshire. If one groups the counties that return double figures together, it is clear that the greatest concentration of finds of matrices is in the east and south east. Norfolk and Suffolk together have 366. The south coast, Kent, Sussex, and Hampshire provide another large concentration. There is another large group in Lincolnshire, Yorkshire and Humberside. A smaller one lies in the Midlands: Warwickshire, Northamptonshire and Nottinghamshire. Obviously the activity of metal-detectorists and the workload of individual Finds Liaison Officers (FLOs) influence this rather than the actual number used in the Middle Ages. The general pattern is interesting and needs further research.

Early work on personal seals was undertaken by Brooke and Postan (1960), and Hilton (1975). Although in legal theory only freemen could use seals, the leases of Ramsey Abbey, Huntingdonshire, indicate that as early as 1,239, villains or unfree members of society, were using seals. It is clear that many of the seal found by metal-detectorists were probably those of unfree men, who might only need the use of a seal once, before it was discarded. There is also evidence (Harvey 1991: 126) that some institutions provided seal matrices to be engraved and supplied for a particular act of sealing. The best discussions of personal seals are by Harvey (1991) and Harvey and McGuinness (1996).

Seals with personal names

Seals with personal names are particularly interesting. Much work has been done by historians of surnames from documentary sources. There are two general surveys (Reaney and Wilson 1997; McKinley 1990). There are seven volumes of local surveys. These are Yorkshire, West Riding (Redmonds 1973), Norfolk and Suffolk (McKinley 1975), Oxfordshire (McKinley 1977), Lancashire (McKinley 1981), Sussex (McKinley 1988), Devon (Postles 1995) and Leicestershire and Rutland (Postles 1996).

Names on seals can be particularly revealing. Since many seals have been reported from Norfolk and Suffolk, this article will concentrate on those counties, and add other examples. Richard McKinley's database for his Suffolk and Norfolk volume was 18,500 for Norfolk and 17,000 for Suffolk, making a total of 35,000. The number of seal matrices in the PAS database for Suffolk and Norfolk

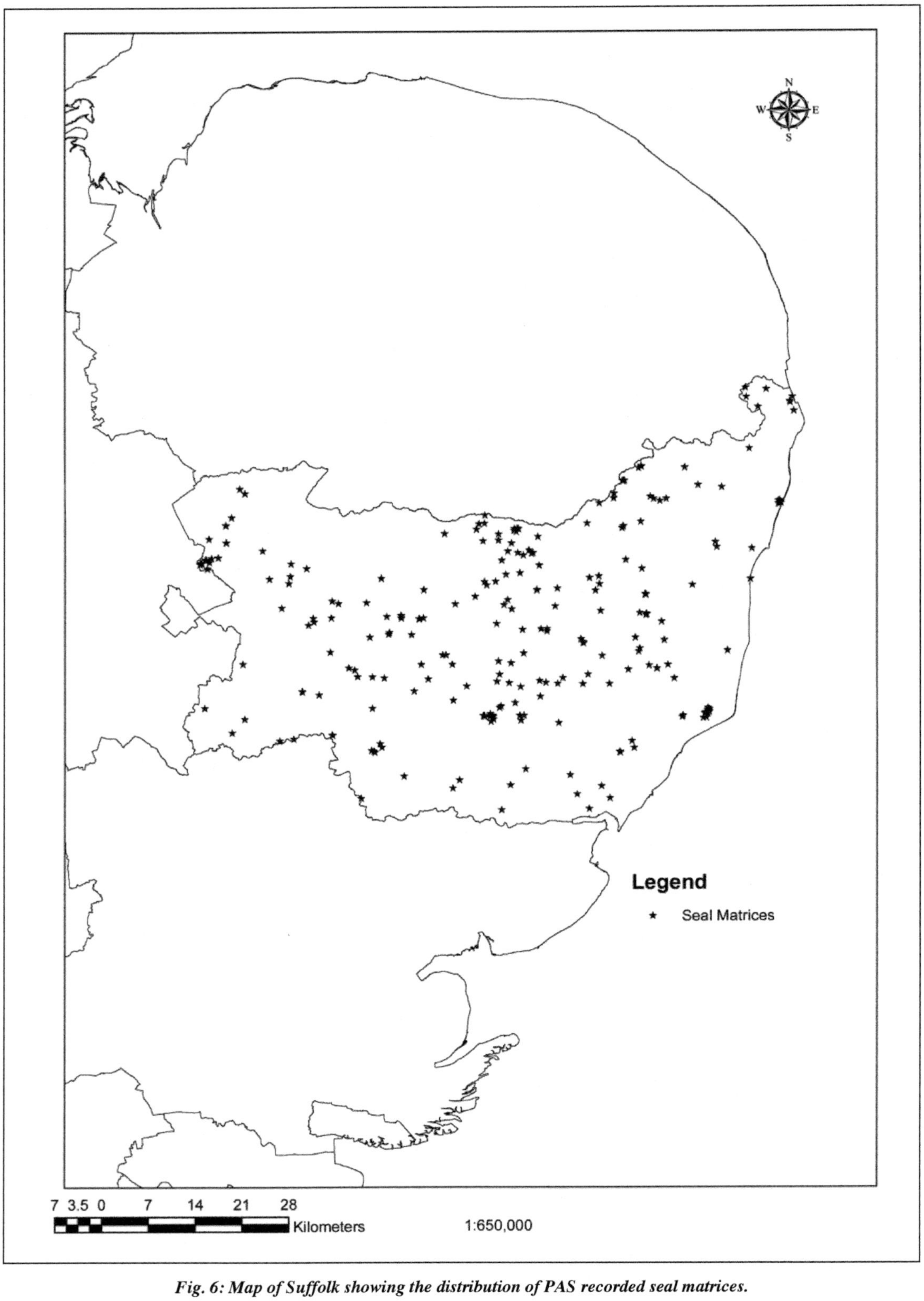

Fig. 6: Map of Suffolk showing the distribution of PAS recorded seal matrices.

(366), is about one third of 1% of the names recorded in contemporary documents. Looking at the Suffolk seals by categories, there are 125 seals with personal names, of which 101 are male and 24 female; one could deduce a 20% use of seals by women as opposed to men. Twice as many women's seals are pointed oval (vesica-shaped) as opposed to men using this shape.

Some inscriptions indicate relationships. The use of *filius* (abbreviated *fil*) such as William, son of Ro, found at Cockfield, Suffolk (SF-7455) and or daughter (*filia*) such as Olivia, daughter of John D, found at Nettlestead, Suffolk (SF-F6D250), and wife (*uxor*) such as Agnes, wife of John, found at Little Waldingfield, Suffolk (SF-41A894), or widow such as the seal of Ivoie, relict or widow of William, found at Freckenham, Suffolk (PAS: SF-1363). An interesting seal for family relationships is the double-sided seal of John and Sylvia Everard (see above, Fig. 1). Such double-sided seals tend to be male on one side and female on the other - probably husband and wife. Tax return records indicate there was a Robert Everard living in Blaxhall, Suffolk, in 1327.

Names of women are recorded such as Clarice, Amice or Agnes, although none of the excessive and much-to-be-deplored elaborate personal names of the late 13th century appear on the seal matrices (Postles 1996, 79-89). There is a great variety of women's names, and seal matrices provide more of an insight into a different level of social naming than the documents. Some ladies use two names such as Isabella Jane Palande (WAW-7EE083; Fig.7).

The 13th-century seal of Clarice the New Man or Newcomer (TAR 1998/9: 71-72, no. 165; SF-8922; Fig. 8) appears odd to us, since she is surnamed new man rather than new woman. This is likely to indicate that her surname was hereditary. Newman was often used as surname or a bye name for a serf, so this must indicate a fairly low status, although of sufficient resource to need a seal for a charter. It may be dated before 1260-70 since it was found with two other matrices at Thwaite, Suffolk with a coin hoard dated to 1260-70 (*TAR* 1998/9; 71-72, no. 165).

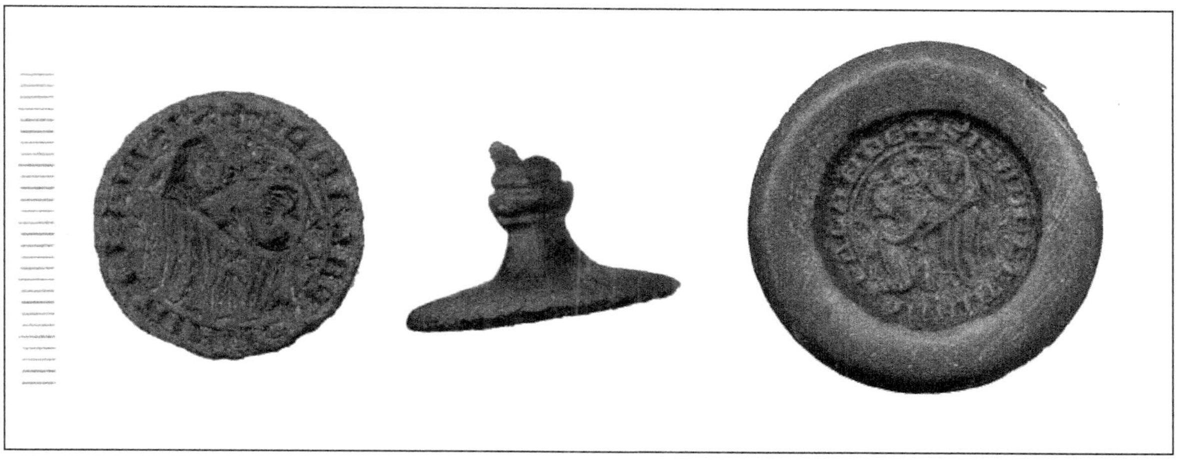

Fig. 7: Matrix and seal of Isabella Jane Palande (WAW-7EE083).

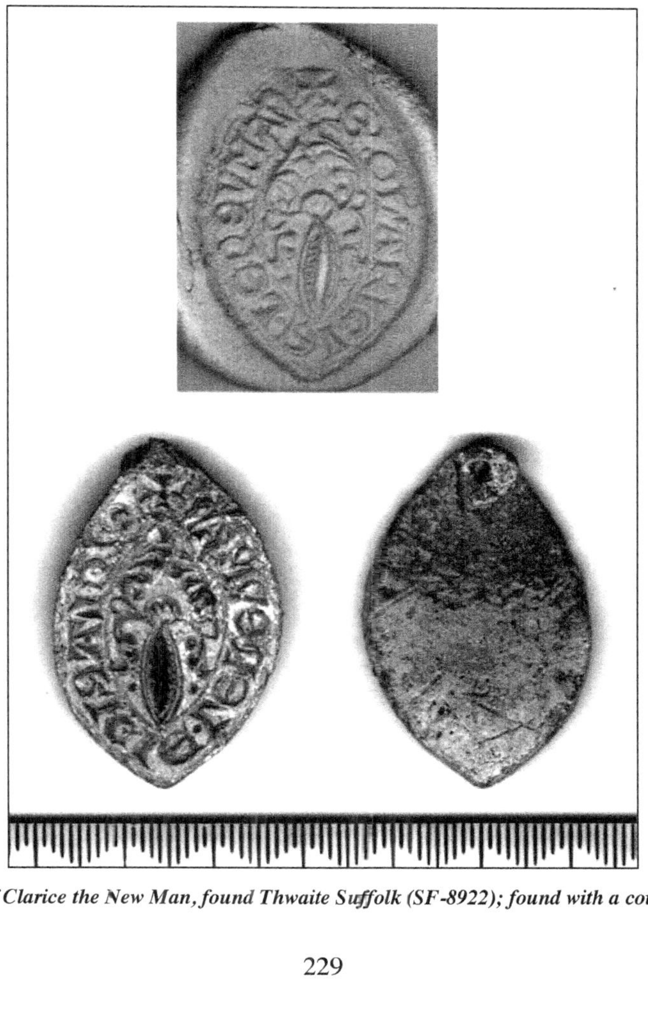

Fig. 8: Seal and matrix of Clarice the New Man, found Thwaite Suffolk (SF-8922); found with a coin hoard dated to 1260-70.

Fig. 9: The other seals from the Thwaite hoard.

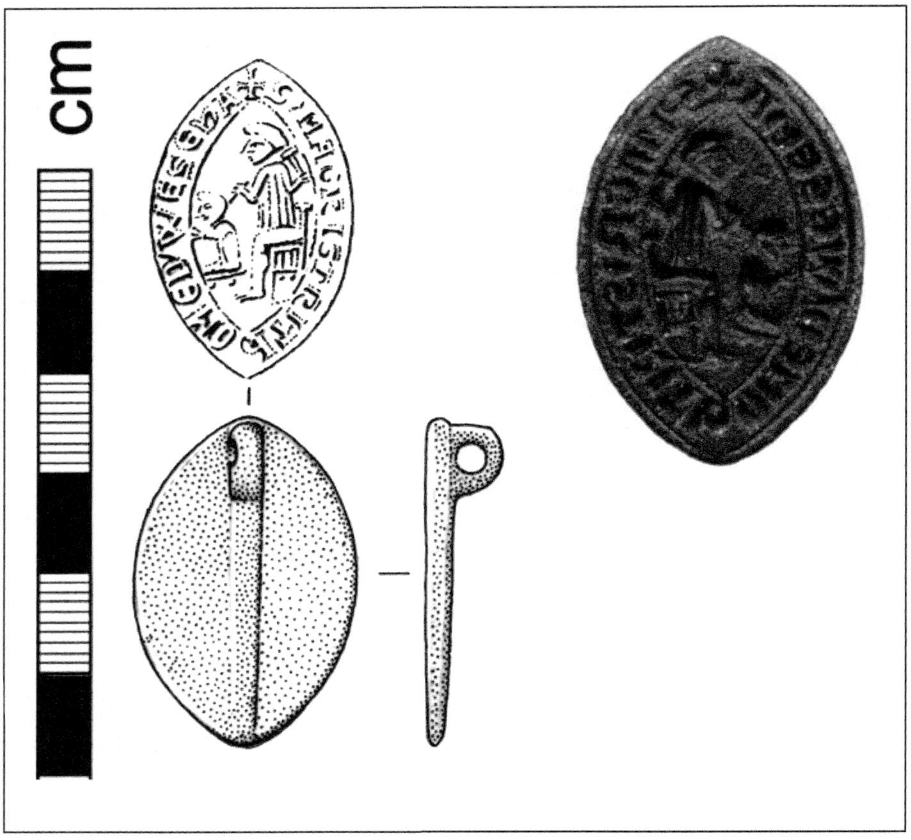

Fig: 10: Seal and matrix of Master Thomas of Weseham (HAMP-56E6E3).

One of these three seals is circular, and refers on one side refers to the owner, identified as Sevalli… (surname missing), and the other side has a pattern in relief surrounded by the inscription *Ave Maria Gratia Plena*, suggesting that the seal had a double use, both as a seal and an amulet to hang around the neck (Fig. 9). Many lead or lead-alloy personal seals of the late 12th and 13th centuries are difficult to date accurately.

A second group of names is based on features of the landscape. The seal of Alicie Atewatere (Alice Atwater) was found near Reigate (SUR-354A35; *PAS Southeast Regional Newsletter* 3 2006).

The third form of names relates to occupation or status, such as that of Ricardi le ferur (PAS: WMID-763). This is for Richard the Farrier or blacksmith, and shows his hammer and a horseshoe beneath.

A more puzzling seal is that of Master Thomas of Weseham (HAMP-56E6E3; Fig. 10). The name gives no indication of the occupation, unlike the scene in the centre of the seal. Three suggestions have been made. First, that he was a master mason. Second, a surgeon, and the scene shows a surgical operation such as trepanning. Third, that he was a schoolmaster. Carole Rawcliffe (pers. comm.) commented: 'the detached legs (which belong to the 'patient') would confirm that the standing figure is creating a stone image or images. In any event, I very much doubt that a surgeon of the status of Thomas de Weseham would have commissioned a seal with such a theme - not least because it shows him performing a manual operation: top-flight surgeons were extremely conscious of their social position and would have elected to be depicted with either a book or a lancet. Thomas was apparently knighted for his services to the King, and would have adopted this form of address. If the seal were to pre-date his knighthood, he would surely be *chirurgus* rather than *Magister*, which is customarily the address of a physician (although not invariably). Most surgical treatises warn against operating on the skull unless absolutely necessary'. So perhaps he was a master mason, but, if so, it is unusual for a master mason to be shown both seated and in such a pose.

Seals can add much to the study to the general picture of the use of occupational surnames outlined by Thuresson (1950) and Fransson (1935). The seal of Benedict the Baker (Fig. 11) found at Dunwich, Suffolk in the 19th century shows the need to take account of older finds. Its unusual nature suggests that it may have been used by Benedict to stamp his bread as well as his documents. Other Suffolk examples are Richard le Dicher (SF-1283), Adam le Hauberger (mailshirtmaker) (SF-7507), William le Carter (SF-464D58). The interest of both carter and ditcher is that, according to McKinley (1975: 6), there is a relative scarcity of agricultural occupational names in Suffolk sources between 1250 and 1350 (McKinley 1975).

Fig. 11: Seal of Benedict the Baker from Dunwich, Suffolk.

The fourth type of surname derives from the place of origin of the person, known as topographical or locative. William of Hereford (see above) provides a good example. Surnames derived from place names can provide evidence for migration. The subject is fraught with difficulty when dealing both with documentary sources and seals, since place names are capable of different interpretations. For Suffolk, it is clear that many locative surnames relate to short movements within the county. But there are examples of much longer distances moved. McClure explored the complex problem of analysis of this subject, which is due to the large proportion of 'ambiguous place-names' in England (McClure 1979: 167-82). The seals on the PAS database reflect this. For some seals, in addition to the locative surname, there is also the find place, so that one knows both from where the person or family derived their surname and also where it was lost. For instance, from Suffolk, Adam of Vinenest (probably Wenhaston) lost his seal (SF-77DC93) at Great Barton; and Robert Varin of Fr seal (SF-8A8C25) was found at Freckenham; Agnes Lofholm's seal (SF-9531) was found at Barton; the seal of Robert de Brocfor (SF-1689) was found in Thwaite, but relates to a man of this name who lived in the adjacent parish of Wetheringsett cum Brockford.

Just as Geoffrey of Hastings lost his seal in Austria, so there are cases of foreigners losing their seals in England. Suffolk offers two cases: Claus Kieken, seal with a merchant's mark, found at Parham (SF-2261B2) and that of Peter of Coninc (the Flemish word for king) found at Gedgrave (SF-31B113). Both finds indicate the strong relationship with Flemish and German merchants in Suffolk and Norfolk.

Jewish seals are very rare, and in England should date from before the expulsion by Edward I in 1296. There is always the possibility that some could be uncovered. An interesting seal is the seal of Rachel Spinster (PAS: SF-7817; Fig. 12) found at Fornham St Martin, Suffolk. Edward Martin has suggested that this should be read as 'Seal of Rachel' with 'NEO' possibly meaning 'I spin' and therefore the seal of Rachel the Spinster, or 'NEOV' from *necvitas* meaning 'serf', and perhaps finishing in *Benedicti* meaning 'of Benedict'. Rachel is not a common name in the Middle Ages and appears to be restricted to Jews. If however Rachel was the serf of Benedict, it is difficult to see why she had her own seal. This is an enigmatic and possibly quite important seal.

The PAS database also gives the opportunity of analysing the choice of image on the seal by the possessor, which has already considered for occupational names.

Heraldic seals, such as Walter of Thornton (referred to above) offer much new evidence on the use of heraldry not included in the rolls of arms and heraldic manuscripts. While Walter's seal has acceptable heraldry, that of John... (surname uncertain; BH-257E82) has informal heraldry based on the merchant's mark which surmounts it. A simpler use of pattern is shown by the use of fleur-de-lis, in which different versions of the flower can be compared. The seal of Peter Fitz William of Newball, Lincolnshire (*TAR* 1998/9, 71, no. 164) is of silver, and shows the top end of the market, while the other lead seals of men, such as William... (SOMDOR-C80253), Richard Heremon (WAW-AAC936) and William Braid (WMID-3835) use slightly different variants.

Fig. 12: Seal and matrix of Rachel spinster (SF-7817).

Fig 13: Matrix of Mary of Hertford (SOMDOR-B4FC92).

Images chosen by women can also be studied. Found at Cerne Abbas, Dorset (Fig. 13) is the seal of Mary of Hertford with a stag or hart at the centre (SOMDOR-B4FC92), which shows the use of a rebus on a name. However, Alice Vercore, (WMID-6064) chose a masculine symbol of a tilting helm with the crest of a bird above, but with flowers on either side.

Some men have enigmatic devices. William of Hereford (see above, Fig. 3) has a person wearing a three-quarter length garment with numerous folds. One arm is out stretched holding a horizontal platform on which lies a book, the other hand what appears to be a horn. Below, the out stretched arm, in front of the figures knees are three fleur-de-lis-like symbols. Above the head of the figure in the corner there is a six-pointed star.

Matthew Vickery (or possibly 'vicar') of Ivychurch (KENT-4911; Fig. 14) shows a standing man with lance and a shield. Was he a soldier of God? Or did he see himself as a spearman, as opposed to the equestrian image of the knight which was so favoured in the 12th and 13th centuries by his social superiors. Found at New Romney, Kent, perhaps might it represent a member of the 13th-century Kent home guard against the possibility of French invasion?

There is much work still to be done in this area. There are the very interesting series of seals which are impersonal, such as the seals with romantic scenes, those with squirrels, or those hunting images, or the fool with the inscription 'I am useless' (*Ie suy inutile*) or that of the duck with the inscription '*vas vas va*' (SOMDOR-2D8983) which is surely is an onomatopoeic representation of the sound of a duck.

Fig 14: Matrix of Matthew Vickery (or Vicar) of Ivychurch (KENT-4911).

An example of research on such impersonal seals is shown by birds attacking duck with '*Alas ie su pris*' on which such valuable work has been done in Sussex by Liz Andrews-Wilson and Christopher Whittick in relating the use of a seal matrix found in Sussex of that size and with that inscription which was used to seal this charter of 1373 conveying land in Magham Down about ten miles from the findspot of the matrix (*PAS Southeast Regional Newsletter* 3 2006).

An important recent survey of the iconography of personal seals is the study by Elizabeth New (2002: 47-68) of 'Christological personal seals and Christocentric devotion in later medieval England and Wales'. This deals with images such as the Pelican in its piety and Lamb of God, sacred monogram, Crucifixion, Christ in Majesty and in Judgement. All her three hundred examples were taken from the published catalogues of record offices and there is a very interesting study to be undertaken to compare her analysis of personal seals with those devotional characteristics with those in the PAS database.

But where one can be certain who owned the seal, one has the great opportunity of determining the personal patronage of the images of secular art. For instance Richard Remvild (SOMDOR-504; Fig. 15) has a seal with addorsed birds, which is very similar to a design used on medieval tiles. This is common on other materials such as textiles (the western use of the device was derived from eastern textiles). The occurrence on a seal is an interesting example of the spread of the motif. What is even more interesting is that the design was particularly popular on tiles made and use in Wessex, the same area where the seal was found.

Fig. 15: Seal of Richard Remvild (SOMDOR-504).

The seal of Isabella Jane Palande (WAW-7EE083; Fig. 16) shows a lover kneeling before his beloved who holds a chaplet of flowers. This may be compared with similar scenes on 14th-century French ivory mirror backs such as that in the Victoria and Albert Museum (V&A, no. 217-1867; Barnet 1997: no. 55).

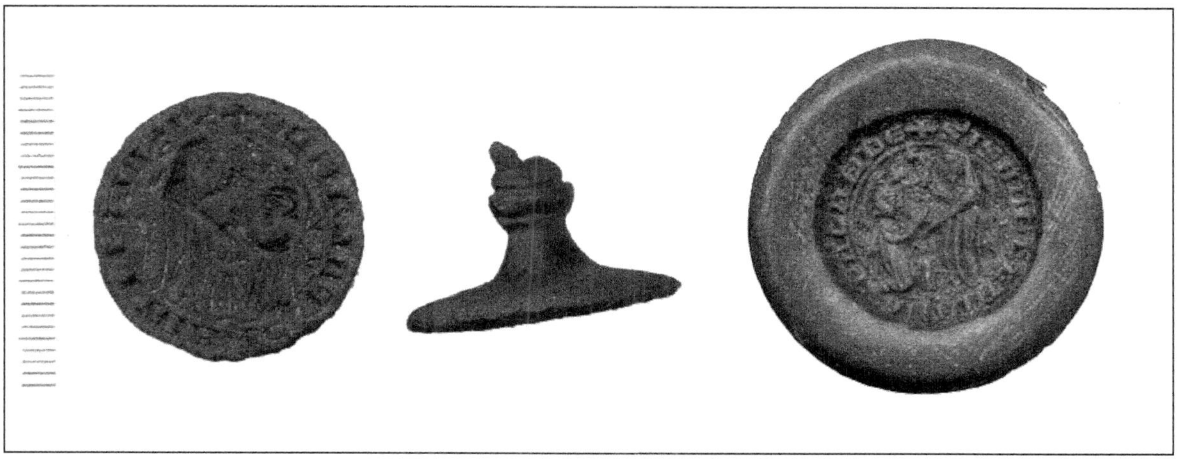

Fig. 16: Matrix and seal of Isabella Jane Palande (WAW-7EE083).

Conclusion

There is clearly much to be done in analysing different types of seal matrix, their distribution, variation and forms of cancellation, and then plotting them against time and space. There is also much to be done on the use of the types of letter forms for dating. The unique quality of seals is their relationship to written sources and sometimes actual documents. A subject of considerable interest is the use of language on the seals, whether Latin, French or English, and the meanings and distribution of seals in different languages. Two useful studies on the linguistic background are Short (1980) and Lodge (1992).

Photographs and impressions are essential. Each seal that has an intelligible personal inscription needs to be analysed not only in the archaeological context of the discovery, but also in the historical context of the locality, to discover what one can about the person and where he came from and why he lost his seal there. By doing so, one can gain an insight into the names and status of such ordinary people, and the way in which they wanted themselves shown in both symbol and art.

Acknowledgements

Many thanks to James Robinson (British Museum) and all the FLOs past and present, particularly Liz Andrews-Wilson, Angie Bolton, Helen Geake, Naomi Payne and for their loan of impressions from seal matrices, to Daniel Pett for his help with the photographs, and to Geoff Egan and Michael Lewis for their editing.

Bibliography

Barnet, P. 1997, *Images in Ivory: precious objects of the Gothic Age* (Princeton University Press, Princeton).

Brooke, C. N. L. and Postan, M .M. (eds.) 1960, '*Carte Nativorum*, Northants', *Record Society* 20, xlii-iii.

Cherry, J. 1996, 'The silver seal of Geve of Calston', *Wiltshire Archaeological Magazine* 89, 134-36.

Cherry, J. 1997, 'Der siegel stempel des Geoffrey von Hastings aus Grossau bei Raabs/Thaya, NÖ', *Mittelalterarchäologiein Österreich* 13, 21-22.

Cherry, J. 2002, 'The Breaking of Seals', in Andersen, M. and Tegnér, G. (eds.), *Middelalderlige Seglstamper i Norden*, Roskilde Museums Forlag, 81-97.

Cherry, J. 2004, 'Seal Matrices: past present and future', *The Monmouthshire Antiquary* 20, 51-60.

Friedenberg, D. M. 1987, *Medieval Jewish seals from Europe* (Wayne State University Press, Detroit).

Frannson, G. 1935, *English Surnames of Occupation, 1100-1350* (C. W. K. Gleerup, Lund).

Guinness, A. F. 1995, 'Non armigerous seals and seal usage in 13th-century England', *Thirteenth Century England* 5, 165-77.

Harvey, P. D. A. 1991, 'Personal seals in 13th century England', in Wood, I. and Loud, G. A. (eds.), *Church and Chronicle in the Middle Ages: essays presented to John Taylor* (Hambledon Press, London), 117-27.

Harvey, P. D. A. and McGuinness, A. 1996, *A Guide to British Medieval Seals* (British Library, London).

Hilton, R. H. 1975, *The English Peasantry in the Later Middle Ages* (Oxford University Press, Oxford) [reprinting of 1953, 'Gloucester Abbey leases of the Late Thirteenth Century', *University of Birmingham Historical Journal* 4, 1-17].

Linenthal, R. and Noel, W. 2004, *Medieval Seal Matrices in the Schøyen Collection*_(Hermes, Oslo).

Lodge, R. 1991/2, 'Language attitudes and linguistic norms in France and England in the 13th Century', in Coss, P. R. and Lloyd, S. (eds.), *Thirteenth-Century England*, IV, 73-83.

McClure, P. 1979, 'Patterns of migration in the late Middle Ages: the evidence of English place-name surnames', *English Historical Review* 32, 167-82.

McKinley, R. 1975, *The Surnames of Norfolk and Suffolk. English Surnames Series* 2.

McKinley, R. 1977, *The Surnames of Oxfordshire. English Surnames Series* 3.

McKinley, R. 1981, *The Surnames of Lancashire. English Surnames Series* 4.

McKinley, R. 1988, *The Surnames of Sussex. English Surnames Series* 5.

McKinley, R. 1990, *History of British Surnames* (Longman, London).

New, E. 2002, 'Christological personal seals and Christocentric devotion in later medieval England and Wales', *Antiquaries Journal* 82, 47-68.

New, E. 2006, 'Signs of community or marks of the exclusive? Parish and Guild seals in Later Medieval England', in Burgess, C. and Duffy, E. (eds.), *The Parish in Late Medieval England. Harlaxton Medieval Studies*, 14, 112-29.

Portable Antiquities Scheme, Southeast Regional Newsletter 3, 2006.

Postles, D. 1995, *Surnames of Devon. English Surnames Series* 6.

Postles, D. 1998, *The Surnames of Leicestershire and Rutland. English Surnames Series* 7.

Postles, D. 1996, 'The distinction of gender? Women's names in the 13th century', *Nomina* 19, 79-89.

Redknap, M. 2000, 'Aberavon, Port Talbot: medieval seal matrix', in Bland, R. F. (ed.), *Treasure Annual Report* 1998-1999 (DCMS, London), 73-74.

Redmonds, G. 1973, *Yorkshire West Riding. English Surnames Series* 1.

Roth, C. 1953, 'A medieval Anglo-Jewish Seal?', *The Jewish Historical Society of England Transactions*, ser. 1951-2, XVII, 283-6.

Short, I. 1980, 'On bilingualism in Anglo-Norman England', *Romance Philology* 33, 467-69.

Syzmanski, I. 2005, 'Seal matrices: recent Yorkshire discoveries', *Yorkshire Archaeological Journal* 77, 143-67.

TAR 2008/9 = Bland, R. F. (ed.) 2000, *Treasure Annual Report* 1998-1999 (DCMS, London), 73-74.

Thuresson, B. 1950, *Middle English Occupational Terms* (C. W. K. Gleerup, Lund).

Searching with a Fine-toothed Comb: combs for humans and horses on the Portable Antiquities Scheme database

Steven P. Ashby and Angie Bolton

To many users of the Portable Antiquities Scheme (PAS) database, hair combs might seem an unusual focus for study. They are not commonly found by metal-detectorists or other members of the public, and the number recorded on the database (23 at the time of writing) is diminutive in comparison with the numbers recovered as part of controlled excavations (around 200 combs and fragments are known from the excavations at 16-24 Coppergate, York alone). This disparity relates to the fact that the vast majority of Roman to post-medieval combs were manufactured in organic materials such as bone and antler, and their often poorly preserved remains (offering little resistance to the plough) are unlikely to be found by any but the most keen-sighted of detectorists.

Why then, devote a paper to the study of the small quantity of combs on the PAS database, given the far larger numbers known from elsewhere? While the database sample is small and cannot be taken as representative of the UK corpus as a whole it is an interesting subset. Indeed, the combs represented on the database differ markedly (in raw materials, form and ornament) from the majority discovered through archaeological excavation. This is probably a result of the differences in methods of collection. This volume, celebrating as it does the 10th anniversary of the PAS, seems an appropriate venue for a discussion of these objects, as it provides the opportunity to consider some of the potential for future study and understanding of these combs. One of us (SPA) has a specialism in hair combs of the medieval period, while the other (AB) recently recorded an Iron Age example (WAW-250340). It thus seemed sensible to pool our ideas and resources and assess what could be gleaned from the small but interesting sample.

Apart from a particularly fine and well preserved Roman example from Northamptonshire (NARC-242E72) and a number of more poorly preserved Anglo-Saxon to medieval examples, bone and antler combs are poorly represented on the PAS database (for the reasons outlined above). Readers with an interest in the bone and antler combs typical of the British Isles are referred to the syntheses by Ashby (2006), MacGregor (1985: 77-95), and Tuohy (1999). Herein, our intention is simply to focus on a few combs of particular interest.

An Iron Age comb of bronze from Warwickshire

The first comb of interest is a cast copper-alloy comb from Tanworth-in-Arden, Warwickshire (WAW-250340; Fig. 1) dating to the late Iron Age. The comb was found in 2006 by Russell Peach and is an exceptional example of Iron Age metallurgy, measuring only 64 mm long by 53 mm high and featuring complex cast ornament. It is extremely unusual, with the only parallel known to the authors on display in the Bibracte museum (in the French province of Saone and Loire) (Sally Worrell, pers. comm.), though even this differs in important respects from the PAS example.

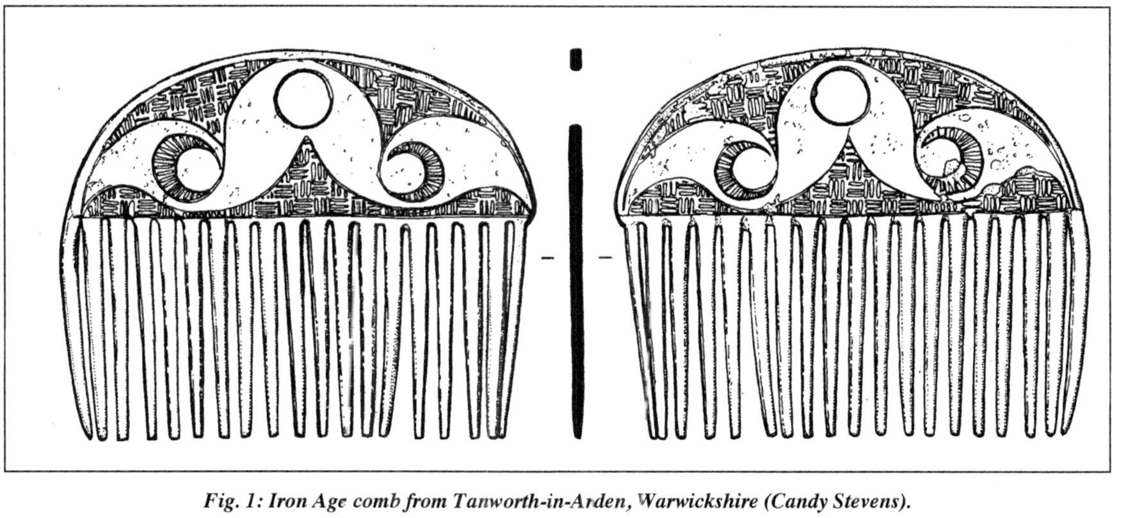

Fig. 1: Iron Age comb from Tanworth-in-Arden, Warwickshire (Candy Stevens).

The Tanworth-in-Arden comb is made of copper, tin (tin content is between 12-15% which is in the upper range, but could be partly due to tin enrichment at the surface) and arsenic (a minor element often found in Iron Age bronze) (Mary Davis pers. comm.) and is cast in a single piece. It is sub-rectangular in profile, with a shallow plano-convex back. Nineteen teeth are intact, but originally there were twenty; the missing tooth was broken in antiquity and the comb re-shaped to hide the break. A large decorated field lies above the teeth, and on both faces this field is filled with cast 'mirror-style' ornament with the armadillo motif being predominant on a cross-hatched background, within a plain border. At the centre of the field lies a circular perforation of 7.2 mm diameter, presumably intended for suspension, and it is notable that this feature is incorporated into the design, suggesting careful planning prior to casting. Further decoration is apparent on the comb ends.

The comb is perhaps most notable for its decoration, which bears considerable similarity to that seen on late Iron Age (*c.* 40-70 AD) mirrors (see for instance Jope 2000: pls. 240, 242, 246-47), spoons and terrets (*c.* 25-75 AD), and is considered to be of Insular (British or Irish) origin rather than Continental (Adam Gwilt, pers. comm.). Direct comb parallels are few, and the only comparable metallic example (from the museum in Bibracte) differs in ornament, form and tooth gauge. The latter feature is particularly important, as it may suggest a difference in function.

Thus, the utility of the comb is not certain. The coarse tooth gauge might lead one to propose a use as an equestrian grooming comb (Sara Wear, pers. comm.), as has been assumed for large, ornate, coarse-toothed combs of later periods (see, for example, the "*pferdekämme*" from Birka: Ambrosiani 1981: 68-69). In contrast, the comb may simply have been an unusually coarse hair or beard comb. It was discovered on the periphery of the Iron Age mirror distribution across southern England. Its findspot and decoration may therefore suggest that it was used in association with mirrors. The comb may have been used primarily for display as a form of jewellery or dress accessory, and may even have had a purely symbolic role (see below). Of course, these alternatives are not mutually exclusive and such a comb may have a multitude of meanings and purposes, contingent on the contexts in which it was used.

The comb's use of 'mirror style' ornament is particularly interesting. One might ask why two objects of different form would share similar ornamental traits. Could one propose that the Iron Age comb and mirror were in some way conceptually linked? It might well be that such objects were manufactured and used together, forming part of a 'grooming set', or there may have been more symbolic or even eschatological concerns involved. With this in mind, it is notable that Pictish sculpture in Scotland very frequently features 'mirror' and 'comb' symbols, and that one very rarely appears without the other. Such sculpture probably dates no earlier than the 4th or 5th centuries AD (Smith 2003: 113) and is thus considerably removed from the Tanworth comb in both time and space, but the possibility of a shared understanding of 'mirror and comb' as part of a conceptual framework is intriguing.

What could this meaning be? One possibility, first mooted by Andrea Smith (2000, 2003) in her study of combs in Pictish sculpture, is that they formalised the relationships between tribal leaders. Thus, in the 4th and 5th centuries, the carved depictions of combs in Pictish sculpture stood for the combs exchanged between the Anglo-Saxon and Pictish elite as diplomatic gifts. Arguably, combs played an important role in the maintenance of such alliances in the face of common enemies to the south (Smith 2003: 113-14).

Smith supports this concept with documentary evidence for the exchange of mirrors and combs of precious metals in Anglo-Saxon England during the early 600s (*ibid.*; Bede, *HEA* II.11), while there is evidence that similar objects were exchanged between members of the ecclesiastical elite as late as the 8th century AD (Sorrell 1996). Silver combs have been reported from Viking-Age hoards of precious metals (Graham-Campbell 1987: 337-38), and large antler combs from this period may also have been exchanged in this manner (Ros 1992; Ashby 2006).

It is thus clear that there was a long-lived early medieval tradition of combs being used as diplomatic gifts. Whether it is possible to push the origins of this tradition back into the Roman period, or even the pre-Roman Iron Age is a moot point, but there is no reason to rule out such a possibility. It is accepted that reciprocal gift exchange played an important role in the maintenance of social and political relationships in prehistoric Europe (Mauss 1925; Gosden 1985; Creighton 2006: 14-45). Combs were clearly part of the repertoire of Iron Age material culture and their apparent scarcity might well be suggestive of a particular high status. Moreover, there is reason to suspect that items constructed in high cost materials, and designed expressly for the purpose of grooming a subject, held status associations. Indeed, the use of such objects may have been bound up with concepts of the identity and the self, or even of religion and the magical properties of hair. The existence of such beliefs and associations is well established in ethnographic study (Berg 1951; Leach 1958; Hallpike 1969; Derrett 1973) while there are also traces in early medieval and later literature and archaeology (Smyser 1995; Bartlett 1994; Venclová 2002; see Ashby 2006 for a review).

Alternatively, if combs such as the Tanworth-in-Arden example had equestrian associations this does little to downgrade their status; it is well known that horses have been prized possessions for much of human existence and their burial in the Iron Age is suggestive that equine veneration or respect has its origins in early antiquity. In this context, objects associated with the grooming of horses may themselves have attained a level of prestige, as carts and chariots clearly did (Dent 1985).

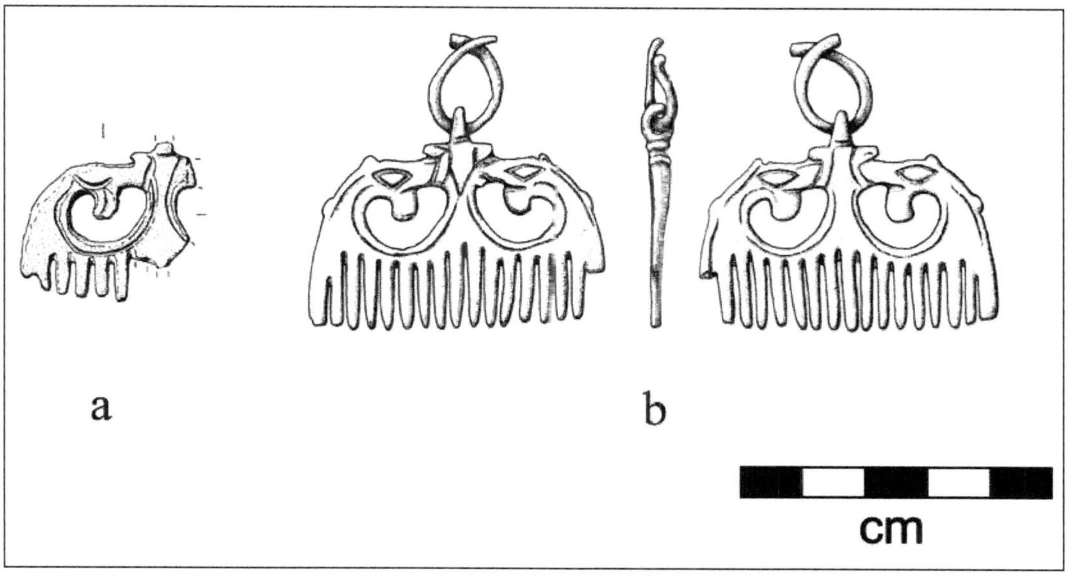

Fig. 2: Viking Age comb pendants from a) Brampton, Norfolk (Sue White) and b) South Lincolnshire (Pat Walsh).

Clearly, these ideas are at present little more than speculation. The situation is rather opaque and will only be elucidated through further research, but the fact that the Tanworth comb has been recorded with the PAS has opened up the area for further enquiry, and as such it is an extremely important find.

Two early medieval bronze comb pendants of Baltic origin

In 2003, Steven Ashley recorded a fragmentary copper-alloy openwork comb from Brampton, Norfolk (NMS-1801; Fig. 2a; Ashley and Paterson, in Geake 2003: 209). This example contains a pelta-shaped opening, with a central-stalk dividing the ornament into two zoomorphic heads. The comb preserves the remains of a suspension loop at its crest, confirming its use as a pendant.

A better-preserved example was recently recovered by a metal-detectorist in South Lincolnshire and recorded by Steve Ashby in 2007 (NARC-B3E1B5; Fig. 2b). This example, measuring only 47 mm long, is decorated with Ringerike-style zoomorphic ornament, the primary theme being a pair of in-turning zoomorphic heads, with the animals' necks represented using openwork casting. A use as a pendant is suggested by the presence of a perforation for suspension at the top centre of the comb, through which is threaded the remains of a large copper-alloy suspension ring, or perhaps the basal loop in a chain.

These artefacts are extremely unusual finds for the British Isles. Indeed, early medieval metal combs of any type are rarities in England, Scotland, Wales and Ireland. The authors know of a bronze example recovered during early 20th-century excavations at Whitby (McIntyre 1929), and there are reports and descriptions of silver combs from the Cuerdale and Broch of Burgar hoards (Graham-Campbell 1985: 246-53; Graham-Campbell 1987: 337-38; Smith 2000: 184; Smith 2003: 114). These combs are broadly contemporary with typological dates for the South Lincolnshire and Brampton examples (the Cuerdale hoard was deposited *c.* 1005 AD, while the Burgar hoard has been dated to the late 8th century, see Graham-Campbell 1985: 257), and they are consistent with a use in gift exchange (see above). However, in the Burgar case the artefact itself is now lost, while the Cuerdale comb is fragmentary. The significance of the PAS examples, then, is clear.

In detail, the form of these combs (or comb-shaped pendants as they are more properly termed) is only closely paralleled in the area around the Baltic Sea. Here, bronze examples can be dated to the centuries immediately following 1000 AD, and seem to be based on slightly earlier bone prototypes. They are known from northwest Russia, Finland, Latvia and Lithuania, with rare examples from Estonia and Sweden (presumably arriving by means of the Baltic's thriving trade network). Furthermore, zoomorphic ornament is not uncommon on comb-shaped pendants in this region (Luik 1999: 156), and all in all, one can be fairly confident that the PAS examples represent artefacts displaced (by trade or travel) from this part of north-east Europe.

Most interestingly, many examples have very short teeth, while there are examples from Finland and Latvia that lack teeth altogether, suggesting that their key role may have been as dress accessories or symbols, rather than functioning toilet implements. Indeed, there are also a number of medieval axe- and knife-shaped pendants from the Baltic area, and it may be more appropriate to see the comb pendants in question as part of this tradition, rather than as combs in and of themselves. Several Baltic examples are known from hoards, while burial evidence demonstrates that such combs were worn close to the chest, shoulder or waist, with one particular example suspended on a chain only 50 mm long; far too short to allow use in personal grooming while attached. Indeed, some may have been suspended on a chain between two brooches, while still other examples may have been used as part of elaborate head-dresses (*ibid.*: 158-59). Their role within a repertoire of items used in personal display thus seems assured; their use was not restricted to that of a simple grooming tool.

Notwithstanding the above, bone comb pendants of similar form do show evidence of use wear on their teeth (*ibid.*: 158). Such 'beading' would not be visible on copper alloy examples, but it is of course possible that they were also used in this way. In sum, the situation is ambiguous, but it seems certain that these comb pendants had an important role in display. This must have been particularly true in Britain, where such items would have been truly exotic and communicated powerful messages of identity and ethnicity (see below).

The presence in late Viking Age England of combs of undoubted northern European origin is interesting. Given the legacy of Norse contact in other regions (northern Scotland in particular, see Barrett 2003), one might assume that close ties between Britain and Scandinavia were maintained into the 10th and 11th centuries. However, this does not seem to be the case for northern England, at least on the basis of artefactual evidence. For example, the paucity of Scandinavian imports identified in Viking Age levels at York has been commented on previously (Richards 2000: 121), while the bone and antler combs from the settlement show closest affinities with Irish material (see Ashby 2006).

In this context, artefacts that show close associations with Scandinavia are noteworthy. A small number of 10th- to 12th-century bone and antler combs excavated at sites including York, Lincoln and Northampton have been identified as being of undoubted northern European manufacture (see Ashby 2006) and betray the presence of individuals with close Scandinavian connections. The copper alloy combs recorded with the PAS can surely be added to this group. They are of particular interest, as they can be linked with eastern Scandinavia and the Baltic, and thus add nuance to the traditional model that draws lines between Viking Age Britain and Norway and Denmark. Some level of contact between Britain and the eastern Baltic in the late Viking Age and medieval period is uncontroversial, but this concept has frequently been overlooked in synthetic works.

Notwithstanding the above, it is clear that these combs are among a very few indicators of north-eastern European contact, and it is necessary to consider the means by which they may have reached Britain. Indirect (down-the-line) exchange seems unlikely, given their idiosyncrasy and the powerful ethnic symbolism that may have been a corollary (see below). Direct trade with the region is conceivable, but if this occurred on any scale, then the scarcity of such combs in England relative to 'insular' and Anglo-Scandinavian types requires explanation. An alternative dispersal mechanism is reciprocal exchange; metal combs in particular may have been exchanged between members of the political elite of the respective regions as diplomatic gifts (see above). Their rarity, even in north-eastern Europe, might support such a model. However, perhaps the simplest explanation is that they reached England as the possessions of migrants, merchants, mercenaries, political envoys or other travellers.

As the possessions of migrants from the Baltic region, or items acquired by travelling Anglo-Scandinavians, these combs say little about large scale political or economic networks. Rather, each comb is best understood in its own terms, rather than as part of the group. While context information is important in the construction of object biographies (Appadurai 1986; Hoskins 1998; Gosden and Marshall 1999), and such data is not available for the present examples, it is nonetheless instructive to reflect on the role that they may have played upon reaching English shores.

It is certain that such combs acted as symbols of identity. There is reason to believe that bone and antler combs were used in this way (Ashby 2006), but the copper alloy examples represent a greater investment in raw materials, were clearly suspended as a visible dress accessory, and, if the archaeological record is reflective, were less common than their bone equivalents. They must, therefore, have been extremely visible fields for the display of identity, be it age, gender, status, ethnicity or political affiliation. Being so different in both form and material from Anglo-Scandinavian combs, and unlike any pendants in circulation in the Danelaw, they must have been highly conspicuous in the public arena and would have actively communicated powerful messages of 'the other'. Nonetheless, certain aspects of the pendants would have been familiar to the Anglo-Scandinavian audience. The Ringerike beasts of the South Lincolnshire pendant would, even in an unfamiliar context, have been recognisable motifs, redolent of the broad 'Scandinavian' artistic milieu. Thus, the messages constructed by the use of such a pendant were complex, multi-faceted and mutable, and above all conditioned by social context.

Discussion

What then, can we learn through the study of the combs from Tanworth-in-Arden, South Lincolnshire and Brampton? On the basis of its 'mirror-style' ornament, the Tanworth example seems likely to have been manufactured in the British Isles, while the Brampton and 'South Lincs' combs were produced in eastern Europe. Furthermore, the dates of manufacture of the two forms are separated by around 1000 years. This chronological and geographical disparity precludes any detailed comparison in terms of distribution or function, but some general observations are perhaps appropriate.

If nothing else, the combs appear to show a longevity or recurrence of the comb as symbol. That is to say that in both Iron Age and medieval contexts the manufacture and materials seem at odds with the combs' sole use being as a simple toilet implement, devoid of status or identity-based associations. That is not to say that their role in grooming was insignificant; indeed, it may be this very act (whether it is the grooming of people or horses) that lent them their great symbolic resonance. It is difficult to claim any direct line of influence from the late Iron Age to the early medieval period; the combs clearly arise from culturally discrete traditions. Nonetheless, the social significance of grooming and associated paraphernalia is well attested for the Roman period (Eckardt and Crummy 2006), while arguments have also been made for combs having a particular social significance in the Anglo-Saxon (Williams 2003) and Viking Age periods (Ashby 2006). It therefore seems that the comb, as an object of hygiene (and thus closely associated with ideas of the human body), and as a highly visible dress accessory, has repeatedly been utilised in a symbolic manner. The precise means by which it was exploited were complex and variable; it has acted as a field for both private and public display, has been used in the construction and manipulation and identity, and has been exchanged as a means of establishing and consolidating alliances and allegiances. Our understanding of such communication and negotiation must be drawn from knowledge of the context in which these exchanges took place, and it is therefore neither possible nor desirable to draw detailed comparisons or parallels between the ways in which the combs discussed above were used. Nonetheless, even if the meaning of the ornamental comb was shifting and variable, its recurrence down the centuries is of note in itself.

Conclusions and future work

In this short article it has not been possible to do any more than outline some interesting issues raised by the recovery and preservation by record of a few unusual finds. Nonetheless, it has been shown that objects on the PAS database have the potential to contribute to debates regarding social, as well as economic issues (see papers elsewhere in this volume for the latter), even when sample sizes are small. The role of small finds in the development of archaeological thought is not limited to the production of chronologies or distribution maps, neither is it necessarily precluded by the absence of detailed stratigraphic data. The number and diversity of finds on the PAS database make it an invaluable resource for archaeological investigation (particularly in rural areas) and continued targeted interrogation can only lead to further illumination.

Postscript

Since this article was written, a small number of further copper-alloy comb pendants have been identified. These include an example of unknown provenance, but reported to Kevin Leahy (Ref: North Lincolnshire Museums 2483; thanks to Jane Kershaw for bringing this to our attention), and one from Mareham on the Hill, Lincolnshire, identified by Adam Daubney (PAS: LIN-DD07D2). The Lincolnshire clustering may in part be related to recovery bias, but is interesting. Notwithstanding, these objects seem to be a little more common in the British Isles than previously thought. Given their clear associations with eastern Scandinavia, their presence in the British Isles is interesting, and should they continue to be found, may tell us something of the organisation of Baltic and North Sea trade and travel. We await further discoveries.

Acknowledgements

The authors would like to thank the finders of the combs mentioned in this article and would also like to extend their gratitude to all those that have commented on the combs and the article itself, including Mary Davis, Adam Gwilt, Jody Joy, Heidi Luik, Sara Wear and Sally Worrell. Particular thanks to John Naylor for his editorial comments. All errors remain the authors' own.

Bibliography

Ambrosiani, K. 1981, *Viking Age Combs, Comb Making and Comb Makers in the Light of Finds from Birka and Ribe*. Stockholm Studies in Archaeology 2 (Stockholm).

Appadurai, A. (ed.) 1986, *The Social Life of Things: commodities in cultural perspective* (Cambridge University Press, Cambridge).

Ashby, S. P. 2006, *Time, Trade and Identity: bone and antler combs in northern Britain c. AD 700-1400* (unpubl. PhD thesis, University of York).

Ashley, S. and Paterson, C. 2003, 'Brampton', 209, in Geake, H., 'Portable Antiquities Scheme', *Medieval Archaeology* 47, 202-17.

Barrett, J. H. 2003 'Culture contact in Viking Age Scotland', in Barrett, J. H. (ed.), *Contact, Continuity and Collapse: the Norse colonization of the North Atlantic*, Studies in the Early Middle Ages, 74-111 (Brepols, Turnhout).

Bartlett, R. 1994, 'Symbolic meanings of hair in the Middle Ages', *Transactions of the Royal Historical Society, sixth series* 4, 43-60.

Bede, *Historia ecclesiatica gentis Anglorum*, ed. and trans. L. Sherley-Price, *Ecclesiastical History of the English People*, 1990 (Penguin, London).

Berg, C. 1951, *The Unconscious Significance of Hair* (Allen and Unwin, London).

Creighton, J. 2006, *Britannia: the creation of a Roman province* (Routledge, London).

Dent, J. 1985, 'Three cart burials from Wetwang, Yorkshire', *Antiquity* 59, 85-92.

Derrett, J. D. M. 1973, 'Religious hair', *Man* 8, 100-3.

Eckardt, H. and Crummy, N. 2006, 'Roman or native bodies in Britain: the evidence of late Roman nail-cleaner strap-ends', *Oxford Journal of Archaeology* 25 (1), 83-103.

Gosden, C. 1985, 'Gifts and Kin in Early Iron Age Europe', *Man* 20, 475-93.

Gosden, C. and Marshall, Y. 1999, 'The cultural biography of objects', *World Archaeology* 31, 169-78.

Graham-Campbell, J. 1985, 'A lost Pictish treasure (and two Viking-age gold arm-rings) from the Broch of Burgar, Orkney', *Proceedings of the Society of Antiquaries of Scotland* 115, 241-261.

Graham-Campbell, J. 1987. 'Some archaeological reflections on the Cuerdale Hoard', in Metcalf, D. M. (ed.), *Coinage in Ninth-Century Northumbria, the Tenth Symposium on Coinage and Monetary History*, British Archaeological Reports, British Series 180 (BAR, Oxford), 329-44.

Hallpike, C. R. 1969, 'Social hair', *Man* 4, 256-264.

Hoskins, J. 1998, *Biographical Objects* (Routledge, London).
Jope, E. M. 2000, *Early Celtic Art in the British Isles* (Clarendon Press, Oxford).
Leach, E. R. 1958, 'Magical hair', *Journal of the Royal Anthropological Institute of Great Britain and Ireland* 88, 147-64.
Luik, H. 1999, 'Kammikujulised luu- ja pronksripatsid Eestis', *Eesti Arheoloogia Ajakiri* 3, 131-59.
Mauss, M. 1925, *Essai sur le don. Forme et raison de l'échange dans les sociétés archaïques*, Année Sociologique, 2nd series (Paris).
MacGregor, A. 1985, *Bone, Antler, Ivory and Horn: the technology of skeletal materials since the Roman Period* (Croom Helm, London).
McIntyre, J. 1929, 'Anglian comb from Whitby', *Yorkshire Archaeological Journal* 29, 350.
Richards, J. D. 2000, *Viking Age England* (Tempus, Stroud).
Ros, J. 1992, 'Antler and bone handicraft in late Viking Age and early medieval Sigtuna', in Hall, R. A., Hodges, R. and Clarke, H. (eds.), *Medieval Europe 1992, York: Medieval Europe 1992*, Preprinted Papers Volume 7: Art and Symbolism (York), 157-62.
Smith, A. N. 2000, 'Material culture and North Sea contacts in the fifth to seventh centuries AD', in Henderson, J. C. (ed.), *The Prehistory and Early History of Atlantic Europe*, British Archaeological Reports, International Series S861 (Archaeopress, Oxford), 181-88.
Smith, A. N. 2003, 'From the small green isles to the Low Countries: artefactual evidence for contact around the North Sea basin in the Later Iron Age', in Downes, J. and Richie, A. (eds.), *Sea Change: Orkney and Northern Europe in the later Iron Age, AD 300-800* (Pinkfoot and Orkney Heritage Society, Balgavies), 111-16.
Smyser, H. M. 1965, 'Ibn Fadlan's account of the Rus with some allusions to Beowulf', in Bessinger, J. B. and Creed, R. P. (eds.), *Franciplegius: medieval and linguistic studies in honor of Francis Peabody Magoun, Jr.* (New York: New York University Press), 92-119.
Sorrell, P. 1996, 'Alcuin's "comb" riddle', *Neophilologus* 80, 311-18.
Tuohy, T. 1999, *Prehistoric Combs of Antler and Bone*, British Archaeological Reports, British Series 285 (John and Erica Hedges Ltd, Oxford).
Venclová, N. 2002, 'The Venerable Bede, druidic tonsure and archaeology', *Antiquity* 76, 458-71.
Williams, H. 2003, 'Material culture as memory: combs and cremation in early medieval Britain', *Early Medieval Europe* 12, 89-128.

Lightning Source UK Ltd.
Milton Keynes UK
UKOW07f0226121017
310723UK00004BA/21/P